DESIGN IN ARCHITECTURE

DESIGN IN ARCHITECTURE

Architecture and the Human Sciences

GEOFFREY BROADBENT

Head of School of Architecture,
Portsmouth Polytechnic

JOHN WILEY & SONS

London · New York · Sydney · Toronto

Library of Congress catalog card number
71–39233

ISBN 0 471 10583 X

Reprinted in litho by Ceuterick, Printers since 1804

Brusselse straat 153   B 3000 Louvain (Belgium)

Contents

Acknowledgements

A book of this complexity could not have been written without the help of many people, and this help has taken many forms; intellectual stimulus in the generation, evaluation and refinement of ideas, practical help in the mechanics of book production, the granting of permissions to use material from existing publications.

Given this complexity, it seems invidious to mention individuals, and I apologise in advance to those who have been left out. My initial interest in the *how* of architectural designing was stimulated by colleagues on the teaching staff at Manchester University, especially Dennis Thornley, Derek Buttle, James Harris and James Bell, whilst my ideas on the subject have been much developed in discussions with other colleagues: teachers, researchers, and students at other institutions, especially John Tarn and John Page at Sheffield, Juan Bonta, Joe Wang and Tony Ward of my research staff at Portsmouth Polytechnic. I cannot single out individuals from the teaching, administrative and technical staff there now, but their contributions have been very great.

I have also enjoyed the stimulus of certain multi-disciplinary groups in the exploration of ideas; the Ascot Design Group, formed with Roderick Males, the Design Research Society and the RIBA Research Committee whose Research Award in 1965 encouraged me to focus down on certain areas within a very broad field. From these exploratory groups, Jane Abercrombie, George Atkinson, Brian Foss, Alex Gordon, Clive Wooster, Chris Jones, Tom Markus and Barry Wilson have helped in particular to crystallize my ideas, whilst their theoretical foundations have benefited greatly from ongoing discussions on RIBA Research policy with Bill Hillier, John Musgrove and Pat O'Sullivan.

My ideas have been sharpened further by feedback from my own students, from lectures in many places throughout Britain, France, Germany and Spain, in North and South America, from my contributions to various conferences, especially the Birmingham Symposium of 1965 (Gregory, 1966), the Ulm meeting of 1966 (Ulm Group 4, 1967), the Portsmouth Symposium of 1967 (Broadbent and Ward, 1969) and EDRA 2 (Archea and Eastman, 1970) and to various journals, in particular the Architects' Journal, the RIBA Journal, and the A.A. Journal in its various manifestations. Certain material in the book has been adapted from its original publication in those forms.

Finally, and like anyone who feels impelled to write, I acknowledge an enormous debt to my family: Barbara, Mark and Antony. I will not repeat here the platitudes on this topic which appear in most first books for that, in a way, would generalize their contribution too much. Suffice it to say that I laid unreasonable demands on them between November 1967 and September 1970 by writing, not one first book but two. Yet in addition to all that this implies, Barbara actually learned to type so as to convert my rather squalid drafts into publishable manuscripts.

Introduction

This book represents five years of exploration. When I started the research on which it is based, in the middle 1960s, architecture was in a fairly critical state. Few new buildings really pleased the users and the architectural profession as a whole was viewed with considerable suspicion by the society it was supposed to be serving. There was much talk of conservation on the grounds that *any* old building preserved was likely to be better looking, better constructed and more comfortable than anything the average architect could put in its place. There seemed to be a serious split between architects and their public as to what new buildings should be like (see for example Nairn, 1966), not that the former could actually agree among themselves.

Some architects believed with Gropius (1956) that the 'one-off' building, designed for a particular client by an individual, was an anachronism—indulgent self-expression on the latter's part which seemed to them socially irresponsible. They advocated instead a standardized approach in which the factory-made components of prefabricated systems were designed for transportation to site and assembly there, to form 'functional' buildings in which the architect's own tastes found no expression whatever. There was no place in their somewhat puritanical scheme of things for the architect as purveyor of delight, so that whilst their responsible attitudes were much to be admired, the buildings they produced failed conspicuously to please.

Others, without denying entirely the architect's right to self-expression in design, felt that he ought to offer this as one among several equals within a design team. Effective team working would demand an access of management techniques; there was much talk of the designer's responsibilities in terms of efficiency, productivity and cost control. If the efficient and economical buildings thus produced proved depressing to look at, well, that was too bad—a rather trivial penalty for putting first things first. I even proposed an amendment to Vitruvius's categorization of the qualities which architecture should possess (in Sir Henry Wotton's translation). This found a certain currency amongst management orientated architects (see for example Gordon, 1968).

'Well building hath five conditions; commoditie, firmness and delight—on time and at the right price.'

That seemed comprehensive enough at the time but, on reflection, proved not to be enough, being at once too simple from certain points of view and much too complex from others. No building, as far as I know, ever really delighted its users if it proved grossly incommodious, that is too small or otherwise unsuitable for their needs. Its first and obvious purpose was to contain their activities, to provide rooms or other spaces in which these activities could be pursued (in most cases) conveniently and in comfort. Nor would they be particularly happy if the building fell down or showed other evidence of lacking firmness. Certainly they would be highly displeased if it cost too much or took too long to build.

So I came to the unexpected conclusion that in terms of commoditie, firmness, time and cost, 'well building' had only one condition—the much-abused delight. Delight as the fundamental condition for architecture had been abused in two ways. It had been abused by those—managers and systems-builders—who deplored the pursuit of delight for its own sake and, conversely, by those who still strove for delight of a kind but saw it only as a visual matter. They overlooked, or forgot, that the ancient writers on architectural theory from Vitruvius onwards had attached considerable importance to the delights of commoditie and firmness, that their own concentration on visual delight was a legacy of the nineteenth century empirical, picturesque theories. Buildings were supposed to delight if they looked good, conformed to some currently fashionable imagery, subscribed to certain conventions of visual order and so on. If they delighted in this sense, then one was supposed to ignore practicalities such as the roof leaking, that they got too hot in summer or too cold in winter, or that they cost too much. Yet the alternative, systems/ management view, that appearance was not important, seemed to me to ignore a fundamental fact in the relationship of man to buildings: that whether we like it or not people experience them by means of their senses. In addition to looking at them, they touch them, hear sounds, feel warm or cold within them. Each building even has its characteristic smell. In other words it stimulates the senses in general, including several senses which had been forgotten in the concentration on visual delight, and not only that but the *only* information we receive directly from buildings comes to us by these sensory channels.

Rasmussen (1959) had touched on this matter, but clearly there was much to be learned from perceptual psychology (in for example Allport, 1955). I started to look at the implications and discovered the essential premises which underlie most theories of perception—that what one perceives consists of a transaction between what is 'there' physically in the 'real' world, stimulating one's sensory receptors, and the thoughts or ideas which one has already inherited at birth or, more particularly, learned from one's past experience.

This raised a number of fundamental issues about man's relationships to architecture; it began to explain why you feel cold in my sitting room whilst I feel warm enough: your experience of temperature is different from mine, and I know almost subconsciously where it is best to sit. It also explained why you *like* some buildings whilst I like others, why our disagreements can be violent, and why, occasionally, we can even agree. The building itself, the object of our perception, is constant, a physical *thing* which is quite unchanged by our perceiving it. But the lifetime of experience which, respectively, we bring to the perceiving of it, is different for each of us and this accounts for the differences in our perceptions of it.

It was one thing, however, to realize that man's relationships with his buildings are perceptual ones and quite another to utilize this fact in designing. To use it in designing, one had to set up certain concepts against which the building itself could be judged in perceptual terms—concepts which brought together man as a perceiving organism and the environment within which he did his perceiving. Several pointers were available as to how this could be done. Some of them are described in Chapters 8 and 9, and others lay within the physical conditions in which I wrote the book. My garden in Southsea is a small, paved, walled affair facing south. It is possible, for six weeks or so in the summer, to live there very comfortably, eating, working and relaxing; one could even sleep without benefit of any building, except for reasons of security and visual privacy. But I am hardly tempted to work there in the winter; I prefer to use one of the rooms in my house where, because of the structure itself, together with the built-in services (lighting, heating and so on) my family and I can recreate on, say, a December afternoon environmental conditions in terms of heat, light and sound equivalent to those we enjoy outside in June.

The building and its services control the physical climate. They act as a set of 'filters' between a given, external environment and the activities we want to perform; they enable us to set up conditions within which certain activities can be carried out conveniently in comfort and, occasionally, with delight. Clearly the spaces which buildings contain have to be big enough—but not too big—for the activities they are to house; their sizes and shapes are important and so, in terms of convenience and comfort, are their physical relationships with each other. We may have to move from one room to the next, but clearly there are limits to adjacencies of this kind. We shall have to decide which rooms must be next to each other and which can be further away. Locational planning decisions we take in this way will determine the ease with which people move not only from room to room, but from building to building, street to street and so on. In determining the ease with which people can move from place to place, we may well affect their behaviour and thus their social relationships.

Clearly, therefore, one could go a long way towards designing buildings (or even architecture) by establishing what activities they were to house, the space standards and environmental conditions which these activities required, the resources available for building with, the physical conditions obtaining on the available site, and reconciling these four things by means of the building itself—an environmental filter between man and his environment.

In building we shall also be dealing with resources in terms of land and materials. Labour will be expended in extracting, working, transporting and assembling the materials. Each of these processes will add to its value, and the building itself will certainly add value to the site. Capital, therefore, will be invested in its production and the building, once completed, may well be a source of revenue.

We can describe the building, therefore, as an environmental filter, a container for activities which locates them at a particular place, or a capital investment but these, individually and collectively, will not be enough.

At certain times and in certain places, building did originate as an environmental filter (see Chapter 2), although in much recent building—the curtain-walled office slab, light and dry, systems-built housing—this primary function seems to have been forgotten, or played down to such an extent that the buildings barely function from this point of view. Yet they certainly represent capital investment.

However, as Deffontaines (1948), Raglan (1964) and Rapoport (1969) remind us, architecture—even the house—offers something yet again. Raglan in particular concentrates on its religious origins, whilst Eco (1967) suggests that any symbolic marking of *place* ought to be called architecture. Primitive man chose a particular stone, or a grove of trees, as a place to meet or to worship; his choosing of place was itself an architectural gesture, and architecture since has always had this symbolic function, whatever else it may have had.

Given these possible origins, we might easily fall into the obvious trap of trying to distinguish between 'building', that which acts simply as climatic filter, and 'architecture', that which offers a symbolic marking of place. Pevsner (1943) took this view, suggesting that Lincoln Cathedral is architecture whilst a bicycle shed is mere building. But this seems to me a rather precious distinction; both structures modify the climate and both structures also mark certain places on the earth's surface, dedicating them to specific human use. They have other things in common, which may be even more significant in this particular discussion. Each displays evidence of conscious design decision in which the human intellect obviously has been involved; they display straight lines, curves and right angles such as do not appear in nature, organized into geometrical patterns of symmetry, repeated rhythms and so on. In other words, they display patterns of visual order which it is usual to call architectural.

Not only that; both cathedral and bicycle shed enclose space, using the available materials, according to their inherent properties, with economy and precision. Yet they differ in one important respect. The cathedral's essential structure, to use Pugin's terms (1841), is *enriched*; that is, covered with ornament whilst, apart from a coat of paint, the bicycle shed most probably will be unadorned. It is easy therefore to assume that the bicycle shed is 'functional' whilst the cathedral, because of its enrichments, self-evidently is not. But the bicycle shed may be rather a poor one which fails to support the bicycles properly, or allows rain to drip on their seats. Many so-called 'functional' buildings have failed in just such simple respects; their roofs have leaked or, more particularly, they have let in too much sunlight, too much solar heat, too much traffic noise. They have *failed* to act as environmental filters. The *only* thing that was functional about them was their appearance. Lincoln Cathedral too can be desperately cold in winter but in terms of lighting and acoustic control, not to mention planning, it functions rather well—as a cathedral.

It may be, therefore, that by any reasonable definition the cathedral is *more* functional than the bicycle shed, and there are other differences. The cathedral, to put it crudely, is a richer piece of design than the bicycle shed. It presents conspicuous evidence that more ways of thinking were expended in its design than in the case of the bicycle shed. Not only does it have a more complex structure (the province these days of the engineer) but the enrichment displays, or seems to display, quite different modes of design thinking. If one pursues this view to its conventional conclusion, the engineer designs the essential structure whilst the architect adds something over and above which is not strictly necessary and which, at worst, costs the client a great deal of money.

More and more over the past two hundred years, the various functions of building design have been separated out. As the theory of structures developed, so the engineer became a separate practitioner whose work, on the whole, could be quantified. He believed himself, for this reason, to be doing a tougher job than the architect, and so, as they too emerged, did the quantity surveyor, the heating, ventilating and electrical engineers. The architect's task gradually shrank; he was left with the 'soft-edged' aspects of building design, those things which could not be quantified but relied instead on his skill and judgement as an aesthete and a gentleman. He was concerned, above all, with matters of form, proportion, colour and texture—the raw material, as it were, of visual delight.

Increasingly, however, it seemed probable that these too could be quantified. Colour, for instance, could be specified in terms of hue, value and chroma; experiments could be set up in which psychological response to colour could be quantified, and thus a further aspect of the architect's remaining task would be eroded. Form, proportion, texture and so on could follow so that the architect might be left, literally, with nothing to do.

Curiously enough, the device which makes such quantification possible, the computer, seems likely also to rehabilitate the architect or, at least, the architectural mode of thinking. This, as Christopherson suggests in quite another context (1963), may be different from the engineer's. Typically, the problem of crossing a river may be put to engineering students in the following terms: 'Given a suspension bridge of this span, weight and shape, with cables of this material, how thick would the cables have to be ?' That would be put to them as a *design* problem but, as Christopherson says, the basic design decisions have already been taken; the problem really should have been put as: 'How would you bridge this river ?' Yet that still pre-empts the idea that one should use a bridge; the equivalent question to architectural students might well have been: 'Here is a river so many metres wide, it flows at such and such a rate; so many cars per hour are trying to get from north to south, so many others from south to north, how shall we cross it ?' In this form it becomes a strategic problem, calling for reserves of imagination, ingenuity and creativity which are simply not tapped by questions of mere cable-sizing.

Yet the designing of cables, not to mention columns and beams, can now be programmed and thus made the subject of routine computation, as can the equivalents for cost, the design of heating, ventilation and lighting systems. Those who in the search for 'tougher', more 'certain' jobs opted for the quantitative aspects of design are increasingly likely to find themselves redundant. But the architects' 'soft-edged' skills—those which require personal judgement in the study of human needs—are becoming valuable again. *They* determine what the computer is programmed *with*. They will have to be exercised over a much broader range than the architect tradition-ally retained for himself. He will have to concern himself with far more than visual effect, 'enriching' the essential structure of the building. As a first step, he might look at the users of his building as perceiving organisms. Each of them will perceive his buildings by means of their senses; they will see, hear, feel warm or cold and otherwise experience what he has done. The decisions he takes in designing will have a direct effect on what they perceive.

But the psychology of perception suggests that whether we like it or not, and whether we agree with them or not, other people will bring their personal experience to bear in the perception of our buildings and that may vary greatly from person to person; what each feels to be light enough, warm enough and quiet enough—these personal views and wishes certainly will make it difficult, if not impossible, to set up absolute standards in these matters. Other people will also bring personal values to bear in judging the building as a whole, not merely monetary values, but values also in terms of symbolism, of what buildings ought to look like, what other buildings they seemed to resemble, whether they appeared bright and cheerful, dignified, efficient and so on. People will read such meanings into our buildings whether we want them to or not, however 'functional' or aesthetically neutral the architect tries to make them, just as they read equivalent meanings into the ways each of us personally dresses, grows his hair and so on. The tweed-jacketed scientist who claims never to think about the 'style' of his clothes is projecting just as much of an 'image' as the sharp-suited city gentleman or the long-haired, bearded hippie. Each is advertising to the world the place he believes himself to occupy within, or even outside, society. Buildings project images in precisely this way and however 'functional' we want our architecture to be, we cannot avoid our responsibilities for deciding what those images shall be.

So, in addition to discussing the building as a container of activities, a modifier of the physical climate, a changer of land-value, we have to consider its cultural implications. The way we choose to dress is determined by certain social, political, economic and even moral pressures, not to mention aesthetic ones, and these together form a cultural climate. We operate as designers within this climate too, and there is a two-way interaction. Every judgement we make is determined, to some extent, by pressures from the cultural climate, whilst the results of our decisions in terms of projects designed, of buildings built, themselves act on the cultural climate, causing certain aspects of it to be modified.

It is clear, therefore, that the design of architecture finally can never be a matter of completely automated decision. It is doubtful whether design in any field can ever quite be that, although many people, for what seem to be *aesthetic* reasons, are anxious that it should. They point to the range of techniques which have become available to the designer, from ergonomics, operational research, systems analysis, information theory and certain other disciplines which originated, or developed rapidly, during World War II, and which depended for many of their applications on the extensive use of computers. They offer powerful tools for decision-making—when one has data in quantifiable form—and their proponents can point to many areas of designing from the original atomic bomb to undersea housings and manned lunar vehicles, which would have been quite impossible without the access of these techniques.

There is much to be said for this argument. The initial purpose of architecture as we have seen, is to modify the physical climate so that certain human activities can be carried out conveniently and in comfort. If techniques are available which have enabled man to survive on the sea-bed, or on the surface of the moon, by modifying their essentially hostile climates, then clearly the architect is acting irresponsibly if he refuses to apply them to the simpler, but still unsolved problems of modifying the climate at the surface of the earth. Some architects, such as the Archigram Group (1965) have wanted to apply the technology, say, of undersea housings to building on the ground, but that would be vastly expensive and the structures thus produced would be over-elaborate for the climate control problems which the earth's surface presents. They would also waste many of the earth's increasingly precious resources. Others, more subtly perhaps, have tried to adapt not the objects themselves but the techniques used in their design, to the design of less complex things such as buildings. There have been several attempts to abstract from operational research, systems analysis and so on, design processes for use in other fields (see Asimow, 1962; Jones and Thornley, 1963; Gregory, 1966; Broadbent and Ward, 1969; Jones, 1970; and Moore, 1970).

Nevertheless they do not solve the fundamental problem, for however excited one may be by the quantitative techniques which were used in designing, say, the atomic bomb or the Apollo spacecraft, the initial decisions to make and drop the bomb, to land a man on the moon, were taken by human beings for political, *cultural* reasons. As we have seen, such cultural reasons also play their part in the design of architecture. Some of them *can* be quantified—their quantification occurs in the various human sciences, physiology, psychology, and sociology. It seemed reasonable, therefore, to see what these also had to offer the designer.

It became clear, however, that beyond all this were many things in architectural design which could not be quantified. They were matters of imagery, values, identity, sense of place, which the human sciences had only begun to tackle. Eventually, as might have been expected, my study expanded into a manuscript of some 300,000 words about half of which was concerned broadly with the development of architectural values within a history of designing, and the other half with the human sciences, their input into design and the development of design methods within which they could be utilized. That proved too much for a single publication, for apart from sheer physical size the argument was too complex to be presented between the covers of one book. Yet there was a natural division and it seemed reasonable that the two parts should be published as separate books—the present volume, therefore, is concerned largely with design techniques, and the study of design values will be published separately.

Finally, this is a text book, assembling in one place material from the various disciplines which, recently, have made new contributions to design. That is why certain topics, such as statistics or human science techniques, are treated at a fairly basic level. Most architects and students of architecture will be unfamiliar with their terminology and their modes of application. I have tried to explain these and to indicate what confidence we, as designers, might place in their findings. In each case, however, I can merely introduce the subject, whilst trying to indicate appropriate sources of further information. To each specialist, no doubt, my treatment will seem inadequate, biased and in some cases downright misleading. That is because, in each case, I have tried to look at the subject as an architect, concerned with design decisions, trying to abstract from it those aspects which seem most relevant in design. It is for designers to judge my success and failures but these finally will depend on the extent to which my book helps them generate another new architecture, more concerned with human needs than design ideals, and more amenable to changes in human use than the last one seems to have been.

CHAPTER 1

The Architect as Designer

We could investigate the architects' contribution to architecture in several ways—by looking at what they have designed and trying to establish what kinds of processes produced such products, by watching architects in action as a more direct way of establishing the nature of the processes they use, or by looking at architects themselves to see what kinds of people they are, in the hope that this will throw some light on the ways in which they design.

Each of these methods has certain advantages and certain disadvantages. Buildings which look similar may have been designed in quite different ways. We may be misled if we try to deduce the architect's processes from his products. Our presence may disturb the architect if we try to observe him in action, for reasons which we shall discuss in Chapter 7, so that too will be misleading. We shall start by looking at the architect himself and the things which psychologists have said about him. .

There are difficulties in this approach because, although the architect has become a favourite subject for psychological research, the research itself is subject to the vagaries of psychological fashion, to the conflicts which have arisen between different factions in psychology, to the application of methodologies which may be profoundly satisfying to those who use them, but which finally tell us very little that *we* want to know about the architect.

Most psychologists like to think that the architect's chief problem is one of 'creativity'—whatever that may mean. Liam Hudson (1966) describes it as a psychological 'band-wagon', and it seems to mean many things to many people. In an architectural context, it tends to suggest 'artistic'. One thinks immediately of a Gaudi, or a Frank Lloyd Wright, sketching busily with a 6–B pencil, probably on the back of an envelope. Popular definitions of creativity in other fields too suggest that above all it means something far removed from practical. Often it is simply a matter of being different for the sake of being different. Frank Barron, an American psychologist, says (1958): 'By his imagination man makes new universes which are nearer to his heart's desire'—not a bad aim and perhaps the only one, ultimately, which man can set himself and, if we take it literally, the architect ought to play some part in it. Barron and his colleagues of the Institute of Personality Assessment and Research at the University of California, Berkeley, have undertaken, under the direction of Donald MacKinnon, the most massive survey yet into the nature of creative people. MacKinnon and Hall were very anxious to test architects, for reasons we shall consider in a moment, but even here the psychologists' use of the word creative and the architects' seem rather different. It may be helpful, therefore, if we list some of the meanings which people in different fields have attached to this rather curious word. The most common appear to be those shown in Table 1.1.

Table 1.1

ARTS	To paint an 'original' picture, write an 'original' poem, piece of music and so on.
SCIENCES	To formulate a new theory or postulate a new hypothesis.
TECHNOLOGY	To solve a technical problem in a new and more 'elegant' way. Elegant in this sense means simple, efficient and economical.
PSYCHOLOGICAL TESTING	To generate the richest possible permutation on a given set of ideas.

MacKinnon's definition (1962a) seems to combine something of all these, and he suggests that 'creativeness', essentially, fulfils at least three conditions:

'It involves a response or an idea that is novel or at the very least statistically infrequent. But novelty or originality of thought or action, while a necessary aspect of creativity, is not sufficient. If a response is to lay claim to being part of the creative process, it must to some extent be adaptive to, or of reality. It must serve to solve a problem, fit a situation, or accomplish some recognizable goal. And thirdly, true creativity involves a sustaining of the original insight, an evaluation and elaboration of it, a developing to the full.'

If we translate this into architectural terms, we certainly seem to see in it the 'artistic' architect looking for novel and 'statistically infrequent' responses at the level of the whole building. Yet many highly skilled professionals would be profoundly disturbed at the thought that such a response has any place in architectural design today.

Indeed many architects now approach design from a diametrically opposite point of view. They look to the social sciences for generalized statements of human needs, and try to satisfy those needs by standardized solutions to the architectural problems they raise. Few of them realize that in doing so they are following Le Corbusier, who suggested in *Towards a new architecture* that *standards* should be established as a basis for design:

'A standard is established on sure bases, not capriciously, but with the surety of something intentional and of a logic controlled by analysis and experiment. All men have the same organisms, the same functions. All men have the same needs.' (trans. Etchells, 1923)

And he goes on to suggest that if these common needs are established, by means of 'logical analysis and precise study', and satisfied by equally rational means, then new forms of architecture will develop which may well 'have a strange look at first sight'. In other words, he suggests that rational analysis will throw up buildings which are statistically infrequent in terms of appearance because they have been designed to satisfy what is statistically frequent in terms of human need.

At this level, then, MacKinnon's first condition of 'creativeness' is of doubtful value in considering architectural design, but there are other possibilities. Suppose, for instance, that we take a technological view on creativity—that it is a matter of solving technical problems in new and more 'elegant' ways. Surely that has a place in anyone's vocabulary of architectural design techniques, however rational they may think themselves? Indeed it has been one of the tragedies of systems building, as developed so far, that no one paid much attention to the creative aspects of detail design. In CLASP, for instance, the detailing is unbelievably crude—one has only to look at the ways in which windows are fitted into the steel frame, or corners negotiated, to agree with Reyner Banham that the 'clip joints' are indeed 'ill met' (Banham, 1962). The problem here, of course, is that the architects who developed CLASP were attracted to the project *because* they considered themselves non-creative and, conversely, creative architects would have nothing to do with it, because they found the whole idea of systems in building inhibiting. So CLASP became an assemblage of bits and pieces, each designed rationally in itself, but lacking any kind of consistency because no one in the team was capable of the creative gestures needed to transcend the immediate problem and produce an overall solution which was elegant in the technological sense—simpler, more efficient and cheaper.

So MacKinnon's first condition of creativeness may be suspect if we consider it only at an 'artistic' level, but it is certainly relevant if we bring in the technological meaning as well. And his second condition, concerning the creative response's relationship to the problem, and to reality, is much nearer the mark. An architect, after all, designs real buildings to go on real sites for real clients and MacKinnon's third condition—that his creative response must be related to the problem if it is to make any sense at all and 'involves a sustaining of the original insight, an evaluation and elaboration of it, a developing to the full'—is surely what design is all about. It is a matter of hard work, of forcing an idea through. As Thomas Alva Edison said, 'genius is one per cent inspiration and ninety-nine per cent perspiration'.

So whatever one's view of the nature of the architect—rationalist, empiricist, or something else—there is a great deal in MacKinnon's definition of 'creativeness' that has some bearing on his work. It so happens that the Institute's research was concerned with painters, writers, physicians, biologists, economists and anthropologists (Barron, 1958). They particularly wanted to test architects, as a control group, on the grounds that architects represent one of those domains of creative endeavour in which the successful practitioner must be *both* artist and scientist. MacKinnon quotes Sir Henry Wotton (misattributing the idea to Ruskin) that 'well building hath three

4   *Design in Architecture*

conditions, commoditie, firmness and delight'—as evidence that architectural creativity is cross-cultural in nature. One feels he might also have quoted Vitruvius, whose definition is rather more comprehensive. Writing on the nature of the architect Vitruvius says:

'Let him be educated, skilful with pencil, instructed in geometry, know much history, have followed the philosophers with attention, understand music, have some knowledge of medicine, know the opinions of the jurists, and be acquainted with astronomy and the theory of the heavens.' (trans. Morgan, 1914)

As a matter of fact, MacKinnon's architects were complete all-rounders too. Certainly they were not far behind Vitruvius's in range of abilities. At the end of the tests the psychologists were most impressed by the architects' 'juggler-like' ability

'to combine, reconcile and exercise the diverse skills of businessman, journalist, psychiatrist, educator, and psychologist'.

But in addition to testing a group of 40 'creative' architects, MacKinnon and Hall also tested 43 'Architects II' who had fewer pretensions to creative distinction, although each had worked at some time with a member of the first group, and 41 'Architects III' who were very ordinary practitioners. It so happens that the 'creative' group was the hardest of the three to build up. They were subject to more searching tests than the others, and MacKinnon describes the selection procedure in some detail (1962b), but there were some notable refusals including the redoubtable Frank Lloyd Wright.

At first sight, we ought to be very pleased that on the *Gough Adjective Check List* (1954) the creative architects, as a group, proved to be highly attractive personalities. But all this test amounts to is that each psychologist selects from a list of 300 adjectives those which he thinks best describe each subject under test. Still the architects came out of it very well and 100 per cent of the 'creative' ones were considered 'alert, artistic, intelligent and responsible'. Each of the adjectives used to describe 80 per cent or more of them was highly flattering even though, as Dr. Abercrombie pointed out (1965), there are some nasty adjectives on the list too, such as 'dull, sulky, spineless and vindictive' but none of these apparently applied to the creative architects in any significant number.

They also came out well on Block's *100-item Q-sort* (1961), another consensus of psychologists' opinions. The first seven items in their collated list read:

1. Enjoys aesthetic impressions; is aesthetically reactive.
2. Has high aspiration level for self.
3. Values own independence and autonomy.
4. Is productive; gets things done.
5. Appears to have a high degree of intellectual capacity.

6. Genuinely values intellectual and cognitive matters.
7. Concerned with own adequacy as a person, either at conscious or unconscious level.

Only the last of these casts the slightest doubt on an otherwise impeccable profile of personality as seen by the psychologists. The impression of thoroughly decent and effective members of the community was confirmed by other, rather more carefully controlled tests, such as the *California Personality Inventory* (Gough, 1957). In this test the score for Architects III in particular was remarkably even, with a high drive for independent achievement, a high capacity for status and a great interest coupled with responsiveness, in the inner needs, motives and experiences of others. As we might expect the creative architects differed somewhat from the Architects III on this test. They were higher in social presence, in self-acceptance, in psychological mindedness (whatever that is) and in flexibility. But they were rather lower in sense of responsibility, in socialization, self-control and tolerance, in wanting to create a good impression, in sense of community and in conformity. In other words, they were slightly more anti-social.

Dr. Abercrombie sums this up by describing MacKinnon's architects, not to mention those she knows, as being made of 'sugar and spice and all things nice' (1965), which is very gratifying for us. But one cannot help feeling that to some extent MacKinnon *wanted* his architects to be nice. As we have seen, Hudson was suspicious of some testers because they did not seem to like the people they were testing—but the reverse obviously can be true as well. MacKinnon clearly is happiest with 'creative', well-adjusted people who are open to experience, and one is reminded of Gordon Allport, in another context (1954), who believes implicitly that it is 'better' to be tolerant than to be authoritarian. In many ways, his tolerant person resembles MacKinnon's 'creative', but his tests seem rather less well documented. Allport's descriptions of his personality-types are loaded with emotional overtones too: they confirm his own prejudice (in favour of flexibility) very clearly, and yet it seems to me that by describing his 'opposite' they throw a good deal of light on to the kind of person that MacKinnon and his colleagues were looking for.

The tradition of personality studies in which Allport worked was initiated by Fromm (1942), Maslow (1954) and others. One can understand the urgency with which psychologists of Jewish origin sought to tackle the problem of anti-Semitism during World War II, and certainly one can sympathize with it. The key publication in this field was *The Authoritarian Personality* of Adorno and others (1950). They were concerned, in particular, with Fascist authoritarianism but the tests they developed have been used for testing other kinds of rigidity, too. Allport, particularly, was interested in race relations and on the whole he uses the word 'prejudiced' to describe the people he was studying.

As we might expect, Allport traces the development of his prejudiced personalities from childhood. Often the child *adopts* prejudiced attitudes from his parents but the way they treat him may also have profound effects. If they are harsh with him, repressive or domineering, if they neglect him, or if they are inconsistent (sometimes permissive, sometimes rejecting and sometimes over-indulgent) they may inhibit his ability to come to terms with the world and with himself. A person who has been so damaged, according to Allport, will exhibit the following characteristics:

Ambivalence towards parents—a love–hate relationship in which a subject knows that his parents were unjust, mean or cruel but at the same time feels unable to criticize them.

Moralism—the prejudiced person feels the need of a rigid moral code, insisting on cleanliness, good manners and conventional behaviour. This is attributed by Allport to strict toilet-training in infancy and to a code of behaviour by which most of the child's impulses are considered wicked and punished accordingly. When he reaches a position of authority himself, he sees it his duty to punish other people who transgress his personal code and he may devote a great deal of energy to detecting such lapses in those around him. It is the mechanism of Puritanism.

Dichotomization—perhaps with moralism, the most potent indication of prejudice. This 'two-valued logic' is a necessary over-simplification for the prejudiced person; it enables him to classify behaviour immediately as 'good' or 'bad'. He tends to think that there are two kinds of people, such as the weak and the strong, and that there is 'one right way' of doing anything.

Need of definiteness—is another aspect of the same mental processes. Allport believes that cognition itself—the way a prejudiced person *knows* about the world in terms of perceiving, remembering, imagining, conceiving, judging and reasoning—is different from cognition in the tolerant person. He *needs* to know things definitely; he cannot tolerate ambiguity of any kind; he can never admit he is wrong or that he 'doesn't know'. As Allport says: 'Prejudiced people demand a clear-cut structure in their world, even if it is an inadequate structure. Where there is no order, they impose it. When new solutions are called for they cling to tried and tested habits. Wherever possible they latch onto what is familiar, safe, simple, definite.' In MacKinnon's terms, they are non-creative. Allport offers two explanations for this. One is that the prejudiced person has a very confused self-image. The ego itself cannot offer a safe anchorage point, so he must impose an outer definiteness on the world. The other theory holds that the parents of prejudiced persons forbade them many things. Rewards were delayed, or never even offered; the child, therefore, developed an urge for immediate and definite answers. Ambiguity puts the reward in doubt, better therefore to adopt concrete, definite modes of thinking even if they tend to rigidity.

Externalization—because things do not always conform to the rigid structure which he has imposed on the world, the prejudiced person believes that he has little control over his destiny. Things happen to him from 'out there' and he cannot participate actively in their control. 'They' attack him and he has to defend himself.

Institutionalism—naturally, if one is searching for support and order, it can be found in institutions—teams, clubs, societies, lodges, schools, churches and so on.

They save the trouble of making personal decisions because they codify the rules by which one must behave. On the whole, according to Allport, the prejudiced person is more devoted to such institutions than the unprejudiced, he is trying to find institutional safety and security, so he likes to become a member of a group.

Authoritarianism—one of the most easily recognized characteristics of prejudice: personal freedom makes for unpredictability, indefiniteness and change. In order to avoid such disorder, the prejudiced person looks for hierarchies—power structures are definite, easily understood and dependable. Strong leaders lead to an authoritative, orderly and powerful society—the prejudiced person, asked to name his heroes, is liable to choose Napoleon, or even Hitler, whereas the non-prejudiced person may suggest some great artist, scientist or humanitarian. Allport believes that this need for authority reflects a deep distrust of human nature—people are seen as guilty, evil or dangerous until proved otherwise.

We have seen already that in some ways Allport's prejudiced person is the 'opposite' of MacKinnon's creative. The latter was high in self-acceptance and in flexibility, low in conformity and desire to belong to groups. This tendency conflicts with the pressures which act, increasingly, on the architect to work in groups. It is such an important topic that we shall devote a later chapter to it but, for the moment, let us just hint that the motivation of those who talk most about the need for group working may itself be an indication of prejudice. We shall also see that, in the art of designing, dichotomization can have very inhibiting effects and above all the successful designer needs— at certain stages—not merely to tolerate ambiguity, but to use it actively as part of the process.

Allport finds it difficult to describe the opposite of a prejudiced personality. *Tolerant* he thinks sounds rather flabby, a matter of negative acceptance, whereas he is looking for something much more positive. His unprejudiced individual will be on friendly terms with all kinds of people; he will make no distinction in respect of the familiar categories of colour, race or creed, and he will actively *approve* his fellow men. It may be significant that the English language has no single word to describe such a person and certainly very little research has been done on him. He will accept his parents as real people, appreciating their virtues and recognizing their faults. His judgements generally will be far more subtle than the simple black *or* white of the pre-judiced personality. As Allport says:

'The greater mental flexibility of the tolerant person (even in childhood) is shown by his rejection of two-valued logic. He seldom agrees that "there are only two kinds of people: the weak and the strong'; or that "there is only one right way to do anything." He does not bifurcate his environment into the wholly proper and the wholly improper. For him there are shades of grey. Nor does he sharply distinguish between the roles of the sexes. He does not agree that "girls should learn only the things that are useful around the house." '

Naturally he can tolerate ambiguity; in school and in later life the tolerant person can cope with situations which are not clear-cut. He does not need definite instructions; he has no particular desire for precise structured situations. That again has strong implications for the designer.

One important distinguishing feature of the tolerant person is his ability to project himself into someone else's situation—an ability which Allport calls *empathy*. In one revealing experiment pairs of students were asked to talk to each other informally about some common interest. The pairs were matched for age, sex and so on, but one of each pair was highly authoritarian, the other highly tolerant. Each was then asked to answer questions on the discussion as he thought the *other* might answer them. As we might expect, the high authoritarians projected their own attitudes on to the other person and filled out answers for him which were really their own, whereas the tolerant individuals summed up their opposite numbers and·not only answered the questions as authoritarians might in general, but with considerable sensitivity to their particular partner's attitudes. One thinks for a moment of the architect taking his brief.

Allport's explanation is that the prejudiced person cannot trust his own judgement; he has to force other people into the structure he has formulated for himself; he resorts to stereotyping. The tolerant person, on the other hand, sees things realistically: if an unpleasant situation seems to be threatening he can sidestep it, and this frees him to observe very closely the characteristics of the actual person to whom he is talking. He can even assess himself realistically, and is not afraid to admit the discrepancies between what he would like to be and what he really is. Asked to describe the ideal person for a particular task, the tolerant person will often describe personality characteristics he himself does not possess, whereas the prejudiced person will describe someone very like himself—as he sees himself to be. Naturally, we should expect tolerant self-insight to include the ability to laugh at oneself; but according to Allport, this self-insight of the tolerant has other implications too:

'Several investigators have called attention to a general *inwardness* in the personalities of tolerant people. There is interest in imaginative processes, in fantasies, in theoretical reflections, in artistic activities. Prejudiced people, by contrast, are *outward* in their interests, given to externalizing their conflicts, and finding their environment more absorbing than themselves. Tolerant people have a desire for personal autonomy rather than for external, institutional anchorage.'

In many ways, therefore, Allport's tolerant personality matches MacKinnon's creative one. He is a thoroughly pleasant individual and able, above all, to see the other person's point of view. But are creative architects really like that? Peter Blake presented thumb-nail biographies of this century's greatest architects in *The Master Builders* (1960) and none of them seems to fit the pattern. His character sketch of Wright, for instance, describes him as 'arrogant, strident, full of conceit'. Blake excuses this on the grounds that Wright was a very sensitive person, a country 'hick' trying to defend himself, who was 'deeply conscious of what people thought and said of him, intensely conscious and deeply hurt by what he considered to be insults regularly hurled at him by the city slickers.' And Le Corbusier too, according to Blake, was 'cold, suspicious, pugnacious, sarcastic (but quite humourless about himself), and arrogant'. In private, however, he displayed another facet of personality to those who knew him well: they found him 'a man of tremendous charm, wit, and great warmth; of scholarship, vision and superb taste'. Similarly Blake describes Mies van der Rohe as 'massive', granite-faced, elegantly dressed, gentle, fantastically self-disciplined, taciturn and shy to the extent that he found speech-making painful. Very different, then, are these great men from MacKinnon's 'civilized, dependable, friendly, pleasant and resourceful' Architects I.

There is, of course, a glib explanation for this: that because they were exceptional these great men were different in kind from other architects— and even from MacKinnon's creative architects. We remember too that Frank Lloyd Wright refused to take part in MacKinnon's tests. But Macfarlane Smith (1964) believes anyway that good architects are likely to be 'unsociable, humourless, severe, aloof, suspicious, cool, reticent, misanthropic, calm, cold, calculating, self-centred, shut-in and fanatical'—which certainly seems nearer to Blake's descriptions of Wright, Le Corbusier and Mies. Smith believes this is so because great architects are likely to possess high spatial ability which I shall attempt to describe later, and spatial ability, according to Smith, is found particularly in people of marked *schizothymic* personality. This is a matter of possessing schizoid tendencies, within the limits of 'normality', in which the intellectual aspects of life are dissociated from the emotional. That is why the schizothyme tends towards self-sufficiency, reserve and intolerance, and why he may appear to withdraw from intense human interactions.

Smith contrasts the *schizothyme* with the *cyclothyme*, adding a further dimension to our consideration of personality. The cyclothyme will be 'sociable, (a) good mixer, lively, sprightly, quietly humorous, emotional, understanding, tender-hearted, kindly, soft, alternating between cheerful and sad.' The 'cycles' which the term implies are alternations of excitement and depression and just as the cyclothyme will be more sociable than the schizothyme, so he will be higher in verbal reasoning ability. Macfarlane Smith bases his classifications of people quite simply on their appearance. At first sight, that seems trivial but he brings some evidence to bear that schizothymes tend to be *ectomorphic* or *mesomorphic*. Cyclothymes, by contrast, tend to be *endomorphic* in shape, with a large trunk, protruding abdomen and short legs. They are relaxed, slow, amiable and need to discuss whatever problems they have with other people.

Few of us match these types exactly but we can all be plotted within the triangle which they define. Smith produces detailed evidence from

Kretschmer, and others, which suggests that the majority of great mathematicians and physicists have been schizothymic in temperament, whereas men of letters tend to have been cyclothymic. The schizothymic scientists naturally look for systematization and order. They tend to formulate concepts and favour abstract patterns of thought. They are prone to engage in philosophical and metaphysical speculation. Most of the great revolutions in science were initiated by men of this type whose enormous concentration enabled them to 'fix' their attention, and to focus all their mental energies on to the solution of a specific problem. But there have been cyclothymic scientists too, men who showed enormous versatility—'a preference for empiricism and observation, a distrust of systematization and philosophical speculation, and an inclination to the easy popularization of knowledge.' This observant empiricism, according to Kretschmer, is particularly valuable in biology, chemistry and medicine.

The refreshing thing about Smith is that he actually seems to *like* his schizothymes whereas MacKinnon, Allport and the others dismiss the equivalents in their terminology as non-creative, prejudiced and so on. It will not surprise us to find that Smith classifies the following architects as schizothymes—Le Corbusier, Frank Lloyd Wright, Mies van der Rohe, Gropius, Inigo Jones, Mackintosh, Nervi, A. W. Pugin, Saarinen and Wren—all this the result of somatyping from pictures and reading such biographies as are available. He claims further that all those architects and artists who have shown a consuming interest in *form* for its own sake, for abstraction and for conformity with classical canons have been schizothyme, whereas those whose work is characterized by delight in sensuous experience have been cyclothyme. So Smith hints at two kinds of creativity, one of which comes from the free, easy, friendly cyclothyme and the other from the tight-lipped, severe and forbidding schizothyme. It will not surprise us that they seem to match our empiricist and rationalist approaches to design.

The most sensitive description of these two types, or their equivalents in other terminology, is that of Liam Hudson. He uses the words favoured by Getzells and Jackson (1962), who speak of *convergers* and *divergers*. Hudson began, with his Ph.D. thesis, by trying to distinguish between the abilities of arts specialists and science specialists. As far as he could see, the former tended to have a verbal bias of ability, whilst the latter tended to numerical or diagrammatic ones. He elaborates his findings in *Contrary Imaginations* (1966):

'The typical historian or modern linguist had, relatively speaking, rather a low IQ, and a verbal bias of language. He was prone to work erratically on the intelligence test, accurate at times and slapdash at others; and his interests tended to be cultural rather than practical. The young physical scientist often had a high IQ, and a non-verbal bias of ability; he was usually consistently accurate, and his interests were usually technical, mechanical, or in life out of doors.'

The scientist, of course, with his IQ and consistent accuracy is the *converger* whilst the historian with his relatively low IQ and slapdash habits is the *diverger*. Hudson relates these terms to yet another pair used by Getzells and Jackson, 'High IQ' and 'High Creative'.

His argument is based on the kind of tests used by psychologists to detect these characteristics. The High IQ, Hudson's converger, will respond effectively to questions of the following kind:

Brick is to house as plank is to . . . orange, grass, egg, boat, ostrich?

There is one correct answer, and the subject will *converge* on to it. This will be true of any test in logical reasoning, whether it is verbal, mathematical or even diagrammatic. But a 'creativity' test, by contrast, might ask:

How many uses can you think of for a brick?

Some people can think of only one or two rather conventional uses such as building a house, whilst others can think of dozens, some of them highly original. These are the *divergers*; they respond to 'open-ended' questions with evident enjoyment whether they are concerned with *uses of objects*, the *meanings of words* or even with *drawing*.

Hudson found some interesting differences between his convergers and divergers. The latter naturally were inclined to throw up more and more elaborate ideas on open-ended tests; they peopled the streets in their drawings whereas convergers left them empty, but divergers also produced far more responses which suggested violence to other people. When a converger produced such a response, however, it was likely to be very violent indeed, and completely lacking the humour of some divergers' violence. As we might expect, convergers tended towards authoritarian rigidity of attitude and social conformity. Hudson says:

'Convergers are more likely to approve of being obedient, and having a low opinion of themselves; and to disapprove of being independent of parents. They are more likely to approve of accepting expert advice, and having set opinions; more likely to disapprove of being highly imaginative, and of artistic sensitivity. They are more likely to approve of mixing well socially, of being a good team member, of being personally neat and tidy, and of being well mannered; and to disapprove of "arty" clothes and bad language.'

Unlike MacKinnon, however, Hudson does not write off his convergers as being essentially non-creative. He considers the relationship of his convergence/divergence to 'creativity', in fact, and questions the easy assumption that divergers are potentially creative, and convergers potentially not—a view which certainly is held by MacKinnon. Hudson draws on the work of Roe (1951–1953), MacKinnon (1962) and McLelland (1962) to support his doubts, and finds that Roe's study of creative scientists, in many ways, was more searching than MacKinnon's. Roe points out most forcibly the 'ubiquity of the contrast between a concern with people and a concern with things' (quoted Hudson, 1966) and, as we might expect, her psychologists and anthropologists were interested in people, her biological and physical scientists in things. The latter also tended to show an emotional 'withdrawal' or 'estrangement' which seems to have manifested itself quite early in life. McLelland (1962) attempts to define the origins of this emotional withdrawal and, like Allport, puts it down to fear of parental authority. His scientists anyway tend to come from puritan homes although few of them maintain an interest in religion into adult life. They seem to turn, in fact, from their puritanical upbringings to science as an *alternative* way of life (Hudson, 1966). One of the most telling pieces of evidence in McLelland's argument relates to the use of metaphor in descriptions of nature. Compared with non-scientists, his scientists showed a marked preference for anthropomorphic metaphors when describing inanimate things. In other words, they thought of non-human things in terms of human feelings—possibly as a substitute for their unhappy relations with real people.

This was revealed most strongly in a *Thematic Apperception Test* in which McLelland's scientists were shown cards depicting certain dramatic human situations. They were asked to interpret the feelings of the people in the pictures and to tell stories about them. The scientists tended to dislike this task intensely, as one physicist said: 'That is most objectionable. We will carry out an analysis. I have all sorts of blocks because people are so un-reasonable it always makes great difficulty for me' (McLelland, 1962). Their difficulty, to a great extent, stemmed from an unwillingness to tolerate ambiguity. Accustomed, as they were, to precise analytical procedures, they could not let themselves go in dramatic story-telling. They were worried constantly by individual details which did not seem to fit the pattern of the rest, and Roe's scientists had the same problem; one of them was quite unable to make up stories, even for telling to his own children.

The point at issue, then, is whether our architects ought to be interested in people or in things. If they are interested in people they may be cyclothymic, divergent, verbal, imaginative, empirical in their approach and anxious to satisfy human needs. If they are interested in things they will tend to be schizothymic, convergent and interested in philosophical abstraction for its own sake and in 'perfect' architecture. My own view is that whatever the nature of the architect, his building is eventually going to impinge on the senses of other people. They will experience it with their senses, and no amount of sophisticated abstraction or philosophical argument will persuade them that they are comfortable in a building when their senses tell them it is cold, damp and ugly. Yet I can see the necessity for both kinds of architect— and for all the possible variations in between. Indeed architectural progress is likely to result from the tensions which build up when the two are in constant interaction with each other.

Allport's descriptions might help us detect which we are but one of the most revealing indications is thrown up by Roe and MacKinnon between them. Roe's scientists (and like Smith, she seems to have favoured the 'unsympathetic' types) were intensely and unequivocally masculine. They disliked poetry, although admitted to listening to music, and many of them had outdoor interests concerned with nature or with sport. MacKinnon's architects, on the other hand, were exceptionally high in femininity. As he puts it:

'In the realm of sexual identifications and interests, our creative subjects appear to give more expression to the feminine side of their nature than do less creative persons. If one were to cast this in Jungian terms one would say that these creative persons are not so completely identified with their masculine persona roles as to blind themselves to or deny expression to the more feminine traits of the anima. For some the balance between masculine and feminine traits, interests, and identifications is a precarious one, and for several it would appear that their presently achieved reconciliation of these opposites of their nature has been barely achieved and only after considerable psychic stress and turmoil.'

Stringer (1967) and others confirm this refusal of certain creative people to be bound, by group conventional views, as to what interests are properly masculine and what ought to be considered feminine. He also points to the stress this creates for women art students, who find it difficult in most art schools to define their sexual identity. This may be one of the major reasons, he suggests, for the fact that so far no woman artist, ever, has been accepted on exactly equal terms with the best of her male contemporaries. If we were to sum up the architect's sexual identification, therefore, we might use Susan Sontag's terminology (1967). He may be androgynous but not, we hope, epicene. This blurring of distinctions between the sexes is, of course, a particular kind of ambiguity, perhaps the most fundamental of all. It is not the least of the creative diverger's problems but, as Hudson says, there has been very much less research into the nature of the arts specialist as compared with the scientist. He quotes Bereiter and Freedman (1962) who summarize the artist's characteristics: concern with people, sociability and sensitivity to their emotions. Hudson suggests, however, that this may not be what it seems. He believes that divergers, too, have their own system of defences. Just as the converger is worried by 'messy' situations, so the diverger is worried by precise, logical argument. He is often very bad at it, and sees it as a trap. As Hudson puts it, 'In caricature: the converger takes refuge from people in things; the diverger takes refuge from things in people.' His willingness to *show* his emotions, where other people keep them hidden, may indicate weakness too. He may be too effusive about it, which suggests a certain hollowness; and he may use trivial analogies as a substitute for logic. It may even be that he too is hiding his true emotions behind an adopted pose. Again as Hudson puts it:

'The diverger sometimes has the air of a boy whose real feelings are buried, or lost, and who reassures himself of his capacity for pleasure by a reiteration of its external signs. He may express an emotion, yet drain it as an actor does, of its proper experiential content. The diverger feels more freely than the converger, but not necessarily more fully.'

Hudson poses the arts man's dilemma in its most extreme form—in the case of the novelist. His stock-in-trade, of course, is human relationships and his interest in other people, therefore, is extremely acute, but he does not see them as relating to him personally as real people with whom he interacts but as the raw material with which he works. In itself, that may be relatively innocuous but the politician takes it a stage further, for he actually *manipulates* real people. Again, Hudson generalizes:

'the scientist searches for control over things which he treats as though they were people; the arts man searches for control over people which he treats as though they were things.'

In short, according to Hudson the equating of diverger with creative man is too glib. He believes that creative work will come from *both* convergers and divergers but the nature of their personalities will determine what field they choose to be creative in. The arts seem to offer more room for individuality and for those with a consuming interest in *people* as opposed to an interest in *things*. Architecture, of course, is concerned with people *and* things, which is why we have to look for much more complex personality-types than any two extremes.

One of the tests in Mackinnon's battery begins to hint at this complexity, because it is concerned with people's interests—in people or things, arts or sciences and so on. And unlike most of the other tests it was not so much concerned with the ends of spectra—such as creative/non-creative—but with a complete spectrum of ideas, in six categories. It was the Allport–Vernon–Lindzey *Study of Values* (1951) which takes major fields of human interest, as defined by the German philosopher Eduard Spranger in his *Types of Men* (1928). Certainly it has its limitations; the values expressed are *cultural* values and therefore superficial in some respects. But certainly in architecture we are much concerned with cultural values and Spranger's classification is a useful one. In Allport, Vernon and Lindzey's version the categories are as follows:

THEORETICAL—concerned with a dominant interest in abstract truth within the fields of philosophy, mathematics, physics, chemistry and so on. The theoretician will be interested in human behaviour, in books, in knowledge for its own sake; he may not believe in God and his hero will probably be some great scientist.

ECONOMIC—emphasizing utility and practicality with interests in money, market conditions, real estate, standards of living, business and organization. His hero might be a great industrialist, such as Henry Ford.

AESTHETIC—interested in poetry, architecture, music, ballet, modern painting, literature, sculpture, the past, and placing high values on pageantry, beauty, sensitivity, harmony and design. Tends to be selfish; his hero will be some great artist.

SOCIAL—concerned with human rights, altruistic, unselfish, desiring to help others in welfare work, voluntary service, counselling, care for the sick and aged. Heroine might be a great reformer, such as Florence Nightingale.

POLITICAL—interested in government, administration, leadership, forming public opinion, debate—with a strong desire to influence others. Plays games to win, pits himself against nature, seeks prestige. Hero would be a great man such as Napoleon.

RELIGIOUS—faith and membership of a particular religious group do enter into this category, but it is much more concerned with spiritual revelation, reverence, spiritual aspiration and communion. Searches for a cosmic purpose and seeks to understand the meaning of the universe as a whole.

None of us is wholly one of these and we may combine elements of them all in one make-up; but one of them will probably dominate and others may be hardly represented at all. Some of these categories seem very well defined; political and religious, for instance, both transcend the limitations of party or denominational membership. It is particularly unfortunate, therefore, that aesthetic values should be defined in such trivial and specific terms. The results of this test (Table 1.2), nevertheless, indicate certain trends which are of interest in this context.

Table 1.2

Group Under Test	Value						
	THEO.	ECON.	AESTH.	SOC.	POL.	RELIG.	
TYPICAL AMERICANS							
Male:	44	43	35	36	44	37	(Anastasi,
Female:	36	37	43	42	37	44	1961)
ARCHITECTS I	51	28	56	30	40	35	(MacKinnon,
II	48	36	53	30	39	34	1962)
III	47	38	48	29	39	40	

Significantly, all three groups of architects placed aesthetic and theoretical values well above average, economic values well below. One could explain the difference between rational and empirical designers in terms of a conflict between aesthetic values and theoretical. Yet in devising his categories it was not Spranger's intention to suggest that, in any aspect of human affairs, one set of values was in any way 'better' than the others. He saw them in fact as interwoven, each enhanced by interaction with the others. Progress in human affairs depends on just this interaction and where any set of values is missing —one suspects that religious values tend to be weak at the moment—the fullest possible interplay cannot take place and progress tends to be stultified (Spranger, 1928).

So the *Study of Values* indicates very clearly why most of the other tests, in terms of simple dichotomization—creative/non-creative; open-minded/closed-minded; divergent/convergent; tolerant/authoritarian and so on—are over-simplifications. They simply do not help in revealing the incredible richness of attitudes which is evident in the work of creative architects throughout history. The *Study of Values* helps us to understand some of the reasons for conflict between those who think that architecture is simply a matter of value for money and those who think it should enrich human experience: between those who believe that any building outside the fields of housing, hospital design and schools is immoral and anti-social and those who build cathedrals; between those who see the built environment as a device for making men 'better' and those who think of it in abstract mathematical terms. It helps us understand that each of these conflicting attitudes can be held by intelligent and sincere people; none of them is 'right' and none of them is 'wrong'. Each is necessary if architecture is to be developed by the fullest possible interplay of ideas. If it does nothing else, therefore, the *Study of Values* helps us understand that personality is a very complex matter indeed and confirms that the situation in psychological testing generally is far from satisfactory.

It is even less satisfactory when we look at the designer's professional abilities, as distinct from his other personality characteristics. MacKinnon expected his architects to be high in spatial ability, sense of colour, design and so on; but the tests he used in these connexions were, to use Hudson's words again, 'insultingly trivial'. An architect spends a great deal of time, during the act of designing, manipulating three-dimensional entities in many ways. Some architects can visualize 'in their heads' the most complex interlockings of shapes and spaces, others need sketches, and others again use three-dimensional models as spurs to their imagination. Some architects can walk, in their imagination, around buildings which they have not even designed yet. Others visualize an abstraction of the building which possesses its spatial characteristics but has no solidity—a kind of X-ray image. Some think of routes and others of spaces and there is no indication that any of these leads to 'better' architecture than any of the others, but the simplest of them is far more sophisticated than anything the psychologists were able to test.

As we might expect, the architects did score high on geometrical tests. In the *Gottschald Figures Test* for instance (Gottschald, 1926), where the subject has to pick out simple geometric figures from the larger and more complex ones in which they are embedded, the architects' score was the highest of any group. MacKinnon considers it a test of ability to analyse and reorganize spatial patterns but, compared with the meanest exercise in three-dimensional planning, it seems very naïve. A *Mosaic-Construction Test* too seems extraordinarily simple compared with the problems which face the designer every day. In this the subject is presented with a selection of 1-inch squares, in 22 colours, from which he is asked to make an 8-inch × 10-inch mosaic. The mosaic is then rated by a panel of 'experts' for overall artistic merit, good use of colour, good use of form, originality, warmth and pleasingness. From the published examples (MacKinnon, 1962A; Barron, 1958) it seems that a subject scores high on creativity if his mosaic, first of all, is asymmetrical. A large number of colours is favoured too, on the assumption that a creative person will seek richness of effect and can tolerate a degree of complexity which verges almost on chaos.

The Welsh *Figure Preference Test* is based on similar assumptions. The subject is presented with a series of 3-inch × 5-inch cards on which figures are drawn in black ink. Some of these figures are simple and geometric— straight lines, circles, squares, zig-zags. Others are much 'richer'—freehand scribbles often verging on the child-like. As we might expect, creative people tend to prefer the scribbles. Barron first tried them on a group of painters, who described them as vital and dynamic; the painters looked for asymmetry and complexity, and displayed a positive aversion for the simple geometric figures. MacKinnon's creative architects showed very similar tendencies; their mean preference, compared with certain other groups, was as follows: artists 39·1; architects I 37·5; writers 31·5; architects II 29·5; women mathematicians 27·0; architects III 26·1 and non-artists 13·9.

The difficulty with these tests of aesthetic judgements is that they are based very firmly on the aesthetic prejudices of the testers. It is, of course, simply a matter of fashion that asymmetry should be preferred to symmetry, whilst 'overall artistic merit, good use of colour, good use of form, originality, warmth and pleasingness' certainly beg many questions. So, for that matter, does a preference for scribbles over simple geometrical drawings. These tests, therefore, help us very little to understand what the architects' special abilities really are.

On a high-level test of verbal intelligence, however (*Terman's Concept Mastery Test*) (1956), the architects' score was well below that for creative writers; certain groups scored as follows: military officers 60·3; electronics engineers 94·5; undergraduates 101·7; creative architects 113·2; research scientists 118·2; women mathematicians 131·7 and creative writers 156·4. MacKinnon concludes that a certain minimum standard of verbal intelligence is needed which varies between the professions, but above that level increasing intelligence does not indicate increasing creativeness. Indeed he states quite flatly, 'It is just not true that the more intelligent person is necessarily the more creative one.' (1962)

Yet, irrespective of how a designer actually works, there are certain things which clearly he must do. He must take instructions from his client as to what the building is for; he must observe and survey the site to see what shape it is; he must consider what resources are available and decide how they can best be deployed. As a first approximation, therefore, we might say that the architect must be capable of thinking in the following ways:

1. Rational thinking (about the nature of the site, the available resources and so on).
2. Intuitive or creative thinking (about what these results of rational thinking imply for the building form).
3. Value judgements (as to the relative importance of these various and sometimes conflicting factors).
4. Spatial ability,
   and—in order to make their design intentions known to other people—
5. Communication skills.

It so happens that MacKinnon tested his architects for the first three of these activities. In many ways one's personal balance between them determines how one will approach a problem, and they form part of a comprehensive test known as the Myers–Briggs *Type Indicator* (1958).

This is based on certain ideas contained in Jung's influential work on *Psychological Types* (1923) in which he speculates on a possible system of polarities against which personalities can be assessed. Best known of these polarities is his distinction between *extroversion* and *introversion*. An extrovert, by Jung's definition, is one who adapts quickly to his environment, who likes to manipulate objects and makes quick, but haphazard, perceptions. An introvert, on the other hand, is reflective and thoughtful, tending to shyness and mistrusting anything which is unknown; but he wants his own way and will attempt to master a situation. It will not surprise us that over two-thirds of MacKinnon's creative architects were introverts (1962).

Jung distinguishes four fundamental functions of the psyche which he calls sensation, thinking, feeling and intuition. Sensation, as we might expect, includes all perception of the external world by means of the sense organs; thinking is the function of intellectual cognition, and the formation of logical conclusions; feeling, according to Jung, is a function of subjective evaluation; and intuition is perception by way of the unconscious, or the perception of some unconscious content (Jung, 1923). These four categories are elaborated somewhat in the Myers–Briggs test, and expanded into three pairs of polar opposites.

The first of these pairs concerns the individual's propensity, when faced with a new situation, for perceiving or judging. Most people show a marked preference for one of these ways of coping with the situation, and Mac-Kinnon's sympathies are clearly with perceiving. As he says: 'An habitual preference for the judging attitude may lead to some prejudging and in any case, to the living of a life that is controlled, carefully planned and orderly'—

non-creative, in his terms. And he goes on: 'A preference for the perceptive attitude results in a life that is more open to experience, both from within and from without, and characterized by flexibility and spontaneity.' The implications of this are clear and possibly unexpected. If, in a particular circumstance, it is necessary to observe the facts objectively and to give an unprejudiced decision, the judging type will be less able to give it than the perceiving type. The judger will bring his preconceptions to bear, in accordance with the structure which he, personally, has projected on to the world; he will attempt to regulate the new experience against these preconceptions. But the perceiver will be open to the new experience, able to assess it without bias, sensitive to its subtleties and able, therefore, to be much more objective about it. As we might expect, MacKinnon found that 58 per cent of his creative architects were perceptive types and only 40 per cent judging types, whereas 81 per cent of his architects III were judgers and only 17 per cent of them perceivers.

The second preference in the Myers–Briggs scheme contrasts Jung's sensation and intuition. Most people—75 per cent in the United States—concentrate on existing facts as perceived by their senses. The other 25 per cent perceive intuitively; they look for future possibilities, for links and bridges between what is 'there' and what may be generated from it. One would expect the creative architects to be alert to future possibilities, but even MacKinnon was surprised to find that 100 per cent of them perceived in this way. Against this, 84 per cent of his architects II perceived intuitively and only 59 per cent of architects III.

Thirdly in the Myers–Briggs scheme is a contrast between Jung's thinking and feeling. Thinking-judgement, of course, is a matter of logical processes whereas feeling-judgement is subjective and personal. This dichotomy is very close to some of the others we have considered—scientist versus artist and so on. Artists, perhaps, tend to prefer feeling-judgement whereas engineers tend to thinking-judgement. MacKinnon thought of his architects as artist-engineers and he was obviously delighted to find that, on this scale, his architects I and III were each divided, precisely, into 50 per cent for thinking and 50 per cent for feeling.

One suspects that even on this test certain well-known architects would have performed very differently. Mies van der Rohe certainly has expressed preferences for judging, sensing and thinking whereas Wright and Le Corbusier seem much less consistent. We shall return to this point in a moment but, meanwhile, let us look at the question of spatial ability. There is much dispute among psychologists as to whether it is possible to isolate some specific ability, such as spatial ability, and to consider it separately from general intelligence. Many psychologists believe that intelligence *is* a general matter: a person is intelligent or he is not. But others prefer to isolate individual factors in the belief that high performance in one does not necessarily imply, and may inhibit, high performance in another. Spearman (1927) classified a possible range of abilities into the hierarchy shown in Figure 1.1. Whether one agrees with this grouping or not, at least it helps to explain why Mac-Kinnon's creative architects need not be exceptionally high in traditional intelligence tests, which are based almost entirely on verbal/educational factors. It even helps us to understand Plato's prejudice against rude, mechanical devices—again, his intellectually respectable geometer would confine his thought processes to the *V:ed* group; certainly he would not wish to be associated with any kind of *manual* work.

There have been many attempts over the last fifty years to define the nature of this spatial ability. Macfarlane Smith summarizes them. He himself thought of it as a special aptitude which would be manifest in the ability to perceive simple objects, such as milk bottles or Bunsen burners, and to draw

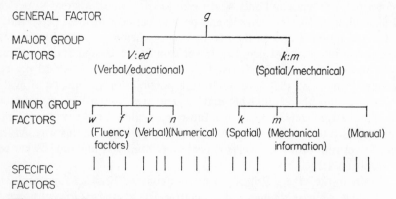

Figure 1.1—Hierarchical structure of human abilities (see also Spearman, 1927, Vernon, 1950, and Macfarlane Smith, 1964)

their shapes accurately, especially in terms of proportion. Michael, Guilford, Fruchter and Zimmerman attempted to synthesize the results of research in this field in 1957, and formed three groups of factors which seemed to have some bearing on the problem. They are:

SR–O—Spatial relations and orientation, which is a matter of looking at a pattern and understanding how the elements within it are arranged. One's own body is used as a frame of reference and as the stimulus pattern is moved into different positions, one understands, by comparison with one's body, that the various elements within the pattern still hold the same relationship with each other.

V—Visualization, a more or less complex pattern consists of certain elements, and one is asked *mentally* to rotate, twist, turn or invert one—or more—of them. The instructions are quite specific and follow a definite sequence. After these various mental manipulations one is expected to recognize the element in its new position, even though its appearance may be greatly changed.

K—Kinaesthetic imagery is a matter of relating the movement of objects to sensations of movement within one's own body. The kinaesthetic sense itself relates to the way in which sensory receptors in the muscles, joints, tendons—or even in the inner ear—are stimulated as one's body moves; kinaesthetic imagery is a matter of relating the movements of *objects* to these personal, bodily sensations. At the simplest level it may be concerned only with discriminating between left and right, with respect to the location of one's own body, but it is significant that when describing man's relationship with the site Le Corbusier wrote in terms of him 'always turning right and left, whirling around.'

It can hardly be doubted that the architect's stock-in-trade consists of the ability to manipulate spaces and volumes in three-dimensional space and the various factors described in this analysis of spatial ability certainly seem to have some bearing on the matter. But the case for high spatial ability as an alternative to verbal or numerical fluency is certainly not proven.

But in all this it almost seems that certain tests were used because they happened to be available and because they were thought, in a very general way, to be appropriate for the testing of designers. Yet no psychologist seems to have found out, or even tried to find out, what the architect actually does when he is designing. Ideally, of course, one would observe the designer 'in the act', monitoring his mental processes and analysing the various sketches, diagrams and other visual material he prepared while he was doing it.

Gordon (1962) describes how a psychoanalyst-inventor was asked to design a new kind of altimeter, monitoring his own thought processes as he did it, by making notes and talking into a wire-recorder. This exceptional individual was able to do what was asked of him very well, but others have found similar tasks extremely difficult. As we might expect, the act of describing what one is doing, while one is actually doing it, tends to interfere with one's performance. As Henry Moore once put it, 'It's like riding a bicycle. Once I stop to think how I'm doing it, I can't do it any more.' Introspection, therefore, is an extremely risky way of analysing the actual process of design.

It would be easier, of course, to take a behaviourist line in such an investigation, in order to observe what the designer can be seen to do—the sources of information he consults, the notes and sketches he produces and so on. Clouzot's film of Picasso in action (1956) indicates a possible approach to such analysis. Picasso works in ink, on translucent paper, which is filmed from behind so that although we do not see the artist's face, or his hands in action, the picture seems to grow, spontaneously, before our eyes. He produces a series of rather trivial sketches and a rather large painting which displeases him so he tackles the same subject again from a different point of view. In almost every case the approach is similar. Picasso starts with a geometrical abstraction consisting either of lines or of areas of colour. Suddenly, the abstract pattern suggests to him (and usually to us at the same moment) some natural object which is then transformed into something else, to which it is analogous. In the simplest case he starts with three circles to which stalks and leaves are added, producing a bunch of flowers. This becomes a waterspout from the nostrils of a rather playful whale. Head and feet are then added to the whale shape, turning it into a cock and now, just as it seems complete, the whole thing is obliterated with opaque colour, leaving certain elements in the surface decoration of the whale-cock's body clear, as the eyes, nose and mouth of a rather sad faun.

In this case it is easy to be seduced, by the richness of the associations which Picasso throws up, into becoming creative oneself in front of his creative act. The stages I have described are clear and unmistakable, but some of the more complex examples in Clouzot's film allow so many interpretations that it is virtually impossible to deduce what was going on inside the 'black box' which is Picasso's brain. And a similar analysis of an architect at work would be even more complex. The nearest equivalent, probably, is the investigation which Livingstone Lowes (1927) undertook into the perceptual origin of two of Coleridge's poems, *The Ancient Mariner* and *Kubla Khan*. Lowes worked his way through Coleridge's notebooks, reading all the books the poet himself had read—accounts of Cook's voyages and so on. He found that, to a remarkable extent, Coleridge's compositional processes consisted of an unconscious combining and rearrangement of the material he had recently read. No such systematic analysis has ever been undertaken of an architect at work although, as we shall see, certain clues of this kind are available in one or two notable cases; but the complexity of such a task would be enormous, especially when (as happens almost always in architecture) other people too are involved in the generation of combinations and the choosing.

Such analyses have been undertaken by Levin, Purcell and Wang, which will be described later, but these are not enough for a generalized description of how the architect works. There are certain things in common, however, between the working methods of Wright, Le Corbusier, Mies van der Rohe and others, as described in Chapter 2, and we can abstract from their accounts the ways of thinking which they seem to have used. These may offer clues as to their particular abilities as architects. Wright and Le Corbusier certainly took great care in observing the site—Wright in terms of its physical structure and climate, Le Corbusier in visual terms as a system of masses with a centre of gravity. Wright, like Mies, then looked at the available resources, in terms of materials, money and techniques of construction, and conducted physical experiments with the last. All three, in various ways, used a *grid* as a means of organizing their plans, and none of them says much about how he investigated the user's needs. Wright, certainly, speaks of a mystical 'ground' to his thinking, concerned with aesthetic and social traditions, and as Banham shows (1969), he cared very greatly for the physical comfort of those who would use his buildings. Le Corbusier's user-needs are a matter of the routes which they will take through his building, and Mies hardly seems to care about them at all. On balance then these psychological analyses have not been particularly helpful, yet they do point the way to some interesting conclusions. Supposing we describe the caricature of a personality which lumps together all the characteristics which have been used to describe the uncreative, authoritarian, convergent, closed-minded schizothyme. Apart from his general problems in matters of human relationships he would have particular problems in design. He would need precise and definite instructions before he could start work at all, and often these are not available. He would believe that there was 'one best way' of solving the problem and he would look for an 'ideal' solution. Above all, he would find it almost impossible to listen with sympathy and understanding to the client's exposition of his needs. In other words, he would impose his ideas on other people, irrespective of what they really wanted, although these ideas in the first place would be derived from some system of authority. He might seek the authority of a group, which would save him the anguish of personal decision, and it would be an exclusive group aimed at keeping other people out. He would tend to be interested in things rather than in people, and in abstract design systems rather than in real buildings. In the act of designing itself he would be unable to tolerate any kind of ambiguity; he would commit himself quickly to a solution or even adopt a preconception, instead of allowing ideas to develop gradually. He would, of course, take a puritanical view of architecture, despising the aesthetic component and concentrating essentially on value for money. However, lastly, according to Smith, he would be very high indeed in spatial ability.

If we draw the opposite caricature—creative, tolerant, divergent, open-minded and cyclothymic—we shall find that he also has problems as a designer. He will be highly individual, to the point of eccentricity, always fighting authority, and so tolerant of ambiguity that he cannot commit himself to anything. He will be able to see all points of view simultaneously, sympathetic to the views of others to such an extent that he has no views of his own, unable to force an idea through and will look for the easy way out. Eclectic, versatile and distrusting systematization of any kind, he will not have the ability to sustain a logical argument, but will be able to generate so many ideas that none of them has any special significance. There is, however, a sinister side to all this: he may tend to treat people as things, and delight in manipulating them. If he finds himself in a group, he may seek to dominate it, over-dramatizing situations and looking for sensory effect to the point of sensuousness. His abilities generally, according to Smith, are more likely to lie in the direction of verbal fluency than in spatial ability.

So, clearly, either extreme will have difficulties as a designer. To summarize these, the convergent architect will tend to formalize a system and to stick to it through thick and thin; he will impose the ideas implied by this system on other people, irrespective of their real needs. On the other hand, the divergent architect will be so sympathetic to other people's views that his work will tend to inconsistency. He will tend to play around with half-baked ideas and to lack the necessary drive to force a conclusion. Few of us, in fact, will match either of these caricatures exactly—we shall find ourselves in some position of mediocrity between them. What we really need, therefore, is some means of transcending personality, of adopting the characteristics of the diverger at certain stages in design, and of the converger at others when this seems more appropriate. One way of achieving this interplay between convergence and divergence might be to bring different personalities together to form some kind of group. But again, we need some mechanism to ensure that the worst features of convergence and divergence do not inhibit the workings of the group. A great deal of thought, in the last few years, has been devoted to devices which will help us do this, under the general heading of systematic design method. It originated anyway in the efforts of certain philosophers, early in this century, to penetrate the mechanisms by which we think in everyday life, as well as in design. However, just to confirm that the two kinds of thinking are involved in any real creative act, let us draw on the experience not of a philosopher but of a poet, Paul Valéry, who understood very clearly the interactions between them:

> 'It takes two to invent anything. The one makes up combinations; the other one chooses, recognises what he wishes and what is important to him in the mass of things which the former has imparted to him. . . . What we call genius is much less the work of the first one than the readiness of the second to grasp the value of what has been laid before him and to choose it.' (quoted Hadamard, 1945)

He is right of course, although we might deplore his use of the word 'invention'—which suggests the making of something out of nothing which, as we shall see, is not possible for the unaided human mind. But Valéry's chooser is a kind of censor, a converger who may or may not recognize a good idea when he sees one. He has much greater power, therefore, than the divergent ideas-generator—if we may so call him—and Valéry does not exaggerate when he describes genius as 'the readiness of the second to grasp the value of what has been laid before him'. If the chooser's work is so important, we should do well to pay particular attention to it, and our problem therefore is much more than one of 'creativity'.

CHAPTER 2

The Architect at Work

Having looked in some detail at what the architect is, or at some of the things psychologists have found him to be, we are now in a position to see what he does, to consider the ways in which he exercises his various abilities. There have been several studies of the architect at work, notably by Levin (1966a, b and c, 1967), Purcell (1971) and Wang (1971), but these have been concentrated on his skills as a decision-maker which, for our present purposes, has certain limitations. All creative people, all professionals, whatever their field of activity, have to make decisions; certain techniques of decision-making may be useful to them all, and we shall consider some of these in Chapter 10. However, we want to concentrate for now on the skills which are unique to the architect as distinct even from other kinds of designers and planners, let alone decision-makers or administrators from even more remote fields. The architect, certainly, will have to exercise skills of locational analysis (putting things in the most appropriate places) but so will town planners and geographers. He will be concerned with structures, servicing and environmental control, but so will several other specialists in the building design team. He will exercise his judgement over matters of cost, but so will the quantity surveyor, over matters even of interior design, which will require from him the skills of the artist. So, if we try to separate out those skills which are unique to the architect, we shall find that they are concerned with spatial ability and, in particular, with his capacity for visualizing, or otherwise generating, the three-dimensional forms of buildings, interior spaces, and the spaces about buildings. It seems to me, after a detailed study, published elsewhere (Broadbent, forthcoming), that architects generally have used four distinct ways of generating three-dimensional form which I have described as pragmatic, iconic, analogic and canonic, in chronological order of application. This is not the place to describe them in detail so I shall summarize their salient features, their historical origins and some of the ways in which they have been used. For the most part my descriptions will be based on archaeological evidence, and this is open to differences of interpretation. These need not distort the classification as a whole, nor is it merely a historical matter. I intend to show its continuing validity, and vitality, in later sections of the book.

Pragmatic Design

The earliest designers seem to have taken a highly practical view of their task, using whatever materials lay to hand, establishing by trial and error what the materials could do and then seeking them out for conscious putting to those uses. There was nothing remarkable certainly about picking up a flint and using it as a tool, except that someone was the first to do it. An ape might have done the same but having used it once, to achieve some immediate objective, the ape would throw it away as being of no further interest (Clark, 1967). Neolithic man learned to recognize that a certain flint could be used as a scraper, another as a chopper, a third as an axe and so on. Not only that; he discovered also that a particular flint would make an even better scraper if it was chipped and shaped. After that it was not just a matter of *finding* tools and weapons by chance, but of looking for suitable stones and working them until they were right.

His approach to building seems to have been similar. Man as we know him emerged about 40,000 years ago, using flint for tools and weapons and living, whenever he could, in the mouths of caves. He was a hunter however and, from time to time, his hunting expeditions took him far away from home. He needed rest and sleep; he had to protect himself from wild animals and, above all, from the elements: so he took to building shelters. Little remains of these shelters, but sites have been excavated in various parts of Europe and various reconstructions have been proposed. Some of these are highly con-jectural—beautiful designs based on rather slender evidence—but A. L. Mongait's reconstructions of mammoth-hunters' tents are reasonably con-vincing, taking into account the evidence of excavations in southern Russia (Mongait, 1961).

The materials available to these early builders appear to have been most unpromising: small stones, some spindly trees and, after that, the bones, tusks and skins of the mammoths, i.e. all that was left after the edible parts had been consumed. The hunters seem to have scratched an oval depression in the ground, some 11 metres long, and to have erected a framework over it consisting of tree-trunks, branches and the mammoth tusks, two of which together could make an effective arch. This was then covered with mammoth skins, weighted down at the perimeter with stones and mammoth bones, thus keeping out the worst of the weather and affording some protection from prowling animals. But the hunters needed more than that: the climate of the steppe could be extremely inhospitable so they built fires inside the tent (three hearths were found) thus effecting a further modification of the physical climate, once the tent itself had kept out the wind and rain, or snow.

A number of essential points emerge from this early building: that the basic reason for building was to modify the given climate as offered by 'wild nature', so that certain human activities (in this case rest and sleep) could be carried out conveniently and in comfort. All buildings, finally, do this—they effect a reconciliation between man's needs and the climate as offered by a particular piece of ground. That is still the fundamental reason for building: the site as offered fails to provide a suitable climate over an adequate part of the year, for the things we want to do.

There is more to it now than modification of the physical climate. The building also, whether we like it or not, will modify, and be modified by, certain cultural climates—social, political, economic, moral, aesthetic and so on. We shall consider these in detail later. So, given this broader concept of climate, the building's purpose *still* is climatic modification.

The mammoth-hunters' tent (Figure 2.1) reveals certain profound truths about the nature of architecture. It also suggests that the first way of achieving

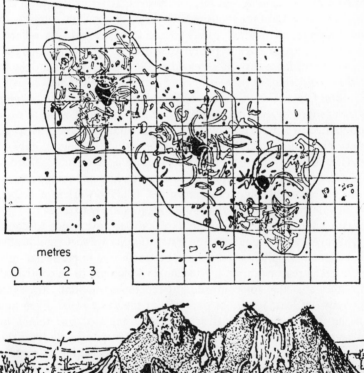

metres

0   1   2   3

Figure 2.1—Mammoth-hunters' tent; upper palaeolithic earth-house from Pushkari near Kiev, *c.* 40,000 years B.C. (from Mongait, 1961). Plan above and reconstruction below

three-dimensional built form was by trial and error, taking the available materials and putting them together in a way which seemed to work. Pragmatic design was the earliest way of building but we still use it in certain circumstances—particularly when we are trying to find the ways in which new materials may be used. For example, so far there is no real theory of air houses. Architects and students in many places have taken sheets of polythene or PVC, welded them together in some dome- or vault-shaped form and inflated them with air pumps. Many of them have discovered by trial and error that, like the mammoth-hunters' tent, the air house needs weighting down at its perimeter if it is not to blow away, or leak.

Once a way of building became established, it was often used in substantially the same form for thousands of years. This is true, certainly, of the mammoth-hunters', tent which as a building form seems to have been used extensively in Europe over a period of some thirty thousand years. The mechanism by which a form is repeated in this way, over great distances in space and long periods in time, is open to dispute. Some archaeologists, notably Gordon Childe (1925), favour a *diffusionist* view that each technique— whether of tool or weapon making, of house building or of making works of art—originated in a particular place, at a particular time and was spread by successive cultural contacts over the earth's surface. Others, notably Levi-Strauss (1963), favour a *structuralist* view that each technique was discovered many times, in many different places, because the human brain, given certain problems to solve with comparable resources, tends to work in characteristic ways which determine the kinds of solutions it is likely to generate.

This is a vital argument and both explanations have much to commend them. However, even if one opts for a structuralist view, it cannot alter the fact that particular building forms have been repeated in particular cultures. There are many reasons for this. The climate which has to be controlled and the resources available for controlling it remain substantially the same for long periods—at least for tribes that stay in the same place. Even nomads tend to have fixed forms for their portable dwellings: one thinks of the Indian's *tepee*, the great black tents of the Arabs and certainly the Eskimo's *igloo*. In the nature of things no historic·igloo survives, but this particular pattern of dwelling seems to have been used by certain Eskimo tribes for their winter quarters over four or five centuries at least. Every member of the tribe knows, or knew, how to build an igloo. He could cut blocks of snow, place them in a circle, often tapered so as to form the basis of a spiral, and then pile other blocks up and over to form a dome. He then filled the gap between blocks with loose snow and the igloo would be complete, affording excellent protection from wind and driving snow. If the igloo was to be used all winter, possibly for family accommodation, then he might line the inside with skins, draped from the snow dome and thus trapping a layer of still air. This effected further climatic modification so that, given sufficient heat-sources in the form of oil lamps and human bodies, internal temperatures of 20°C could be achieved. Illustrations of a snow house, or igloo, are shown in Figure 2.2.

Forde (1934) catalogues vernacular dwelling types from many parts of the world and in each case a particular way of building makes effective use of the

Figure 2.2—Snow house or igloo; Davis Strait (from Boas, 1888)

available resources, in terms of stone, plant or vegetable matter, hair, skin and so on, to effect certain modifications of the given climate. As one might expect, the house-forms in cold climates are designed as far as possible to conserve heat, whilst in warm countries structures tend to be open, with provision for through-draughts and sometimes, as in the case of the black tents, adjustable according to wind direction.

Iconic Design

This match between a climate to be controlled and the resources available for its control would be sufficient justification in itself for the repetition of a house-form once it has been proved to work, but there are other pressures too which lead to conservatism. For one thing, house-form and pattern of life become adjusted to each other. A number of families may cluster and link their igloos together so that social interactions are possible throughout the long winter. In Borneo and in certain parts of Polynesia the whole tribe may live together in a long-house, whereas the black tent of the Arabs is designed with separate accommodation for men and women. There is mutual adaptation, therefore, between house-form and pattern of living, between way of life and house-form. Alexander (1964) dismisses adaptation in this context as 'mere hand waving'. Most westerners, however, would realize its force if they tried living and sharing the established way of life with the inhabitants of a long-house, or even an igloo.

There are other pressures too for retaining an established way of building. A craftsman spends long years acquiring the skills and aptitudes of his craft, learning the nature of his materials, care for his tools and so on (Sturt, 1923). Once he has become a master of his craft these traditional ways will be built deep into his consciousness; he will have acquired patterns of coordination between hand, eye and brain which he will not wish to abandon; his interest will be in passing on these secrets to another generation. Given this tendency for individual crafts to remain fairly constant, there will be strong pressures for the entire pattern of building to remain constant too. There are also cultural reasons as to why a pattern of building should persist. Some tribes have legends which describe the fabled origin of some building form; others have work songs which, as Alexander says (1964), describe the materials one should search for, where to find them, how to shape them, how to put them together and so on, thus representing the first formalized design processes. So again, a way of building is built deep into the tribal consciousness and, because each member of the tribe has a fixed mental image of what a house should be like, we shall call this *iconic* design.

Analogic Design

New words are formed mostly by the use of analogy. If a child knows that the plural of *bean* is *beans* it is logical for him to assume that the plural of *deer* will be *deers*. He has taken a word he knows, a usage with which he is familiar and generated a new word by combining the two. New visual forms frequently arise by analogous processes. Breuil (1952) assumes that the earliest cave painters identified the forms, for example, of bison or deer in stains, projections or recesses in the rock (rather like reading pictures in the fire) and reinforced the outlines of these forms in pigment, thus intensifying their analogic qualities and making them obvious to others. This method of generating new forms does seem fundamental to the human mind. One can support the diffusionists here, and it probably arose spontaneously as a technique in many places. However, its first application to formal architecture, as far as we know, took place in the vast funerary complex which Imhotep is reputed to have designed for King Djoser at Saqqara near Memphis (*c.* 2800 B.C.). Imhotep's task was to provide permanent buildings on an unprecedented scale (Figure 2.3); the only permanent buildings in the Nile Valley up to this time had been *mastaba* tombs of sun-dried brick, flat-topped and with sloping sides, themselves a formal analogy with the heap of stones which burial shafts had come to be covered with—a pragmatic device to prevent the sand blowing away. Houses and other buildings tended to be prefabricated of light timbers, or bundles of reeds smeared in mud and lashed together. Such structures could be taken down and moved easily when the Nile floods were imminent.

Imhotep, therefore, had no precedent for permanent building on this scale and his technique, repeated many times throughout the complex, was to look at existing building forms and carve them on to solid stone. The outer wall of the complex, for instance, is built of limestone blocks, much larger than the bricks of which familiar walls had been built. So on these blocks is carved the jointing pattern of sun-dried bricks. The only way into the complex is through a half-open door, complete in every detail, with boards, hinges and so on, all carved in solid stone. Elsewhere, segmental-headed temples repeat the forms of prefabricated huts, with mud-and-reed columns carved faithfully into stone. The tomb itself was covered by a large square mastaba which was extended several times, both horizontally and vertically, so as to form a substantial pile visible from the exterior. Smaller mastabas were piled on top in diminishing stages thus forming the so-called step pyramid, the first of all pyramids to be built in ancient Egypt.

Imhotep's use of analogy extends from the forms of the buildings them-selves to applied decoration, such as capitals carved in the forms of lotus buds or flowers, crestings in the form of cobra heads and so on. What is not clear, however, is the mechanism by which these analogies were drawn. It is highly unlikely that Imhotep would build, say, a prefabricated hut so that dimen-sions could be transferred directly from it on to the stone copy. It so happens, however, that the first architectural 'drawings' have been found elsewhere at Saqqara. These too are dated as approximately 2800 B.C.; one of the best preserved consists of a limestone chip, an *ostrakon*, some seven inches across, on to which a curve is drawn in ink (Figure 2.4) with vertical lines extending below it and certain figures which can be interpreted as dimensions in the Egyptian system of measurement, cubits, palms and fingers. If one charts a baseline with vertical offsets spaced one cubit apart and dimensioned from

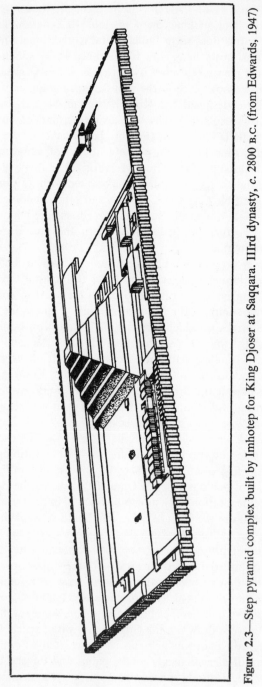

Figure 2.3—Step pyramid complex built by Imhotep for King Djoser at Saqqara. IIIrd dynasty, *c.* 2800 B.C. (from Edwards, 1947)

the baseline, then a curve may be drawn through the points thus plotted similar in form, but some twelve times larger than the curve on the drawing itself. The drawing was actually found near a monumental stone, carved in a saddle-back to the larger curve (Clarke and Engelbach, 1930).

This implies, and the implication is a highly significant one, that instead of starting work immediately, handling real materials in pragmatic or iconic fashion, a *designer* prepared the drawing first as an earnest of his intentions; he may even have tried out several curves in drawn form before choosing one, thus conducting his pragmatic experiments in the form of a simulation or drawn analogue before committing himself to a particular case. However,

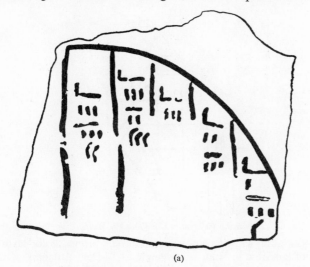

(a)

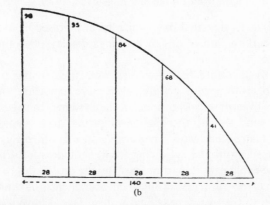

(b

Figure 2.4—Ostrakon (limestone flake) some 180 mm long.
(a) Defining a curve by coordinates. Probably an architect's diagram from Saqqara, IIIrd dynasty, *c.* 2800 B.C. (from Clarke and Engelbach, 1930);
(b) scale drawing of the curve indicated in (a)

once the designer starts thinking and drawing away from the site, several things happen. He becomes interested in the drawing itself as a satisfying object in its own right. Among other things, he has to be sure that it will fit on his limestone chip, papyrus or other available drawing surface, so he begins to draw grids, axes and other devices by which the size and shape of the drawing can be determined *before* he starts the detailed design. In one case, the designer of a landscape scheme, a grove of tamarisk in front of a temple at El-Deir el-Bahari (*c.* 2100 B.C.), became so fascinated by the regularity and symmetry of his grid that he forgot in his enthusiasm that he had encroached on to an adjacent site (Figure 2.5). The grove as actually planted

Photography by Egyptian Expedition, The Metropolitan Museum o, Art.

Figure 2.5—Ostrakon showing landscape architect's proposals for laying out a grove of tamarisk in front of a temple at El-Deir el-Bahari. XIth dynasty, *c.* 2100 B.C. (from Clarke and Engelbach, 1930)

(and excavated) lacks this final row, which he also erased from the drawing, so one of the earliest known design drawings displays also the first architectural mistake.

It seems likely therefore that drawings were used in the translation of known visual forms to new usages and, even more important, that the drawing itself begins to impose conventions on the designer, to suggest order and regularity of a kind which otherwise he might not have envisaged, and to mislead him in many other ways. The curious pose in which Egyptian figures often occur—head in profile, eye facing front, shoulders full frontal, hips in profile—may be explained, in part at least, by the artist's desire to plot what he *knew* to be correct, in terms of linear measurements, of the three-dimensional figure, on to the two-dimensional wall surface. I have used the rather inelegant term *analogue takeover* to describe this phenomenon; similar problems certainly arise in language, where the availability of particular words determines the kinds of thoughts which can be expressed; and whatever design analogues we use, be they drawings, three-dimensional models, computer programmes even, the analogue itself will almost certainly impose its own conventions on our designing and thus distort what we may have intended to do.

Analogic design, with or without the use of design analogues, is still the most potent source of creative ideas in architecture. Frank Lloyd Wright described a number of examples in connexion with his work: water lilies or mushrooms as analogies for the structural units of the Johnson Wax Company's administration building (1936) and Tower (1951); his own hands in prayer for the Unitarian meeting house at Madison, Wisconsin (1951). Le Corbusier also drew an extraordinary range of analogies in the generation of his chapel at Ronchamp (1953), including the shell of a crab. We shall consider these, and other examples of analogy generation in creative architecture, in Chapter 17.

Canonic Design

We have seen already that once the designer prepared drawings before he started work on site, the drawing itself acquired a particular fascination for him; he developed a concern for pattern, for order and regularity, which was often expressed in the form of an overriding grid. Egyptian artists seem to have used grids for other purposes too: networks of fine lines are visible on many hundreds of wall paintings and unfinished carvings. There has been much debate as to the original purpose; some archaeologists believe that they were simply *mises aux carreaux* (grids used in transferring a composition to the wall from an original sketch); or the grids of proportional systems— canonic grids (Figure 2.6).

However, Edgar (1906) observed that they rarely occur in first class work, such as that in the tombs of the kings. The implication here is that first class artists could draw directly on to the wall, but that second raters needed, or their clients insisted on, the support of proportional systems. There is evidence certainly that Egyptian archaeologists of 600 B.C. or so penetrated deep into Djoser's tomb and measured the wall reliefs, deriving from them a proportional system which later came into general use. And this work, presumably, had the authority of Imhotep himself, who by that time had acquired legendary status as, among many other things, the Egyptian god of medicine.

Certainly a proportional system will provide the designer with authority for a great many decisions about the shape of a figure, the size and shape of a façade, a window, a doorway and so on, which otherwise would depend on his personal judgement. Some designers—and it may be a matter of personality—lack confidence in their own ability to make judgements of this kind; they look for the *authority* of a geometric system. This appeal to authority received a massive boost from Greek mathematicians, such as the Pythagoreans (*c.* 550 B.C.), and philosophers, especially Plato (*c.* 428–348 B.C.). Plato, in particular, envisaged a structure for the universe based on the four elements of earth, air, fire and water, each made from regular geometric solids (Figure 2.7) which in their turn were formed from equilateral or isosceles triangles (Figure 2.8). Plato's ideas seem to have found little direct expression in Greek classical architecture largely because he was writing (*c.* 360 B.C.) some 2½ centuries after its conventions had been established in,

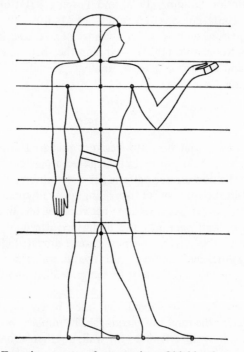

Figure 2.6—Egyptian canon of proportion. Old kingdom version (after Lepsius—*Denkmäler aus Ägypten und Äthiopen*, Berlin, 1849)

say, the archaic Doric temple (*c.* 600 B.C.). The orders themselves implied a canonic system, with their fixed proportional relationships between column diameter, height, spacing and so on.

Curiously enough, Plato's geometry acquired particular importance for architecture during the middle ages when, as Frankl shows (1946), it formed the means whereby the three-dimensional forms of the great cathedrals were generated from the plan. Morgan (1961) describes further applications in his *Canonic design in English mediaeval architecture*, whilst Wittkower (1962) has described *Architectural Principles in the Age of Humanism* (the Renaissance) almost entirely in canonic terms. I have suggested elsewhere that many

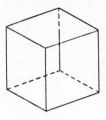 THE CUBE
formed of 6 squares
(24 isosceles triangles)
representing the
element EARTH

 THE TETRAHEDRON
formed of 4 equilateral
triangles representing the
element FIRE

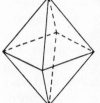 THE OCTAHEDRON
formed of 8
equilateral triangles
representing the
element AIR

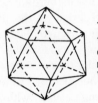 THE ICOSAHEDRON
formed of 18
equilateral triangles
representing the element
WATER

Figure 2.7—Plato's four primary bodies

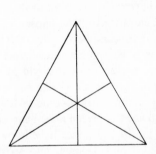

Plato's tetrahedron, octahedron
and dodecahedron are formed
from equilateral triangles. The
60° angle of medieval ad
triangulorum proportion derives
from these.

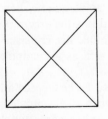

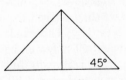

Plato's cube is formed from
isosceles triangles. The 45°
angle of medieval ad
quadratum proportion derives
from these.

Figure 2.8—Plato's derivation of the triangle and square which form the
faces of his primary bodies from the 60° and 45° triangle respectively

people, consciously or not, seem to define architecture as building which shows evidence of canonic proportional systems in its design. Certainly, enthusiasm for this approach has by no means abated, as the current interest in modular systems, dimensional coordination and systems building demonstrates.

These, then, are the four basic ways of designing, or types of design, in sequence of their origin. This chronology also implies an increasing sophistication, with pragmatic design as the most primitive way of designing and canonic as the most intellectual. That is true, but it does not mean that the later ways of designing superseded the earlier ones or that each was used exclusively at a particular time. An extensive survey (Broadbent, forthcoming) suggests that throughout recorded history creative architects have used them in combination, although usually with a certain emphasis on one or other of them.

One can infer this from their work but it can be misleading. Given, say, an enthusiasm for canonic systems, one can *prove* that one's chosen canon was used in the design of the Parthenon, of Chartres Cathedral or of the Barcelona Pavilion, by taking plans, sections and elevations of the chosen example(s) and plotting one's proportional grid and/or canonic diagonal across them (Scholfield, 1958 and bibliography). It may be necessary to distort the odd detail, thicken up a line here and there or even draw the grid at different scales, but if such adjustments are applied intelligently, one can make the salient features of almost any building fit almost any canonic system.

It is equally easy to draw analogies, to say that Wren *must* have known of St. Peter's when he designed St. Paul's, that Wright *must* have known about Japanese architecture when he designed Unity Temple, and so on. It is tempting, in other words, to see visual analogies where analogies need not exist, but the converse is also true. Many architects resent this drawing of analogies especially when one refers to other buildings in describing their work. They seem to believe that, somehow, this diminishes their 'originality', even though (as we shall see in Chapter 16) analogy generation is the most potent form of creativity. Thousands of examples show, however, that although the analogy itself may well be trivial it is the architect's handling of it, playing with it to realize its full potential, his criticism and possible abandonment of it, which reveal his true skill as a manipulator of three-dimensional form.

At this stage, therefore, we shall have to eschew speculation; we shall credit the architect with analogy generation, canonic manipulation and so on, only where he personally has admitted it. In other words, we shall appeal to accounts by architects themselves of their actions in design. Many such accounts exist: I have analysed examples by Vitruvius, by mediaeval designers such as Suger of St. Denis, Villard d'Honnecourt, Roriczer (Figure

2.9), the Milan Cathedral architects; by Renaissance architects such as Brunelleschi, Alberti and Palladio; and by twentieth century architects including Aalto, Gropius, Mendelssohn, Mies, Nervi and Neutra, not to mention the most prolific of all, Frank Lloyd Wright and Le Corbusier (Broadbent, forthcoming). Whilst the terminology varies greatly from one architect to another, and from one account to another, the devices they used in the generation of three-dimensional form can all be described in terms of pragmatic, iconic, analogic or canonic design.

Obviously there are difficulties in using such accounts. They vary in depth,

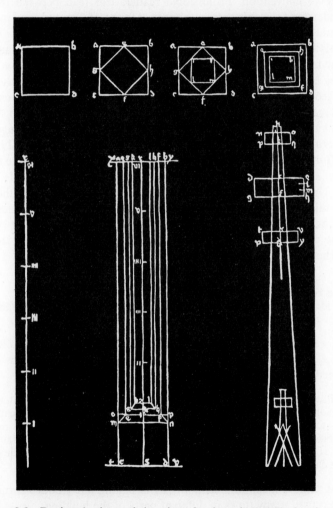

Figure 2.9—Roriczer's plan and elevation of a pinnacle (1486?) showing the method of halving the area of a square from Plato's *Meno*

purpose, clarity and even in honesty. Some of them are little more than fiction, devised for expedient reasons. Many are post-rationalizations—descriptions of events in ordered sequence which can have little to do with what actually happened during the process of designing, intended merely to justify the architect's decisions in reaching a final design. In this respect they seem very like those scientific papers which also, as Watson points out (1968), consist of polite fictions from which personal animosities, chance encounters and happy accidents have all been eliminated, thus giving the impression of a logical, ordered sequence of events which the scientific community accepts as a matter of convention. Professional readers can read between the lines. They understand the conventions, approved forms of discourse and methodologies, and thus they are aware of the subtler implications. My four types of design also offer a set of primitive conventions against which we can understand the finer points (unstated in these accounts) of designing. I have chosen examples by Frank Lloyd Wright and Le Corbusier to illustrate their uses, on the grounds that their accounts will be familiar already to most architectural readers.

Wright described his approach to the design of several buildings in his *Autobiography* (1937) with particular reference to Unity Temple (1911), the Larkin Building (1904) and the Imperial Hotel, Tokyo (1915–22). He brought a particular preconception to bear on the design of Unity Temple (Figure 2.10), a Unitarian church, so that his first step was to persuade the building committee that they needed a *room* in which men could meet rather than a conventional church with steeple, a puny 'finger' pointing on high, which he considered a rather sentimental insult to God. Having thus persuaded them, Wright started work immediately:

'That ROOM; it began to be that same night.
Enter the realm of architectural ideas.
The first idea—to keep a noble ROOM in mind, and let the room shape the whole edifice, let the room inside be the architecture outside.'

There was, however, one very practical constraint. The whole building, to 'church' 400 people, was to cost only $45,000 and this, in Wright's mind, determined his choice of material, concrete, which was cheap.

'. . . . But even concrete . . . meant wood "forms" and some other material than concrete for the outside facing . . . Plastering the outside would be cheaper than brick or stone but wouldn't stick to concrete in our climate. Why not make the wooden boxes or forms so that concrete could be cast in them as separate blocks and masses . . . And the block-masses be left as themselves with no "facing". That would be cheap and permanent.'

He could achieve maximum economy by designing one wooden form which could be reused many times in different parts of the building:

'Therefore a building all four sides alike looked like the thing. This, in simplest

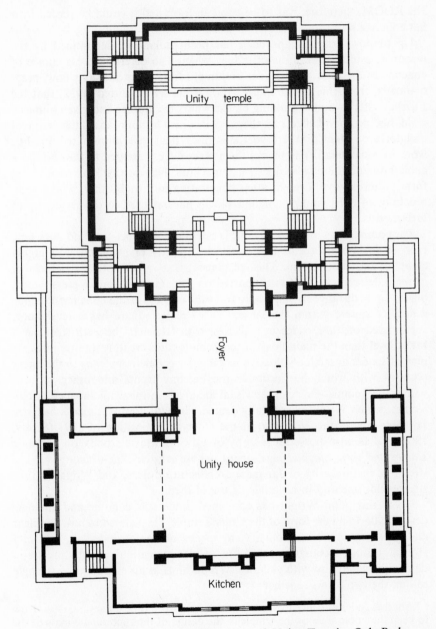

Unity temple

Foyer

Unity house

Kitchen

Figure 2.10—Frank Lloyd Wright; plan of Unity Temple, Oak Park, Chicago 1911

terms, meant a building square on plan. That would make the temple a cube, a noble form.'

His ROOM, therefore, was to be cubic in form and it could be roofed by a flat concrete slab.

Up to now Wright's approach has been pragmatic, determined by the resources available in terms of money which also determined his choice of concrete as the basic material for building. Many other decisions flow, pragmatically, from this initial choice. Wright himself admitted (1932) that the Froebel 'gifts', wooden building blocks which his mother had given him as a child, had profound effects on the ways in which he approached the design of architecture. MacCormac (1968) describes their relationship to Wright's work in some detail. The blocks themselves were presented to the child in a cubic box and there were rules for unpacking them so that square or cruciform patterns were formed, often penetrating into each other, whilst combinations of cubic and rectangular blocks naturally led to the setting up of tartan grids.

The composition of Unity Temple is essentially Froebel-like, and the whole exercise for Wright seems to have been a matter of geometry in a highly complex and subtle form. This, of course, is a rather specialized form of canonic design. The roof is supported on four massive square piers which, placed some distance in diagonally from the corners of the cube itself, define a smaller square within the larger. This smaller square has a level floor, surrounded on three sides by galleries, with 'cloisters' beneath them, at a lower level than the main floor of the Temple, thus creating a fairly intricate play of spaces in section. Wright's rectangular geometry extends to the linear patterns with which he decorates the balcony fronts and other surfaces within the Temple. One can see visual analogies in this with Japanese architecture, which Wright incidentally denied. He had, however, seen a half-size Japanese house, the *Ho-o-den*, at the Chicago Exposition of 1893 (Scully, 1961) and he also possessed a copy of Edward Morse's book on *Japanese Homes and their Surroundings* (1886), whose scratchy line-drawings tend to stress the rectilinearity of Japanese architectural forms, and Wright in turn stresses this linearity in his analogic use of them.

Up to this point Wright has combined pragmatic, canonic and analogic design in deciding the form of the Unity Temple. He planned to link this clear and consistent piece of geometry, by means of an entrance hall, to Unity House—a long, rectangular room for 'secular recreation', equally precise in its geometry and also with galleries. Wright hints at his exasperating struggle to link the two forms together:

'Another series of concentrations—lasting hours at a time for several days. How to keep the noble scale of the temple in the design of the subordinate mass of the secular hall and not falsify the function of that noble mass? . . . some minor concordance takes more time, taxes concentration more than all besides. To vex the architect, this minor element becomes a major problem. How many schemes have I thrown away because some minor feature would not come true to form.

'Thirty-four studies were necessary to arrive at this as it is now seen. . . . The fruit of similar struggles to perfect them all as organic entities—I wish I had kept.'

Such struggles are the substance of any creative work, whether in architecture, painting, sculpture, music, poetry or even the writing of prose. One *knows* that somewhere, deep within the mass of one's disparate and unorganized material and inherent within it are organizing principles—perhaps a single structure—against which the whole can be organized. One searches for that structure, probes, tests, tries out different possibilities; one broods, worries, loses sleep until finally the principles are discovered and the structure is revealed. The idea of such a struggle, I suspect, would be unintelligible to anyone who had no experience of real creative work; it extends far beyond the facile generation of 'creative' idea. It might consist of several organizing principles subsumed within an overriding structure; in the case of Unity Temple, Wright's concept of a cube and the rectangular geometry thus generated, proved extremely fruitful. His problem after that was to bring the Temple itself and Unity House, products of different organizing principles, within the same structure, thus achieving consistency between the two disparate parts of his building.

Wright seems to have had a similar struggle with the Larkin Building. According to his *Autobiography*, his original design consisted of a central open well with a staircase and surrounding corridors—an analogy almost with traditional preaching-house forms, although the Larkin Building itself pre-dates Unity Temple by seven years. The building also contained a system of ducts for ventilation and other services, but these were related rather awkwardly to the building structure. Even so, this rather unsatisfactory design was taken to the stage of a plaster model, for submission to the client, before Wright suddenly realized that staircases and ducts could be much better integrated by shifting them both to the corner of the building and wrapping one around the other, thus achieving a true integration of structure and services. One might describe this as the pragmatic manipulation of forms.

Wright's account of the Imperial Hotel in Tokyo begins with a more general question as to what, in the design of any building, comes first. He answers himself as follows:

'The ground, doesn't it. The nature of the site, of the soil, of the climate comes first. Next what materials are available in the circumstances—money being one of them—with which to build? Wood, stone, brick or synthetics? Next, what labor, or means of power, is available in the circumstances? Manual, machine, or both?' (Wright, 1937)

Again, then, it is a thoroughly pragmatic approach. Having marshalled his resources he comes 'well in toward the processes of thought that properly employ science in the erection of an organic building', but this is not enough;

he also looks for an element of creation, of 'inspiration', which is to give life
to the whole. So:

'We start with the ground.
This is rock and *humus*. A building is planted there to survive the elements. . . . the
ground already has form. Why not begin to give at once by accepting that? Why
not give by accepting the gifts of nature?
Is the ground a parcel of prairie, square and flat?
Is the ground sunny or the shaded slope of some hill, high or low, bare or wooded,
triangular or square?
Has the site features, trees, rocks, streams, or a visible trend of some kind?
Has it some fault or a special virtue, or several?' (Wright, 1937)

So, essentially, the site itself is the starting point of design. In the case of the
Imperial Hotel the site was in the middle of Tokyo, across the park from
the Imperial Palace; it was 500 feet by 300 feet, 'composed of sixty feet of
liquid mud overlaid by eight feet of filled soil'. In other words, he was building on a swamp; but Wright took advantage of this to accommodate another
feature of the site: it was subject to earthquakes and early on, therefore, he
decided that his building should float on the mud, 'as a battleship floats on
salt water', which would cushion it from earthquake shocks. In order to float
it must be light and it must have 'tenuity' so this, together with a need for
fire-resistance, determined the materials—steel and concrete for the foundations, a light, workable lava called 'oya' for the walls, and a copper-covered
roof.

Wright spent a year acquiring the necessary data and testing a flexible
foundation, formed of eight-foot pins of concrete, two feet apart, thus setting
up a canonic grid on which the structure and services were planned. As for
the brief to which he worked, the hotel itself was required because western
visitors to Japan found it difficult to 'live on the floor' as the Japanese did and,
for social reasons, they could not be entertained in Japanese homes. But
Wright saw the profound aesthetic traditions of Japan as part of his 'ground';
he could draw analogies with Japanese forms: 'I wanted to show the Japanese
how their own conservation of space and the soul of their own religion,
Shinto . . . might, in the use of all materials, take place as effectively for them
indoors in sound masonry construction when on their feet, as it had taken
place for them when they were down upon their knees in their own inspired
carpentry' (Wright, 1937). He intended to show how the services could be
built in (plumbing, electrical and heating) without violating the architectural
qualities of the spaces he was making: 'I intended to make all these appurten-
ance systems a practical and aesthetic part of the building itself.'

To ensure stability in the frequent earthquakes, he decided that each floor-
slab should be cantilevered from a central support instead of being supported
at its edges: 'So the cantilever became the principal feature of the structure
and a great factor in shaping its forms throughout as the floor-slabs came

through the walls and extended into various balconies and overhangs.'
Because tradition was also part of his 'ground', Wright decided that the
building was 'going native'; it would have to be designed so that it could be
done better by hand methods than by machinery. The flat planes and straight
lines which he had used in America would have to be modified. During the
process of building he learned a great deal from the Japanese craftsmen;
preconceived details were modified to suit their methods of working. So
Wright's ideal of an 'organic' architecture was realized, or at least realized in
part.

Le Corbusier's generalized account of his design process occurs in *Vers une
architecture* (1923); I have retained the original title because Etchell's translation as *Towards a new architecture* (1927) is notoriously misleading. So, for
that matter, is his use of the word 'axis' for Le Corbusier's *axe*. To English-
speaking readers this suggests the axis of Beaux Arts planning, which Le
Corbusier described as 'an architectural calamity'. It is quite clear from the
context that he had in mind the 'axis' which a person forms for himself in the
act of moving from place to place; I shall use the word *route* for Le Corbusier's *axe*. He writes:

'A route is perhaps the first manifestation of mankind, it is the medium of every
human act. The toddling child sets out a route, man striving in the tempest of life
traces a route for himself. To establish order is to start work. Architecture is based
on routes.
   Arrangement is the hierarchy of routes, therefore it is the hierarchy of aims, the
classification of intentions.
   Therefore the architect assigns objectives to his routes. These focal points are
the wall (solid, sensory stimulus), or light, space (also sensory stimulus).'

As we might expect, where the focus of a route is to be a wall, then that wall
is curved to provide a more varied sensory stimulus.

Le Corbusier even describes a complete design process starting with the plan:

'A plan is to some extent and in some ways the concentrated essence, like an
analytical table of contents. It contains, in a form so concentrated that it seems
crystal clear, like a figure in geometry, an enormous quantity of ideas and a motive
power.
   Right from the start, the plan implies methods of construction . . . .But keeping
strictly to the question of architecture. . . a plan proceeds from *inside to outside*,
for a house or a palace is an organism comparable to every living thing. I shall
speak of the architectural *elements* of the interior, I shall pass on to arrangement.'

Sometimes Le Corbusier walked on to the site which, as he says, is never seen
in bird's-eye view like a drawing-board plan, but from eye-level, by a man
standing on the ground. Nor is his vision static. His eyes are always on the
move and he too is by no means static; he moves around from left to right,
sometimes turning right round. Walking across the site:

'He is interested in everything, by the centre of gravity of the site. In a flash, the
problem extends itself into the environment. Neighbouring houses, distant or

nearby mountains, the high or low horizon, these are formidable masses, which take account according to their cubic volume.'

Their apparent mass varies according to what they are made of:

'... the elements of the site take effect by virtue of their cubic volume, the density and quality of their materials, each carrying well-defined and different sensations (wood, marble, tree, grass, blue horizons, near or distant sea or sky). The elements of the site rear up like the walls of a room, decked out in the power of their cubic coefficient, stratification, material and so on. Walls and light, light or shadow, sad, gay, serene and so on. These are the elements we have to compose with.'

If one is to design so as to fit properly into the context, one must think of the exterior of the building as an interior of the site.

So finally, having worked out the plan on the basis of circulation patterns and having determined the relationship between the building and its environment, comes the moment of synthesis. For the plan is a plan of battle:

'The battle follows, and it is the great moment. Battle is joined with the impact of masses in space and the morale of the troops derives from the sheaf of preconceptions and the driving intention. Nothing exists without a good plan, everything is fragile, and cannot endure, everything is mean, even under a clutter of opulence.'

Perhaps the most controversial statement here is that the designer must have a 'sheaf of preconceptions' to act as a driving force in the act of designing, a view which he shared with Wright. Yet Le Corbusier himself habitually showed the use of such preconceptions; one of his last works, the church at Firminy, is based on a preconception dating from over thirty years earlier, of a centralized volume some three times higher than its width (Mills, 1964).

In the 1920s, however, his preconceptions normally took the shape of a proportional grid, formed of the 'regulating lines' to which he attached so much importance. He had already put such lines to use in his Purist painting, and in *Vers une Architecture* he describes their application in building:

'In order to build well, and distribute your efforts to advantage, in order to obtain solidity and utility in the work, units of measure are the first condition of all. The builder takes as his measure what is easiest and most constant, the tool that he is least likely to lose, his pace, his elbow, his finger.'

By thus imposing a geometrical order, the builder makes clear that his work is the result of human cerebration, 'For all around him, the forest is in disorder with its creepers, its briars and the tree trunks, which impede him and paralyse his efforts.' It has a further effect too: 'By imposing the order of his foot or his arm, he has created a unit which regulates the whole work; and this work is on his own scale, to his own proportion, comfortable to him, *to his measure*. It is on the human *scale*. It is in harmony with him; that is the main point.' His plan, therefore, is going to be based on a canonic proportional system. There is more to it than that, however; he also has structural reasons for designing in this way, resulting from certain preconceptions which he developed during the 1914 war.

During the early months of the war, there had been much devastation of villages in Flanders and the so-called *Dom-ino* house was intended to provide a rapid means of reconstruction. Le Corbusier argued that as far as possible rubble and material from ruins should be re-used, stones calcined by fire or briquettes made from the rubble and other building waste. As one could not be certain of their bearing capacity some means must be found to support the floors independently of the walls. Drawing on his experience with Perret, he

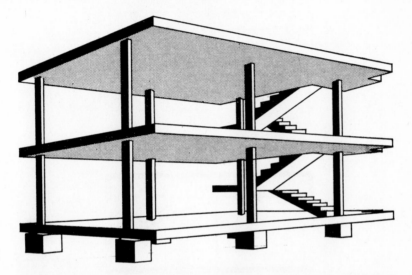

Figure 2.11—Le Corbusier's *Dom-ino* house form in which reinforced concrete floor-slabs are supported on reinforced concrete columns, with cantilevered stairs, 1914 (adapted from Le Corbusier, 1929)

adopted a proprietary method for his *Dom-ino* skeleton (Figure 2.11), consisting of concrete posts supporting concrete floors. These were formed of T-beams, with hollow tiles as permanent shuttering and, most important of all, top and bottom surfaces of the floors would be perfectly smooth with no projecting beams or protrusions of any kind. Given this basic structure, walls could run anywhere, in any suitable material, independently of any supporting function. As Le Corbusier says:

'One had therefore a structural system—skeleton—completely independent of the functions of the house plan. This skeleton simply carries the floor and the stair-case. It is made of standard elements, combinable with each other, which permits great diversity in the grouping of houses.'

It was of course a pragmatic decision, determined by the materials and methods of construction. As for detailed planning:

'Windows and doors must have their dimensions corrected; carriages, limousines have proved to us that man can pass through very restricted openings and that one must calculate the position to a square centimetre; it is criminal to build W.C.s of four square metres.'

So he started to design much smaller ones. In one version of the Citrohan house (1922) the water closet is placed in a tiny curved compartment placed diagonally in one corner of the building, and contained within the bathroom (Figure 2.12). The bath too is located diagonally, and the wall against which

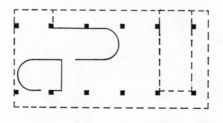

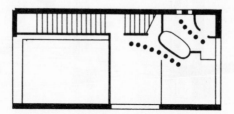

Figure 2.12—Le Corbusier, Citrohan house-type, 1922–27. Supported on concrete *pilotis* with freely curved walls at ground level and a 'bath wall' at second floor (adapted from Le Corbusier, 1929)

it is placed wraps round its curved ends. This device, diagonally or straight, which we might call the *bath wall*, was to become one of Le Corbusier's favourites in planning. It occurs, for instance, in the villa at Vaucresson (1922) which otherwise is a curious attempt to break away from symmetry. The Artist's House project of 1922 contains another characteristic device; the dog-leg staircase with a semicircular landing which is used here for both internal and external effect; we shall call this an *apsidal staircase*. This was actually used in the Ozenfant house (1922) where, on the mezzanine floor at least, it is reflected by a similar curve on the landing (Figure 2.13). The water closet here is contained in a tiny semicircular apse off the bathroom and the bathroom itself is placed in the external angle of a larger L-shaped room. Le

Corbusier curves the internal angle of this L in a quadrant so that its two arms are connected again. An equally difficult planning problem arose in some of the houses at Pessac (1925) where a small bedroom in the corner of a large one meant that the latter had to be approached through a narrow corridor (Figure 2.14). In other words, Le Corbusier devised a set of planning icons—fixed forms—which he could bring to bear on the design of his later buildings

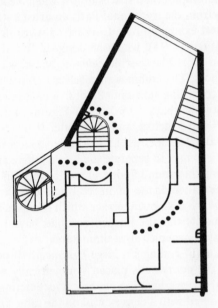

Figure 2.13—Le Corbusier, Ozenfant house, Paris 1922, showing use of 'free' curved walls to facilitate circulation and an 'apsidal' staircase to overcome certain planning problems (adapted from Le Corbusier, 1929)

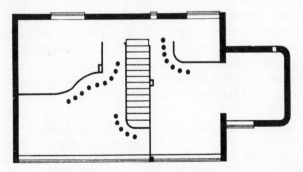

Figure 2.14—Le Corbusier, house at Pessac (1925), third floor plan showing free curves, including a 'grand piano' wall to improve circulation (adapted from Le Corbusier, 1929)

to be used in conjunction with his structural (pragmatic) preconception (the *Dom-ino* shell), and his canonic planning grid. Within this grid he threaded the route which a person might take in moving into and through the building. Salient points on the route were marked by incidents—walls or other devices to indicate changes of direction—whose curves, on the whole, were devised from his planning icons. Whenever possible, he liked to incorporate the three-dimensional relationship of high spaces to low which he knew from the work of Loos, and also from the traditional Parisian artist's studio.

Perhaps the finest example of Le Corbusier's work in this manner is the villa at Garches (Figure 2.15), which he designed for Michael Stein (1927). Structurally, at least, it is a large-scale *Dom-ino* house, with concrete columns and hollow tile floors. The columns themselves are arranged according to a modular pattern, consisting substantially of five bays in each direction. If we number the longitudinal bays 1 to 5, as in Figure 2.15(a), they are respectively 5, 2·5, 5, 2·5 and 5 metres, and if we letter them A to E laterally, they read 1·25, 4, 3, 4 and 1·25 metres. Le Corbusier relates these to the Golden Section, which he also uses to generate the height; there are four layers in his 'sandwich' including the ground floor and roof terrace. In the original design, which has now been altered, the main reception areas are contained on the first floor, one of which is an open terrace which occupies bays 4, 5: C, D and E. Diagonally opposite this the kitchen occupies bays 1: A B, and C. The rest of this first bay is occupied by a dining area.

The ground floor (b) contains a large entrance hall occupying bays 3, 4 and 5: B and C; the doorway is placed symmetrically within bay 4 and is protected by a large, overhanging canopy. On entering, however, one is immediately confronted with a convex wall on the same axis—Le Corbusier's first focal point—but apart from the on-bay columns, there is no further indication of symmetry. There is a piano-shaped opening to the first floor over one's left shoulder, and a wall splays diagonally from the left towards the convex wall one faces. These devices serve to deflect one towards the staircase which rises to one's right, with an apsidal landing halfway up. One arrives at the first floor (c) in the library, passing the ends of low, parallel bookshelves, and is deflected by the balustrade of the piano-shaped opening towards the main living area, which occupies bays 2, 3: C, D and E. Diagonally across from this one is confronted again by a convex curve, which screens the dining area from the rest.

Figure 2.15—Le Corbusier, Villa Stein at Garches (actually Vaucresson) 1927, showing use of *Dom-ino* construction (pragmatic design) and a canonic planning grid (a) through which *routes* are plotted from the ground floor entrance (b) to the first floor reception area and dining space (c). Le Corbusier also makes iconic use of features from earlier designs such as the apsidal staircase and, on the upper floors, bath walls, grand piano walls and so on (adapted from Le Corbusier, 1929)

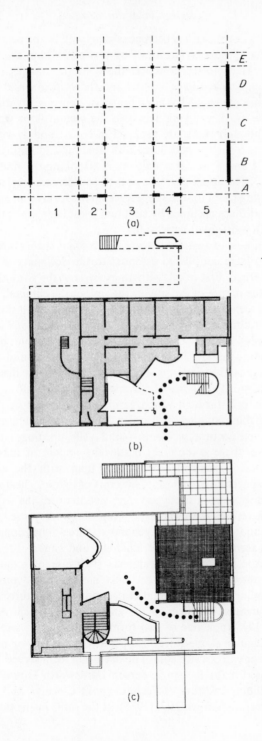

(a)

(b)

(c)

So far then, Le Corbusier has been consistent with his principles; the house forms a sequence of spaces, strung along a route, within the confines of a regulating grid. Henceforth, however, the concept changes. The house is divided, virtually, between bays 3 and 4 and the vertical circulation depends on an apsidal staircase which has risen for service purposes, within bays 2 and 3. This now rises further, giving access to the second floor where the main bedrooms and boudoir suites are grouped in bays 1 and 3, with bathrooms between. There is a further bedroom, with boudoir and bathroom, over the library in bays 4 and 5; it has a balcony overlooking the first floor terrace occupying bay *C*. The apsed staircase rises to roof terrace level and axial with it there is a dressing room for the sun terrace, in the form of an apsed hammerhead. Bays *A* and *B* are occupied by staff and guest bedrooms; the latter have a bathroom with a diagonal bath wall.

Let us attempt now to abstract from these accounts the features which their authors seem to have considered essential to the designing of architecture. Both seem concerned, first of all, with an analysis of the site—the ground, as Wright put it, 'the nature of the site, of the soil, of the climate'. Le Corbusier too looks for its 'centre of gravity'. This preoccupation with site is confirmed by accounts of Aalto and Mendelssohn in action (Fleig, 1963 and Whittick, 1940, respectively). Next Wright considers the available materials and resources, including money, forms of labour, equipment and so on, whilst Le Corbusier takes the *Dom-ino* frame as given. They display different kinds of pragmatism. The choice of a frame construction allows Le Corbusier to use a canonic grid through which various routes must be plotted as the means of establishing architectural order. These routes determine the positions of certain architectural incidents—solid walls, openings and so on—and finally, of course, there is the great battle, the impact of masses in space. Wright seems less concerned with routes than with the environmental qualities of the spaces he is enclosing, in terms of lighting, heating and so on, and with the integration of these servicing systems with the structure itself.

It is clear, therefore, that whatever terminology they used, the ways in which Wright and Le Corbusier generated three-dimensional forms can be described in terms of pragmatic, analogic and canonic design although as one might expect of *creative* architects their use of iconic (repetitive) forms was not very great. Others certainly have repeated *their* forms but, among the founding-fathers of twentieth century architecture, Mies van der Rohe had the greatest predilection for an iconic approach. Almost all his buildings after 1945 took one of two forms, both built of steel and glass—the open, rectangular single-storey hall, and the square, or nearly square, multi-storey tower with service core. The open-hall form served him for many purposes. He used it for the single-person Farnsworth House (1950), for a chapel at the Illinois Institute of Technology in Chicago, and for an entire school of architecture, Crown Hall (1955), at the same institution. The multi-

storey tower served him for apartments (Lake Shore Drive, Chicago) and for
offices (the Seagram Building, New York, 1958). In each case, the 'fit' of
form to function is minimal for, as Mies himself said (1960), functions may
change rapidly and a neutral form can be adapted to many purposes.

Mies's iconic forms were derived in the first place by pragmatic methods.
He spent some time in the early 1920s experimenting with various materials—
brick, concrete, glass and so on. Sometimes his experiments were genuinely
pragmatic; in 1919 he designed an office building for the Friedrichstrasse in
Berlin, by making most of it in thin strips of glass pressed end on into plasticine at slight angles to each other, thus presenting a faceted form, 'to avoid
the monotony of over-large glass surfaces'. In other cases, when he was
designing in concrete or brick, he understood the nature of his materials so
well that there was no need for direct experiment. The form of his Concrete
Office Building (1922) is dictated directly by the materials; given concrete
columns, for instance, it is reasonable to place them in a regular (canonic)
grid; given concrete floor slabs, it is reasonable to cantilever them beyond the
outer row of columns, but their edges will need stiffening so it is reasonable
to turn them up as edge beams.

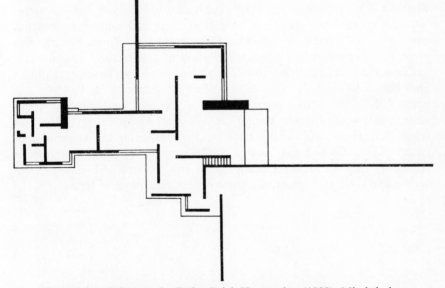

Figure 2.16—Mies van der Rohe, Brick House plan (1923). Mies' designs
of this period represent a pragmatic attempt to let the materials generate
the form. In this case a *mass* material, brick, is used to make space-
dividing planes—one of the clearest attempts in the history of architecture
to use planar construction. The house designs which Mies actually realized
in this way lack the abstract clarity of his plans because the planes of
brickwork carry through, above and below the windows; thus the distinction between plane and opening is confused (after Johnson, 1945)

The Brick House project of 1923 (Figure 2.16) is equally true to its material. Given the rectangular form of bricks, it is reasonable to use them in building walls—straight planes of material meeting in T- or L-shaped junctions. His drawings for this project show every brick in place, with meticulous attention to detail as to how they should be bonded at the corners.

But eventually Mies chose steel and glass as his ideal building materials, on the grounds that as production techniques were developed so these materials, above all, would become increasingly cheap. Yet the actual details of their use, the ways in which they were jointed, details of corners and so on were worked out afresh for each project, often through the use of full- or half-scale models—a thoroughly pragmatic approach. But he also used a canonic approach. As he says in the case of the IIT campus:

'. . . I put a grid over the whole campus; that was more a mechanical help. *After that we had not to speculate where we put our columns.* We put our columns on the crossing points of the grid, all the way through . . .' (Mies, 1960) (my italics)

which is probably the most succinct apologia for a canonic approach in the entire history of architecture.

It should be clear then that whatever else they did in the act of designing, whatever other decisions they made, the founding fathers of modern architecture combined the pragmatic, iconic, analogic and canonic approaches whenever they needed to generate three-dimensional form. Clearly this generation of form is by no means the whole of architectural design, but it has been the least susceptible to analysis which is why we have concentrated on it here. Obviously the form itself is of no significance if the building as a whole fails to satisfy user-needs in terms of planning, space standards, environmental control, costs and so on. We shall be concerned with these issues throughout much of this book but, in considering the welter of analytical technique which has become available to us, we ought to remember constantly that the architect cannot solve any problem of building design without, in some way, generating three-dimensional physical forms.

CHAPTER 3

New Attitudes to Design

If pragmatic, iconic, analogic and canonic design between them can account for all the ways in which architects have generated the three-dimensional forms of buildings in the past, why should we look for new ways of designing? The obvious answer is that whilst the generation of form is important, indeed vital, there is far more to the design of architecture than that. We saw in the last chapter that locational analysis (putting things in their proper places), structures, services and environmental control, cost analysis and so on, are essential functions in the design of architecture. They too have to be taken into account. All buildings, as we have seen, control the physical environment, however crudely they do it; all buildings have a plan form which determines the location of things; all buildings have a structure of some kind; all buildings cost money, or use other resources. There is nothing new in this; it has been true of all buildings throughout history. Why then should there have been a sudden access of new design processes and of techniques for use in these processes?

One can answer this in several ways. A cynic might say that *because* certain new techniques, with a highly complex jargon, have become available from Operational Research (O.R.), Systems Analysis and so on, some designers have felt compelled to use them. They would say, in justification, that the American Space and Missiles Programs represent the highest peaks so far of man's technological achievement, that in pursuit of these programs certain new techniques were devised, that these techniques proved spectacularly successful in the design of rockets, space capsules and so on, that buildings might become equally efficient if these techniques were used in their design. Nevertheless we should realize that even these add nothing fundamental to the four basic ways of design. They simply present us with new materials which we can use pragmatically in design, new analogies such as those which the Archigram Group and others have drawn with space capsules (and undersea housings) but above all with new forms of simulation, design analogues and even new canons to use. We might agree that whilst achievements in these other fields have grown increasingly more sophisticated the design of buildings seems to have got progressively worse, in terms of fitting human need in quite specific ways such as room size, insulation from traffic noise, *quality* of daylight penetration and so on, not to mention aesthetics; for this reason alone it might be sensible to try out every possible new technique in the hope of some improvement.

55

A cynic of a different kind might go on from this to point out the increasing interest, at high political level, in conservation of the environment, including the built environment. He might argue that nothing we design now seems to approach, let alone equal, say, the Georgian house in terms of comfort and convenience. He might even suggest that, given new methods of heating and electric light, *any* old building conserved will almost certainly be better than anything we, as architects today, can put in its place.

There is truth in all this, but the reasons, finally, for approaching design in new ways are deeper than any of it; they are determined by shifts in philosophical attitudes which are not exclusive to architecture, but pervade the whole of our culture and, most specifically, its science and technology. These have had profound effects on the way we think—Morton White (1955) had good reason for calling this *The age of analysis*. We can explain these changes best with reference to certain shifts in the philosophy of science which Goodall (1965) describes as first, second and third science; these represent, respectively, the science of the Greeks, Renaissance science and certain newer sciences developing now from biology. His terminology seems to me confusing, but his categories are useful, especially if his second or Renaissance science is divided into two parts.

In Greek science, and Euclid's is the supreme example, one postulated a set of axioms, self-evident truths, from which a series of theorems could be inferred. One thus built up a self-consistent system, a perfect, abstract structure which may or may not enable one to draw valid analogies with the imperfect structures of the real world. Aristotle built up his complete *Organon* —a classification of the world's entire knowledge—in this way, and it is the method still of some mathematicians and philosophers; it was also the method of our pioneer modern architects as we can see from Wright's 'internal space is the reality of the building', Le Corbusier's 'the plan is the generator' and other similar aphorisms. It is also the method of certain types of research, and much of what I have written in this book is based on it.

Renaissance science, by contrast, was empirical. One observed what was happening in the real world so that instead of running free to form self-consistent systems one's axioms, or hypotheses, were tested against reality. As Galileo put it, 'for I know . . . that one concludent experiment sufficeth to batter to the ground . . . a thousand . . . probable arguments'. A hypothesis, in any case, will be couched in terms of mental images based on what one knows of the real world, and will think in terms of 'atoms like billiard balls, forces like muscular tensions, masses like weight and so on' (Waddington, 1969). We set up a *model* based on things which are familiar to us within the world we know, and use this model as a way of explaining things we do not know, cannot see or which in other ways are beyond our experience.

In its early phases Renaissance science was a matter of observation and hypothesis. One observed the planets in motion and built up a mass of data as to their positions at various times of the year. Kepler tested various hypotheses against this data as to the nature of their orbits and concluded that elliptical orbits, around the sun, most nearly fitted the observed facts. In doing so he certainly 'battered to the ground' Aristotle's concepts of planetary motion deriving, as they did, from a self-consistent set of abstract axioms. Kepler thus built up a model which not only 'explained' planetary motion, but allowed prediction to be made about all future states of the planets. The aim of most scientists ever since has been to find equivalent predictive models for other natural phenomena.

This method of observation and hypothesis is still used in astronomy, descriptive biology, observational ecology and so on; it reveals, or confirms, that certain things do happen but on the whole it cannot tell us why. Frequently we want to know the causes of things or, more likely, which of several possible causes has the greatest observable effect. We form a series of hypotheses about possible causes and set up experiments in which each of them in turn can be varied in strength, combined in pre-determined ways with others, or even eliminated altogether. These are our *independent variables* and we observe their effect on the phenomena under investigation, the *dependent variables*. We can thus determine which of the possible causes has had the greatest effect.

The experiment therefore (Chapanis, 1959) is a set of *controlled observations* under *artificial conditions*, in which certain *variables* are manipulated deliberately so as to confirm or disprove our *hypotheses*. In Popper's more sophisticated view (1963) we set out to disprove our hypotheses or theories on the grounds that if they survive the experiment, and repetitions of the experiment by others, then we have a right to hold them until more potent hypotheses come along. Experiment in this sense is the fundamental tool of traditional research and we shall link it with observation to describe Goodall's second, Renaissance, science.

Our present technology presents overwhelming evidence that these methods work for physical objects, machines, engineering or building structures and so on, but difficulties seem to arise when we employ them in the study of human affairs. Our models tend to be over-simplified. We *can* devise hypotheses about human behaviour by analogy with billiard balls. We can think of them responding mechanically to whatever stimulus we give them, but after a while such models become inadequate. People refuse to behave like machines and if we press the analogy too far curious things start to happen. The experiment itself starts to change what people do.

This may be explained with reference to Goodall's third science of systems and processes which I shall describe in detail later. The dichotomy between first and second science is fundamental to philosophy; it is the conflict between what our senses tell us about the world outside ourselves and what seems to be true from our own experience. One can illustrate this simply with optical illusions, simple drawn patterns which have the curious property that what we perceive is substantially different from what is actually 'there', measurable, physically on the paper. The best known of such illusions, the Muller–Lyer, consists of two lines, equal in length, one of which is terminated by arrows converging inwards and the other by arrows converging outwards (Figure 3.1). Most Europeans and those who have inherited a European culture see *AB* as longer than *CD*, and Gregory (1963, 1966) has suggested an ingenious explanation for this. That need not detain us here—it is bound up with our having 'learned' to see things in perspective—I have simply used this example to show that in certain circumstances there may be a substantial difference between what actually *is* there and what we believe to be there.

Plato wrote at length about such differences in *The Republic* (Cornford, 1941), in *Parmenides* (Warrington, 1961) and elsewhere; certain later philosophers have attached overriding importance to evidence as received by the

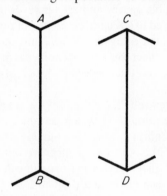

Figure 3.1—The Muller–Lyer illusion

senses—we call them *empiricists*—whilst others were concerned with what they *knew* to be true as a result of reasoned thinking—we call them *rationalists*. Rationalism proper started with Descartes, Leibnitz and Spinoza, who believed that at best the senses give a distorted image of reality. As Descartes put it (1637): 'How often it has happened to me to dream at night that I was here, in this place, dressed and seated by the fire, when all the time I was lying naked in my bed . . .' The more he thought about it, the more difficult it became to decide whether he was awake or dreaming that he was, so how could he possibly trust the evidence of his senses when at any given moment they may be deceiving him.

Nevertheless, whether he was asleep or awake certain entities continued to exist. He looked at his hand; it may be the real thing or it may be an illusion but its colour, shape, size, texture, relationship to his arm and so on, remain essentially the same. Colour, therefore, he thought of as a universal entity, so with shape and size, the number of fingers, the space they existed in, the time through which they endured and so on. Sciences such as arithmetic and geometry dealt in universal entities such as these, with relations between objects, rather than the objects themselves; such sciences, therefore, possessed universal truths which were manifest and indubitable. One might argue that Descartes conceived the idea, say, of a triangle because he had seen a figure or a number of figures to which the name triangle was attached, but he dismissed this explanation on the grounds that other figures could be conceived which no one had ever seen 'but of which (he could) demonstrate various properties touching their essence as (he could) in the case of a triangle.' As Aristotle had demonstrated, one could build up an entire abstract structure for the universe by rational contemplation alone, which would be complete and consistent in itself. This universe, in fact, might seem so rational that the world as perceived by the senses would appear confused and unintelligible in comparison. The only 'real' world, therefore, would be that which one had imagined.

It is significant from our point of view that Descartes derived his *rules* of rational thinking with reference to architecture. He says of his own thoughts:

'. . . one of the first that came to my mind was that there is often less perfection in what has been put together bit by bit, and by different masters, than in the work of a single hand. Thus we see how a building, the construction of which has been undertaken and completed by a single architect, is usually superior to those that many have tried to restore by making use of old walls which have been built for other purposes.'

Clearly Descartes had little respect for team working, nor had he much eye for picturesque irregularity. He continues:

'So too, those old places which, beginning as villages, have developed in the course of time into great towns, are generally so ill-proportioned in comparison with those an engineer can design at will in an orderly fashion that, even though the buildings taken severally often display as much art as in other places, or even more, yet the disorder is such with a large house here and a small one there, and the streets all tortuous and uneven, that the whole place seems to be the product of chance rather than the design of men who use their reason.'

So in town planning also, Descartes preferred the new, fortified towns such as Nancy (1588) and Charleville (1605), conceived as they were by the mind of one engineer, to such ancient towns as displayed, in the tortuous patterns of their narrow streets, the evidence of growth and change over the centuries.

He did more than speculate. He took this imaginary model, of the architect in firm control of a unified piece of design, and tried to apply the designer's methods (or what he conceived to be the designer's methods) to the ordering of his own thoughts. He worked out a set of *rules* by which his own thoughts might be disciplined; they are as follows:

'The first rule was to accept as true nothing that I did not know to be self-evidently so; that is to say, to avoid carefully precipitancy and prejudice, and to apply my judgements to nothing but that which showed itself so clearly and distinctly to my mind that I should never have occasion to doubt it.

The second was to divide each difficulty I should examine into as many parts as possible, and as would be required the better to solve it.

The third was to conduct my thoughts in an orderly fashion, starting with what was simplest and easiest to know, and rising little by little to the knowledge of the most complex, even supposing an order where there is no natural precedence among the objects of knowledge.

The last rule was to make so complete an enumeration of the links in an argument and to pass them all so thoroughly under review, that I could be sure I had missed nothing.'

It is salutary for us to note that already, in 1637, the basis was available on which all rationalized and systematized design methods have since been built. Nor is this the only debt we owe to Descartes, for he also invented coordinate geometry, by which the position of a point in space is expressed in terms of coordinates in three dimensions of length, breadth and height. The co-ordinates, of course, are usually called 'Cartesian' after their inventor and so for that matter is the method of solving problems by breaking them down into their smallest components, even though it had been known to the Greeks.

Rationalist attitudes were brought directly into architecture by theorists such as Laugier (1753), who believed that buildings could and should be designed by rational method—breaking the problem down into its smallest components, 'solving' each of these separately and then synthesizing a 'grand' solution. Laugier also derived 'from first principles' what he took to be the fundamentals of architecture: columns, beams and pedimented roofs. As I have shown elsewhere (Broadbent, forthcoming) the rational tradition in architecture extends directly from Laugier, through such romantically classical architects as Schinkel, to Mies van der Rohe.

Empiricism, by contrast, maintains that all human knowledge derives from sense-experience; that no other knowledge is possible. To a newborn child, for instance, the world is a 'booming, buzzing confusion' (attributed to William James) within which, eventually, he learns to recognize, say, his mother's face. Locke introduced this idea of the mind as a *tabula rasa*, 'white paper, void of all characters, without any ideas', and asked the obvious question: 'how then comes it to be furnished?' According to Locke, we 'build up' ideas such as 'yellow, white, heat, cold, soft' and so on, and then attach words to them. Once ideas have been formed, we can operate on them in various ways by such pressures as thinking, doubting, believing or knowing, thus building up our understanding. Ideas become associated in the mind often by rational connexion but sometimes by chance or custom.

Other empiricists such as Hume developed Locke's idea of associations further: they could arise, according to Hume, from three causes—from resemblance, in which the imagination runs easily from one idea to another rather like it; from contiguity, in which ideas occur together, in time or place, and are thus recalled together; and from cause and effect, where the existence of one is a necessary prelude to the existence of the other. This leads him naturally to a discussion of the probabilities with which a particular cause will lead to a particular effect.

Hume (1739) and Berkeley (1709) in particular took the implications of what Locke said to their logical conclusion. If our knowledge of the world is limited to things perceived by our senses, then how can we be *sure* that we perceive anything at all, apart from our own ideas or sensations. As Berkeley put it:

'. . . it is indeed an opinion strangely prevalent amongst men, that houses, mountains, rivers, in a word all sensible objects have an existence natural or real, distinct from their being perceived by the understanding . . .'

So nothing exists unless someone is looking at it! Not that this need worry us directly, as designers. Ayer, Price, Warnock and others have suggested that we never see or otherwise perceive any material object *directly*. We perceive our own 'sense data', ideas, impressions and so on; that is why we are deceived, say, by optical illusions. But Austin (1962) shows with great subtlety, that the argument itself is a play on words. The empiricist philosophers make obsessive use of certain words, such as 'real', in specific, private and over-simplified meanings; but 'real' means different things in different contexts. A real photograph, for instance, is real only in the sense that it is printed on photographic paper by photographic processes; but it is a *representation* of the real person—not that this need confuse anyone apart from an empiricist philosopher. It is impossible, therefore, to lay down criteria in general for distinguishing the real from the not real. The question does not even arise unless one is actually in doubt, in which case one must make the distinction according to circumstances, and according to the particular problems to which the distinction gives rise.

Again, and as Hipple shows (1957), there are direct links from empiricism into architecture through such eighteenth century writers on philosophy and aesthetics as Addison, Burke, Sir Uvedale Price and Richard Payne-Knight. They were concerned with the ways in which landscapes, and buildings, stimulated the human senses, and the architecture of sensory delight which developed from their theories is known as the Picturesque. Repton and Nash were its greatest exponents but our current preoccupations with the sensory environment have a great deal in common with Picturesque attitudes.

It seems highly unlikely that the conflict between rationalism and empiricism will ever be resolved, nor need that worry us either, for it is a highly productive debate. During its course the fundamental attitudes which rationalism and empiricism express have taken many guises; some of these have developed latterly with particular reference to the human sciences, sociology and so on. They have also played their part in the development of architecture. We shall consider the implications in Chapter 4, but let us say for now that the rationalist designs architecture which is complete and self-consistent as a system, usually in canonic terms (see Chapter 2), whilst the empiricist designs for the stimulation, and even delight, of the senses (seeing, hearing, heat and cold, together with several others) of those who will use, or otherwise experience his buildings.

This suggests a simple dichotomy but, like most such dichotomies, it is over-simple. For one thing empiricism and rationalism have been trans-mogrified over the centuries; their direct descendants in the twentieth century have been behaviourism and phenomenology respectively.

Behaviourism is exemplified for most people by the experiments (experiment of course is an empiricist device) which Ivan Petrovitch Pavlov (1849–1936) started with dogs in the 1890s. In the best-known of these he measured the flow of saliva in dogs. 'Saliva flows,' as Pavlov says (1903), 'when some-thing is given the dog to eat or is introduced forcibly into his mouth. Both the quantity and the quality of the saliva . . . is strictly dependent upon the quantity and quality of the substances brought into the dog's mouth.' He calls this simple physical process a *reflex*. But saliva began to flow when under certain conditions the eyes, ears or other sense receptors were stimulated, even though there was no food or other direct salivary stimulus actually within the dog's mouth. Pavlov called this phenomenon—action of the salivary gland when some other sense receptor was stimulated—a *conditioned reflex*. Experiment has shown that many of the things which Pavlov found of his dogs are true also of human beings. J. B. Watson (1878–1958) defined a similar empiricist approach to the study of human affairs which he called *Behaviourism* (1924).

It seemed to Watson and others that ideas such as 'soul' and 'conscious-ness' were holding psychology back and delaying its acceptance as a true science. The first tenet of behaviourism, therefore, is that 'consciousness' as such does not exist; there is no such thing, even as a 'mind' (see Ryle, 1949). They attempted a new formulation in terms which Watson describes as follows:

'Why don't we make what we can *observe* the real field of psychology? Let us limit ourselves to those things that can be observed, and formulate laws concerning only these things. Now what can we observe? We can observe *behaviour—what the organism does or says*.'

One can even measure it. The unit of measurement, the 'measuring rod' as Watson describes it, was as follows:

'Can I describe this bit of behaviour I see in terms of "stimulus and response"? By stimulus we mean an object in the general environment, or any change in the tissues themselves due to physiological conditioning of the animal, such as the change we get when we keep an animal from sex activity, when we keep it from feeding, when we keep it from building a nest. By response we mean anything the animal does—such as turning toward or away from light, jumping at sound, and more highly organised activities, such as building a skyscraper, drawing plans, having babies, writing books and the like.'

In its extreme forms behaviourism holds that all behaviour is related to patterns of physical connexions in the nervous system and to the conduction of energy along nerve paths. Some connexions are innate and others are acquired as the result of experience; the latter are what Pavlov called *conditioned reflexes*. Every aspect of human behaviour, therefore, is a 'function' of some condition that can be explained in physical terms. On the whole, behaviour is determined by conditions outside the person and these conditions form the *independent variables* of behaviourist experiments. The acts of behaviour thus stimulated form the *dependent variables* and the behaviourists' aim is to establish *relations* between the dependent and independent variables of such reliability that they become matters of scientific *law*. Having discovered these laws, the behaviourist hopes to *predict* human behaviour with a certainty equivalent to that with which astronomers can predict the motion of the planets. It may be possible to predict those things which are determined by certain mechanisms within the body, but the behaviourist looks also for those things which all men inherit at birth and which underlie the enormous variations one observes in human behaviour. He concludes that because of these variations man's inherited equipment cannot include any instincts, capacities, talents, temperament, mental constitution or other such characteristics as vary from man to man. Certainly we inherit differences of stature, of structure, of skin pigmentation, but even these are subject to modification according to the environment in which one lives. And with few exceptions, determined by his physiology, man's response to stimulus will always be determined by things he has learned from the experience of living in an environment which normally includes other people.

The achievement of behaviourism has been prodigious: it has led directly to modern learning theory, to programmed teaching and so on. On the face of it behaviourism offers an ideal set of tools for measuring the effects of buildings on human beings, but unfortunately it is deeply flawed. Some of its flaws stem from the inherent difficulties of observation and experiment (see Rosenthal, 1966). Padgham (1965) points out that all physical measurement is subject to error, due to misreadings of apparatus and so on. There are physiological limits, finally, to the accuracy with which we can read scales and dials and there are psychological reasons also, as Abercrombie said (1964), as to why, by a tilt of the head or some other involuntary movement, we look for the reading we wish to see. Apart from that (as we shall see in Chapter 7) *any* attempt to measure human behaviour will add to the subject's experience and thus affect that behaviour.

Even more important perhaps, there are philosophical objections some of which Daley outlines (1969). She points out, with some force, that whilst behaviourism claims to be neutral—a set of techniques by which stimuli can be presented, responses observed and analysed so that correlations between the two can be established—the intention itself reveals a particular attitude, that human beings, essentially, are nothing more than machines. This has ethical implications and although she does not quote Watson (1924) the following admission, I think, would confirm her worst fears:

'The interest of the behaviourist in man's doings is more than the interest of the spectator—he wants to *control* man's reactions as physical scientists want to control and manipulate other natural phenomena.' (My italics)

Watson, certainly, was writing of man as the subject of experiments in his laboratory but once the aim has been realized there, it is but a short step to wanting to control, say, man in society by behaviourist means. Watson's most distinguished successor, W. B. Skinner, actually wants to do just that (1971). The behaviourist architect too will want to design buildings which *force* people to live in certain ways.

Behaviourism represents a latter-day empiricism, as we have seen, whilst phenomenology is a clear development of rationalism. Its precepts were first stated by Edmund Husserl in a series of lectures (1907), since published in English as *The idea of phenomenology* (1964). They marked a considerable shift from an earlier position, as outlined in *The philosophy of arithmetic* (1891), in which Husserl had tried to reduce philosophy to an exact science based on laws derived from psychology and to be called *psychologism*, in which logic and mathematics were to be restated as psychological generalizations about the ways in which the human mind works. His intention, therefore, was almost more behavioural than that of the behaviourists.

Husserl had felt increasingly uneasy about this. The intention itself seemed to be based on a circular, and self-justifying, argument. He needed certain rules of logic to reason this way but the derivation of those rules required the use of the rules themselves, which was patently absurd. Yet he had to start with something and that something, for Husserl, consisted of *a priori* judgements. These had nothing to do with the world outside himself, as perceived by his senses. He was not in the least concerned with material objects nor with conclusions derived from his observations of such objects. He was concerned instead with his own inner and private experience, with personal, mental acts such as seeing, hearing, imagining, believing and so on. That in itself seems to me a perfectly reasonable concern. We have no justification for thinking it less 'scientific' to record one's own thoughts than to record one's (possibly illusory) observations of the world outside oneself. However, Husserl was concerned also with the *content* of such acts and with the abstraction from them of universal *essences*. The act of seeing, for instance, consisted for Husserl of two parts: the seeing itself and his *cogitatio*, his personal mental act. The content of that act would consist of *immanent* data, and Husserl's aim was to abstract 'pure' data from it, a universal *essence* which would be quite independent of Husserl himself or of any single cogitation. It would therefore be *transcendent*.

The object of his seeing, initially, might well be an orange but Husserl had no interest whatever in its existence as an orange. To be an object of his seeing, however, it would have to have colour, extension, shape, size and so on. Any object which was susceptible to being seen, even if no actual seeing was possible, would have to possess such properties. Given a number of such experiences, Husserl eventually could identify such universal essences as 'orangeness', 'roundness' or other similar properties. He would thus have completed the simplest, or phenomenological form of reduction. At a higher level he might pursue the universal essence of seeing itself, thus achieving *eidetic* reduction, while at a higher level still he would have to 'bracket out' himself—the person who was doing the perceiving—to achieve a *transcendental* state. Once that state had been achieved it would then be possible to construct a complete new reality, willed into existence by the *transcendental ego*, with new objects and new people with entire, new states of mind.

It is, of course, another self-consistent system, accessible to those who 'see' and unintelligible to those who do not. Husserl could claim that the latter lacked his personal insight. Yet in spite of its complexity and difficulty phenomenology has had a profound effect on the foundation of later philosophies and theories, notably in existentialism and Gestalt psychology. Many people find the clearest expression of existentialism in the novels of Kafka, with their implied threats to the hero (or anti-hero) and impending sense of dread. There is no clearly defined movement or school of existentialism; Heidegger, Jaspers, Sartre and Merleau-Ponty all present personal versions of it, with their concepts of 'authenticity', 'dread', 'freedom', 'nothingness', 'existence', 'commitment' and so on.

Heidegger's version is probably the most coherent. He considered that the essential difference between objects and men is that the former merely *are*, subject to the laws of science, whilst the latter are free to become what they will. A human being can stand outside the present moment of his *being*, recollect the past and predict his possible future. He may have had no choice about his present state of being but there is 'total freedom' to create whatever future he desires. This freedom to create the future is the essence of his *existence* as distinct from the mere state of *being* in which inanimate objects exist. It commits him to a tremendous personal responsibility which leads to the feeling of *angst*, a dreadful anxiety concerning the future. For, until he has created it, this future consists only of *nothingness*; there are no guidelines as to how he should approach it because he has total freedom. Most people are afraid of this freedom; they adopt conventional aims and values, concern themselves with seeking the approval of society, with the acquisition of property and so on. This, for Heidegger, is a state of *inauthentic* being. In authentic existence, by contrast, one is not in the least concerned with these matters: one operates without guiding rules; one *commits* oneself to personal responsibility for one's future and to realizing the opportunities which absolute freedom has to offer.

It is from this point of view that existentialists such as Daley find behaviourism sinister. They fear that the *laws* which behaviourism is trying to discover will divert people towards conventional aims and values, thus making it extremely difficult to exercise the absolute freedom which 'authentic existence' demands. They fear also that buildings designed to behaviourist precepts will force people into the stereotyped patterns of inauthentic existence.

Gestalt psychology also developed from phenomenology, in the sense that it is based on Wolfgang Kohler's personal insights as to what 'must' happen during the act of seeing. Kohler observed that when two small lights, quite close to each other, were flashed in a darkened room, then curious things seemed to happen. If the interval between flashes was long enough then one light only was perceived, one failed to notice their difference in position; if the interval was short then the two lights were perceived as being side by side; but if the interval was around 1/16th second then the observer perceived one light which seemed to move from one position to the other. Kohler explained this apparent movement by suggesting that the brain possesses certain organizing properties, dependent on electrical field forces within which a three-dimensional model is constructed isomorphic (see p. 91) with the form one is perceiving. These organizing forces ensure that any form is perceived as a *whole* and not as an assemblage of parts. He devised a number of experiments to show that if incomplete or complex patterns are displayed briefly in a tachistoscope then eye and brain together will complete or simplify them. He concluded therefore that whenever a form displays insufficient unity it will be transformed, by laws intrinsic to the brain itself, into a satisfactory form. The brain thus prefers 'good' form, simple, well-balanced and symmetrical which, because of this organization, will stand out from its surroundings and be perceived as a 'figure' against a 'ground'. Gestalt psychology, essentially, was developed by Koffka and others into a comprehensive science of mental life, covering (in addition to perception) such topics as learning, remembering, intelligence and so on.

Certain design theorists, notably at the Bauhaus, took this as 'evidence' that the brain prefers simple forms, thus matching their predilections for a de Stijl-like architecture. At the same level, however, one could argue that the brain 'enjoys' the task of simplifying complex forms and is liable to become bored if the challenge is removed. Gestalt psychology raised certain questions about perception, especially visual perception, which have not been answered satisfactorily by any other form of psychology. Its premisses, however, were wrong; we know now that electrical field forces of the kind which Kohler envisaged simply do not exist in the brain. Nor is there any reason why they should. Cybernetics, for instance, can explain perception without the aid of three-dimensional models, isomorphic with what we are perceiving. Nevertheless its idea—or ideal—of *Gestalt*, the organized structure against which a whole becomes much greater than the sum of its parts, has crucial implications for the development of recent system theory. Some of these will be described in Chapter 18.

If Gestalt psychology developed from Kohler's personal insights as to the ways in which the brain structures the information it takes in, so *psychoanalysis* developed from Sigmund Freud's personal insights as to the ways in which the emotionally-charged residues of previous experience affect our conscious behaviour. Freud (1856–1939) received a thoroughly traditional medical education and believed himself always to be an empirical scientist. As a practising neurologist, he came into contact with hysterical patients and sought to explain the causes of their hysteria, realizing that these often lay in events from the past which had great emotional significance. His patients, naturally, were unwilling to discuss these incidents, and often had forgotten them. Freud encouraged their recall by a process of free associations, but there had to be a starting point for such associations. Freud found what he was looking for in his patient's dreams, thus (given Freud's particular interpretation of them) any long, thin object, such as a church spire, or any kind of opening, such as a tunnel, could represent the male and female sex organs respectively.

Dreams, therefore, provided insights into one's past tensions and frustrations, as recorded in the unconscious. Initially in Freud's formulation these tensions and frustrations arose when the *libido* (desire for sensual, sexual gratification) suffered repression by the conscious, moral instincts of the *ego*. Later these were broadened in concept so the conflict occurred between *eros* (the life-enhancing, creative pleasure principle) and *thanatos* (the violent, irrational, destructive death wish).

Eventually Freud's two-part division of mind into conscious and unconscious proved inadequate; he devised a three-part scheme in which the instincts, appetites, predispositions and so on which we inherit at birth became the *id*. As we gain experience of the world, part of this is modified, or develops, to become the *ego*; its intermediary with the external world, whilst a special agency within the ego, which is formed in childhood through dependence on one's parents, becomes the *superego*. One's purpose in life, then, is to satisfy one's instincts, eros and thanatos, which are driving forces behind the basic needs of one's id.

Freud (1932), Arnheim (1954, 1970), Ehrenzweig (1965, 1967), Schneider (1950) and others have all written art criticism from a psychoanalytical point of view, whilst Jung applied *his* personal insights to *Man and his symbols*. Yet there has been little published discussion of architecture against the precepts of psychoanalysis, although the symbolism of spires, openings and womb-like spaces is obvious enough.

Personal construct theory was developed by George Kelley (1955) on the basis of *his* personal insights. It is based on the fundamental postulate that 'a person's processes are psychologically channellized by the ways in which he anticipates events', which Kelley then elaborates in the form of eleven corollaries such as 'a person anticipates events by construing their replications'. You had dinner yesterday and the day before that, so you assume you will have dinner tomorrow. 'Persons differ from each other in their construction of events'. Your expectation of dinner may well be different from mine, and so on.

Stringer (1970) introduced personal construct theory into architectural debate; it may well provide a useful framework for the discussion of design values. Since 1945 also, a potent Marxist phenomenology has emerged, with strong existentialist leanings. Its preoccupations have been social rather than psychological but its extreme exponents (see for instance Pawley, 1971) believe that the architect has no right whatever to determine a building's form, that this is the users' prerogative and that, at most, the architect should offer them technical assistance.

We may take it then that rationalism/phenomenology and empiricism/ behaviourism represent opposing traditions in philosophy which have had profound effects on the development of science. But the aim, finally, of any science seems to be as Laplace put it (1812):

'Given for one instant an intelligence which could comprehend all the forces by which nature is animated . . . an intelligence sufficiently vast to submit these data to analysis . . . it would embrace in the same formula the movements of the greatest bodies of the universe and those of the smallest atoms; for it nothing would be uncertain and the future, as the past, would be present to its eyes.'

That is, the scientist wants to find ways of predicting all possible states of every phenomenon in the universe, by extension of the methods which Kepler and others had devised for predicting future states of the planets. This method, of course, had been vastly extended already by Newton (1642–1727) whose Laws of Motion made it possible finally to deduce the whole of planetary theory and the mechanics on which modern technology has been based. Using these laws one could predict with absolute certainty exactly how a finite body would behave.

Even in Newton's lifetime, however, it was becoming clear to others such as Boyle (1627–91) that the overall behaviour of, say, very small particles acting together, such as those which formed a particular volume of gas, could *not* be predicted with certainty. The relationship between volume and pressure of the gas as a whole could only be expressed in terms of *probabilities*. We saw that Kepler and others observed the motions of the planets, analysed the data thus obtained, suggested (or hypothesized) that a system of elliptical orbits would account for the observed motions, and on this basis derived a set of formulae by which the future positions of the planets at any specified time could be predicted. The aim of most scientists ever since has been to reduce other phenomena of nature to a similar condition, so that they too could feed appropriate data into a set of equations and predict any future state of the phenomenon in question.

Boyle had realized that one could not investigate the relationship between the pressure and volume of gas in terms of certainties, but only of probabilities; Bernoulli carried these investigations further in his *Hydrodynamica* of 1738, whilst during the nineteenth century a number of physicists, Clerk Maxwell, Boltzmann and Gibbs, undertook a progressive generalization of the *statistical mechanics* which their predecessors had initiated. It may well be that individual particles in a volume of gas behave strictly in accordance with Newton's Laws of Motion, but one cannot observe them individually. One can only observe the behaviour of the gas as a whole and this is a matter of probabilities. Clerk Maxwell assumed that in a perfect gas the particles would move around at random and at different velocities. Within a given volume of gas the velocities of the particles would be distributed at random within a particular range. They would not be ordered neatly into zones of low velocity and zones of high velocity particles, but the average velocity in one container of gas may be higher than the average velocity in another, according to pressure, temperature and so on. But if the two containers were linked or opened into one another there would be an averaging out of velocities between the two. Where previously the velocities had been *ordered* between the two containers, they would now be reduced to disorder. This disorder is known as *entropy*, which is measured by Boltzmann's formula: $H = - \Sigma p_i \log_2 p_i$; we shall discuss this in other contexts in Chapters 11 and 18.

As physics tried to probe further into the structure of matter it was realized finally that not only were there limits as to what could be observed, but that beyond a certain level the act of observing itself would change what was under observation. As Heisenberg puts it (1958):

'We can express the departure from previous forms of physics by means of the so called uncertainty relations. It was discovered that it was impossible to describe simultaneously both the position and the velocity of an atomic particle with any prescribed degree of accuracy. We can either measure the position very accurately—when the action of the instrument used for the observation obscures our knowledge of the velocity, or we can make accurate measurements of the velocity and forego knowledge of the position. The product of the two uncertainties can never be less than Planck's constant.

This formulation makes it quite clear that we cannot make much headway with the concepts of Newtonian mechanics, since in the calculation of a mechanical process it is essential to know simultaneously the position and velocity at a particular moment, and this is precisely what quantum theory considers to be impossible.'

Heisenberg concluded this as the result of a *Gedankenexperiment*, a 'thought experiment' for which it was impossible to construct 'real' apparatus. It is only to be expected, however, that the fundamental limits of empiricism should be defined by phenomenological insight. The experiment could only take place in an 'ideal workshop' where any apparatus could be made, however sensitive or complex, provided it did not contradict the basic laws of physics. In this case, he imagined an electron gun, which was capable of firing electrons horizontally into a rather special chamber. It could be illuminated by an ideal source of light which could emit a single photon, or any number of photons, of any desired wavelength. He required a perfect vacuum—a chamber completely devoid of air or any other substance—and an ideal microscope which could offer any desired magnification and could also be turned at will over the entire electromagnetic spectrum, from the shortest of gamma rays to the longest of radio waves. Having imagined his apparatus, Heisenberg went on to imagine a range of experiments. If a single electron were fired into the chamber it would follow a parabolic trajectory, as Galileo had predicted, falling towards the bottom of the chamber by the action of gravity, but without some kind of illumination it would be impossible to observe this trajectory. So he would switch on his perfect light source and fire another electron. The chamber would now be flooded with photons of light and, inevitably, the particle would strike some of these (it would have to if Heisenberg were to see it). As it struck them, or they struck it, the particle would be deflected off course by Compton recoil, so that instead of describing a perfect parabola it would take a zig-zag course towards the bottom of the chamber.

Heisenberg's light source was infinitely adjustable; he could minimize the effects of these collisions by lowering the frequency of the light. Given light of infinitely low frequency (and infinitely long wavelength), it would be impossible to locate the electron precisely. Conversely, given light of high frequency and high velocity, one could locate the point of impact with the particle very precisely but the recoil would be so great as to knock it completely off course. If he chose a middle setting with light of intermediate wavelength and of intermediate energy, then the trajectory of his particle would be disturbed only moderately; its path could be defined in a fairly close approximation. It would never be possible to trace its exact line but at least he would be able to describe a reasonably narrow band within which its trajectory would be contained. He could analyse it, if not in terms of certainties then at least in terms of probabilities. The probabilities of uncertainty, therefore, are based on the average behaviour of particles in the mass.

Niels Bohr extended Heisenberg's Uncertainty Principle to a new and general philosophy, based on physics, in which the certainties of Newtonian

mechanics were to be abandoned for ever. Yet for three centuries, conspicuously successful technological development had been based on Newtonian mechanics; common sense suggested that in the 'real' world, at least,
machines behaved as Newton had predicted they would. And when it finally
came to it, Heisenberg's uncertainty was very microscopic indeed; he had
defined it, in fact, as equivalent to Planck's constant divided by the mass of
the particle. Planck's constant amounts to 10^{-27} units (in centimetre-gramme-
seconds) and as Gamow says (1958), we can, according to this, actually
determine its position to 'within a trillionth of a centimetre and its velocity
within a trillionth of a centimetre per second—or 30 microns per century,'
which for most practical purposes is quite certain enough!

Many physicists, as we might expect, objected very strongly to Heisenberg's
conclusions and especially to Bohr's elevation of them to a general principle.
They removed from physics the solid rock of determinism on which Newton
had laid it, and for this they substituted the quicksands of uncertainty.
Just as certain cynical intellectuals seized on Relativity after World War I
as an excuse for abandoning all standards, so others, since 1945, have seized
on the Uncertainty Principle (or Indeterminacy, as they prefer to call it) as
an excuse for non-commitment, for letting things happen as they will or, in
extreme cases, for total inaction. If the act of observing is going to change
things, then why bother to observe them in the first place? Observation is the
basis of action, so if one cannot be bothered to observe them, then certainly
there is no possibility of acting.

The uncertainty principle clearly has many implications for architecture.
If the act of observing changes what is being observed, how can we ever
collect a client's brief—our questions will change what he wanted. Even if we
could collect a brief and design according to it, the client's observations of
our sketch scheme will lead to further changes; so will the various officers'
observations for planning and other approvals purposes. The whole process
of realizing the design as a building on site will be a sequence of decisions,
observing the effects of those decisions, and making changes accordingly;
so will the clients' eventual taking over and occupation of the building. The
decision to demolish it will be taken in this way—observe the building's
performance and change—finally and irrevocably.

It is not surprising, therefore, that a number of architects have taken the
uncertainty principle into account, or the more general principle of indeterminacy, as a basis for considering strategies to cope with growth,
change, flexibility and ageing in buildings, see for example Archigram (1961–
1965, 1965a), Chalk (1964), Crompton (1964), Cook (1964), Green, Cook
and Crompton (1969), Cowan (1965), Habraken (1960, 1972), Price (1964,
1965, 1966a, 1966b, 1967), Weekes (1960, 1965, 1969a, 1969b) and others.
Their terminology is sometimes confused (see Broadbent, 1969) but their
solutions to these problems show considerable ingenuity.

They also reveal certain weaknesses in the human sciences, which, with a few notable exceptions, have continued to develop as if the uncertainty relations did not exist. Many psychologists and sociologists certainly pay lip-service to it but they continue to devise methods of observation and experiment which fail entirely to take it into account. Yet given the nature of human perception, it seems to me likely that the effects of uncertainty will lead to much greater distortion in experiments on human beings than they ever could in experiments on inanimate objects.

We have seen already that perception consists of a transaction between what is there physically, in the real world, and our past experience as recalled at the moment of perception in the brain. Any experiment on human beings inevitably will add to their experience and the experiment itself will alter their perceptions. That will be true, even, of simply asking questions; the words which the questioner uses will be perceived by the subject and this will affect whatever responses he gives.

We shall consider many examples of such phenomena in a later chapter, bearing in mind that all attempts to introduce analytical techniques into the design of architecture must be seen, not just in the light of uncertainty but of behaviourism and phenomenology as well.

CHAPTER 4

Architecture and the Human Sciences

We saw in Chapter 3 that the architect, in the act of designing, may display rational or empirical attitudes to his task. Often he combines them but occasionally one meets an extreme. The extreme rationalist, for instance, will be concerned with the abstract, self-consistent geometry of his building and, by definition, he will have little interest in the ways in which it impinges on the senses of those who use it. Certain architectural theorists of the mid-eighteenth century, such as Laugier (1753), were rationalists in this sense—they sought to apply Cartesian, or equivalent, method into the design of architecture and this led Laugier in particular to believe that architecture consisted, essentially, of columns, beams and pedimented roofs. All the other elements of building—walls, windows, doors and so on—were 'licences' in his terms and therefore to be avoided. One can trace a direct tradition from Laugier and his contemporaries through early nineteenth-century neoclassical architects such as Schinkel, to our own day (Broadbent, forthcoming). The supreme exponent, of course, was Mies van der Rohe, who succeeded in building a Laugier-like architecture of columns and beams, eliminating even the pedimented roof. He avoided the problem of walls, windows and the other elements of building, by filling the spaces between his columns and beams with glass, thus giving the *appearance* of designing without recourse to licences in Laugier's terms.

The buildings he thus achieved, such as the Farnsworth House (1950) or Crown Hall at the Illinois Institute of Technology (1955) (see Figure 4.1) also confirm that other aspect of architectural rationalism—they contribute rather less to user-comfort in terms of environmental control, than the average greenhouse.

The extreme empiricist, on the other hand, will be concerned with sensory experience to the exclusion of a rational structure, in the philosophical sense. Again one can take a direct tradition from the empiricist philosophers themselves, through aestheticians such as Addison and Gilpin, Price and Payne-Knight (see Hipple 1957) to such Picturesque designers as Repton (1840), Nash (1960) and others. We tend to dismiss them as irresponsible, concerned with visual delight to the exclusion of user-comfort and convenience. We also tend to believe that their Picturesque effects were gained at the cost of considerably more expenditure by their clients than straightforward, honest building would have demanded. I have traced the progress of this view elsewhere (Broadbent, forthcoming) to the Puritan sense of morality and responsibility which Ruskin and others introduced into architecture. Sometimes it is true, but on the whole I believe we have done these architects an injustice. The finest of them were concerned not just with visual effect but with pleasurable sensory experiences of a multi-modal kind.

Take one early, but supreme, example—the garden which Henry Hoare and others built at Stourhead (1743), on the edge of Salisbury Plain. In Banham's view (1962) Stourhead is the finest work of art which was ever created in England (Figure 4.2); one can agree with that, in terms of visual delight alone. However, as Hoare left it, Stourhead also stimulated the senses of smell (from varied planting), hearing (from the controlled play of water,

Figure 4.1—The ultimate conclusion of a rational tradition which originated with Laugier and others in the mid-eighteenth century. Mies van der Rohe's Crown Hall, the school of architecture at the Illinois Institute of Technology, Chicago (1955)

both externally and in the Grotto), heat and cold (Flitcroft's *Pantheon* contained one of the first central heating plants to be built since Roman times) and even the sense of equilibrium (the timber bridge over one arm of the lake was designed to 'give' slightly as one walked across it) (Woodbridge, 1965, 1970).

I have also suggested elsewhere that throughout the eighteenth and nineteenth centuries technical innovation in architecture was largely the work of empiricists and there are signs again now (1970) that an empiricist approach is emerging again. Most environmental scientists are empiricists by nature and few architects would dispute their contention that, among other things, one should design for visual, thermal and aural comfort. Some of us would go further than that, in the belief that the architect should design not just for comfort but for delight. It seems inconsistent that he should design for, say, thermal and aural delight without at the same time designing for visual delight.

However, the founding fathers of twentieth century architecture seem to have been rationalists by nature. Mies was the most extreme of them, but Le Corbusier, Gropius and others certainly subscribed to rationalist ideals. They set up self-consistent systems on the basis of personal insights from time to time; they even tried to formulate self-evident truths or axioms. One thinks of Sullivan's 'form follows function', Wright's 'internal space is the reality of the building', or Le Corbusier's 'the plan is the generator'. At their best, these architects achieved a marvellous fusion between rationalism and

Figure 4.2—The paradigm of empiricist architecture, design for sensory delight. Henry Hoare's Stourhead in Wiltshire (1743)

empiricism (which is particularly true of Wright) but, as we have seen in the case of Mies, the closer they approached to pure rationalism, the less satisfactory their buildings prove to have been, from the point of view of user comfort.

It was bad enough when their rationalism determined the form of the building itself, but at worst it extended also to trying to determine the lives which people should live within it. As Le Corbusier put it:

'Demand a bathroom facing south, one of the largest rooms in the house or flat ... One wall to be entirely glazed, opening if possible onto a balcony for sun baths; the most up-to-date fittings with a shower-bath and gymnastic appliances.

... Never undress in your bedroom. It is not a clean thing to do and makes the room horribly untidy.'

In each case, and there are several others in this 'Manual of the dwelling' from *Vers une architecture*, Le Corbusier has clear ideas as to how people should live, and tries to build them into the house so that people will be forced to live in these ways. His enthusiasm for fresh air and exercise was fostered by Dr. Paul Winter, a contributor to his journal (edited jointly with Ozenfant), *L'Esprit Nouveau*. Now, what if the user wanted a small, private, intimate bathroom; how could he live comfortably in a Le Corbusier house?

Again people *have* to live tidy lives if they are to match the conventions of his architecture: 'Demand bare walls in your bathroom, your living room and your dining room . . .', whilst the final clue as to how people's lives should be ordered by the architect is provided in the following phrase:

'Built-in fittings to take the place of much of the furniture, which is expensive to buy, takes up too much room and needs looking after.'

So for that matter does built-in furniture and it also fixes once and for all the arrangement of the room. Contrast this with that staple of the British furniture industry, the three-piece suite with sideboard, which allows for an extraordinary number of permutations in the arrangement of a living room. Each item is movable and any number of people, from one to five, can arrange themselves comfortably and in convenient groups, sitting side by side, face to face or at right angles to each other. It is difficult to envisage any arrangement of built-in furniture which would offer so many possibilities.

To be fair to him, Le Corbusier did design individual items of furniture such as chairs and he seems to have sensed that his personal predilections may not have been the only basis for design. He appears to have been asking for an empiricist approach, one might almost say behaviourist, to the building up of standards relating to human needs, for use in design. 'By needs,' he said, 'I mean utility, comfort and practical arrangement.' Not only that; he was also quite clear that needs could be established by observation and statistical analysis:

'A standard is necessary for order in human effort.
A standard is established on sure bases, not capriciously but with the surety of something intentional and of a logic controlled by analysis and experiment.
All men have the same organism, the same functions.
All men have the same needs.
The social contract which has evolved through the ages fixes standardized classes, functions and needs producing standardized products.'

If all men have the same organism, the same functions and the same needs, then clearly it should be possible to identify the basic standards for design which Le Corbusier seeks. Once those standards have been laid down, then design itself should become a matter of deducing for a particular building the actual form which the general standards determine. As he says:

'The establishment of a standard involves exhausting every practical and reasonable possibility, and extracting from them every recognized type conformable to its functions, with a maximum output and a minimum use of means, workmanship and material, words, forms, colours, sounds.'

Such standards exist, he believes, in painting and sculpture, 'the great standards of the heart', and they also exist in the motor-car industry, where simple function (to travel) and a complicated series of aims (comfort, resistance, appearance) have forced, he says, the 'absolute necessity' of standardization. So all motor-cars have the same essential arrangement.

Nor was Le Corbusier alone in this desire to establish standards. Gropius presents his case for standards in *The New Architecture and the Bauhaus* (1935):

'A standard may be defined as that simple practical exemplar of anything in general use which embodies a fusion of the best of its anterior forms—a fusion preceded by the elimination of the personal content of their designers and all otherwise ungeneric or non-essential features. Such an impersonal standard is called a "norm", a word derived from a carpenter's square.'

He is less precise than Le Corbusier who wanted to define his standards in mathematical terms and indeed Gropius only resorts to mathematics in those rather doubtful diagrams by which he proves to his own satisfaction that, given the same daylight angle (30°), ten-storey blocks allow one to pack more flats at a greater density, on to a given site, than do three-storey blocks and that they also afford a better daylight angle (17° 50') than three-storey blocks.

Gropius's much maligned successor as Director of the Bauhaus, Hannes Meyer, also looked for fundamental standards on which architecture could be based:

'Thinking of building in functional and biological terms as giving shape to the living process leads logically to pure construction; these constructive forms have no native country, they are the expression of an international trend of architectural thought. Internationality is a virtue of the period. Pure construction is the basis and characteristic of the new world of forms.
1. sex life
2. sleeping habits
3. pets
4. gardening
5. personal hygiene
8. car maintenance
9. cooking
10. heating
11. insulation
12. service
These are the only requirements to be considered when building a house.' (Meyer, 1928)

Curious that no one in Meyer's house ever indulged in reading, writing, conversation, listening to the radio or most of the other activities which might be assumed under the general heading of 'living'. Yet even in this list Meyer expressed his priorities for a particular time and place. For many people in many parts of the world 'car maintenance' is impossible because there is no car to maintain. Others might find 'pets' or 'gardening' to be quite irrelevant and, finally, Meyer looked for more fundamental standards even than these:

'All life is an urge towards harmony. Growing means striving after the harmonious enjoyment of oxygen + carbon + sugar + starch + protein. Work means our search for the harmonious form of existence.'

Once one reaches this level of generalization, there is little left of a philosophy to help the designer make decisions when he is faced with real design problems. Meyer's own successor as Director of the Bauhaus, Mies van der Rohe, had an even pithier comment to make of it: 'Life is oxygen + carbon + sugar + starch + protein . . . Try stirring that together,' said Mies, 'it stinks.'

Meyer's conception of standards extended beyond architecture to the whole of a culture or, rather, he sought to relate architectural standards to cultural standards:

'The standardization of our requirements is shown by: the bowler hat, bobbed hair, the tango, jazz, the Co-op product, the DIN standard size and Leibig's meat extract. The standardization of mental fare is illustrated by the crowds going to see Harold Lloyd, Douglas Fairbanks and Jackie Coogan. Grock and the three Fratellini weld the masses—irrespective of class and racial differences—into a community with a common fate. Trade union, co-operative, Ltd., Inc., cartel, trust and the League of Nations are the forms in which today's social conglomerations find expression, and the radio and rotary press are their media of communication. Co-operation rules the world. The community rules the individual.'

Meyer's list, as it happens, points out the difficulty of establishing standards in this way, for none of these products survives in precisely the form in which he knew it or with the ubiquity which he implies. The bowler hat, jazz of the 1920s and Harold Lloyd's films do survive as the cult objects of minority groups; the Co-op, Leibig's and DIN are still operative but their products and standards have changed out of all recognition. In other words, Meyer's examples represented standards only for one cultural group (western Europe and America) at a particular moment in time (the mid-1920s).

It seemed necessary, therefore, to look for more fundamental standards of the kind which, say, behavioural psychologists had begun to pursue. Meyer had actually invited psychologists (although largely of Gestalt persuasion), sociologists and other human scientists to the Bauhaus (1927–28)—an initiative which Gropius seems to claim as his own in *The New Architecture and the Bauhaus* (1935) and *The Scope of Total Architecture* (1956). Others too, such as Richard Neutra, see the human sciences as contributing to *Survival through design* (1954), and in the 1960s there has been an increasing amount of traffic in the other direction. It has become almost fashionable for psychologists and sociologists to take a specialist interest in environmental research and design.

The motives, largely, are political, starting with a generalized concern for the environment. Sometimes, however, the reasons are more specific, as declared by Cohn-Bendit and others in their statement entitled *Why sociologists?*, which triggered the Parisian student revolt of May 1968. They suggested that Mayo, in his famous observations at the Hawthorn factory in 1927 (in Roethlisberger and Dickson, 1941),

'. . . closed the epoch of . . . speculative systems concerning society as a whole and opened the glorious era of empiricism and of "scientific" data-collection. At the same time, in selling his services to the management of an enterprise, Mayo initiated the age of the large-scale collaboration of sociologists with all the powers of the bourgeois world . . .'

In other words, the sociologists' skills were being used to promote the interests of management, to find ways of increasing productivity and so on. Cohn-Bendit and his colleagues go on to say: 'industrial sociology seeks, above all, the adaptation of the worker to his work'. This from a phenomenological point of view is intolerable and it seems to many of those who hold such views that environmental design could offer them opportunities for exercising their skills in constructive ways, by trying genuinely to find out what people *want* rather than manipulating them to accept what is offered. As we shall see, there are difficulties in this but the intention is admirable enough and, for now, we ought to encourage it.

Yet problems arise immediately from causes which Cohn-Bendit and his colleagues touched on. Sociology, for instance, had been a rational matter, initially. Its founding fathers, such as Saint-Simon (1720–1825), Comte (1798–1857)—not to mention Marx (1818–83) and Engels (1820–95)—had brooded on the nature of society and set up models which (for them personally) explained its structure and functions and the mechanisms of social change. Saint-Simon for instance believed, like his contemporary Laplace, that a general theory of the sciences could be set up, against which (given the appropriate data) all future states of any given system could be predicted. Comte took his model from Newtonian mechanics, thinking in terms of social statics and social dynamics, whilst Spencer was much given to biological analogies.

A number of fundamentally different models have been developed in sociology. Buckley (1967) identifies five: the mechanical model, the organic model, the process model and the two equilibrium models of Parsons and Homans. Inkeles (1964) on the other hand, identifies six, which he describes as: evolutionary/developing; structural-functional; physical science/mathematical; organismic; equilibrium; and conflict models. We may collate their descriptions in the following manner.

1. *Physical science models.* Comte's aim initially had been to set up a *social physics* in which society could be seen as an astronomical system in which human beings were attracted by mutual attraction or differentiated by repulsion. One could thus apply the laws which were proving so successful in

physics and engineering to the study of man himself. Now clearly, the models against which physics was developed, concepts such as space, time, attraction, repulsion, inertia, force, power and so on, arise in the first place as a result of human experience; they were things which men 'felt in their bones'. It is not surprising, therefore, as Buckley says, that ' . . . we find conceptions of *moral or social space* in which social events occur; *position* in social space, and a *system of social coordinates* defining man's position in it . . ., *attraction* and *inertia* of individuals and groups, the latter regarded as a *system in an equilibrium* of *centrifugal* and *centripetal* forces'.

The question at issue is (given that these concepts originated in anthropomorphic analogies): can they really be applied, with any conviction, to the study of society as a whole? At best they are drawn at the wrong level and at worst they introduce a phoney precision into the discussion of social affairs which may well be misleading even where it is not downright harmful. As Inkeles puts it:

'The precision of expression which characterizes physical science, with its dimensions of space and time, its forces and vectors, greatly tempt those who weary of the ambiguity of so many sociological terms, the vagueness of the relations specified between variables, and the indefiniteness of the conclusions reached.'

It is a refuge, in fact, for habitual convergers; but it has other, rather more sinister implications. In Inkeles' words:

'The most obvious, and most often cited, explanation for the appeal of the physical science model is that the success of physicists and chemists has given their approach an aura of power and prestige so great that people are inevitably attracted to it.'

2. *Evolutionary models.* In these society is seen as progressing, by definite steps, towards a final stage of perfection. Comte thought in terms of three stages which he called conquest, defence and industry, whilst Spencer and Sumner used a kind of 'social Darwinism'—survival of the fittest—to justify their attempts to block social reform. Marx and Engels presented the best known of evolutionary models, based on five great modes of social being: firstly a primitive Eden which is usually forgotten in accounts of their work; secondly, Slavery in which the exploited are actually owned; thirdly, Feudalism in which the workers are still exploited but no longer owned; fourthly, Capitalism, a depersonalized exploitation in which the worker is subject to the routine of the factory so that production and marketing may be maximized; and finally, Socialism in which no one is exploited and the individual is encouraged to develop towards a state of self-realization. Each stage carried within itself the seeds of its own destruction and would be succeeded inevitably, by the next stage higher on the scale of evolution.

Durkheim assumed an evolutionary process in which successive stages are marked by the ever increasing division of labour, whilst Sorokin believed that societies evolve from an ideational phase in which truth is based on faith, through a stage of sensate culture in which truth is revealed empirically, to an idealistic culture in which the two are synthesized and demonstrated by reason.

There have been other, later and even more sophisticated evolutionary models but, as Inkeles says, they have been largely abandoned now if only because after certain events of the twentieth century no one can seriously believe that society *has* evolved.

3. *Organismic models.* These depend on analogies with living organisms, with particular reference to structure and function. They are concerned in particular with the ways in which societies are maintained and carried forward, even though their individual members change with each new generation. If the evolutionary approach is concerned with social change the organismic approach tries to understand how society is working, as a system, at a particular moment in time. Spencer in particular was fond of drawing analogies of this kind; he was well aware that they could be drawn too far and should be limited to matters concerning the relationships of wholes and parts, but he persisted nevertheless in drawing them further than they could bear. It is easy to say that societies (or even cities) are born, grow, reach maturity and die, to draw analogies between traffic and circulation systems, between communications networks and the nervous systems, but Spencer's mistake, according to Deutsch, is that he failed on the whole to choose the appropriate level at which to draw his analogies. His analogies were drawn between societies and single organisms, whereas for many purposes it would have been better to draw them with whole species.

3A. *Equilibrium models.* Those of Homans and Talcott Parsons are special cases of the organismic model in that they draw on more sophisticated concepts, such as homeostasis, to explain the ways in which society defends itself, say, against juvenile delinquency in much the same way as the body takes action against infection. It is clear, as Inkeles says, that society sometimes fails in this; it cannot maintain itself in a state of near equilibrium; the pressures to change are too great and if a society does not yield to them it will die. Mills and others oppose these equilibrium models directly with a conflict model. They suggest that the true state of society is not one in which agreement is reached by consensus but one in which progress depends on an endless struggle between the privileged and the deprived, with the latter struggling constantly to secure advantages for themselves.

4. *Mathematical models.* Since World War II, with the increasing availability of computers, sociologists, like so many other people, have turned increasingly to the building of mathematical models. The work generally

starts, as Inkeles says, in one of two ways. A researcher observes that time and again his results seem to follow a given form; Bales, for instance, noticed in his study of small groups, almost invariably, that 45 per cent of all acts were directed towards one person; that acts were directed towards other individuals in decreasing numbers; and that about 6 per cent of all acts were directed to the man who received least attention. Bales found, moreover, that the observed pattern fitted fairly closely a harmonic curve. It became possible, using this curve, to predict the pattern of probable interactions for other groups of up to eight people.

Frequently, however, there is no ready-made model of this kind and the sociologist has to construct one; this clearly has its difficulties. Simon (1957) has shown that a great many social processes can be modelled in *stochastic* terms, that is to say in terms of sequences within which the probability of a given event depends to a large extent on preceding events. City size, income, word frequencies and other linguistic phenomena can all be modelled in terms of stochastic processes.

Nevertheless mathematical modelling carries a number of hidden dangers. Like the behaviourist, the mathematical modeller tends to think that his techniques are 'neutral' but the fact that one is using a model at all is a declaration that one has chosen to see the world in a particular way. Simon develops this idea:

'First . . . we do well to avoid *a priori* philosophical commitments to models of particular kinds—whether they be probabilistic or deterministic, continuous or discrete, analytic or set-theoretic . . .

Second, we must not expect to find the models we need ready-made in a mathematics textbook. If we are lucky, we shall not have to invent new mathematics, but we are likely to have to assemble our model from a variety of new materials. For this reason, we should be wary of borrowing, in any wholesale fashion, analogical models from the natural sciences. Analogies there will undoubtedly fit . . . but it will be safer to notice them after we have developed our theories than to attempt to employ them as a basis of theory construction.'

However, models are one thing and techniques are another. The Nanterre group (Cohn-Bendit et al.) suggested rightly (although they got their dates wrong) that sociology had moved away from rational speculation to become an empirical science and empiricists, as we have seen, tend to think of their techniques as 'neutral'. Durkheim (1858–1917) tried to discover 'social facts' by collecting data on, say, *Suicide* (the subject of one of his most well-known books), analysing it statistically so as to plot the *rates* at which suicides took place, comparing these rates for different social groups and thus detecting any *social* implications of variations in the rates.

Max Weber (1864–1920) finally saw the difficulties of both the rational position (which seeks 'insights' without really demonstrating *how* its models actually fit the facts) and the empiricist position (which becomes so bound up with demonstrating the existence of connexions that it hardly ever attempts to show *why*). Weber tried to resolve this by setting up theoretical models *which could be tested* but describing them at the same time in terms of an individual view—ascribed to a hypothetical observer in a specific historical context. He had no use for the ideal type or even for the statistically average, asking the highly pertinent question as to what relationship the average frog would have to all the particular frogs which a biologist observes.

Curiously enough, this view was also put forward by Hitchcock and Johnson in their highly perceptive book on recent (1932) trends in the architecture to which it gave a name: *The International Style*. International style housing, they say:

'. . . implies preparation not for a given family but for a typical family. This statistical monster, the typical family, has no personal existence and cannot defend itself against the sociological theories of the architects. The European functionalists in their annual conferences set up standards for ideal minimal dwellings. These standards often have little relation to the actual way of living of those who are to inhabit them . . . Too often in European *Siedlungen* the functionalists build for some proletarian superman of the future. Yet in most buildings the expressed desires of a given client are the most explicit and difficult functions . . . The idealism of the functionalists too often demands that they provide what ought to be needed, even at the expense of what is actually needed. Instead of facing the difficulties of the present, they rush on to face the uncertain future.'

Yet some things *can* be established statistically, standardized and used as the basis for design. We know that human tissue is damaged by exposure to excessive heat or cold. There is a very high probability indeed that any man would die if he were exposed overnight, unprotected, to a temperature of minus 50°C, or one of plus 200°C. We could move in from these limits and establish the ranges outside which 90%, 80% . . . 10% of men would die. We could even establish the ranges within which 10%, 20%, 30% of men would feel comfortable although, clearly, it will never be possible to establish a simple temperature at which everyone, dark-skinned or light, brought up at the Equator or in the Arctic Circle, would feel comfortable.

Clearly such studies are the province of physiology. It seems, therefore, that *some* of the human sciences *can* present the designer with useful information. Before we decide which these are, however, we ought to look at an extensive range to see what possibilities are available. A tentative list in alphabetical order might read as follows:

Anatomy: systematic description of the body, usually under the headings describing ten major systems—skeletal, muscular, integumentary (skin), circulatory, respiratory, alimentary, urinary, nervous, endocrine (glandular) and reproductive.
Anthropology (physical): comparison of different races in anatomical and anthropometric terms.
Anthropology (social): comparative study of complete human societies in different places, from the point of view of social structure, social function and social change.

Anthropology (structural): attempts to apply the methods of structural linguistics to the study of kinship or other aspects of social anthropology (Malinowski, Radcliffe Brown, Levi-Strauss).

Anthropometrics: direct measurement of the human head and body against a check-list of those dimensions which have been found useful in certain kinds of research; e.g. stature, waist, girth, weight, etc. Statistical analysis of those dimensions.

Archaeology: study of what survives from the physical environment within which people lived in the past; examination of tools, weapons, pottery, buildings, tombs and so on, dated according to distribution (where they were found geographically), stratification (the depth at which they were found) and their relationship to other materials; association (the things they were found with) and typology (comparison with other artefacts about which details are already known).

Demography: observation and recording of births, deaths, disease, etc., and their statistical analysis as indicators of living conditions within a community.

Ecology (human): study of man as an organism in relation to his physical environment; effects of geographical location, climate, degree of shelter, food supply, interactions with other species, etc., on growth, size and development of other physical characteristics.

Ergonomics: method of establishing standards in which certain aspects of the physical environment (independent variables, such as illumination levels, noise levels, temperature, air movement, etc.) are subject to controlled variations. The effects of these variations on human performance are measured in terms of 'comfort', output, efficiency, etc., (the dependent variables) analysed statistically and used in the drawing of inferences about human performance in general or as a basis for design (Murrell, McCormic).

Ethnography: descriptive study of peoples and their distribution, physical characteristics and relationships with each other.

Ethnology: historical ethnography, concerned with customs, culture and so on.

Ethology: according to Mill, 'the science of the formation of character', but more recently used to describe studies in animal behaviour, especially those concerned with territoriality, aggression, etc., (Lorentz, Ardrey, Hall) and their relationships with human behaviour (Morris).

Linguistics: the descriptive, comparative or other study of *language* (the common tool of communication between members of a community) and speech (an individual's use of language). *Diachronic* linguistics deals with changes over time in a particular language whilst *synchronic* linguistics compares different languages at the same point in time. *Structural* linguistics (Saussure, etc.) is concerned with the ways in which words are related to each other in language, either by their positions in sentences (*syntagmatic* relations) or in terms of shared meanings, rhymes etc., (*paradigmatic* relations), on the assumption that such relationships are common to all languages because of certain fundamental structures in the brain. *Generative grammar* (Chomsky, etc.) assumes that such mental processes predispose one to learn language in such a way that the sentences one utters are grammatically correct.

Parapsychology: study of events for which direct empirical evidence is not available, such as thought-transference, telepathy, haunting, communication with the dead, and other forms of extra-sensory perception (Rhine).

Pathology: study of the changes which have occurred in the structure of the body as a result of disease; assessment of any treatment the patient may have received, as an aid to deciding further treatment; deduction as to cause of death.

Physiology: systematic, structural analysis of the ways in which different parts of the living organism are adapted to each other, and of their interactions and functions.

Psychiatry: treatment of mental disease by methods including psychoanalysis, but including also shock treatment, drugs and so on.

Psychoanalysis: belief that descriptions of the nervous system in physiological terms do not explain its unconscious workings; use of 'psychical apparatus' described by Freud to account for these unconscious workings. According to Freud, the predispositions, appetites, etc., which we inherit at birth together form the *id*. As we gain experience of the world, part of the id develops to form the *ego*, its intermediary with the external world. A special agency within the ego is formed in childhood through dependence on one's parents; this is the *super-ego*. One's purpose in life is to satisfy one's instincts, the driving forces behind the basic needs of one's id. In particular, one has to satisfy two basic instincts—*eros* which aims at binding things together, particularly in sexual love—and *thanatos*, the 'death wish', which aims at destruction (Freud, Jung, Adler).

Psychology: originally the study of *mind*, but many psychologists now would deny the existence of mind, preferring to think of psychology instead as the study of *behaviour*. Typical concerns of psychology are the study and correlation of abilities, especially those contributing to intelligence; the measuring of personality traits in terms of physiological and social factors, effects of heredity and/or environment on personality; function of the nervous system; individual development, motivation, feeling and emotion, value systems; physiology and psychology of perception, especially in terms of vision, learning, memory and other cognitive processes (Osgood, 1953; Woodworth and Schlosberg, 1954; Miller, 1964).

Social psychology: observation of people in groups and of their effects on each other in terms of output, efficiency, well-being, and in other respects.

Sociology: the study of society—as distinct from the individual—in terms of all that happens to human beings by virtue of their reactions to each other (Ginsburg, 1955). These reactions may be observed, described and classified under three major headings: social structure, social function and social change. Under structure, for instance, one might study the various units of social organization, family and kinship, various kinds of social or working groups, larger groups such as the neighbourhood, the city and so on. The study of social functions might include those factors which tend to hold groups together: political, legal, economic, administrative or institutional, not to mention co-operation, control and discipline. Social change might start with defiance and conflict, it will be concerned with differentiation, stratification and mobility within society (Inkeles, 1964; Broom and Selznick, 1955; Green, 1956).

Clearly these sciences differ greatly in scope, methods and aims. They differ greatly in degree of rigour and the extent to which they can help the designer with positive results. Many of them in any case are still embryo sciences, anxious above all to establish their respectability as true sciences. General surveys of their applications into environmental studies have been presented by Craik (1970) and Proshansky, Ittelson and Rivlin (1970). But difficulties arise because some of their practitioners seem far more anxious to demonstrate their grasp of a methodology than to produce results which are usable in design. They collect large quantities of data and submit it to minute analysis, without really stopping to think what their analyses are for.

These and other problems have been discussed, often at considerable length, by psychologists such as Wells (1965a and b), Rohlen (1967), Sommer (1967), Canter (1970), Stringer (1970) and Lee (1970 and 1971), by sociologists such as Broady (1966, 1968), Guttman (1966), by architects such as Manning (1967), Rapoport (1969), Broadbent (1970) and Marcus (1970). The RIBA Research Committee (1970), also Hillier (1970), have had much to say on the subject and it has formed the substance of conferences at Dalandhui (Canter, 1970), Kingston (Honikman, 1971) and of the Environmental Design Research Association (see Chapter 13).

CHAPTER 5

Models

We used the word *model* in Chapter 4 to describe each of four basic ways, physical, evolutionary, organismic and mathematical, which had been used as a basis for describing society. Model in this sense means a rather elaborate analogy, or assemblage of analogies, and clearly this is different from the conventional meanings of model which refer to three-dimensional representations on a reduced scale, of buildings, ships, aeroplanes and so on, to people or objects which are good of their kind and therefore worthy of emulation, or to young ladies who pose for artists, photographers or act as walking clothes-horses. Model in this new sense derives its meaning from the analogies of which it is composed; it enables us to represent ideas which otherwise would be difficult, or impossible, to comprehend. No one can *see* society or know exactly what it is made of, how it fits together and so on. We can only begin to understand it by comparing it with other things which we do know and which seem to resemble it in certain respects. A model, therefore, is a complex analogy and one which has been chosen specifically by its user to describe the structure of something.

It is difficult to decide exactly when an analogy becomes a model and equally difficult to distinguish between models, analogies, *mappings* and *simulations*. These seem to have much in common and we might say, provisionally, that analogies exist before the user even notices them. Faced with a particular problem of representation, he casts around and realizes that a particular analogy will be appropriate in the explanation of his concept. Certain kinds of model are little more than this, such as those objects and persons which are seen to be good of their kind and therefore worthy of emulation. Others have to be made by the user for the specific purpose of explaining his concepts; that seems to be true also of analogues, mappings and simulations. *Analogues* seem, on the whole, to be physical objects (drawings, models, laboratory apparatus); *maps*, in geography at least, tend to be drawings whilst *simulations* seem to be numerical in nature, although distinctions between them are by no means hard and fast.

As we saw in Chapter 4, Spencer compared transport systems with the circulation of the blood, thus using the latter as an elaborate analogy—a model. He could have drawn a map showing traffic routes, set up an analogue in which traffic was represented by liquids flowing along pipes or, if he had been living in the twentieth century, a simulation in which traffic was represented by numbers in a computer program. We looked at some of these ideas in Chapter 2 where we found that pragmatic and iconic design were supplemented at a particular moment in history by analogic design (using drawn analogies) and that this caused a decisive shift in modes of designing, so that instead of manipulating real materials on site the designer used his analogues to manipulate concepts which could be translated afterwards into reality. We also saw that in their first recorded uses by the Egyptians, the drawn analogues began to 'take over' from the designer, to impose their own conventions and generally to distort his ways of thinking.

This is true even at the simplest level of using analogies to generate new words in language. A child knows that the plural of cow is cows and, applying the same usage, assumes that the plural of sheep is sheeps. In other words, the analogy itself has inbuilt structure which determines the ways in which the child will use it. Saussure (1906), Wittgenstein (1921) and others have analysed in detail the limits imposed by such structures on the communication of meaning by language, and we shall look at some of the implications in Chapters 7 and 11.

What is true of analogy in language is also true of any kind of analogue, model, mapping or simulation, be it a drawing, a model, a written description or a computer program. It will distort the very concepts it has been set up to clarify. The chief reason for this is that no analogy, analogue, mapping, model or simulation can ever present a one-to-one relationship, complete in every detail, with what is being represented. There would not be much point in setting it up if it could.

Markus (1970) suggests that one of the major barriers to useful research in architectural psychology stems from the fact that models of people do not exist which adequately relate the environment to bodily, psychological, social and verbal behaviour. Such a model however, if it did exist, would be as complex as the world itself. It would be just as difficult to understand the simulated human being's behaviour in the simulated environment as it is now to understand the real human being's behaviour in the real environment. The model would have a further disadvantage: the fact that it was a model would mean that, by definition, it *was* a distortion of the facts. Our understanding of, say, society *can* be improved by drawing analogies with living organisms; we can think of the ways in which societies grow and mature by analogy with the ways in which animals or species evolved. Nevertheless, at best these are incomplete models, useful for some purposes and misleading for others.

No model can ever be complete, correct and universal in its application. We build a model because we want to focus down on certain aspects of a problem; my perception of what is important may well differ from yours. It is likely, therefore, that we shall build different models, which is not to say that mine is right and yours is wrong. We may gain new insights from comparing them; you will have stressed things which I ignored, and vice versa.

Nor should we necessarily seek to combine them. This would lead to a lowest common denominator, thus blurring our focussing on different aspects which was the strength of our original models and which led to the value of comparing them.

It is possible of course to have models of models, models of simulation, analogies of models and so on. Using the broadest of possible definitions, the written descriptions in Chapter 4 were *verbal* models, written down, of the physical, organic and other *models*—elaborate collections of analogies— which certain theorists had used as a basis for understanding society.

The use of model in this broader sense stems initially from Operational Research (O.R. for short, see Chapter 10). Churchman, Ackoff and Arnoff in their early (1957) *Introduction to Operational Research* identify three types of model: iconic, analogue and symbolic. By its definition, an iconic model 'looks like' what it represents: photographs, paintings and sculptures may provide iconic models of people, objects or scenes. A toy car is an iconic model of a 'real' car just as an architect's 'model' is of a building. Such a model, clearly, displays a specific relationship to what is being represented and in particular its various dimensions will be scaled down or, in certain circumstances, scaled up (one can imagine, for instance, an iconic model of an atom).

However accurately it represents the original, an iconic model can never share *all* its properties. An iconic model of a building may be the same shape as the original but made of quite different materials. A concrete building may be modelled in polished hardwood with its windows represented by dark veneers laid on. Such a model, beautifully made, may be more appealing to the client than a scaled-down representation in the colours, textures, transparency and so on, of the original. One *chooses* which properties to represent according to the purpose of the model.

Sometimes it is inconvenient or even impossible to make an iconic model of a particular object, process, event or system, and in such cases, analogue models may be used instead. The various properties of the original may be represented by properties of quite different kinds in the model. A map, for instance, is an analogue model in this sense; roads and political boundaries will be represented by lines, different kinds of land use by different kinds of hatching or colour, different heights by contours and so on.

A graph too is an analogue model in this sense representing properties such as time, number, age, weight, or cost; the first of these could also be represented by sand flowing in an egg timer, by hands moving round a clock face, by successive events on a tape recording and so on. The national economy has been represented at the London School of Economics by means of a bath into which water flows at controlled rates (representing income) and out again through holes of specific sizes in specific positions (representing expenditure). It has also been represented in terms of electric currents flowing within an analog computer. These are all analogue models and they have certain advantages over iconic models in that things which change with time can be represented within them. Most analogue models can be applied in more than one situation, whereas an iconic model always represents a single case.

All the examples we have looked at so far have been described in terms of words. Models can also be made in terms of numbers or of symbols from logic; this is true obviously of time, number, age, weight and cost. It is also true of locations on a map, or even of the forms of buildings which can be described in terms of points in space, located by a system of coordinates (see March and Steadman, 1971). Symbolic models consist of equations or sets of equations, expressing relationships between the entities which one is trying to model. The mathematical models of society which we considered in Chapter 4 included symbolic models and symbolic models generally are the basis of computing (see Chapter 15). We shall be looking at several disciplines in Chapter 10 (Operational Research, Systems Analysis and so on) which depend almost entirely on symbolic model-building techniques. Many of these techniques have been adopted in systematic design method, which accounts for the enthusiasm which many designers now show for building symbolic models.

However, the O.R. definitions of model seem to me unnecessarily restricting; others have classified models in quite different ways; Chorley and Haggett (1967), for instance, catalogue some of these. Models for them may be *descriptive* or *normative*; that is, concerned with describing reality from a particular point of view, or with indicating what might be expected if certain clearly defined conditions are fulfilled. Descriptive models can be *static* (i.e. constant over time) or *dynamic* (i.e. concerned with things which change over time). They may be used to provide a structure against which data can be classified or they may even be used in experimental design. Normative models, on the other hand, will be used to describe an unfamiliar situation (unfamiliar that is, in time and/or space) by drawing analogies with a familiar one. They may be used therefore for prediction.

Models can also be classified according to what they are made of. Chorley and Haggett identify two groups—*hardware, physical or experimental* models on the one hand and *theoretical, symbolic, conceptual or mental* on the other. These overlap to some extent the O.R. classification into iconic, analogue and symbolic models and the latter, in their mathematical guise at least, can be further subdivided into deterministic (dealing with things which occur in a logical, causal chain) and stochastic (dealing with things which occur at random).

Echenique (1968) collates these and other classifications of models into a simple and useful system, plotting them within a cubic space of which the three dimensions are: 1. What the model is made for. 2. What the model is made of. 3. How time is treated.

This seems to me clear and reasonable; with slight modifications it provides a splendid structure against which the nature and use of models can be discussed (Figure 5.1). Echenique's first dimension includes the following four uses for models: description; prediction; exploration; and planning. These uses of models are self-explanatory, but I find it useful to be more specific by identifying three basic functions for models: descriptive, concept structuring and exploratory. These can then be subdivided further. Descriptive

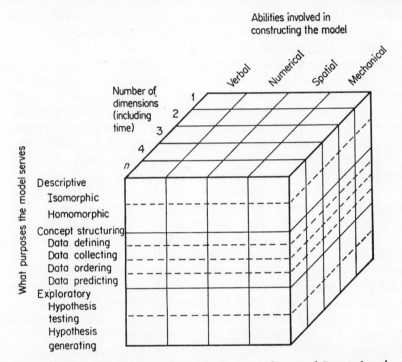

Figure 5.1—A classification of models (from *Architectural Research and Teaching*, Vol. 2, 2)

models, for instance, can be of two kinds—*isomorphic* and *homomorphic*. These are further, and rather unfortunate, terms from O.R. which describe ways of 'mapping' the original on to the model. An isomorphic model has a one-to-one relationship with what is being represented. An exact model of a building with every brick and tile in place, showing every door knob, window catch and so on, would be isomorphic in this sense. That is not the only kind of isomorphic model; a model might be isomorphic in respect of certain properties but not in respect of others. A geographer's map, for instance, might be isomorphic with the countryside it represents, from a geometrical point of view. Every point, curve, conventional symbol on the map, each element in fact, occurs in the geometrical relationship with other elements, which matches exactly the relationship of corresponding elements in the actual countryside.

The map is isomorphic at a particular *resolution level*. At other resolution levels, however, it is not isomorphic with the countryside. At a higher resolution level, the relationship will be homomorphic, that is, applicable in one direction only. There will be many elements in the countryside and relationships between them which, according to scale, are not represented on the map—individual houses, trees, or even blades of grass. Homomorphic relationships, therefore, are many-to-one reductions. A small-scale plan will be a homomorphic reduction of the building.

Predictive models are concerned, as the name implies, with forecasting the future and they occur in several forms which will be described in detail later. As Echenique says, they tend to be extrapolative—based on observing what has happened in the past and what is happening now (persistence, trajectory and cyclic prediction, see Chapter 10)—or conditional—if x occurs, then y will follow (associative and analogue prediction, also in Chapter 10).

A great many models, as we have seen, are concerned with concept structuring and these serve several purposes. They may be used to formulate the rules by which we recognize what is of interest to us (data defining), they may provide a check-list or other framework against which data can be collected (data collecting), or they may provide the framework against which data, once collected, can be analysed and otherwise put into order (data ordering).

Models can be used in testing hypotheses. Watson (1968) has a marvellous description of the way in which a physical model finally confirmed that DNA *could* exist in the form of a double helix. Lastly, a model may be built in the hope that the process of its building will actually *generate* the hypothesis.

Echenique divides his third dimension, how the time factor is treated, into two parts, which are usual in O.R. It seems to me that this could be enriched by using this dimension to express space/time relations in 1, 2, 3, 4, . . ., n dimensions. However, it is his second dimension, what the model is made of, which offers the greatest possibility for development. Echenique extends the O.R. classification to include icons, analogues, words and mathematical functions. In other words, he divides the symbolic models of O.R. into two kinds. This four-part classification seems to me almost a homomorphic reduction of the six-factor classification of human abilities attributed to Spearman (1927) in Chapter 1 (see Figure 1.1): fluency factors; verbal; numerical; spatial; mechanical information; manual. If we ignore the extremes, fluency factors and manual skills, we are left with four media of expression which also represent four basic ways of making models: verbal, numerical, spatial and mechanical. Every time we describe a concept we do so in one of these model forms; we decide what the model is for but (and this is the crucial point) we actually make the model verbally, numerically, spatially or mechanically, according to our personal abilities. Other things being equal, I tend to use words because I have a certain verbal fluency, but you may tend to use drawings, because you are high in spatial ability, to make (iconic) 'models' because you possess mechanical skills or to formulate mathematical models because you are high in numerical ability. My narrative, therefore, can be described as a one-dimensional, verbal, descriptive model (1VD); your drawing is a two-dimensional, spatial descriptive model (2SD); your iconic model is three-dimensional, mechanical, descriptive (3MD); and your mathematical one, let us say, is four-dimensional, numerical, predictive (4NP).

The cube itself might generate, say, $4 \times 4 \times 8 = 128$ kinds of models, some of which have never been used. The further point, and most important of all, is that each type of model has its uses and, what is more, no single type is inherently 'better' than any other. Given such a structure for plotting models against, one can disagree profoundly with Plato who, according to Plutarch, inveighed with great indignation against Archytas (significant name) and Menaechmus who tried to solve certain problems in geometry by means of mechanical models, thus 'destroying and perverting all the good there is in geometry'. Not only did they employ empirical (Plato calls them 'sensible') methods instead of rational ('incorporeal' and 'intellectual'), but they also used 'such bodies as require much vulgar handicraft'.

There were social reasons in Plato's time for abhorring vulgar handicraft —such work as would only be undertaken by slaves—but western culture ever since has preferred intellectual exercise to practical, a snobbery which certainly extends to the present day. It is one reason for the prestige which numerical models possess in certain circles, why it seems more respectable to devise and manipulate a mathematical model which has no practical application than it is to use a mechanical model for solving real design problems.

Mathematical models, however, also enable whole new classes of problems to be tackled which are not susceptible to solution in any other way. This is particularly true where human needs have to be taken into account. Some design theorists, such as Ward (1967), Jones (1971) and Alexander (1971), suggest that mathematical models are inherently *inhuman*, that by definition that which is human must be passionate and irrational. One can understand their reservations and it may be as we suggested in Chapter 1, that those who delight in analysing abstract relationships between *things* also tend to treat *people* as abstractions. Nor will the objectors—and one must also include Janet Daley (1968, 1969)—be content with an assertion that the techniques themselves are 'neutral', that one may use them in a human *or* inhuman way. They simply dislike the idea that people, either individually or in the mass, can be represented by numbers, and nothing will assuage their fears.

In the last analysis they may be right. But we are concerned with relationships *between* people *within* the built environment and as we shall see in

Chapter 9, the relationship of human behaviour *to* the built environment is quite another matter. Given the same room, individuals will behave in quite different ways; the room itself, to a large extent, *will* be neutral. One may describe it therefore in mathematical terms with no violence whatever to the dignity of human beings. And this is true of the whole built environment, of all the objects which man makes and surrounds himself with. Yet even there, it seems to me, there is a scale of appropriateness. Different classes of objects require different kinds of models.

Echenique (1971) and others have suggested that at city planning scale, or at least in urban research, the *only* appropriate models these days will be mathematical models. The problems themselves are so vast, the quantities of data so great, the interrelations between various factors so complex, that they could not possibly be handled without recourse to the computer. Given also that the city itself is in a constant state of change which must be represented in the model, that for strategic planning at least the city must be modelled mathematically, the argument seems to me entirely convincing. Certainly one will use other kinds of models in realizing the plan once it has been conceived, but even so there may be real dangers in presenting a model of the city in physical terms as a three-dimensional spatial model. Planning committees and the public at large, not to mention the planners themselves, become notoriously attached, or antagonistic, to the actual forms which such models present; they tend to 'freeze' development of the city in a particular state.

However, if mathematical models of this kind are appropriate in studying the city as a whole, they may equally be inappropriate in the analysis and design of objects at other scales. One would hardly expect the manufacturer of cutlery to go ahead in the production of a spoon on the basis of a mathematical model, even if the model showed that ergonomically it 'fitted' the hands, lips and tongues of, say, seventy per cent of the adult population. He would want to handle it and even use a prototype—a three-dimensional, spatial, descriptive model, a sample which could be shown to production, marketing and other staff who could then evaluate it against their own, vastly differing criteria; and just as the prototype spoon is essential, so the prototype city is impossible.

Architecture, fortunately, falls between these two scales; that is one of its fascinations. The individual components of building may be treated like the spoon, the overall plan of a building complex like the city, whilst the various scales of architectural reality in between will each need different kinds of models.

Models then will have to be set up in various ways, but certain overriding principles govern what must be done. Model building itself embodies four distinct phases. One decides first of all what has to be modelled—in other words, the subject of analysis or design (see Broadbent, 1963). One may have an existing model—a theory or hypothesis—as to the structure of one's problem; we shall describe such a structure for man-building-environment relationships in Chapter 18. If the problem is new or unfamiliar then we shall have to look in the first place, as we have seen, for analogies which help us towards understanding. We should then be in a position to choose the *kind* of model which will serve our purposes best and we can go on to build it using the various components (words, numbers, objects in space) which our chosen medium of model making makes available. Having made the model, we shall have to test or validate it, but the nature and rigour of our validation will depend on what type of model we have made and what we are going to use it for.

Descriptive models may be compared with the reality they attempt to describe and with other people's descriptions. As we have seen, they can never be complete and the best they can do is to describe the object as we see it. Data structuring models can be tested, initially, against the data which is available. If they can absorb it all, order it intelligibly and encourage its retrieval, then they are probably satisfactory. The real test comes when new data has to be fed in. If our model can cope with this then we shall leave it unchanged, but if it cannot then we shall have to redesign the model.

The most critical kind of model in terms of validation is the predictive model. A predictive model which distorts the structure of the problem will be useless for, however good one's data, one's predictions will be false because the model itself has falsified them. One validates a predictive model, in principle, by analysing known solutions to similar problems and feeding data from them into the model. If the model's prediction parallels what actually happened with a reasonable degree of precision, then one assumes that the model itself is good enough for one's purposes. Churchman, Ackoff and Arnoff (1957) suggest four ways in which the adequacy of the model can be questioned, which we might modify for our purposes as follows:

1. Check that the model actually represents all the variables in which one is interested. The speed of traffic, for instance, might be affected by number of cars, width of road, number and kind of intersections: these are all likely to be accommodated in a mathematical model. But it will also be affected by nature of road surface, time of day, weather conditions, skill of drivers—and these may well have been ignored. Models often include only those things which are easy to represent, but if one is to use them successfully then one must be aware, at least, of what is missing and what effects it *may* have had on the performance of the model.
2. Check that all the variables which have been built into the model are actually relevant. Again, it is easy to build in certain variables because data on them is readily accessible—one uses it because it is there—but its inclusion *may* diminish the effectiveness of the model. It is fairly easy, for instance, to measure sky luminance and to average them out. Figures obtained on this basis were used to determine the 2 per cent daylight factor (see Chapter 7). However, if windows are regarded as a source of visual stimulus rather than a source of light (Markus,

1967), then their size will be quite unrelated to sky luminance. Variations in luminance will simply lead to variations in visual stimulus but one will not need to quantify them.

3. All models, as we have seen, present distorted views of what is being represented but the distortion may vary greatly, in magnitude and effect, from one variable to another. If one is using the model in predicting, therefore, one must be aware of what these distortions are and what their effects are likely to be. Some of them may be scale effects. Suppose, for instance, one has made an interior model (3SD) of a concert hall with the surface colours and textures of its various materials scaled down appropriately. One cannot measure its effects on music reproduced within it and use these directly to predict the acoustic performance of a real hall unless the music itself is 'scaled down', that is, speeded up proportionately. One cannot place any iconic (3SD) model of a building into a wind tunnel and produce directly usable information about the building's likely effects on wind speed, direction, the build up of vortices and so on. The performance of the model in the wind tunnel will depend on its scale in relation to wind tunnel size, surface treatment, rate of flow, way in which the surrounding environment is represented, ground roughness and so on (Langhaar, 1951, 1964). Equivalent problems arise when one tries to use models in the prediction of acoustic performance, lighting and so on.

4. Even if the model itself were completely accurate (fully isomorphic in the terms we have been using) it could still fail to predict effectively if wrong or inaccurate data were fed in. The data which we feed, say, into structural models, will carry very high probabilities indeed, as we have seen, but that may not be true of data which results from social surveys for instance, for reasons which again we shall examine later.

The most effective way of validating any model, clearly, is to feed into it data relating to some known conditions and to see how accurately it would have predicted what has been observed to happen in reality.

CHAPTER 6

Statistical Methods

We saw in Chapter 4 that, whilst it is probably impossible to predict the behaviour of a single human being within the environment, human beings for certain purposes can be treated like particles in Bernoulli's volume of gas; in other words, their behaviour in the mass can be observed, analysed statistically and used to predict their probable future behaviour. Durkheim derived his social 'facts' in this way and a great deal of work in the human sciences is based on similar premisses. Such an approach, of course, is anathema to the phenomenologist and certainly to the existentialist. It detects the existence of conventional aims and values, investing them with authority of a very particular kind. As we shall see, the data on which such analyses are based is often suspect; at best it is indeterminate, at worst it may be incomplete, biased or otherwise distorted. Yet the computational methods by which it is processed may be so complex and so rigorous in themselves, that they invest the information thus produced with a spurious authority. One gains the impression in any case (Hudson, 1967) that many human scientists are so fascinated by these processes that they hardly care about the data even, and have no interest whatever in the human beings it is supposed to be about.

One must not deny the value of techniques merely because from time to time they are grossly misapplied, and there are other reasons too for discussing the nature of statistical methods in that several new disciplines, Ergonomics, Operational Research, Information Theory and so on, are statistically based, and these, as it happens, are the disciplines from which systematic design methods in architecture have emerged.

The first known statistician, John Graunt of London, had been a haberdasher before he took to analysis of human affairs and presumably his experience in selling buttons helped him develop certain rudimentary methods of classification. In 1662 he published the *Natural and Political Observations upon the Bills of Mortality*, a small book in which he attempted to reduce 'several great confused *Volumes*' of figures relating to births and deaths in the City of London 'into a few perspicuous *Tables*.' He simply took parish registers from 1604 to 1661 and reduced the information they contained on 'notorious' diseases, casualties, difference between males and females, and so on, to a series of tables. Of 229,250 people who died in one twenty-year period, about one-third were children under four or five years old; two-ninths died of acute diseases, only 70 of 'chronical diseases'; the incidence of 'notorious diseases' was much smaller than Graunt expected, '1306 died of apoplex, 134 of gowt, 51 of head-ach, 67 of lethargy, 158 were lunatique and 454 died sodainly' (quoted Newman 1960).

Suppose however that Graunt's material had become available, say, to an insurance company who wished to make use of it in the most effective way. Their interest, clearly, would be in using it to predict the numbers of years which their policy holders, in various categories, could be expected to live. It would not be enough, therefore, to know that one-third of the deaths in Graunt's sample were children under the ages of four and five. They would have to know how likely it was that a child, say, of 4 would live to be 10, 20

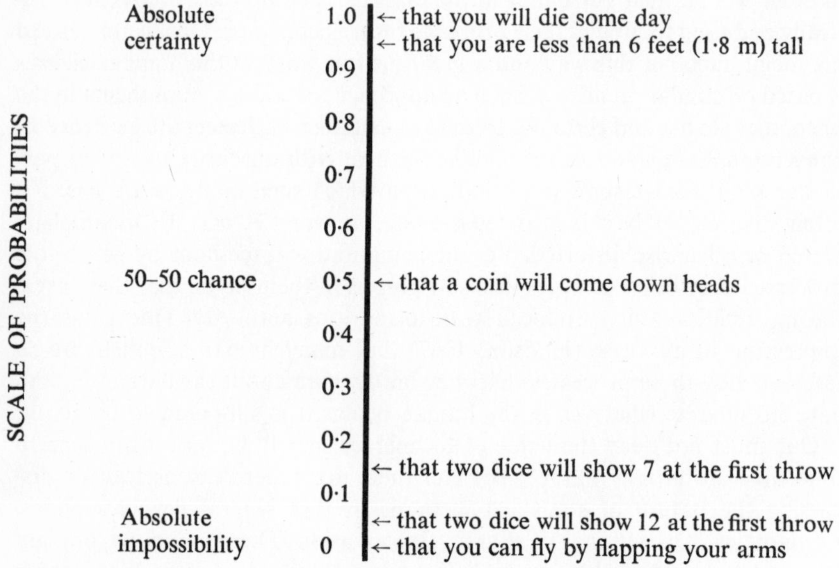

SCALE OF PROBABILITIES			
Absolute certainty	1.0	← that you will die some day
		← that you are less than 6 feet (1·8 m) tall
	0·9	
	0·8	
	0·7	
	0·6	
50–50 chance	0·5	← that a coin will come down heads
	0·4	
	0·3	
	0·2	
		← that two dice will show 7 at the first throw
	0·1	
Absolute impossibility	0	← that two dice will show 12 at the first throw
		← that you can fly by flapping your arms

Figure 6.1—Scale of probabilities (adapted from Moroney, 1951)

and so on. In other words, they would be concerned with *probabilities*, attempts to bring chance events under some sort of order.

That, as we saw in Chapter 3, was one concern of the empiricist philosophers who considered the probabilities with which one event would follow another. The mathematical study of probabilities had been initiated in any case by Pascal and Fermat in 1637 at the instigation of the Chevalier de Mere, an inveterate gambler, but the real foundations of probability theory were laid by Laplace (1812).

The probability that any event will occur lies somewhere along a scale which extends between absolute impossibility—usually expressed as (probability) $p = 0$—and absolute certainty, $p = 1$. The scale may be drawn as in Figure 6.1 (adapted from Moroney, 1951). Probabilities are determined as Laplace suggested, by means of a simple calculation:

$$\text{Probability } (p) = \frac{\text{Number of times event has happened in the past}}{\text{Total number of trials}}$$

Laplace laid down a set of *General Principles of the Calculus of Probabilities* in which he defines probability as 'the ratio of the number of favourable cases to that of all cases possible.' As a first step, one decides whether each of the cases is equally possible; if they are not, then one determines their respective possibilities. It is particularly important to see if they are independent or not; if they are independent, then the probability of their combined existence is the product of their respective probabilities. The probability of throwing any chosen number with a single die is $1/6$, whilst that of throwing the same number with two dice is $1/6 \times 1/6 = 1/36$. This raises an interesting question because, at first sight, the probability of throwing any possible number with a pair of dice will be $1/11$ (each die will fall in one of six positions and their combined totals can amount to any number between 2 and 12 inclusive),

Table 6.1—Standard table of probabilities in dice games (using two dice)

Point (outcome)	Probability	Point (outcome)
2	1/36	12
3	2/36	11
4	3/36	10
5	4/36	9
6	5/36	8
7	6/36	7

whilst Laplace's calculation suggests that it will be $1/36$. In fact the probability of throwing any particular number with two dice will vary according to the number. For instance, 2 can only be thrown in one way—both dice must show a 1; and similarly 12 can only be thrown in one way—both dice must show 6. The probability of throwing 2 or 12 is indeed $1/36$. But 7 can be thrown in several ways—by combinations of 1 and 6, 2 and 5, or 3 and 4— nor does it matter which die shows which. The probability of throwing 7, in fact, is $6/36$ and the Standard Table of Probabilities in Dice Games reads as shown in Table 6.1.

If, after a long run of throwing a pair of dice, we found that the outcomes were substantially different from these, then we should have reason to believe that one of the dice, at least, was loaded. In that case we can use the evidence of the past to shed a certain light on the future.

If the dice are true, however, there is no way of using evidence from the past to predict the future in any particular case. If we were tossing a coin, for instance, and it fell down heads a hundred times in succession, we should consider this extraordinary and, similarly, if we drew a white ball from an urn which contained a million black ones and only one white one, we should consider that extraordinary, but there would be nothing remarkable in drawing the number 475813 from an urn which contained a million numbers. So, as Laplace says, the more extraordinary an event, the more we need to see it supported by strong evidence. The probability that some future event will happen can be obtained by adding the probabilities of each possible cause; where one has *all* the data then the probabilities can be calculated accurately. This is rarely the case; more often than not we have part of the data and difficulties certainly arise when two people each have different parts. Suppose, for instance, there are three urns, A, B and C, one of which contains only black balls whilst the other two contain only white balls. You are asked to predict what colour of ball will be drawn from urn C and, in the absence of further information, you will have to say that the probability of its being black will be one in three. But I know also that urn A contains only white balls, so I estimate the probability of drawing a black ball from C as one in two. Suppose we have drawn a ball from C and it proves to be black; I shall know with *certainty* that urn B contains white balls, but you will only believe that if you trust me when I state that urn A contains only white balls; in other words, you will have to decide what *confidence* to place in my evidence.

That is a trivial example but problems of this kind arise in designing every day. There has to be mutual confidence, for instance, between architects, engineers and quantity surveyors; between designers even and social scientists. We may prefer to place more confidence in the 'hard' advice of, say, the structural engineer rather than the sociologist. However, no designer can ever deal in certainties.

There is no law of nature, or even of physics, which says that steel for use in building must be rolled into straight I-sections and formed into rectilinear frames except that it is convenient. There is something inherently arbitrary, therefore, about the way in which the engineer's problem is set up before he starts designing. Nevertheless, having committed himself to a steel frame, he proceeds to design the individual members; in the case of a beam, for instance, he needs to know its span, the nature and distribution of loading and the method of end fixing. He will possess simple formulae by which he can calculate bending moment, shear force and other relevant characteristics, and he will be aware of legislation relating to factors of safety. He will also have tables which provide him with performance data on the various sections available. All this looks completely determinate and the engineer himself may even think it is and that if he feeds the correct values into his equations then, inevitably, the proper result will present itself and his beam will perform as designed.

However, that is by no means certain. The standards to which he refers have all been established by experiment; beams were loaded until they collapsed and the strength of the material itself, its behaviour in the form of I-section beams, has been tested many times. As we saw in Chapter 2, such matters have always been established pragmatically before a mathematical equation could be devised which seemed to match the observed behaviour.

Each sample of steel is unique, however; one can only gain a general idea of how steel performs by testing a large number of samples and calculating an *average* of their performance. In other words, it is a statistical matter and, given the techniques of statistics, one defines the *probability* with which a sample will perform in the expected way. But it may still be flawed. If that is true of a steel sample it is also true of an actual beam—again one can merely state its expected performance within the average performance of such beams and the probability that a given beam will meet these expectations. Nor is this the only aspect of the design in which probabilities are involved. All the materials, methods of assembly, workmanship, are encompassed not by certainties but by probabilities; this is true of the loading, both the structural loads and the loads imposed by use. Even if one knows that a certain room is going to be used as an office one hardly expects its entire floor to be covered with heavy filing cabinets; the statutory loadings which one has to meet are based on the probability that it will not be so loaded. So the engineer's certainty, when we come to examine it in detail, turns out to be an illusion. As Werner Heisenberg puts it (1958):

'. . . we must remind the reader that in everyday life all of us encounter statistical laws with every step we take, and make these laws the basis of our practical action. Thus, when an engineer is constructing a dam he always bases his calculations on the average yearly rainfall, although he cannot have the faintest idea when it will rain and how much of it at a time. When speaking of statistical laws we generally mean that a particular physical system is known completely.'

When we start to examine human affairs and the effects they have on building the situation is even less certain. Beams and loads at least are inanimate; our observations have very little effect on them; but the sociologist's observations *may* have changed the behaviour of the people he was observing; his samples will be even less reliable than the engineer's, and his predictions, finally, will not be rendered any more determinate by the accuracy and complexity of his mathematics. Like the engineer, therefore, he will be dealing in probabilities in so far as he is actually making predictions, and that will also be true of the quantity surveyor (whose estimates of costs will be a matter of probabilities), the heating engineer and so on. Just as the structural engineer bases his estimates on the results of probabilities of experiments and his experience of the ways in which buildings have behaved in the past, so the quantity surveyor and, increasingly, the heating engineer base *their* estimates of future performance on the measurement of recent buildings.

Statistics is concerned with far more than probabilities. It also deals with frequency distribution (the number of buttons Graunt had of each kind), with measures of central tendency (the kind of which he had most) and with various specialized laws of average (the mean, the median and the mode). Clearly these are valuable in design as helping us find, for instance, the numbers of people who are likely to be comfortable in a particular chair, with a particular level of illumination and so on. It also deals in correlations

Table 6.2—Frequency distribution of the heights of 2,960 American Air Force cadets

Class limits (mm)	Frequencies	Cumulative frequencies	Cumulative percentages
1980–2009	1	2,960	100·0
1950–1979	2	2,959	100·0
1920–1949	7	2,957	99·9
1890–1919	42	2,950	99·7
1860–1889	87	2,908	98·2
1830–1859	226	2,821	95·3
1800–1829	358	2,595	87·7
1770–1799	522	2,237	75·6
1740–1769	575	1,715	57·9
1710–1739	467	1,140	38·5
1680–1709	377	673	22·7
1650–1679	208	296	10·0
1620–1649	68	88	3·0
1590–1619	17	20	0·7
1560–1589	3	3	0·1

—with the ways in which one event affects another—with the relationship, for example, between illumination level and reading speed.

We will look first of all at measures of a central tendency. We may take the case of air force cadets as measured by Randall and others for the American Army Air Force. Now, clearly, it would be possible to *count* the young men and even to number them. Like buttons on a tray, they exist as *discrete variables*—one cannot have a group consisting of 17·5 young males, except perhaps for philosophical purposes. Their heights are a different matter; it is theoretically possible that differences between them will be so infinitesimal as to defy measurement. Like temperature, height is a *continuous variable* and, again like temperature, we have to find some way of indicating which value we are concerned with within the infinite range of possibilities. In the case of temperature, we have agreed a scale against which different values can be plotted. The intervals in this scale are determined by many things, such as the accuracy of our measuring instruments, the degree of accuracy we need for practical purposes and so on. A temperature of 17°C is indicated on our scale, and so is 18°C, but we can, if necessary, record a temperature of 17·5°C. We also know that in passing from 17° to 18°, the

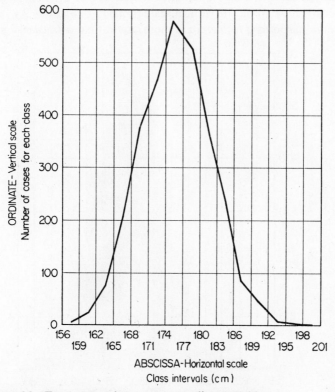

Figure 6.2—Frequency polygon corresponding to Table 6.2

temperature at some point actually is 17·5031°, but we rarely have instruments accurate enough to measure it.

So whenever some phenomenon occurs in continuously variable form, there can, theoretically, be an infinite number of values. We have to find ways, for the purposes of statistical manipulation, to group them into *classes* and that may even be necessary with discrete variables if they are too small. If Randall had taken *class intervals* of 1 cm, he would have had some 45 classes which would have been fairly difficult to handle, and unnecessarily detailed for his purposes. So he grouped them into classes at 30 mm intervals and it is usually found, in practice, that in the investigation of human characteristics, some 10 to 15 classes are adequate. It so happens that the inch of imperial measure provides an ideal interval for measuring many human dimensions.

The information has been displayed as a table (Table 6.2), but it could have been shown as a *frequency polygon* or a *histogram*. The frequency polygon is simply a graphic representation of the same information, plotting the *class* intervals along the horizontal scale (*abscissa*) and the number of cases for each class interval on the vertical scale (*ordinate*). (Figure 6.2.)

For some purposes a *histogram* is more useful than a *frequency polygon*;

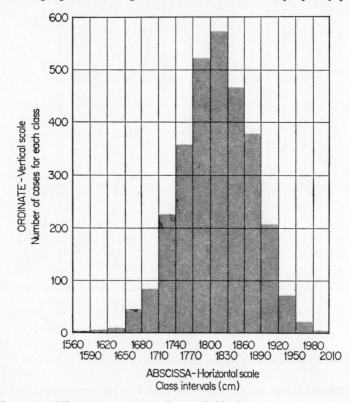

Figure 6.3—Histogram corresponding to Table 6.2

the frequency distribution is still represented graphically but by means of vertical bars or columns (Figure 6.3). If all the bars are the same width, and they usually are, then the relative size of the class interval is represented by its area = height × width.

In all three forms of display the frequency distribution can be expressed as a percentage of the total rather than the number of cases. It is quite permissible, in a histogram, to cut out classes at either end of the abscissa which contain no numbers; this does not distort the information in any way. It is a different matter, however, if one tampers with the vertical scale, or ordinate. If one cuts out the zero line and starts higher up the histogram, it is possible to exaggerate the effects of class differences. This is often done for political purposes whereas if the full height of the histogram is shown such differences may appear to be negligible.

The histogram displays very clearly one of the most important truths in statistics—that the concept of 'average' is too simple. There are at least three ways of finding out what the majority of a population do; these are described as the *mean*, the *median* and the *mode*.

THE MEAN—or arithmetic mean—is what most people understand by 'average'. It is the most elegant measure of a central tendency, the easiest to define and the easiest to calculate. The mean is found by adding up the values of all the items and dividing the total by the actual number of items. In our example the concept of *mean* is irrelevant. It could be found by totalling *all* the heights in the sample—which ranged from 1,560–2,009 mm —and dividing by the number of subjects, and it would probably come to 1,764 mm.

THE MEDIAN is the central item in the entire set. If there is an odd number of items, it is the one in the middle; if there is an even number of items, it is midway between the central pair. In our example there are 15 classes between 1,560 and 2,009 mm inclusive and the median is 1,770–1,799 mm.

THE MODE is simply the value which occurs most frequently. We can spot this easily from the table, the frequency polygon or the histogram; it is 1,740–1,769 mm.

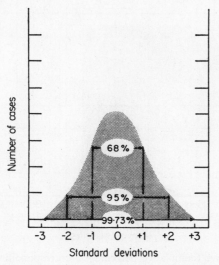

Figure 6.4—Properties of the normal curve (Gaussian distribution)

Each of these values, therefore, is a specific measure of *central tendency* which can be used in particular circumstances. If the distribution is reasonably 'normal' then the median, or the mean, might be appropriate (the median is that value which exceeds half the cases, and is exceeded itself by the other half); whereas if the distribution is at all 'skewed', i.e. weighted towards one or other of the extremes, it may be more reasonable to use the mode.

'Normal' distribution, in a statistical sense, is *Gaussian* distribution, named after the great German mathematician, and it takes the form of the familiar 'bell-shaped' curve (Figure 6.4).

Dispersion

Having dealt with measures of a central tendency, we know the average height of Randall's population, his air force cadets, but that is not enough. It is clear from the histogram that a very large proportion of them were between 1,780 and 1,830 mm high; they clustered within 50 mm of the median. Clearly this would be of interest to clothing manufacturers, chair designers and so on; but what about the extremes; should we not take them into account also in determining the overall range of clothing sizes or seat heights that should be manufactured?

We might, for instance, take the extreme figures 1,560 mm for the shortest man and 2,009 mm for the tallest. That would give us a *range* of 449 mm

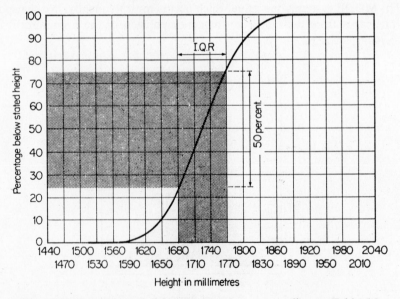

Figure 6.5—Ogive (cumulative percentages) corresponding to Table 6.2, showing I.Q.R. (inter-quartile range)

and clearly no manufacturer or retailer could afford to stock suits covering all this range. It was a matter of accident, in any case, as to exactly what sizes the tallest and shortest happened to be—the *probability* that the individuals concerned would arrive for measuring would be very low indeed.

It is more useful, therefore, to work out a range in terms of *quartiles*, and we have gone some way towards this already in locating the *median*. The median represented that value for nought around which 50 per cent of the population fell above, and the other 50 per cent below. We can extend this principle by subdividing further the upper and lower halves, thus finding *quartiles*, so that 25 per cent of the population fall above the *upper quartile*, and 25 per cent fall below the *lower quartile*. The majority of the population —commonly 50 per cent—will then fall within the quartile range (Figure 6.5).

Standard Deviation

Whilst the mean, the median and the mode are essential concepts in statistics, as measures of the central *tendency* there are many other things which can

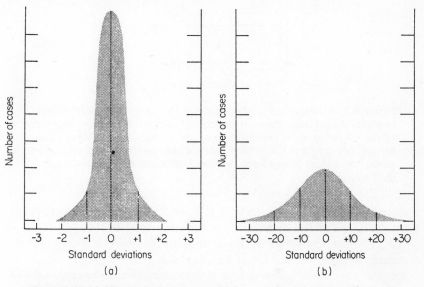

Figure 6.6—(a) Homogeneous group with low standard deviation. (b) Variable group with high standard deviation

be analysed once the distribution has been plotted. Even if the curve itself is symmetrical, it can still tell us a great deal.

In Figure 6.6(a) the mean has the great majority of values clustered about it, whereas in Figure 6.6(b), the mean itself has a low value and there are many deviations from it. These can be measured in terms of the *standard deviation* which is calculated as follows:

1. Measure the deviation of each value from the mean.
2. Square each of these deviations, and calculate the *mean* of all these squares.
3. Find the square root of this *mean*.

The *standard deviation*, therefore, is the square root of the mean values of the squares of all the deviations from the distribution mean. As an example, given a set of numbers 8, 7, 9, 6 and 10, their arithmetic mean is 8, and their

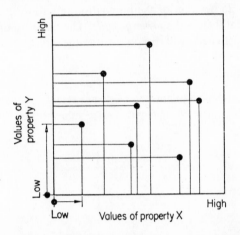

Figure 6.7—Correlations applied. During the course of an experiment or observational study, different values will be recorded for those properties of the subject(s) under investigation which are variable. Different values for any two properties (e.g. height/weight; temperature/comfort) can be plotted on a chart of this form and conclusions can then be drawn about their relationships

respective deviations from 8 are 0, 1, 1, 2 and 2. The squares of these deviations are 0, 1, 1, 4 and 4; added together, they total $0 + 1 + 1 + 4 + 4 = 10$ . . . and the mean of these squared numbers is 2 . . . so the standard deviation for this set of numbers is 2.

But this and similar relationships between variables can be expressed as a *coefficient of correlation* between those variables (Figure 6.7). There are many ways of expressing such correlations but the commonest is the 'Pearson product-moment coefficient of correlation' for which the symbol is *r*. Two things may be absolutely related; as one varies so does the other in an exact correlationship. In this case the correlation will be described as 'perfect positive' and will be given a value of $+1\cdot00$. But the magnitudes of correlations may range from this towards zero, which is the absence of any correlation

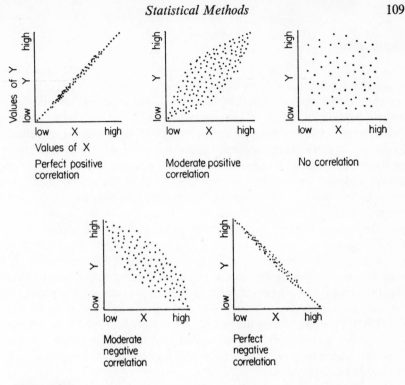

Figure 6.8

whatsoever, through various negative values to —1·00, which is 'perfect negative' correlation (see Figure 6.8).

The characteristics which are being correlated may exist:

1. in each member or group (our relationship of height and weight was such a case) or
2. within quite different things existing at the same time (e.g. the temperature in England and the number of overcoats worn in Germany).

Correlations are very easy to plot but they must be interpreted with great sensitivity. There is a comparatively high positive correlation between the number of radio and television licences issued in England between 1930 and 1956, and the number of deaths from coronary artery disease (Yudkin, 1957). But it would not be true to say that one is the direct and only cause of the other. There is also an inverse correlation between the number of overcoats worn in Germany on a particular day, and the temperature in England. Again, one is by no means the *cause* of the other but both are the result of a third factor, the northern winter. At best, a perfect correlation indicates that the relationship between two events is worth investigating.

Significance

When the heights of Randall's young men were plotted in the form of a histogram they approximated fairly closely to a normal distribution. In other words the observed results conformed, within limits, to the expected theoretical distribution. Sometimes, however, the observed data fails to match one's theoretical expectations. The difference may, or may not, be *significant*. Significance, in this sense, can be measured and tests of significance form an essential part of statistical method. These depend on a comparison between the observed figures and such departures from the theoretical results as one might expect to occur by *chance*. If the observed divergence could only have happened by chance once in a thousand times, then clearly any observed divergence is very important. We can express a ·001 per cent level of *confidence* in it. If the divergence can be expected once in a hundred times, then our level of confidence will be ·01 per cent; for once in twenty, it will be 5 per cent; for once in ten, 10 per cent and so on. Where, according to the laws of chance, the difference is likely to occur for more than 5 per cent of observations then any observed difference is regarded as not significant or, at least, its significance is not proven. Where the probability is 5 per cent, observed differences are regarded as probably significant, and as it diminishes below 5 per cent, then the difference is regarded as increasingly significant. 1 per cent, in fact, is regarded as *significant*.

One of the most frequently used tests of significance, in this sense, is the χ^2 (pronounced ki-squared) test which was developed by Pearson (1900) on a theoretical basis devised by Helmert. It is used where observations of similar characteristics in different samples have led to different results, to test the significance of these results on the assumption, initially, that there should be no significant difference between them. To operate the test one takes the observed value for each observation (0), subtracts the expected value (E), squares the result and divides by the expected result. The full equation, therefore, is:

$$\frac{(0-E)^2}{E}$$

This calculation is performed for each observed value and the results are added to give χ^2

$$\chi^2 = \sum \frac{(0-E)^2}{E}$$

There is one complication, however. One's theoretical expectations on tossing a coin are that it will fall heads 50 per cent of the times and tails 50 per cent of the times. But for a given set of observations it might fall 60 per cent heads and 40 per cent tails. In other words, the two possibilities are mutually exclusive; the results fall into two classes (C); the *degree of freedom* (D.O.F.) in the observations is 1. For a single row of observations such as this the D.O.F. is given by $(C — 1)$. The significance of the result, clearly, is affected by the D.O.F.; and it is given, finally, by the χ^2 table, which takes into account both χ^2 and D.O.F. for the given set of observations. In practice the χ^2 test can be used when three or more classes are available, each of which contains five or more members. One might tabulate these as follows:

Class   A   B   C
Number in class   5   7   6

The χ^2 test can also be used where two or more samples have been obtained in three or more classes.

Class   A   B   C
Sample 1.   5   7   6
Sample 2.   6   5   7

In this case the D.O.F. calculation takes account both of columns (C) and rows (R)

$$\text{D.O.F.} = (C — 1)(R — 1)$$

In a typical χ^2 calculation one prepares first of all a data table on the pattern shown in Table 6.3.

Table 6.3—Data table for χ^2 test

Class	A	B	C	Row total
Sample 1.	a	b	c	$a + b + c$
2.	d	e	f	$d + e + f$
Column total (C)	$a + d$	$b + e$	$c + f$	Grand total (N)

One then prepares a χ^2 table, taking each entry in order $a, b, c, \ldots$ (Table 6.4). Suppose, for instance, we wish to test the effects, if any, which different arrangements have on the production of drawings in the office. We have three classes of facilities:

1. drawing board on high table, draftsman standing;
2. drawing board on low table, draftsman seated;
3. drafting machine, adjustable to taste.

We also have two samples of draftsmen:

A. qualified architects;
B. qualified technicians.

Design in Architecture

Table 6.4—χ^2 table format

Observed numbers (0)	Expected values $\dfrac{R \times C}{N} = E$	Differences $(0 - E) = D$	D^2	$\dfrac{D^2}{E}$
a				
b				
c				

We measure productivity in terms of A2 size drawings (or equivalent) produced by six draftsmen of each kind, for each facility, in one week (Table 6.5).

Table 6.5

Class	A	B	C	
Sample 1.	9	6	2	17
Sample 2.	11	5	5	21
	20	11	7	38

Table 6.6—Example of χ^2 tabular calculation

0	$P \times N = E$	$(0 - E) = D$	D^2	$\dfrac{D^2}{E}$
9	$\dfrac{1}{6} \times 36 = 6$	3	9	$\dfrac{9}{6} = 1{\cdot}5$
6	6	0	0	$\dfrac{0}{6} =$
2	6	−4	16	$\dfrac{16}{6} = 2{\cdot}66$
11	6	5	25	$\dfrac{25}{6} = 4{\cdot}16$
5	6	−1	1	$\dfrac{1}{6} = 0{\cdot}16$
5	6	−1	1	$\dfrac{1}{6} = 0{\cdot}16$

D.O.F. $= (C - 1)(R - 1) = 2 \times 1 = 2$ $\chi^2 = 8{\cdot}64$

The χ^2 calculation can then be completed in tabular form (Table 6.6). If we refer to the standard χ^2 table, we find that for a D.O.F. $= 2$ and $\chi^2 = 8\cdot64$ the observed differences in productivity could be expected on slightly more than 1 per cent of occasions. A significant difference, therefore is proven.

CHAPTER 7

Human Science Techniques

Having outlined the nature of statistics, we can now consider the application of statistical techniques in the human sciences. Let us look first of all at one of the most direct of the human sciences, one which is less ridden with conflicting theories and polemics than the others, that is ergonomics. Ergonomics is a form of applied research, which has been developed to study the interrelations and interactions of men and machines. When design was a pragmatic affair a *fit* eventually developed between man and the tools, weapons, furniture and buildings which he made for his own use. As Endholm says (1967), the Egyptians knew, around 1500 B.C., how to make a chair which for seat height and slope of back was 'better' than anything produced for a further three and a half thousand years. The Windsor chairmakers knew how to make a comfortable seat, for one person, out of solid timber. A man would sit on a bank of clay, and the chair seat would then be carved to match the impression which he left on rising. Queen Victoria's children each had a personal chair, made to size and labelled with his name. Why, then, has it become necessary recently to invent this new field of research?

The answer, as with so many of these new disciplines, lies in weapons design. Before World War I, the equipment and machines used by the fighting services were relatively unsophisticated. During that war new kinds of weapons, such as aircraft and tanks, came into widespread use and they were designed, on the whole, for maximum mechanical efficiency. If that meant discomfort and strain for their operators, it was too bad and it was certainly true that, between the wars, labour was readily available and there seemed to be plenty of time; it was most economical, therefore, to train men to fit the machines. But, already, towards the end of World War I, it had been realized that although no one paid much attention to the comfort of men in battle, production in the factories could be increased if conditions of work were improved. An Industrial Fatigue Research Board was set up (Murrell, 1965) and men trained in the human sciences went into the factories to study men at work. Their approach was rather different from that of the management planners, e.g. Gilbreth in America, whose *Motion Study* (1909, 1917) was based on intelligent observation of people at work rather than on controlled experiment. Throughout the 1920s the Industrial Fatigue Research Board worked in close collaboration with the National Institute of Industrial Psychology and, in 1929, it became the Industrial Health Research Board—

114

indicating a human change in emphasis. However, in the 1930s, industry itself was in an unhealthy state with rising unemployment; the effective use of manpower seemed less important than the process of selection from the large pool of superfluous labour available.

With the outbreak of World War II the situation changed again. The new weapons were very complex indeed; men were subjected to enormous stresses and, what is more, the majority of them were conscripted; they had to be trained quickly. It was necessary to establish, as far as possible, the limits of human performance, and to redesign the weapons so that large numbers of conscripts, coming in all shapes and sizes, could use them efficiently. Research groups were established at Oxford, Cambridge and Dayton, Ohio, and the armed services kept in close touch with these groups. Multi-disciplinary teams were set up, of engineers, industrial designers, psychologists, physiologists and, above all, statisticians. The latter in particular were essential to the exercise because, if the machines were to *fit* the enormous variety of human types who would use them, it was essential that large numbers of men should be measured, in order to establish central tendencies and standard deviations. The study of human performance and of man/machine relationships gathered great momentum and after the war it was seen that much would be lost if each specialist returned to his own discipline. It became necessary, therefore, to identify their combined interests in such a way that they could continue to contribute to it with a real sense of purpose. So in 1949 Murrell and others arranged an inter-disciplinary meeting of anatomists, physiologists, industrial medical officers, industrial hygienists, design engineers, work study engineers, architects, illuminating engineers and so on, out of which the Ergonomics Research Society was formed. The word *ergonomics* itself was coined from the Greek, *ergos* (work) and *nomos* (natural laws) (Murrell 1965). Curiously enough, American research workers in the same field have found it unnecessary to invent a new name for their study; they use two ordinary words instead and call it *Human Engineering* (McKormick, 1957).

The ergonomist, or human engineer, is concerned with people and with the things they use; like the psychologist and the sociologist, he has to find some way of relating two kinds of information which are different in kind from each other. He describes the physical, measurable characteristics of things, such as their length, breadth, weight, location, the number of them and so on, as *parameters*. Bross (1953) says that this word is 'merely mathematical jargon for a symbolic quality, such as L, which may be associated with some measurable quality on the real word such as length. That is fairly straightforward, but there is some confusion over two other terms which ergonomists and others tend to use. McKormick (1957) and Chapanis (1959) call the physical things which can be changed during the course of an experiment, such as the design of a dial, the colour of a painted surface, the height of a seat, the level of illumination, temperature and so on, *independent variables*. Each may be varied separately, as the experimenter chooses, which is why they are called independent. For the same authors, *dependent variables* are those over which the experimenter has no control, such as the performance of people, their sensitivity of touch, their attitudes, physiological processes and so on. In other words, these are the things which the experimenter is trying to test and they may change as the physical parameters and independent variables are changed, but the experimenter cannot change them directly. Others believe that these meanings should be reversed, that as the experimenter has no control over the behaviour of people, just as he cannot control the vagaries of the weather, these are the true independent variables. As we shall see, such confusions have arisen in many of the new disciplines.

Whatever the terminology (and it hardly matters as long as each author actually defines his terms) the intention of classifying the properties of a man-machine, or other system, is that they shall be measured. In other words, they shall be plotted against some kind of scale. It is easy to see that when things have been measured physically, and therefore have numbers attached to them, they can be put into order on some kind of *scale* starting, say, with the smallest and working to the largest. Things which are not so easily measurable, such as matters of opinion, can also be put on to scales. S. S. Stevens (1951) distinguishes four types of such scales: *nominal, ordinal, interval* and *ratio*.

NOMINAL SCALE represents the simplest way in which objects can be put into order. Each of them is given a number, much as a football player is given a number, and the objects *may* be put in order of their numbers. There is no significance in this, and the numbers could be interchanged without its having the slightest effect, but there is another type of *nominal* scale in which, with a large number of objects, all those having the same characteristics are given the same number. This, of course, leads to enormous complications in the logic of classification (see Set Theory) but a simple rule removes most of the difficulties: 'Do not assign the same numeral to different classes or different numerals to the same class.' Beyond that, as S. S. Stevens says, 'anything goes with the nominal scale.'

ORDINAL SCALE arises from the need not just to *number* things, but to rank them in some kind of *order*. The sergeant-major's 'tallest on the right, shortest on the left' is an example of ordinal scaling and, once things have been placed in order, the scale can be used, unchanged, for many types of operations. Stevens suggests that *most* of the scales used in psychology are of this type, and many operations performed with them are therefore 'illegal'. The point about ordinal scales is that, although the *order* of objects is known, the intervals between them are not; some may be very large and some may be very small, but on the ordinal scale they all *look* the same. Typical ordinal scales would be 'hardness of minerals, quality of leather, lumber, wool etc., pleasantness of odour.'

INTERVAL SCALE maintains the order of objects, and also defines the intervals between them. Stevens quotes the two scales of temperature—centigrade and Fahrenheit. In both cases, the marks on the thermometer are equal, and they denote equal volumes of expansion in the mercury. But the zero point on each scale is quite arbitrary, and a numerical value in one scale is converted into an equivalent value in the other scale by means of an equation: $x^1 = ax + b$. But 22°C is equivalent to 72°F and I with my Fahrenheit thermometer am not three and a half times as hot as you with your centigrade. Periods of *time*, on the other hand, can be expressed in such ratios; two months *are* twice as long as one, although calendar *dates* have similar limitations to temperatures. However, one date can be subtracted from another, and the number of *days* can be manipulated by ratio. The essence of interval scales, therefore, is that they have no *zero* although they may be related to one by means of a constant. Typical interval scales are temperature, energy, calendar date, intelligence and other tests of human ability.

RATIO SCALES are the absolute scales of physics and, to be absolute, they need a zero point. Number itself is a ratio scale and in physics two types of ratio scale may be distinguished: *fundamental* and *derived*. Fundamental scales are matters of direct, physical measurement—length, weight, electrical resistance, whereas derived scales are mathematical functions obtained from these, such as density, velocity or elasticity. Once a ratio scale has been set up, its numerical values can be transformed to another scale (e.g. feet to inches) by multiplying each value by a constant (e.g. 12). Once an absolute zero has been set up all types of statistical manipulation are possible.

One of the major problems of all the human sciences is that human affairs in general can rarely be plotted on ratio scales. Often it is barely possible to use even an ordinal scale and a great many spurious conclusions are reached because once an ordinal scale has been set up it is manipulated as if it were an interval, or even a ratio, scale. This has been particularly true in psychology and sociology: once we start to examine these in detail, then certain difficulties arise. Markus says (1970):

'There are difficulties of language, and of orientation. There are divisions between experimenters and those who employ social survey techniques, between those wishing to measure physiological response (e.g. pupil diameter, sweat rate or galvanic skin response) and those who prefer to go direct to measures of performance (e.g. error on standard visual tasks) or behavioural patterns or choices: and between all these and those who attempt to measure the strength of concepts, attitudes and evaluative judgments about environment by semantic techniques.'

Now, clearly, all these techniques are valuable in the human sciences; the fact that these practitioners disagree with each other simply leads to productive tensions between them. The question that interests us is whether results obtained in these ways can, or should, have any effect on what we design.

To reiterate, our task as designers of architecture is to reconcile the needs of certain human activities with a given climate by controlling that climate through the medium of building. The building will be real, physical and three-dimensional; it will enclose spaces which are appropriate, in terms of space standards, environmental control and so on, for the activities which are to take place there, and it will also contain various means by which the user can move or otherwise communicate from space to space.

Experiment in human science, by definition, will involve the setting up of artificial conditions in which certain variables within the environment—heating, lighting, sound conditions, the presence or absence of other people and so on—can be treated as independent and their effects monitored on the subject of the experiment. This monitoring, as Markus says, may take several forms; in particular one may measure physiological response or performance.

Even setting up the experiment will lead to difficulties (Edwards, 1965; Chapanis, 1967). The classic example, I suppose, is the work of Weston and others in the 1930s on school day lighting. This was undertaken for the Medical Research Council and certain assumptions were brought to it: that most people have congenital defects, however slight, in their visual systems and that, for this reason, if school children habitually read under inadequate lighting conditions their eyes will be damaged. Not only that; it was also assumed that daylight was inherently 'better' than electric light for this purpose.

It was on this basis, therefore, that Weston and his team undertook a comprehensive series of studies on visual acuity in children which will be described later, in Chapter 8. Weston's work was thorough enough and he was careful to point out its probabilistic nature. It was taken however that Weston had defined a reasonable minimum level for the worst position in the classroom (now 100 lux); the problem then became a matter of relating this to the actual design of schools. The difficulty, of course, was that sky luminance varies from summer to winter, dawn to dusk, according to the state of the weather, cloud cover and so on.

Sky luminance had, however, been monitored at Teddington (National Physical Laboratory) for many years and figures could be extrapolated for probable luminance throughout an average year. This level exceeded 5000 lux for 86 per cent of the time in which schools are occupied (09.00 to 16.00 hours) and 5000 lux, therefore, was adopted as the luminance level of a standard overcast sky. The child's desk would be illuminated at the working plane, to the required standard (100 lux) if from that position he could see 2 per cent of a standard overcast sky, and thus the 2 per cent daylight factor was devised which became a mandatory constraint on the designers of schools with the Education Act of 1944 (Min. of Ed., 1959).

Because a standard was available, and it seemed to be based on hard data, it was applied in isolation with results which have been summarized by Musgrove (1966), Manning (1967) and the RIA Group (1970). Its immediate effects on design, as summarized by the latter, are that with an 8 ft ceiling (2·4m) the 2 per cent daylight factor can be achieved only up to depths of 16 ft (4·8 m) from the window; if one wants a deeper room, it also has to be higher. One could, of course, use roof lights or clerestories if the form of the building otherwise allowed it.

Rooms which satisfy the requirement naturally have a large window area in relation to unglazed wall and they may have a high rate of external wall even to internal volume. As the RIA report goes on to say:

'. . . large areas of glazing produce sky glare discomfort under certain conditions of sky luminance, irrespective of orientation. High brightness sky may be the area of greatest luminance usable from inside the room, causing serious visual distraction and a serious reduction in visual acuity. If in addition, the windows admit direct sunlight, excessive luminous contrasts can result, reducing visual acuity still further, and possibly producing reflected glare from specular surfaces, and so still greater visual discomfort.'

In addition to this, if the room is entirely side-lit, there will be such a difference in the quantity of daylight between the window wall and the far side of the room that, in order to relieve the apparent gloom, blinds may be drawn and electric light used instead.

In terms of lighting alone, then, the experimental studies lead to some unexpected results and when one considers the effects of large windows on other aspects of the environment, further problems arise. As the RIA report puts it:

'. , . the larger the "proportion" of glass in external walls, the greater will be the effects of solar over-heating and radiation and/or convective cooling producing greater heat losses through the fabric by conduction and radiation, greater heat gains due to radiation, larger building air temperature swings, greater difficulties in thermal control, and more complaints of unsatisfactory thermal environment.'

Again 90 per cent of the noise which penetrates into the building from external sources comes through the windows (Lewis, 1970): over half of this arrives via the cracks around the edges of windows so that from this point of view also unless these are sealed, which implies air conditioning, the windows should be kept as small as possible.

Far from leading to improvements in school design, therefore, the daylight factor has led to actual deterioration in standards, for certain environmental variables, compared with traditional school building. There were several reasons for this. Most obvious is the fact that a single variable, daylighting, was abstracted and made the subject of laboratory experiment. One would expect this to be the case on theoretical grounds alone for, clearly, in the working environment, *all* the variables (environmental, structural, social and psychological) act and interact simultaneously. Not only that, but the human being is acting as a multi-modal, sensing organism. The various senses are stimulated simultaneously; each perceptual act is a transaction between stimulus and experience. That experience is being augmented continuously by every act of each of the senses: what one sees is being modified continuously against what one has seen, has heard and is hearing, has felt and is feeling, has smelt and is smelling, and so on (Dean and McGlothlen, 1965).

Research into synaesthesia, the interchange of experience between senses, is still in its infancy and, whilst a good deal of poetic insight into the subject is available (McKellar, 1957) and most of us have experience now of sound-light shows, if only on television, enough is known to suggest that the person who feels cool because the wall is painted blue may not be deceiving himself (Wenner, 1954).

Clearly the various parts of the building interact in analogous, if much less complex, ways. The founding fathers of modern architecture forgot entirely that in divorcing the function of support (by using the steel or concrete frame) from that of spatial separation (by using light partitions or glass) they were losing not only the supporting function of the wall, but its environmental control properties also, in terms of sound control, thermal control (including its heat storage capacities) and so on.

It is clear too that the external environment acts as a whole in this sense, that the building itself changes the micro-climate, affects traffic patterns, social interactions and so on. We shall have to be absolutely certain as to what we are trying to do, therefore, if we abstract *any* variable from the man/building/environment relationship and make it the subject of experiment. Not only that, but the experiment itself will be subject to indeterminacy. By taking people out of the environment and placing them in the laboratory we shall add to their experience and thus *may* change their responses. They will bring experience to bear on the experiment itself, and this certainly will help determine their responses.

There are inherent difficulties then in applying the results of *experiments on people* into environmental design. Clearly experiment has a great deal to offer in the development of building materials, structures and environmental control systems, and will continue to do so into the foreseeable future, but it is difficult to see how experiments involving people, whatever their value in supporting sociological, psychological or social hypotheses, can have any value in setting up standards for environmental design.

The difficulties become even greater when one starts to *ask* people what they want. As Roethlisberger and Dickson (1939) put it:

'It is commonly supposed, although there is very little evidence to warrant such an assumption, that there exists a simple and logical relationship between what a person says and what he thinks.'

La Pierre (1934) provides the classic example of inconsistency between verbal response and behaviour. He travelled across the United States with a Chinese couple staying in hotels and eating in restaurants. Later he questioned the managers of these establishments as to whether, in principle, they would accommodate Chinese guests. Over 90 per cent said they would not! Kuttner and others (1952) carried out a further study which also suggests that those who express racial prejudices verbally do not necessarily act according to their convictions in face-to-face encounters with members of the despised race. So we cannot take verbal responses at face value, even though a great deal of ergonomic, psychological and sociological research is undertaken as if we could.

That becomes clear when one considers the number of techniques which have been developed for *measuring* verbal response. They are used in a wide range of the human sciences, from ergonomics (comparing, say, physiological response with verbal) to market research (finding out what kinds of consumer goods people seem to want). Before we look at techniques for measuring verbal response in detail, we ought to look at a typical application in architectural psychology. Canter (1967) describes such an application with reference to a study of the preferences which people expressed for working in offices of different sizes. His study moved through six stages:

1. *Is there a problem?* This is a matter of asking people what they *think* they want. In this case, out of 1,180 people asked, 44 per cent said they would prefer to work in an office for about four people and only 1 per cent wanted to work in an office of eighty.

2. *Can the problem actually be studied?* Do the people's attitudes to other things correlate in any way with their preferences in this particular case, e.g. do people who prefer small offices also like large windows? Again Canter asked questions, and analysed the results. There were strong correlations between people's attitudes to room size, their relationships to other people in the new building, their enjoyment of their work, and their satisfaction, even, with the lift service.

3. *Does the variable have much effect on what people actually do in real life?* Even if people say they prefer small offices, do they work badly in large ones? Canter thought that extroverts might work better than introverts in large rooms, but he could detect no relation between personality, measured in this particular way, and room size. But both extroverts and introverts seemed to work less well in the larger rooms.

4. *Does the variable have much effect on what people say, or feel, about their jobs in real life?* Canter was surprised to find that people became happier on three important counts as room size increased: they felt that communications between themselves and management were better, in both directions; they had a greater feeling of being in the 'right' job and they were much less disturbed by noise and other distractions within the room.

5. *Can these surprising results of 3 and 4 be checked under strictly controlled laboratory conditions?* Laboratory tests on students confirmed: (a) that extroversion/introversion has nothing to do with performance in rooms of different sizes, and (b) that distractions such as noise do *not* affect performance in simple clerical work.

6. *What new problem has the study thrown up?* (or back to square one); in this case, there seemed to be considerable discrepancies between what people *said* they did and what they actually did. This suggested more detailed investigations into relationships between verbal behaviour and actual performance in the building itself.

There are difficulties, obviously, in applying the results of such research into architectural design. If it really is true that 44 per cent of people prefer to work in 4-person offices, and 1 per cent in 80-person offices, do we then design a building in which these preferences could be satisfied? In the first place, this would determine the minimum size of organization we should design a building for, i.e. 8,000, so that 1 per cent of the employees could be accommodated in an 80-person office.

However, one must remember the fact that people's preferences change. They adapt, habituate and otherwise begin to prefer conditions which they could not envisage preferring until they had experienced them. This is not invariably true. Some people will *not* adapt, say, to a change of office size, and what is the morality of trying to force them?

None of the human sciences individually has a monopoly of observation techniques, but it will be convenient to describe a number of them with reference to applications in anthropology, sociology and marketing, which is where they were developed. Madge too (1953) has summarized the methods available for conducting a social enquiry under the headings of observation, the interview, experiment and the use of documentary evidence. The latter ranges in type from personal documents, official records and statistics to newspaper reports. Naturally they vary in reliability and there are dangers too that one might pick out only the information which tends to support one's case. Observation too has its difficulties: the presence of the observer may disturb people so they behave self-consciously, and thus the observer will never know how they would have acted if he had not been there. If in the interests of greater accuracy he tries to get too close to them, his subjects may well be even more inhibited. Harrison (1947) advocates the unobtrusive *overhearing* of what people say when they are unaware of the observer's presence. Apart from that, the observer will naturally bring his own predilections and biases to bear in his perception of his subjects.

Some authorities suggest that all these difficulties can best be faced by the participant observer, a term first used by Lindeman (1924) which describes a technique originated by the anthropologist Malinowski (1922) in his western Pacific studies:

'I began to take part, in a way, in the village life, to look forward to the important or festive events, to take a personal interest in the gossip and the developments of the small village occurrences . . . Quarrels, jokes, family scenes, events usually trivial, sometimes dramatic, but always significant formed the atmosphere of my daily life, as of theirs.'

Lindeman describes the technique:

'*Participant observation* is based on the theory that an interpretation of an event can only be approximately correct when it is a composite of the two points of view, the *outside* and the *inside*. Thus the view of the person who was a participant in the event, whose wishes and interests were in some way involved, and the view of the person who was not a participant but only an observer, or analyst, coalesce in one final synthesis.'

However careful he is, the participant observer will disturb people by his questioning, interviewing and form filling, and this must be taken into account when his results are collated. Many people will be suspicious of him; they may even give him silly answers. Yet if he identifies himself too closely with the people he is investigating, he may find it difficult to pull out when his work is complete. These and other difficulties explain, as Sprott says (1958), why so much social research centres on school children and criminals; they may be approached fairly easily and they are in no position to complain.

As Madge says (1953), the method *par excellence* of social science is the *interview*, which he defines as 'purposive conversation'. In this particular context, it will be a 'meeting undertaken to collect information' and, if one wishes to ensure that useful information will be collected, then it will probably be associated with its 'half brother', the *questionnaire*. It may be, of course, that the interviewer does not really wish to collect useful information. The *counselling interview*, as its name suggests, is a development of Freudian psychoanalysis, in which people are encouraged to talk freely with a view to developing insight and personal understanding. *Any* interview may help the subject in this way, even if that was not specifically intended, and there have been cases where the interviewer's obvious care and understanding did a great deal for his subject's sense of well-being. Mayo's famous 'Hawthorne experiments' were one instance of this and similar effects may be detected in reports of surveys at Park Hill in Sheffield and Lasdun's Cluster Blocks in Bethnal Green.

The interviewer is in search of specific information; he will probably structure his questions by means of a questionnaire, and this will take careful preparation. Questions will have to be framed in language which the subjects are likely to understand; and in particular the questionnaire itself should be planned so as to control, as far as possible, distortions which the questioner's own predilections are likely to introduce, bearing in mind that these can influence the subjects in many subtle ways—the intonation of a question, a raised eyebrow, a smile or other non-verbal indicators can all help determine the response. A good questionnaire will contain certain means of identification—a title, serial number, names, places, dates and so on—although in certain cases these may have to be coded so as not to bias the respondents. It will provide space for information on the respondent (age, sex, marital status, occupation and so on) and possibly even his name. It will also contain control questions on simple factual matters, or certain questions repeated and rephrased as a check on the respondent's veracity.

The subject matter of the questionnaire might consist, first of all, of an introduction, an explanation to the respondent as to what the questionnaire is for, why he has been selected to answer it and how the material will be used. In setting up the questionnaire in the first place one ought to have some idea of how the information is going to be analysed; this will help one to ask relevant questions and to formulate them in usable ways. There is clearly a difference between questions which ask people about their *behaviour* and those which merely encourage them to express an opinion; both may be useful, but one should be clear as to which is intended and how to distinguish between them.

The questionnaire itself will form the basis of a *focussed interview*, a form which was first described by Merton and Kendall (1946). The characteristics of such an interview are its non-direction. Merton and Kendall suggest a range of techniques by which the interviewer's personal bias can be played down; *specificity*, in which the interview is focussed on a small and relevant range of the respondent's experience; *range* which describes the degree to which the interview with a particular person confirms or refutes the hypotheses on which the questionnaire was set up; *depth* which describes the intensity of personal feeling which particular questions seemed to evoke. The questions themselves will have to be selected with care. The least specific kind will be *unstructured* or *open-ended* questions; such a question might read: 'What strikes you particularly about living in this house?'—which might release in the respondent a pent-up diatribe about its deficiencies, a word or two of praise for the architect or complete indifference. *Semi-structured* questions obviously will be rather more specific and they may take one of two forms. In the first of these the questionnaire will indicate a particular topic, but the question itself may be rephrased according to circumstances, by the interviewer himself. In the second type the question itself may be carefully phrased to encourage a free response: 'How does this house differ from the one you were in before?' Finally, there are *structured* questions and these again may take two forms: *multiple choice* questions and *dichotomous* questions. A multiple choice question will be accompanied by a series of possible answers and the respondent must choose one of these. Clearly the list of answers will have to be complete, even if that means including 'none of these' or 'don't know', and it will have to be shown to respondents. For this reason the interviewer might have this list in several arrangements, so as to avoid biasing his respondents from the positions of the various answers on his list. The dichotomous question reduces all possible responses to a yes/no form, which is by no means the case with open-ended questions.

This brings us finally to the inherent dilemma of questionnaires, and therefore of interview construction. The unstructured question gives the respondent free rein; he can say what he likes, within limits, and *what* he says is presumably prompted by his inner compulsions. The dichotomous question, on the other hand, puts ideas into his head; it suggests answers to him about things he may never have thought about, and even if he had prior opinions they may well be distorted by being forced into one answer or other of the yes/no pair. Dichotomous questions make things easy for the interviewer and easier still for the statistician, but unstructured questions may have such wide ranging answers and imply so many things that they can hardly be analysed at all. It is in fact a classic case of indeterminacy.

However, the problem goes deeper. Canter (1969) has shown how once data is available from interviews and questionnaires another kind of indeterminacy arises when one tries to analyse it. He is concerned with attitude scales and with the precision, robustness, validity and reliability of such scales. As an architect one may be concerned, for instance, with the degree to which children will be disturbed by noise in the school classroom, the degree to which this will affect their studies and the precautions one should take in the actual design and construction of the school to ensure that extraneous noise is kept to an acceptable level. Clearly this level will depend on many things: the kind of teaching which is going on, the other kinds of stimulus and distraction which are affecting the children and, above all, the tolerance for noise which they have built up over their years of experience of living in houses, working in schools and otherwise existing in environments where they may or may not have been disturbed by noise.

The psychologist sees it rather differently. He is concerned, above all, with building up a *scale* against which the children's attitudes to noise can be measured by asking questions which may *seem* to be measuring other things but which have in common the essential feature that the children's answers to them are affected, to some degree at least, by their attitudes to noise. This is a technical matter; the psychologist is looking for a *pool* of questions which, on statistical analysis, prove to be *homogenous*, that is, which measure the same closely defined thing—in this case attitudes to noise. He is not in the least concerned with the problems of indeterminacy in such questions which we discussed earlier, or with the fact that people do not always say what they think. The information he produces, therefore, is unlikely to be of direct use to the designer.

For reasons suggested in Chapter 4, the designer is likely to be faced increasingly with material from the human sciences which is couched in the language of attitude scaling and factor analysis. If he is to assess its validity for design purposes, as distinct from 'validity' in the human scientists' sense, he would do well to familiarize himself with the jargon. Four types of attitude scaling are in general use: social distance scaling (Bogardus, 1925); Thurstone scales (1929); Likert scales (1932); and factorial scales (Cattell, 1952).

The first of these may be useful, say, in measuring racial prejudice in terms of whether one would admit Canadians, Chinese, Negroes and so on, to close kinship by marriage, to one's club, street or to some other position on the scale, of which the furthest extreme is 'would exclude from my country.' There is no guarantee that the various items *are* homogenous in the sense which other scale-constructors find necessary, that the intervals between them are equal, or even that people would agree that the order in which they are placed is a reasonable one, from one end of the scale to the other. Social distance scales seem to work quite well, however, and may be accurate enough for rough and ready application to design.

Thurstone was concerned with equal-appearing intervals. As a first step in applying Thurstone's method, one collects a large number of items (100 to 150 possible attitudes to the subject) by reading the literature, from pilot interviews and so on. Each of these items is then printed on cards or slips of paper and a number of 'judges', perhaps 50 or so, are asked to place each item into one of 11 categories, from most favourable to least favourable. One then prepares a cumulative-frequency graph (see Chapter 6) *for each item*, from which one determines the median and the inter-quartile range for that item. One then decides how many items one wants to use in the attitude-scale itself and selects an appropriate number from the 100 to 150 or so available. If one decides to use 20, for instance, one might choose those whose medians—or whose individual cumulative-frequency graphs—are nearest to 1·5, 2·0, 2·5 and so on. The median itself is then taken as the value, on the scale, of that particular item.

The 20 item scale is then submitted to the subjects of one's survey, who are asked to agree or disagree with each statement. It is likely, on the whole, that they will agree with very few of them. If a subject takes, say, a mildly positive attitude, he is likely to disagree with all the items which express strongly positive, neutral or negative attitudes. One then adds up the median values of all the items to which he has given positive answers and thus obtains that subject's personal score.

The validity of Thurstone scales obviously depends on the degree to which the subjects under test resemble the judges used in setting up the scale. Most researchers use students for this purpose, but the scales thus set up may be highly unsuitable for use, say, with school children or old-age pensioners.

Likert scales are much easier to produce than Thurstone scales but there is a reasonable correlation between the two. Likert eliminated the need for judges by trying out his scales on a number of subjects, usually around 100, who were asked to work through the test themselves. This could then be improved as a result of the trial run. Likert listed a number of statements up to, say, 150, with a three, five or even seven point scale against each, varying from strongly agree to strongly disagree. 'Strongly agree' may be scored high or low. It does not matter much as long as one is consistent. Strong agreement with certain items *may* contradict the general tenor of one's answers as a whole. In the examples shown, strong agreement to 1 may be quite incompatible with strong agreement to numbers 5 and 6.

The pilot study would soon reveal if there were incompatibilities in the scoring and if necessary the score for number 1 could be reversed in the final total. Likert's particular concern was with unidimensionality, making sure that all the items in a given set actually measured the same thing. He ensured this as far as possible by item analysis in which, at the end of the pilot study, the totals for each item over all subjects are added together and a grand total is also obtained. It is possible therefore to correlate the total for each item with the overall total, minus that for the item in question. It will then be possible to eliminate items which have a low correlation with the pool as a whole, thus purifying the test for use in the field.

Canter (1969) uses a simplified Likert scale to measure children's attitudes to classroom noise. He listed 20 possible noises and asked 200 children to

Table 7.1—Likert scale (adapted from Canter, 1969)

	Cannot hear them at all	Just hear them	Hear them clearly	They are loud	They are very loud etc.
1. People fidgeting		x			
2. Things being dropped			x		
3. Feet tapping				x	
4. Whispering			x		
5. Coughing			x		
6. Desks banging etc.					x

say how loud, in their experience, these noises usually sounded: the first six items that appeared on his list were as illustrated in Table 7.1. Being able to hear them, of course, is not the same thing as being distracted by them but there are possibilities, obviously, of correlating the results with actual physical measurements of noise in classrooms using sound-level meters and even of correlating these measurements with *attitudes* to noise.

It may be that such tests are misconceived, that whilst people are prepared to agree or disagree quite strongly with items within them, nevertheless they raise questions which otherwise would not have seemed important. This of course is true of all attitude scaling. Not only that, but an individual's total may be made up in many different ways: given 10 items, for instance, a total of 35 could be made up of 5×6 and 5×1, 7×4, 2×3 and a 1, and so on. It may be therefore that two identical scores have quite different meanings. The scale, therefore, is not reproducible but it does offer a reliable, if rough and ready, ordering of people's responses to a particular attitude. Moreover, with these five or seven point scales they allow quite fine shades of meaning to be expressed. Questions too can be subtly worded so that their implications are not obvious. This enables unusual aspects of the attitude to be explored. Semantic differential (Osgood, Suci and Tannenbaum, 1957) is a form of Likert scaling which has a particular appeal for architects because it plots concepts eventually into a three-dimensional semantic space.

Scalogram analysis was developed by Guttman and his associates (1950) and it depends on the fact that in certain areas opinions can be plotted along a scale with which most people would agree, which is *ordinal* and *cumulative*. Suppose, for instance, one takes attitudes to pre-marital sexual experience; one could plot certain items along a scale and anyone who agreed, say, with item 3 would also agree with the two items to the left of it. Some people would go all the way to the right and agree with everything, but most of them would have a 'cross over' point beyond which they would not be prepared to

Table 7.2—Guttman scale; sample answers

Subject	Item					
	1	2	3	4	5	6
1	/	/	/			
2	/		/	/		
3	/		/	/		
4	/					
5	/	/	/	/	/	/
6	/	/	/	/		/

agree. One could use the same method to see how good they were at mathematics, what they owned in the way of household goods, and so on.

Guttman's aim, primarily, was to achieve an ideal scale pattern which would be completely reproducible. He would set up a scale for validation by several hundred respondents. A small sample of their answers could be represented as shown in Table 7.2. Positive answers for each *item* have been totalled and the table is now recast to place these in descending order (Table 7.3).

The table is then redrawn again so that the *subjects* are reshuffled to place that with the highest number of positive answers to the left, and so on (Table 7.4). In a 'perfect' scalogram, the heavy line would step diagonally from bottom left to top right and *all* answers above and to the left of it would be positive. In this case there are two 'errors'—answers which do not correspond to this pattern—and these detract from its reproducibility, which Guttman measures as follows:

$$R = 1 - \frac{\text{number of errors}}{\text{number of responses}}$$

and where this figure drops below 0·9, Guttman considers the scale unsatisfactory.

Initially, there may be several dozen items in a scalogram. These may be tried on one or more samples of 100 subjects each: items which resulted in error would be dropped and so would those with which less than 20 per cent and more than 80 per cent of subjects agreed, thus reducing the scale eventually to 8 or 10 items.

Table 7.3—Guttman scale; items reshuffled in order, descending from the left

Subject	Item					
	1	3	2	4	6	5
1	/	/	/			
2	/	/		/		
3	/	/		/		
4	/					
5	/	/	/	/	/	/
6	/	/	/	/	/	

Table 7.4—Guttman scale; subjects also reshuffled

Subject	Item					
	1	3	2	4	6	5
5	/	/	/	/	/	/
6	/	/	/	/	/	
3	/	/		/		
1	/	/	/			
2	/	/		/		
4	/					

Guttman's methods have come in for severe criticism on the grounds that, even if one achieves a high 'index of reproducibility' in Guttman's terms, there is no guarantee that the scale is testing anything worthwhile; success depends almost entirely on the operator's wisdom in selecting suitable items for his analysis.

When trying to attach scores, say, to R items, Guttman's method would simply place them with great reliability in some kind of specified order. Likert's would allocate marks to each item within a range from 5 to 60, whilst Thurstone's could also allocate marks but within a range from 0 to 100. Neither of these would be quite so reliable as Guttman's; thus, as Canter says, 'the investigator must decide whether in his own particular case he wants great reliability or great precision.' A further case of indeterminacy!

It is clear then that these ways of measuring attitudes leave a great deal to be desired. They are open to faulty design, to errors in sampling, to a high rate of refusal in those invited to respond and even to bias on the parts of both the operator who sets up the scales and the interviewers who administer them. The respondents themselves may be ignorant of what is being discussed, think it unimportant or have highly personal reasons for not wishing to discuss it. They may misunderstand the questions, find that none of the indicated responses matches their own attitudes, find that their attitudes change *because* the questions are being asked (effect of indeterminacy), give answers which they think the interviewer wants to hear or give tongue-in-cheek answers for the hell of it. There may be bias in the recording or decoding of the answers and errors also in the statistical analysis or final interpretation.

Most operators of such tests have a touching faith in statistics to get them over these difficulties. They claim that if their sample is large enough (Pearson suggests a minimum of 200 subjects for the application of his method) errors in response from whatever cause will be self-correcting. Obviously this ignores the insidious effects, say, of indeterminacy, that the questions themselves will suggest answers to the subjects. Even more remarkable is the rather touching confidence which many testers place in checking the tests themselves for *self-consistency*.

These internal checks are concerned with the *reliability* and the *validity* of the test, both of which terms are used in a rather special sense. A test is said to be reliable if the results obtained from it are consistent: if the same respondents were asked to complete it twice, then there should be a high level of correlation between the two applications. There are three ways of checking reliability by 'split-half', 'alternate-forms' and 'retest' methods which are almost self-explanatory. In the split-half method, for instance, the items are arranged in ascending order of difficulty and the test is then applied in two parts; one part is formed from the odd-numbered parts and the other from the even-numbered, and scores for the two halves are then correlated.

Validity tests on the other hand are concerned with what the test actually measures, as distinct from what the operator set it up to measure or even what he thinks it measures. A test is assumed to measure *anything* that can be correlated with its results and this can lead to surprising conclusions, especially if correlations which occurred by chance are assumed to be causal. Conversely a number of tests may have been set up to measure quite different things and yet their results can be intercorrelated. Eysenck, for instance, found that measures of opinion on sovereignty, abortion law, corporal punishment and religious education could be correlated, concluding therefore that certain common attitudes underlay them all.

The abstraction of such common attitudes, or factors, has become an obsession with some psychologists who find considerable satisfaction in discussing personality or other human characteristics in these terms. In many cases they refuse to give names to these factors on the grounds that names, such as prejudice, introversion and so on, carry certain connotations and

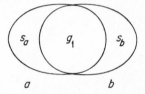

Figure 7.1—Venn diagram showing the common element in two correlated tests

thus the abstract beauty of their various factors is destroyed. As Hudson says, their preoccupation with statistics enables them to discuss such matters without any of the difficulties or embarrassments of getting involved with real people.

The logic of factor analysis was first presented by Spearman in 1904. He assumed that a correlation between any two items such as questions in a psychological test implies three things. There will be a factor which is specific to each item, and a third factor which is common to them both. Given items a and b for instance, the common factor will be g_1 whilst the specific factors will be s_a and s_b respectively (Figure 7.1). Spearman then went on to correlate two other items, such as p and q. These also had a common factor g_2 (Figure 7.2) and it was possible also in many cases to go further than this, to correlate the two (or more) common factors g_1 and g_2, thus deriving a factor G which was common to *all* the items (Figure 7.3). That is precisely what he did, as we saw in Chapter 1, in the analysis of human abilities, verbal, numerical, and so on, from which he derived the general factor G, representing overall intelligence. This may be represented in the form of a Venn diagram (Figure 7.4). Each item, therefore, will be made up of two components—that which is unique to the item itself (its *specificity*) and that which it shares with others (its *communality*).

It may be that tests **A** and **B** have factors x, y and so on in common. The correlation r between tests **A** and **B** then can be calculated as follows:

$$r_{ab} = x_a x_b + y_a y_b + \ldots + z_a z_b$$

Such correlations can then be plotted in the form of a matrix in which each appears twice above and below the diagonal. A set of (fictitious) results might read as shown in Table 7.5.

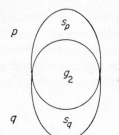

Figure 7.2—Venn diagram showing the common element in two other correlated tests

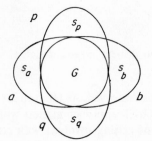

Figure 7.3—Venn diagram showing the common elements in four correlated tests, in this case Spearman's *G* factor

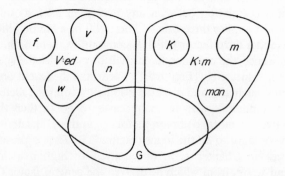

Figure 7.4—Venn diagram representing the hierarchical structure of human abilities shown in Figure 1.1 (page 20)

In other words, the correlation between tests **A** and **B** is 0·63, between **A** and **C**, 0·52, and so on. It is possible by very devious processes to derive whatever factors exist in common between tests: one has to start by *guessing* the communality of each test, possibly by taking the highest correlation value in each column. This is written in the appropriate diagonal cell, between the empty brackets.

One may know the values of these communalities from a previous computation, but even so, factor analysis is an extremely laborious business. Guilford (1954) describes a 22-step process which, for a pool of 20 items,

Table 7.5—Matrix showing correlations between five (hypothetical) tests which have a common factor

	A	B	C	D	E
A	( )	·63	·52	·08	·33
B	·63	( )	·35	·00	·21
C	·52	·35	( )	·56	·57
D	·08	·00	·56	( )	·48
E	·33	·21	·57	·48	( )

Table 7.6—Factor matrix showing for each item the amount of communality which is attributable to factors x and y

Item	Factor	
	x	y
A	·9	·1
B	·7	·0
C	·5	·7
D	·0	·8
E	·3	·6

would start with the computation of 190 correlation coefficients. This is not the place to describe a technique in detail, although Hotteling, Kelley, Burt and Thurstone have all devised methods (see Guilford); the latter also attaches great importance to factor-rotation. One can prepare a factor matrix **F** in which the communality of each item attributable to factors x and y and so on, is plotted in the appropriate column (Table 7.6).

A simple two-factor matrix such as this can be represented diagrammatically as a two-dimensional space, using the factors as orthogonals against which the various items can be plotted, together with vectors from the point of origin O. This is shown in Figure 7.5(a), with the upper right-hand quadrant enlarged in Figure 7.5(b).

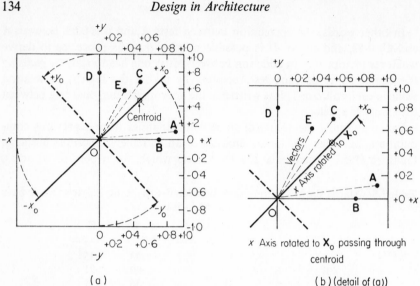

(a)   (b)(detail of (a))

Figure 7.5 (a) and (b)—Geometric representation of the five items (psychological tests) in two-factor space. Vectors **X** and **Y** represent the common factors x and y, whilst vectors **A, B, C, D** and **E** represent the five correlated tests. The *centroid* represents the 'centre of gravity' of these tests within the frame of reference defined by xOy. If the x axis is 'rotated' until it passes through the centroid, the communality which is attributable to factor x can be removed from the correlation coefficients; factor x can then be identified, Once factor x has thus been identified, a second centroid can be found for factor y and so on

It will then be possible to find the centroid of these items, their centre of gravity in relation to the frame of reference xOy, and to draw a reference axis Ox_0. This is the original axis Ox_0; one can then draw a second (temporary) reference axis for factor y, Oy_0, orthogonal, that is at right-angles to the Ox_0 axis, after which one can remove from the correlation coefficients all the communality which is attributable to factor x, thus identifying factor x. Once this has been achieved, one can find a second centroid for factor y, and so on.

The factors thus revealed (x, y, z and so on) may, or may not, be given names such as those we discussed in Chapter 1: tolerance of ambiguity, ambivalence towards parents and so on. Some psychologists prefer not to do this, on the grounds that each of us attaches certain meanings to such words already and we are therefore liable to blur the edges of what has been defined so clearly. This is a perfectly legitimate view for the research psychologist who may well be concerned, above all, with demonstrating his grasp of a methodology to his fellow psychologists rather than with producing usable results.

The designer may well be tempted to take psychologists' findings, such as the following, at face value; 'There is no correlation between introversion/extroversion and preference for office size' (Canter, 1967). 'Analyses of variance . . . indicate that the assessment of scale model rooms is very similar to the assessment of full-size rooms (for "gloom" and "pleasantness")' (Lau, 1970). Yet they are true only in a limited, technical sense, using very specific definitions of the concepts in question. One has to be aware of precisely what the psychologists mean and how they have arrived at their conclusions, before acting on such statements in design.

Finally, let us remember the grave reservations which Liam Hudson has expressed about these statistical approaches to psychological problems (1967).

The tests themselves, he believes, are trivial; they have developed very little since the early years of the century and, instead of devising ever more subtle tests, the testers themselves have concentrated on increasingly refined analyses of the results. The fine analysis of coarse information, however, can be grossly misleading. Even apart from that, this preoccupation with statistics indicates a bias on the part of the testers themselves; they are fascinated by statistics, and hardly interested in people at all. As Hudson says:

'They seem happiest when people are at a safe distance. Many testers seem, too, to have cut themselves off from other aspects of their culture: they display no special knowledge of books, painting, music, science, politics, administration or any other aspect of intelligent life in the world at large.'

To which we might add architecture. So, in building a complete and self-justifying system, the testers have often neglected inconvenient evidence and confirmed instead the results they wanted to find.

CHAPTER 8

Basic Needs

As a first step in this deeper investigation of human needs we shall look at the individual and his relationships with the building. That in itself will be complex enough, but nothing like so complex as his relationships with other people and the effects that these relationships will have, or ought to have, on the design of the building itself. Since our first consideration of the mammoth-hunters' tent in Chapter 2, we have thought of the building as, among other things, a device which modifies the climate, a filter between the external environment and the users within. It enables the climate to be modified to such an extent that the users will be comfortable. We will take such a user, therefore, and consider what his needs for comfort really are.

Clearly his relationship with the building will be a perceptual one, a set of transactions between the stimuli his senses receive and his previous experience; and these, acting together, will determine his reactions to the building. We looked at certain aspects of this relationship in the Introduction, and in particular at the ways in which stimuli are received by the senses, but there is much dispute as to how the other half of the transaction, one's previous experience, has been formed. The behaviourist would say that it had all been *learned*, as a result of previous stimuli, whilst the phenomenologist would point to innate ideas as the basis for organizing such experience. Watson wrote of the 'boomerang-like' way in which certain reflexes operate; we breathe because that is the way we are made. Others such as James (1890) have called these things we do because we cannot help it, *instincts*, and instincts have no place in the behaviourist scheme of things. There is no *real* dispute over something as fundamental as breathing: we can *call* it a reflex if we want to, or an instinct. It makes little difference. Eating, too, is something we must do if we are to stay alive: so the question, really, is concerned with whether other characteristics such as a need for sexual expression, the drive to defend one's territory and so on, are fundamental in the sense that breathing is.

Many writers claim that they are, and there has been a tendency recently to draw analogies with bird and animal behaviour. Each species of bird builds its nest in a certain way; young birds migrate over enormous distances to places they have never been before; salmon return to the river where they were spawned; many birds and animals mark out and defend their territory, sometimes to the death. Tinbergen (1953, 1957), Marler (1965), Crook (1961) and Brown (1963) have studied in great detail the territorial behaviour of

136

certain kinds of birds, and Lorenz's work (1955, 1966) in this field is by no means inconsiderable; but none of this proves, for instance, Ardrey's contention in *The Territorial Imperative* (1966) that aggressive behaviour is innate in human beings, that it is ineradicable and that the need to express it accounts for a good many of the less savoury incidents in human history. A considerable literature has grown up, in fact, which casts grave doubt on the work of Lorenz, Ardrey and Morris (see Montagu, 1968) and because one supposed instinct is thus shown to be based on rather suspect premises, there is a growing belief that the behaviourists may have been right in dismissing the idea of instinct completely.

However, Fletcher (1968) performs a useful salvage operation on the doctrine of instincts. Earlier theories certainly seemed to have been demolished by behaviourism, cultural anthropology, psychoanalysis and so on, but Fletcher concludes that certain characteristics of the human body and mind *are* established by heredity, including the structure of the body itself, certain complex internal processes—nervous, visceral and so on—and the various reflexes. No behaviourist, even, would quarrel with these physical attributes but Fletcher then adds certain fixed patterns of reactions, in which existing motivational states are triggered by external stimuli—certain kinds of exploratory behaviour which he calls appetitive, not to mention certain cravings and emotions.

Fletcher quotes Drever's definition of instinct (1917):

'. . . instinct, physiologically regarded, is a congenital predisposition of the nervous system, consisting in a definite, but within limits modifiable, arrangement and coordination of nervous connections, so that a particular stimulus, with or without the presence of certain co-operating stimuli, will call forth a particular action or series of actions; this predisposition, biologically regarded, is apparently due to the operation of natural selection, and determines a mode of behaviour, which secures a biologically useful end, without foresight of that end or experience in attaining it.'

Fletcher's list of instincts proper, or *primary instincts*, consists of: breathing, eating, drinking, maintaining comfortable temperature (keeping warm, keeping cool), sleeping, waking, caring for comfort of body surface, fearing, excretion (defaecation, urination), general activity, bodily and mental (play, curiosity, hunting) and sexual activity (eroticism and 'courtship', sexual 'fighting', parental activity and home-making). To these he adds a further list of *general instinctive tendencies*: pleasure-pain, attachment-avoidance, positive and negative ego-tendencies. Finally he suggests that a whole range of secondary impulses occur, which vary according to the environment in which one was born but which occur in two forms: inhibitions and aspirations; clearly these will have to be *learned*, as the behaviourists supposed they would.

Whatever one calls them, it is useful to define a set of primary necessities which must be satisfied if the human organism is to survive. One *must* breathe, eat, drink and excrete, otherwise one will die, as one will in extreme temperatures. With rare exceptions resulting from brain injury, one must also sleep and wake. Given a reasonable climate, with adequate natural resources, the human being can do *all* these things without the benefit of building. We might say, in fact, that building merely extends the range of places on the earth's surface at which these things become comfortable.

There is no real evidence that beyond these instincts extracted from Fletcher's list any others necessarily need be satisfied. Take the instinct which Freud and others seem to have considered absolutely crucial, that complex of urges which Fletcher calls sexual activity. Wright (1969) and others have suggested that it is by no means basic, citing the example of priests, nuns and others who have chosen a celibate life and whose orgasmic mechanism 'falls more or less into permanent misuse.' Certainly there is little evidence of their indulging in 'courtship', sexual 'fighting', parental activity and home-making and, as Wright says, they may well *perceive* a beautiful woman as a soul to be saved and not as a stimulus to eroticism. It *may* be also that they are none the worse for this denial of a supposed instinct. Even for the rest of us, Beach (1956) and others have shown that organic factors, such as the secretion of hormones, simply predispose us to arousal, *if* an appropriate stimulation occurs. It is a socio-cultural matter, precisely that phenomenon which D. H. Lawrence loathed so much, 'sex in the head.' As Wright puts it (1969):

' ... sexual arousal is ... associated with imagination and with the mind, cultural influences (whether friends, art, comics, advertisements or entertainment) can condition one to feel sexual arousal even before the relevant stimulus takes place ... Sexual appetite, then, is a habit by which one has *learned* to expect pleasurable arousal and orgasm in certain kinds of situation.'

If this is true of an instinct which, at first sight, seems so basic then it suggests that one should also question such other apparently basic instincts as general activity, play, curiosity, hunting and so on.

Suppose then we start to satisfy those of Fletcher's instincts which are necessary for survival. We shall find, inevitably, that they can *all* be served in an equable climate without further modification of buildings. If buildings had been necessary in the first place, then the human species could not have developed and survived. Most of those characteristics which we think of as human had developed before man started to build.

A completely sealed building, in fact, might well inhibit the first of those instincts, breathing, although it may facilitate achievement of the others. First, and most obviously, it will make it easier to care for the comfort of body surfaces, although even in this we shall usually have undertaken a first modification of the indigenous climate by wearing clothes. This too will assist in Fletcher's related instinct of maintaining comfortable body temperature, although that is a complex matter of *homeostasis* as man, in common with all land animals, can adjust to radical changes in temperature. As air temperature at the skin drops, so the metabolic rate increases and thus the internal environment of the body remains constant. Clearly there are upper and lower limits to this and the effect of building, on the whole, will be to maintain our temperatures within these limits. By 'evening out' the environment in this way, most buildings will also facilitate sleep. The building may or may not provide places where eating, drinking and excreting can take place although often there is a statutory requirement to provide for the latter. Unlike breathing and maintaining temperature, these are discontinuous activities—there may be advantages in moving to another place, or even to another building, to do them.

So buildings, evidently, play a disappointingly small part in satisfying man's basic instincts. Any building inevitably isolates man from the 'natural' external environment; this has led to much speculation by Morris (1969) and others about the deleterious effects of housing man in the 'concrete jungle' or *The human zoo.*

At first sight the argument is a sound one. Let us suppose, for instance, that palaeolithic man (man the hunter) represents the prototype and ideal state of man. He walked upright, made tools and weapons which he used in hunting animals faster than himself. Clearly his life was regulated by nature; he lived near water, he could make fire and he seems to have migrated seasonally. His hunting obviously took place in the open air; it necessitated a great deal of physical activity, not to mention aggression, and it involved collaboration with others. Certain kinds of tribal and taming relationships therefore seem to have developed but, given the evidence of tools, dwelling places, art and weapons, one can speculate as to just what the characteristics were of such a way of life. Just as Laugier derived his fundamentals of architecture by speculating what the first buildings *must* have been like (see Chapter 4), so one can derive the fundamentals of human living by speculating what the life of a stone age hunter must have been like. Let us call this the *atavistic* life and rhapsodize about man's relationship with earth and sun, not to mention fire and water. If we take this as our model we shall conclude, inevitably, that the further we depart from atavistic living, the less satisfactory our lives will be. We shall advocate buildings then which encourage close communion with nature; we might look, like Wright, for a hearth deep inside the house with the magic glow of fire or alternatively, like Mies, we may provide a simple glass box so that grass, trees and sky can be seen from inside the building with little interruption from the structure itself.

Clearly any argument which allows and even leads to such fundamentally opposed solutions is suspect, and certainly it is not particularly helpful. The atavistic argument, in fact, is flawed. Man above all is an adapting animal (Dubos, 1966); that is the secret of his success in dominating the environment, including other species. He adapted to stone age hunting, but he also adapted to   Greek and even eighteenth-century civilization. The choice of *any* single period in his development, of any particular culture as representing the ideal of how man ought to live, is clearly an arbitrary one. Palaeolithic man, for instance, had long arms and fingers which could grip, both legacies from his ancestry in the forest as a tree-dweller, swinging from branch to branch. One might just as well say that tree-dwelling represented the essence of 'humanness', and that our streets too should be lined with branching posts by which, emulating our remoter ancestors, we could swing from place to place in a true concrete jungle.

Surely out of all this, it should be possible to salvage some fundamentals which will help us in the design of buildings? If it were possible then we should expect *all* buildings to be much more alike than they are. There is one clue, however, which comes not from ethology or anthropology, but from psychological experiment. When an individual is confined to a darkened room, which is also well-insulated against external noise, then *according to the conditions of the experiment* strange things happen to him. In *extreme* cases subjects report hallucinations; for one very small group, subject to experiment by Hebb at McGill University,

'. . . subjects reported a variety of visual experiences as having occurred during their confinement. The simple form of visual experience was shifts from light to dark, dots, lines, or simple geometric patterns. All fourteen subjects reported seeing such things. A more complex visual experience was seeing something like "wallpaper patterns" which eleven subjects reported.' (quoted Vernon, 1963)

These and other studies also suggest that during the first day or so of sensory deprivation (SD) one tends to sleep a great deal. Between periods of sleeping one's powers of concentration increased. One can solve problems that previously had proved intractable and achieve penetrating insights which, sometimes, are of real value; but, according to Vernon, this applied to about half the subjects—the other half found it very difficult to concentrate. They would try to close down on an idea, which would seem to evaporate; there was no discipline in their thought processes. Of those whose thinking showed dramatic improvements initially, about two-thirds found later that this was not maintained. One reason for this, which many of them stated, was that their thinking processes would have been better if some other person could have been present. It seemed to them pointless to go on thinking when there was no one else to discuss their ideas with.

Only very small numbers of people have been subjected to SD experiments and the results are by no means consistent, but at least they confirm what we *want* to believe about man in relation to his environment and it is possible to draw some comforting conclusions from them. As Noble said (1963):

'Normal consciousness, perception and thought can be maintained only in a constantly changing environment; where there is no change a state of "sensory deprivation" occurs. Experiment has shown that a homogenous and unvarying environment produces boredom, restlessness, lack of concentration and reduction in intelligence (sic).'

That, presumably, depends on how one defines intelligence! However, Noble uses this to plead for variety in buildings and specifically in office buildings:

'The sort of variation that we often demand instinctively on aesthetic grounds, has a sound physiological and psychological basis. A change in environment stimulates our built-in devices to perceive and respond rapidly to significant events and efficiency is thereby increased. It is worth paying for variety.'

That may or may not be so; most of the SD subjects, after all, attach more importance to the stimulus of *other people* than to stimuli from the environment, but Noble seems to be supported by no less an authority than Professor Vernon (1963):

'I believe that the human being cannot long endure a completely homogenous situation no matter how good or how desirable it is. What is homogenous soon becomes boring and undesirable. Caviare and champagne may be very desirable for breakfast, but not for long as a steady diet. No matter how positive a thing may be, it loses value under unvarying use. Man's appetites soon become jaded, so that he ever seeks new gratifications or, failing this, finds increasing complaint with his status quo.

If by his achievements man becomes bored with it all, even if that all is most desirable by ordinary standards, he will look for change even if he has to destroy his present circumstances; if he cannot build new and differently, in order to depart from the old, he will rid himself of it so that a change is effected.'

If that is so, then clearly the built environment *can* offer relief from boredom, and stimulate man's jaded appetites. The question is, however, what sort of stimulus is needed? And how much? A single window, open to the sky, will destroy the condition of complete SD. It will admit daylight, changing minute by minute in quality and quantity, and it may admit noise. Confinement in a windowed room, therefore, is a very different experience from confinement with full sensory deprivation.

The opposite of sensory deprivation, of course, is sensory stimulus and from this point of view it is usual to consider five basic senses: seeing, hearing, touch, taste and smell, although it is possible to describe some thirty. That would over-complicate the issue but Hochberg (1964) presents a useful classification:

1. *The distance senses:* seeing and hearing.
2. *The skin senses:* touch, warmth, cold, pain, and the closely related chemical senses of taste and smell.
3. *The deep senses:* position and motion of muscles and joints (kinaesthetic), the senses of equilibration (vestibular), and the senses of the internal organs.

Whereas the traditional list contains taste, which is hardly relevant in the consideration of architecture, Hochberg's list contains others which are clearly important but which we rarely take into account, such as smell, the kinaesthetic and vestibular senses. It is unusual to consider *smell* in the design of buildings, yet if we ignore it strange things may happen. Each building has its characteristic smell; we may assume that any building user wishes to be free of *unpleasant* smells in the external environment—the smells of abattoirs, tanning factories, breweries (although some would disagree), not to mention road and rail traffic. The most effective way of keeping them out is to keep the windows closed, but that may not always be possible.

Even so there are other sources of smell inside the building. Cooking is one, perhaps the only one that has really been taken into account. Le Corbusier, after all, advised that one should place the kitchen at the top of the building, so that its smells would not permeate the rest. However, there is a further internal source of unpleasant smells which, delicately, we might label 'personal'. It has been a problem for many years in unventilated assembly buildings, gymnasia and so on, but one which has become particularly acute with new ways of heating buildings; St. George's school at Wallasey, for instance, derives its heat from three sources: from solar heat gain, and a whole wall is glazed to this end, from the electric lights and from the bodies of the people inside. To make sure that these heating sources would be quite adequate, Emslie Morgan, the designer, had a substantial amount of polystyrene insulation built into the external walls. From the point of view of heat and cold the system is very successful, but one's first impression in entering the school, as Manning (1969) and others have observed, is the overwhelming stink. There is some evidence that regular users of the school adapt, or at least habituate to this smell, but if in taking his major design decisions the architect had borne in mind the demands of all the relevant senses, then he would have built in mechanisms to take account of smell. Those may have consisted of a massive ventilation plant and if they had, then the costs of such a plant might well have exceeded the cost of a conventional heating plant. So back to square one.

We have seen that the kinaesthetic senses (position and movement of the muscles and joints) are vital to our perception of space, and help us define our relationships with the spaces we occupy. We shall have to bear them in mind, therefore, when we are designing and curiously enough they help us define certain things about design which, up to now, have remained rather hazy. Sullivan's ubiquitous dictum, 'Form follows function,' raises one obvious question which is 'How closely?' Knowledge of the kinaesthetic senses helps us answer that question quite specifically. If we consider, say, a typist sitting at her desk, then we shall see that at certain levels the degree of ergonomic precision with which we design will have to be very high indeed. Her fingers, for instance, will have to be placed within, say, 5 mm of the appropriate keys if she is to type at all effectively. The height of her chair will not be so critical. We might establish, after a massive anthropometric survey, that 50 per cent of people will be comfortable if the chair seat is 44·5 cm high. If our typist is one of the lucky 50 per cent, then all will be well. Even if she isn't, it will still be possible for her to sit on the chair; it may be 1, 2 or even 3 cm too high or low for her but she will still be able to work, and given the possibility of adjustment, which most office chairs possess, she is highly likely to get it wrong, from the ergonomist's point of view. So whereas her relationship to the typewriter keyboard must be a very precise one indeed, her relationship to the chair is rather less critical. If we consider the route she takes across the floor from office door to desk, many times in the course of each day, then we shall find that this varies from occasion to occasion and maybe by several metres. There is no reason at all why a

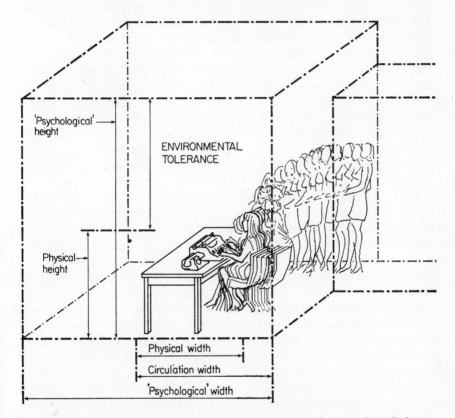

Figure 8.1—Environmental tolerance. No activity takes up the whole volume of space available to it. Considerable tolerance must be allowed between the users, their equipment, furniture, etc., and the space which encloses them. There are physiological and psychological reasons for this, concerned with variations in human dimensions, patterns of movement and perceptual expectation. The architect's task, more often than not, is to *design* this tolerance rather than to design a form which fits the function closely

precise route should be plotted for the activity of walking across the floor (Figure 8.1).

For many other activities too, the *fit* between an activity and the space it occupies may, indeed must, be very loose indeed. There have been many analyses, by time-lapse photography, of people performing certain tasks; some of the most revealing examples however were taken at the Bauhaus (Moholy-Nagy, 1947) such as the well-known one of *Man putting on a shirt*. Light bulbs were attached to salient points of his anatomy (knees, elbows, head and so on) and their traces recorded on a photographic plate. They indicate a pattern of movement in three dimensions rather more accurately than a conventional time-lapse photograph and, if form really followed function in this case, one could build for the man a resin and glass fibre shell, based on data measured from the photograph (a stereo pair of photographs would enable even more accurate measurements to be taken). However, suppose one were to make such a shell and ask the man to use it again to put on another shirt. The sleeves may be 1 cm longer than before and his pattern of movement, therefore, may be substantially different. The shell would not fit the man's actions this time, nor for that matter would it fit any other person performing the same activity. If the man were to use the shell on more than one occasion or if other people were to use it, then we should have to build in a considerable *tolerance* between form and activity.

If we take another simple activity, such as walking down a corridor, we find that the tolerance between a tall man and a corridor of average height, of only 1 metre wide, amounts to some 300 per cent of his silhouette. Le Corbusier recognized this when he designed the corridors of his Citrohan houses to the dimensions of those in the railway carriages of the Compagnie Internationale des Wagons-Lits. Yet even these prove to give a tolerance of some 200 per cent around the man's silhouette (Figure 8.2).

Few architects think it necessary either, to consider the sense of equilibrium. Yet those of us brought up in western culture bring specific expectations to our perception of buildings in this sense. Most of the buildings we know have substantially horizontal floors and ceilings and substantially vertical walls. Certain 'primitive' tribes have no such expectations and just as the Zulus with their experience of living in circular huts perceived certain optical illusions differently from ourselves, so one might assume that they bring different expectations in terms of equilibrium to buildings. They, like us, will normally expect floors to be horizontal, but they will not bring expectations of vertical walls or ceilings. Our expectation of horizontal *and* vertical suggests two things. When we intend to build thus we had better be accurate about it, although the degree of unease which one experiences when faced, say, with a framed painting which is hung slightly askew is known to vary greatly from person to person. In building we ought to satisfy those who feel these things to an extreme degree, otherwise they will be miserable, whereas perfect vertical and horizontality will in no way disturb the rest of us.

It also suggests that we could make much more use than we do of *intentionally* skew surfaces for particular sensory effect. The main debating chamber of the United Nations Building in New York has walls which seem to be caving inwards—the symbolic implications were noted with glee by early critics of the design—but so has Le Corbusier's chapel at Ronchamp and, what is more, its floor is dished too. The experience of walking across a

Citrohan House corridor

Figure 8.2—This 1·8 metre man is walking down a 1-metre wide corridor; the tolerance between his silhouette and the corridor itself amounts to some 300 per cent of his cross-sectional area. The dotted lines represent the minimum corridor size devised by Le Corbusier for his Citrohan house at Stuttgart (1927), based on a railway corridor. Even there, the tolerance is some 200 per cent

slightly dished floor is an extraordinarily subtle one. It is, of course, multimodal: in addition to the sense of equilibrium it also stimulates with a subtle *frisson* the kinaesthetic senses and the sense of sight. In other words, if we take into account a sense which is usually neglected, it leads us to new and creative conclusions as to how we might design. A similar *frisson* was intended by Lord Snowdon, Cedric Price and Frank Newby when they designed the aviary at London Zoo in Regent's Park. Here the bridge by which the public pass into and through the aviary was designed in such a way that it could deflect, in certain parts, ever so slightly as one walked across it.

Further difficulties will arise if we ignore the kinaesthetic senses in the design of buildings; these will be treated in more detail in Chapter 19. Ideally, then, we might analyse the human organism's relationship to its environment in terms of all the relevant senses (Figure 8.3), thinking of it in systemic terms so that all their possible interrelations and interactions are taken into account.

This has not, however, been the traditional approach in environmental research. Instead of this, research has been *molecular*, that is to say, concerned

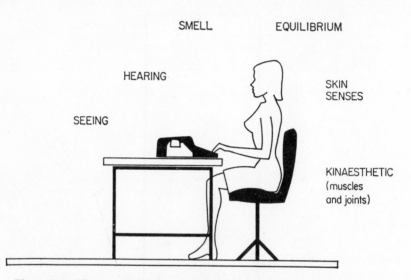

SMELL   EQUILIBRIUM

HEARING   SKIN SENSES

SEEING

KINAESTHETIC (muscles and joints)

Figure 8.3—The user is bombarded with information about her environment continuously by these six perceptual channels. Most architects design for seeing; they are aware too that hearing can raise problems, also the skin senses (heat and cold). Few, however, design for smell, for equilibrium (to confirm our sense of stability) or for the kinaesthetic senses, even though these can help us decide what degree of ergonomic precision will be required in a particular circumstance

with fragments of the environment deliberately isolated so that they can be controlled under experimental conditions; environmental 'facts' separated out as Durkheim found it necessary to separate out his social 'facts'. The *Architect's Journal: Environmental Handbook* (1968–69) provides a comprehensive summary of recommendations for environmental standards, formed by bringing together the results of research which has been fragmented in this way. Significantly enough, its basic classification is based, not on the human senses, but on the building fabric and its services installations. Table 8.1 compares this approach with Hochberg's classification of the senses, in so far as that is relevant.

Two things emerge from this. The *Architect's Journal* classification is hardware-based and it may well inhibit a more fundamental approach based on the systemic interactions of the human senses with the built environment. It is only fair to point out that the *Architect's Journal: Handbook of the building fabric* (1971–72) is written from a thoroughly environmentalist viewpoint. Secondly, a great deal of research has been carried out in certain fields and very little in others. The reasons for this become clear when one considers the relative ease with which certain kinds of research can be done. These two points can best be illustrated with reference to a particular field

Table 8.1—Table showing the ways in which some user senses are treated comprehensively and others ignored in the hardware-based approach to environmental control

User senses	Building environment: form and fabric	Building environment: services installations
Distance senses: Seeing	1. Climate and topography 2. Sunlight: direct and diffused	9. Electric lighting
Hearing	5. Sound	(communications service)
Skin senses: Warmth and cold	3. Air movement and natural ventilation	8. Heating installations, mechanical ventilating and air conditioning.
	4. Thermal properties	
Smell	6. Hygiene	
Deep senses Kinaesthetic Equilibrium	7. User requirements	

based on the sense of seeing, for it is in this field that molecular research has had its greatest successes (in terms of one servicing mode) and its greatest failure (in terms of systemic interaction with other environmental fields).

Artificial lighting, as we saw in Chapter 7, is particularly susceptible to finely controlled experiment; one can arrange light emitters, working surfaces and subjects very accurately; the emission of light can be controlled within very fine limits and illumination at the working surface can be measured with great precision. This affords exceptionally fine control of the independent variables; one can take careful measurements also of the dependent variables. These might include the accuracy with which people can read certain type faces under different lighting conditions, their ability to distinguish fine detail or even their colour preferences. Small wonder therefore that an enormous amount of data has been collected on preferred illumination levels and on other aspects of lighting.

One of the first such studies was undertaken by Luckiesh and Taylor in 1922; they found that the percentages of adults choosing different illumination levels for reading were as illustrated in Table 8.2. Obviously it would have been possible to draft recommendations for, say, office or school lighting using these figures and such recommendations were indeed drawn up on the basis of H. C. Weston's later, and more sophisticated, work for the Medical Research Council (Weston, 1962). He was concerned with the way in which different tasks made different demands upon sight and with the avoidance of visual strain, and he concluded that there are close interrelations between the two; that the physiological structures of the eye and its controlling muscles are such that, whatever the nature of the visual task and whatever the lighting conditions, they must adjust constantly so as to give the sharpest and clearest possible picture of the task. Strain occurs when the muscular system is pressed too hard for too long, and this will

Table 8.2—Adult preferences for different illumination levels established in early (1922) experiments by Luckiesh and Taylor (approximate conversion from foot candles)

Lux	100	200	300	500	1000	2000	5000	10000
Percentages	11	18	32	20	17	1	1	1

occur even with 'normal' eyes if one concentrates on fine detail under inadequate illumination. Few eyes in any case are 'normal'—most of us suffer from slight errors of refraction or other anomalies. So Weston sought to establish by experiment (c. 1935) suitable levels of illumination for different visual tasks; he concluded that the performance of such tasks depends on one's ability to see, that the rate at which one performs them will increase with the logarithm of the illumination level up to very high levels, and that the proportion of mistakes will decrease as the illumination is increased.

In one particularly influential set of experiments, he sought to establish the relationship between illumination level and the time it took school boys to read algebraic equations in a text book—a task which was considered typical of their normal school work. In one case they were asked to read black figures on white paper and, with an illumination level of 1·0 lumen/square foot, they took an average of 141 seconds to complete it. At 5·0 lumens, they took 133 seconds, at 10·0 lumens, 128 seconds, and at 50·0 lumens, 118 seconds. The Ministry of Education required a level of 10 lumens/square foot, at which level, as Weston says, one might expect the school boy's performance to be about 7 per cent less than the possible maximum as observed in his experiments.

Weston set up a family of curves relating visual performance (speed and accuracy) to illumination on the task-object and the size of the object itself. This size was expressed in terms of the angle subtended by the object in the eye, in minutes of arc—a fairly arbitrary measure of such tasks, as colour, contrast and other factors would also be important. Nevertheless Weston's figures provided a useful basis for specifying illumination levels for different tasks, and the Illuminating Engineering Society (IES) adopted it, expressed in terms of detail, size and 'lightness'. One could, in theory, provide lighting conditions in which a specified task could be performed with maximum efficiency—100 per cent performance. However, Weston simplified his method by advocating a 'broad band' approach, specifying levels between 100 per cent and 90 per cent of his theoretical maximum and, on this basis, Weston's proposals were accepted by the Illuminating Engineering

Table 8.3—Comparison of recommended illumination values for general office work in different countries (lumens per square foot, approximately)

France	1961	(minimum)	30
		(recommended)	60
Germany	(draft 1962)		12 to 25
Britain	(1961)		30
Sweden	(1962)		30 to 100
U.S.A.	(1959)		100 to 150
U.S.S.R.	(fluorescent)		20 to 30
	(incandescent)		7·5 to 15

Society (1961). If one accepted 90 per cent performance, then discrepancies of up to 30 per cent in illumination levels would make hardly any difference.

As Musgrove points out (1966), however, the IES Code of 1961 omitted the safeguards which Weston built so carefully into his system, and recommended *fixed* levels instead. What started, therefore, as admittedly 'soft' data was hardened into firm recommendation and credited with a spurious objectivity which its author never claimed. The dangers of such 'objectivity' are made blatantly obvious when one compares illumination levels recommended in 1965 *for similar tasks* (in this case general office work) in different countries (from Manning *et al.*, 1965)—see Table 8.3.

The difference between maximum and minimum recommended values is very great (7·5 to 150 lumens/square foot) yet there is no reason to suppose that the methodology was more or less precise in one country or another. Of course, there are good *perceptual* reasons for the recommendations to vary so much; in each case the subjects of the experiments came to their task with *experience* of previous lighting conditions. Tinker (1943) realized that one's performance will be conditioned by the illumination level to which one has already adapted. He conducted a series of experiments in which readers adapted to certain illumination levels and were then asked to *choose* an optimum level for reading. Subjects adapted to 8-foot candles chose 12-foot candles as the optimum, whereas those adapted to 52-foot candles tended to choose 52 as the optimum level. Such experiments, therefore, will *inevitably* prove indeterminate. The act of measuring people's preferences will change them.

In optimizing on a single criterion one inevitably takes decisions which affect the other senses; the human body cannot agree to ignore the evidence of any of its senses whilst in the building itself, virtually every decision which is taken has some effect, however slight, on its environmental characteristics. It is common, for instance, to ignore the effects of structural decision on environmental standards. We select a structural type and then design it for maximum structural efficiency. Yet if we choose a steel or concrete frame, then its heat and sound insulation properties are vastly different from the equivalent properties of a solid brick or concrete wall.

It may be that from a *lighting* point of view the 2 per cent daylight factor is successful. Certainly the various surveys (Manning *et al.*, 1965; Langdon and Keighley, 1964; Langdon, 1966) suggest that artificial lighting is the most satisfactory feature of present day office design. In Langdon and Keighley's survey, for instance, measured satisfaction with the amount of light available ranged between 90 per cent and 70 per cent and it fell only rarely below 60 per cent. Yet when the levels themselves were actually measured, they reached IES recommendations in only a minority of offices. Most people were satisfied when the general level of illumination for office work reached 15 lumens/square foot; above this level there was very little correlation between illumination and user satisfaction. Lynes (quoted Manning *et al.*) suggests that the obvious conclusion from this is that where actual lighting conditions have been measured against theoretical criteria, such as the IES Code, then invariably they have proved to be inadequate. However, where the users of such lighting have been asked to assess it subjectively, then invariably they have found it satisfactory. In other words, there have been clear and obvious discrepancies between recommendations based on experiment and real-life situations (see also Wells, 1965, 1967; Rapoport and Watson, 1968).

Sommer (1967) confirms this:

'Perhaps the greatest difficulty in applying the experimental method to design problems is that people tend to avoid poor environments when they have the opportunity. Throughout the animal kingdom, flight is the most common reaction to threat. Yet people in psychological (to which one might add sociological) experiments remain seated in their chairs despite abuse, unpleasantness, illogicality and boredom. Subsequent interviewing reveals that they have committed themselves to remaining in the experimental situation . . . the fact that the experiment will take only an hour or two, is one of the major differences between the laboratory and the outside world. One can tolerate the dentist's drill for thirty minutes, while not wanting this as one's daily portion for life.'

One would expect this for several reasons: the experiments on which standards are based, as we have seen, are bound to be indeterminate; the experiment itself adds to the subject's experience. In isolating a single environmental variable one inevitably distorts the effects of interactions between the various sensory modes. Yet one could envisage a range of experiments in which users' real requirements were measured systemically in the working situation. The *audimeter*, for instance, is available; this is a device used in audience research for television. It is built into the set and records automatically when the set is turned on, which channel it is tuned to and for how long. Clearly a simplified device of this kind could be used to monitor lighting —when the artificial lights were turned on, for how long and so on. If the sky luminance were also measured at the time of switching on, then one could measure user needs in this respect very accurately indeed—within a particular cultural group.

There are some things, however, which are not measurable at all in this physical, physiological sense. They are matters of opinion, belief, custom. Most people, for instance, *believe* that daylight is a 'better' source of illumination than artificial light. They feel it is essential to their well-being and believe there are physiological reasons as to why it should be 'better' for their eyes. Hopkinson and Longmore (1959) go further; they suggest that the Scandinavian neurosis known as 'Lapp sickness' is an extreme example of daylight deprivation and go on to say: 'This kind of evidence is by no means conclusive, but if one wants to believe that daylight is necessary for human well-being, it reinforces that belief.'

A more subtle indication of people's belief in daylight was found in Manning's study. Clerical workers in the CIS Building at Manchester were asked to estimate how much of the illumination at their work place was contributed by daylight and how much was artificial. Naturally this varied greatly according to their position in the open plan office. At the same time the total illumination was measured and compared with the contribution of artificial lighting alone, which was measured after dark. People near the window estimated that 75 per cent of their illumination was natural; the figure in fact was over 80 per cent. Twelve feet or so from the window the estimates were very accurate, at about 55 per cent daylight; but further into the room wide divergences were found. At 16 to 19 feet, the estimate was 53 per cent as against an actual 44 per cent, whilst at 50 to 75 feet the estimate was about 27 per cent of daylight, as against an actual 3 per cent. In other words, people deep in the room *wanted* a much higher percentage of daylight illumination than they actually received.

Manning and his colleagues put this down to 'attitudes or prejudices.' They go on to say:

'It is likely that these attitudes are based upon some common factor, perhaps custom, or experience of older and less successful lighting solutions, such as small windows or poorly designed or manufactured electric light fittings. Whatever this common factor might be, it appears to be of little consequence in environments such as the one examined, where the individual is not able to distinguish the existence of conditions which in fact infringe these sensibilities.'

However, as we have seen, people *will* bring their 'attitudes or prejudices' to the building. Their past experience is an essential part of the perceptual translation and one ignores this at one's peril. Why should we *want* to ignore these deeply held beliefs? Far from inhibiting progress in architectural design, they are the stuff of which progress is made. For if we actually succeeded in satisfying people's expectations, systemically, in terms of *all* their sensory modes, accommodating *all* these requirements in terms of seeing, hearing, their skin senses and smell, their kinaesthetic senses and their sense of equilibrium, then the building would be truly revolutionary and quite unlike anything they had seen before.

If we take only the more obvious sensory needs, it will be possible to sketch in some of the characteristics which this building will have. Suppose, for instance, we think of the sky *not* as a source of constant illumination, which patently it is not, but as a source of constantly changing environmental stimulus, which patently it is, then we shall want to allow people their windows. If the windows are too big, then we shall present ourselves with other problems. Langdon and Keighley report that most people were comfortable as far as air temperatures were concerned, in winter at least, at between 64° and 72°F (17·8° and 22·2°C), with a much shorter range of 'optimum comfort' between 66° and 67°F (18·9° and 19·4°C). That is as may be but air temperature, after all, is only one of five variables against which thermal comfort can be measured (Bedford, 1958).

In summer, however, the situation was quite different. Over 40 per cent of office users complained that their working environment was too hot. This figure increased to 49 per cent for offices which faced south-east to south-west, but it was only 27 per cent for offices facing north-east to north-west. Again where south-facing offices had 90 per cent glazing or more, then 55 per cent of the occupants said they were uncomfortable whilst, given the same orientation but with a glazing area of between 40 and 90 per cent, then only 44 per cent complained. So clearly on south-facing facades at least, the windows all have to be small (see also Chrenko, 1953; Teichner, 1967).

Of all the environmental factors noise, according to Langdon and Keighley, caused the most disturbance in the offices surveyed by the Building Research Station (BRS). In their view it constitutes a major interference with work and living. They attribute this to three causes: the increasing use of machinery in offices, particularly automatic data-processing machinery; the rise in urban traffic levels; and the use of light construction and continuous glazing, which offers hardly any obstruction to the passage of noise. In general, 45 per cent of office users were bothered by traffic noises, but on major thoroughfares the figure rose to 65 per cent. This has unpleasant side effects. For instance, in offices facing south generally, 43 per cent complained of overheating and stuffiness in summer whilst again on major thoroughfares, where traffic noise rendered it impractical to open windows, 57 per cent complained.

Internally generated noise had rather different effects. Most of it was confined to machine and typing rooms and here, significantly, complaints about external noise fell off. In large clerical areas the chief sources of noise were conversation, the movement of trolleys and chairs, the opening of filing cabinets and the use of stamps and punches. These too generated quite high noise levels: 60 to 77 dB in open areas, rising to 80 to 95 dB in certain rooms. There were few complaints about noise between rooms, however, presumably because internally generated noises and traffic noise both tended to mask it. Staff at all levels were disturbed by noise and expressed dissatisfaction with noise conditions, but the acceptable level varied somewhat according to the job they were doing. Machine operators, for instance, could tolerate 76 to 78 dB whilst clerical workers would only accept 60 to 63 dB. Again experience had obviously played its part in determining their expectations. Tolerance was also determined, to some extent, by the nature of the noise, continuous noise being more acceptable than fluctuating. The level of machine noise tended to be high, but it was continuous; clerical noises reached a lower level but the sudden opening of a filing cabinet, scraping of a chair on the floor and so on, could cause instant annoyance. That is probably why rooms with a generally low noise level were also considered unsatisfactory; there would be nothing to mask intermittent noise from outside.

The most effective way of tackling these problems, according to Langdon and Keighley, would be to reduce noise at source. Office machinery should be redesigned, with particular attention to mechanism and casing because any attempt to absorb or mask machine noises once they have escaped can only be makeshift. Failing that, the office itself could be planned in such a way that noisy machines were isolated and quiet activities planned together. Planning might also be the answer to traffic noise although the building fabric itself could do much to reduce its penetration. They advocate a return to heavy construction, with reduced fenestration, fixed double glazing and full air-conditioning.

Unlike Weston and his generation of researchers, Langdon, Manning and their associates based their findings on the observation and questioning of *real* people in real buildings. Whilst they investigated each environmental variable separately (lighting, heating and so on) their subjects' experience was in the total environmental context, thus their views on lighting were formed *whilst their other senses were also being stimulated in a systemic way*. Furthermore, the evidence of the various senses operates systemically too. Given that people *want* windows to the external environment, evidence from lighting, heating and sound control studies suggests that these windows had better be small, and located in heavy external walls. It simply needs a Le Corbusier to express these findings in highly charged emotional language, and we shall find ourselves with a new *style*—based on sensory needs.

If we try to define the attributes of 'normal' building according to the philosophy of this book, we shall find that normal building will modify the indigenous climate at a particular place so that certain human activities can be carried out conveniently and in comfort. Their physical relationship and the movement patterns between them will also be facilitated within an ambience such that the cultural group which is to be housed will be able to adapt to it without undue stress. This will require an external envelope which separates adequately the internal ambience from the external environment in terms of: heat control; light control; sound control; smell control.

Heat control will involve the thermal capacity of the building fabric itself. Mass (or heavy planar) construction will absorb heat from the environment and from the heating system. It will thus act as a 'thermal flywheel'; temperature swings will be slow and relatively small. Light and dry construction will have a low thermal capacity; heat absorbed from the environment will be absorbed by the mass of air within the building; there will be no 'thermal flywheel' effect, thus temperature swings will be rapid and large. Such construction will require extensive, quickly adjustable and rapidly responding heating and cooling plants. Heat control will also require: (a) control of heat loss by the use of insulating materials in the external envelope and small, or double glazed, windows; (b) control of solar heat gain. BRS studies suggest that unshaded windows in south facing elevations should not exceed fifteen per cent of the total wall area. Where larger windows are used, various expedients may be used, such as screens, louvres, projecting fins, canopies and 'eyebrows'.

Light control will involve a carefully selected balance between natural and artificial lighting. Many authorities suggest that in order to control sky glare, solar glare, solar heat gain and external noise, windows should be kept as small as possible and used only to provide views of the external environment, with permanent supplementary artificial lighting (PSALI), which can be carefully designed for each activity in terms of direction, 'quality' and illumination values. Where windows are used for illumination, their undesirable effects can be controlled by louvres, canopies, etc., by deep splayed reveals reflecting daylight into the room, by use of windows on adjacent walls, views of ground and buildings outside (rather than open sky) and by light coloured surfaces within the room. Where PSALI is accepted, rooms can be much deeper and the building shape can approach cubic form (which is economical from a circulation and heating point of view) and thus certain sites can be used more effectively.

Sound control will involve: siting the building as far as possible from external noise sources; use of screen walls and, to some extent, planting; use of heavy external envelope (mass or planar) which encloses the building completely, including the roof; complete sealing of all air paths between sound source and activity to be protected—this depends on good workmanship and careful detailing. Sound reduction generally correlates with weight per unit area of structure and on continuity of enclosure; these are easy to achieve in heavy construction (mass or planar) but extremely difficult in light and dry.

Smell control will involve complete sealing of all air paths between smell source and activity to be protected. If the provision for sound control is adequate then adequate smell control will be achieved. If this is not possible then some form of air extraction may be used.

CHAPTER 9

Social Needs

In addition to showing the extent to which sensory deprivation, under certain conditions, may lead to hallucinations and other phenomena arising from one's inner experience, the experiments reported by Vernon and others suggest that the most important stimulus of all in the environment outside oneself will be *other people*. Most of Vernon's subjects reported that when they were not asleep, the first day of sensory deprivation was excellent for concentration. They could focus attention, clearly and precisely, on a very specific problem; some of them indeed solved problems which had proved intractible in ordinary circumstances, but this did not last. From the second day onwards their attention started to wander in mildly unpleasant ways. Having set themselves simple tasks, such as learning the alphabet backwards or remembering the multiplication tables, they found themselves getting stuck repeatedly at certain points. They all thought their thinking processes might have been sharpened *if someone else had been there* so that their problems could be discussed; they wanted a 'listener'. Vernon thinks they might have been satisfied by a fictitious listener—a microphone and speaker circuit with no one actually listening at the other end—but their comments suggested that, rightly or wrongly, the subjects thought of other people as an essential part of the environment if they were to avoid boredom and do any kind of productive work.

So in addition to considering the individual's sensory needs we shall want to consider his relationship with other people and such relations, of course, are the subject matter of sociology and social psychology. We have looked already at various theoretical approaches to sociology and at the range of techniques which social scientists use. It will be useful now, therefore, to look at some examples to see what kinds of information research from the social sciences has made available into design.

Unfortunately, there is no general agreement between social scientists as to how far the built environment *can* influence human behaviour. Festinger, Schachter and Back (1950) are quite clear that it has a considerable effect, so are Caplow (1950), Lee (1957, 1963, 1967, 1971) and Richards (undated). Richards, for instance, describes a particular case in which interpersonal relations, the efficiency and satisfaction of a group of office workers were all affected greatly by changes in the physical environment. Lee (1957) found that children who walked to school, and thus connected school and home in a coherent *schema*, had a higher 'index of adjustment' than those who went by bus or taxi, for whom there was no clear and direct escape route if they felt like going home.

Festinger and others looked at relationships between proximity and friendship in ex-service students' housing at the Massachusetts Institute of Technology (M.I.T.). In one case twelve pre-fab houses were grouped around a cul-de-sac, whilst in the other a two-storey naval barracks had been converted to give five flats on each floor. In each case people seemed to make friends with their next-door neighbours, were less interested in those even two doors away and had hardly anything to do with people only four doors away. Of the people who lived in the cul-de-sac, those at the ends whose houses faced outwards had hardly any friends within it, whilst those from within, who interrelated as a group, tended to develop group opinions in matters such as local politics.

Some very large conclusions have been drawn from these very tiny groups. One should also remember that Festinger's students were all ex-service; they shared similar experiences from the past and equivalent ambitions for the future. A high potential for friendship existed *before* they were thrown into proximity. All we know from these observations is that when people were housed physically in such a way that because of proximity they were likely to meet, potential friends became real friends and this was most likely to happen with those they met most often. One would expect this to happen whenever potential friends are thrown into proximity; and the converse might happen with potential enemies! However, the choosing of people to be placed in proximity is a function of housing management; there is nothing much the architect can do about it, short of aiming at such a narrow economic spectrum or providing his houses with such extreme symbolic values that the imagery will appeal only to a set of potential friends. He might possibly plan three houses, or apartment blocks, equidistant from each other, in triangular formation, but it would be impossible to achieve equal distances with any greater number of units. He might arrange entrances, lifts and staircases so that people could choose *not* to meet each other on entering or leaving but otherwise, and literally, there is *nothing* more he can do about deciding who shall meet whom.

Other social scientists in any case, such as Webber (1964), Hare and Shaw (1965), Broady (1966, 1969) and Gans (1967), take a much more sceptical view as to whether the built environment *can* affect human behaviour and well-being. Gans points out differences between *potential* environment and *effective* environment. Physical built form is merely potential environment; it will accommodate many possibilities, suggesting even that certain kinds of social behaviour would be appropriate. The effective environment, however, will result from interactions between this physical environment and the users. They will perceive it, bring experience, values, beliefs, patterns of social interaction, their culture, to bear on it; there is much more to the effective environment, therefore, than can be determined by a physical arrangement of buildings alone.

Broady (1966) defines, and attacks, a concept which he calls *architectural determinism*, quoting one expression of it as follows: 'The architect who builds a house or designs a site-plan, who decides where the roads will and will not go, and who decides which directions the houses will face and how close together they will be, also is, to a large extent, deciding the pattern of social life among the people who will live in these houses.' He refutes this, with reference to Festinger's study on student housing and to other examples in which physical arrangement seems to have had little or no effect on people's behaviour. One of these concerns a university which, to encourage informal interchanges between staff and students, provided a comfortable coffee lounge between junior and senior common rooms. No one used it because at that time differences in age and status, function and responsibility inhibited any desire on the part of staff and students to meet informally. For the idea to work at all, the people themselves would have had to be redesigned, either by pressure from the university authorities (administration) or by general changes in social structure.

The evidence therefore is conflicting. Each sociologist, as we might expect, collects examples which support his case. On balance it seems reasonable to agree with Rapoport (1971): 'That there are some clear effects of design on behaviour and satisfaction seems undeniable . . . That they are less than designers have believed seems likely'. All we can do is to try and define more closely some of the things they can and some of the things they cannot be.

The prototypes of all such studies, as we saw in Chapter 4, were those conducted by Mayo and his colleagues of Harvard University, for the Western Electric Company in 1927 (Roethlisberger and Dickson, 1939) at the company's Hawthorne works at Cicero, Chicago. The most relevant of these so-called Hawthorne experiments, from our point of view, took place in the Relay Assembly Test Room; five girls (an extraordinarily small sample to base such massive conclusions on) skilled in the assembly of small telephone parts, were chosen to work in this Test Room, well away from the main Relay Assembly Department so that, among other things, they lost regular contact with their former colleagues. Nor were they selected at random. Two of the girls were personal friends, known to be 'co-operative' with management and thus amenable to observation. They were asked to choose the other three.

Mayo and his colleagues hoped to discover the ways, if any, in which working conditions lead to fatigue. The room itself, as a physical space, remained constant but such things as temperature, humidity and lighting conditions were varied, not to mention hours of work and sleep. The girls were examined from time to time at a local hospital. Their work was highly repetitive, consisting of assembling telephone relays, but it demanded considerable skill;

there was no conveyor belt and each girl could work at her natural pace. Temperature and humidity were read hourly and an observer was stationed in the room to monitor and record what happened each day.

Tests were consecutive; on average they lasted about eight weeks but there was considerable variation. Normal working rates were established during three initial periods and the actual tests then began. The first four were concerned with the effects of rest breaks; the total weekly output actually increased as the rest breaks were lengthened, even though the working week itself was reduced by some 5 per cent. There was no rise in productivity when the working day was shortened but the most surprising, and often quoted, result was that when a test was repeated, output proved to be some 20 per cent higher than it had been previously under similar conditions. There seemed to be a general upward trend in output irrespective of the sequence in which tests were applied so that no direct correlation could be found between output and working conditions. That, of course, has been a disappointment ever since to those who believe in architectural determinism.

Mayo tested several hypotheses to account for this unexpected result. The five girls were paid in accordance with their *group* output and this may have led to the building up of a group 'spirit'; when five other girls in the main Assembly Department were put on similar rates, their output also went up. It may be that as a group these other girls wanted to show that they could do as well as the Relay Assembly Test Room group. The most plausible hypotheses seem to be, firstly that the Test Room girls really had welded themselves into a cohesive team and this worked more effectively, secondly that the observer, acting as supervisor, had shown interest in them personally thus increasing their motivation, the so-called 'Hawthorne effect', and thirdly that changes in the sensory environment (lighting, temperature, ventilation and so on) irrespective of what they were, provided positive sensory experience as distinct from sensory deprivation, and that this in itself led to increased output.

Our interpretation, naturally, will vary according to what we are trying to prove, but one thing is clear: the environment for each member of the group consisted of three things—the sensory environment itself with variable physical conditions within a fixed room shape, and two distinct social environments comprising respectively, other members of the team, which henceforth we shall call *users*, and the observer-supervisor who, for want of a better term, we might call *management* or *administration*. The room itself, as a physical *space*, had no effect whatever on variations in output; it was the single constant among a host of variables. The *variations* of sensory conditions seem to have had some effect, but we do not know how much and the *two* kinds of social environment certainly had their effects, although we are not really sure as to how much we should attribute to each.

There was no conscious attempt in the Hawthorne experiment to submit the girls to conditions of positive discomfort. Heating, lighting, ventilation and so on, all stayed within limits we might describe as 'comfortable' or even 'pleasurable'. Yet there is evidence that even beyond such limits, for certain sensory modes at least, performance in certain tasks need not suffer, nor presumably will it improve either. Hovey (1928) wanted to investigate the effects of a *distracting* environment on people's behaviour, so he asked 171 people to complete two intelligence tests under conditions which Sommer describes (1966):

> 'The first form was filled out in a quiet room, the second in a room with 7 bells, 5 buzzers, a 550-watt spot light, a 90,000 volt rotary spark gap, a phonograph, 2 organ pipes of various pitches, 3 metal whistles, a 55-pound circular saw mounted on a wooden frame, a well-known photographer taking pictures, and 4 students doing acrobatics. Sometimes there was quiet in the latter room, but at other times several of these distractions were operating simultaneously.'

On the evidence of these two tests, the group performed just as well on the tests in his noisy room as they did in the quiet one.

Maslow and Mintz (1956), on the other hand, investigated the effects of physical environment on people's *judgement*. They conducted an experiment in which psychology students were asked to rate ten photographs of different people, for 'energy' and 'well-being' or 'fatigued' and 'displeased' along a six-point scale. There were thirty-two students altogether and they were divided into three groups. One group looked at the photographs in a 'beautiful' room—a comfortable study, furnished (according to the experimenter's judgement) with elegance and taste. The second group saw the same photographs in an 'ugly' room—a cleaner's store containing brooms and buckets, which had not been swept for some time—whilst the third group looked at them in an 'average' room—a professor's study which was neat and tidy but by no means elegant. The results of the experiment seem almost too good to be true. Subjects in the 'beautiful' room gave ratings for the ten photographs which were well within the 'energetic' and 'well-being' range; those in the 'ugly' room gave ratings in the 'fatigued' or 'displeased' range, and those in the 'average' room gave average ratings.

Yet the experiment itself was a double bluff (Mintz, 1956). The examiners themselves, in the 'beautiful' and 'ugly' rooms, were being examined although they did not know it. Maslow and Mintz tested each of them in each of the three rooms, ostensibly for practice. In addition to this, the examiners were asked to test themselves at the end of each session, as a check on the reliability of the scale. The experiment as a whole was spread over three weeks, with two sessions per week making a total of six sessions in all; the author worked in the 'average' room during each of these sessions, but the other two examiners alternated between the 'beautiful' and the 'ugly' rooms. It was found that the examiners gave consistently higher ratings when they were in the 'beautiful' room and this was consistent throughout the three weeks. They took longer over the tests in this room too, enjoyed the work, felt it to be important and wanted to go on with it, but in the 'ugly' room they finished the tests quickly, complained of monotony, fatigue and headache. Mintz credited them, in fact, with feelings of discontent, hostility and avoidance generally, but although they seem to have been quite conscious of these differences (they had in fact discussed them) they were surprised nevertheless to find just how much their judgement had been affected by the physical environment within which it was made.

Unfortunately, and in spite of studies by Payne (1970), Wools (1970) and others, this is the *only* evidence that the social sciences have offered so far, that people's *feelings* might be affected directly by their physical environment. It would be true to say also that most architects *aim* to give people elegant rooms, or at least average ones. It would be a strange architect indeed who designed a room for people to live in, or even to take psycho-social tests in, which resembled in any single particular a broom cupboard. Sociological experiment, therefore, seems to be of limited use as an aid to design. The observation of social structure may be another matter. Here, at first sight, we discover the essential basis of every client's brief. For, whether we are designing a house for an individual family or the development plan for an entire city region, we shall be concerned with the ways in which people interact, and, ideally, the pattern of their interactions will determine the relationships of various elements in our design.

Let us take the most basic unit of all social interaction, the face-to-face group (see Sprott, 1958; Abercrombie, 1960; Argyle, 1965, 1967). This consists, as the name implies, of a number of people who have come together for some purpose which can only be fruitful if they can actually see each other. They have actually *moved* from some other place to be in a room, or other space, where they can arrange themselves in some physical relationship with each other. They may have moved from one continent to another, one country to another, one city to another, one neighbourhood to another, one building to another or one chair to the next. Whatever the distance and complexity of their movement, their present proximity and physical interrelationship could not now be taking place without it. At this point, however, they need ask no more of the room than that it is big enough to house them and the activities they wish to pursue, and possesses an internal climate which visually, thermally and aurally offers them comfort, if not delight. If the architect offers them this, then it may be the best he can do. He provides a place where they can meet and after that they decide personally how to interact.

There have been attempts to investigate in detail people's spatial needs in relation to each other. In his *General Psychology* (1938) Stern puts forward the appealing view that each of us is surrounded by a 'personal bubble' of space and, if this is so, then clearly it helps determine the physical distances at which we prefer to see other people. Altman and Lett (1967) suggest that these relate to 'onion skin' theories of personality, in which one exposes different layers of one's psychological self to different people, so that different levels of interaction occur. As one's relationship to another person changes, so 'boundary phenomena' occur at the point where an 'onion skin' is peeled away and new kinds of interaction occur. But within the new zone of inter-actions one's own motives may be very different from one's partner's. One may wish to intensify it, whilst one's partner may tend to shy away.

One anthropologist's view is presented by E. T. Hall in a series of publica-tions (1959, 1963a, 1963b) and most particularly in *The Hidden Dimension* (1966). He is concerned with *proxemics*, the individual's structuring of the space immediately outside himself, which may be effected consciously or unconsciously. Hall classifies relationships between people in terms of four

Table 9.1—Table of social distances (from Hall, 1966)

1. Intimate distance.	
close phase—up to 6 ins (150 mm)	
far phase—6 ins to 18 ins (150 mm to 450 mm)	audible whisper
	intimate utterance
2. Personal distance	
close phase—18 ins to 30 ins (450 mm to 760 mm)	
far phase—2½ ft to 4 ft (760 mm to 1·200 m)	moderate voice
	personal involvement
3. Social distance	
close phase—4 ft to 7 ft (1·200 m to 2·200 m)	impersonal business
far phase—7 ft to 12 ft (2·200 m to 3·650 m)	formal business
4. Public distance	
close phase—12 ft to 25 ft (3·650 m to 7·300 m)	loud voice planned for-mal discourse
far phase—25 ft and over (7·300 m and over)	public utterance
	political expression

basic 'social distances', from *intimate* distance (less than 18 inches or 0·45 m) to *public* distances (12 feet, 3·65 m, or more). As we might expect, intimate distances are reserved for intimate contacts, whereas public distances occur on formal and impersonal occasions. Modes of communication naturally differ according to distance. At intimate distances, which may involve body con-tact, thermal and olfactory cues may play their part, not to mention the kinaesthetic ones which contact implies; so for that matter may visual and aural cues, whilst at public distances it may be only the latter cues which are involved.

Hall (1966) identifies four significant distances which he associates with sensory experience of many kinds, including shifts in voice (see Table 9.1). We may or may not agree with Hall and certainly there is no evidence of rigorous experiment in his work, but his figures may be supported to some extent by figures for speech interference levels (SIL) as illustrated in Table 9.2. The effect of lower speech interference levels may be extrapolated accurately enough for most purposes by trebling the distances for each 10 dB drop in SIL, from which one might conclude that for *really* private conversation, one should take one's partner into a foundry and shout at her from 300 mm!

The point of all this is that all of Hall's conversational levels up to, and including, social distance can be accommodated in a 10-foot (3·0 m) room, although some of the conversation may have to be across the diagonal! The

Table 9.2—Speech interference levels (from Aldersey Williams, 1969)

SIL distance	Voice level and distance for work intelligibility	Nature of communication
45	Normal voice at 3 m	Relaxed conversation Telephone use satisfactory
55	Normal voice at 900 mm Raised voice at 1·8 m Very loud voice at 3·6 m	Continuous conversation in work areas Telephone use slightly difficult
65	Raised voice at 600 mm Very loud voice at 1·2 m Shouting at 2·4 m	Intermittent conversation Telephone use difficult
75	Very loud voice at 300 mm Shouting at 800–900 mm	Minimal communication —pre-arranged vocabulary Telephone use impossible
85	Shouting at 300 mm	

users will decide for themselves if they *want* to be very close and there is nothing the architect can do to stop them.

The fact that they find themselves in the same room working together, relaxing or otherwise engaging each other's company may be their own choice or, more likely, it will result from decisions taken by the managers, or administrators, of the building. Gullahorn (1952), Byrne (1955, 1961), Hare and Bales (1963), Patterson (1968) and many others have been concerned with the effects of propinquity on human relationships at this level, but they fail to make the point that propinquity itself is a matter of how management chooses to use the building rather than a function of the building itself. As Rapoport says (1971), these studies are more concerned with the complex interactions which occur between personality, physical arrangement, prestige, social circumstances and certain other variables.

Nor is there anything the architect can do about the ways in which people choose to interact, their topics of conversation and so on, although they may initially exchange a few pleasantries about his room. Goodman (1964) has shown how even the simplest furniture arrangements have highly complex socio-cultural determinants, whilst Duffy (1969a, 1969b) and Joiner (1971) discuss the ways in which people arrange furniture in their offices so as to define 'public' and 'private' zones within which their preferred spatial relationships with other people will be respected. The arrangement is *their* choice; the room, unless it happens to be some wildly eccentric shape, has little effect on that choice.

Hall (1959, 1966), Goffman (1959, 1961, 1966, 1969), Barnlund and Harland (1963), Lipman (1968, 1970), Sommer (1969) and Fast (1970) have all considered the ways in which people choose to place themselves physically in terms of spatial relationships, for the purposes of social interaction. Sometimes this is fixed by the building itself: Hazard (1962) has shown how in a courtroom, for instance, spatial arrangements are highly stylized and expressive of clearly defined social and functional relationships between judge, accused, counsel and so on; but in most cases, and especially where the furniture is movable, architecture is 'neutral', as Peter Cowan confirmed in studies which he undertook at the Bartlett School of Architecture (now School of the Built Environment), at University College, London. These have been published in various forms, of which *Studies in the Growth, Change and Ageing of Buildings* (1964) is probably the most comprehensive. They grew initially out of an investigation into hospital planning which showed that few medical buildings fulfil their functions properly for more than a limited time. Changes in medical practice, or even social changes, ensure that most hospitals are in fact out of date before they are completed. By definition, one cannot know what the change is going to be and in terms of actual building therefore, in physical terms, it is extremely difficult to cater for it.

Cowan took a rather subtle, if inexact, approach. He plotted a wide range of human activities starting, he says, with the 'five senses and ranging up to large group activities such as dances and conferences.' He then plotted these activities on to a chart showing room sizes from about 4 square feet (0·370 square metres) to 10,000 square feet (920 square metres), against the number of activities which each room size could contain (Figure 9.1). The smallest room, he thought, might accommodate about ten different basic activities, but from this point the curve rose rapidly to about 200 square feet (18·5 square metres), at which point it levelled off abruptly. Beyond this point quite large increments in floor area made very little difference to the number of additional activities which could be obtained.

As a technique, of course, it begs several questions. What, precisely, is an activity in these terms? Clearly it is more than an individual matter and quite large numbers of people may be involved. Then again, how does one know that the list of activities is comprehensive? Thirdly, and most important, does one allow for the fact that a room may be too big for an activity? In other words, ought not there to be some tapering off? Does one count four hundred people attending a dance as one activity or as four hundred?

However, these are mere quibbles and the chart itself is so revealing that as it stands it provides us with some extremely useful information. In order to validate it, Cowan plots against it the actual percentages of room sizes provided in four new hospitals. He finds that they are skewed far to the left,

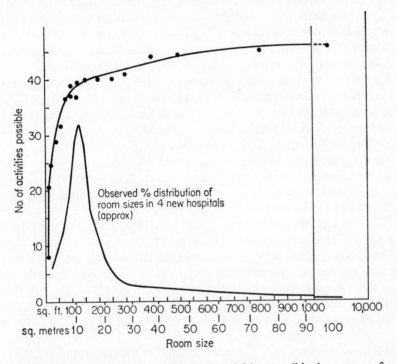

Figure 9.1—Approximate numbers of activities possible in rooms of different sizes (from Cowan, 1964)

that 30 per cent of the rooms are around 150 square feet (14 square metres) and that less than 1 per cent are 1,000 square feet (92 square metres) or over. He concludes from this that a majority of human activities can be housed in spaces of under 200 square feet (18·5 square metres), whilst a very large proportion will be served by rooms of 150 square feet (14 square metres).

Given Cowan's room of about 150 square feet (14 square metres) then, one could carry out an extraordinary range of activities. Given reasonable environmental control, it could be used as a living room, dining room, bedroom; it would be rather generous for a kitchen or a bathroom. It could be used as a study, seminar room, small classroom, office, waiting room or even a small workshop. As Cowan says it would satisfy 70 per cent of the activities in a hospital and altogether some 70 per cent of human activities in general. There is even more to it than that. Clearly activities which can be housed in the same room size are, to some extent at least, interchangeable. Suppose, for instance, that one planned a city centre building in which all the rooms were of 150 square feet (14 square metres). If Cowan is right, then clearly it could be used for almost anything. If one wanted to use it for a hospital, for instance, then one would have to plan, say, one additional block in which the activities requiring non-standard spaces could be housed and one's highly flexible design would be complete. By implication, the same basic building could be used for a university, as an office block, a hotel and so on.

Given any one of Cowan's standard rooms then (and even if they were all about the same size they could vary in shape, mode of decoration, furnishing), the users could choose precisely what they wanted to do in it, from making love to committing murder. There is nothing the architect can, or should even want to, do about dictating their choice. Musgrove, Doidge, Rawlinson and others (1970, 1971) have shown that the greatest inhibition to using a room for many purposes is the name which attaches to it. Their studies of room classification at University College, London, suggest that if one stops labelling spaces 'staff room', 'tutorial room' and so on, thinking of them instead of so much serviced space, then their usage would be much more flexible and economical. Hawkes and Stibbs (1969, 1970a–d) have also developed techniques for analysing rooms in these ways.

That is true of the room as a finite entity, an enclosed space of given length, breadth and height, with windows and doors in particular places; for once it is built, each room will be *as* fixed, but no more fixed, than the Test Room in Mayo's Hawthorne experiments. Temperature, humidity, lighting and other environmental conditions will be variable and so, in most cases, will the arrangement of furniture.

It is no coincidence that with a few exceptions the studies published so far on the social implications of architectural space have concentrated on the arrangement of furniture, with some mention of room size and shape. This is true of Hole and Attenburrow (1966), Lipman (1969), Sommer (1969) and others. Clearly the arrangement of furniture *does* have a profound effect on the ways people can interact, but if the furniture is movable they can *choose* how to arrange it. This suggests, at least, that Le Corbusier was wrong when he said (1923):

'Demand . . . Built-in fittings to take the place of much of the furniture, which is expensive to buy, takes up too much room and needs looking after.'

But compared with the built-in fittings such furniture is changeable within the room and encourages rearrangement at will; it can be moved from room to room, or from house to house easily and any piece or pieces can be replaced when it has served its purpose or when one tires of it.

Sommer summarizes a great deal of work which he and others have done into spatial behaviour within buildings, in a book entitled *Personal Space* (1969). He takes the view, which has also been stressed in the present book, that architecture must enclose space in which certain activities can take place comfortably and efficiently although he presents this as a personal discovery and fails to acknowledge the many architects who have preceded him in this

Table 9.3—Percentage of student preferences for seating arrangements for different social purposes (from Sommer, 1969)

Seating arrangement	Condition 1 (conversing)	Condition 2 (co-operating)	Condition 3 (co-acting)	Condition 4 (competing)
(corner arrangement)	42	19	3	7
(opposite sides)	46	25	32	41
(diagonal)	1	5	43	20
(same side, far)	0	0	3	5
(same side, adjacent)	11	51	7	8
(distant ends)	0	0	13	18
Total (as Sommer)	100	100	100	99

belief. His particular concern is with the ecology (relationship of organism to environment) and ethology (study of behaviour) of small groups. Much of this is concerned with furniture—the way people arrange themselves around tables for different kinds of discussion, the way students located in different positions in the classroom contribute, or fail to contribute, to the discussion; and he then considers a series of 'special settings'—hospital wards and day rooms, classroom spaces (with particular reference to classroom layout and student participation), design for drinking, student residences and so on. Table 9.3 shows the preferences Sommer found among students who were asked to choose seating arrangements for different social purposes.

Sommer's findings are of interest for several reasons. They suggest that face-to-face contact may take several forms; there is no 'optimum' arrangement for any particular condition. Some of his students were concerned about *eye contact*: sitting opposite one's partner forced one into it, whereas 'catty-corner' arrangement 'allows staring into space and not into my neighbour's face.' Above all, Sommer's investigation shows that if one provides a table and a couple of chairs people can choose how they wish to sit and that is of vital importance. It confirms, as so many of these ecological studies do, that provided one gives people choice in the arrangement of furniture and plans the room in such a way that freedom of manoeuvre is possible, then one has done just about all one can to encourage effective social contact.

Experiment, therefore, seems to be no more satisfactory in establishing people's social needs in building than it was in establishing their physiological needs. There has, however, been a great deal more *observation* of people's

Table 9.4

Living rooms for meals and general use	170–180 square feet (15·8–16·8 m²)
Living rooms for general use only	150 square feet (14 m²)
Dining rooms or separate dining spaces	100 square feet (9·2 m²)
Kitchens for cooking and meals	110–115 square feet (10·2–10·6 m²)

social interactions in the physical environment. This of course is a historical matter and one or two rather slight recommendations seem to be forthcoming.

One of the most comprehensive reviews of user studies is to be found in the work of two BRS sociologists—Hole and Attenburrow's *Houses and People* (1966). They took a number of house types and interviewed groups of people, totalling 4,000 altogether, living in different places and in these different types, after which they compared the responses of the different groups. As a first step they collected data on what people actually do in their houses; British housewives, for instance, spent an average of 4 hours per day preparing (and presumably eating) meals, 2½ hours on housework, 1½ hours on laundry and 2 hours on child care. Evening activities such as reading, writing, sewing, knitting, watching television and so on were also analysed. They then looked at different house plans and found that preferred sizes for the different rooms seemed to be the ones shown in Table 9.4. In many ways, however, these were less critical than room shape, and there was an overwhelming preference for square, or nearly square, rooms, except in the case of dining kitchens in which case the two areas, for working and meals, can be easily separated. Hole and Attenburrow plot the percentages by which people expressed their *dissatisfaction* with various room shapes; the room shapes themselves are indicated by shape ratio, i.e. a ratio of 1 : 1·4 means that the room was almost one and a half squares long (see Table 9.5). The longer rooms, apparently, produced difficulties of several kinds. Sometimes it was difficult to place furniture satisfactorily or to move about the room, especially if guests were present. Room shape, of course, is related to furniture arrangement and there were overwhelming preferences for certain furniture-types.

Hole and Attenburrow have little to say on what the people they studied would really have done if they could have chosen. Their subjects were drawn from a very restricted social group whose aspirations extended no further than putting their names on the housing list, being allocated a house and furnishing it to the best of their ability. So their vision of what was possible extended no further than furnishing their present house more lavishly, but certainly in conformity with the local conventions. Asked what they would

Table 9.5

Room type	Shape ratio		
	1·0 to 1·2	1·2 to 1·4	over 1·4
Cooking and dishwashing	9%	12%	17%
Cooking and meals	4%	22%	10%
Meals, cooking and general purposes	9%	14%	35%
Meals and general purposes	5%	9%	29%
General purposes	4%	9%	13%

really like to have, given unlimited money, 66 per cent mentioned some particular item of furniture or floor covering and about one-third mentioned a piece of furniture they had seen already in someone else's house, in a showroom or exhibition. Again, nearly half mentioned a house they knew already, tenanted by friends or relatives; there were few aspirations to middle class standards and, on the whole, these were seen to be completely out of reach.

From the researchers' point of view, the furniture and arrangements they saw seemed very much alike but the occupants, on the other hand, could detect many subtle personal differences and insisted that they 'had their own taste.' Nevertheless one-third of them admitted that other people's houses were their primary source of furnishing ideas; one-third mentioned magazine articles but a quarter of this third suggested that these were not really relevant: 'They are all right if you have lots of money but no good for ordinary folks like us.' Two-thirds mentioned shop windows and exhibitions as general sources of ideas. At the time (1956) display in these shops was restricted to massive, high gloss furniture and the shopkeepers claimed buyer-resistance to new types of furniture; most of them wanted furniture similar to that which relatives had bought.

Hole and Attenburrow detected certain principles in the selection and arrangement of furniture although there was no question of a theoretical background in terms of colour, texture and so on. They thought in terms of furniture groups, the three-piece suite, the dining suite and so on, grouped the suite within the room and then 'set it off' with curtains, floor coverings, ornaments and so on.

This rearrangement of furniture represents one way of modifying the environment *within* the room, but there are other possibilities. The room itself was substantially unchanged in the Hawthorne experiment even though conditions within it were modified considerably. The modifications in this case were largely environmental, changes in lighting and thermal conditions, but many other kinds of change are possible, some of them temporary or superficial, others permanent and fundamental. Superficial changes, such as rearranging furniture, may suggest specific temporary use, e.g. chairs arranged for discussion purposes. Changes in furniture arrangement, decoration, lighting and so on, may lead to apparent changes in the size and shape of the room. Any changes may embody cultural indicators (intended or accidental) as to how the room can, or should, be used (Table 9.6).

All these are *possible*, technically, with any room but are often not carried out because the *administration* of the building will not allow them to be. This is true, for instance, of local authority housing. There are things which tenants are not allowed to do. There may be restrictions on the building as regards fittings, such as fixing shelves to the walls, but the range of things which are not permitted may go very much further than that, from erecting sheds in the garden to keeping certain kinds of pets.

This suggests a powerful tool for examining relationships between users and their buildings. If we observe *all* the changes they have made to a particular building, from adding an extension to changing a lampshade, we shall learn a great deal about where the building failed to match their requirements. If we measure the physical conditions they thus provide for themselves (in terms of heating, lighting, sound control) then we shall learn a great deal about their sensory needs; if we record furniture arrangements, movement paths, both within the building and across our beautifully planted lawns, we shall learn a great deal about their social needs. We shall transcend the difficulties which arise when people say one thing and do another (see Chapter 7). We shall avoid the indeterminacies which distort all observations and experiments with people; our observations will *not* change the building. It will be possible, therefore, to develop tools which enable us to learn a great deal about relationships between people and their buildings, whilst avoiding the inherent difficulties of social science and psychological method.

We shall have difficulties too, which brings us to the true cause (or so it seems to me) of most serious 'misfits' between people and their buildings, in the many changes which they wish to make but do not make because they are not allowed to. In other words, the third factor in the Hawthorne relationship constrains them—that which we called administration.

Table 9.6

	Temporary	Medium term	Long term
CHANGES IN FURNITURE	Move existing furniture, change arrangement	Bring in new furniture, including lamp-shades, carpets, etc.	
CHANGES IN FITTINGS AND/OR FINISHES		Bring in new fittings, built-in furniture, etc. Repaint, paper visible surfaces. Changes in colour/texture may affect apparent size	
CHANGES IN SERVICES	Open/close blinds/curtains. Move standard/table lamps, convectors, fan-heaters, etc. Turn heating, ventilation fans up/down Turn radio, record player, television on/off	Replace lamps/tubes with different values Bring in new standard/table lamps, convectors, fan-heaters, radio, record player, television	Replace/install new services—lighting, heating, ventilating Replace/install heating and/or sound insulation
CHANGES IN STRUCTURE			Open up new/block up old doors windows, etc. Add new space division—walls, partitions etc. Remove existing space divisions —walls, partitions etc.

All users of buildings are constrained by administration, using that word in the broadest possible sense to describe any person or group of people who decide what may or may not be done within a building or to the building fabric. Administration determines who shall work together in a particular office (Figure 9.2) thus helping, at least, to decide whether love or murder will be committed. Administration determines the date at which heating will be switched on in the autumn and switched off again in spring, what size of light bulbs will be fitted, when the building will be redecorated and what colours will be used. Administration, in the form of the headmaster, lays down rules as to how pupils and teachers shall behave in school, which entrances the pupils may use and on which side of a corridor they must walk,

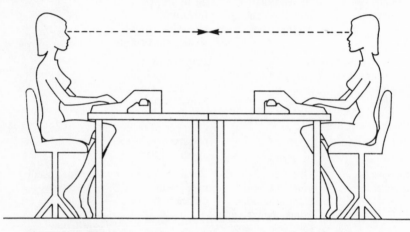

Figure 9.2—These two typists have been put to work in the same room by administration but they, personally, choose what kind of social relationship to enjoy

which staircases they will go up and which they will go down. At another level, administration in the form of an education committee determines how the headmaster may use his school. Administration determines who will live next to whom in a block of flats, who will live in solitary confinement in prison. It even determines, in the form of some planning committee, whether or not a private owner can open a new window on to a room which he finds dark. One can think of hundreds of other ways in which administration, in this broad sense, determines the uses of buildings. It is nonsense, therefore, to think of direct, causal connexions between built form and human behaviour, except at the grossest, physiological level. The Hawthorne experiments revealed once and for all (and with all the sinister implications which Cohn Bendit and his colleagues attributed to them) the power of administration (or management) to determine human behaviour in buildings.

Often, of course, the users themselves constrain each other in ways which enlightened management deplores. Lipman (1968) reports his investigations into patterns of behaviour in the sitting rooms of three old people's homes. As he says, it is unlikely that research of this kind, from the perspective of only one discipline, will reveal data that the architect would consider necessary for use in design. He adapted a participant observer technique described by Hyde and York (1948) in which, once the staff and residents of a home had accepted his presence, he actually sat in the room with the residents, noted who was sitting where, who spoke to whom, and so on. He then questioned certain of the residents about their seat preferences and also obtained information about status gradations among them. He presented a formal questionnaire to those residents who could answer it, thus obtaining data about their last occupation, their friends among fellow residents, activities, feelings about privacy and the sharing of sitting rooms and so on. He found, as one might expect, that the furniture arrangements were considered to be fixed, each resident had a favourite chair and the position of that chair was a matter of status, this in spite of Welfare Department policy and house 'rule' that no chair should 'belong' to a particular resident. Residents would speak of 'their' chairs and would assault occupation, or even attempted occupation, by someone else, with verbal invective or even physical attack. Management in this case seems to have been more 'humane' than the users. Lipman cites seven other studies which confirm his findings on persistent chair arrangement and selection.

It may be as Simmel (1955) and Coser (1956) suggest, that some social conflict is desirable; it may indeed have a therapeutic effect on old people. The question really is as to how far one can, or should, try to stimulate such conflict by designing the building in a particular way. One still needs to know what the architect can do about it. Part of his dilemma is revealed by research such as Canter reports (1970) into students' preferences for seating arrangements in seminar rooms. Canter's aim was to observe which seats students tended to choose in seminar rooms. Various permutations of formal/informal arrangements were tried; the tutor stood close to the front row of seats or distant from it, and so on. Given a formal arrangement—seats in straight rows, and a 'close' tutor—students tended to sit at the back rows. Given an informal arrangement—seats in semicircles and a tutor standing centrally— the students tended to sit on either side of an imaginary centre line. There were certain subtleties in their choice which Canter does not mention: given a door to one side, they tended marginally to sit on that side, and no doubt also if the room had had a window, that too would have affected their choice.

Where does this lead us? If, after an extended series of such experiments, it was shown that students always preferred certain positions in seminar rooms, could we go on to design rooms containing only those preferred positions? Of course not. The experiment tells us nothing about the room itself and it certainly will not help us to design a better one. It confirms what we knew already: that movable furniture encourages choice of arrangement, formal or informal, and also enables us to conduct experiments such as this. That is all.

Sommer (1969) presents an equivalent problem:

'If one finds that French Canadian students are able to tolerate closer presence than can their English Canadian counterparts, does this mean that a Quebec architect can (a) use a smaller room for the same number of students, (b) double the number of students in ordinary size classrooms, or (c) attempt to change the students' spatial preferences by increasing the distances between chairs?'

He concludes that the answers must be given in terms of goals, objectives and values rather than in the form of technical specifications. However, someone—the architect—finally has to make decisions as to the sizes and shapes of rooms. Goals, objectives and values will only help him so far; the lines he draws on a plan *are* technical specifications for a room, with goals, objectives and values built in.

In terms of direct fit to human need the architect can do two things. He can enclose spaces which in terms of size, shape and environmental solutions are appropriate to human psychology and physiology. He can then arrange these spaces in such a way that physical movement between them is facilitated or inhibited. That is all. If he wishes to do more—to ensure a closer match between users, their needs and their buildings—he will have to take up building management or (and this seems to me far more sinister) to redesign administration and users themselves so that they begin to reflect his own personal, social and political convictions.

CHAPTER 10

New Problem-solving Techniques

We have been concerned in the last nine chapters with some of the problems which human psychological and social needs present the architect with. It will now be appropriate to look at some of the new techniques which have become available for problem-solving. We shall examine these general characteristics before we apply them specifically to architecture.

The Greek philosophers, Plato, Aristotle and others, were concerned with processes of thinking and decision. So, for that matter, was Descartes and indeed many of the procedures have a specific origin in his work. Certain twentieth century philosophers and psychologists have also been concerned with these things. Some, as we might expect, have been rational in their approach whilst others have been empirical. Some have examined the processes of rigorous analysis whilst others have sought to explain the processes of imagination. Reading some of these accounts, one is led to believe that they are the province of different kinds of people who seem remarkably like the *convergers* and *divergers* of Chapter 1. Paul Valéry, with considerable insight, has suggested that a truly creative act needs both. He envisages two personalities in dialogue, one creative and the other critical. So if the act of designing is to be productive we may have to find some way of combining, or rather alternating two quite distinct kinds of thinking. Valéry thought that two people would be involved: 'one makes up combinations, the other one chooses' and, if that is so, we shall need some means of ensuring that each can contribute what he does best. There may have to be some structuring of the dialogue between them so that the one knows when, and in what form, to present the combinations he has generated to the other. In practice this structuring may be simply a matter of habit. If two people work together long enough, they begin to know each other's quirks and fancies; each understands what the other can do and there is no need to formalize the arrangement. However, if we examine the idea of formal structuring, in the design situation, we shall find that it has other, unforeseen by-products.

In setting up such a structure in the first place, we shall start by assuming that the diverger and the converger can each do best the things which come naturally to his personality type. Divergers, as we saw, can cope with ambiguous situations, with incomplete instructions; they will tend to throw up more and more elaborate ideas when it comes to making up combinations, but they will tend to be rather slapdash. Convergers, on the other hand, will approach their task of choosing with cool logic; they will look for precision

175

and order in their task of focussing down on the 'one best' solution to the problem. As we very well know, there are many techniques in logic and mathematics which will help the converger in his task. Cartesian *Method*, in fact, is a precise formulation of convergence. In other words, once we have isolated the *choosing* aspects of the design task we can bring a whole battery of techniques to bear which will help us to do it effectively. Other techniques too have been developed to encourage divergence—we shall describe some of them in Chapter 16. So again, once we have isolated the making up of combinations as part of the design task, we can bring in techniques which help us to do this better too.

So this simplest possible formulation of a design sequence into two distinct parts—the making up of combinations and the choosing—has some very serious implications indeed. If techniques are available for encouraging the convergent to be even more convergent or the divergent even more divergent, why should they not also be used to encourage a change-over, at the appropriate point, from one to the other? Valéry's structure suggests that, during the process, divergence gives way to convergence so, having generated combinations by methods which come naturally to him, why should the diverger not then use techniques from logic and mathematics to help him in the task of choosing? In other words, it should be possible to build up a design process which transcends the limitations of a particular personality type and allows him to 'cross over' to the other way of thinking whenever it seems appropriate. There have been many attempts to compare these ways of thinking. One very interesting comparison was undertaken by Max Wertheimer, founder of Gestalt psychology, in the study of *Productive Thinking* which was published after his death in 1943. He outlines, first of all, the operations of traditional logic:

definition
comparison and discrimination
analysis
abstraction
generalization
forming close concepts
subsumption, etc.
forming propositions
forming inferences
forming syllogisms, etc.;

and he suggests that the ability to carry out these operations is generally seen as a mark of intelligence. Among its other virtues, Wertheimer sees it as important that traditional logic concentrates on the basic difference between mere assertion, beliefs and exact judgements, between hazy concepts, hazy generalizations and exact formulations; its emphasis is on proof and on stringency and rigour in each individual step in thinking. But it has one overwhelming disadvantage: it cannot lead to creative results—it is not, to use Wertheimer's term, *productive* thinking. Inductive logic as developed by Bacon and others is simply an extension of traditional logic which, according to Wertheimer, emphasizes the following operations:

empirical observations
careful gathering of facts
studying problems empirically
introducing experimental method
correlating facts
developing crucial tests.

This, too, is convergent although experiment may lead to creative results, if only by accident. Wertheimer contrasts traditional and inductive logic with associationism which had moved a long way since the days of Locke and Hume. Hume's association of ideas by resemblance, by continuity or by cause and effect, had given way in the science of behaviourism, to association by stimulus and response. Koch (1964) suggests that behaviourism was really looking for a *decision procedure*, by means of which real progress could be made in psychology. The operations of the behaviourist sequence, according to Wertheimer, were:

association, acquiring connexions—bonds on the basis of repetitions, role of frequency, or recency
recall from past experience
trial and error, with chance success
learning on the basis of repeated success
acting in line with conditioned responses and with habit.

In other words a problem would be solved by recalling previous examples, by the mechanical repetition of what has been learned by rote, or by chance discovery in a series of blind trials and errors.

That, for Wertheimer, was no real improvement on traditional logic, even though it may occasionally throw up productive ideas. However, he tried to improve on both by presenting a creative thought-process based, as we might expect, on Gestalt psychology. Wertheimer's description of productive thinking is concerned with organization into wholes and with relationships between the parts of a problem. Thinking, he suggests, consists in:

'. . . envisaging, realizing structural features and structural requirements; proceeding in accordance with, and determined by, these requirements; thereby changing the situation in the direction of structural improvements.'

So one concentrates on gaps in the argument, superficialities and disturbances, which are corrected with reference to the overall structure. One tries to detect the structural hierarchy, to separate peripheral features from those which are essential to the structure and, generally, to look for structural rather than piecemeal truth. He demonstrates his technique with reference to a series of problems of which the following is typical (see Figure 10.1): the circle represents a window above the altar of a church, and during redecoration the painters have been asked to gild the two areas above and below it. These are formed by drawing vertical lines, tangent to the circle, and of the same height as the window itself. Beyond these, half circles are to be added top and bottom to complete the figure. The two areas thus defined above and below the window are to be covered with gold leaf, and Wertheimer's problem is to find how much gold will be needed. If one follows his advice and concentrates on the overall structure, instead of on the parts ,the problem is very simple. But he cites five typical responses, some of which involve quite sophisticated mathematics. As we shall see, this kind of approach,

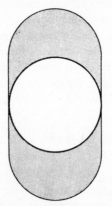

Figure 10.1—Given that the areas above and below the window have to be gilded, how much gold leaf will be required? (adapted from Wertheimer, 1943)

not to mention techniques derived from psychoanalysis, is useful where real creative thinking is needed, but at the moment we are more concerned with combinations of convergence and divergence.

Wertheimer mentions several such approaches:

'e.g. the approach of Hegelian and Marxist dialectics which emphasises dynamic development in their doctrine of "inherent contradictions" with the three steps of thesis, antithesis, and synthesis; the broad development of logistics or mathematical logic (Whitehead, Russell et al) which enriches the topics and operations of traditional logic by the study of the logic of relations, relational networks, considers forms of conclusions other than syllogisms; phenomenology (Husserl) which stresses the viewing of essentials in "phenomenological reduction"; pragmatism (especially John Dewey) with its emphasis on doing and acting, instead of mere ghostlike thinking, on future and on actual progress';

not to mention, of course, his own approach. Of these, the most promising— from the point of view of synthesis between convergence and divergence—

is that of John Dewey. And it is relevant to design in particular because, un-like some of the others, it consists of 'doing and acting' rather than 'mere ghostlike thinking'.

Dewey's conclusions are presented in the form of a book called, appro-priately enough, *How we Think* (1909); it includes his *Analysis of a Complete Act of Thought* (Chapter 6), based on the consideration of three examples, which he describes as: *practical deliberation* (whether to go by car, subway or elevated railway to be in time for an appointment); *reflection upon observation* (the purpose of a pole projecting horizontally from the upper deck of a ferry boat: it turned out to be for navigation purposes); and *reflection involving experiment* (why is it that bubbles appear round the mouth of an inverted tumbler which has just been washed in hot soapy water?).

He concluded that in each case the complete act of thought was a *five* phase event, in logically distinct steps, from the first awareness of the problem to its final application. We may summarize the phases of his 'complete act of thought' as follows, drawing on his examples where necessary:

1. *The occurrence of a difficulty.* A difficulty may occur in very definite form, so that the mind begins to speculate at once on its probable explanation. Or it may manifest itself first as a feeling of unease, followed by a gradual realization, after further investigation, as to what the problem really is. In Dewey's example the *end* was known (to arrive for his appointment on time), and the available *means* were known too (the three modes of travel), so his problem was '*the discovery of intervening terms*' harmonizing the one with the other. His third problem is similar—he has observed the behaviour of the bubbles, and decided it is odd; he is familiar also with the established laws of physics, so again he seeks a means of reconciling the one with the other.

2. *Definition of the difficulty.* Some difficulties present themselves all too clearly; they shock us and need no further definition. But where the difficulty is ambiguous or vague, where it is something 'queer, strange, funny or dis-concerting', it will need critical observation so that we can clarify the *specific* nature of the problem. 'In large measure,' Dewey says, the existence or non-existence of this step makes the difference between reflection proper, or safe-guarded *critical* inference and uncontrolled thinking.' If this stage is not completed, deliberately and thoroughly, then conclusions will be generated more or less at random. Dewey cites the case of a doctor in the act of diag-nosis. The patient may tell the doctor what *he* thinks is wrong, but the doctor must suspend judgement until he has martialled all the evidence. 'The essence of critical thinking,' according to Dewey, 'is suspended judgement; and the essence of this suspense is inquiry to determine the nature of the problem before proceeding to attempt its solution. This, more than any other thing, transforms mere inference into tested inference, suggested conclusions into proof.'

3. *Occurrence of a suggested explanation or possible solution.* Dewey reviews the possible *possible* solutions he envisaged for each of his problems; the various ways of travelling, the ideas that the navigation boom would be a flagpole, an ornament or a radio aerial; the relevant laws of physics. He concludes that in each case, *suggestion* was at the heart of *inference*; it involves going from what is *known* to what is *unknown*. And in one of the key statements in the whole of his argument, Dewey suggests that: 'Since inference goes beyond what is actually present, it involves a leap, a jump, the propriety of which cannot be absolutely warranted in advance . . .' It has come to be known, of course, as the *creative leap*, the central feature of any act of imagination. We shall return to it in a later chapter. But Dewey points out also that the suggestion which arises from this creative leap is merely an *idea*. It is tentative and may well be abandoned later. Synonyms for it, according to Dewey, are *supposition, conjecture, guess, hypothesis,* and (in elaborate cases) *theory.* Not only that, but suspended belief implies the existence of alternatives or rival conjectures and indeed, if the 'best' conclusion is to be reached, it will be essential to cultivate divergently 'a variety of alternative suggestions.' This, again, is crucial to Dewey's method, that only in exceptional cases will it be possible to converge down on to the 'one best' solution; that in normal circumstances, one should always cultivate solutions in variety—one should be divergent.

4. *The rational elaboration of an idea.* Having developed a range of ideas it will be necessary to take each one and develop its *implications* in relation to the problem. This, according to Dewey, is *reasoning*; for just as the idea is inferred from the given facts, so the idea itself is a basis for reasoning. Here one becomes convergent again. In the case of Dewey's navigation pole—he had the *idea* at one stage that it might be a flagpole. But reasoning from this idea, he concluded that a flagpole should have been vertical, and his pole was horizontal. Similarly given the *idea* that it was an aerial, the rational elaboration of *this* idea would suggest that an aerial should be as high as possible on the boat. But given the idea that it was a navigation pole, the rational elaboration of this seemed to fit *all* the observable, relevant facts in the case. So reasoning provides for Dewey the intervening terms which reconcile the means and the end, the problem and its solution.

5. *Corroboration of an idea and formulation of a concluding belief.* Reasoning can show that *if* an idea is adopted, then certain consequences will follow, but this is *only* a hypothesis, and before it can be adopted finally, it must be tested. Sometimes as in the case of the navigation pole mere observation is enough, but in other cases, experiment is required. As Dewey puts it: '*conditions are deliberately arranged in accord with the requirements of an idea or hypothesis to see if the results theoretically indicated by the idea actually occur.*' And, of course, the essence of an experiment is that it should be re-

peatable. If, then, the experimental results agree with the theoretical predictions and it is clear that only the conditions under which the experiment is conducted could yield such results, this may be taken as proof that the conclusion was correct—until further evidence indicates that it should be revised.

Graham Wallas, in contrast (1926), describes four *stages of control* in a complete act of thought, which he calls:

1. *Preparation:* the conscious accumulation of knowledge, dividing the field of enquiry by logical rules and adopting a definite 'problem attitude'.
2. *Incubation:* in which one avoids thinking about the problem, either by detailed concentration on other things or by relaxing entirely from conscious thought by engaging in some kind of activity which does not require it.
3. *Illumination:* a sudden successful leap which may be preceded by a train of associations and an awareness in 'fringe consciousness', an 'intimation' that success is at hand.
4. *Verification:* the idea is validated and reduced to exact form.

Yet Wallas's four stages have a great deal in common with Dewey's five stages: Wallas's preparation looks much like Dewey's definition and Dewey's explanation is much like Wallas's illumination; they both describe it in terms of a creative 'leap'. I find Wallas's incubation convincing whilst Dewey's two final phases ring truer than Wallas's verification. All in all, they seem to be describing similar sequences of events, but dividing them into units of different length and focussing down on different aspects of them.

Such thought sequences, as we have seen, seem to apply to every scale of problem, from deciding which way to travel by public transport to formulating a minor theory on the behaviour of soap bubbles. Dewey and Wallas both describe in effect a *decision sequence*: a person senses a difficulty, defines it, incubates possible explanations, has creative insights, elaborates them and puts one of them into practice. Both sequences as they stand have been adopted in many circumstances and modified to others. Peter Drucker, for instance, distinguishes a five-phased decision sequence in *The Practice of Management* (1955) which resembles Dewey's in many respects:

1. Defining the problem.
2. Analysing the problem.
3. Developing alternative solutions.
4. Deciding on best solution.
5. Conveying decision into effective action.

Similar decision sequences are to be found in Operational Research, a study of decision procedures which developed during World War II.

Operational Research

Newman (1960) describes some of its origins:

'Mathematicians discussed gunnery problems with British soldiers in Burma; chemists did bomb damage assessment with economist colleagues at Princes Risborough . . . generals conferred about tank strategy in the Italian campaign with biochemists and lawyers; a famous British zoologist was key man in planning the bombardment of Pantellaria; naval officers took statisticians and entomologists into their confidence regarding submarine losses in the Pacific; the high command of the R.A.F. and American Airforce shared its headaches . . . with psychologists, architects, paleontologists, astronomers and physicists.'

In other words, the amateur warmakers put their civilian specialisms at the service of professional soldiers and airmen and many of them brought a scientific outlook to problem solving, with particular reference to the mathematics of probability.

In many cases they failed, but they also had some spectacular successes. Morse and Kimball describe some of them in *Methods of Operations Research* (1951), including several ways to hunt a submarine. Sargeaunt (1965) describes one of these as 'the classic early application of O.R.' which was concerned with the setting of depth-charge fuses, dropped by aircraft on to diving submarines. It had previously been assumed that the aircraft would be spotted long before it could fly over the submarine and that, consequently, the submarine would have had a chance to crash dive to a depth of 50 or 100 feet. On this basis, all fuses were set to fire at 100 feet and, during the action, there was no time to reset them. The percentage of 'kills' was very low indeed; there was no time to experiment by trial-and-error (which would have been expensive in submarines), so a team of scientists was detailed to investigate the problem and to apply scientific method to its solution.

They started by collecting all the available reports of encounters between aircraft and submarines (we may call this 'data collection'); they then *analysed* this information and found that a surprising number of submarines actually stayed on the surface. These were 'sitting ducks', easy to locate but difficult to destroy with a depth charge which exploded 100 feet (30 m) below the surface. Conversely, *any* submarine which had succeeded in diving was extremely difficult to locate; the team therefore concluded that maximum success could be achieved if the fuses were set to fire at 25 feet (7·6 m). As it happened, this was impossible, the fuses were designed *not* to go off above 35 feet (10·6 m), but even at that setting, the number of 'kills' more than doubled. Once the design of the fuse itself had been modified to allow for the higher setting, the rate of 'kills' increased dramatically, by 700 per cent. Naturally the submarine crews were aware that *something* significant had happened, but they thought that the amount of explosives in the depth charges had been doubled! The simpler explanation never occurred to them.

Churchman and his colleagues (1957) describe one decision sequence for

Operational Research, and Sargeaunt (1965) describes another (Table 10.1). They have much in common and some differences; Churchman speaks of *a* solution, Sargeaunt of 'varying circumstances'. Nonetheless they both envisage the use of the mathematical model as a device by which the solution(s) may be synthesized. Ver Planck and Teare (1954) describe some of the ways in which such models can be constructed (summarized in Asimow, 1962). In the first place, as Churchman and Sargeaunt both say, it is necessary to state or formulate the problem. It may be a matter of taking some familiar object and improving its performance in some respect. In that case we have to state the nature of the improvement; it should then be possible to identify the parts of the design which need to be changed. However, certain constraints will affect the possibilities of change; these may be quite specific matters concerned with the nature of materials, the laws of physics and so on, or

Table 10.1

CHURCHMAN	SARGEAUNT
1. Formulating the problem.	1. Statement of the problem involved.
2. Constructing a mathematical model.	2. Collection of relevant data.
3. Deriving a solution from the model.	3. Analysis of data to provide a model of the real-life situation, and checking the validity of the model.
4. Testing the model and the solution derived from it.	4. Manipulating the model to estimate what will happen under varying circumstances.
5. Establishing controls over the solution.	5. Selection of the optimum course of action.
6. Putting the solution to work: implementation.	6. Continuing check on the validity of the model in the light of fresh data.

they may be much more tenuous, matters of opinion and belief. Once a mathematical model has been constructed the various parts can be related numerically. In other words, the nature of the design and its desired performance can be written as a series of equations. In the first instance, it may be necessary to write a separate equation for each part of the problem, but later some of these may be combined and once the equations have been written, it will be possible to insert different numerical values for each variable. In this way, the performance of the object may be predicted under a wide variety of conditions—Sargeaunt's 'manipulation of the model to estimate what will happen under varying circumstances'. The results of these manipulations can then be tested against the criteria laid down initially, so that the 'optimum course of action' may be selected.

Again, a great many techniques have been developed under this heading of operational research and some of these, at least, have proved attractive to some designers. Some of them, such as decision theory, have been developed as integral parts of design method and will be considered in detail elsewhere. Others, which will be described here, are important sources of design methodology but so far they have not been assimilated fully into the design process itself.

They all depend in some way on setting up models of what is being investigated: the terms iconic, analogue and symbolic model originate in O.R. (see for example Churchman, Ackoff and Arnoff: *Introduction to Operational Research* (1965)). As we saw in Chapter 5 this classification is barely adequate for our purposes but the vast majority of O.R. techniques would be described in our terms as numerical, one- or two-dimensional (sometimes including time) and data predicting.

Linear Programming

Linear programming is perhaps the most frequently used of all operational research techniques. It is based on the fact that, in many problems, when the relationship between variables is plotted on a graph it proves to be linear. In many cases, for instance, if one doubles the resources one may also double costs, and profits. Many kinds of problem can be approached in this way; typical of them are:

(a) Finding out how a particular set of parts can be manufactured at minimum cost.
(b) Allocating the available capital between different kinds of new equipment.
(c) Finding the cheapest mix of available raw materials to match a given set of criteria.
(d) Dividing work between different teams.
(e) Crop rotation.
(f) Allocating scarce materials or products.
(g) Locating new plant, offices, warehouses and so on.
(h) Transportation problems.

Problem (h) represents a special case and we shall consider it separately; in order to demonstrate the general principles of linear programming, we shall consider an architectural application of (b).

Let us suppose we have to design an estate of ten tower blocks, each ten storeys high and containing 96 flats. For reasons of orientation, and for variety, there are two types of block: type *A*, which contains 60 3-bedroom flats and 36 2-bedroom flats; type *B*, which contains 72 3-bedroom flats and 24 2-bedroom flats. It is a matter of housing policy that, as far as possible, two-thirds of the flats should be 3-bedroomed and the remainder 2-bedroomed. The problem is to decide how many blocks of each type should be built on the estate. The total number of flats on the estate will, of course,

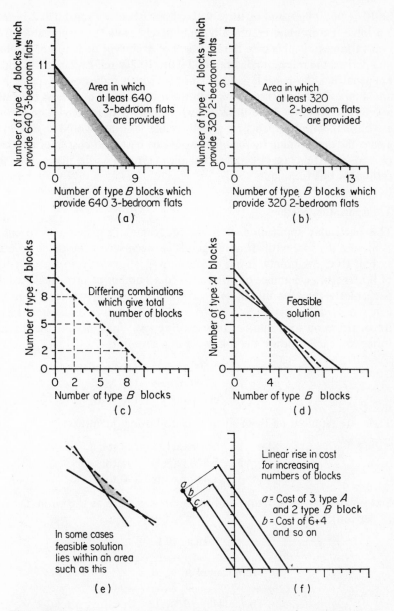

Figure 10.2—Linear programming method. Given two types of flat block, how many of each type must be built to house a particular population?

be $10 \times 96 = 960$, and of these 640 will be 3-bedroom and 320 2-bedroom. To solve the problem graphically, one merely plots the given values for the two variables—in this case the numbers of each type of flat in each block—and derives the relevant constraints. Figure 10.2 is self-explanatory, and it so happens that the feasible solution in (d), which indicates 6 type *A* blocks and 4 type *B*, actually coincides with the total number of flats as indicated in (c). But it may not have done, in which case a triangular zone would be established, within which a range of possible solutions would lie, (e). In such a case the determining factor often would be cost, and cost lines also can be plotted—see (f). Gass (1958) and Handley (1962) describe many other applications of this technique.

Transportation Method

This particular application of linear programming is designed to cut to a minimum the cost of distributing goods between several despatch points and several receiving points. It has obvious applications, say, in the distribution of bricks from a number of brickyards to a number of sites and it would be particularly relevant in the case of systems building where, for instance, concrete cladding panels were to be made in a number of different factories for distribution to a number of sites. Suppose, for example, that three factories can each produce the following in a given time:

Factory *A*:   1,600 panels   (100 tons)
         B: 1,200 panels   (75 tons)
         C: 800 panels   (50 tons)

These are required on three sites in the following quantities:

Site   1:   640 panels   (40 tons)
       2:   1,520 panels   (95 tons)
       3:   1,440 panels   (90 tons)

Sixteen panels weigh 1 ton, and transport costs are as shown in Table 10.2 (£ per ton):

Table 10.2

From factory	A	B	C
To site 1:	9	12	6
2:	6	7	4
3:	8	1	2

One might start to solve the problem by selecting the cheapest transport route—factory *B* to site 3—but, apart from any other consideration, the total output of this particular factory is inadequate for the total demand of this particular site. One might also try to eliminate the most expensive routes, and an initial solution to the entire transport problem might read as shown in Table 10.3.

However, by working upwards from the lowest transport cost, factory B to site 3, we have landed ourselves in difficulties with transport from factory A to site 1, which costs £9 per ton. So one might recast the table—the changes

Table 10.3—Initial solution

Transport from factory	A	B	C	Total
Transport to site 1:	40 tons @ £9 = £360	0 tons @ £12 = £0	0 tons @ £6 = £0	40 tons @ £360
2:	60 tons @ £6 = £360	0 tons @ £7 = £0	35 tons @ £4 = £140	95 tons @ £500
3:	0 tons @ £8 = £0	75 tons @ £1 = £75	15 tons @ £2 = £30	90 tons @ £105
Total	100 tons @ £720	75 tons @ £75	50 tons @ £170	225 tons @ £965

Table 10.4—Revised solution

Transport from factory	A	B	C	Total
Transport to site 1:	*0 tons @ £9 = £0*	0 tons @ £12 = £0	*40 tons @ £6 = £240*	*40 tons @ £240*
2:	*95 tons @ £6 = £570*	0 tons @ £7 = £0	*0 tons @ £4 = £0*	*95 tons @ £570*
3:	*5 tons @ £8 = £40*	75 tons @ £1 = £75	*10 tons @ £2 = £20*	*90 tons @ £135*
Total	*100 tons @ £610*	75 tons @ £75	*50 tons @ £260*	*225 tons @ £945*

are noted in italics in Table 10.4. The process is repetitive and other solutions may be even cheaper; one finds these by 'iterative' procedures for which, of course, the computer is ideal.

Network Analysis

Some of the best known O.R. techniques are those concerned with network analysis. They were developed on the basis of wartime experience. During the 1939 war, it became abundantly clear that production could be seriously delayed when certain parts were in short supply and subject to long delivery periods. So methods were developed of setting delivery dates by working forward from the pattern of current shortages (Sargeaunt, 1965). Critical path scheduling (CPS or CPM) was developed from this and, later, more sophisticated methods which take account of probability, under the general title of PERT (Program Evaluation and Review Technique). The RIBA Handbook (1965) sums up these methods as follows:

PERT: Program Evaluation and Review Technique: developed for the United States Navy, 1957/58; originally concerned more with 'events' than activities; also uses three time estimates for each activity, optimistic, likely and pessimistic.
CPM: Critical Path Method: similar but more concerned with activities, and uses one time estimate for each. Critical Path Methods (plural) is the name used by the Building Research Station.
CPA: Critical Path Analysis and
CPS: Critical Path Scheduling are names used for similar methods.

Other names which Duckworth lists are:
PEP: Program Evaluation Procedure
LESS: Least Cost Estimating and Scheduling
SCANS: Scheduling and Control by Automated Network;

and de Hanika mentions:
RAMPS: Resource Allocation and Multi-Project Scheduling, an extension of PERT by which limited resources may be allocated between a number of separate projects.

The first step in network analysis is to identify individual activities within the overall project. The RIBA Handbook (1965) defines an activity as a task which takes time and usually consumes resources. Its starting and finishing

Table 10.5—Activities involved in building a house

Ref:	Activity description	Starting event No.	Finishing event No.	Estimated completion time
A	Order bricks	0	1	1
B	Order plant	0	2	7
C	Order concrete	0	3	1
D	Strip site	2	5	1
E	Excavate	5	6	2
F	Deliver concrete	3	6	3
G	Lay foundations	6	7	3
H	Deliver bricks	1	7	14
I	Design and order joinery	0	4	14
J	Build walls	7	8	10
K	Build floors	8	9	5
L	Build roof	9	10	4
M	Deliver joinery	4	10	14
and so on.				

points are known as *events*. Once the activities have been defined, they can be placed in logical sequences; in a building operation, for instance, excavation will precede the laying of foundations, and the foundations must be poured before work can start on the walls. One prepares, first of all, a table, estimating the time which each activity will take. Part of the table for building a house might take the form shown in Table 10.5.

Once such a table has been prepared it can be translated into the conventions of network analysis, in which each activity is represented by an arrow, whilst the events which mark its start and finish are marked by circles—some possibilities are shown in Figures 10.3 and 10.4, whilst a complete network for the house which is started in Table 10.5 might be drawn as shown in Figure 10.5. On this chart (Figure 10.5), the earliest and latest times for, say, event 6

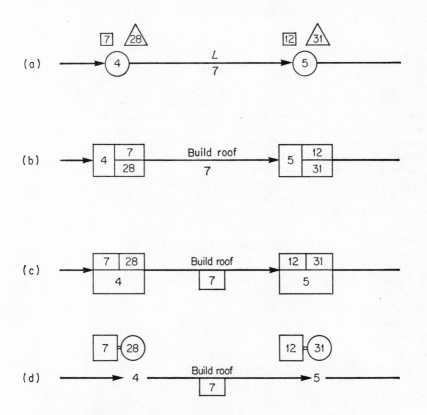

Figure 10.3—Activity *L*, build roof, presented in four typical notations. It starts with event No. 4, finishes with event No.5 and takes 7 days. Event No. 4 could start, at the earliest, on day 7 and finish, at the latest, on day 28. Equivalent starts for event No. 5 will be 7 days later.

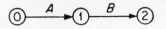

Activity B follows activity A, and cannot occur until A is completed. Event 1 marks the end of activity A and the beginning of activity B.

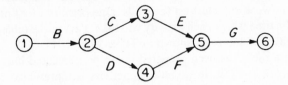

In this case, event 2 marks the end of activity B and the beginnings of both activities C and D. Events 3 and 4, on the other hand, represent the beginning of activities E and F, both of which end in 5. Activity G cannot start until E and F have both been completed.

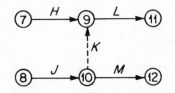

Here, two paths of activities are running in parallel. H ends in event 9, which also marks the start of activity L and, similarly, J ends in 10, which marks the start of 11. But in this case, activity L is also dependent on event 10; it cannot start until activity J is completed. The relationship, however, is not reciprocal and event 10 could start before event 9. Activity K is simply there to indicate a sequential relationship; it does not consume either time or resources, and then it is called a *dummy* activity.

In practice, the chart is capable of carrying much more information than this simple form would suggest. It is possible, for instance, to plot the estimated completion times against each activity, and to add these progressively, to form *event times*.

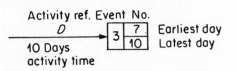

We may draw a chart, therefore, in the following form:

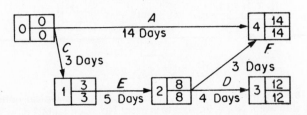

Figure 10.4—The network originates in event 0; events are then plotted sequentially

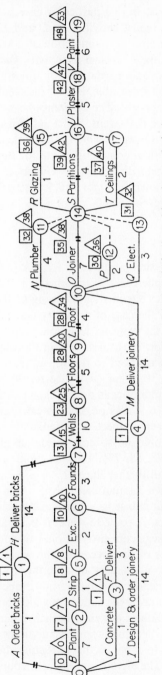

Figure 10.5—The complete network showing the critical path, indicated by the symbol ─╫─

vary by as much as 6 days. In this particular case, activities *C* and *F* are estimated as taking 4 days, whilst activities *B, D* and *E* will take 10 days. The spare time available therefore for completion of activities *C* and *F* amounts to 6 days. Such spare time is known as activity *float*. The earliest time for any event is obtained by totalling the activity times which lead by the longest path to it, whilst the latest acceptable time for the event is obtained by working backwards from the final event. The difference between these two times then is known as the *slack* for that event. Some activities will have no *float*, and there will be no *slack* in the events which connect them; any overrun on these activities will affect the final completion date for the project, and the time-path which connects them, therefore, is known as the critical path. It is marked on the chart shown in Figure 10.5. Battersby (1964) and Lockyer (1964) both describe developments of network analysis and critical path technique.

Monte Carlo Method

One particular kind of simulation in O.R. is known as the Monte Carlo method. As its name implies, this is concerned with situations in which events occur at random, as they do in dice-throwing or the spinning of a roulette wheel. Duckworth cites the case of a factory manager who thought he was losing custom because the external telephone lines seemed to be in use so much that some customers rang off in despair of ever getting through. So the switchboard operator was asked to record, in minutes, the times when one, two and all three lines were engaged. The results were tabulated, and by simulating a series of random calls during the peak period (3.00–5.00 p.m.), entirely by paper exercise, it was possible to calculate the probability that a customer would have been connected immediately, or on a second attempt. The chances that he would be so connected, on successive days, were (in percentages) $97\frac{1}{2}$, $87\frac{1}{2}$, 78, 88, $77\frac{1}{2}$, 100, . . ., and so on. It was clearly unnecessary, then, to install further lines.

De Hanika illustrates a manual method of simulating the distribution of goods from a central warehouse to a series of branches, and from there to a large number of retailers. A roulette wheel is marked up to indicate retailer demand, with various segments proportional in width to known demand, obtained by the analysis of past records. The wheel is spun many times to simulate the behaviour of retailers in ordering goods. A similar wheel is marked to indicate the known demand from branch warehouse to central store, and to take account of the time-lags which have been experienced in the past, between the date at which a branch indented for goods, and its eventual delivery. This wheel too is spun many times and, between them, the two wheels can be used to simulate this particular distribution system under a variety of conditions. The digital computer, of course, is an ideal device for simulation of this kind, especially as it can be programmed to generate random numbers.

Queuing Theory

Queuing theory, as its name implies, is concerned with waiting of some kind; in fact it is concerned with waiting of any kind. Obviously it has some bearing on traffic problems—one may queue for a bus, and cars may proceed along a single carriageway in the form of a queue, their speed limited by the slower driver. One may queue for service in a shop and in industry queues are of enormous importance. Sometimes they are merely irritating, as when workers queue for their pay; at other times they are inefficient, as when the same workmen queue for materials or tools at the store. Even the sales manager's order book is a queue (of customers) and so is the production line. Queuing theory therefore has a great deal to offer the designer who is concerned with efficient planning. As in most O.R. techniques, it is a matter of setting up a mathematical model of a situation. Duckworth (1965) bases his model on 'traffic intensity' which is determined by dividing the main service time by the mean interval between successive arrivals. In other words, this model will take into account the rate at which people join the queue and the average time it takes for one of them to be served.

In each case, it is important to plot a *cumulative* average, which eliminates the effect of extreme intervals, long or short. A succession of arrival intervals might read:

2 5 8 4 6 3 7 5 6 8 7 4 3 2 6 7 5 6 5 8 4 (seconds, minutes, etc.).

One adds the first two intervals, and divides by two; one then adds the first three intervals and divides by three, and so on:

$$\frac{7}{2} \quad \frac{15}{3} \quad \frac{19}{4} \quad \frac{25}{5} \quad \frac{28}{6} \quad \frac{35}{7} \quad \frac{40}{8} \quad \frac{46}{9} \quad \frac{54}{10} \quad \frac{61}{11} \quad \frac{65}{12} \quad \frac{68}{13} \quad \frac{70}{14} \quad \frac{76}{15} \quad \frac{83}{16} \quad \frac{88}{17} \quad \frac{94}{18} \quad \frac{101}{19} \quad \frac{109}{20} \quad \frac{113}{21}$$

which read in decimal notation

3·5, 5·0, 4·7, 5·0, 4·6, 5·0, 5·0, 5·1, 5·4, 5·5, 5·5, 5·2, 5·0, 5·0, 5·2, 5·2, 5·2, 5·3, 5·5, 5·4

which leads to an average interval between arrivals oı

4·68.

Duckworth shows that the average service time could be calculated similarly (e.g. 3·50) and the traffic intensity then would be, say:

$$\frac{3·50}{4·68} = 0·748$$

and, conversely, the average waiting time per customer would be found by the formula:

$$\frac{1}{1-p} \times \text{mean service time;}$$

in our example the mean waiting time would be:

$$\frac{1}{1 - 0.748} \times 3.50 = 10.81 \text{ minutes.}$$

For values of traffic intensity below about 0·5 and a service time of one hour, the mean waiting time will be under three minutes, but it will rise to 5 minutes for a value of 0·8; and to 25 minutes for a value of 0·95. These values, of course, are for one queue and one service point, but more complex queues can be simulated. Queuing theory is appropriate for problems concerned with:

The number of machines which one operator can work.
Servicing in batches, such as passenger lifts, casualty wards, rubbish collection, traffic marshalling.
Restaurant and canteen servicing.
Self-service cafeterias, production lines.
Fluctuating power demands.

See also Morse for further applications.

Value Analysis

This is an industrial technique by which the cost of the *elements* within a product is examined critically in relation to their utility. Fallon says (1964)

'Value analysis/value engineering is a functionally orientated scientific method for improving product value by relating the elements of product worth to their corresponding elements of product cost in order to accomplish the required function at least cost in resources.'

It is concerned, in the first place, with *functions* rather than with elements, so it is not merely a matter of replacing a simple component by a cheaper one, with no real change to the product as a whole. Each component is assessed in terms of what it *does* and the cost of this particular function; by this means the structure of the product itself is brought into question. The components are termed 'utility originators' and each 'utility originator' costs money. Its *performance* can be assessed in relation to this cost and the aim, of course, is to achieve the maximum utility for the minimum cost. In other words, it is a matter of striving for the greatest possible 'value', and 'value' is determined by the ratio—utility : cost (it may also be determined by the ratio of input : output).

In industry, value analysis is carried out by an inter-departmental team: design, production, buying, marketing and so on. The team considers whether a given function may be achieved more cheaply and its chief attack, of course, is directed against the inertia which attaches to an existing design which, in other respects, seems satisfactory.

The value analysis process may be divided into six stages:

1. Preparation phase (stating the problem);
2. Information phase (getting the relevant facts);
3. Evaluation phase (definition of the function of the product);
4. Creative phase (find less costly ways of performing the same function);
5. Selection phase (scanning a set of alternatives);
6. Implementation phase.

Decision Theory

Decision theory, according to Bross (1953), developed from the application of statistics into agriculture, industry and commerce. New theories were developed, particularly with reference to the inspection and testing of products, so that, in the years just before and during World War II, a new concept began to emerge, which he calls *Statistical Decision*. In addition to statistics, it drew on experience from many other fields, particularly theory of games, cost accounting, information theory, logic, economics and 'almost anything else you care to name' (Bross, 1953). However, it may be summed up, without too much over-simplification, as the application of scientific method to decision-making.

We ought, first of all, to define what decision-making is. It is assumed, in the first place, that we wish to take some course of action and that several possibilities are open to us. It is further assumed that we can *choose* between these possibilities, which begs a great many philosophical questions. Without this assumption, there would be no decision theory, so it will suit our purposes to subscribe to it. Some decisions anyway will be automatic; I do not choose to breathe, and if I put my finger on a hot stove there will be no philosophical problems involved in deciding to withdraw it (Hall, 1962). Yet even this simple example raises the fundamental dichotomy of decision theory which is concerned, always, with two different classes of things. On the one hand, there are the physical characteristics of the system—in this case, the hot stove and my finger. On the other hand, there is a system of *values* which may be very complex—I value my finger end and should not wish to see it damaged for many reasons, concerned with its function or its appearance; certainly I should not wish to feel pain.

Hall points out (1962) that inevitably, in specifying the physical performance of a system, we speak in terms of what we want it to do. We may express its intended performance in terms of inputs, transformations, outputs, boundary conditions and so on, but all the time we are concerned with a piece of equipment that we need to perform a job which we think ought to be done. We are, in fact, setting up a value system. In the early stages of, say, a product-design job, our value system will be set up in terms of some, or all, of the following criteria:

Profit which, after all, is the motive for most industrial production. The actual profit requirement for any specific product can be specified very closely indeed. The *market*, of course, is an important factor in the profit function, as is *cost* which will determine the economic feasibility of a product. Capital and running costs will both be important for manufacturer and consumer.

Quality may be measured in many ways. The quality of a television picture can be measured objectively in terms of the number of scanning lines and so on, but eventually it will be judged subjectively by those who see it. In many other fields, too, it may be necessary to set up physical design objectives on the basis of psychological testing, even though consumer reaction, eventually, will be intensely subjective.

Performance objectives may be of this kind, but they also cover such criteria as *systems reliability*, which may be expressed in terms of probability that the system will operate in the environment for which it is designed for longer than some specified minimum period.

Competition may be an important spur in defining the objectives of a system, whether it is commercial or military.

Compatibility with existing systems may also be very important, especially where large amounts of capital have already been sunk in some commercial or military enterprise.

Flexibility refers to the ease with which a system may be adjusted or modified to take account of expansion or changing use. It may or may not conflict with *permanence* which in itself is difficult to measure and which cannot take account of unpredictable technical advances.

Elegance is often seen, by engineers, as a function of simplicity which in itself is very subjective.

Safety is also difficult to measure, and must be set against the actuarial values which insurance companies put, say, on the loss of a limb.

Time is one of the most important criteria of all, especially in competitive situations. It certainly interacts with profit, cost variables, the state of the market and so on. Quality almost certainly will be a function of design and development time, so will flexibility and maybe even elegance.

Hall's list, then, begins to indicate the complexity of a value system initially derived entirely from trying to define, as objectively as possible, the physical performance of a system. At once the list raises difficulties. For one thing, many dimensions are involved—Hall lists over a dozen and there may be others. What is much more difficult is that these dimensions are different in kind; there is no one scale against which they may all be measured. Profit and cost certainly are measured against the value of money, which is measured by *ratio* scales (see Chapter 7) but it is extremely difficult to measure certain ethical, social, philosophical and psychological concepts against such scales although, as we shall see, attempts have been made to do so. Houses, after all, are valued for rating purposes which is a matter of equating such intangibles as quality, amenity, comfort and so on with hard cash.

There is a further complication, too, in the making of decisions. Sometimes a given choice will result, invariably, in certain consequences. If I decide to press the 't' on my typewriter, I am reasonably certain that a 'q' will not appear. We may call this a decision made under conditions of *certainty*. If I toss a coin, on the other hand, there is no such certainty that it will fall heads. There is, however, a probability of 0·5 that it will fall in this way and I am aware of the probability, but my decision to call 'heads' was made under conditions of *risk*. It so happens that probability was involved also in the case of my typewriter; as Hall says: *Certainty is a special case of risk in which the probabilities are 0 or 1.* Lastly, of course, many decisions have to be made under circumstances in which the probabilities are not known; we say that these are made under conditions of *uncertainty*. A further variable in the making of decisions is concerned with the number of people involved. We shall have something to say on group working and its advantages over the individual for certain purposes in Chapter 17.

So now we are in a position to set up a Decision-Maker, for which Bross

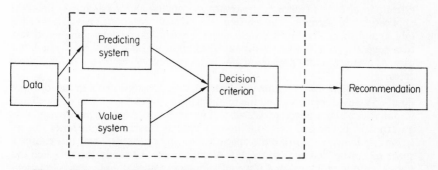

Figure 10.6—The Decision-Maker (after Bross, 1953)

has prepared a Block Diagram as shown in Figure 10.6. In order to make use of it one collects, first of all, the available data on which the decision is to be based—in other words a list of possible actions. This is fed into the *Predicting system* from which one obtains a list of possible outcomes for each action, and the probability (certainty, risk, uncertainty) for each one. The data is also fed into the *Value system* from which one obtains a second quality—the *desirability* of each outcome. At this point then, given a list of possible actions, the two systems have thrown up the following information:

1. A list of outcomes for each action.
2. A probability associated with each outcome.
3. A desirability associated with each outcome.

Of these the list of possible outcomes is by far the easiest to obtain. We can use all the resources of simulation, model-building, experiment and test which are available to us from O.R. and design but, in the last analysis, it will be a matter of prediction. Bross (1953) outlines a series of prediction techniques each of which, no doubt, is much more reliable than the proverbial crystal ball:

Persistence prediction is based on the fact that for certain practical purposes circumstances do not change. One might predict the behaviour of certain individuals by observing the consistency with which they hold certain prejudices and habits. Once their personality characteristics are known, there is no reason to suppose that they will change. Bross suggests that the persistence prediction of weather is about 75 per cent effective. To forecast tomorrow's weather, one simply describes today's. In certain circumstances, persistence prediction is useless. Skill in playing the stock markets, for instance, depends on predicting *changes*.

Trajectory prediction is a matter of observing trends, particularly in the short-term. One might observe that, on successive days, the noon temperature was 10, 11 and 12°C. It might be reasonable to predict that on the following day it would be 13°C but there would be obvious difficulties in long-range forecasting on this basis.

Cyclic prediction depends on the lesson of history. It was first used in predicting astronomical events (eclipses, the return of comets) and it has highly practical applications in farming (the pattern of seasonal variation), navigation (tide tables) and so on. To be effective it needs a great deal of data going back, say, over several cycles, unlike persistence prediction which merely needs the latest case, or even trajectory prediction which can be undertaken on the basis of three cases.

Associative prediction is a matter of observing relationships between two or more events. Pavlov's dogs observed the relationship between the ringing of a bell and feeding time, and a good speculator will observe the relationships between, say, government policy and the condition of the stock market. Sometimes the relationship is *causal*. I strike the space bar on my typewriter, and this causes a space to appear between words. But often it is not; certainly Pavlov's bell did not *cause* food to appear and if we mistake mere associations for causal relationships, we shall find ourselves in considerable difficulties. Yet most prediction in everyday life, not to mention politics, economics and so on, is associative. And often it is a matter of extremely complex associations between many, apparently unrelated things—a political assassination in America, a wage-freeze in Britain, a technological break-through somewhere else.

Analogue prediction is perhaps the most potent of all, because it can take so many forms. It is based on the inherent properties of analogy, that two things which have certain properties in common are assumed to be alike for properties about which knowledge is limited to one of them (see Chapter 16). We may take available analogies—Bross compares the nations with atom bombs to small boys with sticks of dynamite, and predicts the fate of those nations by analogy with the fate of the small boys; but one may set up analogies too, which is where the techniques of O.R. and design generally come into their own.

Hindsight prediction is certainly the most effective (Bross says it is 100 per cent successful), if the least understood of all forecasting devices. It is the prediction of an event *after* it has occurred—the province of radio and television pundits, newspaper columnists, economists, and especially politicians. It is also the method of much technological forecasting. One keeps in touch with certain research laboratories and predicts that these current products will become ubiquitous in ten or twenty years' time. All one needs, according to Bross, is the ability to make ambiguous (or even contradictory) remarks within the context of a generalized I-told-you-so method.

These techniques between them can help predict the various possible outcomes for each variable and, in certain circumstances, they may help predict their relevant probabilities. Bross describes several probability devices, of which the simplest is the *Direct system*. This is a matter of collecting data on a large number of cases and of codifying their outcomes. He wants to know, for instance, if it is going to rain within the next hour—the sky is heavily overcast so he searches his memory for past situations of a similar kind, consults his friends, a meteorologist, all the available experience stored up in books and journals. He is, in fact, following a procedure:

1. Collect data on previous, similar situations (calling each one a case).
2. List the outcomes for all previous cases on which information is available.
3. Classify the outcomes and count the number of times each type occurs.
4. Calculate the probabilities:

$$\text{Probability of outcome} = \frac{\text{Number of occurrences of outcome}}{\text{Total number of cases}}.$$

In addition to searching past records, one may set up experiments as one would in predicting the probability that a coin will fall heads. This experiment, of course, is repeatable. The first ten flips *might* land tails but, as the number of cases increased, so one would expect the results to cluster, with increasing density, around a probability of 0·5.

The probability of the various outcomes is one thing, their desirability quite another. Desirability, of course, is a question of values and values are very difficult to assess. As we have seen, it may be possible to reduce all values to the level of economic value, but this in itself has several facets. Hall (1962) describes *market value, value-in-use* and *imputed value* as closely related concepts within the general field of economic value. Market value itself may be defined as money price, which is a matter of social contract. It is derived empirically and after a few weeks' house-hunting anyone can predict, with reasonable accuracy, the market value of a particular house. This estimate, in fact, is its *imputed value*. Market values are transferable—my house would still be *worth* a certain sum, even if I were to give it away and if it were not for one serious flaw the *market value* system really would be a powerful means of unifying all the other value systems; but unfortunately the value of money changes. As Hall says, to measure the value of things by their *market value* is rather like trying to measure dimensions with a rubber scale.

Nor is *value-in-use* much more accurate, for this is a matter of utility to the individual which is subjective. It is not even transferable in the way that market value was, for if I did give my house away I could not also give with it the enjoyment I had in living there. That would be a matter of *psychological* values which, according to Hall, reside in any sort of *interest* or *appreciation* of an object. It involves feelings and, ultimately, the desires, tendencies or needs which underly such feelings; but to be of use in a system of values such feelings must be measured for intensity. To some extent this is possible, but only within the limits of *ordinal* scales (see Chapter 7). Bentham's *Utilitarianism* is based on the assumption that one could weigh any course of action in terms of the pleasure or pain it would produce for each individual in the community. A balance sheet was to be drawn up, on which pleasure and pain were plotted against eight variables: intensity, duration, certainty, uncertainty, time of occurrence, fecundity, purity and number of persons affected. Pain would weigh against the minus side of the ledger, pleasure against the plus. Any proposed course of action could be tested against this and, naturally, preference would be given to those actions which weighed heavily on the positive (pleasure) side of the ledger.

This obviously has its difficulties, as have other attempts to quantify value systems such as that of Churchman and Ackoff (1954). They assume that given a set of objects one can put them in order, say, A, B, C, D. They assume further that one can assign numbers to them, between 1·00 and 0, indicating the intensity of one's preference. We might guess, roughly, at:

$$A \qquad B \qquad C \qquad D$$
$$1·00 \quad 0·85 \quad 0·75 \quad 0·20$$

But then we consider our preferences further, and conclude that really we prefer A to the sum of B, C and D taken together. So we reassign values:

$$A \qquad B \qquad C \qquad D$$
$$1·00 \quad 0·65 \quad 0·20 \quad 0·10$$

We then consider the relationship between our preference for B, and our preference for C with D, and so on. So finally we find ourselves with an *ordinal* scale which indicates certain relationships between items, but is not constrained enough to guarantee a proper *interval* scale.

Von Neumann and Morgenstern (1953) have a slightly more sophisticated version of the same idea. They assume that an order of preference can be put on the various possibilities and that preferences can be stated also for combinations of events and stated probabilities. Given five items, A, B, C, D and E, one then states, for instance, whether one prefers B to a 50–50 chance of getting A *and* C. If one prefers B, then one concludes that B is closer to A than to C in one's overall scale of preferences. By working through one's preferences and their combinations in this way, it is possible to construct a true *interval* scale—always assuming that one's predictions of probabilities are accurate.

So far, we have considered the way in which data is presented to Bross's Decision-Maker and the roles within it of his predicting system and his value system. The third component of the Decision-Maker itself is the

Decision criterion and again Hall (1962) has some pertinent things to say about this; so far, we have assumed that the criterion is a *statistical* matter. However, as Hall says, very few decisions, in engineering or elsewhere, are made entirely on this basis and many (such as the decision to remove a finger from a hot stove) are *automatic*. Automatic decisions, in fact, are probably the most common of all, and next most common are *trial-and-error* decisions which previously we have called pragmatic. These depend on rapid learning and on memory and they also require a rather vast pool of experience; but where possibilities can be tried and modified very rapidly, as in the case of the digital computer, trial-and-error methods are still very satisfactory, under the guise of *iterative* procedures. As we have seen, pragmatic methods have many advantages: they tend to be simple and, above all, they tend to spark off creative ideas, especially where real materials are used and put together in new ways by accident.

Hall's fourth decision criterion is the *appeal to authority* which, as he says, takes many forms:

'Its use may indicate an alternative to reason, as when the ancients used an assortment of gods, devils, spirits and muses to show the best way. Its use may signal the shirking of responsibility, or mental laziness, when one applies an established company policy, or passes the buck up or down a line of organization. It may be the sensible thing to do, as when one consults an expert or an established textbook. Finally, appeal to authority may be the required thing to do, as when one consults the law to avoid wrongdoing.'

Authority itself may be based on arbitrary power, backed up by 'persuasiveness, guile, gall, or naked economic or physical force.' As Hall says, generally it is to be abhorred. Other kinds of authority are based on *intuition*, which ranges in logical status from simple emotionalism to a form of rigorous scientific reasoning which has been telescoped into an instant of time. Authority anyway ought to be constrained by some *ethical* system and Hall advocates in particular a stoic ethic which, translated into systems engineering, means '*to want what we can get*' instead of worrying about things which are beyond our grasp. In other words, it is a matter of understanding the environment within which one is designing, its possibilities and its'limitations. And finally, Hall appeals to *mathematical criteria* as the final authority in design.

So, following Bross, let us now apply the Decision-Maker to a very simple example. He is sitting in his easy chair one evening, about 6.00 pm, deciding whether or not to take the car to the office next day. If he does, he is likely to be back home again at the same time on the following day, but he *might* have an accident. On the other hand, if he goes by bus it will certainly be cheaper but he will probably be late. He can attach cash values to each of the criteria in this decision problem—the alternative costs of journeys, the value of being home early, the cost of an accident; and he can attach probabilities too, on the basis of previous experience. So he draws up a table, which takes the form of Table 10.6.

Having plotted the table, it is now possible to ask a series of questions. Taking each action in turn, for instance, one might abstract:

1. The most *probable* outcome, and its desirability;
2. The most *favourable* outcome, and its desirability;
3. The least favourable outcome, and its desirability.

On the basis of question 1 he would certainly choose to *drive car*, whereas 2 and 3 would both suggest *take bus*. Bross then prepares a balance sheet for each mode of transport over 1,000 days, and on this basis, by car one expects to arrive home early 850 days, at a total cost of £300, whereas by bus one

Table 10.6—Decision table (after Bross, 1953)

Action	Drive Car			Take Bus	
Cost of action (£)	−0·30			−0·15	
Outcomes	Arrive home early and without incident	Arrive home late due to traffic delays	Accident	Arrive home early and without incident	Arrive home late due to missed connexions
Probability of outcome	0·850	0·145	0·005	0·100	0·900
Desirability of outcome	0·00	−1·00	−50·00	0·00	−1·00

would arrive home late 900 days at a total cost of £150. On the other hand, one would have had five accidents by car; Bross shows how this, and several other criteria, can be taken into account in making the final decision.

Theory of Games

This really is an extension of decision theory, in which one's choice of action is determined by the possible alternative actions of an opponent playing the same game. Vajda (1961) describes its origin in Borel's notes on the so-called Fundamental Theorem, elaborated by von Neumann and Morgenstern in 1944. They were concerned, in the first place, with competitive games but soon saw that the theories derived therefrom could be applied in other fields, such as economics, not to mention combat and warfare; they have even been applied into set theory and topology. A *game* in this sense is a set of rules which determine what a player may do, what is to be won and who wins it, depending on what the players have chosen to do. A game consists of a series of *moves* and Vajda describes a simple one, in which two players, *A* and *B*, each put down a penny, head or tail, without showing it to the other. The pennies are then uncovered, and if both show the same side, *A* pockets them, whereas if they show different sides, *B* pockets them. This is a *two-person* game and one player wins what the other loses; the sum of their gains and losses is zero, hence it is called a *zero-sum* game. It is fundamental to the idea of a game in this sense that a player's gains or losses depend not only on his own actions, but also on the actions of his opponent. It is difficult to cope with more than two players in Games Theory, but it is possible to envisage a fictitious third player who takes no active part in the game, but is merely there to make or receive payments which are not passed directly between the

Table 10.7—Pay-off matrix

		Player *Y*			
		A	*B*	*C*	*D*
Player *X*	*a*	4	2	3	4
	b	2	−3	1	0
	c	6	−2	3	2
	d	2	−6	4	1

two players. Vajda mentions also the possibility of *n-person* games, but does not describe them in detail.

For *two-person* games, it is possible to set out in the form of a table the results of one's own, and one's opponent's possible choices (see Table 10.7). The table is known as a pay-off matrix and, in this particular case, it is written from the point of view of player *X*. If he chooses strategy *c* and player *Y* chooses his strategy *A*, player *X* stands to gain 6 units. But if player *Y* chooses strategy *B* instead, then player *X* stands to lose 2 units. There is, however, a *minimax* rule in Theory of Games, by which one minimizes one's maximum loss. If player *X* chooses strategy *a*, he is certain to gain at least 2, and he may gain 4. For player *Y*, of course, the signs in this table would be reversed. He stands to lose by playing every strategy but *B*; in this case his maximum loss would be 2, but he stands to gain 2, 3 or 6.

So the safest bet for *X* is to play strategy *a*, and the safest bet for *Y* is to play strategy *B*; they coincide on square *aB*, which is called the *saddle point* or solution to the game; all two-person games, in which one player gains what the other loses, have such a saddle point.

CHAPTER 11

Communications

One of the most thorough applications of statistics into human affairs has occurred in the field of communications, a study which can be defined in many ways but which is concerned, fundamentally, with the ways in which information is passed from one person to another. Cherry (1957) suggests that, among other things, communication is essentially a social affair, a matter of *sharing* certain elements of behaviour, or modes of activity, and that this sharing depends ultimately on the existence of rules which are understood by everyone engaged in the communication. Speech and writing are obvious modes of communication; so for that matter is drawing but, as Cherry says, these are not the only ones:

'Social intercourse is greatly strengthened by habits of gesture—little movements of the hands and face. With nods, smiles, frowns, handshakes, kisses, fist shakes, and other gestures we can convey most subtle understandings. Also we have economic systems for trafficking not in ideas but in material goods and services; the tokens of communication are coins, bonds, letters of credit and so on. We have conventions of dress, rules of the road, social formalities, and good manners; we have rules of membership and function in business, institutions and families. But life in the modern world is coming to depend more and more upon "technical" means of communication, telephone and telegraph, radio and printing.'

With the development of communication facilities, the social unit has grown from village to town, to modern city state; McCluhan (1964) put the same idea more poetically when, in showing that the communications device itself imposes its inherent structure on what is being communicated, he coined the slogan, 'The Medium is the Message.'

All this is of vital importance to the architect because, literally, he spends almost his entire working day in tasks which in general terms may be described under the heading of communications. Table 11.1 results from the analysis of a group of architects at work in the offices of Building Design Partnership at Preston; the observations were of several kinds, including questionnaires and filming by time-lapse camera, and the results present a fair record of how the average young architect spent his time in that particular office at that particular time. His seniors, obviously, would be engaged in different things; they might attend many more meetings and do far fewer drawings, but they too would spend most of their time communicating, or being communicated to. Even if the office eventually were to install every possible kind of electronic aid, so that all aspects of design were computerized,

Table 11.1—Percentages of time spent in various activities by a young job architect. (Based on figures provided by Building Design Partnership, Preston.)

Drawing and associated activities:

Drawing and lettering	19·2%
Measuring	2·3
Selecting colour scheme	1·2
Erasing	1·7
Searching for pencil	1·6
Sharpening pencil	0·3
Setting up work space	2·7
Colouring prints	3·9
Obtaining prints or drawing paper	0·4
Folding prints	0·1
	Total 33·4

Information-seeking:

Referring to catalogues	1·2
Referring to drawings	1·9
Referring to specifications, bills of quantities	0·6
Checking specialists' drawings	0·1
Searching for drawings	2·3
Searching for other information	0·9
Other information away from work place	0·6
	Total 7·6

Discussion and verbal communication:

Discussing with colleagues or admin.	14·5
Internal telephone	0·5
Consulting quantity surveyor or heating and ventilation engineer	1·7
External telephone	4·0
Discussion with contractor, client or rep.	0·7
On site or visiting client	8·3
Admin. or design session	1·4
	Total 31·1

Letters and written communications:

Dictating letters	1·0
Writing letters	1·0
Signing letters	0·3
Reading correspondence	1·0
Making notes	1·0
Preparing reports, specifications, financial	1·1
Writing schedules	0·3
Costing work, filling in time sheets or expenses sheets	0·6
	Total 6·3

Thinking	9·5
	Total 9·5

Continued overleaf

Table 11.1—continued

Miscellaneous:
    Calculating   1·0
    Walking about   2·8
    Waiting   0·4
    Personal   2·3
    Other   5·6

Total 12·1

100%

from the collection and storage of data to the production of drawings and other contractual information, the architect's tasks would still be concerned largely with communication—but he would spend more time communicating with machines than with people.

Certainly this would involve a considerable redistribution of his communications tasks. Presumably he would no longer spend as much time erasing, or searching for a pencil; the total time for drawing and associated activities (33·4 per cent) might indeed be reduced. Discussion and verbal communication would certainly increase and so for that matter would information-seeking; for, given the possibilities of computerized data storage and retrieval, the temptation is to store so much more information that the area of search is correspondingly greater. Letters and written communication might stay as they are (6·3 per cent) and thinking, one hopes, might even increase. If, in fact, one takes thinking as self-communication, then the only activities which cannot be classified as producing, communicating or referring to information are the 12·1 per cent of 'miscellaneous' activities which, no doubt, would stay substantially the same.

So if the architect now, and for the foreseeable future, spends 87·9 per cent of his time in communication of one sort or another, then clearly it is a topic of vital importance to him. He might learn a great deal, therefore, from the analysis which has been undertaken in the past forty years under the general heading of Communications (or Information) Theory.

As we might expect, the first people to take a serious interest in the efficiency with which messages could be transmitted were communications engineers. When messages are being sent over wires and each second costs money, it is particularly important that as much information as possible be passed with the greatest possible accuracy in the minimum time. Whatever the communications system, it is extremely unlikely that the message received will be an exact replica of the message which was sent in the first place. Parts of it inevitably will have been lost or misunderstood, and when one considers all the possibilities for distortion, it is quite remarkable that any message ever gets through in anything like intelligible form.

The amount of it which will get through can be studied in terms of probability; information theory, in fact, is the statistical study of communication. It is based on a *systems* view of the 'communications channel', the name used for any device or assemblage of devices by which information is passed from its original source to its final destination. Any communications channel, whatever its form—radio, television, cinematic, spoken, written, printed, photographed, drawn and so on—can be represented by the same block schematic diagram which was worked out, initially, to represent a telephone channel. Its essential elements are the three shown in Figure 11.1.

We will assume for our purposes that the information source and information destination are human brains, and the purpose of the channel is to pass messages from one brain to another. We may take it also that the source's intention, essentially, is to pass information to the destination so as to change the state of the latter. This suggests immediately that if the destination knows already what the source is going to say, then there will be no point in passing information; but there is more to this than intentions for, if the destination knows the source's intentions, it will be technically impossible for

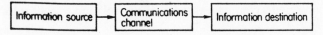

Figure 11.1—Essential elements of the communications channel (based on Shannon and Weaver, 1949)

communication to take place, for communication depends, essentially, on the destination's *uncertainty* as to what the message is going to be. It will be impossible also for communication to take place if the destination has no means of understanding the source's message. In many cases source and destination share a common *language* and, in communications terms, language consists of a set of signs, or symbols, and a set of rules for using them. Written or spoken language, for instance, consists of words; these are signs, of which a finite number exist in a dictionary of that language. If transmitter and receiver both have copies of that dictionary—or understand its contents—then messages can be built up which consist of words selected from the list. To put it crudely, the source will have an idea of what it wants to communicate; it will choose the most appropriate words, pass them along the communications channel, the destination will then assimilate those words and, with luck, it might reconstruct some semblance of the source's original idea.

The *accuracy* of such communication will depend on many things. Source and destination will both bring their experience to bear on the words which are actually chosen. Their understandings of each word may have certain things in common and certain points of difference. My use of the word 'big' will depend very much on context—a big mouse will be a great deal smaller than a tiny elephant. So, immediately, in trying to communicate we hit directly upon a perceptual problem which in itself *ought* to make accurate communication almost impossible. There are other problems too. It may be that the language itself is lacking the words I need to express my ideas with clarity. Let us take a particular restricted case, which illustrates the point beautifully and, incidentally, summarizes most of what we have said about communication so far.

Nelson's famous signal at Trafalgar, as every schoolboy knows, read: 'England expects that every man will do his duty.' What is not so well known is that Nelson originally asked his Flag Officer, Pascoe, to signal 'England confides that every man . . .'—*'confides'* in this sense, meaning 'is confident'. In communications terms, flag signalling was a language. There was a set of symbols—the flags—and a set of rules for using them. Each flag represented a letter of the alphabet, or a number, whilst the signalling manual contained a dictionary, each word of which could be represented by three flags. Other words which were not in the manual had to be spelled out, letter by letter. There were also rules as to how one distributed the various sequences of flags over strategic points in the rigging of the ship—in other words, the manual contained a comprehensive set of symbols and a set of rules for using them.

Pascoe, however, was using the new manual of *Telegraphic Signals and Marine Vocabulary*, prepared by Sir Home Popham (1799) and this did not contain the word 'confides'. He suggested to Nelson, therefore, that a substitute word 'expects', which was in the manual, would save a great deal of time in transmitting the message. It has also been recorded (Warner, 1958) that Nelson's message failed to communicate anything to his sailors—they knew the content of his message before he transmitted it; in communications terms it was *redundant*.

Already, this simple example has introduced a number of complications. Everyone who seeks to communicate shares some of Nelson's problems. If the source of the message is a brain, for instance, it will be incapable of transmitting messages unaided, apart, perhaps, from telepathically. The business of translating ideas into words will consist, in part at least, of mechanical processes; the production of sounds by vocal chords, palate and other parts of the mouth, the movement of hands and fingers in writing or typing. These processes of translating the message into a form which can be transmitted are known as *encoding*, and at the further end of the channel an equivalent, reverse process of *decoding* takes place, in which the physical forms of words are translated back into ideas. In the case of a telephone channel, the encoding and decoding are at least two-stage affairs. The source initiates the message, encodes it into words and encodes it further into a pattern of sounds. These are picked up by a microphone and translated into electrical impulses which may be transmitted along a wire. In this case, then, we might call the microphone a *transmitter* and, again, there is a corresponding device at the far end of the channel in the form of an earpiece, a *receiver*. Our three-part channel, therefore, has now expanded into seven.

There is a further complication however in that each of these elements in the channel is subject to *noise*, which is the communications engineer's term for anything which interferes with the accurate transmission of the message. It is easy to see how this originated in the disturbances which can take place in a telephone line—crossed wires, crackles, hisses, electrical disturbances and so on. These can never be eliminated entirely, for however carefully the channel is designed there will always be some residual noise in the circuits, caused ultimately by the statistically random, Brownian motion of the electrons themselves. One can understand too why the background disturbance to individual conversation at a cocktail party should be called noise; in many ways this resembles the random perturbation which is characteristic of noise in the telecommunication sense. It may come as a surprise, at first, to realize that a drawing too can be noisy for, given the definition that noise is anything which interferes with good communication, a drawing may be noisy if it is folded, blotchy, covered with tea stains or faded. It will be noisy if the lettering is too small, the lines too thin for effective printing or the dimensions inaccurate. It will be noisy also if the architect used symbols which are not part of the agreed language between source and destination.

That suggests that one should think very carefully indeed before one uses anything other than conventional signs or symbols in communication and certainly communication will be difficult enough if one sticks to these alone. As we saw from Nelson's problem there may be no word, or symbol, to describe exactly one's initial idea. One distorts the message immediately in choosing from the available list of signs. We may call this distortion *semantic noise*. Having been distorted at source, the message will be subject to all the vicissitudes of noise within the channel and when it reaches the receiver it will be subject to further noise. For in the process of decoding, as we have seen, it is highly likely that receiver and destination between them will attach rather different meanings to the signs from those which the source intended. The receiver, destination, in any case, may have a considerable desire to remain in its existing state, or to choose its own future state; it may not want to be communicated with. So we may call noise at this point *perceptual noise*. Our schematic diagram, therefore will have to include these new elements, and will now take the form shown in Figure 11.2.

Having set up the mechanical channel by which communication can be effected, it might be helpful to clarify the question as to what can be communicated. Even if source and destination—or, at least, transmitter and receiver—share the same language there is still no guarantee that the selected signs will *mean* the same things to both of them. Meaning, essentially, is a question of the relationship between a sign or symbol and the object or

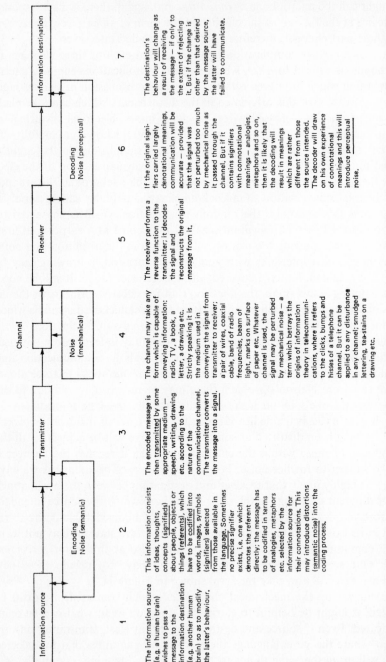

1	2	3	4	5	6	7
Information source	Encoding Noise (semantic)	Transmitter	Noise (mechanical)	Receiver	Decoding Noise (perceptual)	Information destination

Channel

1. The information source (e.g. a human brain) wishes to pass a message to the information destination (e.g. another human brain) so as to modify the latter's behaviour.

2. This information consists of ideas, thoughts, concepts (signifieds) about people, objects or things (referents), which have to be codified into words, images, symbols (signifiers) selected from those available in the language. Sometimes no precise signifier exists, i.e. one which denotes the referent directly; the message has to be codified in terms of analogies, metaphors etc. selected by the information source for their connotations. This may introduce distortions (semantic noise) into the coding process.

3. The encoded message is then transmitted by some appropriate medium — speech, writing, drawing etc. according to the nature of the communications channel. The transmitter converts the message into a <u>signal</u>.

4. The channel may take any form which is capable of conveying information: radio, TV, a book, a letter, a drawing etc. Strictly speaking it is the medium used in conveying the signal from transmitter to receiver; a pair of wires, coaxial cable, band of radio frequencies, beam of light, marks on surface of paper etc. Whatever channel is used, the signal may be perturbed by mechanical noise — a term which betrays the origins of information theory in telecommunications, where it refers to the clicks, bumps and hisses of a telephone channel. But it can be applied to any disturbance in any channel; smudged lettering, tea-stains on a drawing etc.

5. The receiver performs a reverse function to the transmitter; it decodes the signal and reconstructs the original message from it,

6. If the original signifiers carried largely denotational meanings, communication will be accurate — provided that the signal was not perturbed too much by mechanical noise as it passed through the channel. But if it contains signifiers with connotational meanings — analogies, metaphors and so on, then it is likely that the decoding will result in meanings which are rather different from those the source intended. The decoder will draw on his own experience of connotational meanings and this will introduce <u>perceptual noise.</u>

7. The destination's behaviour <u>will</u> change as a result of receiving the message — if only to the extent of rejecting it. But if the change is other than that desired by the message source, the latter will have failed to communicate.

Figure 11.2—Complete information channel with sources of noise, etc., plotted in (based on Shannon and Weaver, 1949)

idea which it represents. At this point, however, we meet a crucial difficulty in all discussions on communication: that the authorities themselves cannot agree as to what the essential terms mean. One is reminded of Shaw, to misquote him: 'He who can, communicates. He who cannot, writes a theory about it.' The simplest discussion on meaning, probably, is to be found in Saussure, the founding father of French linguistics. In his *Course in General Linguistics*, a series of lecture notes edited after his death (1915), Saussure is concerned specifically with spoken language and he says:

'Some people regard language, when reduced to its elements, as a naming-process only—a list of words, each corresponding to the thing it names.'

This is an oversimplification, but nevertheless,

'. . . this rather naive approach can bring us near the truth by showing us that the linguistic unit is a double entity, formed by the associating of two terms . . . a two-sided psychological entity that can be represented by the drawing [Figure 11.3]:

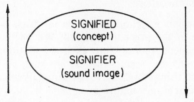

Figure 11.3—Saussure's two-part sign. The signifier is the word or other symbol we use to represent an object, whilst the signified is *both* the object itself and our concept of it (from Saussure, 1915)

Our definition of the linguistic sign poses an important question of terminology. I call the combination of a concept and a sound image a *sign*, but in current usage the term generally designates only a sound-image, a word, for example.'

Any noun may be called a *sign* only because it 'carries' the concept of a physical object; the sound-image received by the senses is only half the sign but it implies the idea of the whole. Saussure's aim, then, is to remove the ambiguity which arises from calling three things by the same name.

'I propose to retain the word *sign*,' he says, 'to designate the whole and to replace *concept* and *sound-image* respectively by *signified* and *signifier*; the last two terms have the advantage of indicating the opposition that separates them from each other and from the whole of which they are parts.'

One of Saussure's most important insights is the realization that this relationship between the two parts of a sign—signifier and signified—is quite arbitrary. With rare exceptions, any pattern of sounds and letters could have been used, initially, to signify a given object. In France, for instance, a certain animal is called *boeuf*; a few yards across the border, in Germany, it is called *ochs*, whilst in England, separated by twenty miles of water, it is called *cow.* There are a few signifiers, it is true, which seem to have a special relationship with their signifieds—onomatopoeic words, for instance, which might denote animal noises. Even these are arbitrary in certain respects. In France, for example, the child's word for a dog is *ouaoua*, whereas in England it is *bow-wow*. Both words have some connexion with the sounds some dogs actually make, but their difference confirms Saussure's contention that ultimately the relationship between signifier and signified is arbitrary.

However—and this is the most important point of all—once a relationship has been forged between signifier and signified, then no one can change it arbitrarily. As Saussure says: 'No individual, even if he willed it, could modify in any way at all the choice that has been made; and what is more, the community itself cannot control so much as a single word; it is bound to the existing language.' He suggests in any case that the signifier is chosen *by language*, that it cannot have been chosen by any other means and that once it has been so chosen, it becomes part of the 'social contract' by which men communicate with each other:

'No matter what period we choose or how far back we go, language always appears as a heritage of the preceding period. We might conceive of an act by which, at a given moment, names were assigned to things and a contract was formed between concepts and sound-images; but such an act has never been recorded. The notion that things might have happened like that was prompted by our acute awareness of the arbitrary nature of signs.'

Once a relationship has been established between signifier and signified, and it has become part of the 'social contract', its origins and the means by which it is transmitted from one generation to the next must be studied in precisely the way that one would study any other social institution. Saussure's scheme has been elaborated in many ways; one of the most useful extensions was presented by Ogden and Richards (1923) in their semiological triangle which

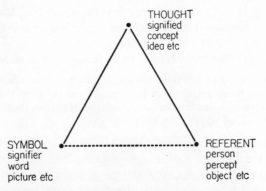

Figure 11.4—Ogden and Richards' semiological triangle in which Saussure's signifier becomes a symbol, whilst his signified is split into two parts, the thought and the referent

in addition to distinguishing between signifier and signified, also adds a third term 'the referent', indicating the person, object, etc., which is being referred to (Figure 11.4).

If words can only have meanings because society has agreed that they should, then individuals within society are bound to use words in those meanings if they are to make themselves understood. The fact that signs are arbitrary might well ensure that their two components maintain a reasonably constant relationship with each other. There is no logical reason why one should prefer *sister* to *soeur* in describing a certain person, and this in itself is an extremely potent reason for retaining whichever one's particular society has chosen to use. Again so many words are available in a given language that unless society itself has changed dramatically any likely thought can be expressed in terms of the available words. An individual user, in any case, will be so concerned with actually using the language that he cannot stop to reflect on how it could be restructured. But above all:

'Language—and this consideration surpasses all the others—is at every moment everybody's concern; spread throughout society and manipulated by it, language is something used daily by all. Here we are unable to set up any comparison between it and other institutions. The prescriptions of codes, religious rites, nautical signals, etc., involve only a certain number of individuals simultaneously and then only during a limited period of time; in language, on the contrary, everyone participates at all times, and that is why it is constantly being influenced by all. This capital fact suffices to show the impossibility of revolution. Of all social institutions, language is least amenable to initiative. It blends with the life of society, and the latter, inert by nature, is a prime conservative force.'

So in certain respects language tends to stay constant with the passage of time, but curiously enough there are other pressures, also concerned with the passage of time, which encourage change in language and this change, according to Saussure, always involves a 'shift in the relationship between the signifier and the signified.' No individual can initiate this change. The original connexion between signifier and signified was established *by language* itself, and changes in this relationship also are caused by language. Sometimes the changes are phonetic, as when the usage of particular words spreads to people who pronounce the *phonemes* of which they are constructed in different ways (a phoneme is the smallest unit of individual speech-sound). New words are formed by analogy with old; given the words decorate, unknown, manageable, one could very well suppose that a further word, undecorable, ought to exist. Children learn words by analogy and sometimes this process of learning itself leads to the formation of new words—sheeps as plural of sheep, skad as past tense of skid. In each of these cases (and Saussure cites others) linguistic change is generated from the substance of language itself; and in all these cases (undecorable, sheeps and skad) the new word is perfectly intelligible —if unacceptable—to anyone who attaches similar signifieds to the signifiers which were used in generating the analogies. That, essentially, sums up the importance of 'social contract' as a means of ensuring that source and destination (or transmitter and receiver), do agree, substantially, on the relationships between signifiers and signifieds of the signs they use. They must agree, in other words, on the *meanings* of the words, symbols or signs of other kinds which form the elements of their common language.

Information theory, however, is not in the least concerned with *meaning* but with the simple mechanics of transmitting messages economically. Indeed, according to Hartley, who first initiated it (1928) the passing of information consists not in transmitting *meanings* but only in transmitting *signs*. Meanings, for him, are subjective things associated with signs. It might have been helpful if he had made Saussure's distinction, that what we transmit are signifiers —associated subjectively with signifieds. Language itself, for Hartley, is 'a set of symbols and a set of rules for using them,' whilst information is 'the successive *selection* of signs from a given list.'

Hartley aimed to show how the transmission of information could be analysed statistically and several of the concepts we discussed earlier in the chapter can be expressed in statistical terms. If information consists of selected signs from a given list, then one can attach *probabilities* to the frequencies with which certain signs will be chosen. As I write this sentence, my freedom in choosing words becomes increasingly restricted; it is highly unlikely, for instance, that the next word will be zebra. *Noise* too can be measured statistically and so, for that matter, can the destination's *uncertainty*. Once Hartley had shown the possibilities, others took up the statistical study of information transmission; Claude Shannon (1948) posed four fundamental questions, which may be paraphrased as follows:

1. How can the amount of information, and the rate at which information is produced, be measured so as to take into account the structure of the message in terms of probability?
2. How can the capacity of a communications channel be measured? Given a particular information channel with a known signal strength, and a specified level of noise, how many information units can be transmitted per second?
3. What makes a coding process efficient? Given the maximum possible efficiency in coding, at what rate can a given channel convey information?
4. What are the general characteristics of noise, and what effect does noise have on the accuracy of the final message? How can the undesirable effects of noise be minimized?

The last two have been answered already, whilst the first two require a more statistical treatment. I have simplified this as far as possible, in the interests of good communication, to an architectural readership.

We can answer Shannon's first question with reference to several ideas which have been discussed so far. There is no possibility of transmitting any information unless the destination is uncertain as to what the message is going to be. The message is going to be transmitted in the form of signs, chosen from a given set or ensemble. We have seen already that the available words of a language form such a set and so for that matter do the letters of the alphabet. If I choose a letter of the alphabet, you are uncertain as to what it is—there are 26 possibilities and I have chosen one of them. We might say, therefore, that your uncertainty is represented by 26 units of some kind. That would not be very helpful because the obvious question is '26 units of what?' So information theory measures your uncertainty in terms of the number of yes–no questions you would have to ask to locate the letter I had chosen. You might well ask at random: 'Is it A, D, Q . . . ?'; but that is un- likely. It would be much more sensible, in fact, to employ the Greek method of *division* which was to continue dividing the alphabet successively into halves: 'Is it before N? Is it before H?', and so on. In that way you could locate any letter fairly quickly; sometimes you would have to ask four questions, and sometimes five.

Let us simplify the problem by taking an ensemble of eight letters— A B C D E F G H. A little experiment, using the method of division, will show that you can *always* locate the selected letter with a maximum of three questions. In other words, your *uncertainty* is three units per letter. If you can locate a single letter out of eight by means of three questions, you can also locate a single letter out of sixteen by means of four questions and so on. So in information theory terms we can state values for your uncertainty (H) as follows:

$$H \text{ (A to H)} = 3 \text{ units per letter}$$
$$H \text{ (A to P)} = 4 \text{ units per letter}$$

It is no coincidence, however, that for the ensemble of eight elements, A to H, your uncertainty (H) should amount to 3 units per letter and that $8 = 2^3$. We are concerned with binary questions, that is questions with two possible answers and for any ensemble of n elements the number of questions (H) will equal the power by which two has to be raised to equal the size of the ensemble:

$$H = \log_2 n$$

Log tables are available, calculated for base 2, and using these tables one can determine the uncertainty for any size of ensemble. Given the alphabet, for instance, $\log_2 26 = 4 \cdot 7$ which represents the average number of binary questions required to locate any letter, selected at random. That is why some- times you would have to ask four questions and sometimes five.

However, letters do not occur at random in written English. It is well known, for instance, that Samuel Morse set up his code by counting the quantities of different letters which he found in a printer's shop. There were

12,000 E's, 9,000 T's, 8,000 A's and so on down to 200 Z's, and these quantities reflected, very roughly, the probabilities with which individual letters will occur. We know now with greater accuracy than Morse that in any sample of written English, it is probable that for every J or Z there will be 131 E's, 104 T's, 82 A's, 80 O's, 68 R's and so on (Edwards, 1964). If we cut up a sample of written English, and then try to guess which of its letters had been drawn, at random, out of a hat, it is 131 times more likely that the letter so drawn will be an E, rather than a J. Given, say, a thousand letters the *probability* that the J, or any particular *one* of the 131 E's, will be selected is a thousand to one—0·001. The *index of probability* for each of the letters mentioned above is for E, 0·131; T, 0·104; A, 0·082; O, 0·080; R, 0·068 and so on. These numbers are very small—they must, in fact, total 1, which is the index of absolute certainty in probability calculations. If we are going to express them logarithmically, therefore, to base 2, we shall in fact be finding *roots* of 2, rather than raising it by various powers. So our logarithm will be negative, and the probability that the ith letter will be chosen is $-\log_2 p_i$. In trying to guess which letter had been chosen at random from the alphabet, the probability that you would succeed with the first question was $\dfrac{1}{4 \cdot 7}$. In trying to guess which letter had been drawn from our 1,000 cut from written English, the probability that it would be E was $\dfrac{131}{1,000}$; T, $\dfrac{104}{1,000}$; Z, $\dfrac{1}{1,000}$ and so on. And given an average sample of written English, one could add these probabilities together thus defining the *information content* of the sample.

Shannon, Weiner and others reinterpreted Hartley's original law in precisely this way to define, not the probability of choosing an individual letter, but the *average* information content of a long sequence of letters:

$$H = -\Sigma p_i \log_2 p_i$$

where p_i is the total number of symbols. This can then be used to define three more important concepts in information theory—Relative Uncertainty, Redundancy and Entropy. To take the first of these:

$$\text{Relative Uncertainty} = \frac{\text{Actual Uncertainty}}{\text{Maximum Uncertainty}}$$

We have seen already that the *maximum* uncertainty involved in identifying a letter selected at random from the alphabet is $\log_2 26 = 4 \cdot 7$ approximately; but if we add together the 26 known values of $p_i \times -\log p_i$, we find the *actual* uncertainty is 4·129, so:

$$\text{Relative Uncertainty} = \frac{4 \cdot 129}{4 \cdot 700} = 87 \cdot 9 \text{ per cent}$$

In other words 87·9% of the letters actually convey some information. Uncertainty must be present in the destination for any information to be passed at all, so if the destination is only 87·9% uncertain as to what the message will be, part of the message is not conveying anything to him. It is *redundant*. And in this case:

$$\text{Redundancy} = 1 - 0{\cdot}879 = 12{\cdot}1 \text{ per cent}$$

It would be possible on the same basis to analyse the content of a typical production drawing. That too exhibits a massive redundancy. Take, say, the accepted symbol for an 11-inch cavity wall. The width of the wall is described three times, by scale, by dimension and by description; the material twice, by hatching and by description; and the cavity also twice by drawing and by description (Figure 11.5). Obviously it would be possible to rationalize the

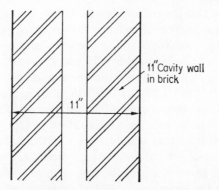

Figure 11.5—Traditional method of describing a cavity wall on a production drawing. This coding has inbuilt redundancies; the material is described twice, the width three times and so on

symbol to reduce the apparent redundancy, yet before we do that we ought to remember two things: redundancy is the means of overcoming noise, and site drawings tend to get very noisy with folds, tea stains and so on, whilst this particular symbol is accepted by social contract in the building industry and we cannot change it unilaterally.

Shannon's formula $H = -\Sigma p_i \log_2 p_i$ looks remarkably like Boltzmann's formula for the entropy of a perfect gas (Cherry, 1957), which refers to the Second Law of Thermodynamics. Those of us who are scientifically literate, by Lord Snow's famous definition, will remember that this Law states: 'systems can only proceed to a state of increased disorder' and that as time passes 'entropy can never decrease.' The classic example, of course, is that of gases in a bottle divided into two connected parts. We may start with a greater pressure in one part than the other but, with the passage of time, the system will tend to even itself out. We started with specific information on the positions and energies of the various particles of gas but with the increase of randomness this knowledge decreases.

Because Shannon's formula *looked* like Boltzmann's, he adopted the same terminology and called the destination's uncertainty *entropy*; but, as we have seen, the destination's uncertainty also is a measure of the information which may be transmitted and Norbert Wiener, therefore, argued the opposite case (1948): 'Just as the amount of information in a system is a measure of its degree of organization, so the entropy of a system is a measure of its degree of disorganization; and the one is simply the negative of the other.' So he calls H, the information content of a message, its *negative* entropy. As McGill and Quastler have suggested (1955) it is supremely ironical that the two leading exponents of *communications* theory should fail to agree on the definition of one of its most crucial terms.

We saw just now that the redundancy of written English is not the same as the redundancy in a random sequence of letters taken out of a hat. That is because certain letters habitually follow one another in written English; if we see a Q, we *expect* it to be followed by a U, and if we saw a sequence of letters which started W, I, N, D, O, we should be in no doubt as to what the next letter might be. The probability that W will occur in this case depends not only on its frequency, but also on what has gone before (Edwards, 1964). So the redundancy of written English is rather greater than 12·1 per cent. The theory of such sequences was developed by the Russian mathematician Markov; a 'Stochastic' process is one which produces a sequence of discrete symbols according to certain probabilities. If these probabilities *depend* on previous events in the series, it is called a markov process and if, in such a process, the influences between letters extend *only* over a finite number of letters, the process is called Ergodic. Ordinary language is an Ergodic process in this sense, and any reasonably large sample is sufficient to represent the whole sequence (Edwards, 1964).

As for Shannon's second question—how one can measure the capacity of a communications channel—this too had worried Hartley and he found that two things were relevant; the *time* available for transmission and the *bandwidth* of the channel itself. Cherry (1963) relates these rather neatly with reference to a gramophone record. Let us suppose that a short piece lasting, say, five minutes is being played on a violin. The actual notes which may be played on a violin, disregarding harmonics, extraneous scrapings and clicks, cover a *bandwidth* of 200 to 3,000 cycles per second. If we now double the speed of the record, our five-minute piece will last only two and a half minutes; we shall hear the same 'message' in half the time. But the *bandwidth* now will be from 400 to 6,000 c.p.s., twice the width of the original. There will now be twice as many frequencies within which to locate each note and each note will be half as long, which will introduce an element of *uncertainty* into its identification. Conversely, the *longer* the notes, the *narrower* the bandwidth and the more certain will be our identification.

In other words there *is* an absolute limit to the amount of information any channel can carry, be it a telephone wire, a letter or a drawing. There is a limit to the number of lines a drawing can carry, the amount of detail which is possible, the fineness at which it is legible. Shannon himself answered this question by writing another theorem:

'It is possible to encode a source of messages, having an information rate H, so that information can be transmitted through a noisy channel with an arbitrarily small frequency of errors, up to a certain limiting rate C, called the limiting capacity.'

This limiting capacity depends on such constraints as bandwidth, noise and so on; Shannon united these in an equation which expresses the maximum capacity of a communications channel: the greatest quantity of information which may be transmitted

$$C = WT \log 1 + \frac{P}{N} \text{ bits}$$

where
W = bandwidth
T = time
C = channel capacity
P = signal power
N = noise power

This suggests that since noise is present errors will be inevitable anyway; it is difficult to see that messages could be transmitted with *certainty*, but what it means in practice is that any attempt to transmit information at a higher rate than C will result in errors whilst at any rate below C, errors will be tolerably few.

There is much more to statistical information theory than this but once its principles had been established by communications engineers, they were adapted and modified in several other fields. Obviously they are of interest to the psychologists and the sociologists studying human interactions; they have also led to new ways of looking at aesthetic problems. In one study (see Brown, 1966) it was shown that regular shapes are easier to perceive than irregular ones. Symmetry, straight lines or lines changing in a regular manner involve less uncertainty than irregular lines with many corners. The information content of shapes can be explored: the shape is plotted on a graph by filling in the appropriate squares; the finer the graph, the greater the degree of detail. A subject is then presented with an empty graph and his task is to guess which squares should be filled and which should be left un-filled. If the number of his correct guesses is high, then one assumes that the shape exhibits a high degree of redundancy, but where the number of correct guesses is low, then the *information* content of the shape is high. As might be expected, straight lines and smooth curves are easy to guess once their direction has been set, but it is difficult to guess where a line ends or what happens at a corner.

Moles (1966) has undertaken a massive study on *Information Theory and Aesthetic Perception* in which he too analyses the relationship between uncertainty and expectation with particular reference to music. He is concerned, as we might expect, with *form*; an organized signal which emerges against a disorganized background of noise. Our perception of a form might be likened to perception of an autocorrelation between the elements which constitute it, and there is a limit to the number of such elements we can apprehend at any one time. In other words, we can distinguish a simple form from the background noise easily whereas, faced with a more complex one, we tend to scan it and to *select* forms *from* the message, on the basis of our past experience and expectations. Naturally, we sometimes find what we want to find instead of what is actually there. A highly complex form with no redundancy is extremely difficult to transmit and equally difficult to receive; and, according to Moles, it will also be devoid of aesthetic value. Aesthetic value is concerned with structures (these give the message intelligibility) and with *symbols*. Symbols in this sense are collections of elements which are known in advance and, of course, their perception depends on the observer's past experience and on his memory.

Given the basic opposition of order-disorder which information theory inherited from thermodynamics, Moles develops several others which he calls *dialectical dipoles:*

Predictable	Unpredictable
Banal	Original
Redundant	Informative
Intelligible	Novel
Simple	Complex

Clearly the left-hand member of each pair transmits little or no information whereas the right-hand member transmits a great deal; but, bearing in mind the difficulties which Moles himself describes in transmitting and receiving complex information, the aim, as far as possible, should be to strike a just balance between the two, according to circumstances.

That, finally, is the message of information theory for the designer. Whatever intention one is trying to transmit, one should choose a language which is known to the receiver—and this will vary according to whether he is client, consultant, local authority official or a member of the building team. Traditionally, for instance, the architect (and certainly the student architect) spent a great deal of time preparing elaborate presentation drawings including, more often than not, a large perspective in colour. Some students were good at this, and used their skill to mask their deficiencies as *architects*—as designers of actual buildings. In this case they introduced not redundancy to overcome the effects of noise, but noise to overcome banality.

Yet the principle, at least, was sound. If the architect is to transmit his intentions to the client, then he must choose a language the client understands; indeed he has a moral responsibility to choose such a language, but few clients understand architects' drawings; they may, just conceivably, be able to see relationships on plan, but this is equivalent to following a musical score, say, to a gramophone record, reading one line of instruments and matching approximately the up or downward trend of the melody. So the architect's task is to convey more to the client than orthographic projection ever could. Obviously perspectives, or more particularly models, will help him communicate more effectively and of course they will have their own intrinsic attraction. The architect, if he is wise, will take advantage of this. It is an essential part of the design process that one builds into the client a mechanism for perceiving what one has done. Good communications at this stage will help direct the client's expectations in ways which are favourable to the architect and as we have already seen he *owes* it to his client to do just this. In other words, he should present the most intelligible and attractive drawings he possibly can, in a language which the client understands. Within that language, one should encode by means of accepted symbols and use them according to the accepted rules. One should know when to introduce redundancy and how much to introduce in order to overcome noise, and one should recognize that, as transmitter and receiver begin to know and understand each other, so the amount of information which can be transmitted will decrease; entropy will set in. In the case of a one-off job for a new client, then uncertainty will be high all round; in the case of the nth systems built house for the same authority by the same contractor, then there will be hardly any uncertainty at all. In other words, information theory confirms many things which we know already, but it helps us to be more precise in their analysis and to be more definite in their application. And whilst information theory itself is concerned with quantity of information, rather than quality of meaning, it provides some of the background, at least, to the study of meaning.

Lady Welby (quoted Ogden and Richards, 1923) defines meaning as the *effect* which the utterer of a sign intends it to produce on the mind of the interpreter. She also distinguishes two other levels of meaning: the first effect of a sign, without further reflection, on a mind qualified to comprehend it, which she calls the *sense* of the symbol; and the final effect which the sign would produce on a mind qualified to comprehend it if circumstances allowed its full effects to be worked out. This she calls the *significance* of the sign.

We may take it then that the function of signs is to signify, and the process of acting as a sign is called *signification*. Beyond this, it is usual to distinguish between the signifying function of signals and the signifying function of symbols. A signal *denotes* something; a proper name is a signal in this sense; it is associated with a concept which 'fits' an actual person. This relationship between person, concept and signal is called *denotation*. It is essential, according to Langer, to distinguish between this and the simpler relationship which exists between symbol and concept, when no object is actually present or even referred to. This is called *connotation* and it is concerned with the concept which a word conveys. Ogden and Richards clarify this difference between denotation and connotation: they say that *denotation* means the set of things to which a sign can actually be applied, whilst *connotation* refers to the properties one looks for in deciding whether an object actually belongs to that set. The ways in which we define these properties have been explored exhaustively by Bruner, Goodnow and Austin in their *A Study of Thinking* (1956).

Langer (1942) gives examples of signals and symbols in these senses. She describes certain natural signs or signals as follows:

'Wet streets are a sign that it has rained. A patter on the roof is a sign that it is raining. A fall of the barometer or a ring round the moon is a sign that it is going to rain. In an unirrigated place, abundant verdure is a sign that it often rains there. A smell of smoke signifies the presence of fire. A scar is a sign of a past accident. Dawn is a herald of sunrise. Sleekness is a sign of frequent and plentiful food.'

If she had been writing a few years later she might have used the word signals for all these signs. Symbols, on the other hand, are man-made signs, used not only to *indicate* objects but to *represent* them. As Langer says, a picture may represent an object; she asks what properties such a picture must have in order to effect an identifiable representation:

'Must it really share the visual appearance of the object? Certainly not to any high degree. It may, for instance, be black on white, or red on grey, or any other colour on any other colour; it may be shiny whereas the object is dull; it may be much larger or much smaller than the object; it is certainly flat, and although the tricks of perspective sometimes give a perfect illusion of three-dimensionality, a picture without perspective—e.g. an architect's "elevation drawing"—is still unmistakably a picture, representing an object.'

A picture may be 'realistic', a very close analogy indeed for its subject, or it may be highly conventionalized, tending towards a diagram which simply represents the relationship between parts of the subject. Yet it is still recognizable as a representation of the subject and it has certain things in common with the more elaborate and realistic representation. They share an essential *concept* of the subject and such concepts, finally, are all that symbols can convey.

We can use words as signs in either sense. We may utter the word 'dinner' in the presence of a clever dog. It will act as a signal that food is on the way and it may well set up a conditioned reflex. Sometimes we use words to communicate with each other at this level, but more often we use them as symbols to convey concepts. As Susanne Langer says:

'We use certain "signs" among ourselves that do not point to anything in our actual surroundings. Most of our words are not signs in the sense of signals. They are used to talk *about* things, not to direct our eyes and ears and noses toward them. Instead of announcers of things, they are reminders . . . they take the place of things that we have perceived in the past, or even things that we can merely imagine by combining memories, things that *might* be in past or future experience . . . they serve . . . to let us develop a characteristic attitude towards objects in absentia, which is called "thinking of" or "referring to" what is not here.'

CHAPTER 12
New Maths

As we saw in Chapter 2, the ideal of canons in design derives, ultimately, from the Greek philosophers. Socrates believed that behind the evanescent and ever-changing world as perceived by the senses there was an order of a mathematical kind and, once this structure was understood, it should be possible to comprehend the world intellectually; but as we know, the geometry of the Greeks was by no means sophisticated enough to enable, say, space to be comprehended in the way that Riemannian geometry shows. The curved spaces of Riemannian geometry enabled comprehension to extend far beyond the possibilities of flat surfaces and three dimensions but its curved surfaces, at least, were of uniform curvature. Other geometries have been discovered, however, which deal not in surfaces of uniform curvature but in surfaces which are bent, twisted, magnified, shrunk or otherwise distorted. They fall under the general heading of *topology*, the mathematics of position (*geometria situs*) and of distortion, which deals not with the bending, twisting and so on themselves, but with the properties of objects which are so fundamental that no amount of such distortions will alter their relationships; in mathematical terms, it deals with the *transformation* of *invariant relationships*.

It originated in the analysis by Euler (1707–73) of a curious problem set for themselves by the burghers of Königsberg, now Kaliningrad in East Prussia. The city is located on an island called Kneiphof and the surrounding banks, where the two arms of the river Pregel meet. The four distinct areas of the city are linked by seven bridges and, on Sunday afternoons, the citizens used to stroll across them. Some of them tried to plan their route, the 'Spaziergang', so that in the course of visiting each part of the city they would cross each bridge once, and once only, returning eventually to their starting point (Figure 12.1).

Euler's method consisted first of all in labelling each area or region of the city A, B, C and D, and when a person moved from, say, A to B Euler denoted this crossing by AB, irrespective of which bridge was actually used. The letters $ABDC$ would denote that the traveller had visited each of the four regions in that order and crossed three bridges in doing so. Eight letters therefore would be needed to denote that seven bridges had been crossed, but certain areas (A and B for instance) are connected by two bridges, so the corresponding notations (AB or BA) would have to occur twice. AC would occur twice too, whereas AD, BD and CD would only have to occur once.

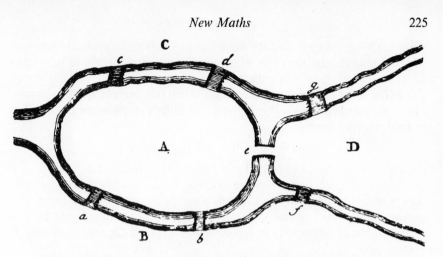

Figure 12.1—The city of Königsberg from an eighteenth-century map

Euler's problem, therefore, reduced itself to stringing these combinations together, in the correct order, within an ultimate total of eight letters. Actually there are five bridges leading to area A; to cross them all one would have to leave it three times and return twice, or vice versa. In a string of letters representing these crossings therefore, the letter A would occur three times. Euler prepares a table (Table 12.1). The last column totals 9, so it will *not* be possible to cross each of the bridges once only.

Euler also produced a graph (Figure 12.2), that is a diagram representing the form of the city. This graph, in fact, had nothing to do with the coordinate systems of algebra, with equations in x and y. It was instead a figure in

Table 12.1—Euler's table of bridges

Number of bridges 7, giving 8 ($= 7 + 1$) letters

For area A: number of bridges = 5,	letter	A occurs	3 times
B:	,,	3	,,	B ,,	2 ,,
C:	,,	3	,,	C ,,	2 ,,
D:	,,	3	,,	D ,,	2 ,,

geometry consisting of points (nodes, vertices), lines (arcs, edges) and the areas they enclosed (faces or domains). His graph has a one-to-one relationship with the city of Königsberg, that is to say each part of the city was represented by some appropriate feature of the graph. Each of the four areas into which the city was divided was represented by a *vertex* marked with the appropriate letter and he linked these points with *edges* representing the bridges and other parts of the route. Just as his table showed that one extra crossing of a bridge would be necessary if he were to return to his starting point, so his graph indicated the same fact in a different way. In the terminology of graph theory, the edges which meet at a vertex are said to be *incident* to it. In his graph of Königsberg, three edges are incident to each vertex, except for *A*, which has five. The edges incident to a vertex (*A*) are numbered *p*(*A*) and described as *local degree* to (*A*); so Euler's graph might be described in the following terms:

$$p(A) = 5; \; p(B) = p(C) = p(D) = 3$$

Each vertex therefore has an odd number of edges; but, as Euler deduced, if one were to follow a path which traversed each edge once only (a cyclic path) then it would be necessary to enter each vertex by one edge and leave it by another, every time one visited it. In other words, each vertex should have an even number of edges; but in the Königsberg graph they were all odd. It

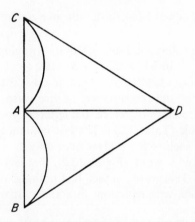

Figure 12.2—Euler's *mapping* of Königsberg in the form of a graph

would not therefore be possible to traverse the Königsberg graph by means of a cyclic path. As Euler put it:

'If there are more than two regions which are approached by an odd number of bridges, no route satisfying the required conditions can be found.

If, however, there are only two regions with an odd number of approach bridges, the required journey can be completed provided it originates in one of the regions.

If finally, there is no region with an odd number of approach bridges, the required journey can be affected, no matter where it begins.'

So even if Euler failed to solve his problem, or rather proved it to be insoluble, he succeeded nevertheless in founding an entirely new branch of mathematics, which has been developed in several ways since his time. One of the most fruitful ways, from our point of view, is in the direction of Graph Theory, and graphs in Euler's sense may be used to represent almost anything which involves *connexion* in some way. We shall find them particularly useful, for instance, in the analysis of circulation patterns; each vertex might represent an activity, or a room, a building or even a town, and the edges connecting them will then indicate routes of one kind or another. These routes might represent the physical movement of people, goods, the flow of information; any of the things, in fact, which have been defined as *throughput* in systems analysis.

So far, however, the most advanced applications of graph theory to analysis of this kind have been found, not in systems engineering but in geography, under the general heading of Locational Analysis and in architecture as *The Geometry of Environment* (March and Steadman, 1971). Haggett (1965, 1967, etc.) classifies the use of graphs under four headings: first, models with a single path; second, models of networks without circuits which are called trees; third, models of networks with circuits; and fourth, models of cellular networks. He considers these last to be different in kind from the first three; they are concerned with lines along which flows are

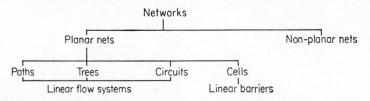

Figure 12.3—Haggett's classification of networks (from Haggett, 1965)

directed, whereas cellular nets consist of containing lines or barriers across which flows may or may not move. Haggett classifies networks as shown in Figure 12.3. Each of these has its uses in design: we shall consider paths, trees, circuits and cells in that order together with several other techniques noting, where appropriate, some of the uses to which each has been put.

Paths

Other things being equal, most of us assume that the shortest distance between two points will be a straight line and that a straight line, therefore, will give us the easiest and most economical route between them.

Losch (1954) was concerned with optimum paths where movement costs varied widely over different parts of the route—land and sea, mountain and plain, and so on. He thought the problem analogous to the passage of light through media with different refractive indices. Transport overland is usually more expensive than sea transport and, given the appropriate costs, it should be possible to decide which of several ports to use on a given coastline, or even where to build a new port. Again, the least-cost route across a range of mountains will be neither straight over the top nor right round one end, but along some compromise path that lies between the two (Haggett, 1965). In each of these cases the easiest route, and certainly the shortest in terms of time, may be round the obstacle instead of across it. If we are concerned with three points instead of two, it may be quite uneconomical to connect two of them by means of a straight line, Figure 12.4(a), with a spur off to the third. Steiner (quoted Haggett, 1968) found it invaluable to study the angles of a

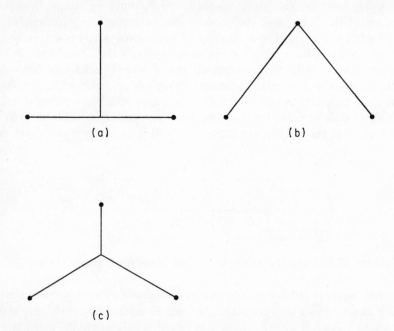

Figure 12.4—Minimum path connexions. Where any three elements—cities, buildings, etc.—are arranged in triangular formation, it may be useful to find the minimum length of path, road, etc., which could connect them. At first sight (a) and (b) show economical connexions between the three points but if the angle at any one of them is equal to, or less then, 120°, then it will be more economical to locate a fourth point so that the three paths meet at 120° as in (c)

triangle which is formed by the three points; he found that if one of them is equal to, or greater than 120°, then the other points should be connected to this one. However, if all the angles are less than 120°, it is more economical to connect the three points to a fourth one, so that three paths meet there at 120° (Figure 12.4). Miehle (1958) extends Steiner's rule to cover large numbers of points and Haggett (1968) quotes his equations relating fixed points and movable junctions.

   The mathematics of such problems is not complex, but it may be tedious;

various devices have been used for solving them mechanically (Morgan, 1968). Some make use of transparent overlays, marked with 120° junctions. Others consist of fixed and movable pegs, with pulleys around which a thread is drawn. When the thread is drawn taut, the movable pegs take up optimum positions for the junctions. But the *soap bubble* method is much more elegant. Pegs about ¾-inch long are mounted between parallel sheets of Perspex, and the model is then immersed in a soap solution (a 50:50 mix of liquid detergent and distilled water will do very well). When the model is withdrawn, soap films are left between the two sheets of Perspex, connecting the pegs in a close approximation to the optimum layout. Eventually the films contract to form minimum links, perpendicular to the Perspex sheets and, with luck, they will retain their formation for up to 24 hours. Frei Otto has used a more sophisticated version of this model, in which one sheet of Perspex with pegs attached underneath is immersed in a bath of soap solution and then carefully lifted to a position above, but parallel to the liquid surface. The films then form between this surface and the bottom face of the Perspex and they will last almost indefinitely, especially if the whole model is enclosed in a Perspex box which keeps it dust-free.

Additional refinements are possible with this model; the distance between planes can be adjusted at will, thereby increasing or reducing pressure within the bubbles and thus changing their configuration. It is not practicable, however, to change the conditions at an individual point (peg) which is possible with the mechanical, thread and pulley method.

Plotting the most economical way of *connecting* a series of points is one thing, but plotting the most economical route between certain of them is quite another. For one thing, there are several kinds of shortest route, and such problems become very complex indeed where large numbers of points are involved, where the network is asymmetric—some links are one way only, or longer in one direction than the other—(Haggett, 1968). There is also a whole class of problems concerned with finding the shortest route which connects a particular set of points in the graph. For obvious reasons these are known as *travelling salesmen* problems; for a particular group of thirteen major cities in the United States, over 479 million 'shortest' cyclic routes have been plotted, and for one hundred cities, 9.3×10^{158} such routes are possible (Haggett, 1965).

The situation becomes even more complicated when some routes are more *expensive* to follow than others. Akers and others have developed ways for building in values for the various branches in a network, based on their capacity and so on (quoted Haggett, 1968). Similarly Ford and Fulkerson (1962) have investigated *minimum-cost flow paths*.

All of these, clearly, have implications for the planning of buildings or, more particularly, groups of buildings such as those of a hospital, a university campus and so on.

Trees

A graph may be drawn in such a way that it has no *circuits*, in which case it is called a *tree*. It is easy to see where the name came from. One starts with a single vertex, A, the *root*, and from this draws edges to several other vertices A_1, A_2, A_3, ...; from each of these one draws edges to further vertices A_{12}, A_{13}, ..., A_{22}, ..., etc. In any tree, there is a single *arc* connecting any pair of vertices and in particular there are no multiple edges. Once it has been established, of course, the botanical analogy can be extended in many ways. A number of trees may be placed together to form a *forest* and the various arcs

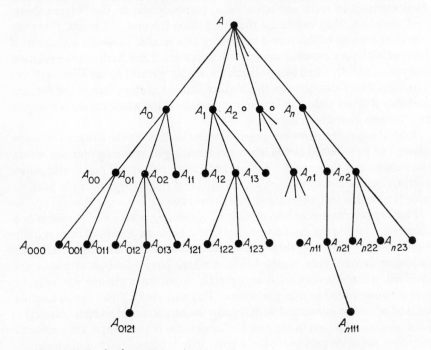

Figure 12.5—A planar tree

in each tree are called *branches*. The last vertex in each branch is called the *terminal vertex* and it is connected to the tree by a *terminal edge*. The simplest tree consists of one edge connecting two vertices and, however far it is extended, a tree with n vertices will have $n - 1$ edges.

In its simplest application, a tree may be described as the 'side elevation' of a sorting process. We might consider Figure 12.5 as representing the preliminary sorting of statements from the brief. A_0 represents the entire client's brief; factors affecting planning may be sorted to A_1; factors affecting structure to A_2; factors affecting costs to A_3, etc. There is, of course, one crucial difference between the sorting process represented here and the one which we consider desirable, in that in the tree diagram each factor eventually finds itself as the terminal vertex of one branch of one tree whereas, in practice, it will be useful if many factors appear in several categories.

One might represent a punched card system by means of a tree. Given 80-column cards, with 12 punch-places in each column, one would draw 12 edges from the root, each terminating in a vertex, 12 edges from each of these vertices, and so on, down through 80 rows of vertices.

As Haggett says (1968) the most important and frequent tree-like form in nature is the river system (a living tree is not a tree, because trees are planar, although a tree could be represented in *tree* form—drawn folded out flat). Although by definition any collection of points connected only by a single path will form a topological tree, the only forms which are of particular interest are those which have a noticeably dendritic structure. 'The accent shifts from location and form . . . to *structure* and *growth*: here questions are directed towards the intricate concepts of network, order and the inter-relationship of its several parts, and towards changes in order and balance over time.'

Horton (1945) analysed streams and rivers in terms of trees, identifying the 'parent' stream and the 'tributary' by means of two rules. Working upstream from the mouth, at any junction of two streams:

(1) the one joining the parent stream at a greater angle is the tributary and
(2) if both streams join at the same angle, then the shorter is the tributary.

Similar 'laws' seem to govern the formation of flow system in quite different circumstances. In the arterial system of the body, as in the stream, the arteries tend to branch at different angles, according to a marked hierarchical system. As d'Arcy Thompson says (1917):

'. . . (1) If an artery bifurcates into two equal branches, these branches come off at equal angles to the main stem. (2) If one of the two branches be smaller than the other, then the main branch, or continuation of the original artery, makes with the latter a smaller angle than does the smaller or "lateral" branch. (3) All branches which are so small that they scarcely seem to weaken or diminish the main stem come off from it at a large angle, from about 70° to 90°.'

Naturally, there have been attempts to determine why such regularity should be found in various natural flow systems. Cohn (1954) studied the problem of supplying blood to a cube divided successively into smaller parts; his expressions for the number of branches, the length and resistance of each branch, and the total resistance of the system to flow, approximated closely to the results obtained clinically. Steinhaus (in Chorley and Haggett, 1967) attempted a similar analysis on two dimensions and he too found that a dendritic pattern enabled him to cover the greatest possible number of points on the surface in the most economical manner. As Haggett says, it is almost as if the tree were 'trying to get away from itself in the manner of self-repulsing magnets strung together . . . or a tree stretching its branches to get as near as possible to the available atmosphere.'

One practical application of trees in planning terms is known as the *connector* problem, which may be considered in terms of cities to be connected by roads, wards in a hospital or colleges in a university to be connected by covered ways. Other applications might be in the connexion of services—electric conduits, heating mains, gas, water or oil pipes. In each case, the problem is to build the whole network as cheaply as possible. In the simplest case, there may be three terminal points, *A*, *B* and *C*. It will be enough to build one of the possible *arcs ABC*, *ACB*, *BAC* and, by inspection, it should be possible to decide which side of the triangle is the longest and leave that connexion out. For more complex layouts too, the cheapest connecting network must be a tree—otherwise one could leave out a link in the circuit and the points would still be connected.

Ore (1963) suggests an *economy rule*. As a first step, one joins the two points with the shortest, and therefore the cheapest, connecting link. One then extends the tree by adding successively the cheapest possible links until all the points have been connected. If at any stage several links appear to cost the same then it does not matter which one is connected. A tree thus constructed is called an *economy tree*. Such techniques have obvious applications in the analysis of circulation patterns for people, traffic, services, sewage and so on. Burberry (1970) discusses some of these in detail.

Circuit Geometry

As we have seen, a tree is a graph which has no circuits. The only way of moving, say, from terminal vertex *A* to terminal vertex *B* is by means of a route from *A*, which takes us back towards the root, to some higher order vertex *C*, and then out again to *B*. If the route involved passing some intermediate vertex more than once, then we must have looped back on ourselves, but once all such loops have been eliminated and we can move from *A* to *B* without passing any vertex twice, then the direct route is called an arc. If the terminal vertices *A* and *B* are directly connected, we shall have not just an arc but a closed loop or path. We shall be able to move from *A*, through the various vertices of the original arc to *B* and then back to *A* again. An arc such as this, which returns to its starting point, is called a *circuit*; and once our graph contains circuits, it is no longer a tree. If circuits are possible, so are other kinds of circular paths.

One can measure the *connectivity* of a graph which distinguishes it from a tree in various ways, and Haggett (1965) has described several of these. One can measure the *centrality* of a particular vertex by counting the maximum number of edges in the shortest path by which that particular vertex is con-

nected to any other vertex in the system. This is its König number as described in Kansky (1963). In a transport system delays usually occur at
intersections, so a vertex with a low König number will be 'near' the centre
of the system in terms of transport time (Figure 12.6).

The connectivity of the system itself may be given by the *Beta* index (Figure
12.7), which relates the number of vertices v and the number of edges e in two
fundamental ways. It is found, quite simply, by dividing the number of edges

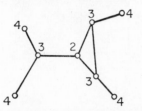

Figure 12.6—Centrality of vertices measured by König numbers

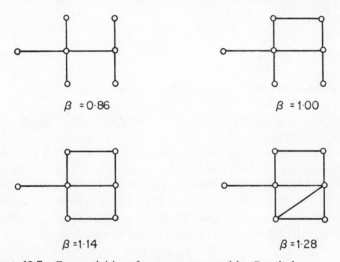

Figure 12.7—Connectivities of systems measured by *Beta* index

by the number of vertices: e/v; and Kansky gives four examples, increasing
in connectivity: they each have seven vertices, but the number of edges
increases from 6 to 9. Where β is less than 1·0, then the graph is a tree; where
β is equal to 1·0, then it has only one circuit; and where β is greater than 1·0,
then the graph represents a complex network.

The diameter of a graph is a rather crude measure obtained by counting
the number of edges in the *arc* between the two most distant vertices. Obviously the diameter increases as more vertices are added to the graph, and
falls as improved connexions are made between them (Figure 12.8).

Kansky uses this concept of diameter to calculate the *shape index* for a network, which is given by C/d, where C is the total mileage for, say, a transportation network and d is the diameter; but the diameter can be measured in several ways. Although the diameter of the most complex graph in Figure 12.8 is 4, there are three possible routes between the two most distant vertices. In a real transport system these might represent substantially different

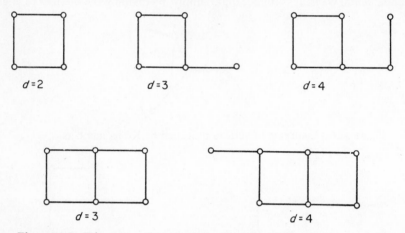

Figure 12.8—Diameters of graphs (after Kansky, 1963)

mileages; and to obtain the diameter Kansky takes not the smallest, but the mean value of these.

A large network may be so complex that these and other measurements cannot be obtained directly from the graph. In that case, one might resort to *matrices* and Haggett (1967) shows various ways in which these have been applied. In one of the simplest, derived from Pitts (1965), one simply plots the number of edges in the shortest path connecting each pair of vertices. This short-path matrix $(A(P))$ might take the following form:

$$A(P) = \begin{pmatrix} 0 & 1 & 2 & 3 & 2 & 3 & 4 \\ 1 & 0 & 1 & 2 & 1 & 2 & 3 \\ 2 & 1 & 0 & 1 & 2 & 1 & 2 \\ 3 & 2 & 1 & 0 & 3 & 2 & 1 \\ 2 & 1 & 2 & 3 & 0 & 1 & 2 \\ 3 & 2 & 1 & 2 & 1 & 0 & 1 \\ 4 & 3 & 2 & 1 & 2 & 1 & 0 \end{pmatrix}$$

Other forms of matrix may be drawn. In Pitts's X matrix, a direct link between two vertices by means of a single edge is indicated by 1, and all other links are indicated by 0. He then raises this matrix to the power of the graph's diameter, in this case 8, plotting to and from each settlement the

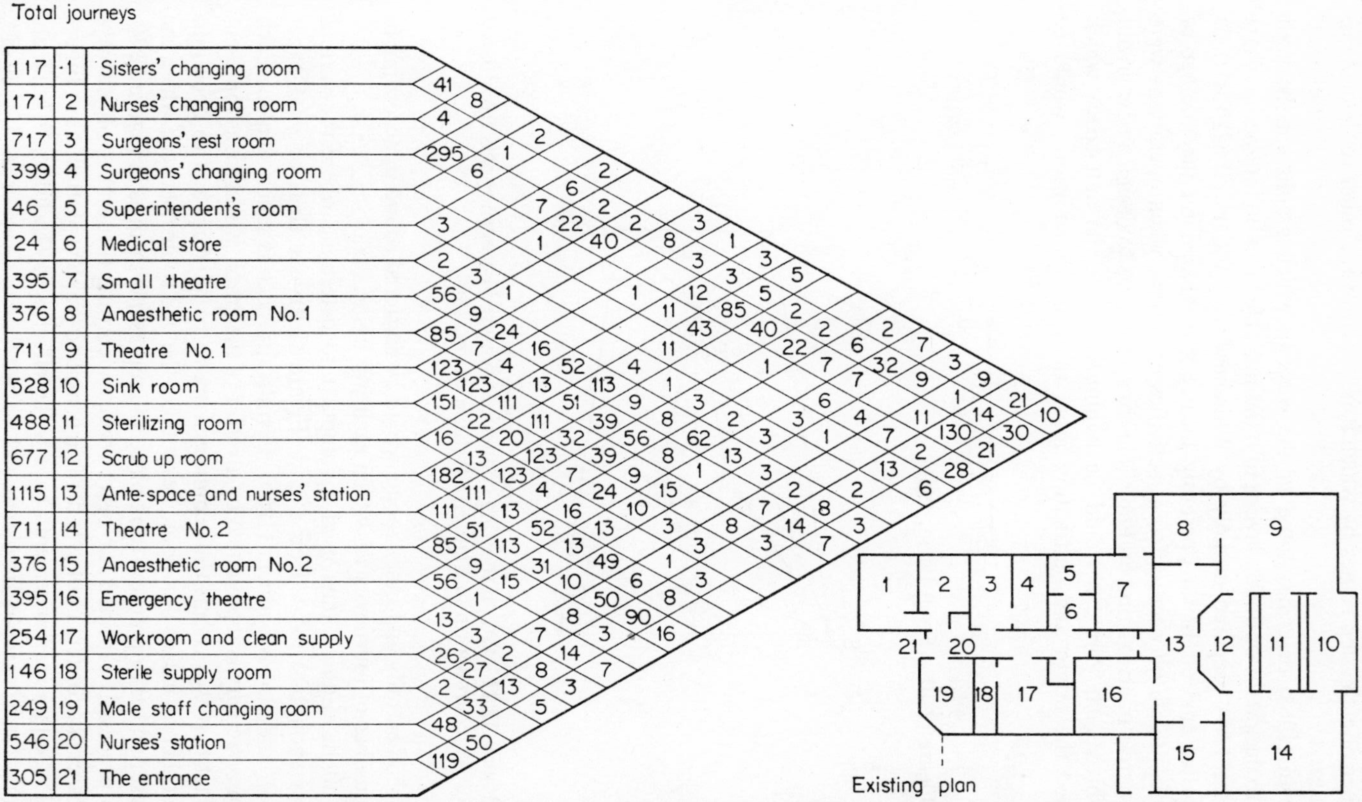

Total journeys

Total journeys	No.	Room
117	1	Sisters' changing room
171	2	Nurses' changing room
717	3	Surgeons' rest room
399	4	Surgeons' changing room
46	5	Superintendent's room
24	6	Medical store
395	7	Small theatre
376	8	Anaesthetic room No.1
711	9	Theatre No.1
528	10	Sink room
488	11	Sterilizing room
677	12	Scrub up room
1115	13	Ante-space and nurses' station
711	14	Theatre No.2
376	15	Anaesthetic room No.2
395	16	Emergency theatre
254	17	Workroom and clean supply
146	18	Sterile supply room
249	19	Male staff changing room
546	20	Nurses' station
305	21	The entrance

Existing plan

Figure 12.9—Association chart showing the numbers of journeys between the different rooms of an operating theatre suite during a typical day's working (from Whitehead and Eldars, 1964)

number of eight-step routes by which it is linked to the other settlements in the matrix.

Levin (1964) describes some of the ways in which graphs can be used '. . . to decide the optimum layout of buildings'. He takes an interaction chart (Figure 12.9) prepared initially by Whitehead and Eldars (1964) for their computer analysis of an operating theatre suite, based on the number of journeys taken between different activities or rooms, when operations were in progress in an existing building. The aim, then, was to design a new layout in which such journeys would be minimized; thus the ante-space which formed the origin and destination more than any other room, would be

F   G

Figure 12.10—(From Levin, 1964)

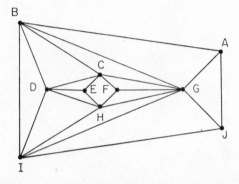

Figure 12.11—Graph showing connexions required between rooms 8 to 16 of the chart shown in Figure 12.9 (from Levin, 1964)

planned centrally and other rooms would be clustered round it, according to the number of journeys with which each was associated.

Whitehead and Eldars used a computer to determine where the various rooms should be located on a grid (Figure 12.9)—see their original paper (1964), and also Broadbent (1966). Levin's approach is much simpler. Each room or activity is represented by a vertex of the graph, whilst edges represent the fact that two rooms thus connected are to be adjacent and to open into each other by means of a door. Levin takes the two rooms between which the largest number of journeys took place and represents them as in Figure 12.10. This process is repeated for other rooms according to number of journeys in descending order, until eventually a complete graph is plotted, as in Figure 12.11. Certain rearrangements have to be effected as the graph is built up, because Levin's graphs are planar and no two lines can ever cross. If they did,

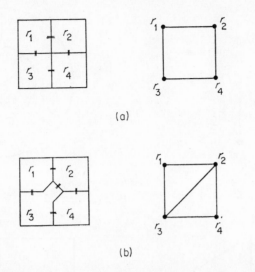

(a)

(b)

Figure 12.12—Plans mapped in the form of graphs which retain essential connexions between rooms. Technically, each graph is a *dual* of the equivalent plan, and vice versa (from Levin, 1964)

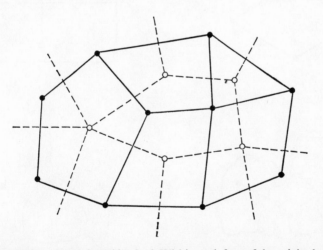

Figure 12.13—A graph and its dual. Within each face of the original graph, including the infinite face, a point is plotted which becomes a vertex of the dual. This new system of vertices is then connected by edges, so that each edge of the original graph is crossed once, and thus the dual is formed. At the simplest level of application the original graph might represent activities (at the vertices) and appropriate links between them (the edges). The dual might then represent a space-separating structure

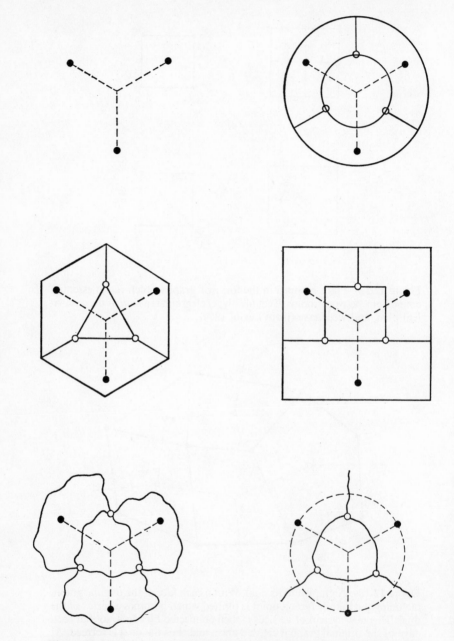

Figure 12.14—A given graph may have many duals; five possibilities are shown here for the same graph (from Cousin, 1970)

then the graph would show a system of room relationships which could not be planned physically, unless one placed another vertex—and thus another room—at the point of intersection. He takes the simple case of four rooms which one wants to plan so that each opens into all the others, as in Figure 12.12(a). In this case each room opens into two of the others. One can even arrange a diagonal connexion, shown in Figure 12.12(b).

Levin describes an elaborate procedure for transforming his graphs into

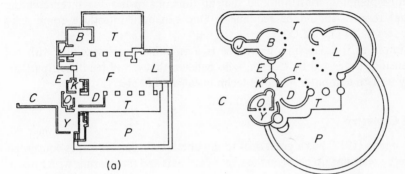

(a)

(b)

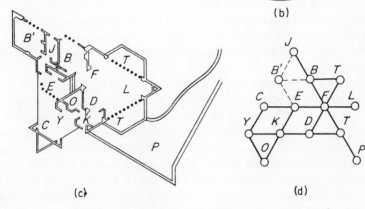

(c)

(d)

B	bedroom	F	family room	O	office
B'	Sundt bedroom	J	bathroom	P	pool
C	car port				
D	dining-room	K	kitchen	T	terrace
E	entrance	L	living-room	Y	yard

Figure 12.15—March and Steadman (1971) show how three Frank Lloyd Wright houses, designed for different clients on different sites, are really duals of the same graph. (*By courtesy of RIBA Publications Ltd.*)

(a) Life 'House for a family of $5,000–$6,000 income', 1938
(b) Ralph Jester House, Palos Verdes, California, 1938
(c) Vigo Sundt House, near Madison, Wisconsin, 1941. (This has an extra bedroom, *B'*.)
(d) Graph of space and room linkages for the three projects

spatial layouts, but he could have used the *dual* graph for this purpose. This is simply a graph drawn in such a way that each vertex of the original becomes a domain in the dual, and each domain in the original becomes a vertex (Figure 12.13). Cousin (1970) pursues this idea in some detail; he points out that once the links, say, between activities or spaces have been represented on the original graph, one can draw the dual in many ways, most of which appear 'organic' in architectural terms although one can introduce various planning constraints so that all domains in the dual—representing actual rooms—should be rectilinear. One can even introduce room sizes (Figures 12.14 and 12.15).

Simple as it is, Levin's technique is a valuable one, especially with the extensions suggested by Cousin, who believes that it will lend itself particularly well to computer graphics techniques (see Chapter 15).

Cell Geometry

Thompson (1917) has a great deal to say about cell geometry. It is concerned with the relationship between the sizes of animals and their forms, with rates of growth, and above all with how they share certain fundamental geometric structures. He shows how simple cells, drops of oil in water, bubbles and other phenomena are all related by principles of surface tension, how the splash from a drop of milk takes similar forms to certain flowers, drops of ink in water, jellyfish.

He has a great deal to say about hexagonal forms, which are found when spherical cells, bubbles and so on are packed together and, most particularly, in honeycomb. His analysis of honeycomb in terms of cell geometry shows the dangers to which earlier analysts succumbed—from Pappus of Alexandria to Lord Brougham—of assuming too much geometrical knowledge, accuracy and sense of economy in the use of wax on the part of bees; but Thompson points out that the hexagons which the bees form are by no means mathematically accurate. The cell walls vary in thickness, the angles are curved and there is some variation in size. Yet it is still not clear how the form comes about. According to Willem (quoted Thompson, 1917) each cell begins with a hemispherical basin, on which the bee plasters wax in a fairly haphazard fashion. Eventually, each bee buries its head in one of the basins, scrapes, smooths and gradually rams home the wax. Gradually the circular cells are expanded to fill the spaces between them, and the familiar hexagonal form is seen. Yet, according to Thompson, that is not adequate as an explanation. If this were all that happened, the cells would be much less regular than in fact they are. He suggests, therefore, that the properties of the material itself must be taken into account, that just as soap bubbles packed together assume a hexagonal configuration, for reasons of surface tension, so wax in its warm and fluid state will assume the same configuration.

As Thompson and others have shown, the hexagon possesses a conjunction of properties which makes it particularly appropriate for many natural (and man-made) forms. In the first place, soap bubbles, cracks in mud or varnish and, most particularly, living cells, tend to meet in Y-shaped conjunctions of threes. It is, of course, the simplest possible conjunction of elements, much simpler, say, than the conjunction of four squares, although the *average*, according to Thompson, is 120°. If this is so, then the polygonal areas themselves, on average, must be hexagons.

Inherent in the nature of the hexagon, therefore, is the property that it will *pack* close together with others of its kind. This is true of the square too, and the triangle, but no other polygonal figure shares it. The hexagon has two further advantages, however, which stem from its approximation to a circle. The circle encloses a greater surface area in relation to its circumference than any other plane figure; the hexagon is closer to a circle than either the triangle or the square, and therefore it is more economical in this respect than either of them. Similarly, the radius of a circle is constant and therefore accessibility from the centre to any point on the circumference (*the maximum radial distance*) is also constant. That is not true of the triangle or the square. The square is about half as efficient as the circle in this respect, whereas the hexagon is about four-fifths as efficient as the circle (Haggett, 1965). It is not surprising therefore that, just as Thompson found it profitable to analyse natural forms in terms of hexagons, Christaller (1933) and Losch (1940) should use the same figure to investigate the geographical structure of human settlements. Nor is it surprising that Buchanan should opt for the hexagon as the most economical format for road patterns in his report *Traffic in Towns* (1963).

Euler's formula may be extended to show 'what regular polygons of equal area may be used to completely fill a plane without overlapping or unused spaces' (Losch, 1954). These are known as *tesselations* and the condition is fulfilled only when:

$$1 + \frac{p}{p^*} = \frac{p}{2}$$

where p is the number of edges at each vertex, and p^* is the number of edges bounding each cell. With regular triangles, for instance

$$1 + \frac{6}{3} = \frac{6}{2}$$

whilst squares and other rectangles ($p = p^* = 4$) and hexagons ($p = 3$, $p^* = 6$) also satisfy the equation (Figure 12.16). O'Keefe points out that irregular tesselation can also be formed from the square, the triangle and the hexagon (Figure 12.17).

As we have seen, of all the regular polygons which allow for such tesselations, the hexagon is the one which contains the maximum area for the minimum edge length, allowing also the greatest accessibility (i.e. the shortest distance between the centre of the cell to all points on its boundary).

However, whilst these properties of the hexagon are of undoubted value when the space to be divided is an unbounded plane, there are problems, as Haggett shows, when the plane itself is small, as it might be in the case of an

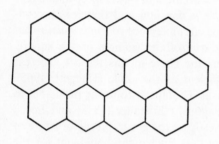

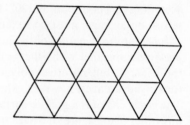

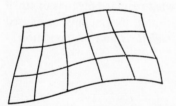

Figure 12.16—Regular tesselations

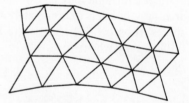

Figure 12.17—Irregular tesselations

island. He applies the essential feature of the hexagon—the vertex with three connecting edges at 120° to each other—and applies this to the island of Formosa which has seven maritime counties, that is to say none of them is completely surrounded by other counties. Roughly, Formosa is an ellipse and on the map there are five places at which three counties meet in a single point. These can be represented by vertices with edges at 120° co-equal angles, and seven of these edges run out, as county boundaries, to the sea. But the other four edges represent internal divisions; Haggett shows that with three counties, one needs no such internal walls, with four cells, one needs one, with five cells two, and so on. Thompson (1942) calls such internal divisions *polar furrows*. With four cells the polar furrow would be a single edge (equivalent to one side of a hexagon), and with five cells it would be two such edges meeting, probably at a common vertex. With six cells various arrangements of polar furrow are possible—Thompson indicates three—and the number of possibilities increases with the number of cells. Bruckner estimates that for 13 cells there are 50,000 possible arrangements of polar furrows, and for 16 cells something like 30 million.

The geometric domes of Buckminster Fuller represent one way of applying these properties to building structures whilst Critchlow (1969) has worked out many permutations of cell-like forms which may be packed together three-dimensionally. Some of them may have architectural applications although one might suppose that the minimum requirement for any cell which is to be so used would be a horizontal floor!

Map Colouring

One of the key problems in topology is concerned with the number of different colours required to distinguish the different countries on a map. Again this may seem remote from architectural design but, in fact, it has important

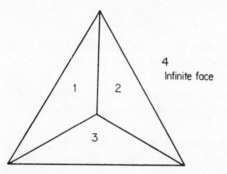

Figure 12.18—Map colouring. Each of the four faces, including the infinite face, requires a separate colour

implications as to the number of rooms, say, which can be reached from one circulation space. The British mathematician Cayley suggested in 1879 that any map could be coloured properly by means of four colours and, although this has yet to be proved, it has led to many important developments in graph theory.

Clearly the tetrahedron graph shown in Figure 12.18 requires four colours, one for each of its faces, including the infinite face. A square graph with four faces meeting at the centre, could be completed in three colours—two colours alternating in the faces within the square, and one for the infinite face. Suppose now we take one vertex in a more complicated graph with any even number of edges meeting in it. This section of the graph could be completed in two colours, alternating round the vertex. If instead of an even number of edges we had an odd number it would be necessary to add one more colour, making a total of three, to complete the odd face.

If we now draw a small circle round the vertex, this will give us an additional, central face, and the original edges will now meet the circle in vertices of *degree three* (Figure 12.19). The three faces surrounding the circle can now be coloured as before—we required three colours for an odd number of vertices—and the circle will require a fourth. Similarly, if we draw a larger circle as the boundary of our graph, the infinite face beyond it could be

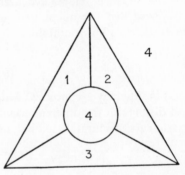

Figure 12.19—A fifth face can be added and, because it does not touch the infinite face, the same colour can be used again

coloured in the same way as the central circle. It is apparent, therefore, that any graph, map or plan, however complex, can be coloured with four colours.

If this is true of colouring, it is also true of spaces opening into each other and therefore it will never be possible for more than four spaces to open directly into each other.

Topology

Just as there is a relationship between the number of vertices and edges of a graph or tree so, like Descartes before him (1640), Euler discovered in 1752 that there is a fundamental relationship between the corners (vertices, V), the sides (edges, E) and the faces (F) of a regular polyhedron, or three-dimensional solid and he defined this relationship:

$$V - E + F = 2$$

For a cube it reads

$$8 - 12 + 6 = 2$$

And for a polyhedron with a hole through it, the formula becomes

$$V - E + F = 1$$

If we made our cube, or any other simple polyhedron, out of thin rubber we could cut out one of the faces and fold the remainder flat out on a plane surface. Their shapes would be distorted, of course, but there would be the same number of vertices and edges and each plane would still form a polygon but there would be one plane less. It has in fact become a planar network, or *graph*.

Once we start distorting surfaces in this way, whilst retaining their essential relationships, we are well into the field of topology, a branch of mathematics which stems, ultimately, from Euler's original problem. It was first developed in Listing's *Vorstudien zur Topologie* (1847) and one of the finest surveys still, is to be found in *What is Mathematics* by Courant and Robbins (1941). They give the proof for Euler's formula and describe the enormous range of possibilities inherent in topological transformation. A plane, square sheet of rubber, for instance, can be stretched into a circle, a triangle or any other polygon, a *C*-shape, a *U*-shape, any shape in fact which does not involve tearing, cutting, or joining up two edges which originally were free.

So it is not possible, as a topological transformation, to form a sphere from a plane sheet of rubber; but if one started with a sphere, it could be distorted into a cube, a tetrahedron or any other polygon, not to mention a saucer-shape, a bowl, a wineglass—any shape, in fact, with one or more depressions in it. Nevertheless it could not be transformed into a cup: a cup has a handle which contains a 'hole'. So to form a cup one would have to start with a *torus*—a doughnut or car-tyre shape containing one hole at the start. The torus could then be pushed and pulled into any form containing one hole, but it could not be used to form a teapot which contains at least two holes, one for the handle and one•for the spout. And so it goes on. The essential point in topology is that each part of the original figure shall correspond to one point and one point only, of the figure into which it is transformed. Any property of the original figure which may be transformed by topological transformation is called a *topological property* of the figure.

One way of testing the topological equivalence of two figures is to test their connectivity. Given two circular figures—a disc and a disc with a hole in it, such as a washer—one could draw a circle on each of them. In the first case, the circle could be 'shrunk' down to a single point within the *domain* of the original disc, but in the second case it cannot for in the shrinking it would pass over the boundary between the domain of the washer and the hole at its centre. The domain of the disc is *simply connected*, whereas the domain of the washer is *multiply connected*; but the washer can be converted into a simply connected domain by a single radial cut, which will allow deformation into a circle again without a hole in it. Similarly a domain with two holes in it could be converted into a simply connected one by two cuts, one with three holes by three cuts, and so on.

One of the most important topological properties of figures is so obvious, at first sight, that it hardly seems worth stating: that if we draw, say, a closed circle on a sheet of rubber, it will always separate two domains, one inside and the other outside itself, whatever topological deformations the rubber is subjected to. It is not so obvious when one considers intricate and convoluted figures instead of simple circles, although Jordan's *Curve Theorem* still holds true:

'A simple closed curve C in the plane divides the plane into exactly two domains, an inside and an outside.

And further: whenever any point P in the inner part is connected to a point Q in the outer part by a continuous curve L, then L intersects C.

However, Jordan's proof was faulty, because it was exceedingly difficult to define such terms as 'inside' and 'outside'.

Set Theory

A further branch of the new mathematics, which is often confused with topology, is described generally as set theory. Strictly speaking, it is not a branch of mathematics at all, but a branch of logic; and even if the nature of its symbolism and the formal way in which it is presented make it *look* like mathematics, there is nothing mathematical about the content. Designers, on the whole, are used to working with visual symbols; it need not surprise us, therefore, to find that as logicians sought increasing precision in their reasoning they found words inadequate, so they invented a set of symbols which enabled them to 'concentrate upon what is essential in a given context', and set rules for using those symbols. Certain mediaeval philosophers had used symbolism of a kind for this purpose, but the first serious study was undertaken by Leibnitz, who was looking for a *universal scientific language* and a *calculus of reasoning.*

If Leibnitz implanted the idea, the development of symbolic logic as we know it today was really the work of George Boole, who taught logic and mathematics at Queens College in Cork. As Boole said:

'That which renders logic possible, is the existence in our minds of general notions —our ability to conceive of a class, and to designate its individual members by a common name . . . Assuming the notion of class, we are able, from any conceivable collection of objects, to separate by a mental act, those which belong to the given class, and to contemplate them apart from the rest.'

He goes on to say that the process may be repeated. We might conceive of another class, and designate other members to it, and so on. Some members may belong to more than one class and, by selecting a particular series of classes, we may eventually identify the one member which belongs to all of them.

Such is the nature of symbolic logic but, since Boole's death in 1864, it has been developed in many ways. Most significant from our point of view is

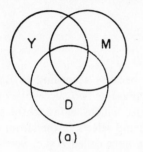

Y = your meaning of the word architecture

M = my meaning of the word architecture

D = dictionary definition of the word architecture

(a)

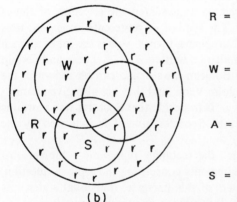

R = the set of all rooms in a building

W = the subset of all rooms which must have windows

A = the subset of all rooms which must have full air conditioning

S = the subset of all rooms which need a high level of sound insulation

(b)

Figure 12.20—Venn diagrams: (b) is a more complex idea, showing the set of all rooms in a building with its various subsets

John Venn's invention of a diagram (Figure 12.20(a)) in which each set is indicated by a simple closed curve.

In spite of its tremendous power the Venn diagram can be exceedingly simple to use in demonstrating some complex ideas (Figure 12.20(b)). The most sophisticated use of set theory in design is to be found in Christopher Alexander's work (1963, 1966) and this is described in Chapter 14.

In conventional algebra an expression such as $A + B = C$ contains two kinds of signifier. The variables A, B and C represent numerical values, whilst the symbols $+$ and $=$ refer to mathematical operations such as addition, equalization and so on. An expression in Boolean algebra may look very similar, but the letters represent simple statements or logical premises whilst the mathematical symbols refer to operations in logic, such as 'AND', 'OR' and so on. One might take the first figure in deductive logic (see Chapter 16):

All men are mortal (statement A)
Socrates is a man (statement B)
Therefore Socrates is mortal (statement C)

and represent it by $A \times B = C$. This is so because according to Boole's *Laws of thought* the term $A \times B$ (or $A.B$) represents two successive operations. One selects all the objects in the universe which belong to the set of things we have decided to call A (i.e. all men) and selects further from these all those which belong to the set of things we have called B (i.e. Socrates); and thus one deduces that Socrates is mortal.

Other algebraic symbols represent other operations in Boole's symbolic logic; thus in $A + B$, the symbol $+$ represents the *aggregation* of all those things which are A or B or both, although originally, according to the conventions which Boole himself used, $+$ represented the selection of things which were A or B but not both. The symbol $-$ represents *exception*; thus if A stands for all men and B for Europeans, then $A - B$ is the set of all men who are not Europeans. This can also be written $B + \bar{A}$. These and certain other logic operations which the Boolean laws define can be shown in the diagrammatic form developed by John Venn, and they are also given names; thus our use of the equation $A.B = C$ to decide that Socrates was mortal is an example of the AND operation—Socrates himself is indicated by the shaded area in Figure 12.21.

In each of these Venn diagrams, the rectangle represents a 'universe of discourse', a *set* of all possible statements concerning the topic in question, whereas the circles represent *subsets* of this universe, individual statements A and B, which are being compared, combined or otherwise manipulated to give a third statement C, which is represented by the shaded area. In the AND diagram, for instance, C is 'true' if both A and B are true; but it is 'false' if A or B, or both A and B are false. Thus one might say:

All birds are black (statement A)
All swans are birds (statement B)
Therefore all swans are black (statement C)

which is perfectly *valid* logic, but nevertheless untrue because statement A is untrue.

In this example each statement is 'true' or 'false'. It is or is not contained within a particular set; there are no halfway positions. Symbolic logic gener-

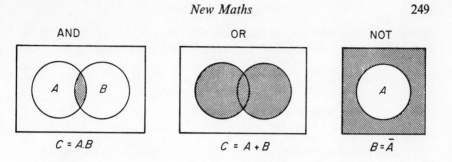

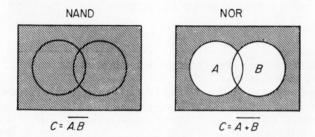

Figure 12.21—Venn diagrams showing various propositions of symbolic logic. Each of these concepts in logic can be represented by circuitry in the computer, and each such 'logic element' has an associated *truth table* which lists all the possible states of inputs A and B, together with their corresponding outputs, C. The truth table for an AND element is as follows:

$C = A.B$	Inputs		Output
	A	B	C
	0	0	0
	0	1	0
	1	1	1
	1	0	0

ally deals in 'two-value' statements of this kind which is why it has been so important in developing the logic of computers. An electronic circuit also can be switched 'on' *or* 'off', thus Boole's *Laws of thought* can all be represented electronically; the *logic unit* of a digital computer contains a number of logic elements (or *gates*) which correspond to the forms described above: *and, or, not* and so on.

In addition to this, the computer can also perform arithmetical operations —addition, subtraction, division and exponentiation (raising numbers by various powers). These too depend on whether a particular circuit is switched 'on' *or* 'off' and thus all numbers must be reduced to *binary arithmetic*; each shift to the left means that a digit is multiplied by 10, so in binary arithmetic a similar shift represents multiplication by 2.

position of digit	0	0	0	0	0	0
represents	16	8	4	2	1	0

thus 000010 represents 1
001010 represents 5 and so on.

We shall return to this shortly, but meanwhile we ought to look at certain developments of Boolean algebra, and particularly *set theory*, in which the membership, or otherwise, of a particular set is expressed by mathematical symbols. A set in this sense means any aggregation of objects which have

Table 12.2

$A \subset B$	all the elements of set A are *contained* in set B
$B \supset A$	set B *contains* set A
$A \cap B$	intersection of set A and set B (those elements which are common to both set A and set B, equivalent to $A.B$)
$A \cup B$	*union* of set A and set B (those elements which are in set A or set B *or* in both, equivalent to $A + B$)

something in common. Alexander (1964) describes several examples. Thus the set of fruit in a dish includes all those objects which possess the essential attributes of fruit. They will be edible, non-poisonous and so on. Within this set there will be various subsets—apples, oranges, bananas, grapes—and within these subsets there may be further subsets—green apples, red apples,

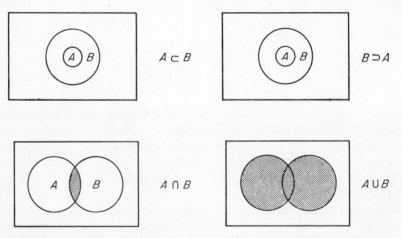

Figure 12.22—Venn diagram showing containment, intersection and union of sets

sweet apples, sour apples and so on. Some of the subsets will overlap; there may be sweet green apples, sweet red ones, sour green apples and so on. Peanc (quoted in Newman, 1960) provides one set of symbols for analysing such sets but his symbolism is by no means generally agreed. The concepts shown in Table 12.2 are typical. These too can be represented by Venn diagrams (see Figure 12.22). These begin to indicate the enormous power of such diagrams for many kinds of analysis.

CHAPTER 13

Development of Design Methods

By the early 1960s, systems engineering, ergonomics, operational research, information theory and cybernetics, not to mention the new maths and computing, were all available to the design theorist in highly developed forms, and several events marked the emergence of design method from these sources as a discipline in its own right. This was seen most clearly at the Ulm school of design, the *Hochschüle für Gestaltung*, where Maldonado and others sought to establish a 'practical anthropology' in which the designer would be integrated very closely into society, operating 'at the nerve centres of our industrial civilization, precisely where industry makes the most important decisions affecting our daily lives' (Maldonado, 1958).

The Hochschüle, in fact, had been founded in 1949 by Inge Aicher-Scholl with Otl Aicher, encouraged by the United States' High Commissioner, as a memorial to members of her family who had been victims of the Nazis. In 1951 they invited Max Bill to become director; he formalized the curriculum, designed the buildings and became head of two departments—architecture and product design.

However, by 1956, Bill's colleagues at the Hochschüle were striving to free themselves from the Bauhaus legacy which Bill brought to it; he was replaced by a Board of Directors with Maldonado as chairman, who pursued a much tougher, scientifically orientated line. Otl Aicher became rector in 1962, to be succeeded by Maldonado in 1964 and Herbert Ohl in 1966. During Ulm's second 'scientific design' stage the 'art' and intuition which Bill had stressed were to be replaced by analytical methodology. One approach to this methodology was described by Hans Gugelot, lecturer in industrial design at the Hochschüle and designer of those cult objects of the 1960s, the *Braun* fan-heater, record-player and other electrical appliances. Gugelot's design method (1963) was as follows:

1. Information stage: one finds out all one can about the firm one is designing for, its production programme, any emphasis or shift of emphasis towards a particular class of product. One must review similar products of other firms and find out generally all one can about the field one is working in.
2. Research stage: one must find out all one can about the *users*; too often, decisions on user 'needs' are made by a committee which, by reason of status alone, is incapable of knowing what users really want. One tries to assess the *context* in which the product will be used; at the same time, one looks into function, possible production methods—especially new processes and developments,

252

3. Design phase: here the designer can be creative; one looks for new *formal* possibilities (Gugelot's own designs, for Braun at least, were all contained in extremely elegant 'little grey boxes'). Where no new formal idea is forthcoming, then one must fall back on variations of existing forms (Gugelot mistrusted this because, as he said, 'I fear that our own work too could be made the theme of such modifications'). During this phase, one must bear in mind the needs of other people who will be involved in making the product.

4. Decision stage: one seeks a favourable decision from sales and production managements. If the design is radically new, then there may be great difficulties in 'selling' it to them. An adventurous sales manager might be persuaded to take a calculated risk, but production can *only* be persuaded by sound, technical argument.

5. Calculation: this is a matter of adjusting the design to specific production standards and if it is done intensively, then the design itself can be utterly spoiled. Production departments often fail to realize that alterations which seem slight to them often have grave formal consequences. There must be continuous two-way communication.

6. Model-making: one builds a prototype, a working model which is a great help in production planning, and helps demonstrate the limits of any technical risk involved.

Gugelot wrote as a practical and highly successful designer; indeed most of the staff at the Hochschüle acted as consultants to industry. Their work had a common emphasis, which was reflected in their teaching methods, in that however rational their functional analysis of a design problem might be, the object itself, and especially its container, finished up as an extremely simple form, usually rectangular, and often grey. Clearly Ulm had learned a lot from the Bauhaus and it was no coincidence that a member of the original *de Stijl* group, Vordemberge-Gildewart, was a member of the Ulm staff. As his obituary in the Ulm journal states:

'Vordemberge-Gildewart limited himself to a few basic pictorial media: exactly defined forms of Euclidian geometry (triangles, rectangles, stripes, straight lines), clear colours, uniform textures. His pictures create an impression of mathematical precision and calculation: he named them deliberately, not "constructions"—for they were not planned mathematically—but "compositions". . . . They embody an artistic tradition which has done much to form the HfG.'

Virtually every product of Ulm displays those same characteristics, from the first complex grid exercises with which students started their course, to the products from typography to architecture which the staff produced. Ironic, perhaps, that the school whose name is associated most particularly with rational methodology could produce the most canonically perfect objects in the entire history of design.

Nevertheless, Maldonado certainly pursued a serious interest in the science of design exemplified in an article which he wrote with Bonsiepe (1964) entitled *Science and Design*. This consisted of a thorough review of the source disciplines, especially vector analysis, matrix analysis, linear programming, mathematical analyses of complexity, such as those by Moles (see Chapter

10), topology (see Chapter 12), cybernetics (Chapter 18), the theory of algorithms (Chapter 16), experimental psychology (Chapter 4) and, of course, anthropology.

As one might expect, this drew on the work of others which in the early 1960s had begun to establish design method as a discipline in its own right. Much of this, curiously enough, dated from 1962 when Morris Asimow produced his *Introduction to Design*, the first book in a projected series edited by James B. Reswick, of the Case Institute of Technology, under the general title of *The Fundamentals of Engineering Design*. Other titles in the series were to be *Reliability in Engineering Design* (Reethof and Queen), *Design with Computers* (Curry), *Communication in Engineering Design* (Rosenstein, Rathbone and 'Schneerer, 1964) and *Creativity in Engineering Design* (Alger and Hays, 1964). He describes design almost entirely in terms of information processes. It consists, he says, of 'the gathering, handling and creative organizing of information relevant to the problem situation; it prescribes the derivation of decisions which are optimized, communicated and tested or otherwise evaluated; it has an iterative character, for often, in the doing, new information becomes available or new insights are gained which require the repetition of earlier operations'. It is no coincidence that concepts referring to *information* which is *communicated* account for no less than 26 of the 64 words in Asimow's description.

His method derives very clearly from systems engineering and, like Hall, he describes two scales of operation, one of which loops within the other. Asimow calls the larger of his two scales of operation, his strategy, the design *morphology* and it comprises the following stages:

1. Feasibility study—Phase I
2. Preliminary design—Phase II
3. Detailed design
4. Planning the production process
5. Planning for distribution
6. Planning for consumption
7. Planning for retirement of the product

The detailed design phase is further subdivided:

1. Preparation for design
2. Overall design of subsystems
3. Overall design of components
4. Detailed design of parts
5. Preparation of assembly drawings
6. Experimental construction
7. Product test programme
8. Analysis and prediction
9. Redesign

Finally he outlines a general process for solving problems which he calls the design *process* and which also has its stages:

1. Analysis
2. Synthesis
3. Evaluation and decision—which is extended into
4. Optimization
5. Revision
6. Implementation

Asimow sees his design *morphology* as the vertical structure of engineering design and his problem-solving procedure (his design *process*) as its horizontal structure. Each step in his morphology contains the sequence of events which he describes as the design *process*. Again there is confusion here, because in all other studies which we have considered so far, the latter has been called the *decision sequence*, whilst the 'vertical' structure has represented the overall design process. Morphology, anyway, savours of inappropriate jargon—it is really a term from biology, concerned with a study of the *forms* of plants and animals, and it comes from the same root as *amorphous*. So from now on, we shall use the term *design process* to describe everything that happens, from the time a problem is first detected to the final completion of the design. According to the nature of the problem, this process will consist of one, or many more, complete acts of thought (in Dewey's sense) which we shall call *decision sequences*.

By the time Asimow's book was published, people other than engineers had become interested in what systems engineering, operational research and the other new fields had to offer in design. The first *Conference on Design Methods* was held at Imperial College, London, in September 1962 and, significantly, its organizers included a professor of Building Science, two engineers (one with an interest in aeronautical engineering), two industrial designers, an artist, a typographer, two architects and an ergonomist. In addition to this range of interests, the speakers also included a town planner, a psychologist, a computer engineer, a professor of logic and a cybernetician. The aim of the conference, as stated by the secretary, Peter Slann (an aeronautical engineer from Imperial College) was

'. . . to bring together people of common interest and purpose, people working individually and in groups in their own special fields of the arts and the sciences, exploring the application of scientific methods and knowledge to their own particular problems, and to break down the barriers that exist between one activity and another, attempting to discover the possible connections that link all creative activities. We had to seek a common language for communications between disciplines especially those hitherto completely unrelated.'

Many of these barriers arose from the fact that each of the new disciplines which seemed relevant to design had its own formidable jargon. To outsiders some of them seemed to have various features in common. Operational research and systems engineering shared certain techniques, so did cybernetics and information theory. Yet, in each case, the respective protagonists claimed that theirs was the original discipline and that the other was an offshoot or a subset which could be contained within it. One gained the impression of tightknit groups, each anxious to preserve its own identity and intent, as far as possible, on keeping the outsider out.

So, whilst the stated aim of the conference was a worthy one, it was fraught with difficulties and its primary finding too was rather misleading. Many of the speakers, from Christopherson who opened the conference to Page who closed it, detected a three-phase sequence at the centre of design method. They called it by various names; Christopherson spoke of

(a) conception
(b) realization
(c) communication

whilst Page used

(a) analysis
(b) synthesis
(c) evaluation

which look very like the central phases of the various decision sequences we have examined from Dewey, Drucker and others. Unfortunately, because the conference proceedings, edited by Jones and Thornley, were published as *Conference on Design Methods 1962* (1963) many people have supposed that these headings represented the central phases of the design process itself.

This need not have happened if Page's wise words summing up the conference had been heeded. He pointed out the fallacy of believing that a design process consists of a single, simple sequence 'straight through from analysis to synthesis to evaluation' because, as he said, 'in the majority of practical design situations, by the time you have produced this and found out that and made a synthesis, you realize you have forgotten to analyse something else here, and you have to go round the cycle and produce a modified synthesis, and so on. In practice you go round several times.' Page understood the essential difference between a design process and a decision sequence; that the former is a way of structuring the order in which a vast number of decisions may be made. Yet since 1962 a great deal of ingenuity has been expended in *trying* to equate the stages of a design process with the phases of a decision sequence. The most notable of these, by Archer (1963) and Mesarovic (1964) are shown in Figures 13.1 and 13.2, whilst Jones described several others in a later article under the heading *Design Methods Compared: Strategies* (1966).

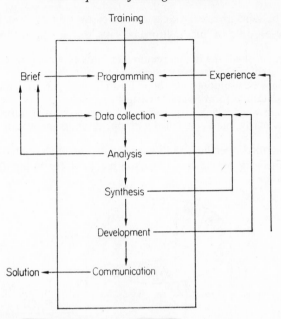

Figure 13.1—Systematic method for designers—an attempt to plot the whole sequence of the design process in a flow chart with feedback loops (Archer, 1963)

We shall discuss certain papers from the 1962 conference under various headings later, notably those by Alexander, Norris and Thornley but the most characteristic, in many ways, was that by Jones himself, which summed up the main stream of design method thinking at that time. His description of aims has been quoted many times:

'The method is primarily a means of resolving a conflict that exists between logical analysis and creative thought. The difficulty is that the imagination does not work well unless it is free to alternate between all aspects of the problem, in any order, and at any time, whereas logical analysis breaks down if there is the least departure from a systematic step-by-step sequence. It follows that any design method must permit both kinds of thought to proceed together if any progress is to be made. Existing methods depend largely on keeping logic and imagination, problem and solution, apart only by an effort of will, and their failures can largely be ascribed to the difficulty of keeping both these processes going separately in the mind of one person. So systematic design is primarily a means of keeping logic and imagination separate by external rather than internal means.'

This aim is achieved, according to Jones, by a system of notation which records *every* item of design information mechanically, and quite outside the memory. One must be careful to separate out imaginative ideas, and designs, from logical statements of information and requirements; he suggests that these might be kept physically apart, perhaps on opposite sides of the same folder. The recording of information, he says, developed in three stages:

1. Analysis in which all the design requirements are listed and reduced to a set of logically related performance specifications;
2. Synthesis in which solutions are found for individual performance specifications and then built up to form complete designs;
3. Evaluation in which alternative designs are tested against performance specifications—particularly those concerned with operation, manufacture and sales.

He then described specific techniques for use at each stage. Analysis will start with a meeting, at which each person reads out the thoughts which occur

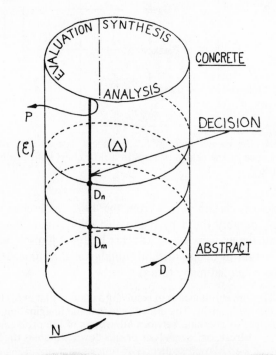

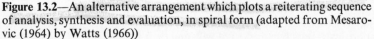

Figure 13.2—An alternative arrangement which plots a reiterating sequence of analysis, synthesis and evaluation, in spiral form (adapted from Mesarovic (1964) by Watts (1966))

to him on first acquaintance with the problem. These thoughts are combined, without any kind of editing or criticism, to form a *random list of factors*; they are then listed down the left-hand side of an interaction chart against a series of categories. The first category is the first factor; it may be concerned with size, cost or some other aspect of the problem, and further categories are generated by checking down the list of factors. Eventually each factor will be allocated to one or more categories and, after various sources of information have been tapped, it will be possible to prepare a further chart within which the *interactions* between categories are plotted. Jones describes various developments from this which are shown in Figures 13.3 to 13.9, based on ways of plotting the same information by means of interaction nets and topological diagrams.

He is now in a position to write performance specifications—*p-specs*—in which the requirements are expressed purely in terms of performance, with no reference to shape, actual materials, design and so on. He compares a design specification with a performance specification:

Design spec: Control panel mounted at 45°;

P-spec: Control panel to be visible from all operating positions.

As a final stage in the analysis, these p-specs are circulated to all interested parties, discussed, revised and eventually agreed.

Jones described various techniques for synthesis, such as brainstorming (see Chapter 17). He points out that systematic design differs from traditional methods at this stage, in that with the latter one works towards a single solution (a sketch design) which is then worked out later in detail, whereas with systematic design one looks for one or more partial solutions to each p-spec. These partial solutions may then be assembled in various permutations to give several combined solutions, from which a selection can then be made. Inevitably, the solutions to some p-specs will conflict with the solutions to others. One can plot their interactions on a chart and thus avoid these incompatibilities. Jones also described a *new solution plot* in which a graph is drawn plotting existing solutions against, say, shape and performance. Naturally they tend to cluster around certain positions on the graph and, given a knowledge of their performance, it will be possible to predict areas in which good new solutions could be found.

Finally, Jones considers evaluation, the various means of detecting deficiencies in the design *before* one is committed to it—as he puts it: '*before* final manufacturing drawings have been started, *before* production begins, *before* the product has been sold, *before* it has been installed and *before* it has been put to use.' As Jones says, any error which is detected after this stage will become progressively more expensive, as more time and money are invested in the design. Evaluation, traditionally, is a matter of experience and judgement but, as design becomes more complex, that becomes less effective. Jones advocates a method of statistical evaluation, based on the following methods:

1. The collection and assessment of available experience and judgement.
2. Simulation, using any available form of model, drawing analogue, computation and experiment.
3. Logical prediction, using interaction charts and nets to 'design' the multiplicity of situations which the product might meet during its working life.

4. Pre-engineering development by means of prototypes—small-scale production, sales and operation before full-scale production, sales and operation are undertaken.

He describes several graphic techniques for analysis which have since become commonplace in design; indeed many designers believe them to be synonymous with design method. The interaction chart and the random connexion diagram are probably the best known of these. Various architectural applications are shown in Figures 13.3 to 13.9.

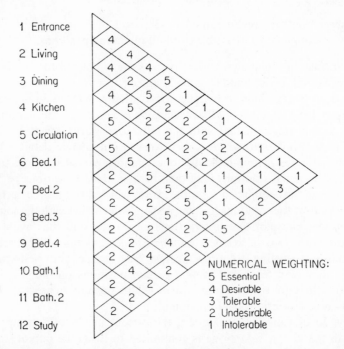

1 Entrance
2 Living
3 Dining
4 Kitchen
5 Circulation
6 Bed.1
7 Bed.2
8 Bed.3
9 Bed.4
10 Bath.1
11 Bath.2
12 Study

NUMERICAL WEIGHTING:
5 Essential
4 Desirable
3 Tolerable
2 Undesirable
1 Intolerable

Figure 13.3—Simple interaction chart showing connexions between rooms. Such charts are often produced with no indication as to what the connexions imply. In this case they refer to ease of movement between rooms and the numerical coding is suitable for computer anaylsis

The Design and Innovation Group organized a conference at the Birmingham College of Science and Technology (now the University of Aston) in September 1965, which was published as *The Design Method* (edited by S. A. Gregory, 1966). Again Jones's paper was devoted to the *State of the Art*, whilst the present author spoke on *Creativity*, but otherwise the conference was concerned largely with industrial matters. There was a Conference/Course at Ulm in April 1966, which was organized by Denzil Nield of the Department of Education and Science, for British teachers of architecture, on the subject of *The teaching of design—Design method in architecture*, at which a series of design method projects, based on systematic methods, was devised for use in schools of architecture. It was followed by a feedback meeting at Attingham Park in November, 1967 (Starling, 1966, 1968). In December 1967 the School of Architecture, Portsmouth College of Technology (now Polytechnic) organized a large conference on *Design Methods in Architecture* (Broadbent and Ward, 1969). In addition to these, a Design Research Society was formed in Britain (London, April 1966), a Design Methods Group (DMG) and an Environmental Design Research

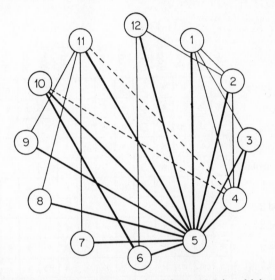

Figure 13.4—Connexions diagram derived from 13.3 in which all links of strength 3 (tolerable) and above are plotted with lines of appropriate thickness. Such a diagram may utilize information from several interaction charts; in this case the dotted lines show that certain rooms (4-10 and 4-11) are connected by their shared need for services (water and waste)

Association (EDRA) in the United States. DMG produces a newsletter and organized a large conference at MIT in April, 1968 (Moore, 1970), whilst EDRA meetings have been held at Chapel Hill (Sanoff and Cohn, 1969), Pittsburgh (Eastman and Archea, 1970) and Los Angeles (Mitchell, 1972). Other groups met on behalf of the Ministry of Public Building and Works in London during 1968 and 1969 to discuss *Computer-aided architectural design* (MPBW, 1969).

For many people, both proponents and opponents of systematic design, these charts and diagrams became the *substance* of systematic design. That was particularly true in schools of architecture where the diagrams themselves, beautifully redrawn, were pinned to the wall in place of the *project* drawings which had characterized final submission under the Beaux Arts system. A highly sensitive architect, such as Eric Lyons, could say to me: 'Design method, ah, yes. That's where they do all those charts and diagrams instead of designing buildings?'

He was right, and we shall look at some of the more extreme examples shortly; but before we do so, we ought to remember that parallel with these developments a number of design theorists were trying, conscientiously, to look at what the designer actually did in practice, and to formalize the design process on this basis.

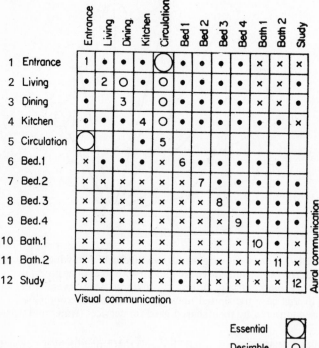

Figure 13.5—The pattern of *functional* links within certain building types, such as houses, is often so complex that a connexions diagram based on them, such as 13.4, becomes too complex for use in practice. It may be preferable in such cases to prepare a chart showing *environmental* compatibility, indicating the degree to which it may be desirable, or undesirable, to see and/or hear from one room to another. The coding system used here allows for immediate visual inspection

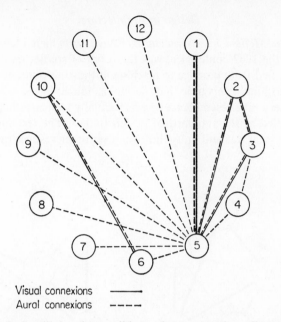

Visual connexions ————
Aural connexions ————

Figure 13.6—It will then be possible to plot a connexions diagram, based on 13.5, which gives a much clearer picture of how the house should be organized than 13.4

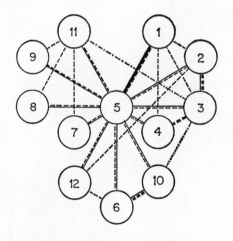

Coding of connexions
Environmental (visual + aural) ————
Functional (communications) ————
Functional (shared services) —·—·—

Figure 13.7—Combination and topological distortion of connexions diagrams, based on 13.6. The most connected space (5: circulation) is plotted first, rooms with strong proximity relations to it are plotted next and so on. Once all the rooms have been plotted, connexions from other diagrams, e.g. 13.5 can be drawn in

The *Design Method in Architectural Education*, which Dennis Thornley described at the 1962 conference, was the result of studies initiated in 1958, when he returned from practice to teaching at the University of Manchester. It was clear to him at this time that 'design 'as taught in the school of architecture had very little resemblance to what actually happened in practice, and he was appalled at the standard of design tuition. The terminology of the Beaux Arts system was still in use but whatever other vestiges remained were

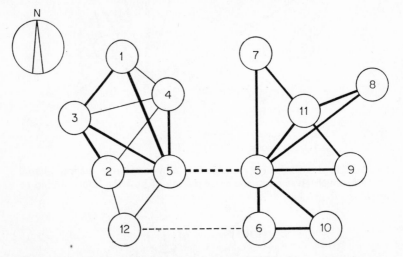

Figure 13.8—Further topological distortion of 13.7, taking orientation etc. into account, e.g. bedrooms, where possible (8, 9) face east, living room (2) faces west, kitchen (4) north, etc. It has been decided also to split the house on to two levels, linked by the circulation (5). One functional link—bedroom (6) to study (12)—may have to be broken

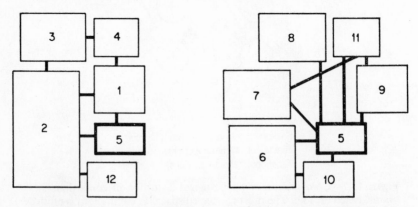

Figure 13.9—Further topological distortion of 13.7 to take account of room sizes. This needs room-separating elements (walls) to make a workable plan

curiously emasculated. Lacking any other authority for what he was designing, the student worked from precedents in photographed architecture—buildings of Scandinavian provenance were particularly favoured. Odd details were culled from here and there and assembled much like Gaudet's elements. The designs *looked* like modern architecture but there was little functional analysis, and appearance (both of the building itself and, most particularly, of the drawing) accounted for very nearly all. All the tutor could do was to compare his prejudices with the student's; there was no rational basis for criticism.

Thornley sought to establish not merely a systematic basis for teaching design, but a new theory of architecture, by thinking out on the basis of his own experience what an architect actually does when he is designing something. The *Method* itself, as outlined in Thornley's initial statement, consisted of seven stages but by the time of the conference it had been reduced to four:

1. The Accumulation of Data
2. The isolation of a General Concept or 'Form'—
   (a) The Essential Purpose of the building
   (b) The Relationship of the Building to the Individual
   (c) The Relationship of the Building and its Occupants to the Surrounding Social and Commercial Pattern
   (d) The Relationship of the Building to its Physical Surroundings
   (e) Economics
   (f) Preliminary Consideration of Spatial and Formal Organization
   (g) Preliminary Consideration of Structural Organization
   (h) The Establishment of an appropriate 'Form' or Generalized Concept
3. The Development of the 'Form' into the Final Scheme—
   (a) Detailed Consideration of Spatial and Formal Organization
   (b) Detailed Consideration of Structure
   (c) The Development of Architectural Values
4. The Presentation of the Final Scheme.

This sequence, first of all, is a design process, in our terms—not a decision sequence. Phase 2 includes the preparation of an outline scheme, which is then considered in detail under the relevant headings during stage 3. That, as we shall see, is an essential feature of the best known design process in architecture—the RIBA Plan of Work (1955). Thornley's Method was intended specifically as a teaching device, against which the tutor could monitor the student's work. Each stage was assessed whereas previously a single mark had been given for each scheme, after assessment of the presentation drawings, and this lent undue weighting to the drawings themselves.

The Method went through various metamorphoses as a result of experience in the Manchester School. One very significant change, instigated by Bell and developed by Buttle, occurred during stage 2, when the student concluded his investigation of the programme by preparing a concise, written design *theme*, which is described as 'a crisp and clear summary of the overall architectural objective'. The substance of Bell's worry was that many students became bogged down in the exigencies of briefing and in studying the practicability of their schemes to the extent that they had no clear aim; architectural values were forgotten. As Thornley says, it became clear from tape-recordings that most of them were far more advanced in their thinking processes and range of ideas than their actual designs would suggest. The solution to this particular problem, therefore, seemed to lie in verbalization; the student was asked to write a summary of his design intentions which, unlike any kind of sketch or model, would not commit him at this stage to any specific organization of forms. The theme itself might state the purpose of the building, and indicate acceptable performance standards. It might indicate the building's relationship with the physical environment and with the user, and it might also state the degree of economic control.

There is no doubt translation into another medium, in this way, will help some designers—presumably those who tend to verbal fluency. The new design analogue will itself help spark off new approaches to the problem; but there is no doubt also that others would find it a grave inhibition; they find verbalization difficult and even irrelevant for their purposes. Similarly, 'form-finding' is described specifically as a graphic activity, in which the major elements are located according to their needs in terms of orientation, aspect access, external relationships and so on. Within this pattern of zoning, individual rooms and spaces are positioned in accordance with circulation requirements. On this basis, a series of solutions is prepared and one of these is selected for development.

The Manchester Method actually forms the basis of the *Process of Design* section in the RIBA *Management Handbook* (1965); the stages actually read:

1. Programming (brief, draft programme, programme)
2. General Study (meaning, form-finding, evaluation)
3. Development
4. Refinement

As we have seen, it is quite specifically a design process as distinct from a decision sequence, but the RIBA *Handbook* contains an alternative, the *Plan of Work*. This was developed, originally, at the War Office and later at the Ministry of Public Building and Works under the general direction of Clive Wooster, and it is specifically concerned with design *team* working. In other words, it is not merely a sequence of events which an architect might work through on his own; it also indicates in considerable detail the contributions which other members of the team might make. In the first place, two kinds of architect are involved (or, at least, two kinds of architect-function)—management and design. And in addition to these, the *Plan* also considers the functions of the client, the quantity surveyor, the engineers (civil, structural, mechanical and electrical) and the contractor. The staging is as follows:

A. Inception
B. Feasibility
C. Outline proposals
D. Scheme design
E. Detail design
F. Production information
G. Bills of quantities
H. Tender action
J. Project planning
K. Operations on site
L. Completion
M. Feedback.

So, like the Manchester Method, the design stages comprise two cycles—a feasibility study (Thornley's general study) and the scheme design (Thornley's development). However, unlike the Manchester Method, it goes beyond the architect's immediate design task through quantities, tendering and so on, to final completion of the building and even feedback (or feedforward, as Markus calls it (1967)) in which lessons learned on one job may be used with advantage on the next. It also contains two cut-off points. There is a statement between stages D and E to the effect that the brief should not be modified after this point, and a further warning after detail design that '*any further change in function, size, shape, or cost after this time will result in abortive work*'.

Each stage in the *Plan of Work* is expanded, diagrammatically, in the form of a precise check-list which tells each member of the team what he ought to be doing. Feasibility, for instance, starts with a meeting at which the following things are to be decided:

1. State objective and provide information:
   (a) First brief; requirements; completion time; cost;
   (b) site data
2. Determine priorities
3. Define roles and responsibilities of team members and methods of communication and reporting
4. Define methods of work, methods of obtaining and recording information
5. Agree sources and presentation of cost information
6. Agree check-list of actions to be taken
7. Agree timetable
8. Agree programming and progressing techniques.

The *Plan of Work*, however, also contains a decision sequence for use during each stage, which it describes as the *cycle* of work:

(a) stating objective and assimilation of relevant facts
(b) assessment of resources required and setting up of appropriate organization
(c) planning the work and setting timetables
(d) carrying out work
(e) making proposals
(f) making decisions
(g) setting out objectives for next stage.

Again, this is more comprehensive than any Dewey-based sequence which would, in any case, be contained in its stage (f)—making decisions. The RIBA *Handbook* also describes a great many techniques which could be of use in design; some of the more important are network analysis, programming and job costing, user requirement study and communications, in many guises. These will be described in the next chapter, together with the appropriate techniques.

The *Plan of Work* was intended, initially, to be an interim suggestion as to how methods of working in the design team may be improved. It was to have been replaced by a much more thorough study which was undertaken between 1963 and 1966 by the Tavistock Institute of Human Relations, but for various reasons the report eventually produced as a result of this research, under the title of *Interdependence and Uncertainty* (Tavistock, 1966) is disappointingly slight. It does however point the difficulties inherent in all design processes which tie the group (or even the individual) to a rigid sequence of events. Certain case studies were examined and, as the report says,

'. . . each time a design decision was taken it set in train a chain of consequences which could and did cause the initial decision to be changed . . . Since the full implications of any decision or action can seldom if ever be forecast with absolute accuracy, a communications system which assumes that they can will simply not work.'

So first of all it is necessary to realize that decisions are *interdependent*. The report continues:

'It was found, too, in all our case studies, that doubts about planning permission, about ownership of land, about approvals and finance bedevilled the briefing and design phases. Uncertainty about the availability of materials and labour upset any attempt to plan an orderly flow of work. Late, faulty and misrepresented information also created confusion.'

So one must recognize too that decisions are *uncertain*.

The Tavistock report takes the three central phases of the decision sequence —analysis, synthesis, evaluation—and applies them at two scales to the process of design and the organization of construction on the building site (the breakdown is as shown in Table 13.1). These would follow each other as two complete cycles; the results of the designer's evaluation would be passed to the contractor as the basis of his analysis. Nevertheless it is not a very convincing breakdown; choice, for instance, is necessary in both cycles. In the designer's cycle it is described as evaluation, which is reasonable, but in the contractor's it comes under the heading of synthesis which is something very different. In principle, however, the intention is a good one and it could be used to extend the two major decision cycles implicit in the *Plan of Work* into three, covering the contracting stages as well. But the Tavistock report goes on, quite rightly, to point out that no design process can be completely linear. It must incorporate feed-back loops of some kind so that new information which is thrown up at any stage may be included in the further

Table 13.1

DECISION SEQUENCE	PROCESS OF DESIGN	ORGANIZATION OF CONSTRUCTION
analysis	collection and classification of data	contractor decides what courses are open to him
synthesis	setting up possible solutions or hypotheses	make a choice from these
evaluation	choice of solution	formulate his choice in terms of a constructive plan

recycling of one of the decision sequences. For instance, information from the contractor's analysis will have to be fed back to the designer's analysis if he is to take the available resources into account. In other words, information from the construction planning stage has relevance to the actual process of design and might well modify it. The difficulty of charting a feasible design process opens the way, in the Tavistock report, for a description of AIDA— Analysis of Interconnected Decision Areas—which is an ingenious method of circumventing many of the problems. It will be described in Chapter 14.

There have been a few other attempts to investigate what the designer actually does when he is designing (see Chapter 2)—as distinct from advising him what he *ought* to do. The most complete, probably, is that by P. H. Levin (a physicist then at the Building Research Station) under the title of *The Design Process in Planning* (Levin, 1966, 1967). He too found that once a decision has been taken there is no indication that it will be implemented. It may be ignored or understood to mean something quite different from what was intended. He uses the terminology of systems analysis (design parameters, dependent and independent variables) and in the case which he studied, which was an exercise in town-extension, the design parameters proved to be matters of area dimension and, most particularly, of location, in terms of map references. As he says, many parameters are interrelated; for instance, 'the total area is equal to the sum of the component areas'. His independent variables are those which the designer *cannot* manipulate—thus confusing our previous definition—the physical and mental characteristics of people, the economic climate and, for that matter, the physical climate. All the designer can do is to predict values for these independent variables, but he cannot ordinarily change them. His dependent variables are dependent, as we might expect, on the values which he has measured for the design parameters, and predicted for the independent variables. They include the number of inhabitants which the town is to house, its gross population density, capital and running costs, journey times and even the frequency of accidents between motorists and pedestrians.

The design process, as Levin observed it, consisted first of all in identifying his three categories, and grouping the various elements on the man/artefact/environment system within them. The designer achieves this largely on the basis of his own judgement and he identifies relationships between them on the same basis. His next task, then, is to predict values for the independent variables, such as a figure for car-ownership in the year 2010 A.D. Some independent variables are less explicit than that; he will also have to predict a value for family size and that will depend on the attitudes to birth control and to overcrowding. In terms of the decision sequence, the activities which Levin has prescribed so far, all come under the heading of briefing and analysis; but his next task approximates to synthesis—he has chosen values for the dependent variables—which will satisfy the various requirements. These values must be selected within certain limits, and Levin describes these limits as constraints; one constraint may be an upper limit on population size, and another may be the corresponding lower limit. A pair of constraints, therefore, will define a tolerable range of values for a given dependent variable, but some ranges may be so short as to admit of only one value. In the case which Levin studied the designers were well aware of the constraints which limited certain of their dependent variables, such as population size, costs and the peak hour traffic in an east–west direction. He found that constraints could also be identified which governed the values of dependent variables and some of these derived directly from dependent variables; for instance, it was laid down that new residential areas should be within two miles of the town centre, and this constraint was determined by transport costs. Sometimes the constraints on design parameters take quite specific, physical form: there may be an impassable barrier to extension in a certain direction and, certainly, no two buildings, or other artefacts, may be located on the same site.

So the next major step was identification of values for the design parameters—in other words, determining the actual physical dimensions of the plan and other forms. This too is a matter of synthesis, but once the values have been identified they are susceptible to evaluation, or, as Levin describes it, to the identification of values for the dependent variables as determined by the independent variable and the design parameters. And the evaluation will continue with an investigation into the consistency of values, relationships and constraints. In the case study, for instance, a value was reached for the amount of land required for expansion (design parameter) which was then checked against two relevant dependent variables—population size and population density. On the basis of this check, the designer concluded that this value for the total new land required did not meet the constraints resulting from the two dependent variables and the population target was reduced.

Lastly, the designer compares different values for the design parameters; in other words, he compares different designs by checking them against the various constraints and relationships. If one design satisfies them all, then that is an obvious choice, but in most cases each design will satisfy some of the constraints and relationships but not others. In that case, one must decide an order of importance for the various constraints, and that will probably be a subjective matter. One must further decide how much the less critical constraints can be compromised.

CHAPTER 14

New Design Processes

The new maths, with a certain amount of statistics, has been almost as influential in the development of new design methods as all the other sources and disciplines put together. Clearly there was a fascination for many rationally inclined theorists in raising design to the highest possible level of abstraction. It may be that the personalities involved, and their particular motivation, were similar to those who practised canonic design in the past. We find the same desire for the abstract purity of a concept, the same tendency to think of people as abstractions (often of a statistical nature) rather than as persons, the same unwillingness to think of a building (or anything else in design) as a concrete, physical thing.

Such views, naturally, are unacceptable to the empiricist who sees the building as a real, tangible thing which modifies the physical environment, and in doing so impinges on the user's senses. He thinks of it in terms of a physical structure (walls, vaults, columns and beams) supporting physical spaces in which physical actions can take place. These spaces will be enclosed by visible surfaces, walls, floors and ceilings, with doors, windows or other openings giving rise to other habitable spaces. The spaces themselves will possess measurable characteristics in terms of the visual, thermal and aural environments; they may well be given names such as 'living room', 'bedroom', 'kitchen' and so on. The empiricist who thinks of buildings in these terms may find it difficult—and certainly unnecessary—to conceive of the building as an abstraction. His ideal, if possible, would be to work again pragmatically —manipulating real materials to full size on the actual site. That is rarely possible now; buildings (and problems) are far too complex, so he will have to *think* about his design first, using analogues or models. It is likely though that, instead of ranging over all the possibilities shown in Figure 5.1 (see p. 91), he will tend to use two- or three-dimensional spatial or mechanical models (see Chapter 5). His design thinking will tend to be analogic or repetitive, and his approach to design will depend as far as possible on comparing his experience of things which he has observed in the real world. His own sketches, drawings and models fall into this category; these will be comparable, in perceptual transaction, with his ever-changing visual, aural, thermal and other sensory experience of real buildings. Some of the finest designers in the history of architecture have worked in these ways and yet, as we saw in Chapter 2, there has been a parallel tradition, in which the abstract geometry of the design analogue seemed even more important to the architect than the sensory stimulus which the building would afford its users. We called this canonic design and, in spite of its limitations from the sensory point of view, the vocabulary of design as a whole would certainly be poorer without it.

It is entirely appropriate, therefore, that today's design rationalists should develop new canonic design techniques; the pioneer in these developments was Christopher Alexander, one of the first to use graphs and set theory in a method which he described to the 1962 conference (Jones and Thornley, 1963) and in *Notes on the synthesis of form* (1964). He could have used these concepts from the new maths as Haggett does, in the form of planning models; graphs, after all, would enable highly complex circulation patterns to be analysed, whilst sets might help in classifying, say, the various activities which the building is to contain, in terms of environmental needs, servicing requirements and so on. However, Alexander preferred not to use them in this way; his aim, quite specifically, was to transcend such familiar concepts as 'circulation' or 'acoustics' on the grounds that, if he uses them, the architect will be hidebound by traditional attitudes and approaches. Alexander and Chermayeff developed this point at some length in *Community and Privacy* (1963). They suggested that conceptual changes were taking place and that words such as 'yard', 'garden', 'kitchen', 'bedroom', already 'firmly anchored in the culture of days gone by', could only be misleading in the search for 'better' solutions. Each of these words, they say, is 'heavily loaded' and makes any number of 'irrelevant images' spring to mind. So they concluded that 'until one stops using popular or generalized words to describe specific objects and events, one will continue to be deceived by the associations with them and fail to arrive at the essential functional aspect of things and places that is the planner's actual concern in problem-analysis and design.'

Of course, they are right. The words they quoted *do* carry residues of meaning from the past. That is an essential feature of the social contract which, as Saussure says, ensures that words carry similar meanings for different people (Chapter 11). Without these residues of meanings, communication would be impossible; we should each use words in different ways; and, as Saussure went on to say, the relationship between a word and the thing it 'stands for' (signifier and signified) is initially arbitrary but, once it has been formed, no one can change it unilaterally. All one can do is to hope for a change in the social contract.

However, if one cannot change a word then, conversely, one cannot change the concept to which it refers. That too is a matter of social contract—the relationship between signifier and signified. We might well succeed in trying to rid ourselves of concepts 'firmly anchored in the culture of days gone by' but if we do, then, by definition, we shall fail to communicate with the rest of society. We shall have broken the social contract. In other words, as architects, we shall fail to give people what they need, because we shall have refused to match their expectations.

People will bring their expectations to bear on our buildings, based on their past experience, whether we like it or not. Nothing we can do can subtract from that experience, although we can certainly add to it, and if we are to make buildings which are acceptable, comfortable and otherwise satisfactory for their users, then these buildings will have to conform, in terms of sensory satisfaction, to the expectations which people bring, Not that this need inhibit our originality. Any new building which is warm enough but not too warm, light enough, and impenetrable enough to sound, would certainly be very different from the majority of recent buildings. If we brought new technologies to bear in solving these problems of environmental control, then it may be dramatically different. But if we are to satisfy these human sensory needs, the building *will* have a physical structure, a physical circulation pattern and environmental control qualities. The only way to avoid these attributes would be to redesign human beings so that their senses, perceptual acts and expectations were vastly different from those of conventional human beings.

Alexander (1964) opened his argument by tracing a history of designing. The earliest design for him, significantly enough, was, in our terms, iconic. He dismissed the need for a pragmatic stage, and considered the capacity of people to adapt to the environment they have made for themselves to be 'mere hand waving'. Iconic design, which he called 'unselfconscious', represents a good 'fit' between building and user, a fit which will not be achieved by analogue design. He recognised the symptoms of 'analogue take-over' when the designer is seduced by the excellence of his own sketches and builds the forms they suggest. The cure for this, according to Alexander, was to take design back into a further stage of abstraction. If the problem is converted into mathematical symbols, then the designer will feel neutral about them; he will perform various operations on them dispassionately and thus end up with a new solution generated, perhaps, without his even being aware of it.

The essential thing for Alexander was that one designs a form, and this form is determined by the context into which it should fit. 'Form' and 'context' together will become an 'ensemble' and, for Alexander, an 'ensemble' could be one of many things—the 'fit' of a tie with a certain suit, the 'fit' of a phrase by Mozart at a certain point in a sonata, the 'fit' of a kettle to the context of its use. Crucial in all these cases is the definition of context, the fact that the ensemble can be divided in many ways. In redesigning a kettle the designer might divide the ensemble in such a way that he finished up by redesigning the entire house. So Alexander reduced the idea of 'fit' to specific terms, taking the case of a metal face which is being tested against a standard steel block. One inks the surface of a standard block and rubs the face against it; any high-spots show immediately and demonstrate the 'misfit' of form to context.

So, by a series of trials and errors, one might eventually achieve good 'fit' but, according to Alexander, this method is too slow and too expensive. His way of synthesizing form built on d'Arcy Thompson's remark that a form is a 'diagram of forces'. Once the context is described in terms of a diagram of forces, then the form will be another diagram, complementary to it. Clearly the levelness of Alexander's metal block *can* be described as a diagram of forces, without the slightest difficulty. That is one thing, but achieving it by the technical means available is quite another.

However, from this simple example, Alexander drew an equally simple conclusion. His metal block was either a good 'fit' or it was not; there were no fine shades of meaning about it. He extended this principle to form a general rule: a form either 'fits' its context or it does not; it is as simple as that. Like Graunt before him, Alexander tried to match buttons, and found that the misfit may be in terms of size, colour, number of holes or any one of a vast number of variables. A 'misfit' in terms of any of these would cause the whole ensemble, the button and its context, to 'misfit'.

The problem with any design, then, was to find the relevant variables. His buttons had size, colour, number of holes as variables, and there were others, but what were the equivalent variables for a house? In the case of an Indian village (Alexander, 1963, 1964), he found 141 misfit variables and some of them seem very curious by western standards:

'3. Rules about house door not facing south;
6. Wish for temples;
7. Cattle treated as sacred; and vegetarian attitudes;
16. Women gossip extensively while bathing, fetching water, on way to field latrines;
78. Shade for sitting and walking.

The difficulty, of course, is that different designers might identify quite different lists of misfit variables. Suppose another designer listed quite different variables for an Indian village, or even a different number of variables. Alexander dismissed such objections; all designers, he said, would achieve the same list sooner or later, although the order of importance they attached to different variables might vary, according to personal predilections. That seems to me a rather pious hope and in practice it may not be true. In *Community and Privacy*, for instance, Alexander and Chermayeff listed 33 basic requirements for a house; it is a revealing experience to write one's own list of 33, for comparison with theirs.

Their first three *basic* requirements (grouped it is true into a particular category) are:

'1. Efficient parking for owners and visitors; adequate manoeuvre space.
2. Temporary space for service and delivery vehicles.

3. Reception point to group [what group?]; sheltered delivery and waiting. Provision for information, mail, parcel and delivery boxes, and storage of parcel carts.'

Not a word, in the first three, about the environmental conditions inside the house, to which many of us would give overwhelming priority. Indeed, of their 33 requirements, 16 are concerned with vehicular traffic in some way, and only 10 with environmental matters. Five of these are permutations on the idea of noise, and of all the 33 only two are concerned explicitly with the business of living. It is a curious agglomeration of requirements which, to me personally, seems extraordinarily unbalanced. I doubt if any other designer would produce an identical list.

Part of the problem, of course, is in deciding just what a variable is. Alexander suggested that if his method were to work, the variables should be comparable in scope and each one should be capable of about the same number of solutions. For instance, one might say: 'maintenance costs low enough', but that really ought to be part of 'economically satisfactory'. One could not use both these statements in the same list of variables, because they are unequal in scope. All he could do then was to suggest that one should resort to judgement and common sense in preparing one's list. Given that the variables were equal in scope, they should also be independent of each other. Each variable should be a complete, self-consistent statement which did not refer to any other, so Alexander's variables must be independent, but not in the usual sense of the term as we saw it used in ergonomics.

He found it useful, as an aid to visualizing this breakdown of the problem into its tiniest components, to use the *tree* of graph theory (Chapter 12). Clearly the root of the tree represented the root of his problem, its division into branches represented the division of his problem into major categories, and each terminal vertex of his graph represented a single misfit variable (Figure 14.1(a)). A conventional solution might be found by solving each misfit variable, in the Cartesian manner, and building up a complete answer by synthesizing these small ones successively. But Alexander was not interested in conventional solutions. The whole point of his method was that one should regroup the misfit variables, work out solutions to each of these groups, and then synthesize these group solutions into a new whole; but by definition one cannot regroup the terminal vertices of a tree. Each one is separate and the only way of connecting them is to go back via a higher branch of the tree. If two vertices belong to remote branches, then it may be necessary to go back to the root. The tree formation, by its very nature, preserves the *original* structure of the problem.

Alexander's answer to this was highly ingenious. He took the tree to represent a 'section', or 'elevation' of his problem, and used the Venn diagram of set theory to represent the same relationships in 'plan' (Figure 14.1(b)). Each branch of the tree was indicated by a subset on the Venn diagram and each terminal vertex, finally, by a point. A Venn diagram too preserves the original hierarchy of relationships between variables, but it is possible to plot *relations* between points in different subsets. So the rigid hierarchy is gradually eroded away.

In practice, Alexander scanned his list of variables and noted interactions between them; but, like the variables themselves, these interactions were difficult to define. In the case of a kettle, he found two variables which clearly interacted:

'The kettle's too small
The kettle's occupying too much space.'

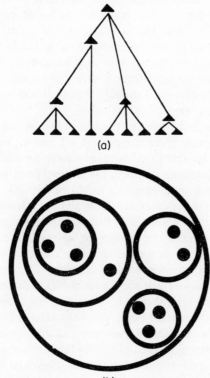

(a)

(b)

Figure 14.1—Alexander *decomposes* his problem into individual 'misfit variables', clusters these into subsets for which group solutions can be found and then recomposes these solutions to form a new whole. He uses the tree of graph theory to present his problem in 'section' (a) for decomposition purposes and the Venn diagram (b) to show how the misfit variables are clustered together to form subsets. (Reprinted by permission of the publishers from Christopher Alexander, *Notes on the Synthesis of Form*, Cambridge, Mass: Harvard University Press, Copyright, 1964, by the President and Fellows of Harvard College.)

Their relationship, apparently, was one of conflict. If one makes the kettle bigger, then it will occupy even more space. In other words the variables are mutually exclusive. In other cases, two variables may be satisfied by the same component of a design; if one takes 1 and 2 in the list of housing requirements from *Community and Privacy* then, clearly, the adequate manoeuvring space for owners and visitors might occupy the same piece of ground as the temporary space for delivery vehicles. On rare occasions they might conflict but, generally, these two requirements concur. So, given his range of misfit variables, with each one plotted as a point on a graph—or even in a Venn diagram—it was possible to plot their interactions by means of appropriate links, or absences of links. He concluded then that 'two variables interact if and only if the designer can find some reason (or conceptual model) which makes sense to him and tells him why they should do so.' However, this still left Alexander with the problem of *strengths* of links. As he said, in one case variables may conflict so strongly that they virtually exclude each other. In another there may be no more than 'a barely discernable tendency for them to concur.' Furthermore, 'an explicitly statistical test would give the interactions a continuous range of values'.

So eventually he opted for three strengths of interaction—positive, negative and neutral. These were given values $+1$, -1 and 0. Alexander's 'labelled' graph could then be translated into a matrix representing *two variable* correlations and Alexander assumed, for no very good reason, that correlations between three or more variables would vanish.

However, that, in many cases, is specifically not what happens. If we take the case of the kettle, Alexander's two variables suggested that size and capacity were in conflict. If the kettle were big enough to hold enough water it would be too big to go on the shelf; but one very good way of reconciling this apparent conflict would be to draw a graph, different from any of those which Alexander uses, in which size (in some critical dimension) and capacity were plotted against each other; one could then use a *third* variable such as cost to decide exactly at what point to compromise between them. In other words, it is a simple example of linear programming (see Chapter 10).

Alexander, however, is interested only in the interactions between pairs of variables. If each interacts also with several others, he treats each of these interactions separately. One of the reasons for this is that in computer applications of the *method*, such as Hidecs (see Chapter 15), it would be much easier to reduce these links to two; the binary operation of the digital computer leads to a further case of analogue take-over. So links, now, may be 'positive' or 'negative'. Nonetheless for Alexander two variables interacted or they did not; it was as simple as that. In the Indian village example, each variable interacted with a dozen or so others, and he isolated groups, or 'subsets', of variables between which interactions occurred; there are twelve such subsets in the village example. Having grouped his variables into subsets, Alexander prepared a diagram for each subset which 'solved' geo-

metrically the problems of relationship which the subset raises. Given, therefore, the whole range of models which, say, Echenique describes (Chapter 5),
Alexander chose to use only those which could be categorized as two-
dimensional/spatial, which seems to me unnecessarily restricting. It also led
to difficulties. Each diagram was a simple geometric expression of what
must be done to make the variables 'fit'. Sometimes a diagram was easy to
draw. In one example (not connected with the village) Alexander investigated
a traffic intersection. He could find the numbers of cars going in each direction and turning from one direction to another. The traffic flow would then
be represented with arrows, pointing in appropriate directions and varying
in thickness according to the number of cars. A wide arrow would indicate
many cars, a narrow arrow few, and eventually this diagram could be translated, with very little change, into the actual plan of an intersection, with road
width proportionate in width to the arrows. There would be a very close
relationship in this case between the diagram, the forces it represented, and
the form which resulted from it.

   In other cases, however, there was no such direct relationship between
variables and diagram, nor could there be. Sometimes it was impossible to
draw an appropriate diagram. How does one represent an abstraction such
as 'cattle treated as sacred', for instance? It is combined in the village example
with eight other variables concerned with upgrading of cattle, protection of
cattle from disease, efficient use and marketing of dairy produce, prevention
of famine if monsoon fails, and so on; these play their part collectively in

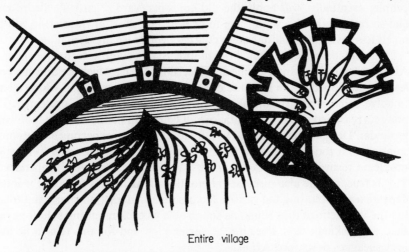

Entire village

Figure 14.2—Alexander's final diagram for the Indian village in which the
diagrams by which various subsets of variables were 'solved' are synthesized to form the overall solution. (Reprinted by permission of the
publishers from Christopher Alexander, *Notes on the Synthesis of Form*,
Cambridge, Mass.: Harvard University Press, Copyright, 1964, by the
President and Fellows of Harvard College.)

Figure 14.2 which is rather beautiful, but has little apparent connexion with practical or symbolic requirements for keeping cattle. Once the diagram has been drawn, however, it exercises, as we might expect, its own form of analogue take-over. Ward (1966) reports an example from the design of office furniture (see Moore, 1969); a major requirement was that the typist should have reasonably quiet working conditions; Ward's diagram for this consisted of a 'cone of silence', and when the craftsman came to make a mock-up of the furniture, he actually made a 'cone of silence' in fibreglass. That difficulty could have been avoided if the method had allowed him to use a verbal or numerical model. Keith Hanson too (1969) has reported on the difficulties he experienced in illustrating similar concepts during the design of a housing project; again, the circle he drew to represent protection from outside noise became the actual plan-form of his housing.

In other words, by moving to a further stage of abstraction, Alexander aggravated the problem of analogue take-over instead of diminishing it; and in leaving the design at this stage, in the form of abstract diagrams, the *method* is rather less help than conventional design methods might have been. They, at least, show relationships between rooms and other parts of a 'real' design, even if they do not show the shapes of the rooms themselves. It is even more difficult to translate one of Alexander's diagrams into a three-dimensional building (beautiful as it may be in its own terms), than it is to translate the other kinds of diagrams which architects want to use, because the diagrams must be translated into the three-dimensional forms to which people, eventually, *will* apply the old concepts 'yard', 'garden', 'bedroom', and so on, whether we want to or not. The effort of translation will be much less severe if we admit these concepts whilst we are designing.

Luckman described at the Portsmouth Symposium a technique named AIDA—Analysis of Inter-connected Decision Areas, which he and his colleagues developed at the Institute of Operational Research, and which seems to solve some of the problems which Alexander's technique presented. He presents reasoned and potent criticisms of Cartesian method on the following grounds: 'Designers have tended to fall into the trap of expecting an optimum solution to a total problem to be the sum of optimum solutions to its sub-problems, regardless of the fact that the sub-problems are highly independent.' This is true, and he also discusses attempts such as Jones's to cater for inter-dependence by plotting the various factors on an interaction chart, and treating the interactions thus found as sub-problems each requiring solution; but that, as Luckman says, does not go far enough and for this reason he and his colleagues developed AIDA.

It is based on the fact that at any level in design from, say, the design of a spoon to the design of a complete city, the problem itself can be expressed in terms of various factors and that for most of these factors several solutions are possible, but the particular solution which is selected for one factor will encourage certain solutions for other factors and inhibit others. Each factor for which a range of solutions may be possible is called a *decision area* and these decision areas in Luckman's description are concerned with specific, definable, concrete things. In building, for instance, decision areas might be:

(i) The state of whole or part of the building, such as height, position, direction of span or colour.
(ii) Individual components of the building, such as window, roof cladding or type of door handle.

As far as possible, one would try to define decision areas within particular levels, and avoid links between decision areas at different levels. There may

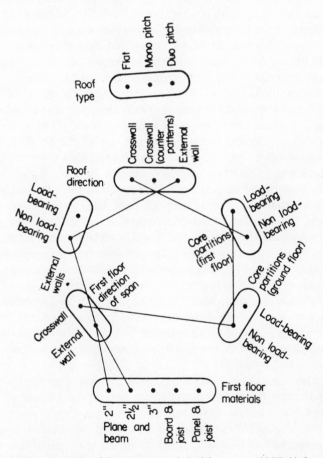

Figure 14.3—Analysis of interconnected decision areas (AIDA) for a terraced house (adapted from Luckmann, 1970)

be links between roof cladding and direction of span, but it is difficult to see how choice of door handle could affect position of building.

Having defined his decision areas, Luckman plots them in the form of a graph; the decision areas are represented as vertices and the connexions between them as edges. He is careful to point out that this is *not* a directed graph. At this stage one cannot forecast the order in which the decision areas should be resolved; this will be determined, eventually, by the form of the graph itself. Once the overall form of the graph has been determined further detail is plotted in.

Each vertex, or decision area, within the graph is then expanded and drawn as an oval, within which points are plotted to represent the various options. Where the choice of a particular option in one decision area will inhibit the adoption of a certain option in another decision area, then the two are linked; as Luckman says, these links represent *incompatibility*. At first sight, it would be more appropriate to link compatible options, but this was tried and the resultant graphs became so heavily congested that they were difficult to follow. By linking incompatible options, Luckman and his colleagues imply also that other, unlinked options are independent of each other.

Once the graph has been drawn, it indicates many things about the structure of the problem. Some graphs naturally decompose into separate networks, each of which can then be tackled independently. Others form 'rings' and these suggest further study before the rest of the graph is explored. Finally a solution is built up by choosing one option from each decision area, in such a way that no incompatible options are used. It may be possible to base the majority of choices on a single criterion, such as cost, which will only be compromised when incompatibilities have to be avoided, but in many cases, the criterion of choice will be different for each decision area; one may require choice based on cost, another on environmental standards, a third on aesthetic criteria, and so on. In such cases, it will be quite impossible to relate the choice of options to any single scale of measurement. Again, some decision areas may be treated deterministically; some others will require statistical decision, whilst others again may be indeterminate, but provided one satisfies the interconnected decisions and the others are genuinely independent, then this discrepancy in decision-types may be a positive advantage. AIDA therefore encourages one to use many kinds of models.

AIDA also lends itself, as we might expect, to computer applications and, as Luckman says, these soon become necessary as the number of decisions and options begins to rise. Given two decision areas with three options each, the number of possible combinations will be 3×3, that is 9. Given six decision areas, half of them with three options and the other half with two, then the number of combinations will be $3 \times 3 \times 3 \times 2 \times 2 \times 2$, that is 216.

Luckman describes the technique with reference to interconnected decisions in designing a small house (Figure 14.3). It becomes clear eventually that the decisions concerning roof (direction of span), external walls, first floor (direction of span), partitions (ground floor) and partitions (first floor) are interconnected. Roof and the first floor could span between cross walls or between external walls; the designer had a choice in these matters according to which of his walls were load-bearing. Luckman's graph shows these and other interconnected decisions.

Certain options were eliminated on grounds of cost, and eventually each of the five central decisions was reduced to two possible options. The number of feasible solutions therefore became 2^5 or 32 theoretically possible solutions. Interconnexions between these reduced the number of compatible solutions to 8. The final selection was based on a cost analysis of these eight. When one considers that even at the second stage the decision graph for seven decision areas contained a potential $3 \times 3 \times 2 \times 2 \times 5 \times 2 \times 2$, that is 720 possible solutions, the reduction is striking, and convincing.

AIDA offers a much more subtle approach to design problems than any Cartesian decomposition, putting forward a framework within which many other techniques may be employed, including the full range of creative techniques (see Chapter 17), especially morphological analysis and many kinds of decision-making from the most determinate of algorithms, through statistical decision to the most intuitive of judgements. It offers potentially a much greater richness in design than the *Synthesis of Form* method; Alexander himself began to move away from this in a later essay entitled *A City is not a Tree* (1966). This is a beautifully written and reasoned essay in which Alexander contrasts his tree with a different kind of graph, a semi-lattice. To make his point, he takes examples from town planning, comparing what he calls 'natural cities', Sienna, Liverpool, Kyoto, which have grown over the years, with 'artificial cities', such as Chandigarh and the British New Towns. He argues, convincingly, that the interrelations between elements in a natural city are much more complex than any tree structure could indicate. The difference, essentially, is that in a tree structure any two subsets are either totally separate or one is wholly contained in the other, but in a semi-lattice subsets overlap and the elements common to both also belong to the collection. The two structures are compared, in 'section' and 'plan', in Figure 14.4.

This simply demonstrates, in topological terms, what most of us sense anyway, that in a 'natural city' things are not neatly zoned and segregated; they overlap, merge and are confused. These are the characteristics which give a 'natural city' richness of texture, variety—and squalor. As an example Alexander quotes the case of a corner drugstore at Berkeley, California, outside which there is a traffic light. In terms of 'tree' planning, which is the working method of all administrators with tidy minds, these things are unrelated—they belong to different sets; but in practice what happens is that, when the light is red, pedestrians waiting idly for it to change look at the papers displayed on the newsrack outside the drugstore. As Alexander says, 'this effect makes the newsrack and the traffic light interdependent; the newsrack, the newspapers on it, the money going from people's pockets to the dime-slot, the people who stop at the light and read the papers, the traffic light, the electric impulses which make the lights change, and the sidewalk which the people stand on, form a system—they all work together.'

So, clearly, the overlaps form an important distinction between a tree and a semi-lattice, but there is more to it than that. According to Alexander, a tree based on 20 elements can contain, at most, 19 further subsets of these 20. A semi-lattice however, also based on 20 elements, can contain over a million

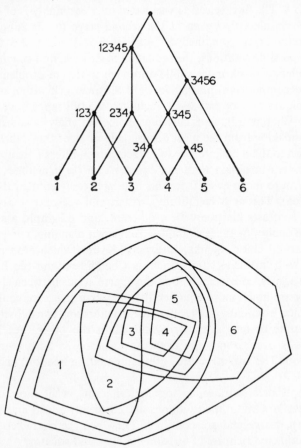

Figure 14.4—Alexander suggests that where a city is structured like a tree (see Figure 14.1(a)) the result will be too artificial. Natural cities tend to grow in semi-lattice form (from Alexander, 1966)

subsets. Alexander proceeds to develop his argument, with great power and beauty, by analysing first a series of 'planned' cities and showing them all, in terms of organization, to have been conceived as trees. Tree thinking is indicated by any tendency to zoning of any kind, the segregation of traffic and pedestrians, the provision of 'special' places for 'special' functions, such as children's play.

In contrast to tree thinking, Alexander instances Ruth Glass's analysis of what actually happened to people who lived in a typical neighbourhood of Middlesbrough. She draws a hard line round their neighbourhood, a line marking sharp discontinuity of building type, income and job type. This neighbourhood contains, among other things, elementary schools, secondary schools, youth clubs, a post office, greengrocer and a grocer selling sugar. She then plots for each of these functions the 'catchment area', the homes of people who use these facilities. None of these catchment areas matches exactly the outline of the neighbourhood and none of them matches each other; nor are they disjoint—they overlap. They represent, in Alexander's terms, overlapping subsets—a semi-lattice.

From this Alexander concludes that planners ought to think in terms of semi-lattices rather than trees, a laudable aim but one fraught with difficulties. Some of these he mentions himself, citing Gestalt-based experiments in perception, in which people, asked to remember and redraw complex, overlapping patterns, tend to simplify them, forgetting in particular the overlaps. He realizes also that many attempts to provide richness and overlap by piling a wide range of functions into the air (under the guise of comprehensive redevelopment) often lead to chaos and confusion; but surely the aim of *planning* for overlap, for semi-lattice structures is a vain one? Richness cannot be planned; it is the result of pragmatic decisions taken over the years by many different people, with different aims and needs. The 'natural cities' he instances—Sienna, Liverpool, Kyoto and even Middlesbrough—have areas which were planned initially, but now they overlap.

A City is not a Tree is a more potent argument than any of Alexander's critics have devised against the 'fit/misfit' basis of his *Synthesis of Form*. When one is concerned with the disjoint elements of tree structures, each element may be *contained* in a set or not—this is a 'fit/misfit' situation; but when it may be *contained* or not in each of six or a hundred *overlapping* sets, its actual state may be, as Alexander suggests, one of a million or so possibilities. The greater the number of sets, the more intricate their degree of overlap, the greater the importance of continuous scales, spectra and shades of grey.

It is curious that in another paper, *From a Set of Forces to a Form* (1966), Alexander describes possibilities for certain much more fruitful approaches to design, which he does not seem to have developed. He suggests that the idea of 'need' is too specific for effective use in design; a building finally results from many *forces*—gravity, the tendency of people to walk in straight lines, and so on. So he replaces the concept of need by the concept of force, suggesting that such forces will work inexorably to determine what *form* an object will take. It is a useful idea, and one which is capable of much development. One could, for instance, distinguish between systems which tend to equilibrium and therefore resist the forces of change, and other systems which will always be in a state of change because their component forces can never be resolved; but, given Alexander's basic idea, the problem of design resolves itself into:

1. Given a system, how can we assess the forces which act upon it and arise within it?
2. Given a set of forces, how can we generate a form which will be stable with respect to them?

Unfortunately he makes no attempt to define how one might identify and assess the relevant forces.

He assumes, however, that they can be assessed, by methods described in *The Atoms of Environmental Structure* (1965/6), and that once they are known they can be analysed in a number of ways. On the whole, he believes that numerical analysis has only limited applications to environmental design. Geometry can be used, say, to define the form of a chute down which goods will slide in the minimum time, to analyse movement patterns in, say, a hospital, and to design load-bearing structures. Next he describes *analogic* methods, although in each case he refers to the pragmatic use of an analogue. He cites the 'centre of gravity machine' in which weights represent proportionately the populations of various cities, the heating loads of departments in a hospital—any quantifiable elements which can be located physically on a map or plan. The weights are suspended in their appropriate positions from strings tied in a common knot which takes up a position at the centre of gravity of the system thus indicating where an airport, a boiler house and so on, ought to be. Alexander also cites Gaudi's inverted models of arches for the Guell Colony chapel using weighted wires and his own (pragmatic) temporary use of bamboo furniture to determine the layout of a room. Again though, Alexander finds such pragmatic analogues have only limited use because none of them (by definition) represents *all* the forces which will be present in the 'real' situation.

Finally Alexander describes his *Relational* method; in this he attempts to transcend the limitations of numerical and pragmatic-analogue methods by finding some means whereby *all* the forces acting on a form can interact. That, he says, depends on finding something which they all have in common and the one thing they have in common is that each is seeking a specific end-state; in other words, each has certain *physical* implications. The physical implications of each force can be plotted as an abstract diagrammatic form, and the diagrams can then be fused to generate a form which represents a fusion of their end-states.

Elsewhere (Alexander and Mannheim, 1962) he describes a sophisticated development of the town planners' 'sieve map' used in locating a highway connecting two towns. As a first step, they prepared twenty-six maps of the area showing such characteristics as earthwork costs, regional development, the cost of land, bridges, road surfacing and substructure, traffic desire lines, user costs, travel times, existing and future transporting systems, patterns of drainage and micro climate, implications for noise, air pollution and so on. In each case, the map was marked black wherever the particular force was favourable to highway development, white where it was not, and with appropriate shades of grey plotted in between. Two or more of these drawings were then superimposed and fused photographically; in one case, for instance, user costs, services and bridge costs were combined in this way until, eventually, all twenty-six diagrams had been superimposed and two black lines remained, of which the darker was selected as the line of the highway.

Clearly there is room for discussion as to how these various factors should have been weighted and difficulties have arisen in some of Alexander's later essays where certainly highly personal views expressed in algebraic or graphic form have been given the semblance of objectivity by the medium of expression itself. The experience of personal loneliness thus led to his concept of *The City as a Mechanism for Sustaining Human Contact* (1967); a desire to move around at high speed by car led to a *Pattern of the Streets* (1966) which conflicts violently with other environmental considerations and so on (Broadbent, 1968, 1969).

A different approach entirely was taken by the Offices Development Group at the then Ministry of Public Building and Works in London. Their Activity Data Method (ADM) was developed under the direction of Ian Moore and published in several forms, notably as *User Requirement Study* in the RIBA *Handbook* (1965), as *Activity Data Method* (1966) and as a worked example *Planning a Major Building Type* (1966). The aim, essentially, was to find a more precise unit of briefing than the schedule of accommodation—a 'shopping list' of rooms, with areas. Moore and his team chose the activity as an appropriate unit, but found it difficult to define; cooking is an activity, so is beating an egg. Eventually they decided that 'an activity is rather like an elephant, difficult to define, but once you've seen one, you know what it is' (MPBW, 1966).

In practice the activities which a building was to house would be listed and an *Activity Data Sheet* prepared for each one. This included:

1. A general description of the activity itself, noting the people involved and the things they used, including furniture and equipment.

2. The space components of the activity in the form of sketches, indicating its overall dimensions and shape.
3. Its environmental requirements against a detailed check-list of air, visual, sound and safety conditions, together with an indication of the services required and other demands on the fabric of the building.

In addition to this, a *link analysis* diagram was prepared in consultation with the users, showing proximity relationships between activities. ADM as a whole offered an interesting basis for briefing, but the link analysis presented difficulties because it over-simplified whilst the check-list of environmental requirements was far too complex and detailed for day-to-day use in practice.

The authors of ADM quickly recognized its deficiencies; Alexander, by this time, was working with the group and *The Atoms of Environmental Structure* (1967), which he wrote with Barry Poyner, is an attempt to overcome them. Any building, they thought, could be absolutely and unequivocally *right* or *wrong* for its users. This was a question of fact not of values. A building could be designed so that its physical geometry provided a perfect fit to the users' needs. This was to be achieved, not by asking people what they wanted or even observing what they did in their existing building—the building itself would inhibit the expression of their real needs. One attempted to find out what people *tried* to do when given the opportunity. This 'operational' version of a need was called a *tendency* and, according to Alexander and Poyner, such tendencies could be readily detected, and tested.

People have a tendency to look out of windows; that can be catered for and so can many other obvious tendencies. So far so good, but people's tendencies also conflict. You tend to park your car in your garage and your guests tend to park theirs in your drive, so you cannot get out: that is a conflict of tendencies. Your own tendencies also conflict. Your chair is becoming uncomfortable; you have a tendency to move, but you also have a tendency to continue reading. A good designer could reconcile these conflicts within you, between you and your guests, between any conflicting tendencies within the man/environment relationship. He would do this geometrically. People tend to collide at a blind corner because they cannot see each other approaching. Yet one has only to draw the right diagram—a curved corner, a transparent corner, a flower tub which they have to walk round—and their conflict will be resolved. The mechanism of reconciliation will be a geometrical *relation*.

Daley (1970) attacked this concept and found it badly wanting. By setting up a mechanism which reconciles people's behaviour, the designer is controlling what they do; and in trying to reconcile people's tendencies he is making implicit moral judgements. Certain tendencies may be desirable: others may be undesirable—the designer cannot be morally neutral in trying to reconcile them.

Alexander developed the *relations* of the *Atoms* paper to form *Patterns*: discrete elements of environmental geometry, such as entrances, activity pockets, workspaces, windows, interview booths, which can be combined in particular solutions (see, for example, Alexander et al 1968). Some of the patterns express more abstract values: small services without red tape, barber-shop politics and so on, but each pattern is represented by a diagram expressing geometrical relationships which can be built physically into the environment. In one case at least, the *Proyecto experimentale* to replace *barriada* (shanty town) housing in Lima (Alexander et al, 1971), the pattern approach has led to subtle and beautifully worked out results but in general it is open to some of the criticism which applied to the original *Notes* method, in that certain environmental values (even elementary ones such as heat, light and sound conditions) *cannot* be represented in terms of geometrical relationships.

On further reflection, Alexander himself (1971) has expressed disgust at the whole *Notes* approach which he describes as a 'painful and drawn out misunderstanding'. One's aim, finally, must be to create beautiful buildings; design method has nothing useful to say about this. The appreciation of any methodology requires a precision of approach which simply will not allow one to achieve the frame of mind in which creative designing can take place. This, finally, is a question of being at peace with oneself; computer-aided design in particular, militates directly against that.

Bruce Archer, in his paper to the Portsmouth Symposium (Broadbent and Ward, 1969; also in Moore, 1970) tries to lay down the foundations for a science of design, as distinct from an actual design process. That accounts for the extreme complexity of his argument, which is greater even than Alexander's, and for his adoption of abstract mathematical notation, and the terminology of operational research, so as to achieve compatibility with the latter and with certain aspects of management science. Some of his techniques derive from these disciplines but he also draws heavily on statistics, systems engineering and the scales of psychological measurements devised by S. S. Stevens. Archer's conscious aim is to provide a common framework against which design problems in any field (architecture, engineering and industrial design) may be perceived, and he is anxious to establish that the 'logic' of designing is largely independent of the thing being designed. Having set up his logical model, terminology and notation, Archer hopes that designers in various fields will use it as a basis for their work thus facilitating comparison between them, and the derivation of more precise general laws for design.

He starts by referring, with evident reluctance, to *values*. When a man discerns that something is wrong, he becomes discontented and tries to do something about it. A particular property of the environment gives rise to a certain desire; the attainment of that desire is described as a *goal*, and the action which one takes in trying to achieve that goal is described as a *goal-directed action*. When the action one should take is not immediately clear, then a *problem* is said to exist; it might be concerned with identifying as closely as possible what improvements are required, identifying the means of achieving these improvements, or identifying both the necessary improvements and the means of achieving them. The problem itself bars one's achievement of the goal; its presence is undesirable and action must be taken to remove it. Problem-solving, therefore, becomes a goal-directed activity.

In most cases, one must resolve the problem before one can correct the undesirable conditions; Archer calls the aims of problem-solving, *objectives*, and the aims of condition-correcting, *goals*. Problem-solving will be a matter of planning, and condition-correcting a matter of implementation. A great deal of planning or problem-solving will consist of redefining the goals which are to be implemented in condition-correcting. The term 'design', according to Archer, consists of conceiving the idea for, and preparing the description of 'a proposed system, artifact or aggregation of artifacts'. So the designer would like to start by describing the proposed system or artifact; but where he cannot describe it immediately, then a problem exists (in Archer's terms). Designing is a goal-directed activity, and usually a goal-directed problem-solving activity.

Having defined design in this way, Archer concludes that *all* the properties required to satisfy the final goal are present in the initial, unsatisfactory condition of the environment; and furthermore, some of the desired properties are adequately provided already. Others are present, but to an unsatisfactory degree, whilst others again are absent, or, as Archer puts it, 'present in zero degree'. It seems strange however that in trying to specify these conditions with such precision Archer ignores the possibility of negative properties—properties which not only fail to satisfy the desired conditions, but actively militate against their achievement. He fails to do this because the analogue he uses to describe the relationships between *objectives* and properties is a correlation chart in which ordinate and abscissa both start from zero.

By Archer's definitions, then, the designer's *objectives* are defined by his value system; they define what properties of the environment must be changed in order to achieve the designer's goals. He then plots a whole range of correlation charts (see Chapter 6), in which the designer's objectives, or goals, (O) form the ordinates (vertical scale) and the properties or conditions of the environment (P), the abscissa (horizontal scale). He then plots along the abscissa various conditions of P: $P(u)$ represents the ideal state of the property in respect of a given objective (there may be an ideal range rather than an ideal point on the scale); $P(l)$ the minimum acceptable state of P; and $P(m)$ the maximum acceptable state of P. Given a linear relationship between property and objective, one can read off directly which state of property *P* will satisfy the requirements of objective *O*. Suppose, for instance, one was concerned with relationships between air temperature and comfort. Comfort would be the objective (*O*), and certain other conditions of the property (*P*), the air temperature, would satisfy that objective. So far then Archer has defined certain rather obvious things about design with a high degree of precision; but then two things happen. First of all he allows a massive analogue take-over; one can write the equation which represents a linear relationship between *O* and *P* in his correlation chart quite easily, and a further equation which allows one to calculate a particular relationship between objective (*O*), and the degree to which it is satisfied by a particular state of property (*P*). Archer, in fact, writes this equation as follows:

$$O(y) = 1 + \frac{P(x) - P(u)}{2P(u) - P(l)}$$

where: $O(y)$ signifies the particular degree of fulfilment of an objective;

$P(x)$ signifies the particular state of a property or condition;

$P(u)$ signifies the ideal state of a property or condition in respect of the given objective;

$P(l)$ signifies the minimum acceptable state of a property or condition in respect of the given objective.

He then plots several other more complex and curvilinear relationships between (*O*) and (*P*): exponential, parabolic and so on. There may be cases in design where such relationships exist, although there are no examples in Archer's description; one suspects, in fact, that he plots these relationships and writes the relevant equations simply because it is possible to do so, and doing so is evidence of a certain mathematical sophistication on his part.

However he then justifies this excursion into mathematics on rather curious grounds, by producing a further equation:

$$O(y) = fP(x)$$

where *f* signifies 'some function of'.

This, Archer says, means 'the degree (*y*) of satisfaction of objective *O* is some function of the state (*x*) of property *P*', and he suggests quite rightly that as an alternative to 'reading out in the mind's ear the full verbal equivalent of each (such) cipher', the equation is much more elegant, but that is not quite the point. Equation and sentence are both rather complex ways of saying some very simple things. In the general case, he means something like: 'Where one's satisfaction with an object depends on a particular physical property, then one's degree of satisfaction with that object depends on the state in which that particular property occurs.' Or, in a specific case, one might want to say: 'I want to boil a lot of water. Kettle will hold more water if it is bigger.' It might be argued that in simplifying to this extent one loses precision, but the precision of Archer's general case is, in fact, spurious.

More often than not one's satisfaction with an object depends, not only on the states in which its individual properties occur, but also on the inter-relations between these states. These tend to be more important than the particular state of any single property. One takes a *systemic* view. Nor is that the only problem which Archer raises in setting up his system of scales, nominal, ordinal, interval and ratio. Stevens was careful to specify the operations which were permissible in each, and to indicate that in many cases psychologists cheated by trying to perform 'illegal' operations, assuming that the scale which was actually available to them had the properties of a more rigorous one which was not.

Archer recognises that the final arbiter in most assessments of design is a human being, with values, opinions, experience and other built-in sources of 'unreliability'. If one asks this arbiter to rank a series of chairs for comfort, for instance, he might put them in some sort of order, thus achieving at best a rather suspect ordinal scale. And if one asked a number of arbiters to rank the chairs in order of opinion, there may or may not be a consensus of agree-ment between them. Given such a consensus, then one still has an ordinal scale, but if they cannot agree, then one finishes up with a mere nominal scale.

Nevertheless, Archer *wants* to achieve an interval—or even a ratio—scale, against which he can plot his chairs for comfort, so he asks his 'arbiter' not only to rank the chairs (thereby achieving an ordinal scale) but to allocate marks on a scale of 1 to 100, thus achieving not only a rank ordering but also some intervals between them. Archer suggests that by this means he has achieved not just an interval scale (which he calls incidentally a rating scale) but a fully fledged ratio scale, on which all computations are possible. 'Within the context of a given design problem,' he says, 'rating scales can be perfectly adequately substituted for ratio scales, providing that the arbiters are correctly chosen and the conditions for judgement are adequately controlled.'

Such sleight of hand in the long run is bound to discredit any attempt to set up a *science* of design. Yet Archer takes his argument further and decides that 'nominal scales are merely rating scales with only two ratings—above the limit and below the limit'. In other words, they are a means of putting things into two lists: acceptable and not acceptable. Archer is perfectly free to apply this meaning if he wants to, but social contract is on the side of Stevens who uses nominal scales merely to give things names or numbers; they are specifically *not* devices for evaluating things.

Having discussed all this with reference to one objective and an associated property, Archer expands his argument to include relationships between two properties and then three. But it is difficult to draw a correlation chart in more than three dimensions; the graphic analogue gives way at this point to a written description: 'the interdependence of the states of the properties,' he says, 'constitutes an *n*-dimensional hypersurface on the realm of feasibility'; and furthermore, 'an important prerequisite for an ultimate solution is that at least a portion of the realm of feasibility should intersect the domain of acceptability'. So be it.

So the act of designing, for Archer, becomes:

1. Agreeing objectives
2. Identifying the properties or conditions required by the objectives to be exhibited in the end result
3. Determining the relationships between varying degrees of fulfilment of their respective objectives
4. Establishing the limiting and ideal states of the properties and hence the domain of acceptability implied by the objectives
5. Identifying the laws controlling the interdependence (if any) of the properties
6. Ensuring that the interdependence of the properties constitutes a realm of feasibility and that this lies, at least in part, in the domain of acceptability
7. Selecting an optimum solution within the arena thus delineated.

Archer then suggests that most design activities involve more than one person, and that the objectives will shift as different arbiters become involved and are able to press their case. He finds the whole relationship between design problems, decision variables and their context extremely complex, using the terminology and block schematic diagrams of systems engineering to represent this complexity. As a result of this, he concludes that the designer's goal should be expressed in terms of *performance*. Given a particular set of design *resources* (materials, processes, finishes and so on) and a particular *context* (the characteristics of materials, prices of commodities and other factors which will affect the design but over which the designer has no control) the design itself will be a set of decisions (materials, processes, shapes and finishes which the designer can choose) whilst its performance will be expressed as a set of performance *criteria*, analogous to Jones's *P-specs*. For a chair, these might lay down certain things it should do: accommodate people within a prescribed range of stature and build, withstand certain structural tests, sell at less than a certain price, earn a given profit at a certain rate on investment.

One would prepare a scale for each of these, indicating the point(s) at which each criterion will be satisfied. Presumably one would draw a scale, say for stature, and then plot on it the range of heights which one hoped to accommodate, another one for build, a third one for weight to be supported, and so on. Archer proposes two more steps for his act of designing:

8. Proposing one or more sets of states for the decision variables, within the scope of the resources; establishing the predicted performance(s),

that is to say, the resulting sets of states of the properties; and ensuring that at least one performance lies within the arena defined by step 7 above
9. Selecting the optimum proposal.

He nowhere describes the mechanism for setting up these scales; the scale for stature, presumably, would be plotted in metres, those for structural tests in kilograms/distance dropped; kilograms/time; kilograms/direction, and so on. Price and profit obviously would be expressed in terms of cash, but Archer nowhere indicates how, given parallel scales such as these, of which the measuring units are different in kind, one relates them to one another. All he suggests is that they 'may be represented arranged in order of importance'.

However disparate they may be both in kinds of units and in numbers of units, Archer plots his scales side by side with the least important objective to the left, and the most important to the right between the same vertical limits, and plots on to each the points representing degree of fulfilment. He then finds it useful to link these points, thus plotting a 'merit curve' against which one can gauge by eye the characteristics of each solution. If the merit curves of several solutions are plotted against the same scales, then the 'better' solution will be the one whose curve lies highest on the chart. Of course the best solution will also score highest on the most important objectives, which will lie to the right of the chart; it will have a positive slope, in Archer's terms. A convex curve will be better than a concave curve because it will indicate that values of intermediate objectives are also tending upwards. Obviously there are difficulties in ranking the objectives; Archer employs his previous trick of allocating values to an ordinal scale against which the objective scales themselves may be plotted in whatever irregular spacing is thus indicated. Such a diagram however, according to Archer, becomes 'excessively complicated' where more than five properties are involved, so he prefers to use a matrix instead.

So far, as he says, Archer has set out a structure for the problem, but he has not been concerned with what the actual solution might be. In any system, he says, the input is varied, according to certain laws, to become the output; the laws themselves may be those of physics, chemistry, mechanics and so on (he also includes sociology, psychology, ethics and aesthetics in his list of disciplines based on laws), but in design, as he says, it is difficult to observe these laws in action; it is much more helpful to adopt the O.R. concept of the black box. One can sometimes determine the effects of a black box with reference to an analogue. Given a known case in which the black box has operated (he cites the example of analysing the action of a river using scale models), one sets up an analogue in which analogous inputs produce analogous outputs, and then observes the output from the analogue with different inputs.

So to convert his systematic model into a design tool, Archer resorts to analogue, using design *drawings*, vector diagrams, block models and so on for this purpose. In other words, he decides what to do first on the basis of his systematic model, does it, with reference to a real design problem using whatever drawings, diagrams, models or other design analogues are necessary to achieve it, then refers back to the schematic model to decide what he should do next. At this stage the outline of his design process has leapt to thirty items, including certain necessary feed-back loops. This is then placed within the context of an entire design/production process which takes the following form:

Phase 1. policy formulation
2. preliminary research
3. sketch designs
4. detailed design
5. prototype construction
6. marketing appraisal
7. production design
8. production planning
9. tooling
10. production and sale.

Then, as we might expect, he repeats the intention of his 1963 process, to prepare a network analysis of all this, a standardized approach to design problems. The misunderstandings implied by this intention are discussed in Broadbent (1968). Finally, Archer relates his programme to the RIBA Plan of Work, finding parallels between the ten phases listed above and the twelve stages of the Plan.

Clearly, there are differences; phases 1, 2 and 3 are equivalent, but the Plan's four stages: D, scheme design; E, detail design; F, production information; and G, bills of quantities, are matched by only one of Archer's— detailed design. The differences between building and other factory-based industries in terms of scale, production methods and so on, are indicated by comparing the Plan stages H, tender action; J, project planning; and K, operations on site, with Archer's 5, prototype construction; 6, marketing appraisal; 7, production design; 8, production planning; 9, tooling; and 10, production and sale. Prototype construction is impossible in building except where small units are going to be built in exact repetition. At the higher levels of abstraction, then, Archer's science of design might apply with equal relevance to architecture, engineering and industrial design, but at the level of implementation his description, if anything, emphasizes the differences in approach and methodology which, historically at least, have separated them from each other.

So far these approaches to design based on the new maths and on statistics have raised very grave doubts. One suspects that certain of their authors were so bemused by the complex notations they had achieved, that they were unable to see how irrelevant they were to the actual process of design. Fortunately, however, examples are available now which suggest that, properly handled, the new maths and statistics have a great deal to offer the designer.

Land Use and Built Form Studies at Cambridge University (LUBFS) developed from the analytical work done by Sir Leslie Martin and Lionel March in preparing the Whitehall plan (1965). It proliferated in three directions, unified to some extent by computer-aided design studies. These were an Offices Study (Hawkes, March and Tabor), a Universities Study (Bullock, Dickens and Steadman) and an Urban Systems Study (Echenique). In each case, the subject of study was viewed as a system of interacting elements, physical objects located in particular relationships with each other. The Urban Study, for instance, was based on the three major elements of which, according to Lowry (1964), a city is composed: basic employment location, residential location and service employment location. It also took Lowry's basic premiss that cities are formed and grow around basic employment, which must be located physically on the ground; its location determines in turn where residential and service employment (shops, schools, etc.) will be located.

Having agreed that the city was formed in this way, the group could then develop a mathematical model taking into account the three major classes of activities to be housed, the land available and the network of transportation connecting the different locations. Once this basic model had been validated, further detail could be built in; basic employment could be divided into primary, secondary and tertiary industries; service activities into schools, shops, offices and so on; residence into housing for different socio-economic groups. Validation of the model naturally depended on the availability of data. It so happened that transport studies, a land-use survey and an employment survey were available for Reading, sufficient for a clear picture to be built up of Reading at a particular moment in time (1962–64). Reading as predicted by the model was compared with reality—in terms of where basic employment, residence and service industries were located, the density of development in each area and so on. The model proved remarkably accurate. This was true of similar though less detailed studies of Cambridge, Stevenage and Santiago (Chile) so that, having been validated, the model could then be used for predicting the effects of new, or alternative, planning proposals. Given the basic conflict in any town plan between desire for space as reflected in low densities, and desire for easy access to other activities as reflected in proximity, the model predicted that the London County Council's abortive new town of Hook would have been low on the former and high on the latter; whilst Milton Keynes would reverse these priorities, but at a higher level of overall acceptability (see Lindsay, 1971).

In their original Universities Study (1968) Bullock, Dickens and Steadman attempted to set up an equivalent model for universities, taking into account the location of teaching, residence and social accommodation, not to mention interrelated factors such as timetabling, travel between residence and teaching sites and so on. They also looked in some detail at questions of cost: capital costs, servicing costs and maintenance costs. Again, once the model had been set up, it had to be validated against the performance of real universities; in this case Reading and Leicester, and the Leicester Polytechnic. The group undertook diary surveys of these three institutions, in which quite large samples of students (750 in all, 400 from Reading) were asked to describe in detail their personal activities, including sleeping, for one week. The diary sheets were 'blank', that is, each student filled in his own times and described the various activities in his own words, thus minimizing some of the difficulties of such surveys as described in Chapter 7. Some 350 separate activities were recorded; these were coded and grouped, for the initial analysis, into categories such as walking, formal teaching, private study, eating, drinking, casual social activities, leisure activities (alone), personal hygiene, domestic activities and sleep—some 46 categories altogether. A comprehensive picture was thus built up of what students actually *do*. This may well be useful in deciding, say, what eating facilities, reading spaces and so on, are really needed in universities the size of Reading and Leicester (both around 4,000), how timetabling affects the utilization of space, and how facilities may be planned for economy in journey times where that is an important consideration.

The LUBFS Offices Study, as we have seen, grew out of work for Martin's Whitehall plan (1965) in which, among other things, the concept of *maximum permissible envelope* was defined. This useful device, under the guise of 'environmental matrix', forms an essential part of the environmental design process which is described in Chapters 19 and 20. Hawkes (1968) described the evolution of building bulk control showing how pressures from architects have led at various times to changes in legislation so that preferred shapes could be built. He quotes Croghan (1965) who showed that such pressures in the late 1940s led to the changes in London County Council practice which allowed the LCC architects to build Le Corbusier-like 'pavilions in the park' at Roehampton. Martin, March and Trace argue in various papers (1966, 1967 and 1968) that *if* daylight penetration is essential—and that is the premiss on which Le Corbusier devised these forms—then low rise, high density housing grouped around square courtyards would be much more *efficient*, not to mention its social advantages.

March (1968) describes possibilities for the mathematical description of building form—vastly extended in March and Steadman (1971)—whilst Hawkes and Stibbs (1971) have applied some of these to the development of a computer model against which the environmental performance of individual rooms or whole buildings can be evaluated. This is a limited study in that it takes existing legislation in respect, say, of daylight factors and tests the proposed building against them. The model as set up cannot be used for testing the legislation itself in the interactive way which, as we saw in Chapter 13, will eventually be necessary. Tabor (1970a, 1970b) has been concerned particularly with the analysis of routes in buildings; his work throws doubt on much of the work which has been done in the optimization of circulation (see Chapter 12).

As a whole then, LUBFS work is one of the clearest indications we have that an abstract, rational mathematically-based approach has much to offer in design. It takes the possibilities of such model-building and unlike, say, Alexander, it applies them to things which are physically real in buildings and cities—location, circulation, environmental conditions, the building fabric itself.

CHAPTER 15

Computer-aided Design

To many designers still, the computer presents a challenge. They exaggerate its potential in two ways: some see it as a threat to their future—the computer will surpass them in designing ability, thus putting them out of work—whilst others invest it with magical properties, believing that any *data* fed into it will emerge in the form of precise and definitive *information*. They behave as if information thus produced is authoritative *because* it has passed through the computer. A third view too is widely held, which is not peculiar to designers, that the computer is somehow degrading, that it will diminish the humanity of all those who associate themselves with it. This view has been presented most forcibly by F. R. Leavis (1970) who resents any suggestion that the computer can enrich human life in any way—

'Most certainly, immense changes are. taking place; most certainly they will go on and accelerate; and, if there isn't any forethought, if there isn't a sustained and organically collaborative effort of life-charged and life-serving human intelligence, most (not almost) certainly the changes will be for the worse.'

He may well be right if we allow over-caution or over-enthusiasm to dictate our attitudes to the computer, but my own view is that if we weigh the issues carefully, assessing those things which the computer can do well and those things it cannot, in comparison with the human brain, if we design new computers so that they can engage in even more effective dialogue with the human brain, then far from changing things for the worse the computer will allow man greater freedom than ever to exercise his 'life-charged and life-serving human intelligence.'

There are direct answers too for the over-cautious and the over-enthusiastic. Lady Welby anticipated the former when she wrote of Babbage's *Analytical Engine* (*c.* 1832), '[it] . . . has no pretensions to *originate* anything. It can do *whatever we know how to order it to perform.*' It is up to us, therefore, to tell it what to do. The second has an even more direct answer, the computerologist's pithy comment, 'Garbage in, garbage out.'

This last point is crucial to my argument. There are certain kinds of design problem for which hard data is available; this may be true, for instance, of structural design. As we have already seen, the engineer does not deal in certainties, but he does deal in high probabilities; thus it is possible to feed statistically-based data into the computer on the strength of materials, factors of safety, loadings and so on, in the knowledge that, provided the *program* is well written, acceptable results will be generated automatically. But for many other aspects of design, hard data is not, and cannot be, available. Even in the eighteenth century rationalists such as Laugier, Perrault and others had come to realize that in matters of proportion, colour and so on, human judgement had to be exercised, and the situation has not changed. As we saw in Chapter 4, there are many aspects of human response, social interaction and so on in which experiments on people actually change their perceptions and, for this reason, in the foreseeable future, vast areas of environmental design will have to be based, not only on physical certainty but on human judgement. One might go further than this and suggest that whenever 'garbage' is fed into the computer it is the result of faulty human judgement. Unfortunately the 'garbage' which comes out will *look* authoritative, neat and precisely printed, its deficiencies masked by the highly technical language in which it is couched, thus granted that spurious authority which computer enthusiasts tend to attribute to it. So in presenting us with the means by which calculable certainties and probabilities can be manipulated on a vaster scale than ever before, the computer also requires that the judgements we feed in should be more sensitive than ever. That 'life-charged and life-serving human intelligence' to which Leavis so rightly subscribes, will have a greater responsibility than ever to ensure that its judgements are soundly based.

Given this intelligence and the computer, our whole approach to client user and environment will be revolutionized. This will apply not only to the design of buildings, but to the ways in which buildings are put together and controlled once they have been put into use in terms of servicing and environmental control. It may happen in time that we shall devote less energy to designing buildings and concentrate instead on the ways in which a computer-controlled building can be made to change itself more easily in use. However, none of this will happen if timid designers continue to fear (or ignore) the computer, whilst computer enthusiasts continue to be so bemused by its complexities that its most trivial outpourings take on—for them—the sanctity of holy writ.

It will be difficult to effect a *rapprochement* between them. The timid designer, rightly, will be put off by the formidable language which computerologists use amongst themselves—evidence perhaps that they need the mutual support which, as we saw in Chapter 1, is provided by an incestuous group. As Chandor points out in his *Dictionary of Computers* (1970), some 3,000 words, phrases and acronyms have been invented, put to new uses or otherwise altered for use in computing laboratories. This brutal violation of Saussure's social contract as to the meanings of words is unprecedented in the rise of any new science unless it be in the parallel and equally jargon-ridden field of space technology. More than any other factor, however, it seems to have led to the rise of the computer mystique, to the difficulties which most of us have in understanding computerologists and therefore to our imputation to them of sinister motives.

Not only that, but the achievements of computer-aided design so far, and on the whole, have seemed to be almost trivial, at least in the field of architectural design. Many people doubt that it has anything serious to offer. This results directly I believe from an almost complete failure in communication which has arisen between computerologists and traditional designers. Few traditional designers have felt the need for computer-aids but some of those who were not very good in traditional terms have thought that they might have a future in computer-aided design. Naturally they hoped that this future would be different in kind from traditional designing so, instead of trying to solve the problems of design as it has been practised, they looked to the computerologists to suggest the kinds of problems which ought to be tackled. Naturally they suggested problems which were easy to program, so that certain classes of problem (such as circulation), which were easy to solve traditionally, have been made more complex than ever they were before. It is common to find, therefore, a trivial aspect of designing given undue weighting, and allowed to dominate other more important factors *because* it can be quantified, a program can be written for it, and the spurious authority attached to it of having been computed.

We should do well to remember, then, that essentially the computer is only a calculating machine and that its use initially was limited, although on a much larger scale, to the functions which slide rules, desk calculators, cash registers and other mechanical devices had previously been used to perform. Before very long it was realized that such a powerful tool could be used for more than calculating. It could be used to process *information*, using the word information in a very wide sense. Thus anything which can be stored in books or other written documents, on film or recording tape, can be stored in the computer. Moreover access to this information can be very rapid; instead of having to hunt, physically, for the appropriate book or file, one can ask the computer for it. The computer will then display the information as required—on a television-like cathode-ray tube, printed or drawn on paper, and so on. The possibilities are endless; clearly both the calculating function and the information function of the computer are of interest to the designer. In addition to freeing him from many routine tasks, they may help him actively in design.

In computer jargon, *information* is that which comes out of the computer, processed as required. The raw material which goes in is called *data*. Data in this sense consists of facts presented in the form of numbers, alphabetical characters, symbols on a drawing, or in any other way which enables values, states or conditions to be expressed in precise and measurable terms. In architectural design, for instance, data might consist of lines or other symbols on a drawing, figures representing costs, the code number of a window type, performance characteristics of a wall panel, the address of a manufacturer, the specification of a concrete mix, a quantity of earth to be shifted, the name of a room, a daylight factor, a reverberation time, the live load on a structure, the colour of a door, and so on.

Such data can be subjected to a wide range of operations within the computer: items can be listed, categorized; calculations can be performed on them; they can be summarized, plotted in drawn form or otherwise processed to form usable information. Compared with other processing devices, including the human brain, the computer is extremely fast in operation; it can store vast amounts of data and can be extremely versatile in use. We shall need to take these things into account if we are to use it intelligently in dialogue with the human brain, for the two are complementary; the computers available so far tend to be good at things in which the human being is weak and vice versa. One hopes that in the design of future computers this complementary function will be further enhanced.

Yet whatever developments occur—and some of them undoubtedly will be unexpected—the underlying principles of computers will presumably remain the same. They have been known for a very long time in any case. Babbage's analytical engine was to have performed all the essential functions of the computer; it was to have had a store or memory for holding numbers, a mill or arithmetical unit for grinding them together, a control unit, input devices for feeding numbers and instructions into the machine and output devices for displaying the results. His *difference engine* already served the functions of the mill, whilst Jacquard (1752–1832) had used punched cards to control the extraordinarily intricate patterns which his loom was capable of weaving, thus presenting a highly versatile input device. Herman Hollerith, a statistician, developed a sorting device for punched cards which enabled him to analyse returns from the American census of 1880.

By World War II some highly complex differential analysers had become available in which gears and shafts were rotated to represent counting, multiplication and other operations on numbers. The mechanical devices which performed these operations were replaced by electrical ones in the earliest electronic computers such as ENIAC—Eckert and Mauchly's Electronic Numerical Integrator and Calculator (1946), in which changing numbers were represented by analogous changes in voltage. Such devices are known as *analog* computers. The analog computer, like the differential analyser, accepts inputs which vary with respect to *time*; wheels rotate and voltages vary with *time*. The easiest operation to simulate in an analog computer is *scaling*—the multiplication or division of one variable by a constant. Adding is easy too but the multiplication or division of two or more variables is rather more difficult. These operations can be achieved by mixed electrical and mechanical devices in which one variable is simulated by changing voltages and the other by using an electric motor to operate a variable resistance.

Analog computers have been used to investigate the thermal performance of buildings. The various heat inputs, from heating plant, light fittings, the human occupants and solar radiation, all vary with time; voltages representing them can be fed into circuits representing the thermal capacity of the building, the paths by which heat is lost and so on. Thus one can observe the thermal performance of the building in this analog form, under different conditions and correct any faults in its thermal design before the building is built. Other kinds of architectural problem concerned with structure, servicing, circulation and so on, have all been represented in analog form, but

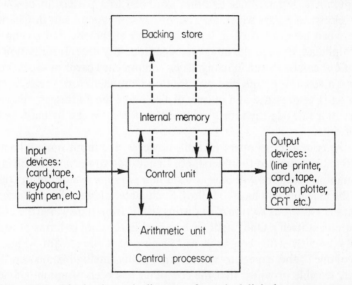

Figure 15.1—Block schematic diagram of a typical digital computer system

although it has many uses, the analog computer also has severe limitations. If it is constructed to form a very close analogy with a particular real-life situation, then its adaptation to represent other situations will be difficult. Slight shifts in voltage also may lead to false results, because different voltages represent different numbers. The analog computer is too inaccurate for many purposes, therefore, and the digital computer is preferred.

The digital computer consists of various components which between them represent the five elements of Babbage's analytical engine—store, arithmetic unit, control unit, input and output devices (see Figure 15.1). In a typical configuration the *hardware* (computer jargon for the physical units of which the computer is built) consists of a central processor and contains an internal memory, an arithmetic and logic unit and the control section. Around this, peripheral units contain the backing store, the computer's long-term memory, and various input and output devices. The latter may take many forms which are listed in Table 15.2. The commonest input device is a punched-card reader which takes eighty-column cards, each column of which can be punched to represent a single character—a letter, number, symbol and so on. These cards, some 18 cm long, are fed into the reader in which a photo-electric head senses the holes and thus generates a pattern of electrical pulses which are fed into the computer. The commonest output device is a line printer which types numbers, letters and other characters on to a roll of paper at speeds of 300 to 2,000 lines per minute up to a maximum of 160 characters per line.

All the input devices of a digital computer are designed to reduce the input data (numbers, letters, lines or other symbols) to a pattern of *binary digits* (bits)—electrical pulses which may be 'on' or 'off'. As we saw in Chapter 12, numbers can be so reduced in terms of binary arithmetic, but so can letters of the alphabet, or even the image on a cathode-ray tube. Information in the form of *bits* can be stored in many ways—on punched cards or tapes (hole/no hole) on a recording tape disc or core in a computer store (pulse/no pulse) and so on. The presence of a pulse will also make the fluorescent material on the face of a cathode-ray tube glow and thus a picture can be built up out of lines of dots.

For the computer to operate at all, however, the input must take a form which it is programmed to understand. In addition to the *data* which is going to be manipulated, one will have to feed in a *program* as a set of instructions which the machine will have to follow. Such material in the form of programs and data is known as *software*, to distinguish it from hardware (the computing equipment itself). One might wish to feed in the data in terms of perfectly ordinary English sentences, such as 'This room is 10m × 8m × 4m. What is its volume?' and expect to receive an equally intelligible answer. This is perfectly feasible provided that the computer has been programmed accordingly. Nor is programming particularly difficult. Some designers prefer programming the computer themselves, whilst others will employ a professional programmer. In either case the first step in programming will be to develop an understanding of what one is trying to do. What precisely is the program meant to accomplish? Often this can be defined in terms of the *input* available for processing, the type of processing which might be appropriate for it and the form of information *output* desired. In other words, one determines which of the many available methods is likely to yield the most satisfactory results, a process of investigation which is known as *systems analysis*. The possibilities will depend to some extent at least on the size and flexibility of the computer system to be used. Once these have been agreed, it is usual to prepare a *flow chart* or a *decision table*. The former is of interest to us as a graphic representation of the operations to be performed because it provides analogies with certain ways in which design processes can be set out. Flow charts may be prepared for the computer program itself at different levels of complexity. An outline flow chart will be used to convert the problem into a series of steps in sequence. It will show all the input and output functions, the way in which the various elements of data are to be processed, how the program itself will be divided conveniently into segments and routines such as input, main and output routines, and so on.

Some problems, however complex, can be solved by arranging a number of operations in linear sequence. Data fed in at one end of the sequence will be passed through these operations, in that order, and the solution will emerge automatically (Figure 15.2). Such a fixed sequence of operations is called an

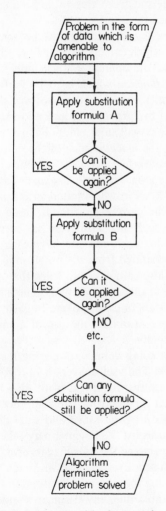

Figure 15.2—Flow chart for an algorithmic procedure

algorithm. Other programs are not so simple. It may be that in plotting the flow chart certain sequences of operations are seen to repeat themselves. In this case there is no need to program each repeat separately. Their repetition can be indicated by *branching* or looping. Other problems again cannot be solved in this way. They need a *heuristic* program, one which operates by trial-and-error so that each attempt at a solution is assessed and successive improvements attempted until an acceptable solution is reached within previously defined limits (Figure 15.3). Once the problem has been analysed in this way and broken down into tiny steps as displayed in the flow chart, it can be *coded* into programming language, written on a coding form or sheet. It will be transferred from this to some appropriate input medium (punched cards, punched tape and so on).

The program will have to take into account the *word-length* of the computer —the number of digits which can be held together for processing as one unit passing into and out of the computer. Each unit must contain a series of digits to represent the *function* which is to be performed on the operands within it (add, subtract, logical shift and so on), the operands themselves (data or other material for processing) and addresses within the computer at which these operations will take place. Each possible operation will be given a number within the *machine code* of the computer itself. Such codes are difficult to use because few people can remember strings of numbers. For this reason, various alpha-numeric *languages* have been developed, such as ALGOL and FORTRAN in which initial letters, abbreviations and so on, are used to represent the various functions. These are much easier to use than machine language, and once a program has been written in one of them it can be translated into machine code by means of a *compiler* and the computer will then be operated from the program in this form.

The languages themselves are easier to learn than machine code, but they may seem cumbersome to the user. Many designers will prefer to communicate in the words of written, or even spoken, English, and if more such 'plain language' programs were available, the use of computers in design would undoubtedly expand rapidly.

The usual method of using computers during the past twenty years has been by *batch processing*. The user delivers his program—a set of cards or a tape—to the computer centre where it is 'run'. It is highly likely that it will have to be *debugged* after the first run. The computer print-out will conclude with the ominous words *program failed* and each defect will be numbered with reference to a failures list. Debugging may take several runs, but once the program has been corrected the user may receive the *output* fairly quickly or he may have to wait hours, even days, for it. When this frustration is added to the tedium of producing the program itself, and of ironing out the 'bugs', then it really is remarkable that any designer should want to computerize his task. Clearly it is the province of enthusiasts. There really is a sense of

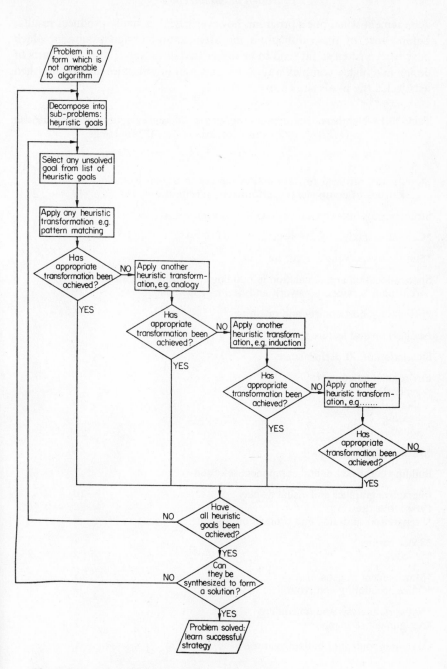

Figure 15.3—Flow chart for a heuristic procedure

achievement when one's program, however trivial, actually produces results; but because of these difficulties the architectural design programs which have been written so far tend to be rather trivial, to 'solve' the easier parts of design in a highly complex way. A rough count of examples in two published lists yields the totals shown in Table 15.1.

Table 15.1—Numbers of computer programs in different categories based on British (MPBW, 1969) and American (CAP, 1970) listings

	MPBW	CAP
Storage and retrieval of information for use in design including catalogues of components, performance specifications, etc.	10	12
Structures against which design data can be classified	8	
*Computer models of city structures	1	6
*Site surveys, contour maps, etc.	1	9
Space allocation and circulation in buildings, including pedestrian, vehicular, services, pipework and drainage layouts	19	39
*Estimating, cost control and quantities	6	7
Auditorium and lecture room design	3	1
Simulation of lift performance	1	2
Environmental control:		
general	1	2
thermal	9	
lighting	4	
sound	1	
*Structural calculations	6	
Building construction and component selection	7	1
Interactive graphics and visual display	10	
Perspective drawing	2	6
*Preparation of design and production drawings	7	4
*Specifications	1	4
*Schedules	2	3
*Management in general	5	
*Office accounting and payroll	1	
*Network analysis and scheduling		5
*Assignment of manpower	2	4
Computer control of buildings in use	1	

* Indicates categories in which specialized lists prepared for town planning, quantity surveying, structural engineering, etc., would contain many more examples.

Other programs, not included specifically in these two lists, include:

calculation of building area, volume, ratio of external surfaces to area and/or volume;
costing of alternative plans;
analysis of space utilization in existing buildings;
plotting of permissible building envelope;
statistics and O.R. techniques in general;
analysis of user activities against time.

These figures are by no means exhaustive, but they do indicate the areas of architectural design which computer enthusiasts (architects *and* non-architects) have thought worthy of attention or comparatively easy to program. Equivalent lists could have been prepared for Australia (see Gero and Brown, 1969), France (IRIA, 1971), Italy (Foti and Zaffagini, 1969), Spain (Camarero, Segui et al., 1972) and certain other countries, but the overall trends would be similar and in particular one would usually find that over one quarter of all published programs, not to mention academic papers about computing, are concerned with space allocation and circulation, one tenth with information systems of various kinds, and a similar number with computerized drawing in some form. Only one twentieth seems to deal with environmental control and, in these lists at least, a similar number with estimating and cost control.

If one also takes into account appropriate programs from town planning (location and transportation analysis) and O.R. itself, then the total percentage available for circulation and space allocation analysis would be even higher, and whilst these *are* important aspects of building design one cannot help feeling that they have attracted so much attention because they lend themselves fairly easily to programming; the analogue has taken over again! Campion (1968), Philips (1969), Willoughby (1970a, 1970b, 1970c and 1970d), Tabor (1969, 1970a, 1970b and 1970c), England (1971) and many others categorize and discuss these approaches in various ways, whilst in CAP (Stewart, Teicholz and Lee, 1970) they are grouped into six categories which, in decreasing order of popularity (numbers in brackets), may be described as: interchange (10); clustering (8); neighbouring (we shall call them adjacency—6); random (4); optimization (2) and vector (2) programs.

Interchange techniques operate by modifying a preliminary plan so as to effect, say, the greatest possible reduction in circulation costs. This initial solution may be generated by the computer or by the human designer; once it has been prepared it can be submitted to optimization procedures in which each element is exchanged, successively, with every other. These successive adjustments can be tested against stated criteria such as minimum cost, minimum circulation distance, and so on, until an 'optimum' solution is found. The best known of such programs is CRAFT (Armour, Buffa, 1963;

Vollman 1964) although it is not the most typical. This Computerized Relative Allocation of Facilities Technique was worked out initially for the location of industrial plant; the aim, at each stage, is to make the 'best' possible move, so as to effect the greatest possible cost reduction. Elements may be exchanged in pairs or in threes and CRAFT identifies the most favourable exchange at each stage by estimating the potential cost improvement for every exchange which is possible at that stage. CRAFT thus converges, eventually, on the 'best fit' solution—that which shows the greatest cost reduction over the initial solution. Lew and Brown (1968), Rohn (1970) and others have described various improvements to the original CRAFT program.

Clustering programs can be used, in principle, to classify objects of any kind into sets or groups whose members have certain attributes in common. They may be used alternately with decomposition programs such as HIDECS (Alexander and Manheim, 1962; Alexander 1963) which separate the elements of a given problem and their interactions in tree (HIDECS 2) or semi-lattice (HIDECS 3) fashion (see Chapter 14). Alexander's *Synthesis of Form* method (1962) is based on decomposition and recomposition in this way (see Chapter 14). HIDECS 2 defines the order in which the elements of a solution must be recombined within a hierarchy; it thus raises all the problems one might expect when binary variables are decomposed, and recombined in tree-like formations (see Chapter 12).

HIDECS-RECOMP (Bierstone and Bernholtz, 1966) takes the output of HIDECS 3, which is in semi-lattice form, and recomposes the various elements into interrelated subsets of the problem as a whole. Unlike the earlier HIDECS programs, which required a certain amount of hand-calculation, HIDECS-RECOMP is entirely automatic. Clustering programs of this kind clearly lend themselves to planning problems, but they can be applied to any kind of problem in which elements are interrelated in some way. It is generally assumed, however, that the various elements of a problem should contribute equally to its solution, with no weighting to emphasize elements which, given other procedures, might be considered more important. In practice, as Kowai says (1968) this may be highly undesirable.

Adjacency programs take into account relationships between, say, activities or rooms in terms of movement between them. Data may be derived from the analysis of an existing building in use, such as the program devised by Whitehead and Eldars in their analysis of an operating theatre suite (1964) .Whitehead and Eldars recorded the number of journeys in the existing suite between rooms and activities on a typical working day (weighted by salary, etc.) so that a surgeon's journey became equivalent to 3·2 student nurses' journeys. These were then plotted in a chart (Figure 12.9) from which it will be seen that the number of journeys varied greatly from room to room, with the highest total of all (1,115 journeys) to and from the ante-space and nurses' station. The rooms also varied in size and it was intended, eventually, to plot them on a 10 × 10 square grid so that, again, weightings were built in; the smallest rooms (e.g. the medical store) were allocated one square and the largest (the two operating theatres) were allocated 6 squares each.

The output from the computer located each element in turn at an appropriate position on the grid, ordered according to number of journeys. Thus the four elements comprising the ante-space were located first, followed by

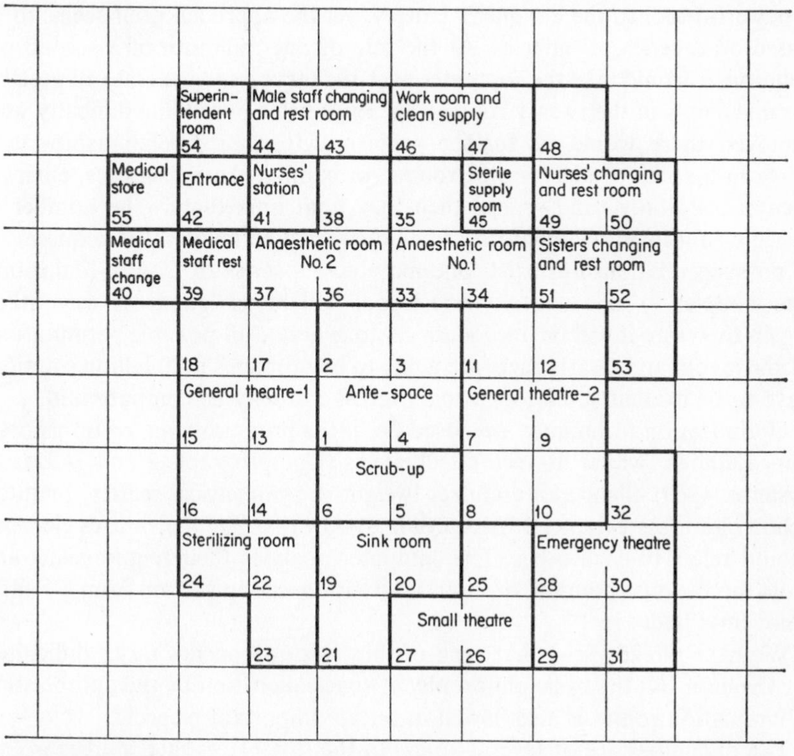

		Superintendent room 54	Male staff changing and rest room 44	43	Work room and clean supply 46	47	48	
	Medical store 55	Entrance 42	Nurses' station 41	38	35	Sterile supply room 45	Nurses' changing and rest room 49	50
	Medical staff change 40	Medical staff rest 39	Anaesthetic room No.2 37	36	Anaesthetic room No.1 33	34	Sisters' changing and rest room 51	52
	18	17	2	3	11	12	53	
	General theatre-1 15	13	Ante-space 1	4	General theatre-2 7	9		
	16	14	Scrub-up 6	5	8	10	32	
	Sterilizing room 24	22	Sink room 19	20	25	Emergency theatre 28	30	
		23	21	Small theatre 27	26	29	31	

Figure 15.4—Whitehead and Eldars' diagrammatic layout of an operating theatre suite

those comprising the scrub-up, the two theatres and so on; the diagrammatic layout thus derived is shown in Figure 15.4 and as one might expect this had to be modified manually to achieve a plan which would actually work. Developments of this technique have been described by various permutations of Agraa, Eldars and Whitehead (1964, 1965, 1968a and b), Phillips (1968) and others. As Beaumont (1967), Tabor (1970) and others have shown, adjacency programs tend to generate wide and deep concentric plans, with irregular perimeters which may be extremely uneconomical to utilize in practice.

Random techniques in theory can be used to generate all the possible layouts with which a given number of rooms can be arranged using pseudo random number, or Monte Carlo methods (see Chapter 10). Examples include ALDEP (Seehof and Evans, 1967) and LOKAT (Sinton and Fosberg, 1969); various constraints can be stated and used as a basis for selecting feasible solutions from the vast mass thus generated. For twenty rooms, as Phillips shows (1968) this might amount to over 6 thousand billion layouts (6×10^{17}), any of which may or may not be usable. At first sight, this adds a powerful tool to the designer's battery, yet the approach itself seems to be based on a series of fallacies. At the rate of one millionth of a second per solution, it would take the computer over 19,000 years to generate all possible arrangements of the twenty rooms; but even if this overriding difficulty were removed there would be further problems. If defined relationships exist between a series of activities or rooms (proximity, shared services, environmental conditions, and so on) then they limit immediately the number of feasible solutions; neighbouring techniques may be much more economical. If no such relationships exist, one may have a series of Cowan-like rooms (see Chapter 9) of which any one layout will be as 'good' as any other. Again therefore it will be uneconomical to generate all possible permutations of the layout and clearly there are going to be problems if 20 billion solutions have to be evaluated, although this process too may be computerized.

Optimization techniques are based on linear programming, or transportation methods, whilst in vector techniques (Comprograph 2 and 3, Design Systems, 1969) client and architect 'weight' a symmetrical matrix, or interaction chart (see Chapter 13) according to how they *feel* the various elements should relate to each other. The computer analyses their requirements and plots the various rooms at appropriate positions along vectors from a central point on a line.

We have already seen that each of these six approaches raises difficulties for the user, but the basic philosophy of space allocation by the optimization of circulation routes is also flawed in certain important respects.

The difficulties are of several kinds. In the first place, such studies isolate one aspect of planning which itself is only part of architectural design. They take proximity, which is only one aspect of planning, without reference to other considerations. They ignore the interactions between planning and environmental control, in terms of aspect, sun path, noise (both external noise and noise generated within the building), economy of service runs, relationship of plan to structure. The concentric, irregular plans which adjacency programs produce are often impossible, and certainly expensive, to build. They ignore such considerations as the relationship of floor area and shape to length of perimeter wall, which will have critical effects, say, on the running costs of services. Willoughby (1971) discusses an alternative approach in which one first designs the building envelope, which at first sight seems a thoroughly classical method or at least one based on preconceptions. But other Cambridge work shows that such preconceptions *may* carry their own economies. On an open site, for instance, a deep one- or two-storey building with a thick, dense, well-insulated roof, might be extremely effective for environmental control (Hawkes, 1971). One may accept such an envelope and locate various activities within it.

Another class of problems arises, as England suggests (1971), from the assumption, implicit in most of these circulation and allocation models, that plans can actually *be* optimized. This presupposes that the organization to be housed will never change, that relationships between activities, departments and so on, can be frozen at a moment in time; in other words, they not only fail to provide in themselves for growth, they may inhibit later changes by matching too closely this prior situation. Not that one can define that situation very closely. One promising approach, as we saw, was to observe an existing building in use, as Whitehead and Eldars did with their operating theatre suite in which journeys were recorded to provide data on movement patterns for the new design. However, an existing pattern of use will inevitably be constrained against the existing buildings; one can never be sure what people would have done in other circumstances; the analysis, in other words, will perpetuate various aspects of the given situation, some of which may be unsatisfactory. Yet because of the way the data was collected, they may be built into the new design. Even greater difficulties arise when one tries to postulate a new and unknown situation without benefit of such analysis. Intentionally or not, one will build values into one's predictions. Whitehead and Eldars weighted their data on journeys so that a single surgeon's journey was taken as equivalent to 3·2 student nurses' journeys. This in itself incorporates a set of social values; the surgeon is 'more important' than a nurse because he earns a higher salary. His time is more valuable and it doesn't matter if the nurse gets tired. Yet if one took this argument to its logical conclusion one would save the surgeon any journeys at all; one would arrange the plan so that he could stay rooted to the spot with the whole operation revolving round him, even if it meant that the nurses had to walk much further. In doing this, however, one would be exposing him to circulatory diseases such as phlebitis and he would find himself, before very long, a patient on his own table, being operated on by one of his colleagues. This slight exaggeration indicates the dangers of feeding suspect values into the analysis of an existing situation, but is it not even more likely that one will feed suspect values into some postulated future?

This is not the only kind of value which may be distorted or lost in programming the computer. Thiel (1961, 1962, 1964), Lynch (1960), Appleyard et al. (1964) and Halprin (1965, 1970) have all been concerned with the environmental values one senses in moving through physical space. Any design process which fails to take these into account may result in buildings which as sensory stimuli are simply unacceptable to their users. Allied to this are the subtle virtues of 'wasted' space such as Hazard described in his study of law courts (see Chapter 9). Such exercises merely confirm the fact that computer-aids throw enormous responsibility on the human designer; his choice of what is worth analysing will itself be a reflection of his values; the data he feeds into the computer will confirm them further; to repeat an earlier quotation, 'Garbage in, garbage out'.

Future developments in computer-aided design, therefore, will most certainly be more fruitful if we pay more attention to what the human being can do well, what the computer can do well, and the possibilities for dialogue between them. This will depend on identifying their characteristics more closely and building on their differences. Several computerologists have attempted comparisons between brain and computer. Table 15.2 combines elements from those by Fitts (quoted Singleton, 1966), Murrell (1965), Chandor (1970) and others.

Table 15.2

	Computer	Brain
Speed of operation	1,000 million or more numbers in one minute	Ten 7-digit numbers in one minute
Accuracy	Complete	Doubtful
Long-term memory	800 million bits (magnetic film store)	15 million million bits
Fastest intake of data	100 thousand characters (numbers, letters, etc.) per second (magnetic tape)	10,000 bits per second (all senses acting simultaneously) 25 characters per second selected data
Fastest output of data	As for intake	25 characters per second

Input devices	card reader
	tape reader
	keyboard
	character recognition
	devices: optical
	        magnetic ink
	voice recognition
	devices (doubtful)
	tape decks
	visual display units
	  with keyboard
	  with light pen
		eyes
		ears
		skin senses: smell
		        taste
		        touch
		        heat and cold
		kinaesthetic senses
		equilibrium
		internal organs

	Computer	Brain
	can also be coupled to measuring devices for electrical energy, heat, light, sound, radioactivity and so on	
Output devices	line printer page printer card punch paper tape punch console typewriter tape deck graph plotter cathode-ray tube	voice production hands, which may operate pencil pen keyboard switches, knobs, ·levers, etc.
Response to stimuli	Responds only to clear, simple stimuli, confused by ambiguous stimuli Digital computer requires stimuli to be presented within a very narrow range	Responds to clear or ambiguous stimuli Eye and brain (also ear and brain) together good at pattern recognition, can distinguish 'figure' from 'ground', isolating wanted signals from unwanted noise. Deals with wide energy range (10^{12}) and variety of stimuli, e.g. eye provides brain with information on hue, value, chroma, location, movement and so on
Cognitive processes	Follows instructions with complete accuracy, performing logical and/or arithmetical operations according to a *program* The program may consist of an *algorithm*; or it may be heuristic	May follow instructions precisely or in haphazard fashion May misunderstand them Analytical processes may be interrupted by creative leaps, thus short circuiting some tedious procedure, or generating a new kind of solution which may transcend all previous efforts, or prove to be completely irrelevant
	Speed, precision and accuracy of arithmetic operations of addition, subtraction, multiplication, division and exponentiation (raising numbers by various powers). Logic operations are largely a matter of comparing numbers or other data according to the	Slow, subject to error in arithmetical operation Logic may be suspect

Table 15.2—continued

	Computer	Brain
Cognitive processes —contd.	conventions of Boolean algebra; the 'and', 'or', 'not' operations and so on	
	The computer may thus decide which branch of a program to take, and draw conclusions from logical premisses (deduction), draw simple analogies and so on. The elements which are being compared must be reduced to the same format. Can draw simple direct analogies (size, shape, orientation, etc.) and this capacity may be extended in future to the generation of creative analogies. All possible analogies will be generated, will need man-made criteria for evaluating them	Perceiving, remembering, imagining, conceiving, judging, reasoning affected by feelings, emotions, motivation and so on

Good at comparing and judging unlike things, at inductive logic and at drawing analogies, metaphors directly relevant to the problem in hand |
| | Good at differentiation, integration | Good at interpolation, extrapolation, prediction, generating grammatical sentences, translating languages |
| | Remembering | Making complex, multimodal decisions

Exercising reasoned judgement |

It is not enough, therefore, to say that man ought to be Valéry's generator of combinations and the computer his chooser between them. For certain purposes it might be the other way round; but if they work together properly, then the dialogue between them must be facilitated.

The ideal for many designers seems to be an *interactive graphic* system in which one communicates with the computer by means of a television-like display and a 'light pen', which is used for drawing on to it. The computer can be programmed to straighten the lines of one's rough sketch, to correct one's perspective, to draw a perspective from plan and elevations, and to rotate the object in perspective so that it can be seen from different points of view. A single perspective can also be 'doubled' to form a stereo pair. One can 'place' standard symbols on the screen to represent doors, windows, wall panels and so on, moving them from place to place as desired to try out different plan configurations. One can ask for further information of these configurations—area, ratio of area to perimeter wall, cost and so on. In some cases the display includes a 'menu' of things one can ask for. One points the light pen at the appropriate word and the display changes accordingly. Clearly this is highly convenient if one is concerned with certain kinds of systems building, the IBIS programme (Gordon, undated) represents one such application, and Campion (1968) suggests that, for reasons of economy, this kind of computer-aided design should be applied *only* to systems building. However, visual display requires a very high storage capacity of the computer and the installation itself is very expensive. It has been used in practice by the West Sussex County Architects Department for certain aspects of their SCHOLA programme, concerned with planning, component selection and cost checking. Eventually it should be possible to check one's design proposals against the building regulations, other statutory constraints, lighting, thermal, and other environmental standards, all within an environmental matrix (see Chapter 19) developed on the interactive display for a particular site. One report (MPBW, 1969) suggests that:

'Development of advanced graphics will provide more realistic and useful visual representations than the current line drawings on cathode ray tubes. It will be technically possible to "walk" through a full scale building at the design stage, the computer providing a 3D image automatically adjusted to the user's viewpoint as he turns his head. Software for computing the visible faces of solid objects in half tones has been much improved recently and computing times for this and similar operations could be speeded with special purpose hardware. Colour has been developed and will soon be available.'

Eventually, perhaps, it might be possible to add other environmental conditions, to simulate the thermal and aural ambience, and to simulate different lighting conditions.

Many interactive graphics programs merely encourage one to generate, canonically, three-dimensional rectangular forms, interpenetrating and overlapping, which may then be enlarged, reduced, projected into perspective, axonometric and so on. INTU-VAL, however, is an interactive graphic development of Alexander's route location method in which the various maps of the area are displayed. Kamnitzer (1969) reports that contours, land values, geology, population, conservation and visual interest have been used so far. Any one of these may be displayed; the designer sketches his proposed route on to the map, including access points, bridges and so on, using a light pen, and then instructs INTU-VAL to display a series of bar charts evaluating the proposed route from various points of view—driving time, cost, safety, visual interest, community service and so on, up to a total of twelve factors of which six will be physical and six non-physical. Given this information, he can then decide how to improve the route. The designer then uses his own judgement to decide which of these factors are important and which unimportant, after which he can relocate the route as necessary, in order to improve its rating in terms of the important factors.

Assessment of visual interest, of course, depends on being able to *see* how the route changes as one drives along it, and Kamnitzer's *City-Scape* has been developed, in conjunction with NASA and the General Electric Company, to simulate this in coloured planes. One 'drives' through it, controlling speed, direction and head-eye movement and further developments should enable rapid modification to be made, including 360 degree, and later complete, spherical projection.

Similar techniques, obviously, could be applied to the simulation of building interiors but unfortunately much of this is potential rather than actual. A good deal of computer animation so far has been rather like a cartoon film. Clearly it is possible to display the equivalent of a single frame in a cartoon film on the cathode-ray tube. It is possible also to display successive frames and for the computer to draw immediate frames between them. One achieves computer animation in this way, but that is not the same thing as achieving a program of such complexity that the designer can 'walk about' inside what he is designing. Undoubtedly this will be possible eventually, just as the rotation of perspective drawing is possible, but it seems to be some way ahead.

Negroponte (1969, 1970) envisages an *Architecture Machine*, which operates in intimate dialogue with the human designer:

'Imagine a machine that could follow your design methodology and at the same time discern and assimilate your conversational idiosyncrasies. This same machine, after observing your behaviour, could build a predictive model of your conversational performance. Such a machine could then reinforce the dialogue by using the predictive model to respond to you in a manner that is in rhythm with your personal behaviour. This dialogue would be so intimate (even exclusive) that only mutual persuasion and compromise would bring about perceptions and ideas— ideas, in fact, unrealizable by either converser alone. In such asymbiosis, it would not be solely the designer who would decide when the machine is relevant.'

Certain aspects of this performance can be achieved already to operate with the subtlety which Negroponte intends, but the machine would have to recognise every gesture, however trivial, and to interpret it in context; it would also have to understand the processes of imagination, analogy, metaphor and so on. This would be essential, as Negroponte points out, if the designer were to be computer-aided, rather than having his personal design processes computerized.

It may be that one's dialogue with the computer in itself becomes such a satisfying aesthetic experience that one becomes more concerned with process than with product. A simple example of this has been presented by Zinovieff (1968) in the form of a device which picks up the tune one whistles into a microphone and submits it to a number of variations—in pitch, speed, volume and so on. In a rudimentary way it composes variations on what one has whistled. One can even envisage a much more sophisticated device which reacts in the way that Negroponte described and leads one into aesthetic experience which is entirely personal—it may even act directly on the 'pleasure centres' which Olds (1956) has identified in the brain. It is highly likely, in fact, that computers will be developed which monitor human reactions, but instead of using them in design we might do better to use them in buildings. Thus one will arrive, say, at one's office in the morning to find the mere shell of a building, the simplest possible form of weather protection, very heavily serviced. One will start to work (talking perhaps, to another person) and various sensing devices in the building will monitor what one is trying to do. Data thus collected will be passed to a central computer which will then instruct certain parts of the building to adjust themselves to one's purposes. If one's conversation is private, then an insulated office will form itself and remain for as long as one needs it. Elsewhere in the building other rooms will form themselves around individuals or groups of people according to their environmental needs. Negroponte's unit has already developed a door, or rather an opening, which 'recognizes' people as they approach it, in terms of height, weight, length of stride, silhouette and so on—the first step, perhaps, towards a fully responsive environment.

We already make responsive environments, to a limited extent, for plants— and computers. The Climatron at St. Louis houses various zones for different kinds of vegetation; the climate in each is monitored and adjusted accordingly. Similar controls are built into various plant houses in the Botanical Gardens at Edinburgh not to mention commercial greenhouses in various parts of the world. The ERNIE computer installation at St. Anne's on Sea contains various climatic monitoring and adjusting devices; certain schools near London Airport have windows which are closed automatically when aircraft noise exceeds a certain level; again, though, full development on these lines seems a very long way ahead. Meanwhile, we shall have to look at ways of making the computer more useful to the designer in the immediate future.

One report (MPBW, 1969) suggests that the development of computer-aided design systems depends on several factors and in particular on freeing the designer from the frustrations inherent in the batch processing of punched cards. Much greater flexibility will be needed and five ways of encouraging this are suggested:

1. The development of multi-access systems in which several users each have a keyboard terminal on-line to a central computer. Standard programs would be available and the user would merely have to type in appropriate data. Such facilities are available already on a limited scale.
2. The development of cheap interactive graphic systems, less demanding on the computer store. Again several users could have graphic terminals on line to a central computer.
3. The development of large, direct-access stores. Such stores exist but the software for large-scale files is not generally available.

4. The development of plain language programs so that users can converse with their computers easily and even suggest modifications to programs which will then be incorporated.
5. More efficient means of letting it be known what programs exist, of interchanging programs, of diminishing incompatibilities which exist between different programming languages and of making sure that those who develop suitable programs are adequately rewarded.

There is not the slightest doubt that brain and computer together are capable of revolutionizing our entire approach to design. Suppose, for instance, that we undertook a thorough analysis of human environmental requirements, monitoring the way in which people live, noting points of stress between themselves and their environment, measuring the environmental conditions which they chose and modified for themselves, submitting the whole of this data to computer analysis and drawing up standards for new environments on the basis of this analysis. We *might* find that this ability to collect all the relevant data, to analyse it fully, to present the information thus derived in such a way that the human designer could make truly reasoned judgements, would lead us to an architecture which seemed reasonably like the best of that we know already. If the Georgian square really is as good, environmentally, as many people believe it to be then this man-made computer dialogue might well lead us back to something very like the Georgian square.

CHAPTER 16

The Design Spectrum

By the early 1950s a whole new range of techniques was available to the designer. They had been developed from the analyses of thinking by Dewey, Wertheimer and others, in fields such as systems engineering, operational research, ergonomics and so on. Information theory and cybernetics had much to offer so that altogether it looked as if dramatic developments would be possible in all aspects of design. Many designers, particularly in the United States, felt that some kind of millennium was at hand. Design could be completely rationalized and would not be held back ever again by individual values, opinions or personal 'creativity'. In the field of weapons design particularly, this seemed to be true. Highly complex programmes were set up involving hundreds of designers, suppliers and manufacturers. Their work was coordinated by methods such as network analysis (CPM itself was developed for the Polaris missile programme); new organizational structures, even, were designed and the results seemed to exceed the most sanguine expectations. In other fields, however, the results were rather disappointing. The act of designing, certainly, became much more complex; the designed object itself rarely seemed 'better' than before and frequently worse. Even in the weapons programme the illusion that total rationality would solve all the designer's problems was finally shattered on the night of October 4, 1957, when the Russians launched their first Sputnik.

As Hudson says (1966), this alerted American opinion, official and otherwise, to Russia's emergence as a first-class technological power. It was quite unthinkable to many Americans that this country of supposed barbarians should beat the most highly equipped and technologically sophisticated nation in the world, at the game of rocket launching. Three and a half years later, and still smarting under this blow, President Kennedy announced on May 25, 1961 that America would land a man on the moon and bring him back safely, before the end of the decade.

The immediate task, however, was to discover, rapidly, the scientific talent which would enable America to equal and to surpass the Russian achievement. In a series of panic conferences in Michigan (Anderson, 1959), Colorado (Gruber et al., 1962), Los Angeles (Steinberg, 1962) and elsewhere, it was agreed that the cure for America's ills lay in the cultivation of *creativity*, that this, and not intelligence, could be taken as the proper indication of a child's potential for development, and that creativity rather than academic ability should be cultivated in schools and universities. These views, in fact, had been

321

held by psychologists long before Sputnik. Guilford (1950), Roe (1951, 1953) and others had already published work on creativity in various fields and there had been conferences on creativity at Utah in 1955, 1957, and a further one in 1959, the proceedings of which were edited by Taylor (1956, 1958 and 1959). Ghiselin's *The Creative Process* had been published in 1954, Osborn's *Applied Imagination* in 1957, whilst the works already quoted by Dewey, Wallas and Wertheimer date respectively from 1909, 1926 and 1945. Sputnik, at least, helped to put all this work into context, and the plea for creativity was at last granted a fair hearing.

Hudson goes so far as to say that since Sputnik creativity has become something of a research 'bandwagon' for psychologists, a boom in the psychology 'industry' of America paralleled only by programmed learning. Like all bandwagons it has excited suspicion; research into creativity has become suspect even though, finally, it *is* a proper study for psychology. Few things, in fact, could be more rewarding for a psychologist than the study of a fine, imaginative brain, operating at its most effective.

The reason for this mistrust, as always, was that things had become polarized. One must either be creative *or* intelligent, rational *or* intuitive—divergent *or* convergent. It never seemed to occur to the partisans of one or the other that a person might be both or, as Valéry rightly says, that both are needed in a fully creative act. There was opposition of another kind too, from those who resented any attempt to probe their creativity. They saw it as a mystery in the mind which it would be dangerous to analyse. Henry Moore once said, 'It's like riding a bicycle, once I stop to think how I do it, I can't do it any more,' and there is some truth in that. We have many accounts of creative activity written *after* the event, such as those in Ghiselin (1954), but anyone who is deeply involved in the creative act will almost certainly resent intrusion at the time and may well resent it afterwards. Gordon (1961) notes that early in the investigations which led, eventually, to his *Synectics* method of ideas-generation, the artists and scientists he questioned about their psychological states during the creative act responded in two ways. Some, he says, welcomed this probing of their inner workings, without any fear that it might destroy their creative capacity; others, however, refused to discuss the (to them) mysterious workings of their minds, although months later replies finally came in from most of them too.

Let us look, for a moment, at where, and when, one is supposed to be creative. The panic over Sputnik implied that if some of the American engineers had been imaginative, instead of merely intelligent and rational, then the United States would have beaten Russia at getting a satellite into orbit. Instead of laboriously calculating everything to do with their rockets, they would have taken a creative *leap*, in Dewey's terms, and come up with a more elegant solution (using 'elegant' in the sense by which we defined it in Chapter 3).

That may or may not be true, but it helps us narrow down the area in which we expect creativity to operate. Given, say, a typical decision sequence— briefing, analysis, synthesis, evaluation and implementation—then clearly creativity plays its part in synthesis. At first sight one would eschew, as far as possible, any suggestion of creativity in briefing; one is looking, after all, for facts. Analysis, by definition, is non-creative and so for that matter is evaluation. Creative evaluation, indeed, suggests that one might be deceiving oneself about the excellence of one's decision. As for creative implementation, well yes, it might be necessary when people have to be persuaded to put a creative decision into action. So let us allow that in this last phase of decision too there may be some room for creativity.

However, the major concentration of creativity, clearly, will be during synthesis—the generation, in variety, of solutions to the problem. This is where the creative leap belongs and, if the evaluation which follows is rigorous enough, then clearly any creative leap will be eliminated in which one has jumped too far. So a properly ordered decision sequence will encourage one to be creative—as wildly creative as possible—during the central phase of synthesis. Yet already we are guilty of over-simplification. We have assumed that analysis and synthesis are separate things, that the one gives way to the other. Abercrombie suggests (1965) that it does not. She is not concerned with creative decision but with an analogous problem of response in the child to a test of spatial relations. In this item from the Frostig Developmental Test of Visual Perception, children are asked to look at a grid of dots, on to which a figure is drawn in line by joining up certain dots. They are then asked to copy the figure on to an empty grid of dots, Figure 16.1. The task is graded according to age and if the child is presented with a pattern which is too complex for him, then two things may happen. Some children try to relate the figure to something they know already. They might say, 'Oh, it's a sort of eight,' and then draw an eight with little or no reference to the figure they are supposed to be copying. Abercrombie suggests that this is an intuitive response, that the child is quite happy to have constructed something which is like the idea in his head, rather than like the original figure on paper; he does not even attempt to check back from his drawing to the original. He synthesizes without analysing, but when the child is further developed he examines the original pattern very closely and tries hard to match it, dot for dot and line for line. The result may be grossly inaccurate still and, at first sight, it looks remarkably like analysis without synthesis. Abercrombie suggests, however, that it is far more likely to result from imprecise analysis. The child may have started at the wrong dot, turned left instead of right, made an oblique stroke instead of a vertical one, and carried on from there. His *construction* is faulty because he has no real grasp of structure based on analysis. As he matures, of course, he will be able to balance analysis with synthesis and to draw increasingly complex figures.

According to Abercrombie, this is true of architectural design too, that one can only synthesize what one has mastered already by analysis. She also makes the important point that analysis can only be mastered in the context of a continued struggle to synthesize—one is motivation for the other. That is one of the reasons why a scheduled design process is misleading: it suggests that one stage necessarily follows from another; but in the instant of designing the two are inextricably interlinked.

So far so good, but we are concerned with more than design. We saw in Chapter 10 that decision sequences in other fields (in operational research, for instance) include a stage equivalent to synthesis—the generation of

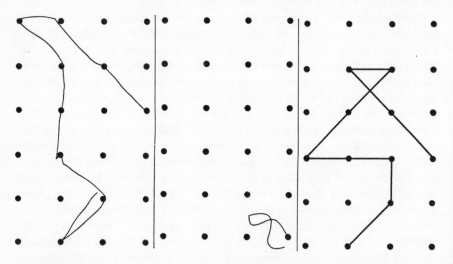

Figure 16.1—Frostig test for the development of visual perception, which Abercrombie (1965) uses to illustrate the interdependence of analysis and synthesis

solutions in variety—which depends on the operation of a mechanism, the feeding of data into a certain equation, the manipulation of variables which results, automatically, in the generation of solutions in variety. In other words, given the fruits of analysis (in both cases a set of data) Dewey takes a creative leap, whereas the operational researcher turns a handle and generates solutions automatically.

We would go further. Beveridge points out in *The Art of Scientific Investigation* (1950) that many great discoveries in science have been achieved, on the face of it, by pure chance. One of the best known examples is Sir Alexander Fleming's discovery of penicillin. He was working with some cultures of *staphylococcus* and had occasion to open the plates on which they were growing several times. They became contaminated with various moulds, and around one particular colony of mould, the staphylococci tended to die. Fleming observed this, as hundreds of biologists before him had observed the results of similar mistakes, and realized that it was significant. The mould was identified as penicillium and it was possible to isolate the substance in it which was killing the staphylococci, and thus penicillin was discovered. As Beveridge rightly says, there is more than chance to such discoveries: the other vital component is a prepared mind, prepared to observe the significance of chance. Briefing, obviously, is a method of preparing and is necessary, therefore, if a mind is to see the significance of the chance event once it has occurred.

So already we have seen three quite different means by which the results of analysis may be converted, by synthesis, into possible solutions: by the fixed processes of mathematics in O.R., by some form of creative leap and by pure chance. The last two, possibly, have something in common and indeed the first and last are not entirely alien for, after all, the computer which can be used to work with undeviating allegiance to a strict instruction can also be used to generate random numbers; they have that much in common. Let us assume for now that the strictly followed rational instruction and pure chance are opposites—the polarized ends, as it were, of a spectrum. It will be a spectrum in which the elements shade into each other finely; at certain points there will be difficulties in distinguishing one from the next. The number of elements will be quite arbitrary, but the magic number seven gives us a good enough working number.

We have already identified the two ends of our spectrum and it will be convenient now to plot some of the others, starting with the mid-point; clearly Dewey's creative leap is both too specific (sometimes it is only a tiny step) and too broad ('creative' might mean almost anything). We need a term which will help us move from the known to the unknown with the minimum of restriction. Cassidy (1962) suggests that in moving from the known to the unknown, constructs may be related in three ways, which he describes as ratio, analogy and metaphor. Their uses are different in the arts and sciences; ratio, for instance, is the *rational*, mathematical way of doing things and as far as possible the scientist will use it; but certain constructs cannot be related in this way, so he resorts to analogy and this, for Cassidy, is 'an imperfect ratio or proportionality.' The artist too (Cassidy writes more of the humanist) tends to analogy, but some of his experiences are so elusive that he can hardly communicate them at all. In that case he resorts to metaphor. Ratio, analogy and metaphor then, might form elements of our spectrum but still we need two more divisions to bring our total up to seven. Let us use the traditional devices of logic, deduction and induction, which will slot very neatly into the gaps in our spectrum. So the full spectrum now reads: algorithm; ratio; deduction; analogy; induction; metaphor; chance. Philosophically it is indefensible. The elements are different in kind; chalk, cheese and bad red herring; music, colour and noise. That's as may be, but we are not looking for consistency in the spectrum; rather for a pragmatic device which *may* help us actively in design. For this purpose, the elements *must* be different in kind, otherwise each would generate the same kind of solution and one device would serve all purposes. As a matter of fact, one of them—analogy—very nearly *does* serve all our purposes: most of the other elements can be taken as special cases of it. But it will be useful to give each of them an identity to show that each special case has particular things to offer. So to make this point we will look at each of them in turn.

Algorithm

Algorithm is a mathematical device for solving a particular class of problems. The word itself is part of our legacy from the Arab world, for Al-Kwarizmi, a ninth century mathematician, was one of the first to write a complete account of the numerical system which the Arabs had learned from the Hindus, using 4, 5, 6, 7, 8 and 9 in the forms we know them now. Some purists, therefore, insist that because it derives from the word for decimal notation we should call it algorism; but having corrupted al-Kwarizmi's name so far, we can hardly quibble at one slight further corruption to algorithm. Whatever we like to call it, the *Theory of Algorithms* was worked out in enormous detail by the Russian mathematician A. A. Markov (1954). He defined algorithm as 'an exact prescription, defining a computational process, leading from various initial data to the desired result.' Its main features, according to Markov, are as follows:

(*a*) It will be *definite*: the prescription for the algorithm will be precise, with no place for arbitrariness, and it will be universally comprehensible.
(*b*) It will be *general*: it will be possible to start from the given data, but the data itself may vary within certain limits.
(*c*) It will be *conclusive*: the algorithm will be orientated towards some desired result, obtained with certainty, provided that the proper kind of data has been fed in.

The algorithm will consist of a set of substitution formulae, a set of simple step-by-step rules which tell one as one works through precisely what to do next. A computer program, of course, takes this form and many people use the word algorithm loosely to describe the flow chart by which a computer program is planned. A simple example is shown in Figure 15.2 (page 305). Clearly many techniques in operational research may be written as algorithms of this kind; and in architectural design, circulation patterns (1), including drainage (2), the design of simple repetitive structures (3), heat loss calculations (4), acoustical calculations (5), choice from a list of components (6), choice of cladding panels (7), have all been computerized and thus expressed in the form of algorithms. However, the algorithm itself, or rather the flow chart, may be used as an analogue for certain aspects of architectural design, such as flow and circulation systems.

Ratio

With *ratio* we move away from the strict inevitability of algorithm, although we are still concerned with mathematical relationships. We are, in fact, concerned with the numerical relation one quantity bears to another of the same kind. The simplest applications of ratio are expressed in the following form:

if 2 is to 3 as 6 is to x, then x must be 9

Mathematically it may be expressed in various ways:

$$2 : 3 = 6 : x, \quad \text{or} \quad \frac{2}{3} = \frac{6}{x} \quad \text{or} \quad 2/3 = 6/x$$

At this level ratio bears a strong resemblance to algorithm, and this is true also of some of the great generalizations in physics, which are often expressed as ratios:

$$E = mc^2$$

where E = energy
 m = mass and
 c = a constant

This, of course, is a formula—one of the key formulae in the shaping of twentieth century affairs, from Einstein's Special Theory of Relativity. Formulae, in fact, and equations are merely complex ratios. Einstein's formula is a pretty tight one, just one constant, c, so it can be described as an algorithm for finding energy: feed in the data (in this case a quantity for the mass), multiply by the constant squared, and out comes energy. In some fields the equations may be much more complex, involving differentials and a range of constants. Obviously such equations are not so tight, they begin to move us away from the strict mechanics of algorithm.

As we saw in Chapters 4 and 5, ratio in the form of proportional canons has been one of the great formative bases of architectural design, and even now its power is by no means diminished. Clearly it applies at many levels. The size and shape of a window are clearly matters of proportional ratios, so are the size and shape of a façade, a room, a plan. Classical, medieval and Renaissance design were largely matters of ratio; so for that matter are dimensional coordination and much systems building today. It is simply the old Pythagorean device of imposing a geometric structure on the world.

Yet ratios may be applied in many ways. In classical systems generally, the proportional relationships between elements remain constant but the sizes of the elements change. A large Greek temple is merely a small Greek temple, identical in form but larger in size. In medieval systems, on the other hand, the sizes of elements stay fairly constant but the proportional relations change. A Gothic cathedral is larger than a Gothic church; it also has more parts.

Deduction

Deduction, technically speaking, is the method of reasoning by inference from premisses which Aristotle described in the *Prior Analytics*. As we saw in Chapter 12, its mechanism is the syllogism, a formal statement consisting of two propositions from which a third one follows naturally. A favourite example, quoted by Russell (1946) is:

All men are mortal (major premiss)
Socrates is a man (minor premiss)
Therefore Socrates is mortal (conclusion)

The major premiss is universally true (at least no case is known of a man who was not mortal); the minor premiss is true of this particular case (i.e. Socrates) and the conclusion too is specific to that case. The general form of this syllogism may be represented:

Premisses: $\begin{cases} \text{all M is P} \\ \text{all S is M} \end{cases}$
Conclusion: all S is P

Yet although the great edifice of deductive logic has been built on these principles and many authorities (e.g. Cohen and Nagel, 1961) take them as the basis of scientific method, the foundations are in fact shaky.

Take the major premiss of our first syllogism: all men are mortal. We cannot *really* be certain of that. We know that almost every man born over a hundred and fifty years ago is now dead; we also know that most men born over a hundred years ago are dead. We know of no case where a man has proved to be immortal; so that although we know with a probability approaching certainty that men are mortal, we cannot be absolutely sure. According to Russell, the only inferences of which we can be certain are those of logic and pure mathematics—also law and theology—but apart from these, all major premisses have been derived by induction and they are matters of probability therefore, rather than certainty. Most deduction is really induction in disguise.

In spite of these grave defects, deduction has its uses. We might define it, for our purposes, as inference by reasoning from a general rule to a particular solution. This clearly has applications in design. In some ways, for instance, it is the mechanism of systems building. One sets up a system of general rules and deduces a particular solution from it.

Analogy

We now reach the mid-point of the spectrum, beyond which we shall be dwelling in regions devoted increasingly to some of the more rarified characteristics of imagination and intuition. There may be some confusion, initially, as to the differences between *analogy* and *metaphor*. Let us see how Fowler defines them in his *Dictionary of Modern English Usage* (1961):

ANALOGY '(log., Gramm); "accordance with proportion." Inference or procedure based on the presumption that things whose likeness in certain respects is known will be found or should be treated as alike also in respects about which knowledge is limited to one of them.'

METAPHOR '(Rhet.); "transferring"—which might be supplemented by an OED definition; 'figure of speech in which a name or descriptive term is transferred to some object different from, but analogous to, that to which it is properly applicable.'

One might also add *analogue* which Fowler doesn't define. It is *not* apparently a common device in rhetoric. The key words here, of course, are contained in Fowler's brackets: *analogy* is a device in logic and grammar—and, be it noted, in mathematics—whereas metaphor is a device in rhetoric.

The essence of analogy, as a device in logic, is that there should be an *important* resemblance between two things; the whole value of the inference by analogy depends on this resemblance. Two objects may resemble each other in many trivial details, without presenting any suitable grounds at all for drawing an analogy. Mellone cites the instance of two boys who resemble each other in a great many ways: height, appearance, strength, accidents of birth in the same town, education at the same school, similar social backgrounds and yet, given all these factors, one could never infer that they were equal in intelligence. To provide a strong argument from analogy therefore, '*the resemblances must be essential and the differences unessential*.'

In logic a single analogy will be inconclusive but a number of analogies, if they all converge on a single point, may be perfectly adequate. Darwin presents a classic instance of such analogical convergence:

'a. In districts of the earth now exposed to glacial action, we find scored or "striated" rocks;
   In such and such a valley in Great Britain we find striated rocks;
   Therefore this valley probably has been exposed to glacial action.
 b. In districts now exposed to glacial action we find perched boulders;
   In the same valley we find perched boulders;
   Therefore this valley probably has been exposed to glacial action.
 c. In districts now exposed to glacial action we find lateral and terminal "moraines";
   In the same valley we find lateral and terminal moraines;
   Therefore this valley probably has been exposed to glacial action.'

(quoted Mellone, 1966)

When analogies converge like this, they leave little room for doubt, even though each taken on its own would be quite inconclusive.

The danger, of course, is that one indulges in *false analogy*—in which, given certain essential *resemblances* between two objects, one forgets the *differences* which are also *essential*. Many people have drawn analogies between the city and the human body, using such terms as 'lungs' for parks, 'cancerous growth' for areas of blight, 'arteries' for main roads. They even speak of its youth, maturity, old age and death; such analogies may be useful for the low level of description they offer but, as Fowler says, they soon get extended beyond the bounds of endurance.

Analogy, then, is a useful device, and one we shall consider in greater detail later. Convergent analogy of the type used by Darwin clearly has much to offer in design and so, by analogy, has the use it is put to in grammar, whereby new words are created by analogy with old. We considered the mechanism in Chapter 2.

Induction

Inductive reasoning is concerned with finding the unifying pattern; given certain facts, we assume that some general principle unites them and our aim is to find the rules by which they are connected and, if possible, to 'explain' this connexion by linking it with other general laws. We seek to *organize* facts which, taken individually, seem isolated, fragmentary and at variance with each other.

Aristotle identified several types of induction. In one of these he was concerned with the mental processes whereby a universal character, or relation, is identified with reference to an actual case or event. Obviously this is a haphazard process and there is another sense in which many others have followed him since. It is a matter of establishing a universal proposition by enumerating *all* the instances which may be subsumed with it. This too has its dangers and Russell (1946) gives an amusing instance of false induction of this form:

'There was once a census officer who had to record the names of all the house-holders in a certain Welsh village. The first . . . was called William Williams, so were the second, third and fourth . . . At last he said to himself, "This is tedious, evidently they are all called William Williams. I shall put them down so and take a holiday." But he was wrong. There was just one whose name was John Jones.'

That was bad luck and sometimes, indeed, one has complete knowledge of all cases, and one's induction is still invalid. The problem is to know how valid an induction may be when one has incomplete knowledge of the instances. At this point it becomes a matter of probabilities, which we have already examined in Chapter 6.

The father of inductive method in science is generally supposed to have been Francis Bacon, as described in Chapter 5, and his *Novum Organon* was intended obviously as a successor to the orginal *Organum*, a title given to

Aristotle's collected works. Bacon set down in detail the steps of inductive method; observe a large number of facts, formulate theories to explain these facts, and test these theories by experiment. Popper (1963) believes this is impossible. He says that one *starts* by forming a hypothesis, which can only be the result of an intuitive guess. Having formed the hypothesis, one deduces logical predictions from it, and these may then be submitted to test by:

(a) comparison of conclusions for internal consistency
(b) examination of logical form of theory
(c) comparison with earlier theories to see if an advance has been made
(d) empirical testing of conclusions and predictions.

Popper's views have had some currency in architectural circles (see Landau, 1965); briefly his argument is this: one cannot invent a hypothesis in the way that Bacon thought one could, by collecting observations, analysing specific cases and ordering them into categories and achieving some huge generalization by analysis of these specific cases. One is bound to be prejudiced at the start. Even if the induction itself were possible, it would be based, inevitably, on distorted information. One cannot collect observations at random; if one tried there would be no basis for selection and one would finish up by accumulating the whole of the world's knowledge. So one *has* to start by deciding what to look for, and this in itself suggests that one has certain views on the subject. In other words, one has a hunch, a hypothesis, a prejudice—something, anything, which acts as a basis for observation and enables one to select from the world just those things which are of interest and relevance.

Popper is not in the least concerned with how one's initial hunch, prejudice or theory was formed. That, he says, is a private matter; we shall disagree with him because the origin of hunches is such a fascinating affair. His method of testing, too, may be suspect. As we saw in dealing with deduction, Russell suggested that laws can *only* be achieved by induction, unless they be in the fields of logic, law, mathematics or religion, and Popper says nothing to disprove this assertion. But, however shaky the foundations on which Popper's tests may be based, if one's hypothesis survives them then the theory is verified. If it doesn't, then the theory is falsified. One can never *prove* a theory; all one can say is that for now it has not been disproved. So science will never reach finality; as Levin once said, in quite another context, 'It's like a blob of mercury, once you've put your finger on it, you find it isn't there any more.' Popper puts it more solemnly:

'Science does not rest on rock bottom . . . It is like a building erected on piles. These piles are driven forward from above the swamp, but not down to any natural base, and when we cease our attempt to drive piles into a deeper layer [or, he might have added, even farther forward] it is not because we have reached firm ground. We simply stop when we are satisfied that they are firm enough to carry the structure for the time being' [and again, he might have added, when we are satisfied that the structure, for now, is big enough].

Metaphor

As we have seen, metaphor is that 'figure of speech in which a name or descriptive term is transferred to some object different from, but analogous to, that to which it is properly applicable'. Certainly, the original Greek word meant 'a transference' but, for Aristotle at least, there was far more to it than that. 'The greatest thing by far,' he said, 'is to have a command of metaphor.' And what is more, he went on to say, 'This alone cannot be imparted to another: it is the mark of genius, for to make good metaphors implies an eye for resemblances.' Schon (1963) finds that people who analyse language tend to circumscribe metaphor too much. For him, language consists almost entirely of metaphor, to such an extent that we do not even notice it. He takes a number of commonplace sentences and underlines the metaphors in each. We can go one better by quoting his explanation and italicizing the metaphors in that:

> '*Focussing attention* on the metaphors *in* ordinary language is like *focussing on* the colour green. We *see* it *everywhere*. It has, too, the effect of immediately *removing the film of obviousness that covers our way of looking* at the world.'

I. A. Richards disagrees with Aristotle in *The Philosophy of Rhetoric* (1936). It is quite wrong, he says, to assume that some men have 'an eye for resemblances' whilst others do not and what is more, 'we all live and speak, only through our eye for resemblances. Without it we should perish early. Though some may have better eyes than others, the differences between them are in degree only and may be remedied, certainly in some measure (. . .) by the right kinds of teaching and study.' Yet, according to Richards, many people think of metaphor as a 'sort of happy extra trick with words', instead of the 'omnipresent principle of language'. Richards, in fact, sees metaphor as fundamental to human communication to the extent that 'we cannot get through three sentences of ordinary fluid discourse without it (. . .) even in the rigid language of the settled sciences we do not eliminate or prevent it without great difficulty. In the semi-technicalized subjects, in aesthetics, politics, sociology, ethics, psychology, theory of language, and so on, our constant chief difficulty is to discover how we are using it and how our supposedly fixed words are shifting their senses.' Furthermore, as he shrewdly observes, the more abstract our thinking becomes, the more we 'think increasingly by means of metaphors that we profess *not* to be relying on, especially as the metaphors we are trying to avoid stretch our thoughts just as much as those that we choose to accept.'

The greatest problem with metaphor is that traditional definitions, such as that quoted above, are confusing and limited. As Richards says, they make metaphor a verbal matter, a shifting and displacement of words, 'whereas fundamentally it is a borrowing between and intercourse of *thoughts*, a transaction between contexts.' A further difficulty is that the term itself, *metaphor*, confuses the contexts between which transaction takes place. If we are to understand the power of metaphor at all, we shall have to separate its constituent parts, the original idea and the borrowed one. Richards devises terms for these: he calls the underlying idea, the principle subject, the *tenor* of the metaphor, which is then described or qualified in terms of the *vehicle*. The *metaphor* itself, of course, is the double unit of tenor *and* vehicle; it conveys far richer meanings than either could alone. The vehicle is more than a mere embellishment of the tenor; vehicle and tenor in conjunction give a far more powerful meaning than either could alone. Moreover, the richness of metaphor lies in the fact that relationships between tenor and vehicle can be infinitely varied; at one extreme the vehicle may be little more than a decoration or colouring on the tenor, whilst at the other the tenor may become almost an excuse for introducing the vehicle.

Richards distinguishes two types of metaphor—those which work through direct resemblance between tenor and vehicle, and those which work simply because we hold common attitudes towards them. It might be enough to draw metaphors between two things merely because *we like them both*. Richards illustrates some of the differences between literal and metaphoric meanings; he takes the word 'leg'. We might speak about the leg of a horse, and then about the leg of a table. A table cannot walk, its legs share only certain characteristics of a horse's; those common characteristics become the *ground* of metaphor. And what of a spider's legs, or a starfish's—or are they arms? Does a chimpanzee have four legs, or two? And what is a wooden leg? It is, of course, both a literal leg and a metaphoric one.

Metaphor is the stuff of poetry, and Richards analyses a couple of lines in which Denham compares the river Thames to his own mind:

> 'Though deep, yet clear; though gentle, yet not dull;
> Strong without rage; without o'erflowing, full.'

The mind is the tenor, the river the vehicle; *deep*, in the context of river suggests 'not easily crossed, dangerous, navigable, and suitable for swimming, perhaps'. Not very flattering descriptions for a mind—here the poet is suggesting 'mysterious, a lot going on, rich in knowledge and power, not easily accounted for, acting from serious and important reasons'. There seems to be little comparison, yet *river* is essential to the metaphor: as the vehicle it controls the mode in which the tenor develops. But, says Richards, try replacing river with a cup of tea:

> 'Though deep, yet clear; though gentle, yet not dull;
> Strong without rage; without o'erflowing, full.'

Obviously one can put the most unlikely objects together, but can one draw a metaphor from them? Richards implies that one can—in certain circumstances.

What is one to make, say, of Marcel Duchamp's stool and bicycle wheel? Richards does not say but on the whole he thinks that when the surrealists put unlikely objects together, it was merely a fashionable aberration. One remembers Lautreamont's phrase, which started it all, 'beautiful as the unexpected meeting, on a dissection table, of a sewing machine and an umbrella.' And André Breton's generalization into, 'to compare two objects, as remote from one another in character as possible, or by any other method put them together in a sudden and striking fashion, this remains the highest task to which poetry can aspire' (*Les vases communicants*). But, says Richards, if we do that, then certain things happen. They trigger 'a general confused reverberation' and the mind strains to connect them; and so, as William Empson puts it, 'statements are made as if they were connected, and the reader is forced to consider their relations for himself. The reason why these statements should have been selected is left for him to invent; he will invent a variety of reasons and order them in his own mind. This is the essential fact about the poetical use of language' (Empson, 1930). In other words the poet challenges his reader to perform his own small creative act, in front of the poem.

The more remote the two things, so Richards says, the greater the tension and 'that tension is the spring of the bow, the source of energy of the shot'. He goes on to say, however, that the strength of a shot is no guarantee of its accuracy. Prolonged and repeated tension will lead to strain or boredom, or both. So on the whole, those strange juxtapositions of the surrealists were self defeating. All they provoked in the end was boredom.

If metaphor was the stuff of surrealism, it is not surprising that many scientists view it with suspicion. Schon attributes this to Locke and other philosophers of the Enlightenment:

'Metaphor and analogy and other "figures of speech" seemed to them confused and obscure, a part of the darkness of the mind in which the immediately preceding centuries appeared to them to live. To admit to metaphor and analogy a central role in human thought, in scientific discovery, would be to let chaos in the back door.'

'This habit of disbelieving in the functional role of analogy and metaphor was . . . a kind of protective device: it permitted the philosophers of the Enlightenment to pay no attention to the metaphors underlying their own thought . . .'

For everything they thought was based, initially and as it had to be, on analogy or metaphor. Mathematics itself is a glorious metaphor for what happens in the real world. Newtonian mechanics is a metaphor, probability is a metaphor, indeterminacy is a metaphor—obviously everything which 'stands for' the real world, represents it or, most particularly, imposes an abstract structure on it, is and can only be metaphor.

Chance

The most famous exhortation to observe the effects of chance in design is probably Leonardo da Vinci's advice to a young painter:

'A WAY TO STIMULATE AND AROUSE THE MIND TO VARIOUS INVENTIONS;
I will not refrain from setting among these precepts a new device for consideration which, although it may appear trivial and almost ludicrous, is nevertheless of great utility in arousing the mind to various inventions.
And this is that if you look at any walls spotted with various stains or with a mixture of different kinds of stones, if you are about to invent some scene you will be able to see in it a resemblance to various different landscapes adorned with mountains, rivers, rocks, trees, plains, wide valleys and various groups of hills. You will also be able to see divers combats and figures in quick movement, and strange expressions of faces, and outlandish costumes, and an infinite number of things which you can then reduce into separate and well-conceived forms. With such walls and blends of different stones it comes about as it does with the sound of bells, in whose clanging you may discover every name and word that you can imagine.' (quoted McCurdy, 1938)

The place of chance in scientific discovery is equally well substantiated. Beveridge (1961) catalogues ten instances in the main part of his book, *The Art of Scientific Investigation*, and considers another seventeen in an appendix. These range from Galvani's discovery of current electricity to Fleming's discovery of penicillin, and include such notable 'finds' as Rontgen's —that certain rays could penetrate black paper. He later called them X-rays. Beveridge goes so far as to suggest that 'probably the majority of discoveries in biology and medicine have come about unexpectedly, or at least had an element of chance in them, especially the most important and revolutionary ones'. This, he believes, is because a discovery which breaks really new ground cannot be foreseen; it is not in accord with present beliefs.

Essential to all these discoveries by chance, of course, is that a trained mind was present which was able to realize their significance. In several of the instances which Beveridge quotes, a laboratory assistant made a mistake: Ringer's assistant, for instance, failed to use distilled water in making up a saline solution, and used tap water instead. As a result of this the heart of a dissected frog continued to beat long after it could have been expected to. Once he knew of the substitution, Ringer was able to analyse the tap water and isolate the salts which were responsible for this increased activity. It is a matter of training one's powers of observation to be on the look-out constantly for the unexpected and to make a habit of examining every clue which chance presents. The scientist who is looking out all the time for convincing evidence will fail to observe the bonus which chance is presenting him. It is a matter of separating out discovery and proof. That is the danger of too much emphasis on one's hypothesis—the danger of Popper's method. If we seek deliberately to ignore everything which is not relevant to our hypothesis, we shall certainly ignore the results of chance. Although a hypothesis, therefore, is essential to the *planning* of an experiment, once the experiment has been set up the hypothesis should be forgotten. Charles Darwin's son wrote of the great man:

> 'Everybody notices as a fact an exception when it is striking and frequent but he had a special instinct for arresting an exception. A point apparently slight and un-connected with his present work is passed over by many a mind almost unconsciously with some half considered explanation, which is in fact no explanation. It was just these things that he seized on to make a start from.'

The point is, therefore, that chance is only one component of the discoveries attributed to it. As Beveridge says, it is a misleading half-truth to speak of 'chance discoveries' or 'accidental discoveries'. As Pasteur said, 'In the field of observation, chance favours the prepared mind.' Chance merely provides an opportunity, which the prepared mind then must recognise and interpret. One must remember that discoveries which now seem significant, and in which chance played a part, were by no means significant until someone recognised them as such. The discoverer has related them to the pattern of existing knowledge, which is why they now seem significant to us. Beveridge lists three difficulties in making discoveries by chance:

(a) Infrequency of opportunity—which is really the only chance component in discovery, and even here the skilful scientist will try out novel procedures which, by chance, may expose them, to the maximum extent, to the risk of encountering a fortunate 'accident'.
(b) Noticing the clue—acute powers of observation will be needed if the unexpected is to be noticed during routine observation of the expected. This requires an exceptional ability to remain alert and sensitive.
(c) Interpreting the clue—this of course, is the most difficult aspect of all, and only the 'prepared mind' will recognise its potential significance.

Beveridge considers a whole range of 'near misses' in the grasping of significance in chance effects. At least one other physicist had noticed evidence of X-rays before Rontgen, but he had been merely annoyed by this. Similarly, others had noticed that staphylococcal colonies were inhibited by moulds before Fleming's notable discovery. Scott says that he thought it merely a nuisance, and suggests that Fleming's discovery was not due to chance, but to perspicacity in seizing on the discovery.

The essence of the prepared mind, then, will be that it is capable of seeing the significance of an apparently trivial observation. It is likely to be a mind filled with relevant but loosely connected data or vague ideas, which simply need a small catalyst to enable them to crystallize. One difficulty, of course, is that a mind so prepared is liable to be sidetracked. The essence of research is to be able to detect the clue which is worth following up. This calls for a certain independence of mind, an ability to free oneself from prevailing conceptions—together with imagination and the widest possible range of experience. On the evidence of some of Beveridge's examples, one should not be put off by ideas which have been dismissed already by others. It is a paradox in discovery that the first person to see an idea may well dismiss it as impracticable and credit, quite rightly, devolves on to the person who later forces it on to a reluctant world. Often, of course, a succession of half-developed 'precursor ideas', as Charles Nicolle has called them, pave the way for the fully developed idea later.

CHAPTER 17

Creative Techniques

Certainly it would be possible, given any problem of transition from analysis to synthesis, to work deliberately along the design spectrum, and there should be an appropriate point of entry according to the nature of one's problem. We saw, in considering the various elements of the spectrum, that those who favour algorithm have tended to concentrate on certain classes of problem: the analysis of circulation, the selection of components, relationship of building volume to perimeter, costs and cladding materials, the design of repetitive structures, and so on. Some of these problems might lend themselves to analysis in terms of ratios and we saw that systems building, in many ways, can be treated as design by deduction. The central mechanism, however, in translating analysis to synthesis (which is not invalidated by Jane Abercrombie's view of the two as complementary aspects of the same process) undoubtedly is analogy.

The use of analogy in this creative sense is described by many people in many different ways. Koestler (1964) invents his own terminology and writes of *bisociation* between two *matrices*. A matrix, in his sense, is a 'frame of reference', an 'associative context', a 'type of logic', a 'universe of discourse', and it is ordered against a *code* of fixed rules, a 'code of behaviour'. Koestler's point is that, given these matrices with their fixed codes, strange things happen at the point where we move from one to the other. Given a matrix which embodies a strict code of rules in the social sense, defining proper behaviour, say the behaviour of a man who is proper to the verge of pomposity, we laugh when he slips on a banana skin. That particular action seems quite out of context within that particular matrix. Koestler's bisociation is simply this crossing of contexts; given other kinds of matrices, then the bisociative act can also be creative.

As we might expect, Koestler has been taken to task for this highly simplified view of creativity. For one thing, his physiology is suspect and for another, he seems to think that *all* psychologists spend *all* their time watching rats in mazes, instead of being concerned with human affairs (Moray, 1963). However, the major difficulty is that *bi*sociation, by definition, is far too limited. Why should it not be *tri*sociation occasionally, or even *dodeca*sociation? In other words, why should he not use the accepted terms, analogy and metaphor, which have the advantage that finally, they seem to mean so much that they hardly mean anything at all?

Before we look at the mechanisms he might use, let us look for a moment

338

at the kinds of synthesis an architect might perform. It is clear that working through any of the design processes we have described so far, or those yet to be described, he will engage in many kinds of thinking (see Chapter 2). All these kinds of thinking can be described in terms of the spectrum, whether he be writing Alexandrian misfit variable, plotting Archer's objectives or dashing off the proverbial sketch on the back of an envelope. Sooner or later, though, he will have to start designing architecture, proposing an enclosure for a certain volume of space, and three-dimensionally dividing the space thus enclosed. All this with an eye to the concrete means available whereby these spaces might be enclosed, their costs, their environmental implications and all the other factors which determine the whole of architecture.

We saw in Chapters 2 and 3 that in history four basic ways of achieving this had been developed; pragmatic, iconic, analogue/analogy and canonic. The first of these deals in the manipulation of real things; if it is honestly pragmatic then there can be no question of analogy or metaphor; it is the real thing itself. But iconic design, clearly, is a type of analogy: one reproduces forms which are known to be satisfactory by a 'process of reasoning from parallel cases; a process whereby . . . words (or other things) are built up on the model of others.' Iconic design, in fact, amounts to a rather exact analogy. Canonic design too has its analogical aspects. It is either repetitive, which also supposes exact analogy, or it depends on the use of drawings—the canonic grid, and other design analogues for the building.

Clearly, too, the technology of building depends a great deal on design by analogy. Structure, construction details, services, finishes, these all develop by analogy from one building to another. Drawings, models, specifications, bills of quantities; these are all analogues for the building. It is quite clear therefore that design could hardly operate without analogy in several forms, but rather than pursue this theoretical argument let us look at what architects actually do at the moment of synthesis. Let us take synthesis at its highest level, the conception of a building *form* which may, or may not, meet the rigours of later evaluation. This, for many architects, is the only worthwhile kind of synthesis, but let us be quite clear that the same mechanisms apply in the design of a structure, a circulation pattern or even a fixing device. Indeed, the difficulty with a great deal of architectural design has been that those who thought themselves creative could hardly be bothered with the simpler technological aspects of building, whereas those who approach such problems from a rational point of view have tended to assemble the fragments of a problem without taking the further step of synthesizing a creative solution.

At the other end of the scale, let us take a very obvious, but rather tragic example: the Sydney Opera House (see Figure 17.1). Utzon's first sketches look remarkably like the sails of yachts, heeling over in the wind, and as Helmer-Petersen says (1959) this creates a striking composition, admirably suited (formally at least) to Bennelong Point in Sydney Harbour. Not only that, but the analogy had certain practical advantages; as Helmer-Petersen goes on to say:

'The great merit of this building is the unity of its structure. One of the most difficult problems of opera house design is to relate the stage tower to the separate and surrounding buildings . . . The solution suggested in this scheme is that the two auditoria should be roofed by a series of interlocking concrete shell vaults, in which the high stage tower is within one of a series of separate shells.'

Looking back from our vantage point now in history, we can see that this, to say the least, was an optimistic view. Yet the jury, obviously, were convinced of the scheme's merits for, in addition to these practical advantages, they thought it the most original and creative submission.

In other words, and whatever happened later, Utzon did precisely what was asked of him; he prepared a competition submission which caught the eye of the jury, and it was selected. If one took an overall view of the competition itself as one massive decision sequence (which of course it was) then Utzon

Figure 17.1—John Utzon's first sketch for the Sydney Opera House (1956). Direct analogy with the sails of yachts heeling over in the harbour

played his part admirably. He took the brief, prepared for him by the jury, analysed it as best he could, synthesized an elegant and complex submission for evaluation. The first point of failure in this sequence, quite clearly, occurred at this stage of evaluation; the jury should have convinced themselves that the Utzon proposal *could* be built, within whatever limits they had chosen to set on time, cost, performance and so on. This suggests further that if the design process includes a rigorous evaluation stage, then one *can* be wild and free, indeed ought to be as wild and free as possible at the moment of synthesis.

A full design process, therefore, will encourage such creative activity; the architects we call creative have sensed this intuitively: at an appropriate moment during the process of imagination, they have allowed their imagination to run free, and on the whole they have tended to work by analogy. There are obvious examples in the work of Wright; the administration building for Johnson and Son (1936) was designed as a series of concrete mushrooms (actually the analogy was with water lilies) which touch each other to form the roof, with glass filling the areas between, to give a decidedly under-water effect. The First Unitarian Church at Madison, Wisconsin (1950) has a triangular form which Wright derived by direct analogy with his own hands clasped together in prayer.

In cold description such analogues seem incredibly naive, and yet they *are* the stuff of imagination. Most architects—and artists—are extremely reluctant to admit the sources of their analogies. They think that such admissions would somehow diminish one's respect for their creativity; but far from it—they will merely confirm that they have brains and mental processes which every other human being possesses. Our respect for them, in fact, might increase if they admitted that, given the *same* mental processes, they are able to make better use of them.

We have already considered the function of the brain in the act of perception which, in a sense, is the converse of the act of creation. A lifetime's acts of perception have submitted to the brain an enormous range of ideas for critical evaluation and storage. In the network of neurones, therefore, there will be an enormously complex development of cell assemblies (engrams). The sum of all these provides the overall knowledge of the brain and where there is a great wealth of expert knowledge the engrams may occupy the greater part of the cortex. Eccles (1958) suggests that some failure of engrams to synthesize or to interrelate *may* be the neuronal counterpart of a problem in search of a solution. He further surmises that the 'subconscious operation of the mind' involves the interplay of these and other engrams in some incredibly intense and complex way. As patterns of engrams interact, repeatedly, they probably interact and congeal in different ways. It is to be expected, therefore, that new patterns will emerge from this subconscious activity. Occasionally one of these new patterns will transcend and subsume the existing patterns and by some sort of resonance, within the cortex, it may intensify and rise to conscious attention. At this point it will come to light as a new idea, to be subjected immediately to the mechanisms of criticism and evaluation.

Le Corbusier occasionally admitted his method of working. In *The Chapel at Ronchamp* (1958) he says:

'The shell of a crab, picked up on Long Island near New York in 1946 is lying on my drawing board. It will become the roof of the chapel . . .'

And so it did, or rather, the roof possesses a strange involuted form which could indeed have been derived by analogy from his little crab shell (see Figure 17.2(a) and (b)).

There are other sources of analogy too. Le Corbusier writes of 'visual acoustics' and one notices the unmistakable bell-shape of the chapel's plan (c). The walls were to be made of salvaged stone, thick, with a window form which is familiar in Arab architecture (one remembers his fascination with this some forty years earlier) in which a tiny opening externally splays back

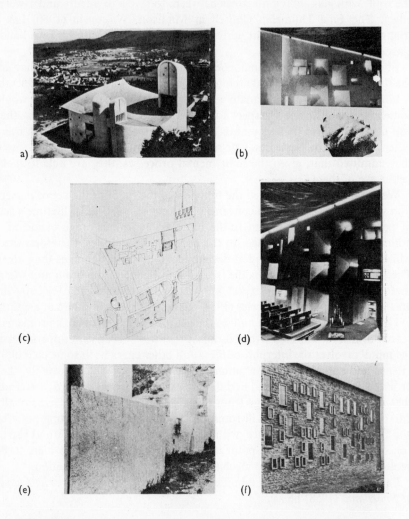

Figure 17.2—Le Corbusier's chapel at Ronchamp (a) (1955). Sequence of direct analogies. The shell of a crab lying on Le Corbusier's drawing board (b), 'becomes' the roof of the chapel; the body of the chapel is bell-shaped (c)—Le Corbusier's 'phenomenon of visual acoustics'—whilst visual images from his years of travel and sketching have also been built in: the deep-splayed windows in thick white walls (d) which he had seen in Arab housing, and ventilation 'funnels' such as those which Stirling photographed on the island of Ischia (e). George Pace may or may not have drawn visual analogies with Ronchamp for his chapels at Llandaff (f), but comparison with Le Corbusier's random windows suggests that the use to which a visual analogy is put *may* be more important than the analogy itself ((a), (b), (c) and (d) from Le Corbusier, 1957; (e) from Stirling)

wide and deep into the wall, so that the small amount of light admitted (with little accompanying solar heat) will be reflected off these splays, deep into the building (d). So determined was Le Corbusier to build this into the building that when it proved impossible for the contractor to build this wall of salvaged stones (hangover from the Citrohan idea?) he had a light concrete frame designed, with tapering columns and occasional beams around which his splayed window shapes could be formed of chicken wire sprayed with plaster. In other words, Le Corbusier was so determined to build this particular analogy that he was content to build it as a stage set.

There are still more:

'I was telephoning,' he says, 'the photograph of the reredos by Boulbon was in front of me upside down. The pentagon hit me in the eyes . . . I trace the working drawing . . . All the internal harmony of the work is in the drawings . . . It is incredible that artists today should be indifferent (even hostile) to this prime mover, this "scaffolding" of the project.'

And this particular analogue suggests for him the basic 'armature' of his chapel doors.

The most remarkable analogy of all was spotted by James Stirling on the island of Ischia—a vernacular cottage with three roof turrets, designed to deflect any passing breeze deep into the living space (e). These turrets were arranged with the two smaller ones back to back, and a large one at right angles . . . and then one remembers Le Corbusier's years of sketching in his thirties.

At first sight this is too good to be true—a simple stimulus-response model of creative ability. Le Corbusier spends a lifetime building up a store of analogies (his years of sketching being particularly fruitful); faced with any design problem, an analogy pops out at precisely the right moment. Obviously it is not quite so simple. One might for instance present a group of students with Le Corbusier's analogies and ask them to design a chapel each. It is highly likely that we should find ourselves with a group of very strange, not to say incongruous, designs. That is likely because the analogies would be foreign to the students, or absorbed only superficially. In Le Corbusier they had become fundamental to his experience, absorbed, compared, contrasted, combined, overlaid by later experience, and changed by new perceptions; but they were there to be called on and, faced with a difficult design problem, Le Corbusier could draw on them.

We too have our stores of analogies, not perhaps as rich as Le Corbusier's, but valuable nevertheless because they are personal. Yet we fail to draw on them. It never occurs to us; they do not seem relevant and instead of that, we content ourselves by drawing analogies with other people's work. It is not surprising, therefore, that a great deal of energy has gone into devising systems which *encourage* us to draw on our own stores of analogies. Some of them are highly effective: it may be that all they do, in the long run, is to free our inhibitions. If we choose, or are asked to work through a set of operations which encourage us to be creative, then creativity, for the moment at least, is acceptable. It is expected that we shall throw up some new and strange ideas and, again, for the moment, they will be taken seriously. Criticism will be suspended, and we shall do things which under 'normal' circumstances we should be rather diffident about. I have described elsewhere (Broadbent, 1966) certain techniques which have been devised for enhancing creativity in three groups:

1. Check-lists
2. Interaction techniques
3. Techniques based on psychoanalysis.

This is not the place to repeat those descriptions, but it might be useful to show the relevance of the techniques themselves to architecture.

Check-lists

Perhaps the simplest of all devices for stimulating creative ideas is the check-list; a list of words—or visual images—which one scans in the expectation that some of them, at least, will trigger off new ideas. In this respect they are rather like the word-association tests of psychoanalysis (Jung) and no doubt a psychiatrist could tell a great deal from one's response to a check-list; but a check-list may, and perhaps should, be a very personal thing, based on the designer's knowledge of what sort of words or ideas will stimulate him, and related to the class of problems in which he specializes. An engineer's check-list may or may not be suitable for an architect and vice versa.

The danger of check-lists is that they tend to become too vague: 'How can we improve this design?' It would be possible to work out a particularly relevant set of questions for any design type, but even a general check-list can focus with surprising precision on to the difficult aspects of a problem. Typical check-lists have been compiled by Osborn (1963), Gregory (1963), Matousek (1963), Eder and Gosling (1965) and others. Osborn's list is extraordinarily detailed, and covers seventy pages of his influential book *Applied Imagination*. One section reads:

'THE VICE VERSA TECHNIQUE—*Transpose* positive and negative? What are the opposites? What are the *negatives*? How about *up-ending*? Should we turn it *around*? Why not *up* instead of *down*? Or why not *down* instead of *up*? How about *reversing* the roles? How about *saying* it in *reverse*? How about doing the *unexpected*? What can be done by way of *surprise*? Why not try the *other end*? How about *building it upside down*? Why not have a light going *upward* instead of *downward*?

Certain parts of this, clearly, could be applied to architecture in many ways. Given an intractable planning problem, for instance, any one of Osborn's phrases (and there are many more) might just conceivably suggest some appropriate modification.

Summerson (1949) suggests that Le Corbusier approached architecture in the perverse kind of way which such check-lists encourage:

'. . . it seemed as if Le Corbusier was deliberately cultivating every perversion and every discord which utilitarian design in steel and concrete had introduced into building. He flouted the appearance of stability; he allowed huge windows to approach within a few inches of the corner of a building.

And he made domestic buildings look like factories! Summerson continues:

'But it was impossible, at the same time, to deny these buildings a certain artistry —a perverse poetry of their own . . . for to him the obvious solution of a problem, however charming, cannot possibly be the right solution. Just as in a painting by Picasso, Braque or Leger, the appearance of a thing is torn to pieces, broken into bits and reconstituted in a ridiculous jig-saw which has, nevertheless, a perfect logic of its own, so a building by Le Corbusier is a ruthless dismemberment of the building programme and a reconstitution on a plane where the unexpected always, unfailingly happens.'

Yet this contrariness has its own inner logic:

'One can, perhaps illustrate his topsy-turvydom by imagining a conversation with the man . . . we observe, naïvely enough, that "the house stands in the garden," to which Le Corbusier replies, "no, the garden stands in the house." We suggest that "a building is, in principle, four walls with windows for light and air," and he replies that, "on the contrary, a building may just as well be four windows with walls for privacy and shade." We put it to him that a park is a space for recreation in a town, and he replies, "not at all; in the future the park will not be in the town but the town in the park." '

How did Osborn describe it? The vice versa technique!

Interaction Methods

Interaction methods take many forms. Guerra (1969) describes one in which line diagrams of various structural types are plotted vertically and horizontally in an interaction chart. Each square of the chart then contains a line diagram which combines two (or more) structural types. Norris described *The Morphological Approach to Engineering Design* at the 1962 conference which is based on the work of Fritz Zwicky at California Tech (1948). It depends on the production of a table or chart in which, first of all, one lists the various *parameters* of the problem. Norris defines parameters as 'what the subject must "be" or "have" ' such as its form, size, material, orientation, quantity, speed and so on. Opposite each parameter he then plots a series of *parameter steps*—ways of achieving what the subject must 'be' or 'have'. One 'assembles' a solution then by taking a single parameter step from each line. His example

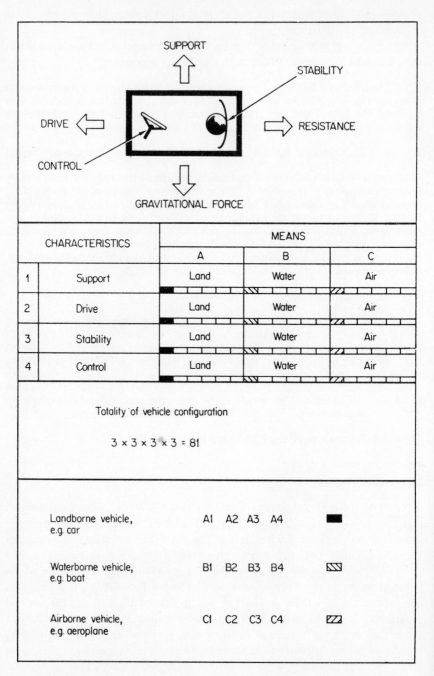

Figure 17.3—Morphological chart of vehicle configurations (Norris, 1962)

of vehicle configurations (Figure 17.3) will make the point clear; it is easy to read off this chart, say, the motor car which achieves support, drive, stability and control from the land, the aeroplane which achieves all four from the air, the hovercraft which may combine two or more of these means. This implies that there are still a great many vehicle configurations within his $3 \times 3 \times 3 \times 3 = 81$, which still have to be invented. Norris sets out the form of a design process, using morphological techniques, of which the main headings are as follows:

Determine terms of reference
Define problem
Carry out analysis and synthesis, using the morphological chart:
    Step 1. Set out field of investigation in chart form:
        (*a*) analysis into parameters
        (*b*) analysis into parameter steps
        (*c*) synthesis of parameters and parameter steps to form chart on
            which parameters and parameter steps describe all possible
            solutions
    Step 2. Determine basis of comparison for choosing best solution on
        following basis:
        (*a*) analysis of terms of reference
        (*b*) analysis of defined problem
    Step 3. Set out assumptions—'sieves' and 'filters' against which solutions
        can be tested
    Step 4. Reduce field of investigation by analysing rows and columns,
        grouping parameters and otherwise eliminating as many steps as
        possible
Present acceptable solutions.

Psycho-Analytical Methods

The most effective creative techniques are brainstorming and Synectics. They promote the generation of analogies (or even of metaphors) and we have already noted the importance of analogies in creative architectural design. Brainstorming and Synectics were designed specifically to promote the *assembly effect* which occurs spontaneously sometimes when several people generate free associations together. They derive, in part, from *group psychotherapy* and there is no doubt that, like such psychotherapy, they *can* promote far deeper probing into the subconscious than any individual working, alone, could achieve. But this is by no means always the case as Taylor, Berry and Block (1958) show in their rather critical paper. The best known of them is 'brainstorming', described by Alex Osborn in *Applied Imagination* (1963) whose check-lists we have already quoted.

Brainstorming

Osborn's first experiment with 'organized ideation' was in 1938, and his first participants named their efforts Brainstorm Sessions. The word is now included in Webster's International Dictionary, defined as: 'To practise a conference technique by which a group attempts to find a solution for a specific problem by amassing all the ideas spontaneously contributed by its members.' The technique itself has been used in some form or another for at least 400 years, by certain Hindu teachers, under the name of *Prai-Barshana*— literally 'question outside yourself'. In practice, brainstorming is simply a technique for generating check-lists, which are then used like other check-lists at all stages of the design process. Osborn believes brainstorming to be effective for several reasons; in particular when anyone puts forward an idea, it not only raises associated ideas in his own mind but also stimulates the associative powers of all the others. There is also the stimulating effect of rivalry, or people trying to outdo each other in the generation of ideas, and there is the important factor of *reinforcement*. When someone else picks up one's idea and develops it, then that, in some ways, is a sign that they approve one's efforts; one is stimulated to throw out further ideas. The key to successful brainstorming lies in Osborn's four basic rules:

1. *Criticism is ruled out.* Adverse judgement of ideas must be held over until later.
2. *'Free-wheeling' is welcomed.* The wilder the idea, the better; it is easier to tame down than to think up.
3. *Quantity is wanted.* The greater the number of ideas, the more likelihood of a useful idea.
4. *Combination and improvement are sought.* In addition to contributing ideas of their own, participants should suggest how ideas of others can be turned into better ideas; or how two or more ideas can be joined into still another idea.

The first rule alone, that *'criticism is ruled out'* can be remarkably effective in liberating discussion whenever a meeting has reached some point of deadlock. It can often be freed again quite easily, by inviting each antagonist to summarize his own case, without criticism from the others. Yet many people find this extremely difficult; they cannot allow anyone to present a reasoned case without interruption. Many speakers also seem incapable of summarizing an idea in one word or, at most, as a succinct phrase. They insist on speaking several sentences, which slows the pace of discussion and causes others to lose interest. Brainstorming in particular depends on the rapid firing of ideas; short phrases even, of only two or three words, may be too long in that they interrupt the momentum which, for effective brainstorming, has to build up.

All ideas are recorded, either on tape or in shorthand—a rapid firing session will keep two secretaries almost frantically busy. Afterwards the list of ideas is typed in wide spacing and circulated to the members of the group, who can then enter any afterthoughts. Finally, a full list of ideas is prepared, and each idea checked for feasibility, preferably by a panel of specialists which took no part in the original brainstorming. It may be that out of seven hundred ideas, only two or three are worth developing but if those are good ones, then the brainstorming will have served its purpose.

There seems to be no limit to size of a brainstorming group. Osborn cites instances of up to 200 participants; I have had successful results with 50, but the optimum seems to be between 7 and 12; an odd number has certain advantages over an even number. Where regular brainstorming is envisaged, the group might consist of a leader, an associate leader, about five regular members and the same number of guests. 'Core' members should be chosen for their facility in generating ideas, and the function of guests is to avoid too much stereotyping in patterns of thought. There may be difficulties if people of vastly different status are present, which underlines one of the basic necessities of brainstorming, that group sessions should be amiable and relaxed—not to say convivial. Osborn reports that many of the best sessions have taken place over a good lunch; the recommended length of a brainstorming session is between 30 and 45 minutes, during which time one can expect at least 100 ideas; in one group the first ten minutes produced 27 ideas, and the next 15 minutes produced 86.

Lastly, and most important, Osborn makes no claim that brainstorming is the answer to *all* ideas-generation problems. He recognises certain difficulties, especially where groups fail to follow the recommended procedures, or expect too much of brainstorming. Furthermore, he stresses that it is no substitute for individual creative thinking and, ideally, would like to see a three-phase sequence:

1. Individual 'ideation'
2. Group brainstorming
3. Individual 'ideation'.

At each phase, far more ideas will be produced if one agrees to the 'deferment of judgement' principle.

Jones (1963) describes a variation on brainstorming, in which each item in a performance specification is read out, after which the participants are 'asked to mention any idea, criticism or solution that comes into their heads, however weird or eccentric it may appear to be'. In another version which Jones has also used, each idea is written on a separate card, and the cards can then be sorted into appropriate categories.

Synectics

Synectics too was conceived as a group activity but, unlike brainstorming, does not rely on the chance build-up of streams of associations within the group. Instead of that, it focusses with some precision on an area in which associations probably will be generated by a system of analogies and meta-phors. It was developed by W. J. Gordon, whose book *Synectics* (1961) is probably the most accessible account, even though many of its recommend-ations are now repudiated in practice; some of the changes are summarized in Alexander (1965). It had become clear to some of his associates that a synectics group worked best when Gordon was leading it; they observed him in action for some time and then formalized his methods for use throughout the firm (*Synectics*, 1964). It may be fortunate, in terms of general use, that this formalization took place after Gordon had emerged from a phase in which he thought that swearing helped free up the mind for creative work (a colleague described him as 'a blasphemous Santa Claus).

Like Morphological Analysis, Synectics is a complete design process in itself, including briefing, analysis ('Making the Strange Familiar'), develop-ment and appraisal, but its most striking feature is the central phase of synthesis—('Making the Familiar Strange'), or seeing the problem in a new light. It does this by a system of analogy generation—although consideration of the design spectrum might suggest that certain analogies approach the condition of metaphor. Three types of analogy are defined:

1. Personal Analogy
2 Direct Analogy
3. Symbolic Analogy;

and between them they are capable of tapping the entire range of human experience, which is why they are different in kind from each other—personal, concrete and abstract.

Figure 17.4—Harold Severud uses personal analogies to encourage a 'feel-ing' for structure in his students (from Severud, 1954)

PERSONAL ANALOGY (see Figure 17.4).—the designer identifies himself with a tiny aspect of the problem in design; 'If I were this beam, how should I feel? What are the stresses acting on me? What is my attitude to the supports? And so on'.

DIRECT ANALOGY—the problem is compared with known facts in another branch of art, science or technology. Synectics quotes the example of Brunel, who, faced with the problem of building underwater constructions, observed a teredo worm forming a tube for itself as it bored into timber. From this Brunel conceived the idea of the caisson.

SYMBOLIC ANALOGY (see Figures 17.5, 17.6 and 17.7)—the designer tries to penetrate to the essence of special meaning which he attaches to the problem, usually verbally, and in terms of a 'binary couplet'. A ratchet, for instance, was described as 'dependable intermittency', a grinding wheel as 'precise roughness'. In one Synectics session the group was concerned with

Figure 17.5—Duchamp's *Nude descending a staircase* (1911) draws a symbolic analogy with the space/time relations of Einstein's Relativity. It represents a three-dimensional person moving through the fourth dimension of time on a two-dimensional canvas

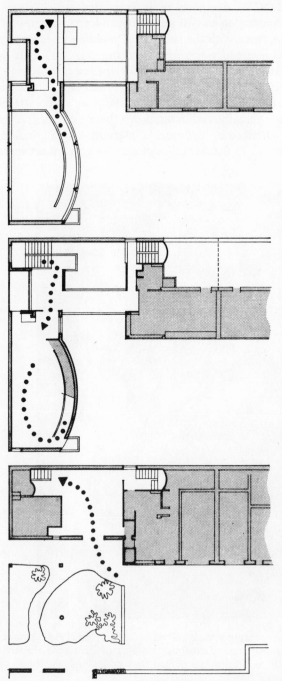

Figure 17.6—The reception suite of Le Corbusier's *Maison la Roche* is planned as a sequence of three-dimensional spaces for the display of two-dimensional paintings, through which one must move along a fixed route in the fourth dimension of time. The symbolic analogy with Duchamp's *Nude* and hence Einstein's Relativity, is clear and evidently intended

solving the problem of an unwanted flame in some complex piece of 'hardware'. This had defied all efforts at rational solution, and proved extremely difficult also for Synectics but, asked the question, 'What is the essence of flameness?' one of the group eventually thought of it as a 'ghostly wall' which opened up a whole range of feasible solutions.

In practice, a Synectics session is conducted systematically by a leader who starts by describing the 'problem as given' to the participants. This is then analysed and discussed, becoming in the process the 'problem as understood'. Attention is then focussed on one aspect of the problem, and the system of analogy generation begins. Often the leader asks a question which can be answered only in terms of personal analogy; if this fails, he may move into the area of direct analogy. A skilful leader will focus attention on a particular area of direct analogy—biology is an extraordinarily rich source of analogies for technological devices, or engineering for analogies to problems in management and human relations. It is, of course, possible to build analogy on analogy: the leader might ask that certain personal analogies be put together to form a symbolic analogy. Having found an appropriate symbolic analogy, he might ask for direct analogies with it. In the case of 'precise roughness', for instance, a strange and fruitful direct analogy proved to be 'the law of averages' because it is precise in dealing with very large numbers, and crude when dealing with a few. The essence of analogy generation is that, having described the problem in precise analytical terms, the group takes an 'excursion' into the irrational, and as one Synectics executive says, 'if you know where you're going, you're not going anywhere.' To sum up, the 'Synectics Flow Chart' takes the form shown in Table 17.1.

Table 17.1—Synectics Flow Chart (letters in brackets indicate standard abbreviations for the various terms)

A. The problem as given (PAG)
B. Analysis and discussion
C. Purge of immediate solutions
D. Problem as understood (PAU)
E. Evocative question (EQ) requiring an answer in terms of one of the analogy types:
  (i) Personal Analogy (PA)
  (ii) Direct Analogy (DA)
  (iii) Symbolic Analogy (SA)
F. Play with analogy
G. Application of analogy to PAU (or PAG), to see if a new viewpoint can be developed.
H. Either:
  (i) develop the new viewpoint and evaluate it
  (ii) if there is no new viewpoint, either:
    (a) repeat E, F, G
    (b) repeat D, E, F, G,
    (c) if G reveals a new aspect of the problem, repeat D, E, F, G

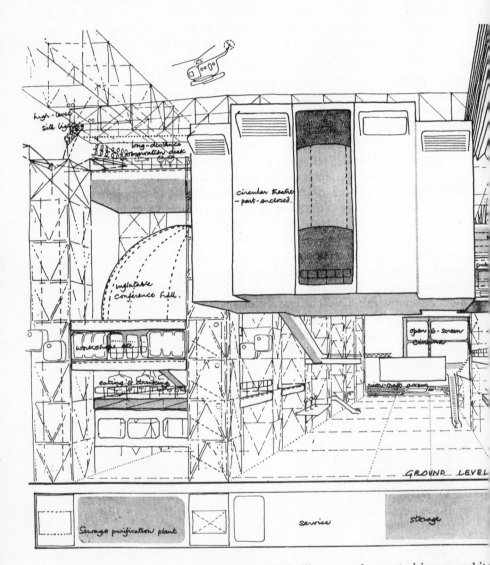

high-level
site lights
long-distance
observation deck
circular theatre
– part-enclosed.
inflatable
conference hall.
workshop 112
eating & drinking
open 6-screen
cinema
GROUND LEVEL
Sewage purification plant
service
storage

Figure 17.7—Cedric Price's Fun Palace (1964), like so much recent visionary archit
In this example a shipyard-like structure supports a gantry crane by which wall p
lar positions, used for a particular occasion, then moved away so that enclosures

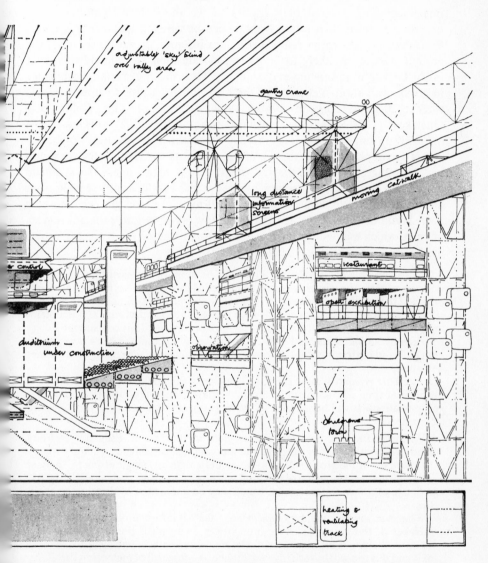

adjustable 'sky' blind over valley area

gantry crane

long distance information screens

moving catwalk

control

restaurant

open exhibition

auditorium — under construction

observation

diorama' tower

| | heating & ventilating track | |

...s on symbolic analogies with feedback principles from cybernetics (see Chapter 18).
...g and other components, inflatable and other structures, can be located in particu-
... for other sets of activities (see Broadbent, 1969).

However, the sparking off of ideas is by no means the whole of design. If we take a simple decision sequence—briefing, analysis, synthesis, evaluation and implementation—then it only applies to the third stage, synthesis. It so happens, however, that group working can be valuable at other stages too. Whenever a task involves remembering, for instance, then a consensus of the group's memory is likely to be more accurate than any individual's; that might be helpful in briefing and, similarly, there might be certain advantages in group evaluation. Yet many of these advantages accrue to several people working simultaneously in parallel, rather than face-to-face. Collins and Guetzkow (1964) call the arrangement from such parallel working a *synthetic* group and of course it is everyday procedure in an architect's office.

It is apparent, therefore, that in certain circumstances the face-to-face group has advantages; in others the individual and in others again the synthetic group. The design of architecture involves processes which could benefit from all three at different times, and much skill may be needed in deciding how they should be related. Collins and Guetzkow (1964) describe the advantages of each, which may be summarized as follows (adapted from a contribution by the author to the RIBA Handbook).

The *individual*, working alone, will always be more economical than any group in terms of time (he can take decisions immediately and has no need to convince others of the worth of these decisions); he may also be more economical in terms of effort. He will not have to divide his time between making decisions and maintaining personal relations with the rest of the group. Tactical decisions should always be taken by an individual and most strategic decisions also will be *initiated* by an individual—the group leader—who notes the existence of a problem and defines its nature.

A *synthetic group* will share certain advantages with individual working in that a majority of time will be taken in decision-making, and very little in maintaining group relations. It will be superior to the individual working alone in the following circumstances:

(a) Whenever the task involves random error in some form. Estimating, of any kind, will come into this category and a consensus of estimates made separately by members of the group will be more accurate than any single estimate. In most cases, a consensus estimate of this kind will also be more accurate than the agreed estimate of a face-to-face group, which may be dominated by certain personalities.

(b) Whenever the task involves *remembering* factual information accurately. Each member of the group will have brought his own expectations to the material as he was taking it in; inevitably, therefore, he remembers one distorted version of it and this too will have changed with time. A consensus of memories, therefore, will be more accurate than the individual or face-to-face group memory.

(c) In creative thinking, in terms of quantity of ideas. It is extremely unlikely under any circumstances that every member of a synthetic group, working independently, will generate the *same* creative ideas as every other and if their ideas are dissimilar, then a consensus of ideas inevitably will be more extensive than any individual contribution. The *quality* of ideas, however, will still be limited by the abilities of the most creative member.

(*d*) Whenever the task involves the *duplication* of effort (developing two or more ideas so that the best can be chosen) or the division of labour (apportioning parts of the task to different individuals so that it can be completed in a shorter time). A large-scale architectural project may involve duplication in this sense, and it will certainly involve division. Again there is skill in apportioning the various parts of the task to those best qualified for them and obviously the design team comes into its own at this point so that the architects, technicians, quantity surveyor, the various kinds of engineer and so on, each take away the things they can do well.

A *face-to-face group* consists of individuals confronting each other, probably round a table, and reacting continuously to each other. It may share the advantages of (*a*), (*b*) and (*c*) above, although in estimating and remembering, a powerful individual may well distort the consensus of group opinion so that in many cases, a synthetic group will be more accurate in these tasks. In creative thinking, however, face-to-face group members may 'spark off' ideas against each other by an *assembly effect* so that, finally, the quality of ideas is higher than any individual could have achieved. Techniques for encouraging this assembly effect were described earlier in this chapter, but each of these depends for its success on the presence of a powerful chairman. It is common also for a face-to-face group to be used as the final arbiter in the *evaluation* of ideas, reports, design projects and so on. The danger here is that such a group will only accept the lowest common denominator thus leading to frustration for those who, individually or in synthetic groups, have fed in truly creative ideas, and to the degradation of the final product which becomes dull and lifeless. The majority of reports from professional institutions, government agencies and so on, bear ineloquent testimony to this effect. The *cost* of a face-to-face group in terms of productivity, will always be higher than the cost of an individual or a synthetic group working for the same length of time, as the following simple equation shows:

cost per decision $= [(P_1 \times S_1) + (P_2 \times S_2) + \ldots + (P_n \times S_n)] \times T$

where P = a person (architect, quantity surveyor, etc.)

S = salary per hour

T = time (number of hours)

Much can be learned about the virtues and deficiencies of face-to-face groups by costing decisions in this way (possibly by the analysis of a tape-recording) taking care also to cost the hidden expenses which occur, say, when certain members of such a group spend a great deal of their (and the group's) time, 'rubbing each other up the wrong way'.

However, if the groups which Collins and Guetzkow describe so clearly are to be applied effectively, then *somebody* must decide how their work is to be interrelated, and who is to belong to each. That somebody may well be an individual. The most effective groups, in architecture at least, have usually been started by individuals. One of the first and finest of all, Tecton, was founded in the 1930s by Berthold Lubetkin. Gropius personally founded The Architects' Collaborative (TAC) whilst the pioneers of school building systems were assembled in the Hertfordshire County Council offices by C. H. Askin. Building Design Partnership was founded by Grenfell Baines, whilst Alex Gordon and Partners still retains its founder's name; only the Architects' Co-Partnership (initially Capon, Cocke, Cooke-Yarborough, de Syllas,

Grice and Powers) seems to have come together in a more democratic fashion. And where one man has been responsible for the initial impetus, then clearly his personality is going to be reflected in the structure of the organization. He will choose his first associates because he believes they can cooperate with him; they will join him because they respect him and wish to take part in what he wants to do. It seems naïve to deny this, if not downright dishonest.

Once the organization is in being, of course, its relationships *may* be so tight-knit that the founder finds it unnecessary to display overt leadership. If his initial selection was good, his own values will be so firmly built into the system that they are expressed automatically.

In the nature of architectural design it is not possible for any architect to wield power without the full collaboration of others. With very few exceptions, the architect *inevitably* works as a member of a group; however strong his personality he still needs a great many other people—architects, technicians, consultants, contractors and so on—to translate his ideas into reality. Curiously enough, one of the few architects to work successfully alone, Walter Segal, has by this means achieved miracles of economy and efficiency in his work—a fact which he attributes, rightly, to the extraordinary consistency which is possible in design decisions of every kind when one person is taking them (Segal, 1968).

Most of the other architects dismissed as *prima donnas* by Gropius, have made a great point of indicating the value which they placed on collaboration with others. Frank Lloyd Wright called his office the Taliesen *Fellowship*; in the book, called significantly *My Work* (1960), Le Corbusier presented long lists of those who worked with him, and acknowledged the importance of his dialogue with them. Lasdun (1965) too has indicated the value which he places on a dialogue with his staff at the start of a job, whilst Coia (1969) has made it known that the creative work in his office is undertaken largely by a team consisting of Metztein, MacMillan and a specific job architect.

It has been proved time and time again that creative ideas are rarely sparked off by democratic discussion between equals. They lack motivation and tend to drift into pleasant but unrewarding chat. It is a fallacy anyway, to suppose that a design group (or team) can ever be democratic. Whether the office is public or private, the members of the group will have been chosen in the first place often against one man's criteria, or at least by people who themselves were thus chosen, and they will have been formed into the group by similar means. So even if he does not chair the group, the members will find themselves together because they have that, at least, in common.

They will also vary in experience, status and seniority, the most effective known curb to equal participation. This will be particularly true in the private office where the man who signs the salary cheques naturally can make his views felt very easily. In the public office too, seniority carries with it inevitable authority, so that altogether we can take it that no design team, ever, can be truly democratic, unless it consists of equals in the early stages of a group partnership such as those who originally formed the Architects' Co-Partnership.

One gets the impression that for some advocates the whole point of group working lies in the exhilaration which they hope to experience when the assembly effect has really taken over. Indeed Middleton (1967) sees active participation as a way of controlling the dehumanization which results from the increasing size and complexity of human enterprises. 'It is,' he says, 'about ways in which the human scale of endeavour and concern can be retained in an increasingly inhuman scale of work . . . Our objectives and the machinery set up to gain them can only get bigger, and more complex, and embrace wider and wider areas.' The problem, therefore, lies in whether this increase in size and scope will result *inevitably* in subordination of the individual to bureaucracy, or whether his active participation in democratic procedures, both as a citizen and as a member of a working group, will compensate for this subordination, or even prevent its happening. Much student political theorizing is tragically naïve on this point. It forgets, for instance, that full democractic representation includes the most reactionary, conservative and retrogressive views, in addition to the most progressive.

Middleton sees a clear distinction between original thought, which for him is a lonely activity, and the testing of hypotheses, a logical process in which, he believes, the group can participate with advantage:

'The setting up of the hypothesis is inspirational, the outcome of intuitive apprehensions by personal memory patterns. The creative moment, as we have seen, is that instant when, sometimes by a supreme effort, sometimes without warning, every factor affecting the total problem and capable of apprehension by the intelligence . . . is held in the mind simultaneously and appears before the inner eye arrayed in a single, synoptic vision. This is essentially a private experience and is not easily to be shared out among a team. Herein lies the special character, the difficulty and the fascination, of collaboration in design.'

Yet he goes on to describe certain fields of endeavour—sport, music, film and television production, journalism—in which tremendous exhilaration is to be found in the 'meeting of minds' within a group. Common to these is a set of constraints. Football has its rules, interpreted by the referee; the team also has a general strategy formulated perhaps by the manager, and tactics for a particular game devised by the captain; within the limits thus laid down, each player is free to improvise, to respond to his colleagues and opponents, to observe the state of play, to sense the tempo of the game, to anticipate what others will do, and so on. In other fields too—Middleton cites music hall, ballet, drama and television—the team is united by a common bond of empathy. This, he believes, is essentially emotional:

'It derives its motive power from the heightened nervous tension engendered by that proximity of disaster which can never be far distant from any live performance.'

One of the finest descriptions of such interactions is to be found in an extraordinarily sensitive book on *Jazz* by Andre Hodeir (1956) in which he says:

'. . . collective creation . . . takes place in various ways, depending on whether one artist, while creating, has in mind some other artist whose own inventiveness will be superimposed on his, or whether several musicians work together, simultaneously and in equal proportions, to bring a piece into being . . . Some contributions may seem fairly modest—that of a pianist who modifies the harmony of a theme, or of a drummer who puts his skill and his rhythmic sense at the service of the soloist he accompanies. However any musician who has played in a jazz band knows the stimulation that can be expected from a harmony that falls just right or a way of playing the cymbals that really swings.'

Nevertheless, here too the nature of what *can* be improvised is severely circumscribed by certain rules. The group, first of all, has agreed on a melody which implies a particular harmonic structure outside of which the players cannot stray. In other words, the melody will be played in a particular key and the improvisation will tend to centre on the tonic, mediant, dominant and octave (doh-mi-soh-doh) of that scale, elaborated by means of grace notes, passing notes, retardations, anticipations and so on. Moreover the rhythm will be fixed, as will the order in which the different players are to take successive choruses. The structure of the piece, in fact, will consist of these choruses preceded by an introduction, with occasional interludes and possibly a coda. That is all.

These conditions are necessary if collective improvisation—or as Hodeir prefers to call it, spontaneous polyphony—is to take place. He limits his study, furthermore, to ensembles of two or more voices, equal in importance, in which no voice is subordinated to its neighbours, and all voices contribute with equal power to the single end, a joint work. Yet even in these tightly prescribed circumstances, total democracy may not be possible, even if it is desirable: 'The band may be dominated by a creative genius whom his sidemen do not always understand, or several personalities of more or less the same stature may get together in a group without achieving the necessary fusion.' So, according to Hodeir, spontaneous polyphony never did produce a really great work; Armstrong's first Hot Five (dominated by the master) shows much greater originality than Oliver's Creole Band, but is unquestionably less homogeneous. And finally, he believes, the homogeneity which such democratic groups display is simply a function of the rules by which they operate:

'Personally, [he says] I believed for a long time in the "genius" of the musicians who were heard improvising together on the best records of oldtime jazz. I thought these works testified not only to a solid tradition but also to a superior level of talent, a kind of almost miraculous prescience. Experience has shown, since then, that a number of students who couldn't even be called especially gifted are able to equal the glorious Louisiana veterans in this domain when they put their hand to the pastime. Miracles lose their aura when they occur too frequently. . . . There is no alternative to concluding that our conception of the difficulties of group improvisation was infinitely exaggerated . . . the New Orleans masters' famous "feel for playing together" can be seen to have depended less on divination than on prudence. . . . It would seem that jazz can expect to speak a perfect collective language only if it is worked out by individuals.'

Suppose, however, that it were possible to transcend all these difficulties in setting up a democratic design group, that it took the form envisaged in the plan of work: architects management function, architects design function, quantity surveyors, structural, mechanical, electrical and service engineers, contractor, and so on. How would it actually work, and how might one expect the results to be different from those achieved by similar people, but working under the dominance of a *prima donna* architect?

The design process, as we saw in Chapter 2, is going to involve many things: collecting information of user requirements and analysing it, collecting information on the site and analysing that, designing the building fabric as a means of reconciling the needs of one against the conditions of the other, and so on. Clearly any form of data collection can be undertaken by a group and if the intake of information has been standardized by means of forms, check-lists and so on, then it can be redistributed for analysis. Once the analysis is complete, then clearly it will be useful if various members of the group come together to report their findings. So far, I suspect, there is no problem but it is at the next stage, design synthesis, that the advocates of group working find themselves out of sympathy with the individual architect.

They seem to think that if architects, quantity surveyor, the engineers, client and the contractor sit round a table at this point, then something magical will happen; the design, finally, will be 'better', more economical and socially more acceptable than if one mind had dictated what should be done. If a design *could* be synthesized in this way, then undoubtedly the experience would be extremely rewarding for those who took part; but is that likely to happen? To answer this, we must look at the people involved, their functions and the abilities they bring to their task. The plan of work envisages two kinds of architects—architects management function and architects design function. What, first of all, is the difference between them?

It has been said, and with some justification, that all architects initially take up their career because they want to be designers. Traditionally at least, they have been taught as designers; the central core of architectural education has consisted of design projects and the students' performance, largely, has been judged on this ability up to, and including, the classification of degrees. If that is so, then in turning to an interest in management, the architect is rejecting his initial motivation, and such a rejection implies that design, for him, was not a very satisfying activity, possibly because he was not very good at it. This, of course, is an oversimplification, for effective design, indeed any effective creative work, implies a high ability to manage at least one's own affairs. This is confirmed by personal accounts, or biographies of Le Corbusier, Stravinsky, Picasso, not to mention a host of writers, all of whom confess to an extremely rigorous personal regime, involving long and regular hours. Indeed, many of them find this regularity the greatest spur to creativity.

That being so, there is no conflict between a design function and a management function—where one's own work is concerned. The desire to manage others is a different matter for, as we saw in Chapter 1, some people find this much more rewarding than doing any kind of physical creative work themselves. We also saw in Chapter 1 that where MacKinnon's creative architects had to work with others, they wanted to dominate the group, but on the whole they were not much interested in such activities. We remember Allport's rigid personalities who sought the support and order of institutions, groups and teams. It saved them the trouble of making personal decisions, gave them rules and codified modes of behaviour; they felt more secure when the authority of the group was behind them. It rather looks as if the creative architects want to get on with the job without too much personal interaction, whilst the non-creative (managing?) architect is more concerned with the group *for its own sake*.

If we look at the other members of the team, they, as we have seen, have chosen professions which *give* them much greater certainty than the architects'. Although we questioned in Chapter 6 the absolute certainty of engineering design, and preferred to think of it as a statistical matter, a matter of high probabilities, nevertheless these other members of the team have opted for definiteness rather than ambiguity and significantly they have chosen to operate mathematically. One could trace a history of professional relationships which showed that whereas in the eighteenth century, say, everyone in building exercised personal judgement, everyone *but* the architect has opted out of this, as far as possible, and chosen to deal in computation instead. Once a theory of structures was available, for instance, certain engineers opted out of value judgement, believing they were doing a tougher and more realistic job because they dealt in design which was determined by calculation. Similar moves occurred with the rise of electrical and mechanical servicing in building; these, as we saw in Chapter 8, have tended to be hardware based; they have dealt with the certainties (or at least the probabilities) of what machines can do, instead of the ambiguities of what people really want. Quantity surveying also can be said to have dealt in a similar way with costs; given the initial guesses which form an estimate, the rest can be computed; the quantity surveyor too believed that his job was essentially more realistic, and more socially desirable, than the architect's.

There is much dispute amongst psychologists as to whether people *choose* such careers because of predispositions in their personality type, or whether the career itself, the mode of education, the colleagues they spend their time with, lead them to play a particular role. Obviously no profession associated with the construction industry has the monopoly of a particular personality type; in each profession there are ranges of personalities which may be plotted against the scales of Chapter 1 and against many other personality variables too. But if we take the carricatures represented by, say, Hudson's convergers and divergers, Smith's schyzothymes and cyclothymes, Allport's prejudiced and tolerants, Rokeach's rigids and flexibles, there is clearly a tendency, confirmed by the surveys of MacKinnon, Rowe and others, for architects to cluster at the 'soft' end of each spectrum, and for engineers to cluster at the 'hard' end.

If that is so, then clearly there will be difficulties of communication. There is no doubt that for his traditional role of value-judger, manipulator of ambiguities and safeguarder of human interests, the 'creative' architect's personality is highly suitable. There is no doubt either that for their roles of computation-based technological realists and watchers of the purse strings, engineers and quantity surveyors also are selected, or have selected themselves, from appropriate personality groups. However, these roles will change, inevitably, with the rise of computer-aided design. The computer, by definition, is a device which can take away from human beings the necessity to do routine computation. For many building types it will be possible to write standard programmes for structure, lighting, heating, cost and so on, so that having applied his judgement to the interpretation of human need, the *architect* will be able to feed in sufficient data to design the building entirely, without reference to any other member of the building team. In other words his insistence on retaining such tasks as involve value judgement, the resolution of ambiguities and the safeguarding of human interests will ensure that he—and not the routine calculator—retains his value in the foreseeable future.

CHAPTER 18

Cybernetics and Systems in Design

Psychology, sociology and the other human sciences have a great deal to offer in the way of theoretical structures against which man/environment relationships can be modelled; they offer techniques for analysing these relationships and, to some extent at least, they offer results from such analyses which may be applicable in design. Ergonomics, operational-research, information theory, the new maths and computing also offer techniques which may be useful in design, yet the impact of research from these disciplines on the designer in practice has been very small indeed. Something, clearly, is wrong.

Difficulties have arisen for several reasons. One is that because there has been no real tradition of architectural research—apart from certain aspects of history—it has been common to bring in researchers from fields outside architecture, physicists, psychologists, sociologists and so on (Broadbent, 1970b). They brought with them their established disciplines and methodologies, together with ideas as to what constituted a 'good' problem; there was no intention, certainly, of solving the architect's practical problems. An 'applicability gap' thus arose between research and practice (RIBA report, 1970).

This was aggravated by the need which most researchers had, for reasons of prestige within their own fields, to demonstrate the rigour with which they could apply research methodology and this, in most cases, meant an empirical, astronomy/physics-based methodology, in which individual factors in the man/environment relationship had to be isolated for observation and/or experiment.

As we saw from the example of lighting research in Chapters 7 and 8, certain difficulties may arise when the designer tries to synthesize the results of such fragmented research. Standards which have been set up, say for lighting, may, if they are to be satisfied, make it difficult or impossible to satisfy standards which have been set up, independently, for heating, sound control and so on. These, and similar examples, account for the resistance which most architects have shown towards the assimilation of research results into practice and to the adoption of new techniques for use in designing. They have sensed a fundamental difference between the researchers' approach—essentially Cartesian—and their own—of 'juggling all the balls at once'.

Increasingly though, scientists in many disciplines are beginning to take an all-round view again, to think in terms of 'wholes' rather than 'parts' and

364

clearly this approach seems far more sympathetic to the traditional architect. As Angyal said (1941):

'In all sciences which deal with living organisms, the need increasingly makes itself felt for a radical reorientation in their foundations. The hope that life could be expressed and understood in terms of the physical sciences has largely been given up and at the same time scepticism has begun to creep in with regard to the possibility of a scheme of human personality.'

This, as Angyal says, was not a new view even then. Aristotle's *Organon* was an attempt to incorporate the whole of human knowledge into one vast scheme. Hegel's system was another. Gestalt psychology had dealt in wholes —J. C. Smutts, one-time premier of South Africa, had invented the term 'holism' to describe such a view, whilst others, such as J. B. S. Haldane and Ludwig von Bertalanffy, had thought of it as 'organismic'. We saw in Chapter 4 that Spencer and others had adopted organismic models of society.

The trouble was, as Angyal said, that these holistic or organismic views tended to be all-embracing, superficial and finally incapable of analysis. As Angyal put it:

'. . . some state that wholes, as such, cannot be studied since scientific investigation presupposes the analysis of the whole into parts, which then makes possible the study of the inter-relationships of many parts.'

Popper, too (1957), has some trenchant criticisms of the holistic view. He questions the possibility of considering even a limited concept like society in holistic terms. If each part is related to every other, and some parts, at least, are related to things outside that particular society, then before very long one will be concerned, as Aristotle and Hegel were, with the whole of human knowledge; but as one tries to encompass any part of it, this vast range of knowledge will be changing in other directions. It will be impossible even to categorize the whole of what is known at a particular moment in time.

Yet these difficulties, according to Angyal, are not insurmountable, the whole *must* be subdivided if we are to analyse it, but there are various ways in which the subdivisions can be effected. If we choose the wrong kind of subdivision, then the whole will be destroyed, whereas other kinds of subdividing may throw its structure into relief. Angyal considers four ways of subdividing a whole, such as a plant, an animal or some inanimate object. One could cut it at random, thus producing a collection of unrelated parts; one could divide it, according to some preconceived and fixed principle that failed to take its inherent structure into account, which would represent a rational approach; one could abstract distinguishable properties from it, such as size, shape, colour, consistency and so on, which would represent an empirical approach; or one could divide the whole *according to its structural articulation*. He takes an example from architecture:

'The parts which will be obtained in such methods are real holistic units, such as, for example, the division of a building into corridors, rooms, windows and doors. The study of such *parts* will be at the same time a study of the characteristics of the *whole*. The door, for example, is not required simply as a quadrangular wooden board, but in relation to its function and adequacy *as a door of the building*, that is, an integral part of a whole . . . the door is something which alternatively permits the connection and separation of a room from another or from the outside—a statement which would be impossible if the door were considered in itself and not as part of a building.'

If the window in Chapters 7 and 8 had been considered in this way, then a good many problems to which it led would not have arisen. One science, traditionally, has dealt in these terms, the science of ecology, which is concerned with relationships between living organisms and their environments.

Knight (1965) traces a brief history of the subject which, as he says, was known in principle to the ancient Greeks. Hippocrates suggested that 'whoever wished to investigate medicine properly, should proceed thus: in the first place to consider the seasons of the year, and what effects each of them produced (for they are not all alike, but differ much from themselves in regard to their changes).' Aristotle too, referred to the habits of animals in relation to the environmental conditions in certain areas, whilst Theophrastus, one of his pupils, was concerned with plant communities, and with the types of plants which were to be found in certain areas. He considered these plant communities in terms of the physical environment in which he found them and wrote about marine aquatic plants and so on. So Theophrastus has some claim to be called the first ecologist and, as Knight says, his work was not surpassed until the eighteenth century when Reaumur published a massive natural history of insects.

Techniques developed rapidly during the nineteenth century: von Humboldt, Agassiz, Darwin, Forbes and Wallace all made crucial contributions. Saint Hilaire coined the term *ethology* in 1859 to signify the relationship between the organism and its environment, whilst nine years later Reiter combined the Greek words *oikos*, meaning 'home', and *logus*, a 'discussion or study', to form *oekologie*, which has since been anglicized to *ecology*. A series of specialisms naturally developed in ecology; one of the first of these, according to Knight, was the study of community—the way in which two or more species, living together, interacted with each other. Mobius tried to define this more clearly in his study of oyster beds (1877): 'Every oyster bed is . . . a community of living beings, a collection of species, and a massing of individuals, which find everything necessary for their growth and continuance. . . . Science possesses as yet, no word by which such a community where the sum of species and individuals, being mutually limited and selected under the external conditions of life have . . . continued in possession of a certain definite territory. I propose the word *Biocoenosis* for such a community.' A great deal of ecology since Mobius's time has been devoted to the study of *biocoenosis* and recently the term ethology has been revived to describe the study of animal behaviour.

Ecology, of course, is an empirical subject, but it is generally agreed that ecological concepts can be interrelated in some form of hierarchical structure, in which the *ecosystem* is taken to include every component of the environment, living and non-living, so that the entire world may be taken as one vast ecosystem. There have been attempts to consider it in this way—Buckminster Fuller's will be familiar to most architects—but inevitably they tend to superficiality. The true ecologist, therefore, tends to concentrate on the ecosystem of a single pond, forest, desert area and so on. In a pond, for instance, he would have to examine the algae, insects, crustaceans, bacteria, seed plants, snails and fish, not to mention their relationships with each other. He would also have to consider *abiotic* (non-living) factors of the environment, such as sunlight, cosmic radiation, temperature, oxygen concentration of the water, mineral content, substrata and so on. Obviously he can concentrate on community ecology, population ecology or some other specialized aspect, but even if he is not particularly interested in the abiotic elements of the environment, he will have to study their more critical interactions with the living organisms.

One way of ordering these studies is to think in terms of the ways in which certain elements at different *trophic levels* in the environment act as food for others; this is called the *productivity approach*. The four links in the food chain are, firstly, raw materials: non-living substances such as sunlight, water, oxygen, carbon dioxide, organic substances such as minerals in the soil and other nutrients used by plants for their growth. The second link is producer organisms, mostly plants, ranging in size from microscopic organisms such as phyloplankton in the water, through grass and shrubs to trees. They generally use available energy from the sun to convert carbon dioxide, water and the other raw materials, by the process of photosynthesis, into carbohydrates, fats, proteins and vitamins. The next link is composed of consumer organisms; these higher organisms feed on the producer, and most of them are animals, in one of the two forms; herbivores such as sheep and cows, consume the producer organisms directly and transform some of the materials into body tissue, thus utilizing the producer organisms indirectly whilst carnivores alternate the characteristics of herbivores and carnivores. Finally, reducer organisms: these consist of fungi and bacteria (some authorities also include insects) which close the circle of the ecosystem by breaking down dead producers and consumers and converting their organic material into raw materials again.

The ecologist, therefore, resists the temptation to indiscriminate holism by concentrating on a single pond, a single square metre of vegetation and observing everything that goes on within it. Its theoretical structure also enables him to examine some highly complex interactions in ways which are subtle enough, extensive enough, and yet which have fundamental and clearly defined limits. That is possible because, as Angyal recommends, this theoretical structure has been derived from the observed relationships of organisms and their environments; it thus repeats the structural articulation which is inherent in those relationships.

However, the organismic model has been developed much further than this in two interrelated new disciplines which are known as *General System Theory* (von Bertalanffy, 1968) and *Cybernetics* (Wiener, 1948). They form part of a general critical shift in science which Goodall (1965) has character-ized as Third Science, to distinguish it from the Rational (based on self-evident truths) science of the Greeks and the Empirical (based on observa-tions and experiment) science of the Renaissance. Waddington (1970) describes certain characteristics of this new science:

'The first of these developments has the increasing tendency of physics to analyse the basic nature of the material world into entities which seem to be radically differ-ent from anything we can experience. The world of billiard ball atomics existing at definite times in simple three-dimensional space dissolved into the esoteric notions of quantum mechanics and relativity . . . Even earlier in origin though slower to have a general effect, was the conception of biological evolution by material selec-tion, which has profound implications about the essential importance of time and process, and also introduces the revolutionary idea that chance and indeterminacy are among the fundamental characteristics of reality.'

General system theory and cybernetics both originated in the study by Cannon (1939) of the means by which the body temperature stays constant, and of other built-in devices by which the body senses changes in the external environment and adjusts itself accordingly, such as the ways in which the volume of blood maintains itself, concentration of sugar, salt, oxygen and carbon dioxide remain constant in the blood, foreign bodies and invading organisms are attacked, and so on. He concluded that such processes do not maintain a simple state of equilibrium; they are basically unstable and dynamic. Cannon described them as follows:

'When we consider the extreme instability of our bodily structure, its readiness for disturbance by the slightest application of exernal forces . . . its persistence through many decades seems miraculous. The wonder increases when we realise that the system is open, engaging in free exchange with the outer world, and that the structure itself is not permanent, but is being continuously built up again by processes of repair.

The constant conditions which are maintained in the body might be termed equi-librium. That word, however, has come to have a fairly exact meaning as applied to relatively simple physico-chemical states, enclosed systems where known forces are balanced. The co-ordinated physiological processes which maintain most of the steady states in the organism are so complex and so peculiar to living beings . . . that I have suggested a special designation for these states, *homeostasis*. That word does not imply something set, immobile, a stagnation. It means a condition which may vary, but which is relatively constant.'

The homeostatic mechanisms of the body require a number of components, interlinked so as to work together in certain ways. There must be some organ (a receptor) to sense changes in the environment which transmits appropriate messages to the brain (the control centre). The brain then decides what to do about it and transmits messages to the other organs (effectors) which can take appropriate action. They do this and the brain needs to know that they have done so, so that when the 'normal' state of the organism has been reached again, the effectors can be instructed to stop their action.

Wiener called such a complete system of components, and the links between them, a *feedback* loop, and it is the basic mechanism of cybernetics. Living organisms contain many such feedback loops, controlling many processes, in addition to homeostasis. Cybernetics draws analogies in both directions between living organisms and machines. Wiener (1950) describes a simple feedback system as follows:

'... a kitten bats at a swinging spool. The spool swings to its left, and the kitten catches it with its left paw. This time messages of a very complicated nature are both sent and received within the kitten's own nervous system through certain nerve-end bodies in its joints, muscles and tendons; and by means of nervous messages sent by these organs, the animal is aware of the actual position and tensions of its tissues. It is only through these organs that anything like a manual skill is possible.'

Wiener and Rosenbluth, in fact, had conducted extensive studies on a particular muscle of a cat's leg, cut from its attachment and fixed to a measuring device so that the action of the feedback loop which controlled it could be determined. Their interest was stimulated by a problem which Wiener faced at the beginning of the war in 1939, which was concerned with shooting down aircraft. The problem of hitting a moving target had been there since men started shooting at each other, but the aeroplane presented special difficulties in that its velocity was very close to the velocity of the missile used to bring it down. It was useless, therefore, to aim directly at the target, one had to aim in such a way that missile and target would come together in time and space at some point in the future. One might begin by extrapolating from the present course of the plane, assuming that it would continue to fly in a straight line. But that would be unlikely, for once one has started firing at him the pilot would be highly likely to take evading action. Yet there would be certain limitations in the course he could take, for given a high starting velocity and a system of control that depends on establishing new patterns of air flow, his new path probably would be curvilinear. One could fire therefore at a calculated distance in front of him, observe the effects of one's shot and adjust one's aim accordingly.

It occurred to Wiener that there were close analogies between the control system he had devised and the feedback loops of living organisms. He and his colleagues coined the term *Cybernetics* (1947) for this study of feedback and control systems, from the Greek word *kybernetes*—a steersman. The word *governor* derives from the Latin version *gubernator* and indeed the *governor* which James Watt designed to regulate the action of his steam engine under varying conditions of load acted in this way. It consisted of two spherical weights, attached by pendulum-like rods to a fixed collar on either side of a vertical shaft. When the shaft was at rest the weights hung down but as it began to rotate (driven by the engine) the weights were swung outwards and upwards by centrifugal action, depending on the angular velocity of the shaft, which in turn was determined by the speed of the engine. There was a second sliding collar around the shaft, somewhat below the fixed one, and connected to the pendulum-rods by other rods so that as the weights swung upwards and outwards, this collar was raised up the shaft. This second collar was grooved and a lever protruded into it which activated the valve controlling the supply of steam to the cylinder. As the engine speed increased, so the angular velocity of the shaft increased, the weights moved further outwards and upwards, the sliding collar rose and the steam supply was reduced. So the engine slowed down, the weights dropped, the collar dropped, the steam valve was opened and so on. The *feedback* in this case tended to oppose what the system was doing already; it was thus a form of *negative* feedback.

The principle has been described in 1868 by Clerk Maxwell, but as Wiener pointed out, other more recent devices embodied equivalent principles. Wiener says that:

'For any machine subject to a varied external environment to act effectively it is necessary that information concerning the results of its own action be furnished to it as part of the information on which it must continue to act. For example, if we are running an elevator, it is not enough to open the outside door because the orders we have given should make the elevator be at that door at the time we open it. It is important that the release for opening the door be dependent on the fact that the elevator is actually at the door; otherwise something might have detained it, and the passenger might step into the empty shaft.'

Wiener describes the control of any device which is based on its actual performance rather than on its expected performance, as feedback. This, he says, involves the use of sensing members, which are actuated by the motor members, and takes the form of *tell-tales* or monitors; their function, fundamentally, is to control within the mechanism any tendency towards disorganization. They produce, in other words, a 'temporary and local' reverse in the expected direction of entropy. There are certain difficulties in this, however. One can envisage a state in which Watt's governor began to oscillate; suppose the engine were going too fast; the weights would fly outwards and up, pulling the sliding sleeve with them. That would close the valve, cutting off the supply of steam so that the engine speed dropped. The weights would drop too, opening the valve again and the process would be repeated, so that instead of maintaining a constant rotation, the governor itself would be responsible for violent oscillation in the speed of the engine. This instability is known as *hunting*. Wiener himself cites the example of a gun which has to be operated in widely varying circumstances. Sometimes the grease is warm, so the gun swings easily and rapidly. On other occasions it is frozen, or mixed with sand; the gun is sluggish. Obviously it is not enough to fire the gun when it *should* be pointing in the right direction, especially if one is aiming at a moving target, so feedback elements are built into the control mechanism which reads the amount by which the gun is behind the position it should have taken.

What Wiener's kitten, his anti-aircraft gun, the homeostatic mechanisms in your body have in common is the fact that they are controlled by feedback

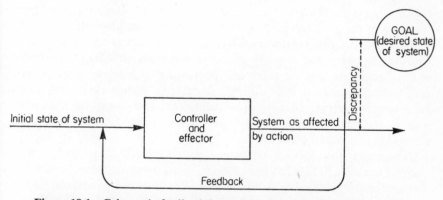

Figure 18.1—Cybernetic feedback loop. Such loops are frequently shown without the goal, but if no goal exists there will be nothing for the loop to feed back. In many cases, e.g. educational processes, the goal will be constantly changing but it will still be possible to measure discrepancies between the present state of the goal and the present state of the system

loops, and that they are goal-seeking (Figure 18.1). In other words, a target is set for each of them, their performance is monitored and fed back to the appropriate control centres, which then determine what should be done next. But there are crucial differences between the different kinds of feedback loops according to how the goal is determined. At the lowest level are feedback loops which maintain equilibrium in mechanical systems; James Watt's governor is a case in point. They take the form of simple causal chains: Watt's engine makes no attempt to control its surrounding environment whereas Wiener's kitten *is* trying to control the spool which is outside itself. Rosenbluth, Wiener and Bigelow (1943) attempted to define *purposeful* behaviour as that which is directed towards some specific goal, the goal itself being some feature in the environment with which the organism is trying to achieve a particular relationship.

Their definition was criticized very forcibly by Richard Taylor, a philosopher who pointed out that to a neutral observer even a rolling stone would seem to exhibit purposeful behaviour in this sense. If this is so we shall have to be very careful in recognizing any behaviour as purposeful, particularly if it is displayed by one of the simpler organisms. Their behaviour may well be due to circular causal chains determined by unthinking processes of survival and reproduction. Taylor suggests that the essential difference between that human behaviour which is purposeful and the behaviour of lower organisms or mechanisms which is not, is that human beings can set themselves non-existent goals; one might search for the Holy Grail. Buckley (1967) suggests that once this distinction is accepted we can define purposeful behaviour more clearly. Whatever the external goal, whether it be the Holy Grail or simple personal survival, the process of search must involve some internal representation of the goal. Once this goal is thus represented internally, one seeks to match the external environment to it and one's activity can be defined as goal-seeking. Men can also set goals for machines providing appropriate internal representation for them and once the goal has been defined their goal-seeking activity is little different from ours. Goal-seeking purposeful behaviour, therefore, consists of matching external events or objects to internal test criteria, and of course, devolves true feedback loops, not just simple circular causal chains.

Cybernetics, therefore, is concerned with feedback loops and control systems, but once its field has been defined, many interpretations are possible. Wiener himself (1948) calls it 'the science of control and communication in the animal and the machine', whilst Couffignal (1956) suggests that 'Cybernetics is the art of assuring effective action'. Pask (1961) discusses these and other definitions, concluding that for the cybernetician,

'His object of study is a system, either constructed, or so abstracted from a physical assembly, that it exhibits interactions between the parts whereby one controls another, unclouded by the physical character of the parts themselves.'

According to Ashby (1965) cybernetics is a theory of machines which deals with what things *do* rather than what they *are*. It is not concerned, therefore, with analyses of their structure, nor are the laws of physics particularly material to it; it relates to the real machine (be it electronic, mechanical, neural or economic) much as geometry relates to the real object. For just as geometry nowadays treats of spaces and forms which cannot possibly be built in the real world in addition to those which can, so cybernetics deals with the functions of machines, only a limited number of which can actually be made to operate. And given a specific machine, cybernetics not only asks what it will do now, but what are all the behaviours it can possibly produce. At this point, it seems to have analogies with information theory, for that too deals with *sets* of possibilities rather than with individual elements within these sets.

Ashby is particularly concerned with the biological aspects of systems; he asks why a rabbit's ovum grows specifically into a *rabbit* rather than into some other living form which might have developed by similar physical processes. The energy required for this transformation is taken for granted in cybernetics which becomes instead a study of the information and control systems by which this energy is directed. The strength of cybernetics according to Ashby, is that it provides a common vocabulary by which engineers and physiologists might understand each other. As he says, some of the most dramatic developments in science, especially during the twentieth century, have developed from the cross-fertilization of two branches of sciences which previously had pursued separate furrows.

Even more significant, perhaps, is its particular value in analysing complex systems. As he says:

'Science stands today on something of a divide. For two centuries it has been exploring systems that are either intrinsically simple or that are capable of being analysed into simple components. The fact that such a dogma as "vary the factors one at a time" could be acceptable for a century, shows that scientists were largely concerned in investigating such systems as *allowed* this method; for this method is fundamentally impossible in complex systems . . . Until recently, science tended to evade the study of such systems, focussing its attention on those that were simple and, especially, reducible.'

But many systems, both living and mechanical, are so dynamic that they do not allow the manipulation of one variable at a time. As one variable is changed so its connexions and interaction with others ensure that they too will change, a fact which, according to Ashby, was first demonstrated by an ecologist, Sir Ronald Fraser, in his experiments on agricultural soils during the 1820s. If this is true of soils, how much more so is it true of the organisms which grow in the soil or those which feed on them, and of the ecological relationships between them.

The parallel concepts of General Systems Theory were developed by drawing analogies between mechanisms and living systems as a whole, with particular reference to their relationship with the environment. A living organism is *open* to the environment whereas most inanimate mechanisms are *closed*. Their characteristics are compared in *General Systems Theory* and as von Bertalanffy puts it (1950):

'A system is closed if no material enters or leaves it. It is open if there is import and export, and, therefore, change of components. Living systems are open systems, maintaining themselves in exchange of materials with environment, and in continuous building up and breaking down of their components.'

This is in contrast, say, to a chemical reaction which takes place in a closed vessel and which must therefore, according to the second law of thermodynamics (Chapter 11) eventually reach a state of equilibrium in which most of the energy available for chemical interactions has been expended, thus reducing the system to a state which is high in entropy.

Theorists, such as Auerbach, have suggested that living systems, by their very nature, avert the menacing effects of entropy within the universe and that this, in fact, is their fundamental purpose. This, according to von Bertalanffy, is an over-simplification. Certainly entropy cannot but increase in a closed system, but it may not increase in an open system. In certain circumstances—according to Schrödinger—a living organism feeds on negative entropy. It imparts complex organic molecules, uses their energy and then returns simpler end-products to the environment. A living system, therefore, maintains itself in a steady state by importing materials which are rich in free energy and thus, unlike a closed system, it can avoid an increase of entropy. Some of its internal reactions, however, will produce an increase in entropy and if the environment is taken into account, together with the system, then the *total* exchange of energy will always conform to the second law of thermodynamics.

The living system itself will tend towards a higher state of order, differentiation and complexity—at the expense of energy won by oxidation and other energy yielding processes. Growth, decay and death all represent approaches to, and slow exchanges within a steady state and each requires the expenditure of energy. As von Bertalanffy describes it (1941),

'Every organic form is the expression of a flux of processes. It persists only in a continuous change of its components. Every organic system appears stationary if considered from a certain point of view; but if we go a step deeper, we find that this maintenance involves continuous change of the systems of next lower order: of chemical compounds in the cell, of cells in multicellular organisms, of individuals in super-individual life units. It was said, in this sense . . . that every organic system is essentially a hierarchical order of processes standing in dynamic equilibrium . . . We may consider, therefore, organic forms as the expression of a pattern of processes of an ordered system of forces. This point of view can be called *dynamic morphology*.'

However, as far as the living organism is concerned, the environment will be indeterminate. Yesterday it was cold, today it is warm, tomorrow it may be cold again. Yet your body maintains its internal temperature within very fine limits. If it did not do so you would die. Alternatively, take the case of an animal in the wild: yesterday there was food, tomorrow there is none. The animal goes hungry but it does not die unless the famine is prolonged, because it can metabolize some of its own fat.

Nevertheless we are still lacking in a rigorous definition of system: Angyal (1941) takes us some way towards this in considering the differences between a system and a relationship. A relationship, according to Angyal, needs only two members, between which relations can be established in terms of position, size, colour, shape or other observable factors. Compound relationships may also be formed in which A is related to B, B to C and so on; but they still do not form a system unless, overriding all these relationships, there is a 'whole' of some kind, within which the various elements are distributed and in which each participates by virtue of its position in the whole. For Angyal, a system is a distribution of members within a dimensional domain. The members are not significantly connected except with reference to the whole.

The crucial differences between a relationship and a system are indicated in Figure 18.2 in which the linear relationship Z, between A and B, tells us nothing about their position in the system, whereas co-ordinates about X and Y enable us to locate them precisely within the whole. There is a *direct* connexion between objects in a relationship; no intermediary of any kind is required; but in a system, the connexions between members may be much

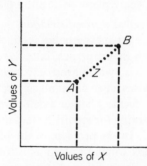

Figure 18.2—Differences between a relationship and a system. The linear relationship Z tells us nothing about the overall positions of A and B within the system contained by X and Y. Coordinates about X and Y enable us to locate A and B precisely within the system

more complex. As Angyal puts it, '*In a system the members are, from the holistic viewpoint, not significantly connected with each other except with reference to the whole.*' It is not enough, then, to consider each part of the system separately; one must view them with respect to a superordinate, more inclusive factor, the system within and by which they are connected. Eventually one will have to *model* the system, and the modelling of systems is an essential part of cybernetics. Beer (1965) points out the advantages of having a multi-disciplinary team in systems analysis, so that each member can suggest suitable kinds of models from his own discipline.

It is necessary now to distinguish between a model of the system itself as a structure and a model of the system's behaviour; some cyberneticians are concerned almost exclusively with the latter. Ashby, for instance, has a great deal to say about the *transformation* which a system might effect. Change is measurable, whether it is change in position of the earth as it moves through space, or change in the colour of a sunbather's skin as it darkens after exposure. Ashby describes a particular terminology for various aspects of such change. In his sunbathing example, for instance, the original pale skin, that which is going to be acted upon, is called the *operand*; the agent or factor of change, in this case the sunlight, is called the *operator*; the change itself, from pale skin to dark skin, is called the *transition* and the final state of the skin, that which it is transformed to, is called the *transform*. This particular transition might be indicated as follows:

$$\text{pale skin} \rightarrow \text{dark skin}$$

In practice a particular operator will induce a number of transitions. 'Exposure to sunlight', for instance will effect

$$\text{cold water} \rightarrow \text{warm water}$$
$$\text{coloured curtains} \rightarrow \text{faded curtains}$$
$$\text{pale and sickly plant} \rightarrow \text{healthy plant}$$

Such a set of transitions is called a *transformation*.

One of the most vital concepts in cybernetics is concerned with transformations effected by a system whose properties, initially, are not known. Such a system is known as a *black box*, which arose as a living issue under wartime conditions when certain devices, such as bomb sights, were sealed and secret. A technician might have to decide whether a defective bomb sight should be scrapped, or was worth returning for repair; he had to test it without opening it up to see what was inside. In the problem of the black box, therefore, the engineer is given a sealed box which has terminals for input and output. He may feed any voltage, shock or other disturbance to the input, and he observes the effects these seem to have on the output. The same kind of thinking—although not, one hopes, the same voltages, shocks or other disturbances—may be applied in the analysis of a human brain, or of an organism such as a rat in a maze and, as Ashby says, it is precisely the way in which a child learns to manipulate, say a door handle, so as to achieve the desired output (an open door).

Ashby describes a conventional procedure for analysing a black box. One assumes that the inputs can be measured; they might be represented by control knobs with pointers and one can thus express *the state of the input*. Similarly, one assumes that the output might be connected to a set of dials, or other form of display, so again one can observe the *state of the output*. One will then conduct a series of experiments (apply different inputs) in a particular time sequence, which can be recorded. It will be quite impossible to repeat one of these experiments exactly, although the only difference between two experiments which are otherwise identical, is that one took place before the other and therefore might have had an effect on it. As one proceeds, one prepares a *protocol*—a straightforward list in which the states of input and output are recorded against time. The input to an electrical black box might consist of a sine wave, whilst to a human black box it might consist of a psychiatrist's questions.

The beauty of black box procedure, according to Ashby, is that no skill is needed on the part of the operator for, if the contents of the box are genuinely unknown, then any random pattern of inputs is as good as any other. In many cases, of course—from electronics to psychiatry—the operator will have had experience of similar black boxes and that will help him select a suitable range of inputs. The experimenter may find, eventually, that certain regularities are observable in the output of the box; its output is repetitive. He will check, then, the inputs which produced these regular outputs and they too may or may not be regular. He *may* find that the system is determinate or, as in the case of the pendulum, he may have to take further variables into account. It may be that the system will never give single-value transformations, in which case he will have to look for *statistical* determinacy, for averages rather than for absolutes.

Klir and Valach (1965) generalize this procedure for describing a system, its behaviour and, as far as possible, the processes within the system which lead to that behaviour. They start with a description of its structure—as far as that can be observed—writing down a *protocol* on the observed relations; they then look for connexions between them. These connexions can be expressed by means of words, diagrams, mathematical symbols, or some other analogue. In other words, they build up an abstract model of the system's structure and/or behaviour. The model, of course, is itself a system and, if its behaviour is equal to the original system's, then it really is a *model* in the cybernetic sense.

The two systems exhibit equal behaviour, according to Klir and Valach, when equal stimuli to both systems always evoke the same responses from both. To test this, part of the input to one system is assigned to the other, with a suitable transformation of relations between the stimuli; this is called *input mapping*. The equivalent manipulation of the systems' outputs is called *output mapping*. The behaviour of system A has the same structure as that of system B if an input and output mapping exists such that system A models the behaviour of system B. Every model of a system is also a model of its own behaviour, but a model of behaviour need not be a model of the system itself—the distinctions between *isomorphic* and *homomorphic* modelling we discussed in Chapter 5.

Isomorphic relations can be expressed in ways other than diagrams. If a stone is thrown vertically into the air, its trajectory can be plotted as a set of points in the air, and these will be isomorphic with a set of points on a graph which, in its turn, can be expressed by means of an equation. Suppose, for instance, the initial velocity of the stone to be 50 feet per second. It so happens that the lines along which air flows past an airfoil (at subsonic speeds) form a pattern which is identical with that by which electric current flows in conducting liquid past a non-conductor, and in many other cases, too, it is possible to detect isomorphs between electrical and physical systems.

It might be possible, where this is the case, to *substitute* the electrical device for the mechanical, or vice versa. Strict isomorphism, in fact, allows that two machines are equal only when such a substitution is possible; but other lesser degrees of resemblance are possible. If we take the case of map and countryside again, the correspondence between one and the other applies at a fairly low level of resolution. According to the scale of the map, each town, each street or each house even, may be represented, but we shall never have a map in which, say, each plant or blade of grass is represented. If we looked at the countryside in such detail, we should distinguish a greater number of elements and relations than the map can possibly show. In this case we should be concerned, not with an isomorphic relationship between countryside and map, but with a homomorphic reduction. Isomorphism expresses one-to-one relationships, homomorphism expresses many-to-one reductions. The isomorphic relationship is symmetrical, it operates in both

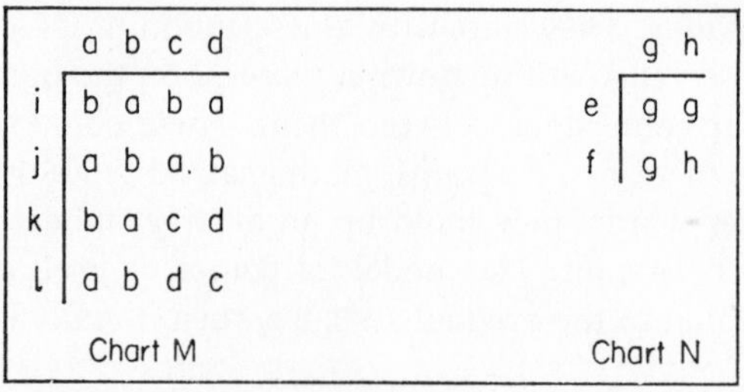

	a b c d			g h
i	b a b a		e	g g
j	a b a. b		f	g h
k	b a c d			
l	a b d c			
	Chart M			Chart N

Figure 18.3—A graphic example of homomorphic reduction. If we think of chart M as divided into four quarters, then its relationship to chart N becomes clear (adapted from Ashby, 1956)

directions; whereas homomorphic reductions are asymmetrical, they operate in one direction only.

Ashby cites the case of two pendulums, one of which is half the length of the other. They are not isomorphic in the strict sense, but if they are measured on separate time scales, one of which has values of twice the other, then they prove to be very similar. He also suggests a graphic example of homomorphic reduction (Figure 18.3). We can see that if we think of the left-hand chart as divided into four quarters, then it bears a very clear relationship to the right-hand one, N.

Clearly this reduction in complexity can be a first step in analysing highly complex systems. As Ashby says, a biologist watching a bird build its nest will hardly give a thought to the detailed activity which is going on in the bird's brain, nor will the anthropologist observing a tribe in council be concerned with the internal activities of each tribesman. One can choose an appropriate level of resolution, and the relationships between various levels can be represented on a *resolution graph*.

Klir and Valach show the fundamental structure of such a graph (Figure 18.4). Each node in such a graph represents a single viewpoint from which a single object may be assessed. The terminal (or lowest) node is always indicated by S_1 and this represents the lowest possible level of resolution; at this level the observer understands the *behaviour* of the system, but has no knowledge of its structural properties. As one passes to a higher node (in an opposite direction to the arrows) so the resolution level increases, and there may be several viewpoints at each level. If one is considering a radio receiver, for instance, one may be interested in the complete circuit at a low level of resolution and in the amplifier, the power supply, and so on, at a higher level. Klir and Valach present a resolution graph in which the interrelationships between various *subjective* viewpoints are represented (Figure 18.5).

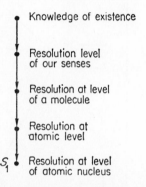

Knowledge of existence

Resolution level
of our senses

Resolution at level
of a molecule

Resolution at
atomic level

S_1 Resolution at level
of atomic nucleus

Figure 18.4—Resolution graph for the analysis of physical systems from the largest scale to the smallest (adapted from Klir and Valach, 1965)

Grinker, Mesarovic (1969) and Emery (1969) have all published essays on systems theory.

Sir Stafford Beer describes in some detail the process of siting a new steelworks in systemic terms, and notes that, initially, management will be faced with a mass of disparate views, often conflicting. Some of them will be based on fact, others on 'inspiration' masquerading as fact; most of them will be factual if something else is true. He calls these 'contingently factual', and they finally specify the system of decision, although they are not really recognized as contingent. Traditionally one would build up a highly complex total decision by adding together a series of minor sub-decisions. A junior metallurgist might suggest that the whole process be based on a certain reaction and, for no very cogent reason, his suggestion might be adopted. The actual siting might be recommended by an economist on the assumption that quite a different technology, but one which he knows well, will be used. Given these and other unrelated components, it is highly unlikely that the final decision will be consistent or coherent.

An alternative process, which Beer suggests, is that one recognizes from the start that one is dealing with an infinitely large number of different integral and high variety alternatives, and one's aim, therefore, is to select one of these. The decision process, therefore, consists not of building up more and more variety but of eliminating more and more uncertainty. Each possible answer can be plotted as a small square within the total decision space, arranged probably in a square array. The aim, therefore, is to range over this decision space as economically as possible so as to locate the square which offers the best possible solution. But, given an array of a million squares, an average search would take one over half a million of them, assuming that

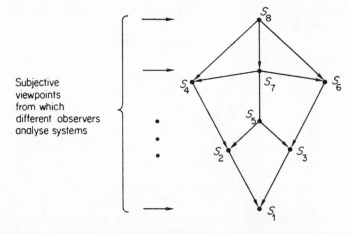

Subjective viewpoints from which different observers analyse systems

Figure 18.5—Resolution graph showing the way in which different observers will analyse a given system from different (subjective) viewpoints. As we saw in Chapter 5, they will also make different models of it (adapted from Klir and Valach, 1965)

there was no means of eliminating various sub-sets of small squares which shared some characteristic regarded as damning.

The squares may be plotted in the first place against a system of coordinates; each side of the overall array will be 1,000 squares long, one can locate any one of a million squares by searching the two coordinates, and this search will involve only 2,000 items. An average search now will only take 1,000 steps. Naturally the search space may be many dimensional; if the decision has n variables, then the decision space will have n dimensions. In the steel-works example, for instance, the decision will include the location of the works, the output in ingots, the range of products, and so on. These, for Beer, are the *logical variables* and their systematic interaction defines the shape and the dimensionality of the decision space.

The required output, for instance, begins to define many other things: the kind of site which is needed for the steelworks, the order of its cost, and so on. The relationships between variables can be expressed in terms of symbolic logic (see Chapter 12) which deals with relatedness, conjunctions and disjunctions, implications and inclusions. We know how many dimensions the decision will have and we can demonstrate symbolically how they will be related. We therefore have its configuration in addition to its dimensionality. The next step is to measure its variety; some, but only some, variables will be binary, such as whether the steelworks is to be associated with an ironworks or not. Others will offer a group of choices such as, given a finite number of steel-making processes, one must decide which of them are to be used, and in what combinations. Given eight such processes, the variety of this decision is eight or, as Beer says, it is a three-bit decision consisting of three binary decisions: $2^3 = 8$.

From this, of course, it is easy for Beer to draw analogies with information theory; he wishes to measure the uncertainty which must be removed in searching for the complete specification which will enable one to make a decision. And it can, of course, be computed by the same equation:

$$H = -\Sigma p_i \log_2 p_i$$

where the p_i is the probability of the ith choices. Where there is a straight choice between two alternatives, then

$$H = -(0 \cdot 5 \log_2 0 \cdot 5) = 1.$$

It may not be an equal choice; there may be a consensus of opinion in favour of one alternative rather than the other: but the uncertainty can still be calculated. One can compute the total uncertainty which has to be removed in reaching a complex decision by summing the uncertainties appropriate to each component of it. Again one can compute the remaining uncertainty when certain parts of the decision have already been taken. When all uncertainty has been eliminated, then $H = 0$; the probability that this is indeed the answer will be 1; in other words the decision has been taken.

For any class of decision problems, it should be possible to plot the average rate at which uncertainty will be eliminated; Beer suggests that it might be a negative exponential decay function. In a particular case, it will be possible to check back from time to time, and if the rate of decay of uncertainty fails to match the curve, or if it changes direction suddenly, then one can be fairly sure that something has gone wrong. In other words, we have an error controlled feedback loop against which the process of decision-taking can be monitored.

Beer finally applies his thoughts on systemic control to the automated factory. In general, he says, automation has been applied only to relatively straightforward jobs involving mass-production with low variety; but a full understanding of cybernetics would allow one to use the computer as a variety generator and thus automation could become much more general. It seems to him just as wasteful to use the computer in standardized routine procedure as it is to use the human being. The same ethical objections do not apply, but economic ones certainly do. The on-line computer ought to be coupled, by sensing devices to what is actually going on in the factory, and its output should also be so coupled. But between times it should be un-coupled in order to stimulate the outcome of possible decisions and to choose between them. In terms of computer technology this is perfectly feasible, but up to now management has not asked for machines which learn by experience and engineers have not offered them. Beer finally presents his personal vision of the future:

'Here is a vast plant, a huge complex interacting system. Its engineers have built control equipment into it, of a subtle cybernetic kind. The plant is, therefore, self-regulatory (we know that trick). It is to some extent self-organizing (we begin to know this trick too). The plant is adaptive to environmental change (we have dis-cussed how this could be done through algenonics (pleasure/pain) loops. But the built-in control systems keep going wrong. The teeth of the cogs drop out, the transistors fail, wires come adrift, whole packages burn out. The engineers, how-ever, have seen all this happen in the brain. They have noted that brains do not continually "go off the air" for maintenance: and so they have copied the brain's trick for handling unreliability, no longer complaining that things sometimes go wrong when manifestly they cannot always go right.'

Beer brings us close to an architectural application of systems/cybernetic thinking, and there have been several other attempts to describe the ways in which these new disciplines will affect the design of architecture. In the United States particularly, they are associated largely with urban 'systems'; mathematical models are set up isolating problems of land use, locational an-alysis, transportation and so on for probabilistic analysis by computer. This usage is certainly familiar in Britain, and McLoughlin (1968) has des-cribed it in some detail, but the word *systems* itself is used far more often in the context of systems building. Unfortunately, by our stricter definitions this too has tended to be non-systematic, in that so much attention has been paid to the problems of components, their manufacture, transportation and rapid assembly on site, at the expense of ergonomic 'fit' to activities (dimensionally coordinated spaces are.often awkward in shape and size), heat, light, sound control and so on, not to mention capital costs and costs in use.

Another popular usage of systems is concerned with information handling; generalized structures—or systems—are devised against which information can be classified, often for computer storage and retrieval. The computer installation itself is called a system, whilst there is a growing, if less specific, interest, in the application of systems thinking to psychological and/or social issues.

I have described these and other usages elsewhere (Broadbent, 1970b), but we are concerned now with more direct applications into architectural design. The key to this, as Angyal suggested, lies in the way one breaks down, for the

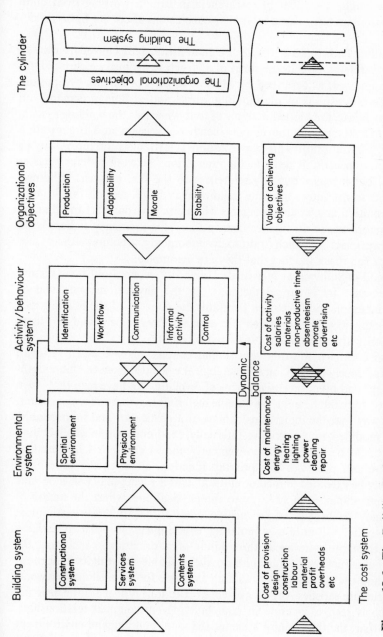

Figure 18.6—The Building Performance Research Unit's conceptual model for the appraisal of buildings in use. It consists of four systems—the building/environmental/activity/organizational systems—plotting interactions between them. When it is folded into a cylinder, interactions can also be plotted between the building and organizational systems; a cost/value system is also incorporated in the lower part of the model (from Markus, 1970)

purposes of analysis, the total man/building environment system, and curiously enough, a number of researchers in Britain working from quite different premisses have come to similar conclusions about its basic articulation.

The Building Performance Research Unit at Strathclyde University worked out an early version of it in the form of a structure against which buildings could be appraised, as described by Markus to the Portsmouth symposium of 1967. Certain aspects of the building fabric, and of human demands on the building fabric, are plotted in terms of four 'systems': the building system, the environment system, the activity/behaviour system and organization objectives (Figure 18.6). This classification is extremely useful within its defined limits, because it deals in the interactions between different classes of factors, but it leaves out any references to the site, adjacent buildings, climate and so on, into which the building may be placed, on the grounds that by definition any 'system' operates within an 'environment' and that the latter therefore needs no further description. This deficiency indicates the primary weakness of such rationally-elaborated structures—their self-consistency can mask the fact that they are incomplete.

Hardy and O'Sullivan, at Newcastle University, worked out their version of the structure by empirical methods, by the physical measurement of buildings in action and developed from this the concept of the building as a climate modifier, a filter between the external environment and the users within (Hardy and O'Sullivan, 1967a and b, 1969).

My own approach towards very similar conclusions was again rational, but based curiously enough, on archaeological evidence, from the mammoth-hunters' tent and other primitive forms of dwelling. We have seen that when man started to build, he put the available materials together to form a shelter, in such a way that the indigenous climate at a particular (and inhospitable) place was modified, thus providing, internally, conditions within which human activities could be carried out conveniently and in comfort. I assume that architecture still possesses this primary function, although the concept of climate may be extended to include cultural, that is social, political, economic and aesthetic climates, in addition to the physical one, whilst the notion of comfort may be broadened to include other forms of sensory stimulus; certain activities will need a 'stimulating' environment. In order to design a building, therefore, one needs three kinds of information; concerning the pattern of activities which it is to house, the available site with its indigenous climates, and the technology of building available for reconciling the two.

This structure satisfies Angyal's essential criterion; it displays the articulation which is seen to operate in man/building/environment relationships. Not only that, the three major systems, the man, building and environment can be further articulated in ways which do not violate the principle; Table 18.1 shows this further articulation in one possible form. There can be little

...environment-as-a-system—are interrelated. The human system wishes to perform certain activities at a particular place, if the environ-ment at that place is incompatible with those activities then a building is designed as a system for reconciling the two.

ENVIRONMENT SYSTEM		BUILDING SYSTEM		HUMAN SYSTEM	
CULTURAL CONTEXT	PHYSICAL CONTEXT	BUILDING TECHNOLOGY	INTERNAL AMBIENCE	USER REQUIREMENTS	CLIENT OBJECTIVES
	The site as given in terms of:	Modifications of external environment to provide suitable ambience for specified activities by means of:	Provision of physical conditions for performance of activities in terms of:	Provide for specified activities in terms of the following needs:	Return for investment in terms of:
Social Political Economic Scientific Technological Historical Aesthetic Religious	*Physical characteristics:* climatic geological topographical *Other constraints:* land use existing built forms traffic patterns legal	*Available resources in terms of:* cash materials labour/equipment *Structural systems:* mass planar frame *Space separating system:* mass planar frame *Services system:* environmental information transportation *Fitting system:* furnishing equipment	*Structural mass:* visible surfaces space enclosed *Sensory environment:* lighting sound control heating/vent	*Organic:* hunger and thirst respiration elimination activity rest *Spatial:* functional (inc. fittings) territorial *Locational:* static dynamic *Sensory:* sight hearing heat and cold smell kinaesthetic equilibrium *Social:* privacy contact	Security Prestige Profit Expansion or other provision for change Housing of particular activities so as to encourage user well-being, motivation, etc.

(G. H. Broadbent, adapted from T. L. Markus: Building-Environment-Activity-Objectives model)

doubt, for instance, that each human being in the human system forms a complete and self-interacting whole. He can be separated from his environment and analysed physiologically, psychologically and so on as an interrelated set of sub-systems—structural, nervous, circulatory, perceptual, but he also forms part of a higher order social system which again can be analysed in many ways.

The building system will affect the way in which he, as an organism, works systematically in so far as it (*a*) leads to the stimulation of his various senses separately—seeing, hearing, smell, heat and cold, kinaesthetic, equilibrium, and (*b*) determines his physical relationships with other people in terms of room size and shape, furniture arrangements, circulation patterns and other means of communication. It *cannot* affect him in any other ways than these, although his sensory experience of the building will encompass all the ways, physical and cultural, in which it has modified the given climate so as to provide conditions for his convenience and comfort. His previous experience of buildings therefore, in terms of environmental standards, aesthetic 'image' and so on will be brought to his perceptual transaction with the building in question and will finally help determine his attitude to it.

The structure also reveals one further point, that provided one takes into account the three major systems, human, building and environment, their sub-systems and the interactions between them, the sequence in which one considers them is hardly relevant. There is no reason to plot a rigidly ordered design process; I have described a possible approach in the Environmental Design Process, which starts with the user's requirements, moves to the physical context and then reconciles the two in terms of a building technology which provides an acceptable filter between them. But that is not the only approach. Most so-called systems building *starts* with the building technology: that is 'given' before the users' needs or even the site are known. The results of this approach so far have been disappointing in terms of environmental conditions, sound insulation, heat control and so on. But if the systemic interactions of building fabric with physical context and user requirements were also taken into account, then this approach would be just as valid as any other.

It seems, therefore, that a systems approach, in its many ramifications, really can be used to help the designer take an overall view of his task. It may help us even to avoid the incipient danger that, because certain factors in design are easily quantifiable, they are given greater weighting in design than those which are not. In other words it gives us a way of structuring the intake of information into design in which all the relevant factors are allowed to play their appropriate part in determining the final design.

CHAPTER 19

An Environmental Design Process

We suggested in the preceding chapter that architectural design could be reduced to a matter of reconciling three systems, the human system, the environment system (that is, everything in the external environment) and the building system itself, subsuming all the interactions which take place between the controlled, internal ambience and the building fabric, in terms of structure, servicing and so on.

Chapters 8 and 9 were devoted to a consideration of what the human system, individual and social, requires of its buildings and we shall have to take this a little further to establish which of its demands, needs and requirements will have to be taken into account in designing the building; but before we do that we ought to consider the three essential systems (human, environmental and building) together and in particular look at the interrelations between them (see Table 18.1, page 385). The advantage of such a scheme is that one can 'enter' the design process at any point. One would expect, conventionally, to start with clients' objectives as stated for a particular project, but the chart shows how, say, a systems building approach is quite legitimate, where a particular building technology exists and is available long before an individual project is commissioned. Similarly, one can envisage conditions in which it may be appropriate to start at any other point on the chart. As long as the six major divisions of the chart are all considered, the order in which they are taken is by no means critical. Unless one is committed to a particular building system, however, it is likely that information will become available most readily in the following order: client's objectives; user requirements; external environment; and given such information, one can then take the necessary decisions in respect of internal environment (ambience) and building technology.

We shall take this order, therefore, as the basis of a complete design process which attempts to reconcile the practices of known and successful architects with the processes available to us from design methodology.

Client Motivation

Physically, as we have seen, the building is a device for modifying climate; if we extend the concept of climate to include social, cultural and even aesthetic matters, then we come close to defining what architecture is. Architecture is building which offers a comfortable—or otherwise stimulating—climate in physical, social, cultural and aesthetic terms. Given this definition, the motivation for designing a new building becomes clear. The client wishes to build because no available space on the earth's surface, enclosed or otherwise, is suitable for his purposes. Suitable means having spaces which are big enough, but not too big, and appropriate in climate, in the comprehensive sense we have just defined, for the things he wants to do.

He may well be doing certain things already—living, working or providing spaces in which other people can live, work, educate the young, heal the sick and so on—in an existing building or buildings. These may be inadequate in many ways, too small in terms of space enclosed, inadequate in terms of the climate they provide, in the wrong place so that physical communications with other essential activities are difficult. Clearly any building which is deficient in these terms will inhibit the activities it houses. People may be uncomfortable, possibly unhappy or even inefficient. If they think this is true, then manufacturers want to build new factories, councils to build new houses and hospital boards to build new hospitals.

Such functional motives for building are comparatively easy to justify and they tend to attract finance. The most potent of these functional motives will be concerned with the value of the building on a particular site which, in commercial terms at least, may be computed from the usable floor area, the revenue obtainable from its use and capitalization on the site and on the building structure itself. Where the value of the land is high, it is likely to have been built on already; but the existing building may be uneconomical in that the structure and circulation occupy a great deal of potentially usable floor area, the building itself has fewer floors than could have been built, and each floor is higher than is now considered necessary. By rebuilding, therefore, it might be possible to increase quite considerably the area of usable floor available on the same site and thus the gross revenue.

However, in doing so, as we have seen, one may well reduce the quality of the enclosed environment, particularly in terms of heat and sound control. That may be reasonable if one's motive is pure financial gain, but one should suspect any argument for demolition and replacement rather than reconditioning of an existing building which is based on other arguments. Financial arguments may even be used to disguise a true but different motivation. Any new building will effect climatic modification, and that may be the client's motivation for building; but he may be more concerned with social, cultural or aesthetic climates rather than the physical climate. Any set of activities requires space, environmental control and a particular circulation pattern, but it may well be that a converted old building will house them better than any new building could. As we saw in Chapter 8 the mass or planar construction of an old building often offers a far higher degree of physical climate control than any framed building could, but it will not satisfy the client's purposes when his real motives are social, cultural or aesthetic.

Social motives might include the direct expression of prestige, power or dominance over one's competitors. Clearly a new building offers more direct evidence of one's ability to consume money conspicuously than any conversion, however appropriate for its purpose the latter may be. Social motives of this kind reach their clearest expression in industry; one builds a new office or factory to excite envy in one's competitors and to establish confidence in one's customers. It may serve as direct advertisement—a fact which the New York authorities recognized in the exceptionally high federal taxes imposed on prestige office buildings such as Lever House and the Seagram Building (see Collins, 1970).

One recognizes similar motives in the client who builds an exceptionally lavish house; like his cars, his paintings and his wife's jewellery, it is a direct expression of his wealth. We may even deceive ourselves into thinking that socially-orientated clients such as the committees which commission housing, schools and hospitals are free of such motivation, but that is not always true. How can one account otherwise for the ways in which certain light and dry building systems, designed to cope, say, with the specific problems of schools in mining subsidence areas, have been approved for other uses such as housing and universities, in which their particular advantages are irrelevant and for which, in terms of environmental standards they are totally inadequate. Clearly the *image* of systems building carries overtones of social responsibility in such cases and housing or university building committees must be *seen* to be socially responsible.

Any decision to build will be a social one; whether he wants it to or not the building will express very accurately the client's place in society. However, social, cultural and aesthetic motives for building are closely bound up with questions of image or, to use the terminology of Chapter 2, with formal *icons*. Inevitably therefore, a majority of clients (and most architects) have strong views about what their buildings will look like. As a crude and obvious example we might take the client who has in mind the icon of a stockbroker's Tudor house. It represents for him such concepts as security, tradition, love of his country and so on. He cannot rationalize these concepts because he feels them too deeply, but they are bound up inextricably with his motivation for building. The architect too has his icons. His are derived from the journals which bind architects together and ensure that they share a set of common values. His icons are concerned with 'functionalism', with the *appearance* of efficiency. The International Style presented just such an icon—the mental image of a building style advocated by Le Corbusier, Gropius, Mies and others—consisting of steel or concrete columns, white walls, large areas of glass and so on. It was anathema to the client who wanted stockbroker's Tudor, or, say, the true 'German' architecture which opponents of the Bauhaus advocated (see Lane, 1968), This 'German' architecture was to have pitched roofs, small windows and certain other characteristics of a particular vernacular. At this level of cultural and aesthetic motivation, both advocates and opponents of the new architecture presented equally specious arguments; they were both concerned with issues of a mystic, philosophical kind which had little to do with architecture. Yet if one applied certain empirical tests, matching examples of each style against our criteria for 'normal' building (Chapter 8), then stockbroker's Tudor or 'German' architecture actually proves to be more satisfactory as far as the user's sensory expectations are concerned, than the International Style.

Let us suppose that a decision to build has been taken, transcending finally any question of client motivation. If all clients and their architects were fully rational and displayed only the highest of motives, then probably few buildings would actually get built. The client, as we have used the term, refers to whoever has commissioned the building and will become its administrator. It may be an individual such as the managing director of a company, two people such as husband and wife, or a committee of some private or public kind. In each case, the client may be totally ignorant in building matters, or he may be highly expert which is increasingly true of certain individuals on building committees.

In some cases the client may also be the user; husband and wife presumably will be building for their own occupation. In other cases he may be user of only a small part of the building; the managing director, for instance, might be a regular user only of his own office. In other cases again, client and user will be quite different people; this will be particularly true where the client is some public committee concerned with housing, schools or other social kinds of building. As we have seen, the client's values, both in commissioning and administrating the building, may be substantially different from the user's; this might be particularly true, say, in the case of a prison, or even where some charitable trust is concerned with building for the recipients of its charity. One can see that in such a case, client's and user's needs might actually conflict; a charitable trust, presumably, will seek maximum value for money whilst the user, particularly if he is infirm or aged, might have specific unusual and expensive needs. It seems likely, therefore, that user needs will provide a surer guide to how one should design than the client's initial motivation.

The pioneers of modern architecture assumed that user needs should provide the basis of their 'functional' brief. There was a conflict, certainly, between what they said and what they actually did, but their intentions at least were reasonable.

User Requirements

Having established the client's motives for building, we shall be in a position to start considering what the building is for. We may think in terms of a building type—office, school, factory and so on; that in itself will give us an overall indication of what we are to house. We can look at precedents including possibly the client's own existing building, and this will give us a more or less detailed idea of the activities which the new building is to contain. They may fall well within Cowan's list of activities which can be housed comfortably in rooms of around 150 square feet (14 metres^2) and we might well proceed from there, providing a range of such rooms with reasonable 'average' environmental conditions. For many purposes that will be quite enough but there may be times when we want to achieve a much more accurate fit between activity and environment. In that case, we can take each activity in turn and record the relevant data on it. As a first step, we shall have to prepare a list of activities; obviously we can ask the client what they will be. He may well name the important ones, but we shall probably find that detailed observation of his existing organization in action suggests others. In particular, it will be useful to trace the sequence of activities by which certain individuals arrive at, enter, move through and leave the building. Having listed the activities, we might want to plot an economic *justification* for each activity. We might, in fact, use an activity questionnaire which could include among other things the following points. What is the product of the activity in terms of: direct profit; indirect profit; social gain; satisfaction of statutory requirements? What is the initial cost of the activity in terms of: demands on structure, space, support, services, and circulation? What is the running cost of the activity in terms of: staff time; demands on structure, space, circulation, services, and maintenance? Any activity which survives this justification obviously deserves to be accommodated.

We can now take the brief for each of these; Figure 19.1 suggests the minimum amount of information which needs to be found in terms of locating the activity within the building. Just what are the needs of an activity, therefore, which will help determine the plan of the building? They may be grouped under four headings: (1) physical space required; (2) environmental conditions; (3) relationship with other activities; (4) effects on structure of the building. The chart itself is, or should be, self-explanatory. It represents, in highly simplified form, those questions from the ADM chart (see Chapter 13) which actually help determine the physical location of an activity within the building. Physical space needs and environmental conditions have been discussed in Chapters 8 and 9.

It is possible, certainly, to consider each activity in isolation and there may be advantages in doing so when we are concerned with environmental, or even structural characteristics; but sooner or later we shall have to consider the distribution of activities throughout the building and this, of course, will be fundamental to the planning, or distribution of activities, in three-dimensional space. Activities may be related to each other in several ways: (*a*) in terms of physical movement from one to another; (*b*) in environmental terms—they may share environmental needs (e.g. air-conditioning) or be quite incompatible in environmental terms (e.g. noise); (*c*) socially.

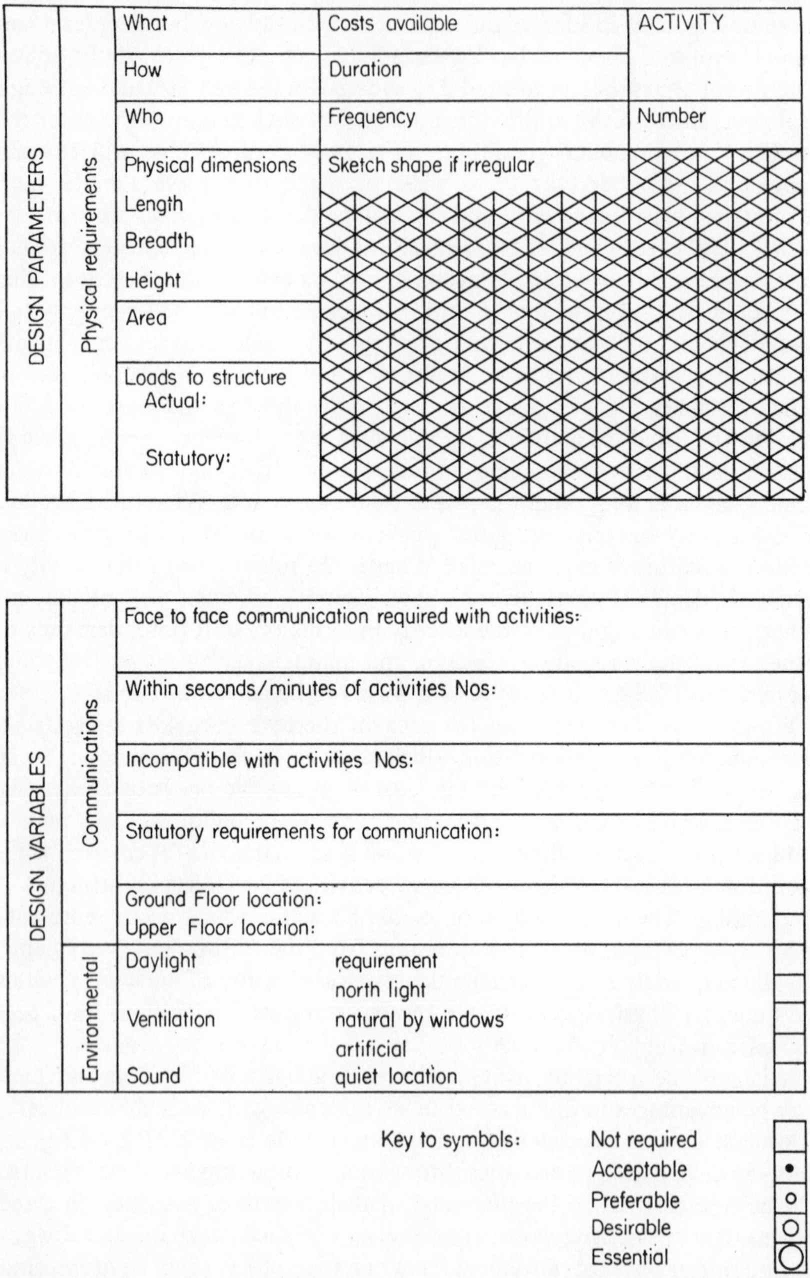

DESIGN PARAMETERS	Physical requirements	What	Costs available	ACTIVITY
		How	Duration	
		Who	Frequency	Number
		Physical dimensions Length Breadth Height Area	Sketch shape if irregular	
		Loads to structure Actual: Statutory:		

DESIGN VARIABLES	Communications	Face to face communication required with activities:	
		Within seconds/minutes of activities Nos:	
		Incompatible with activities Nos:	
		Statutory requirements for communication:	
	Environmental	Ground Floor location: Upper Floor location:	
		Daylight	requirement north light	
		Ventilation	natural by windows artificial	
		Sound	quiet location	

Key to symbols:

Not required	☐
Acceptable	•
Preferable	○
Desirable	◯
Essential	⬤

Figure 19.1—Briefing form for individual activity. This could also be produced as a two-sided filing card

The first of these has been described in many ways, in terms of circulation, movement patterns, spatial sequences and so on. The routes of Picturesque garden architecture fall into this category and so, for that matter, do Le Corbusier's *axes.* Movement itself may be a functional matter, or it may carry symbolic overtones. Where movement is purely functional, then systems analysis (see Chapter 15) offers many ways of plotting it. The block schematic diagram, obviously, may be used to plot the flow of oil through a refinery, but it can also be used to plot the flow of people, say, into a theatre or through an exhibition. Just as oil will be processed and transformed as it passes through the various elements of the refinery, so people may be 'processed' psychologically as they pass through a carefully designed sequence of spaces (Figure 19.2).

Each activity will make demands of various kinds on the building's structure. At the simplest level it will need a horizontal surface, large enough to contain associated furniture and equipment, and it will need enough head room; but as we have seen, the structure itself will have certain environmental characteristics, and it is essential to the environmental design process that these be considered in deciding what kind of structure to use.

Having prepared data sheets on the various activities, the next question is what to do with them. They can, of course, be sorted. That might be a manual business in which, according to selected criteria, one places the sheets in piles. It might be mechanized, or even computerized; Robert Matthew, Johnson Marshall and Partners have used a computer program for sorting the much more complex ADM sheets. But then again we should ask ourselves what the sorting is for. The purpose of the briefing in the first place was to position activities within the three-dimensional space available for building and the sorting too should be undertaken with this end in view.

There are two reasons, finally, for placing an activity in a particular position—or rather, two major reasons, each with many ramifications. The first of these is environmental; as a simple instance of this, other things being equal, one would not place an activity which needed quiet on the noisy side of the building. The other reasons are concerned with relationships between activities, and these two can be subdivided into environmental, functional and circulatory. These are self-explanatory but there are various subtleties we ought to take into account, and techniques of analysis which will help bear them in mind.

At this stage we cannot consider all the environmental implications, because much will depend on the environment into which we shall be building, and this will be the subject of the next section. Suffice it to say, for now, that as part of the process we shall define the block of space available for building into in such a way that it will be possible to allocate positions, for certain critical activities at least. In order to do that, we may need to define a hierarchy of activities, to order them according to some system, in order of

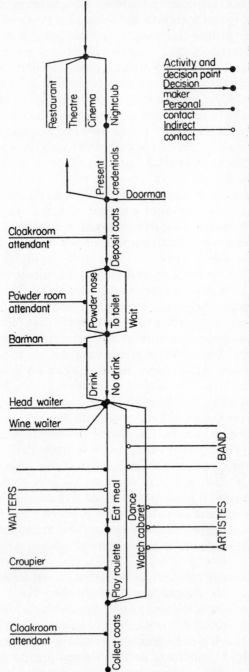

Figure 19.2—Activity and movement analysis of a couple entering a nightclub, plotted in the form of a flow chart. Similar charts could be plotted for everyone else who comes into the club, doorman, attendants, barman, waiters, artistes, croupier, etc., not to mention food, drink, and other goods, so that eventually a complex pattern of interacting flow charts would be built up

importance so that when activities compete for space, as inevitably they will, we shall know how to order their priorities.

Sometimes the hierarchy will be presented to us by the client; it may be the only aspect of the briefing which really concerns him. The difficulty is that any such statement of hierarchy might raise our egalitarian blood. If we modify Le Corbusier's view and admit, at least, that all men have similar organisms, then their needs of the environment, if they are to be comfortable, will be similar if not identical. Clearly, in any building some parts of three-dimensional space will be inherently more comfortable than others; how shall we allocate them? We might take a utilitarian view that our prime concern is the greatest happiness for the greatest number of people. In that case, undoubtedly, we should allocate, say, the typing pool a more favourable position than the board room; but having so expressed our political convictions, it is highly likely that we should also have lost our client. It may be that enthusiasm for the open-plan, *burolandschaft* office stems from egalitarian impulses; if everyone is housed in the same space, then clearly the architect has less responsibility for ordering their hierarchies than when he designs actual rooms, ordered in size according to some social structure. Yet Manning and his colleagues (1965), who were much in favour of such planning, found a much greater feeling of regimentation in staff who had recently been moved to such a building (the Co-operative Insurance Society in Manchester) than they had ever experienced in more traditional offices. This arose in part from the management's desire to keep everything neat and tidy in the open offices, to ban personal effects and to insist on desk tops being tidied every night. As they say,

'The new, more autocratic form of supervision was regarded as being a consequence of the large offices, which it was felt foster a passion for symmetrical layouts and obsessional tidiness.'

The management took a paternalistic view of such matters. One of them said.

'I have concluded that the more perfect one makes the environmental condition the more occupants will complain about deviations from the ideal . . . during hot weather . . . when occupants readily complain if the temperature . . . reaches 74°F . . . a telephone call to neighbouring . . . buildings shows that temperatures of 80°F are being suffered without complaint. The simile of spoiled children comes to mind . . .'

So whatever we do, someone is going to object.

However, as we saw in Chapter 10, certain techniques from decision-making will help us specifically with this class of problem. They can take into account not only the hard financial facts of the case, but people's values as well, and we can apply them with any degree of precision. Suppose, for instance, we take the few environmental requirements which have been shown to influence the position of an activity in the building. As part of our activity brief, we allocated a subjective impression of importance to each of these.

Thus for one activity we might have allocated 'quiet location' as the most important factor of all, whilst another might need strict north light.

Suppose then, by environmental, social or financial criteria we have ordered the activities into an initial hierarchy. We can now begin the next stage of analysis. We could start by grouping them into sets and subsets using, possibly, Venn diagrams (see Chapter 7) and preparing a different one for each environmental condition. As before, the analysis can be undertaken manually, mechanically or by computer; in each case, we shall build up a rich pattern of interconnexions between activities. The crudest, and among the most effective tools for use at this point, are the interaction chart, in one of its many forms, the flow chart and the random connexions diagram (see Chapter 13).

An extremely useful chart, therefore, could be built up of the sequences by which people move into, through and out of the building, and once activities had been plotted in this schematic way, many kinds of analysis would be possible. Instead of simple rectangles, for instance, one might use by analogy the symbols of computer flow charts. The operations box would represent an activity, the decisions box would indicate points of choice along the route and, for major activities, the information symbols (teletype, punched card or recording tape) could be used to feed in environmental information (visual, thermal and aural) as appropriate.

The possibilities of graph theory (see Chapter 12) might be used in analysing the flow of activities and their interrelations; one might find, for instance, that certain activities ought to be planned in tree form, whilst for others circuits might be more appropriate. One could explore the possibilities of networks (Chapter 12), dual graphs and so on. And again, certain techniques from O.R. might be applied at this stage; obviously queuing theory might have a place, but so might linear programming, travelling salesmen and so on. And certainly network analysis would be appropriate where certain activity paths were, literally, critical.

As we saw in Chapter 12, Tabor (1970a, b, c and d) has published a series of papers on *Traffic in Buildings*, including *Pedestrian Circulation* and the *Evaluation of Routes* which throw a good deal of light on these matters. His colleagues, Bullock, Dickens and Steadman, have also shown in their parallel studies of university planning (1970) that we can learn a great deal about the physical planning of rooms, buildings, neighbourhoods, cities and regions simply plotting the ways in which people move from activity to activity and thus from place to place in the course of a day's living. Movement can be measured in terms of time which, clearly, will be a function of distance and mode of transport; many techniques are available (see Chapters 12 and 15) but we should remember that the most *efficient* movement pattern is not necessarily the most effective. Rapoport (1969) cites Hazard on the case of new law courts, in which some extremely efficient planning had led to a gross reduction in circulation area and the distances which people had to walk; but, as he says "the lack of corridors with dim corners where informal conferences and settlements can take place means that many more cases came to trial (they cannot be settled informally out of court); the court calendars tend to become overloaded and this interferes with the administration of justice.'

Some of the more notorious problems of post-war architecture could have been avoided by taking such movement patterns into account. If sequences of activities had been plotted, say, for babies, toddlers, primary school children, teenagers, young married couples, mature couples, pensioners, both fit and disabled, not to mention various categories of people living on their own, then it would have been possible to predict which of them *could* live comfortably in multi-storey flats (such as disabled pensioners who may prefer lifts to stairs) and those who could not (such as families with young children). Flats could have been designed accordingly, and the information made available to housing management, so that it could have been borne in mind in allocating different kinds of housing to different people.

Once activities have been plotted in sequence, many other things follow. Such sequences of course will be vital in the planning of the building; one may think of them as strings of beads and one planning task, at least, is to pack these strings as economically as possible into the envelope available for building; but they cannot be jammed in arbitrarily, because some activities have particular environmental needs. They will have to be placed at specific points in the envelope but the strings must not be broken, so that from these critical activities associated activities remain threaded either side.

There is another problem with these beads; they come in vastly different sizes. Some of them are small, intimate and private whilst others tend to be large, extrovert and public. Their sizes will be determined in several ways. The first determinant of size and probably the easiest to satisfy, will be their functional requirements. We shall have noted, during the activity briefing, what furniture, fittings and so on surrounded each activity, and these will offer clues as to what size of space each will need. It might be fairly easy to plan a cluster of activities, bearing in mind the arrangement of essential furniture and of circulation spaces between. But what of height? Manning and his colleagues (1965) label the height above their typist's head as 'arbitrary' but it is nothing of the kind. As we saw in Chapter 8, she brings expectations to it and we ought to satisfy these expectations. If we did this throughout the building we might finish up with ceiling heights that satisfied most people's expectations and it may be that they would all be the same. Yet the line of enquiry we have been pursuing encourages variations in activity space, and in particular floor to ceiling height, whenever this is appropriate.

We have represented sequences of activities for various individuals by block schematic diagrams, analogous with the diagrams of systems engineering and so on. And the analogy can be pressed further. For just as in the diagram, say, of an oil refinery, each block represents a vessel, machine or other piece of equipment which transforms the oil in certain ways as it passes through, so each block in the diagram which represents the passage of a person through a building represents an activity, contained in a space, which can be used to transform the person, in certain simple ways. We are concerned, in other words, with sequential planning in which the person passes through a sequence of spaces, each of which continues, or contrasts with, the character of the last. The theatre is a familiar traditional example. One enters from the street into a foyer, a relatively large space which nevertheless has a glitter and 'atmosphere' which immediately proclaims its difference from the mundane world we have left outside. We proceed by sequence to cloakrooms, up stairs, to a bar perhaps, and finally along corridors getting smaller and

Table 19.1

Stairs	walking to and from stairs		27	
	on stairs		72	
		total	99	seconds
Paternoster	walking to and from paternoster		30	
	on paternoster		68	
		total	98	seconds
Lift	walking to and from lift		30	
	waiting		105	
	in lift (one stop)		30	
		total	165	seconds

darker as we near the auditorium. Then finally, by contrast with these last, the auditorium itself appears extraordinarily large, bright and otherwise attractive. This may be an extreme example, but the principle is available for anyone to follow and, given an empirical approach to design, the flow diagram itself is a valuable aid in following it.

For many purposes it is convenient to express movement in terms of time, which offers other possibilities of three-dimensional planning than linear distance ever could. It is convenient, for instance, if I press the button on my desk and my secretary appears within thirty seconds. That is possible because her room is next to mine. It is equally convenient if someone I wish to see less often can come to me, or I can go to him, within ninety seconds. That is possible when his room is on the same floor, and it may be possible too for rooms adjacent to the staircase on the next floor, immediately below my office. One set of experiments in a multi-storey building (the Arts Tower at Sheffield University) yielded the journey times shown in Table 19.1 for the

latter situation. Let us assume then that, whatever his motives, the client has decided to build; our next task will be to analyse the site.

External Environment

Our analysis of the site will depend on many things. We may be instructed by the client body to assist in finding a site, in which case we shall base our recommendations on what the building is for. We shall bear in mind, constantly, the fact that the building itself is simply a device which modifies the indigenous climate so that certain activities can be pursued in comfort. If we have defined already what those conditions for comfort are then we shall be able to advise on a site whose conditions need the least possible modification; but that suggests a world-wide search, which is what we ought to make if we take that particular part of the brief seriously. Usually the choice will not be so broad. The location, generally, will be determined by factors other than climate. We are likely to be concerned at least as much with communications, with proximity to raw materials, markets, sources of labour, work, schools, shops or even entertainment. Proximities of this kind are much more likely to determine an initial choice of site than anything to do with unmodified climate. Again, possible sites may, and probably will, be restricted by planning legislation—zones for housing, factories, commerce and so on. Our predecessors, Aristotle, Vitruvius, Alberti and Bacon, knew a great deal about the choices of sites. They and other people working to principles they laid down, seem to have chosen all the best sites anyhow; but we have several advantages over them. If we cannot use a decent site because none is available, then at least we can modify what is offered us—structurally, by means of concrete and other materials they could not use as we do, and environmentally, in terms of the sophisticated services we can now build in. We ought to remember, nevertheless, in choosing any site, that Manning, Markus and others have found that most people when asked, state or imply that one of the most important things about their place of work (and one can extend this, certainly, to include place of living) is that there should be a view out of it. If they attach such importance to this matter of view, then at least we might give them the best we can.

One crucial factor in choosing a site obviously will be cost, or more particularly value, and this can be expressed in many ways. It is likely to be high near the city centre, where the environmental conditions it offers may be at their worst. As Wendt says (1957) it is important to distinguish between the aggregate land values of a particular area, and the specific value of a particular site within it. The value of a particular site will vary according to the size of the market for it, the amount to be spent on urban services within that market, the competitive pull of the particular area, the availability of similar land and the amount of public investment which can be expected in services. Taken together, these help determine the possible gross revenue from the site.

Costs will also be involved in the form of local property taxes, operating costs, interest on capital required for present and future improvements, and depreciation allowance for these improvements. Taken together, these help determine the total expected costs; an estimate of nett annual revenue can be obtained by subtracting these from the gross annual revenue. The actual value of the land can be obtained by dividing this nett annual revenue by the capitalization rate, which last figure can be obtained by combining interest rates, allowances for anticipated risks and one's expectations concerning capital gains.

Moseley (1963) has shown how the building shape itself could be determined according to different patterns of vertical travel. One might plan an office block, factory or many other building types, for efficiency in journey time from one activity to another. One might even plan a town in this way, on the assumption that the journey to work, to shops, or to some form of entertainment is by no means different, in principle, from a journey within the house or the office building. Not that one always aims for economy in journey time. In going to lunch, there may be certain advantages in taking a ten-minute journey thus allowing for adjustment between work and relaxation. A ten-minute journey might encompass many things—a short walk and discussion with someone else, or a much longer journey by car to a more desirable place.

However, economic considerations alone will certainly not be enough in choosing a site. Certain social factors will also be extremely important. Chapin (1966) discusses several of these: the concentration and dispersion of services and of populations, centralization and decentralization, the segregation of populations into distinctive areas, the dominance of certain areas (usually central) and the receding dominance of other areas as one moves to the periphery, the invasion of areas by particular groups which displace those who were originally in possession. Naturally at the macro-scale of planning, these raise all those questions of values, motivation and behaviour which have troubled us considerably at the micro-scale of the individual building.

Complex as the interplay must be between economic and social factors affecting the choice of site, it is highly likely that both will be overridden by planning constraints, by decisions taken 'in the public interest' that the city must and can only be allowed, to develop in certain ways. Chapin identifies five areas in which, by planning, it is hoped to defend the public interest: health, safety, convenience, economy and amenity. The first two of these, of course, are the subject of legislation; in our case the Building Regulations and Town Planning controls.

Economic, social and 'public interest' constraints apply to all buildings whatever activities they are to house. Sometimes planning determines that certain activities shall be located in certain zones of the city although as Alexander (1966), Jacobs (1962) and others have shown, this administrative tidiness may deprive us of the richness we associate with cities which have grown up piecemeal, and whose functions are intermingled in highly complex ways. It may also inhibit the most important reason of all for locating a building in a particular place, that the activities it houses are related to, and must communicate with, activities housed elsewhere in completely different buildings. Very few of us live and spend the entire working day in one particular building. The housewife, say, in Le Corbusier's Unités d'Habitation, could, in theory, spend several months under the same roof; there is no necessity for her to go out into the open air, for everything she needs from day to day is available in the shops which are built into the residential block.

That is an exception, and most of us find ourselves moving from place to place as our activities change during the course of the day from sleeping to washing to breakfasting to working and so on. Chapin classifies all urban activities under three major headings: productive activities, general welfare activities and residential activities.

At this level, then, planning becomes a device for relating activities on a much larger scale than the individual building. One could, literally, take each activity that anyone was likely to perform, from ploughing a field to programming a computer, and plot its relationships with all other possible activities. Early in the nineteenth century it was considered important that the activities of living and the activities of working should be located near to each other, as at New Lanark, Saltaire and elsewhere. One reason for this, certainly, was the paternalistic light in which employers at the time viewed their workers, but it also had certain social advantages and the journey to work was reduced to a minimum. Later as work became noisier, dirtier and generally more unpleasant, planners thought it necessary for work and living to be separated, which led to the idea of rigid zoning in the city; and that led, inevitably, to the many problems connected with the journey to work. Now that many of the more unpleasant jobs can be automated and factories as a whole cleaned up, there is less necessity to separate work from living and in time, undoubtedly, we shall see a new pattern of interrelationships developing. We might aid its development by remembering that during the course of the day, each individual performs a sequence of activities—sleeping, washing, dressing, breakfasting and so on. At the moment, he usually has to perform a superfluous activity known as travelling, between the last of these and starting his day-to-day work. There may be very good reasons why he should, social, environmental and so on, but if we plot his day-to-day sequence of activities on a time basis, at least, we shall be in a position to evaluate the journey to work, to weigh its cost against other, less tangible factors concerned with amenity and to decide, on this basis, how long it might reasonably be.

Assuming now that a site has been selected, by whatever means, how do we set about its analysis? Our task is to record and analyse only such information as will help us in the initial stages of design. We can go further, remembering that our activity briefing was concerned with three things (the physical space available, the communications relationships between activities, and the sensory needs of each activity), to concentrate in our site briefing also on these same factors.

There will be few real difficulties in establishing the spatial characteristics of the site. Obviously we can measure it, survey its surface and even the structure under its surface. The traditional components of a site survey will satisfy our needs quite well from this point of view. We may well use check-lists, but having collected this information the next question is how we use it. Obviously we can draw it on to a plan, with levels or even contours plotted, details of trial holes and so on. Such a plan of course would be a useful document and it might help us to design the building, but to make the best use of it we need to associate it with a much more comprehensive analysis of a three-dimensional kind. Suppose, for instance, that we drew our plan of the site in isometric or axonometric and plotted on to it further information concerned with the *three-dimensional* space available to us, and with the relevant environmental information (Figure 19.3).

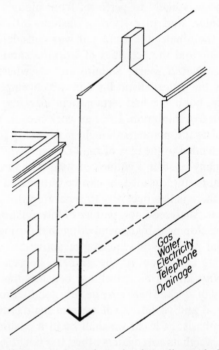

Figure 19.3—Environmental matrix 1: the site, adjacent buildings, services, etc., are modelled in any appropriate medium—two-, three- or four-dimensional, numerically, spatially or mechanically. Thus a drawing, iconic model, digital computer model or visual display is built up to represent the site in three dimensions

There are precedents for such three-dimensional plots; some of the most sophisticated, as we saw in Chapter 14, have been prepared by Land Use and Built Form Studies at Cambridge University. One extremely thorough analysis was conducted by Hawkes (undated) into the nature of 'permissible building envelopes' in London and New York. He analysed successive land-use regulations in the two cities over the preceding sixty years and plotted three-dimensionally the shapes of buildings which the regulations, at various stages,

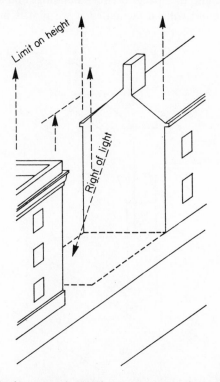

Figure 19.4—Environmental matrix 2: conceptual constraints—legal, planning, financial, etc.—are fed into the model, thus building up a 'permissible building envelope' (see Hawkes, undated)

would have permitted. In 1894, for instance, the London regulations allowed one to build vertically from the edge of the street to a height of eighty feet, after which one was required to splay back at an angle of $63\frac{1}{2}$ degrees so that daylight would be admitted to buildings across the street (Figure 19.4).

Similar plotting of permissible building envelopes indicated that by the early 1950s legislation had changed, after a great deal of lobbying by architects and others, so that Le Corbusier-type 'pavilions in the park' could be built in L.C.C. housing developments at Roehampton and elsewhere. (This research, incidentally, indicates the value to architecture of a historical approach, based on the direct comparison of successive examples. Observation of this kind can be quite impartial, but in this particular instance it threw up a great many social implications concerned with the desire by various architects to build into legislation their personal ideals.)

We too shall need to plot the permissible building envelope for our site and its form can be determined with reference to legislation in terms of building shape, height, the spaces between buildings and so on (Figure 19.5). And obviously its use will be facilitated if we plot it in three-dimensional

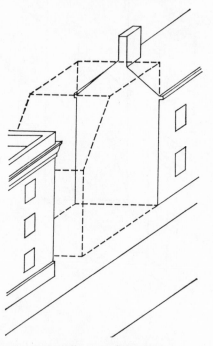

Figure 19.5—Permissible building envelope

form. In other words, it can be drawn on our three-dimensional plot of the site; but we can make it even more useful if we plot on to the permissible building envelope the other kinds of information we recorded for each activity, concerned with movement between activities and with sensory stimuli.

As far as movement is concerned, we shall need to plot around the envelope both pedestrian and traffic patterns, in so far as they are likely to affect our design, bearing in mind legislation concerning access from the site to surrounding roads and so on. As for sensory stimuli, these will fall into the categories we have used already, and again their positions can be plotted on to the three-dimensional drawing. Relevant stimuli to the various senses might be:

Seeing—sun path, buildings, trees, etc., which shade the site from the open sky, attractive views, both natural and man-made, squalid views (presumably man-made) bearing in mind that the view will change considerably from floor to floor and should therefore be plotted for different levels;
Hearing—sources of noise, especially industry, road, rail and air traffic;
Skin senses—sun path (bearing in mind solar heat gain), prevailing wind, rainfall and other climatic information;
Smell—sources of pleasant and unpleasant smell, especially industry (tanning, brewing and so on), road and rail traffic;
Other senses (kinaesthetic and equilibrium) will be much less affected by factors in the external environment, but one should not exclude the effects of optical illusion, both in the landscape and in buildings.

So we build up a permissible building envelope with environmental stimuli plotted round it (Figure 19.6), the *environmental matrix*. This can be plotted at many levels of sophistication. Crudest of all, perhaps, will be a three-dimensional drawing: the site, with the matrix superimposed, plotted in isometric, axonometric or even perspective. This then forms a basis for later stages in the design process. Instead of a simple drawing, the environmental matrix might be a three-dimensional model in perspex, wire or other suitable material, and to any desired degree of abstraction or realism. It might be built on to a contour model of the site, a peg model or other suitable base. But the matrix can also be plotted as a set of coordinates and built into a computer program, or given 'sketchpad' (see Chapter 15) and a large enough computer, it could be presented as a visual display, with environmental stimuli plotted in as much detail as one cared to use.

The purpose of the matrix is to provide, not just the space available for building into, but sufficient indication of where favourable and unfavourable environmental stimuli are located to enable one to plot the activities with particularly critical environmental requirements in the most appropriate places. Chapin identifies nine types of background studies which, taken together, form a complete urban land use study and they might well be useful in plotting the environmental matrix:

1. Compilation of data on physiographic features, mapping of the urban setting
2. The land use survey
3. The vacant land survey
4. Hydrological and flood potential study
5. Structural and environmental quality survey
6. Cost-revenue studies of land use
7. Land value studies
8. Studies of aesthetic features of the urban area
9. Studies of public attitudes and preferences regarding land use.

Sometimes, however, we cannot plot an environmental matrix directly. The concept itself suggests a tight, urban site (restricted therefore, in three-dimensional form) in which we are constrained on every hand by adjacent buildings, trees, open spaces, not to mention the legislation which determines height and other aspects of the matrix's form. Some sites, however, are not like that. There may be hardly any constraints on an open rural site. We may be subject to

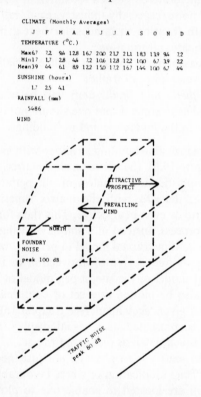

CLIMATE (Monthly Averages)

	J	F	M	A	M	J	J	A	S	O	N	D
TEMPERATURE (°C.)												
Max	6.7	7.2	9.4	12.8	16.7	20.0	21.7	21.1	18.3	13.9	9.4	7.2
Min	1.7	1.7	2.8	4.4	7.2	10.6	12.8	12.2	10.0	6.7	3.9	2.2
Mean	3.9	4.4	6.1	8.9	12.2	15.0	17.2	16.7	14.4	10.0	6.7	4.4

SUNSHINE (hours)

1.7 2.5 4.1

RAINFALL (mm)

54.86

WIND

SITE SURVEY (ENVIRONMENTAL)

Figure 19.6—Climatic, sensory (sources of noise, smell, visual attraction, etc.), social, traffic and other information is plotted on to the permissible building envelope, thus forming the environmental matrix

planning restrictions even there, but suppose the site is a large one and the environmental matrix encloses a volume of space many times the expected volume of the building. Where do we go from there?

For certain building types, one could determine the permissible volume of building on grounds of cost alone, by feeding a suitable cube rate into this three-dimensional grid. The rate itself would vary according to proposed methods of construction, standards of finish and overall building shape. It might be plotted in a series of quantum jumps according to the number of storeys.

We might also employ certain forms of self-limitation which will help us, gradually, to construct a more usable matrix. It may be, as Le Corbusier says, that the site has a natural centre of gravity, determined by its size, shape and the pattern of buildings, trees, hills and other landscape features around it. If there is, then certainly, we ought to be able to detect it intuitively, but if that fails then certain devices might help us. Williams (1954) describes a two-part survey for recording the visual characteristics of sites; in the first part, which is of interest to us, he identifies the three-dimensional characteristics of the site itself and goes on to record the man-made features which have been added to it, distinguishing six basic types of land form:

1. Level or gently sloping or rolling hills
2. Sloping sites, backed by hills or steeper slopes
3. Valley or gorge sites
4. Amphitheatrical or fan-shaped sites
5. Bowl-shaped sites
6. Ridged or hilltop sites.

Once he has described the site itself in terms of these, he goes on to classify the man-made features:

1. Urban textures
2. Green areas
3. Circulation facilities
4. Paved open spaces
5. Individually significant architectural masses, including vertical slab-like, massive and horizontal forms.

This information can certainly be recorded, but then it has to be analysed for use in design. We might do that with sketches, or even sections through the site, or we might use a series of contour models, not just of the site itself but of the whole environment visible from it and preferably made in sections. Given this, we can look across, through and into the site from every conceivable angle, testing the effects of different building masses by modelling them, say, in plasticine.

We should always remember that in different views the building is first seen, always, in silhouette; that its silhouette will be seen in conjunction with the silhouettes of hills, trees, other landscape features and other buildings; and silhouettes can be 'weighed' by that system of visual mechanics which enables one to judge precisely what weight of building mass is required at a particular point, to bring the system into equilibrium, assuming that equilibrium is what we want.

One can thus *design* an environmental matrix in the form of a 'desirable building envelope', but this is only half the story. If one is building in such a situation, it is highly likely that the views *from* the building will be most attractive and in this case no one, yet, has improved on Humphrey Repton's prescription: that one walk on to the site, decide which views one would wish to look out on, and position the main rooms accordingly. In our case, we might take the principle to a finer level of detail, and decide which views are desirable from individual activities.

Yet these methods too might fail, because they depend to a great extent on the judgement, discrimination and sensitivity of the architect. Where those are present, there will be no problem and indeed he will not need this kind of analysis. However, where they are not, he will probably resort to the device which rationalists have used in similar circumstances from antiquity, the two- or three-dimensional canonic grid. Clearly the grid itself *forms* an environmental matrix within which activities can be located. Initially, perhaps, the envelope is ill-defined in size, if not in shape, but the rationalists' answer, given such a grid, is to take as much of it as necessary to house the specified activities, making sure to finish with a rectilinear building to the nearest incremental size on the grid, above or below the actual needs of the activities.

Plotting Activities into the Environmental Matrix

Once the environmental matrix has been plotted, by whatever means, we come to the central phase in design which is the reconciliation of environmental needs for each activity against the environment offered by the site. The analysis of the activity briefings finished with their ordering into some kind of priority, hierarchical, economic, sensory, social or other. It will therefore be possible to take the activities in this order and to plot the first few, at least, into the environmental matrix. Let us take the example shown in Figure 19.7 and suppose that after much discussion it has been decided to give the activity of attending a board meeting the highest priority. We note its environmental needs—quiet location, good view (for when the meeting gets boring) and so on. Our particular environmental matrix presents immediate difficulties. Front and back of the site both face sources of noise (a foundry in one case, traffic in the other) but there is a reasonable view over the road so, on balance, we shall locate it there as the better of two less-than-ideal positions.

We could have located it deep in the core of the building, on the grounds that the activity is intermittent, needs the quietest possible ambience and could take place comfortably in a completely controlled environment; but the directors, in this case, valued the view very highly so we have to locate the activity accordingly. Similarly, we could have located the activity of drawing deep in the building in a fully controlled environment, but the expectations of the draughtsmen, not to mention the directors, were directed towards north light and so we tried to satisfy these as well. It so happens that one location in the matrix, height in the tapered section at the top, offers uninterrupted north light and there is no particular competition from other activities for this particular position. Similarly it is reasonable to locate the activity of entering the building on the street from which most pedestrian traffic will come; reception close to the entrance so that visitors can find it easily; display near reception so that casual visitors can be shown straight to the showroom without penetrating too far into the building and so on.

Certain critical activities seem to have located themselves easily, without

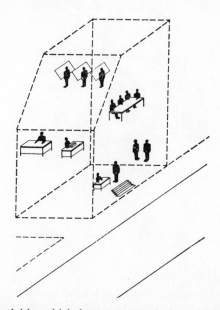

Figure 19.7—Activities which have very particular environmental needs are plotted into the matrix, e.g. the entrance has to be located for ease of access, reception has to be at the entrance and so, for convenience, has the showroom. Three people engaged in the activity of drawing preferred north light—they were placed where they would get it; the board of directors wanted to be free of foundry noise—they are located away from the foundry and, incidentally, enjoy the best view, but they will be disturbed by traffic noise unless further precautions, e.g. sealed double glazing, are built in

much negotiation, but eventually, as further activities are plotted into the matrix, difficulties inevitably will arise. Two activities may compete for the same location. In this case we refer to our hierarchy of activities to determine which shall take priority. In other cases communications will present problems in that a comparatively unimportant activity will have been recorded as linked very closely to two others, rather more critical, which because of their environmental needs have been plotted far apart in the building. We might have to think again about the critical ones, or, if they really are incompatible, duplicate the secondary one. If that is quite impossible, then we shall have to accept the discrepancy as an inevitable defect.

Once the primary activities have been located, it should be possible to plot the secondary ones around them—as we saw earlier—like a string of beads laid and compacted into a box which just fits them. The secondary activities

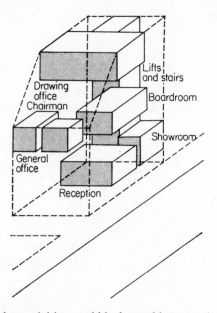

Figure 19.8—Other activities would be located between those with specific needs, according to the circulation and proximity requirements. Eventually all activities will have been located—using theory of games (see Chapter 10) or other O.R. techniques in cases of dispute. Activities will *then* be surrounded by rooms or other spaces; each space will have a floor and walls which must be supported by the structure of the building. This may lead directly to a pragmatic solution for the building form based on the nature of the materials

will be ordered, as far as possible, according to the routes which people take from one to the other in, around and through the building.

Let us suppose now that, given whatever compromise was necessary, we have formed our environmental matrix and all our activities have been located within it. We have been concerned so far with individual activities but not with actual rooms or other building spaces. We are now in a position to design the room shapes in general terms which is the next stage in the process (Figure 19.8). In the early stages of briefing, a number of people were going to be involved in the activity of attending a board meeting. Their environmental needs were similar, they needed face-to-face communication with each other, so it is not surprising that finally they found themselves located together in a particular part of the matrix. So we dedicate this part of the matrix to this particular group activity, in an actual room which we call boardroom. The original brief for each activity will give us some idea of what area of room is necessary, and the directors will have certain expectations as to its probable height. The room we design around them can be any shape which meets the space needs of their joint activity, but their kinaesthetic senses and their sense of equilibrium suggest a horizontal floor, at least, and substantially vertical walls. We shall also find that from the point of view of packing rooms of substantially different sizes together, rectangular shapes offer more possibilities than most others.

And just as a group of people come together in the building because each is performing the activity of attending a board meeting, so another group come together because each is drawing. Again we know the space needs of each, how many of them there are, and we can design a room to fit them. Just as there were conflicts when we were placing the activities into the environmental matrix, so there will be further conflicts when we try to house the activities in rooms, but this approach ensures, at least, that we realize the three-dimensional potential of the space available; room heights, for instance, will be based at this stage on expectations for particular activities; it will be a deliberate compromise if finally we decide that on each floor they must all be the same.

So the activities now are housed in rooms or other appropriate spaces. We can decide just how much, or how little, the various activities should be separated from each other by physical partitions, walls and so on, and how far they should be open—bearing in mind the stated requirements for visual and aural privacy. From this point of view, too, circulation will be counted as activity and must be allocated space accordingly, within or between rooms.

Rooms, circulation and other spaces can be treated now as surfaces, substantially horizontal (for kinaesthetic reasons) and needing support from the building itself. In other words, we have a pattern of loads collected on horizontal surfaces—and the vertical surfaces which separate them. This in itself, may be enough to determine for us what form of structure the building ought to have.

CHAPTER 20

The Derivation of Architectural Form

The environmental matrix, with activities plotted into it, leads us much further than any two-dimensional diagram towards the three-dimensional form of a building, but there is still a considerable translation to be achieved from an abstract pattern of relationships to a physical three-dimensional form. Different architects will approach this translation in different ways, but finally, whatever they do will take the form—individually or in combination— of the four historic *types of design* which we described in Chapter 2: pragmatic design, iconic design, design by analogy and canonic design. Let us consider each in turn.

Pragmatic Design

Pragmatic design was based, initially, on using materials, by trial-and-error to establish building form (see Chapter 2). That use might still apply where we are faced with problems of using new materials, or with using old ones in new ways to achieve greater economy, better performance, or other advantages over their traditional use; but in the nature of things pragmatic design at this fundamental level is unlikely to be an everyday affair now. Other kinds of pragmatism are possible. We suggested that one form of environmental matrix might be a three-dimensional model in wire or Perspex and into this one could slot, literally, three-dimensional blocks of wood, plasticine or polystyrene, representing to scale the spaces which activities might take up. That would simply be a three-dimensional version of the card cut-outs, representing rooms to scale, which many architects still use in planning.

However, pragmatism can still extend much further into design. We understand the properties of materials now, and the ways they are commonly put together in building, but that does not prevent us from allowing these properties, as the earliest builders did, to determine what the building is going to be like. There will be less trial-and-error in our pragmatism, but it will be based on the ways these materials are known to 'work', but materials 'work' in several ways: they have structural characteristics, and our choice will certainly be based on these; but they also have environmental characteristics (some kinds of wall, for instance, ofter better sound insulation than others) and these are not normally taken into account when one is choosing a structure. We shall adopt as comprehensive a view as possible in these

412

matters, and our pragmatic decision on structural type will be based on the following considerations:

(a) The pattern of activities and the distribution of loads from them
(b) The nature of the ground and what it will support
(c) The availability of materials, the possibility of transporting them from elsewhere, their basic properties, constructability and costs, their suitability for working in shop or on site
(d) The availability of labour with certain skills and the possibility of transporting it from elsewhere. The cost of labour in factory and on site
(e) The needs of activities for environmental control within the building in relation to the outside, uncontrolled environment
(f) The required or expected life of the building, related to closeness of fit to activities and the need for flexibility or change within that life
(g) The amount of money available for capital and running costs
(h) Controls on siting and construction imposed by statutory bodies
(i) Nature of the site and surrounding buildings (where there may be some requirement to 'blend in').

Given these clues, we can consider what structural types will serve our particular purpose. As a first step, we might consider the fundamental nature of the available materials. They may be available in solid form as rods, blocks or sheets; or they may arrive on site as something quite different—powders or granules of some kind which may or may not be mixed with fluids (another category of materials altogether) to make formless masses which take the shape of whatever they are poured into (le Good, 1968).

Blocks (usually brick, stone or concrete) may be put together to form solid masses which may or may not contain internal spaces. If they do, then the ratio of internal space to volume of masonry may be very small indeed. As it is increased, however, the masonry will be narrowed down to form walls, or planes of masonry which not only divide the spaces but support the building as well. The structural loading, as far as possible, should be continued along these walls and for the sake of stiffness certain geometrically determined shapes may have to be used. Sheet materials also may be used to form walls or planes, provided they are rigid; they too can act as both space-dividers and structural supports. Timber can be made into such sheets, so can concrete and certain plastics. Certain other plastics, however, such as polythene or PVC are made in very thin sheets, which are by no means rigid enough for such use. They can be used as space-dividers, however, provided they are supported in some way, either by suspending them from a frame of some kind, or making a sealed 'balloon' out of them and inflating it.

Rod materials, on the contrary, can be used very efficiently for structural support but they have no inherent space-dividing properties. The most useful rod materials in building are timber, which has been used to make building frames from pre-history, steel (or, initially, iron) and concrete, a formless mass which can be cast in rod form, but with true rod reinforcement in steel. Rods may be fixed together or, in the case of concrete, cast to form load-bearing structures in which strong materials are used, as appropriate, in tension and compression. They occupy very little space either vertically or horizontally, and for this reason they offer virtually no spatial separation. The structure will form a 'cage' of some kind, into which both horizontal and vertical space-dividers (often of some sheet material) have to be inserted between room and room, outside and inside. If we think of the building only in visual terms, we shall make these space-dividers as light as possible, forgetting that privacy is also an aural matter and that a mass or building has various heat-controlling properties.

These pragmatic thoughts on materials suggest ways of putting them together and we shall find, on reflection, that they can be used in four fundamentally different ways. It will be very rare for us to use one of these ways exclusively in any building, but there may be aesthetic, and even struc-tural advantages, in allowing one of them to dominate. They are:

Providing structural support:
    Mass construction (Figure 20.1)
    Planar construction (Figure 20.2)
    Frame construction (Figure 20.3)

Figure 20.1—Mass construction. The pyramids represent an extreme of mass construction, in which the supporting structure is also space-separating to such an extent that almost complete environmental (heat, light and sound) control is achieved between interior and exterior. The structure ensures that no light and virtually no sound can penetrate, whilst the mass of masonry acts as a heat sink, thus maintaining almost constant temperatures throughout the year

Providing space division:
  Mass construction (Figure 20.1)
  Planar construction (Figure 20.2)
  Skin construction (Figure 20.4)

Mass construction and planar construction occur in both categories; they support the building and divide space, whereas frame construction and skin construction occur in one category each, with little inherent environmental control.

Given these characteristics and their relationship to the nine major factors we chose to consider in determining the structural type, it may be possible immediately to make a choice on the basis of our previous analyses of activity requirements and site. Clearly the decision can be taken with varying degrees of rigour. One may make it by hunch, by simple inspection of the available data, by programming the characteristics of the four structural types into the computer, feeding in data on the particular case and accepting an automatic decision. If, by any of these means, a choice can be made as to the major

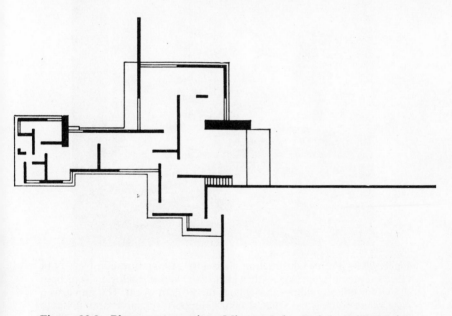

Figure 20.2—Planar construction. Mies van der Rohe's Brick House design (1922) uses a mass material in rectilinear planes, meeting at right angles, which act both as supporting structure and as space-separators. In some cases, the gaps between brick planes are filled with planes of glass; others are left open but in theory at least planar construction shares many advantages with mass construction. Its environmental control properties are similar to mass construction but at a rather lower level

Figure 20.3—Frame construction. Skidmore's Lever House in New York (1952) represents an icon with which many direct analogies have been drawn for office buildings throughout the western world. The frame, as a cage, offers nothing more than structural support; spatial separation has to be added to it in the form of floors, partitions and external cladding. These are supported by the frame and must therefore be as light as possible; their environmental (heat, light and sound) control properties will be negligible. Large areas of glass will encourage heat loss, solar heat gain, noise penetration, etc.; such buildings need comprehensive and expensive servicing systems if they are to be habitable and these consume energy, thus wasting precious resources

structural type, then we can move on to the next stage of the design process. For, given the building shell, we shall be able to predict its performance in terms of modifying the climate of the site and we shall also be able to assess how far it falls short of the stated requirements of the activities. We can further determine what will be needed in the way of services to bring the internal environment up to the required standards and we can relate all these decisions

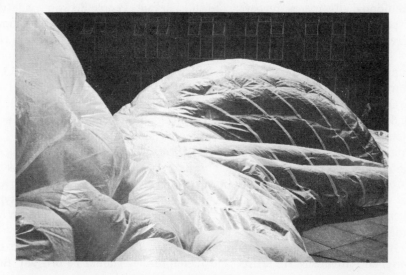

Figure 20.4—Skin construction. Polythene, PVC and other sheet plastic materials are capable of performing minimal space-separating functions but offer no structural support. They can be formed into sealed enclosures, containing air under pressure which supports them, or suspended from internal or external frames to form tents of a highly sophisticated kind. Negligible sound control, light filters through: solar heat and cold may be serious problems but can be overcome by servicing, again wasting energy

to cost. Pragmatic solutions to our problem may take many forms. The comparative appraisal of a suspended skin solution is included in Table 20.1.

These points will be developed in detail later but we have to bear in mind that pragmatic design may well fail. Our building may be such that the odds are evenly weighted between two, or even three of the major structural types. In that case we shall not reach a decision on the basis of pragmatic design, however much we may try to automate and computerize it. Nor will it help us in any way where, for whatever purpose, we want an *imaginative* piece of architecture. All it can give us, unless we are prepared to experiment with new and untried materials, is a further permutation on tried and accepted ways of using known materials.

Iconic Design

Iconic design cannot help us much either. By definition this consists of using tried and accepted forms; historically, it came after design by trial-and-error. Building types and methods of construction were established pragmatically and then repeated because they were known to work in terms of construction and the modification of climate to the activities it was required to house. Its traditional advantages, however, are still relevant. People do know what to expect from iconic design because they have already experienced its kind. Everyone in the building team—client, architect, quantity surveyor, the various engineers, local authority representatives, contractor, subcontractors, suppliers—they all know what the building is going to be like before they start, and communications problems are eased immeasurably.

One knows what to expect in environmental terms; one knows the quantity and quality of lighting, heating, sound control, not to mention the shapes and sizes of spaces, the ways that furniture can be laid out in them, the ways that communications can be made. One also knows what the building is going to be like in terms of *architectural* quality; the appearance will not be a shock to anyone and one can visualize how it will look in context. If a design has proved its worth for housing, schools, hospitals, offices or any other building type then there is no reason to change it. Why then do we put such a premium on originality?

It is simply the result of cultural pressures. People expect artists to be 'original'; architects are artists, and therefore they should be original. But however unsympathetic one may be to this view, there is one very good reason why no building ever can, or should, be an exact copy of another. Every building occupies a site, a unique piece of ground and if it works well on that site then it cannot work so well in every respect on any other site, however close. It may work particularly badly in fact, if an identical building is built next to it.

One thinks, for instance, of Lever House in New York, designed by Gordon Bunshaft of Skidmore, Owings and Merril (see Figure 20.3). When it was built in 1952, it represented a new conception in office building. Bunshaft used something very like our environmental matrix, or at least the permissible building envelope, and concluded that in this case he would not use all the space available. That took the characteristic New York 'ziggurat' form, rising vertically from the perimeter of the site to a height permitted by the zoning ordinance and then stepping back, floor by floor to allow a view of the sky to adjacent buildings. Lever Brothers agreed with Bunshaft that the ground floor should be substantially open, to provide a public garden, to build an open court at first floor level, thus exposing the garden below, and to build a slender tower for their offices occupying only about one quarter of the site in area. Their tower, in fact, penetrated the permissible building envelope slightly but having sacrificed so much in the interest of amenity, they were allowed this indiscretion.

As a pioneer building of its kind, Lever House naturally presented problems. Rain cascaded down its smooth curtain walling and there were problems of water penetration; but on the whole it was a successful building, given the tinted glass, massive air-conditioning and other environmental control devices which American technology and plenty of money could provide. As the first of its kind, Lever House became the iconic prototype for dozens of office buildings elsewhere. Virtually every city in the western world has at least one; some cities such as Sao Paulo seem to consist of very little else. At first the icon was copied in the sincerest form of flattery, as at Castrol House in London; it was also used for other building types, such as the Arts Tower at Sheffield University and certain things became clear. As a building type the smooth glass curtain-walled tower has certain inherent defects. Fronted by wide expanses of paving, it encourages the build-up of vortices so that wind speeds at its base may prevent one even from opening the front door. It may leak as we have seen, but above all the thin aluminium and glass skin offers virtually no environmental control. In particular, there is hardly any sound insulation; there is a massive build-up of heat gain from solar radiation; there are massive heat losses, and the building itself has no capacity whatsoever as a heat sink or reservoir. Add to that the stack effect by which convection currents up lift-shafts and staircases build up to quite considerable speeds and increase the heat gain even more in the upper storeys and one wonders why having built one, any architect should wish to build another.

In the case of Lever House, many of these inherent defects were mitigated, at least, by skilful design and the sheer, lavish provision of services. The layout of ground and first floors, for instance, prevented the disastrous build-up of vortices, whilst the lavish provision of services helped control say, the heat gain and heat loss—at some considerable cost. Many derivations from this icon, such as the Arts Tower at Sheffield, were not so lavishly serviced. They used Lever House —and its successors—as a visual icon forgetting that, to make a viable building, its other characteristics also had to be copied. So there it is possible to measure 97°F in a tutor's room with snow on the ground outside. Other criticism might be made about the provision of lifts; in every case where limited funds have prevented exact copying of the icon, the copy fails. In other words a good deal of adaptation is required to make any copy work, so much, in fact, that design is no longer iconic but analogical.

We can apply iconic design to the small office building. Lever House is hardly an appropriate model, but the same architects' Manufacturers' (Hanover) Trust Company Bank (see Figure 20.5(a)) will serve us well enough. The result is shown in Figure 20.5(b) and it is appraised with the others in Table 20.1.

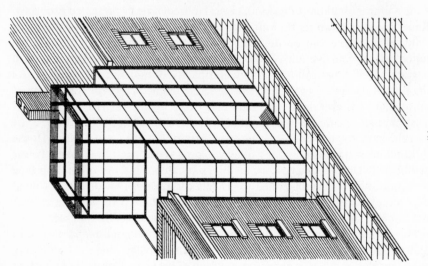

(b)

(a)

Figure 20.5—(a) Manufacturers' (Hanover) Trust Company Bank, New York (Skidmore, Owings and Merril, 1954). This elegant pavilion reverses the usual conventions of bank architecture. Instead of denoting security by the massive use of masonry with the implication that money is kept deep under the ground in massive vaults, the strong room is brought to street level and exposed to the full view of passers-by behind plate glass. Only the most intrepid or foolish of burglars would tackle it under those conditions. (b) A crude and direct solution to the formal problem of our office building, by analogy with the Skidmore bank. A preliminary appraisal suggests that in terms of capital costs, running costs, environmental control, fitness for place, it may not be very good

Analogical Design

As we saw in Chapters 16 and 17, analogy is the central mechanism of creativity and it has been used intuitively by all the architects we call creative at some time or other in their careers, but in most cases, as we saw in Chapter 17, creative analogies have been drawn from fields outside architecture; the crab shell of Le Corbusier's Ronchamp or, even more appropriate in this context of office design, the water lilies of Frank Lloyd Wright's Johnson Wax Factory. Sometimes, as we saw in Chapter 2, the analogue itself takes over; many people have been reminded by the *environmental matrix* with rooms plotted in (Figure 19.8) of Safde's *Habitat* at the Montreal Expo of 1967 (Figure 20.6(a)). A crude analogy with it is shown in Figure 20.6(b). We are all capable of drawing analogies at this level, but a great deal of further understanding is required on the part of the architect if he is to realize their inherent constructibility. If he is this good, the architect will need no instruction from me in the conscious application of analogy; it is the second-class imagination, shall we say, which will need to be stimulated. Yet even there we have much to learn by example from our great predecessors for, almost without exception, they started their creative careers by drawing analogies with other people's work.

I have traced elsewhere (Broadbent, forthcoming) the analogies which Le Corbusier drew with the work of Perret, Mies van der Rohe with the work of Behrens and Schinkel, and Gropius with Behrens and Wright. This process has continued to the next generation. One can see analogies with the work of Le Corbusier in the work of, say, Costa, Niemeyer, Fry, Lasdun, Tange and others. Specific uses of analogies in this way can be traced by comparing Le Corbusier's Jaoul Houses in Paris (see Figure 20.7(a)) with the housing at Ham Common (Figure 20.7(b)) which first brought Stirling and Gowan international acclaim. Le Corbusier had worked out a vocabulary of rough brickwork, concrete arches whose springings appeared as deep, board-marked beams on the elevations and chunky windows within openings which tended to be high and narrow or wide and low. Stirling and Gowan following the tradition of all creative designers in the early parts of their careers, took this formal vocabulary of Le Corbusier's omitting the arches (which had been tiled on their undersides) and refining the rest, so that far from copying the Jaoul Houses, they effected a truly creative analogy with them. We shall draw analogies (Figure 20.8(b)) with Le Corbusier's house for Dr. Currutchet at La Plata (1949) (see Figure 20.8(a)) to suggest a further solution to our problem.

The work of other architects, therefore, is a rich source of analogies and one that cannot be denied. Provided the analogy is an appropriate one, then there is no reason for anyone to deny it; a good analogy of this kind is infinitely preferable to some inappropriate 'original'. Another rich source

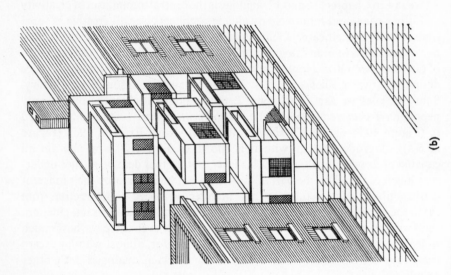

(b)

(a)

Figure 20.6—(a) Habitat, Montreal Expo (1967), (Moshe Safdie). Many people are reminded of this construction in prefabricated concrete boxes by certain of our analytical diagrams, in particular the environmental matrix with rooms plotted in. We shall use it, therefore, as the source of another direct analogy. (b) Direct analogy with Habitat as a solution to the office problem. Preliminary appraisal again suggests problems of costs —both capital costs and running costs— environmental control and so on

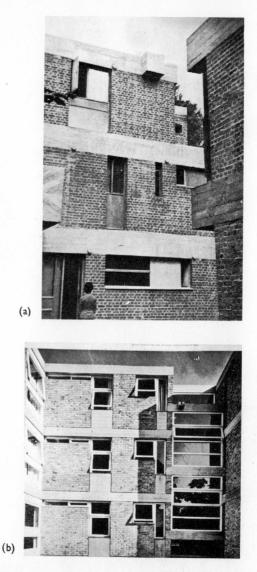

(a)

(b)

Figure 20.7—(a) Le Corbusier, Jaoul Houses, Paris 1954–6. The culmination of Le Corbusier's long exploration towards an architecture of rough-textured materials which started with farm-building projects in the 1930s, included the little country house at Vaucresson (1935) with its *brique brute* fireplace, and finally determined the essential attributes of the style which is known as *Brutalism*. (b) Stirling and Gowan: flats at Ham Common (1958). Careful and intended tribute by two English admirers in which the distinctive features of Le Corbusier's houses—rough brickwork, board-marked concrete edge beams, thick-framed windows in vertical or horizontal slots are 'translated' by a direct analogy into English

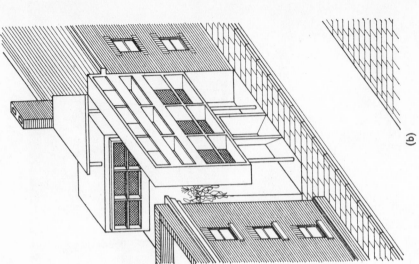

(b)

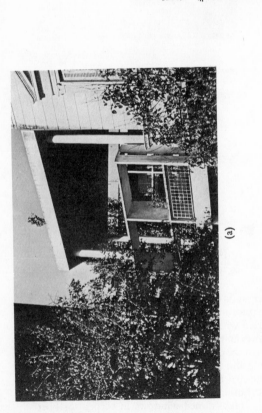

(a)

Figure 20.8—(a) Le Corbusier: house at La Plata, Argentina (1949). Another image evoked by our analytical diagrams, this doctor's house is planned around a route which threads its way up and between concrete columns. Rooms are supported at appropriate places along this route; where no room is required the frame is left open. (b) Direct analogy with the La Plata house applied to the office. Preliminary appraisal suggests almost as many problems as the first two proposals

Figure 20.9—Stirling: Cambridge University History Faculty. A powerful image using attributes of the architecture which Stirling and Gowan worked out for their Engineering Building at Leicester. At Cambridge, however, it seems to have led to environmental problems

Figure 20.10—Better still, use one of Stirling's analogical sources: York House, Manchester, a cotton-sorting warehouse designed by Harry Fairhurst. The cascade of glass—originally between two conventional warehouses—was designed so that daylight could penetrate deep into the building at every floor

of analogy originated in vernacular architecture. Le Corbusier, as we saw, looked at certain kinds of north African housing in drawing one of his analogies for Ronchamp; both Kahn and Gowan have indicated their enthusiasm for Scottish castles, as one would have realized anyway from the Richards Medical Centre in Philadelphia (Khan) and the Churchill College, Cambridge, competition entry (Stirling and Gowan). In Kahn's case, the analogy is confused by his insistence that the towers which surround the

Figure 20.11—A Stirling–Fairhurst analogy applied to the office building. Preliminary appraisal suggests that in terms of costs—capital and running—this may be the best solution so far. It allows great flexibility in environmental control, especially in variation of window-form with all that this implies in terms of daylight control (cascade of glass for the drawing office, small windows for small offices), heat loss, solar heat gain, noise control (double glazing where necessary, deep louvres for the boardroom). It also makes a considerable gesture in the direction of neighbourliness within a Georgian street

square laboratory areas are 'servant spaces' and so they are, or some of them. But if one looks closely at their function (some, after all, are staircases) it becomes clear that many of them project above the laboratory roofs for visual reasons only—to confirm the analogy with the turrets of a castle. Gowan's interest, on the other hand, is demonstrated by the 'curtain wall' of student rooms and the turfed banks which slope up to them, by direct analogy with the motte of a castle.

Further analogies have been found in industrial building; again one can thank Le Corbusier for giving this idea respectability. But increasingly the sources have become, not recent factory building but industrial archaeology. More than most, James Stirling has been extremely reluctant to admit his use of analogy yet the parallels are clear in, say, the History Faculty at Cambridge (see Figure 20.9). The most intriguing of all is York House in Manchester by Harry Fairhurst Senior (1911)—a cotton-sorting warehouse, built between others in Portland Street with a monumental façade to its front elevation and a vast cascade of glass at the rear (see Figure 20.10). Each floor is several feet shorter than the one below and its glazing (an early example of curtain walling) rises vertically and then splays back at 45° to meet the floor above. The intention, of course, was to provide the maximum area of glass so that daylight would be admitted deep into the building for the highly critical activity of sorting cotton.

In our case we might take an analogy with Stirling (see Figure 20.9)—or even better with Fairhurst (see Figure 20.10)—and apply this architectural vocabulary to our problem (see Figure 20.11). This is appraised together with the others in Table 20.1.

Canonic Design

The fourth design type of course is canonic and we could approach this in two ways. One way would be to set up our own canonic system—a two- or three-dimensional grid ensuring modular or at least dimensional coordination in the design and construction. Given the environmental matrix as a basis, with desirable room shapes and sizes already plotted, that might be a highly effective procedure. The basic dimensions of the grid, in all three directions, could be determined with reference to these shapes and sizes; there might thus be a better fit between the grid and the activities than when one starts with the grid itself as a mathematical abstraction. There would still be difficulties in reconciling the grid with actual building components, many of which are made to grid sizes without reference to activity sizes.

The most obvious way of applying canonic design to our problem would be to adopt one of the existing building systems or at least to adapt one, with as little interference as possible to the system itself. Again we shall be in a better position to choose an appropriate system, if such exists, having gone to the trouble of taking an environmental briefing and plotting the environmental matrix. We shall know what environmental standards are needed, heating, lighting, sound control and so on, and again we shall know what sizes and shapes of spaces our activities really need. If a system fails to meet our environmental briefing (as most of them certainly will) then we can reject it as being inadequate for our purposes.

As a matter of procedure we might think it profitable, once we have plotted room shapes into the environmental matrix, to generate solutions in variety as the source disciplines and many design methods advocate. So far, we have generated four such solutions, one each by pragmatic, iconic, analogical and canonic methods. That at least ought to ensure minimum variety, but in practice we shall find that temperamentally, we are attracted to certain of these approaches rather than others. If we believe ourselves creative then we shall tend to work analogically, avoiding iconic design at all costs whereas if we believe ourselves 'rational' we shall probably opt for canonic with occasional excursions, perhaps towards pragmatic. We may find that the procedures of design themselves help suggest what we might do. The analogue can take over at any stage. Once one has plotted room shapes into the matrix, for instance, the drawing itself suggests a particular building form which could be developed analogically, or even iconically.

At this level analogy might seem trivial as a device for generating architectural form, as indeed might the pragmatic, iconic and canonic ways of designing; but they are all we have and the effective use of a tool depends very much on who is using it. I have suggested elsewhere (Broadbent, 1970a) that there are ways of ensuring that in terms of meaning, symbolism and so on, our building is 'relevant' to the time in which it was built. Let us take it for now that we have clothed the rooms plotted into our environmental matrix by a series of possible building shells and our task now is to evaluate them so that one can be selected for further development. They will have certain things in common. We know from our previous analysis in terms of activities, their space and environmental needs, their interrelationships, that from the user's point of view all our solutions will 'work'. This was implicit in the environmental matrix as we left it with rooms plotted around activities. So now we have to apply a series of checks in each case on the building fabric itself to see if that will work, and to see how competitive it is with the other possibilities. The checks in fact can be very simple:

Will it, or can it be made to, stand up? That may be obvious on inspection or may need advice from a structural engineer.
What will it cost? Again we have a reasonably accurate idea of volume and the area of each floor. The use of certain materials is implicit in each solution so it will be fairly easy to estimate approximate comparative costs. Even at this stage it will be useful to estimate both capital and running costs, but we

do not need even that. All we need at this stage is a ranking of our proposals in order of probable cost to help us make our decision; if we can rank probable maintenance costs in addition to probable capital costs, then so much the better.

How will it behave environmentally in terms of heat, light and sound control, paying particular attention to the structure as a device for noise reduction, to control solar radiation, heat loss and to act as a heat sink?

How does it rate symbolically for architect, client body, planning authority and so on?

Given this simple check-list, we can rank the various schemes against each factor, putting the factors themselves in an order of priority to be determined

Table 20.1

	Pragmatic	Iconic	Analogical 1	2	Canonic
	A suspended skin	*B* Skidmore bank	*C* Stirling– Fairhurst	*D* Safde Habitat	*E* CLASP
Structural practicability	1	3	5	2	4
Capital cost	5	2	4	1	3
Maintenance costs	1	4	5	3	2
Servicing costs	1	2	5	3	4
Heat gain	1	2	5	4	3
Heat loss	1	2	5	4	3
Noise control	1	2	5	4	3
Capacity to 'blend in'	1	2	5	3	4
	12	19	39	24	26

by the client body and architect in consultation; is cost more important than symbolism, and so on? The five solutions proposed for our office building might rank as shown in Table 20.1, where 1 equals least favourable and 5 most favourable. Some of these values may be disputed; they would in any case be checked with other interested parties. However, on this particular evaluation, solution *C*, the Stirling–Fairhurst analogy, rates highest on every count.

Nor is this just a stylistic matter, it has very clear cost and environmental implications built in. Once we have selected a form of building against these criteria, we shall then be in a position to forecast its performance. Each of the major structural types, as we have seen, has certain characteristics. The closer one approaches to mass construction, the greater the possibility of sound and heat control without further modification; the level of daylight illumination at various points in the room, given a standard sky, will be such and such, that the penetration of traffic noise is likely to be so and so, and so on. One could go on to predict what standards would be achieved by the building shell itself for the full range of environmental stimuli (lighting, heating, sound control, etc.) after which one could decide what services would be needed to bring these standards to acceptable levels throughout the year. Services in other words, could be seen as *correcting* further the environment as offered by the building shell itself.

Moreover, the corrections could be quantified and costed. One can decide what levels of artificial illumination will be required to make the room just usable for the specified activities after dark, and one can predict both capital and running costs for such an installation. Similarly one can cost higher levels of provision and decide in consultation with the client possible techniques of linear programming—on the most reasonable compromise between cost and the standards to be provided. One might even present alternatives to the client; given this kind of construction, in this situation, interference due to traffic noise is likely to reach a level of n dB in the boardroom. That will disturb normal conversation. For an additional expenditure of £x on double glazing, this interference will be reduced by m dB, and the level will then be acceptable.

There will be occasions when the provision of a particular service affects both the structure and the provision of other services. That, as we saw in Chapter 8, was the case in providing daylight to satisfy the 2 per cent daylight factor. In such a case, one must consider *all* the effects of such a provision. It might even change one's initial choice of structure.

In other words we are concerned with an *iterative* process in which the initial choice of structure is based on cost related to environmental requirements; the chosen structure is modified by services to correct environmental defects, this in turn has effects on cost and structure, so the cycle is repeated as many times as is necessary to achieve the best possible compromise. Further stages in the iteration will be concerned with internal finishes, fittings, and possibly furniture, not to mention external site treatment, until eventually an agreed solution has emerged which can then be put into production. The techniques by which design proposals may be realized have been discussed elsewhere, and notably in the RIBA Handbook of Architectural Practice and Management (1965).

CHAPTER 21

Prospect

It is extremely easy, as many commentators have shown, to predict a future for architecture based on one's own predilections. One sees it as becoming increasingly complex, from a technological point of view; one envisages new materials, new methods of construction, new forms of transport. One predicts that architecture itself will become increasingly irrelevant, that buildings too will disappear in favour of environmental servicing mechanisms. One believes that the architect himself is becoming increasingly irrelevant, that unless he joins a comprehensive environmental design team others will usurp his functions, which are becoming increasingly trivial in any case. If my thesis is correct, these 'predictions' are based on personal predilections, which in their turn will be determined by personality traits. It may be that the personality traits which determine attitudes to architectural design are also relevant in a discussion of predictions. We might even detect rational, empirical and indeterminate attitudes to prediction; certainly there is considerable evidence for the latter. Many architectural educationalists, for instance, believe it impossible to decide what students should be taught because no one knows what job those students will actually be doing in twenty years' time. Prediction, in any case, must be indeterminate; the act of deciding what the future is going to be like will provoke certain attitudes in people and they will set their minds on achieving certain parts of it and on resisting others; the act of predicting will change what can be achieved.

Prediction in any case has notorious, inbuilt difficulties. As Ozbekham suggests (1969):

'It calls for the ability to define goals and norms, to construct sets of concretely envisioned situations, to abstract different alternatives from them, and to choose among such alternatives. It depends upon one's capacity to distinguish what is constant and what variable. Finally, there is the difficulty that to satisfy the above requirements, the resulting construct must be different from the present state of the system and that these differences must embody some good or virtue that the present system lacks.'

A great deal of this book has been concerned with defining goals and norms. These have been concerned with the environmental conditions in which human beings feel comfortable and behave effectively; whilst the great constants of man's relationship with his environment have also been defined —that man builds because he wants to modify the existing climate at a particular place, so that certain of his activities can be carried out conveniently

431

and in comfort; and that when those activities cannot be carried out conveniently where he is, he travels to where they can be carried out. And the variables in man's relationship with his environment, as we have seen, consist of the ways in which climatic modification and travel can be carried out.

A great deal of prediction, naturally, has been concerned with those means and one could group them, very loosely, into three categories—those which are environment-based, those which are building-based and those which are user-based. These of course represent the three interacting systems with which we have been concerned. Building-based predictors—and by building we mean all the things in the built environment—tend to see a bright, not to say dazzling, future, based on increasingly sophisticated technology; environment-based predictors, on the other hand, take an increasingly gloomy view of the ways in which we are despoiling nature by our exploitation and pollution of it. People-based predictors tend to be optimistic or pessimistic according to the respective values they attach to urban or rural life (see Simmel, 1902–1903).

Building- or thing-based predictors have the easiest time of it because they are concerned largely with mechanizing the built environment; machines can be designed to do what one wants them to do, and programmed specifically to do those things, whereas people (and the natural environment) cannot be so programmed. When people and ecological relationships have to be taken into account, one has to allow for different attitudes, perversities and unexpected interrelationships. People may not even want to live the lives which thing-based predictors have designed for them; nature too may respond with seeming viciousness to apparently justified interference by man.

Most thing-based predictors tend to be latter-day futurists. They are fascinated by machines, speed, new methods of transport, the exploitation of new materials and industrial techniques. Thanks to their enthusiasm some of the historic futurist predictions have actually been built, albeit in grossly emasculated form; the Elephant and Castle, Cumbernauld town centre, the Birmingham Bull Ring and other developments pile the different functions of a city high within the intricate, multi-level complexes of buildings—crude and simplified versions of Sant'Elia's original Futurist vision. The theoretical presumptions on which futurism has been based have been greatly extended, by Buckminster Fuller, Reyner Banham, the Archigram Group, Cedric Price and others.

They are concerned with developing new forms of environmental control and new transport systems. Anyone with a little ingenuity (or a morphological chart) can devise a new transport system, vertical or horizontal, airborne, elevated, at ground level or underground, personal or public, powered by steam, the internal combustion engine, electricity or nuclear energy, confined to a fixed track or free-ranging, controlled by human agency or automatic. Richards (1966) describes many such systems, the purposes for which they are suitable, certain problems of interchanging from one to another and the even greater problems of building new forms into existing transport systems, especially within the city centre itself. Transport systems have been a particular concern of the Archigram Group (Warren Chalk, Peter Cook, Dennis Crompton, David Green, Ron Herron and Michael Webb). *Plug-in City*, for

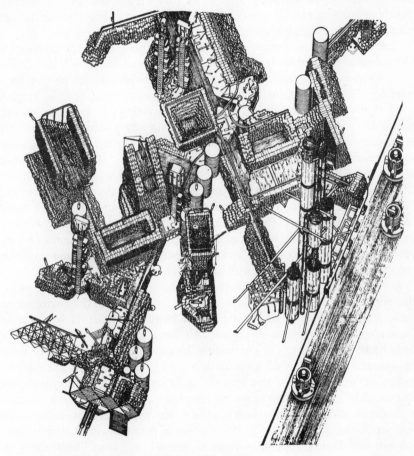

Figure 21.1—Archigram: Plug-in City (1964)

instance (1964), was to consist of a large-scale framework of vertical, horizontal and diagonal tubes within which access ways, energy and communications services were to be contained (Figure 21.1). Highly serviced 'plug-in' units could be hoisted to appropriate positions within this framework by cranes which travelled on rails, and it was an essential part of the concept that these units, and the framework itself, should be expendable. A hotel room might be thrown away after three years, an office unit after ten years and so on. Much of this originates in Fuller's ideas, for since the 1920s he has dreamed of 'throwaway' architecture by analogy with the tin cans, clothes, household equipment and even furniture of the consumer society. One specialized part of Plug-in City was to form a University Node (1965) in which people and goods were transported diagonally and upwards, whilst information moved vertically up to, and down from, the 'silo' or library. Teaching units, of course, would be expendable, 'plugged-in' and replaced as teaching methods changed.

Cedric Price, in his Potteries Thinkbelt (1966) (Figure 21.2) envisaged a technological university (an 'advanced educational industry') for 20,000 students, closely integrated into a community of some 40,000 people, on a rehabilitated triangle of the Potteries, with sides of 8, 7 and $4\frac{1}{2}$ miles long. A good deal of this area would be developed intentionally, as urban sprawl, containing widely spaced faculty buildings within which some teaching would take place, linked by a rail-bus service of which the carriages themselves would contain seminar rooms, self-teaching carrels, fold-out inflatable lecture areas, television demonstration studios and so on. A student, therefore, could attend a seminar or work in his carrel while moving from one faculty area to another. Where formal teaching was required a carriage might be shunted into a siding where the lecture theatre could be inflated. Clearly there is a deep suspicion here of segregating social functions, such as higher education, from the day-to-day lives of 'the people'. There is a deep suspicion too of conventional buildings, and of the architects who design them.

Reyner Banham shares this suspicion and he describes an alternative in the Environment Bubble (1965) in which he wanted to control the environment without benefit of building. This too was based on Fuller. It is a remote descendant of the Dymaxion house. As Banham himself says, man initially had two basic ways of controlling the environment; with one of these he 'avoided the issue', sheltering under a rock, a tree or some structure he had made for himself, and this approach led eventually to architecture as we know it. The camp fire, however, represented quite a different approach to environmental control, one which interferes with the 'local meteorology' and this, for Banham, offers more promising lines of development. A simple camp fire will illuminate a particular circle of ground, and it will also warm an overlapping oval of ground according to the direction and strength of the wind. As Banham says: 'There will thus be a variety of environmental choices balancing light against warmth according to need and interest. If you want to do close work like shrinking a human head, you sit in one place, but if you want to sleep you curl up somewhere different.' So with Francois Dallegret's help, he attempted to devise a super camp fire, a 'standard of living package' consisting of power packs, an adjustable air-blower, lighting, refrigerator unit and cooker, radio, record-player and television with stereo speakers and so on (Figure 21.3).

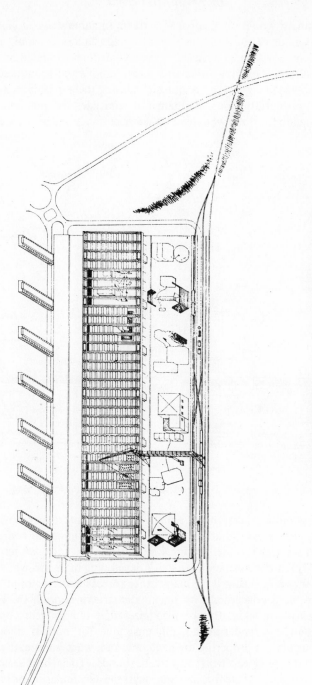

Figure 21.2—Cedric Price: Potteries Thinkbelt (1966)

Ideally Banham would set this package down in some wooded glade, but eventually, as Laugier suggested in similar circumstances, it would start to rain. So Banham envisaged a 'transparent Mylar airdome', inflated by the fan unit and preferably hovering some two metres above the ground so as to allow easy passage from 'inside' to 'outside', closing the gap if necessary with a continuous air-curtain door. Banham also concedes the possibility of a carpeted floor-slab for those who insist on warm surfaces underfoot. Certainly

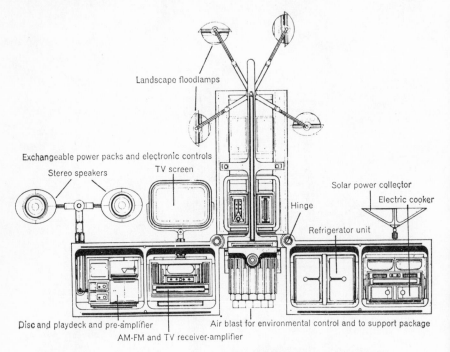

Landscape floodlamps

Exchangeable power packs and electronic controls

Stereo speakers   TV screen

Solar power collector

Electric cooker

Hinge

Refrigerator unit

Disc and playdeck and pre-amplifier

Air blast for environmental control and to support package

AM-FM and TV receiver-amplifier

Figure 21.3—Banham and Dallegret: Standard Living Package (1968)

there are possibilities here, but Banham hopes to improve on what the mammoth-hunters knew—that the most effective environmental control uses structure and services together, acting systematically.

Laing (1967) has gone some way towards developing materials which them-selves act as servicing media. Like many other forecasters of a bright techno-logical future, he is concerned with pneumatic structures, with the building as an inflated plastic skin. But he recognizes that the ambient conditions within such buildings render them highly unsuitable for 'normal' human use. Their sound insulation properties are negligible and, what is more, the curved forms they take tend to focus unwanted sounds. Their heat controlling properties too are negligible for, as Laing says, the accumulation of radiation within the building during periods of sunlight leads to a 'greenhouse effect' whilst there is excessive heat loss when outside temperatures are low, so a considerable heating plant is needed to maintain conditions of comfort within.

One answer to this problem, as Laing suggests, is to make the skin of the building itself adjustable so that it will reflect solar radiation back into the external environment, admit it into the building or retain it there as necessary. He investigated the possibilities of walling materials which were adjustable in this way and concluded that a layered construction in plastic could offer the properties he sought (Figure 21.4). In a typical example the outside skin consists of a glass-fibre net, covered with a highly transparent plastic. The

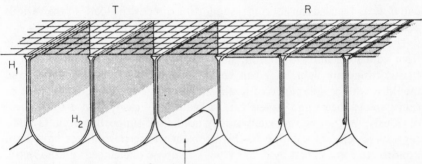

Figure 21.4—Laing membrane. The U-shaped tubes of thin light-transmitting plastic film are fixed to a glass-fibre net which is also coated with transmissive film. Each tube is lined between H_1 and H_2 with a further strip of transmissive film which is half coated with a reflecting layer of metal. Gas under pressure in the U-shaped channel holds this in the transmission position (T) in which case solar radiation (light and heat), etc., is reflected into the building; if gas is pumped behind the movable film, it will assume the reflecting position (R), in which case radiation **cannot** penetrate the skin (see Laing, 1966)

inside surface of this skin is covered with continuous U-shaped channels in highly transmissive plastic, packed tightly together. A strip of transparent film is laid diagonally within each channel U, metallized for half its width, and the channel is inflated with gas on one side or other of this film so that its silvered portion lies either behind and parallel to the outer skin or at right angles to it. The strip thus reflects solar radiation outwards or through the wall into the building. Other of Laing's walling forms achieve similar effects electrostatically, and he claims that by these means he can achieve near 0°C temperatures within an inflatable structure in the Sahara or sub-tropical conditions if necessary in Newfoundland.

A certain amount of energy is needed to pump gas into the channels, but not much, and certainly the idea of a 'dynamic' building which reacts in this way to changing conditions has considerable appeal. The 'ideal' building material, in fact, would do just that, acting like Laing's various skins as structural and servicing medium, but offering higher standards of environmental control. This material will have to be cheap, of course, and we shall want to use it to form the building envelope and to separate the various internal spaces from each other, both horizontally and vertically; we may want it to be transparent or translucent in places, and certainly we shall require high standards of sound and heat control. It seems likely, on the whole, that some sheet material will serve our purposes best and if it can be self-supporting that will be a real advantage. If possible, we should like it to do more than that, to support reasonable loads from the rest of the building and if it can be used for flooring—supporting directly the loads of the various activities—then so much the better.

The best bet, according to Gordon (1968), seems to be some form of plastic resin with long fibres of boron, silicon carbide or carbon bonded into it. Plastic resins are light, they can be made in a wide range of colours and moulded with a wide range of textures; they can be opaque, translucent or transparent; sheets and panels can be made very easily. But a thin panel, obviously, will not be very rigid, it may not be self-supporting even. Gordon suggests an elegant solution to this problem whose possibilities have been explored to some extent by Evans (1969). Suppose one embeds piezo-electric materials in the plastic resin? Rochelle salt or quartz crystals are used in pickups for record-players and when such a material is subject to mechanical strain, as when the stylus moves in a record groove, an electric charge or potential difference develops across some of its faces. This mechanical energy is translated into electrical, and the converse is also true; such a crystal produces mechanical forces when a voltage is applied in a suitable manner. Rochelle salt or quartz crystals are hardly suitable for large scale application but several theorists, including Bernal, have suggested that new *active* materials of infinite stiffness could be developed, from which light compression members could be made; a telegraph pole, for instance, could be as thin as wire. A window cleaner could perform the Indian rope trick easily and aircraft wings could be made very thin indeed. So, given the fairly massive resources which would be needed to develop such materials, our plastic resin panels could be made as stiff as necessary.

Nonetheless that would not solve their obvious deficiencies in terms of environmental control. Their heat and sound insulation properties would be negligible. We might adapt Laing's methods to our purposes, or it may be that they could be brought up to any required standard by embedding further electrodes. It would be relatively easy, for instance, to embody heating coils, possibly in printed circuit form; given internal and external thermostats, or even computer control, these could ensure temperature regulation within the panels equivalent to the homeostasis of a living organism. Sound control also could be achieved by picking up the unwanted noises and feeding them back into the panel so as to vibrate it *off-phase*. If the original noise and its off-phase equivalent from the vibrating panel reached the ear simultaneously, then they would cancel each other out. The panel could be activated in two ways; by attaching a small vibrator (and successful research into this has been undertaken in the Engineering Department at Leeds University) or by building the whole panel as an electrostatic loudspeaker. Both are feasible, although the second solution might be very expensive and there is no guarantee of course that the unwanted noise and off-phase noise from the panel would reach the ear simultaneously. It might be necessary to include a tuning system so that appropriate panels are vibrated for each activity in the room or (and probably a much cheaper solution) individual feedback circuits, consisting of microphone, phase splitter, amplifier and loudspeaker built in for each work station. One can imagine, say, an open plan office or school in which such devices are used. The whole ceiling perhaps is lined with them, and normally they are tuned to cancel unwanted noise; but if someone wants to speak to a colleague at the other side of the room, he simply presses buttons which control the appropriate circuits and whatever he says is picked up by the local microphones (which may even be loudspeakers acting in reverse) and fed to his colleague's work station. A teacher might speak to the whole class in a similar way, or engage in conversation with selected individuals.

As a further refinement the 'active' building panel might be faced with fluorescent materials controlled by photo-electric cells, so that as daylight faded it might begin to glow and emit whatever luminous flux we desired. The active building, then, has considerable potential. It will be very expensive and like many good ideas it may never get off the ground for that reason. The ultimate seems to be the active building of a fairly neutral kind; certainly it is not designed to house specific activities. One arrives, say, in the morning and starts to do something, e.g. answering letters, talking to colleagues, presenting ideas to a client. The building senses what one is doing by various monitoring devices and adjusts itself accordingly, making physical or aurally controlled spaces to suit the needs of the group, turning the lights up or down as appropriate for the reading of fine print, the enjoyment of relaxed conversation, talking on the videophone or watching projected slides.

Several visionaries have envisaged parts of this concept—Price's Fun Palace (1964) was not self-adjusting but at least it was to be changed each day to house a new pattern of activities. Technological forecasting of this kind, on the whole, is extraordinarily easy. One reads it in the popular science journals, not to mention science fiction. Peter Cook (1967) suggests that one keeps abreast of *Scientific American*, *New Scientist* (UK), *Analog*, *Time* and *Paris Match*. These, inevitably, are reporting history, research which has been completed, so if one really wants to 'keep abreast' one visits certain 'think tanks' and research centres from time to time. It is then easy to select, from the ideas and devices one sees, those which *might* become commonplace in ten, twenty or thirty years' time. The fact that one has singled them out thus and published them may lead to wider acceptance than they might otherwise have had. Alternatively, one looks at the most complex mechanisms available and draws analogies from these for architecture. Oil refineries, chemical plants, space capsules, undersea housings and so on, have all been pressed into this particular service. These devices share a common feature; each contains an internal *ambience* whether for chemical substances or for people, which is controlled between very fine limits within an environment which is substantially hostile to the activities within. So one hopes that some day environmental control for human beings at the earth's surface will become as complex and exciting as the most sophisticated of these technological devices.

There is no reason why it should. Many activities even now do not *need* a building, and even where one is required the mismatch between human activities is rarely very great. It can almost always be resolved by traditional building with a number of traditional services; our expectations for ambient comfort are based on these traditional patterns and until these prove themselves inadequate, or new technologies offer themselves which *will* allow better standards, at lower cost, then there is no substantial reason for change.

However, the danger of futurist visions is that they are too abstract; they fail to take account of human interactions. They assume that anyone who wants to live in the permanent solid environment which traditional building provides is somehow reactionary, unimaginative and personally insecure. Banham, for instance (1965), criticizes those Americans who, having opted for trailer caravan living (which is halfway to expendability, after all) should decorate their caravans with Permastone and instant roofing. He believes, quite fervently, 'that if dirty old Nature could be kept under the proper degree of control (sex left in, streptococci taken out) by other means, the United States would be happy to dispense with architecture and buildings altogether'. Price too (1966) believes that 'architects and planners (must) rid themselves of the idea that they are capable, through that which they leave on the ground, of reorientating the past to the advantage of the present.' He thinks it rather pathetic that whilst 'the appearance and performance of clothes, food, furniture, motor cars, and wives/husbands is now considered a subject worthy of only limited-term personal predilection' that is not the case with a house or a town. The architect or planner, according to Price, makes value judgements which ignore the immediate user's needs in favour of an imagery which is designed to appeal to posterity; but not, one might suggest, if they use the environmental design process.

Nor do these advocates of expendable buildings with highly serviced plug-in units pay much attention to what people actually want. Any desire for stability in the environment is dismissed, immediately, as reactionary; and so for that matter is any desire for personal, face-to-face contact. Banham at one time, thought that buildings could be eliminated if people lived in space suits. Others have argued that the videophone, sketchpad and other computer-based communications devices will eliminate almost entirely the need to travel. To do a day's work, one would sit in one's morning bath and press the few buttons which were needed to activate the plant in one's automated factory. Even that would not be *necessary*—computers would be perfectly capable of switching the plant on—but the buttons would represent for the factory manager an equivalent of the egg which his wife mixes into the other ingredients of her packaged cake, in order to justify her existence.

It is conceivable then, that travelling will not be necessary in the future, but the chances are that people will still want to travel. If one examines their reasons, they may prove to be very few. People travel to work at the moment because they have to. On arrival they may tend a machine, pore over a set of papers or engage in some other routine chore. But from time to time they will engage in face-to-face contact with other people. Later in the day, they may travel to the shops, to a theatre, a concert or a wrestling match. At the week-end they may go for a day by the sea, visit some stately home or travel to meet friends. Each time they travel they do so because at the end of the journey there is promise of some intimate, personal sensory experience. They will hear, see, feel and experience directly certain people, places and things which otherwise they could not have experienced. If one eliminates face-to-face contact, then one loses in personal communication the essential nuances of gesture, expression and so on which Argyle (1965, 1967) has described so well, not to mention the 'stroking' (boosting of personal esteem) which Eric Byrne (1966) among others has discussed as often originating in chance face-to-face meetings.

Nevertheless, these objections to architecture, finally, are trivial because they are based almost entirely on visual imagery. The appeal of Archigram, certainly does not rest on the force of its intellectual arguments (they hardly exist), but on the sheer vitality of its graphic presentation. Price and Banham take great delight in extolling the visual delight of areas which, to others, appear merely blighted. Thus Price chooses a squalid area of the Potteries for his 'Thinkbelt' project whilst, given the entire British Isles to choose from for a favourite spot in *Treasure Island* (A.D. 1969) he selected a clearance area in the Manchester slums. Banham too (1968) chose the flat, bleak landscape of the Millwall container port with its occasional asbestos-cement clad buildings, as an example of the powerful and significant environment which new industrial developments could present without benefit of architects. One sympathizes with their mistrust of architects who are concerned with *only* visual values, but one could find powerful enough arguments against such trivialities without resorting to the heavy-handed (visual) satire in which these authors engage.

However, their message essentially is deeper than this. They are concerned with the load of nostalgia which most of us carry around, believing that this, above all, is what prevents us from achieving the proper new architecture which technology makes possible; but as we saw in Chapter 8 there is evidence that many people need signs of stability in their environment, and its absence may be one cause of rigid attitudes. A real danger is that if the plug-in throwaway environment is achieved to any considerable extent, it may have the opposite effect to that which its advocates predict. It may encourage people to structure their lives more rigidly, as a means of achieving personal stability in a world which is in a constant state of flux around them.

Pawley (1968) is concerned with such matters. He suggests that even if the designer tries consciously to produce objects from which all subjective values have been eliminated, the users themselves will 'personalize' these things as soon as they get hold of them. A considerable industry exists, for instance, in the case of motor cars to produce accessories for just this purpose. Function has been 'crowned', but immediately, myth, image and fantasy 'usurp the throne'. 'If the designer cannot express *his* subjectivity the lack is made good by the user: if neither knows how to associate with the object the seller or advertiser finds a way.' He contrasts the plight of an old-age pensioner (designer subject) with the architect (designer object) who is planning a multi-storey office building for the site on which the pensioner's tenement stands. The pensioner 'sits in a squalid room; all around him his furniture is arranged, Edwardian veneered cabinets, tortuously carved tables, high backed chairs. Amongst the furniture is further bric-a-brac in the form of vases, prints and photographs in frames. All these possessions represent the "object evidence" of the pensioner's life, for his relations are all dead and he is alone, using the collection as a barricade against the increasingly cold and hostile world without. His mementoes are living proof of the reality of his former life.'

Pawley produces a wealth of evidence to suggest that the individual populates his dwelling with objects and information some of which, certainly, are of functional value, but others are basically symbolic (Pawley says iconic):

'No outside observer could ever estimate the subjective value of these objects and messages according to an external scale of values, although in the least inventive and most conventional surroundings he might roughly approximate them. The *subjective* value of these objects resides not in themselves but in their interrelation, their sequence and their significance as extensions of the personality of their owner. In other words, they are not really isolated objects but connected molecules in the atomic structure of the individual's own consciousness.'

Unfortunately, the examples which Pawley uses to make his point are not particularly rigorous. He quotes Ardrey's *The territorial imperative* (1967) on the identity, stimulation and security which proceed from possessing territory, quoting Strehlow (1947) on the 'fanatical devotion' of the Arabda people in Australia to birthplace and ancestral home site; Goffman (1961) on the unfortunate effects which 'deprivation of meaningful context' had on certain patients in a mental hospital; Searles's parallel findings that many schizophrenics believe their own disorientation to have resulted from excessive movement of the family from town to town, personal movement from room to room and loss of personal possessions. From this he concludes that behaviour can *only* be understood in the context of the environment within which it takes place.

In applying these thoughts to architectural problems, Pawley cites several examples of the security which buildings bring to people, from the intangible benefits which long genealogy and a family 'seat' still confer on the aristocracy, to the pathetic return of the recidivist to a hospital bed or prison cell which is the only environment he knows well. He points out the inherent desire for permanence which the resistance to any development plan reveals, and the distinction which people make between a house (a 'home', a 'castle', 'security' and so on) and a caravan or prefabricated dwelling which they describe as 'accommodation', 'emergency housing', 'temporary' or 'mobile'. Pawley agrees with Habraken (1961) that the occupant imposes 'meaning' on his environment by the very acts of creating and changing it and from this he concludes that the individual should be encouraged to participate in the making of it. Finally, Pawley describes the *Time house*, his A.A. thesis study for a house which constantly monitors its occupants' actions, recording their speech and filming their movements. It absorbs everything they hear, see, smell, touch and remember; any of this may be recalled instantaneously and thus their subjective memories of events may be supported, at any time, by an objective record of what actually happened.

It is unlikely, then, that the futurist vision will ever be built in quantity because people do .not want it, and there are other reasons too, largely economic. At a trivial level one remembers those splendid plastic bathroom-core units which proliferated at Ulm and elsewhere in the early 1960s. Sensible, rational, they eliminated a lot of messy plumbing and, perhaps even more important, they were superb aesthetic objects; but one never hears of them now because too many vested interests stood in the way of their acceptance. They were not financially viable.

That is true, too, of more visionary forms of transport. Whatever their excellence, which may be considerable, they will not replace the motor car because too much has been invested in the car itself and in the roads, motorways and parking places provided for it. Yet, as many human- and environment-based predictors are reminding us increasingly, the car is one of the most potent despoilers of the environment we have, from the point of view of noise, air pollution, fumes, not to mention the vast tracts of land in town and country which are given over to it. These characteristics are shared by other forms of transport—diesel trains, aircraft (conventional and vertical take-off), helicopters and even hovercraft. Perhaps, after all, we should persuade people not to travel so much.

Such persuasion is the province of the human-based predictors. Until very recently their entire philosophy seemed extraordinarily old-fashioned and fuddy-duddy. They were identified with another, even longer tradition reaching back to Pugin, Ruskin and Morris, who had looked at the industrial city and found it evil. Their postulated return to human values was based on contact with nature, the use of natural materials, hand-craftsmanship and so on, views which were extended by the Garden City theorists, by Wright, Mumford and others. Most of them *were* trying to put the clock back, to oppose technological progress instead of using it to human ends, but recently a series of cogent arguments has been offered in fields outside architecture, which suggest that we ought to look at this 'human' approach again.

There is much confusion though as to what 'human' consists of in a context such as this. For many theorists, as we have seen, it means specifically anti-urban, anti-manmade and otherwise 'natural' or rural. A tree for such theorists is more human than a motor car, which seems to me patently absurd. Georg Simmel (1902-3) throws some light on what seem to him psychological differences between the 'metropolitan' and the 'rural' type of man. These, according to Simmel, depend to a large extent on the ways in which sensory information is processed. His 'metropolitan type of individual' flourishes on 'the rapid crowding of changing images, the sharp discontinuity in the grasp of a single glance, the unexpectedness of onrushing impressions'. His 'rural' man on the other hand thrives on 'lasting impressions, impressions which take a regular and habitual course and show regular and habitual contrasts', all of which, according to Simmel, 'use up . . . less consciousness' than the onrushing stimuli of metropolitan life.

There seems to be some substance in what Simmel says. Eysenck (1953) describes certain observable differences between those he defines as *extroverts* and those he defines as *introverts*; the former are 'quick(er) in everyday life situations, but . . . less accurate than the latter.' They engage in longer periods of eye-contact in the processes of social discourse and they seem, generally, to be *less* roused by external stimuli than the introverts. The introvert, therefore, may have a 'lower threshold of arousal' than the extrovert; he seems to be slower in 'intellectual speed' (Farley, 1966), more sensitive to noise (Smith, 1967), to bright lights and 'loud jazz music' (Weisen, 1965) and so on.

One cannot simply equate Simmel's metropolitan man with Eysenck's extrovert, his rural man with Eysenck's introvert, but the research which Eysenck reports undoubtedly supports, to some extent, Simmel's contention that differences in the processing of sensory stimuli *could* help to account for differences in preference for metropolitan or rural life.

Simmel's types are more than mere sensing mechanisms; they also have attitudes and values determined, in part at least, by the style of life in which they have chosen to live. Simmel's metropolitan man 'reacts with his head instead of his heart'; he takes refuge in 'intellectuality'—'a matter-of-fact attitude in dealing with men and with things'. This is closely bound up with his participation in the 'money economy' which reduces all human interaction to a lowest, impersonal common denominator. He sees little virtue in individual expression, preferring anonymity both in business and in social transactions. He flourishes on a tight schedule—appointments, deadlines and so on—within 'the most punctual integration of all activities and mutual relations' without which 'the whole structure would break down into inextricable chaos'.

Clearly the futurists and their many successors were metropolitan men in Simmel's sense or, at least, they tried to plan urban structures in which Simmel's metropolitan life could be lived at a greater pace than ever before; and whilst few of them have been built, the rate of sensory input which Simmel envisaged has been achieved, and perhaps even surpassed, by modern modes of transport, the mass media and so on.

All this has been achieved in the teeth of intense opposition from Simmel's rural type of man. One has only to think of the *Noise Abatement Society* or the *Anti-Concorde* project to realize how many people live in abject misery because, as rural men at heart, they find themselves living a metropolitan life. That seems to be true of our present-day ethologists, ecologists and Marxist existentialists, not to mention the hippies. Some of the latter have the integrity, honesty and strength of conviction to 'drop out', to live the rural life in communes such as those described by Hedgepath and Stock (1969).

There is a long-standing belief, in English-speaking countries at least, that the rural life is somehow richer, fuller, more honest and complete than the metropolitan life; our most respected novelists, from Jane Austen to D. H. Lawrence and beyond, described its virtues with consummate skill and with such success that a 'cultured' person, by definition, became one who subscribed to the values which they set up. Simmel presents a less attractive but possibly truer picture of rural, or small town, life. He describes the essential features: a profound conservatism, desire to know other people's business, to constrain what they do, to set up barriers against the movement (both of people and ideas) which characterizes small-minded, small-town life. The true metropolitan, in this context, feels stifled, constrained; he misses in particular the *privacy* which the anonymity of city life brings. His difficulties, in fact, are equal and opposite to those which rural man experiences when big-city life impinges on him. We should do well, therefore, in reading any predictions concerning architecture and the built environment, to assess the predictor's own, personal orientation within Simmel's categorization. His metropolitan men, on the whole, will be happy about the future, whilst his rural men will be gloomy, in some cases approaching the suicidal. Typical are:

1. The views of certain ethologists (Morris is a popular example), that at some time in the past, man was better adapted to his environment than he is to the 'concrete jungle' in which—if he so chooses—he finds himself now. This seems to me a highly suspect view. Evolution has left man with certain vestiges of adaptations to many previous environments; long arms and fingers for swinging through the trees, powerful leg-muscles for running across the Steppe; but which of these environments was he 'better' adapted to? And again, if one considers the enormous range of environments, geographical and historical, in which man has *chosen* to live, one realizes that his powers of adaptation are very great indeed (see Dubos, 1965). Where and when can one say that man was living at his best? In some prehistoric cave in southern France? In some Mesopotamian farming community? In fifth-century Athens, fourteenth-century Florence, eighteenth-century Bath? Clearly he adapted to all of these and some people led pleasant and meaningful lives. But then some people adapted to Auschwitz. Unlike the latter, and with very few exceptions, people live in Morris's 'concrete jungle' because they choose to. Nevertheless, such views suggest that we should do well to look at man very closely, from an ecological point of view, and to ease as far as possible his adaptations to his environment.

2. The views of certain economists, such as Galbraith, that the rigid disciplines of mass production are necessary, but that we should divert certain resources away from the production of material goods towards improvement in education and in environmental standards, clean air, the rehabilitation of twilight areas and so on. As we shall see, the possibilities of automation, exploited to the full, may render Galbraith's views on mass production unduly pessimistic, but we shall certainly agree with his diversion of material resources towards improvement of the human condition— once we have agreed what improvement actually is.

3. The views of certain ecologists, such as Fraser-Darling (1969) and Ehrlich (1968, 1970) that the greatest problems for the future in man's relationship with his environment will result from population explosions. They see these as leading inevitably to higher densities of building on the earth's surface, and to increasing demands for material goods. These in their turn will lead to even greater exploitation of the environment for its raw materials, to an increase of factory production and distribution which, with the additional housing required, will lead to increased congestion and pollution. We have already seen that certain forms of construction—such as frames with light and dry cladding—demand the wasteful use of energy to make them habitable. One necessity for these ecologists is to stabilize the birth rate

throughout the world so that it matches and certainly does not exceed the death rate. That in itself will not be enough (Dansereau, 1970; Barr (Ed.), 1971). Already greater tracts of land, water and air are polluted by the waste products of human habitation, some of it indestructible, by the waste products of agriculture, including persistent pesticides such as DDT, by the waste, fumes and noise of industry, including radioactive waste, by the fumes and noise of traffic (road, rail, air and water-borne). At worst manmade toxins such as mine and manufacturing acids, oil and municipal sewage, are pumped into a lake or river to such an extent that it 'dies'. Even where the problems are not so great, one may want to use the water for drinking or even for recreation. Nor is polluted water the only problem: it has been estimated that in America each year some 206 million tons of waste products are spilled into the atmosphere, of which some 95 million tons are contributed by the internal combustion engine. A car's exhaust contains five principal groups of chemicals—carbon monoxide, sulphur oxide, hydrocarbons, certain oxides of nitrogen and tiny particules of lead. These chemicals may combine under the action of sunlight to produce a further range of even more unpleasant chemicals; ozone is a strongly reactive bleach which causes leaves to die, rubber to crack and leads to deterioration in cotton fabrics; peroxyacl nitrate leads to irritation in the eyes whilst nitrogen dioxide will damage lung tissue. It may be that sufficient publicity for these facts will lead public opinion in time to agree that the motor car, like the cigarette, is a dangerous pollutant, and to think again many times before giving over large tracts of countryside and demolishing vast areas of our cities to cater for it. If the purpose of travelling is to gain personal, sensory experience, there is not much point in going at all if on arrival one is confronted with a sea of motor cars.

Eventually, as an increasing area of the earth's surface is built on, we may reduce the number of photosynthesizing plants to such an extent that we find ourselves with insufficient oxygen. Some ecologists believe that already the level of carbon dioxide is building up to such an extent that it forms a heat-trapping barrier around the earth. Thus there may be a rise in average temperatures which, if it exceeds four or five degrees, could melt the polar ice caps. Sea level might rise by 300 feet, thus flooding the world's major cities. Conversely, the dust, fumes and water vapour which are spewing into the atmosphere may form another kind of barrier which keeps out the sun's heat. Thus the planet will cool down, rain will be precipitated, it will freeze, and thus a new ice age will be formed.

Nicholson (1969) believes that modern man has improvised his 'steel and cement wilderness' without any real attempt to find out if it really provides the sort of home which he needs and desires. He suggests that most *intelligent* discussion on the subject, i.e. discussion which agrees with him, has reached pessimistic conclusions and that the world's 'megalopoliticians' are increasingly depressed and frustrated. He suggests that we now have a choice: either we persist with a 'steel and cement' approach which, in his view, will lead either to a catastrophic nuclear war or to a more gradual degeneration through racial and other conflict, drug addiction and so on; or the alternative, as Nicholson sees it, lies in finding a fresh equilibrium between conservation and development for human fulfilment. He believes that human civilization has a double root in nature. Man's character as hunter, fisherman, herdsman, farmer and miner was moulded by the challenge to understand, tame and exploit it. He sees a certain atavistic necessity in this and thinks it unlikely that man will adapt, for a very long time, to a computer-controlled society and to synthesized foods. 'Noise, overcrowding, assault on the senses, pollution of air and water', he suggests, 'induce a sense of claustrophobia which people blindly try to relieve by refugee-like mass movements from the areas which their presence has blighted to others which they are destined quickly to blight in turn.' But nature, unblighted, has very special qualities which make its presence essential to man. 'For nature is more than material natural resources. Its womblike role for man, and its infinite capacity to inspire, refresh and recreate are no less important'—the statement of a truly rural man.

4. The view of certain student activists, Marxist existentialists, whose prophet is Marcuse, that science and technology have resulted in such an unprecedented increase in industrial production that the overthrow of capitalism, which Marx expected, has simply not taken place. Instead of that, the status quo has been maintained, workers have become increasingly affluent and can afford to buy the material goods which they themselves are engaged to produce. Such minute changes as have taken place in society have resulted from the application of scientific analysis to social problems, so technological progress has led, not to the criticism and overthrow of established society, but to its increasingly widespread acceptance. Conflict and rebellion become increasingly unlikely because few people are left to question the status quo. In particular, the workers who ought to be leading the revolt are, on the whole, satisfied with their lot. Conditions improve in the factories and they become increasingly affluent, but they would still be restless if the mass media did not create in them a spurious demand for the goods they produce and which they can well afford.

Marcuse describes the society in which supply and demand have thus been neatly integrated in his *One-dimensional man* (1964) and if he is right, if energy and (dare one say it) wealth are so evenly distributed, then entropy will set in and society inevitably will die. Society therefore needs its irritants and if the workers will not perform their historic task, then the negroes, students and other vocal minorities must. Marcuse's argument, as MacIntyre so brilliantly shows (1970), is flawed, illogical, unsystematic and finally speculative. *One-dimensional man* itself was written at a curious moment in American history when, for once, there was no major conflict between different factions of American society. But that moment has passed and conflict is rife again. That has not, however, prevented Marcuse from becoming the prophet of the student activists and others who feel the need to 'drop out' from society and to 'do their own thing'. Some of them now take the ecologists' view that the greatest evils of industrial society lie in the despoliation and pollution of the environment which, since the industrial revolution itself, seems to have been an essential concomitant of that society. In this, then, they join forces with the ecologists, but there is a difference. Some ecologists at least, are concerned with a balance of nature in which man, as a species, seems to have no part. They will oppose tooth and claw the building of a new reservoir to serve a community of human beings, on the grounds that its building will destroy some unique plant, discourage a rare bird or some other phenomenon of nature. They are entitled to their views, but the new range of environmentalists whose concern is with human values are more likely to press the needs of man rather than the needs of nature; and their argument may be suspect. Fuller (1969) points out that in New York city alone there was enough enclosed space, in 1963, to contain indoors the whole of the world's population—packed rather tightly, no doubt.

Although some of its premises may be suspect, there *is* a 'human' backlash against technology, a search for a post-industrial society which has other manifestations too, but they all depend, finally, on the generation of new attitudes and a sense of responsibility in man's use of the earth's surface. There are obvious answers to the population problem and equally obvious objections to them. The ecologists, Galbraith and Marcuse, from vastly opposing positions, are all asking substantially for very similar things. Unlike their predecessors in human-based prediction, some of them at least are prepared to accept technology for the good things it can do. Our problem, therefore, will be to reconcile the thing-based and the human points of view. One way of reconciling the two may lie in that Cybernetic-Systems approach which we considered in Chapter 18, in conjunction with the computer-aided design and control possibilities of Chapter 15.

Although the software (suitable computer programs) is still very limited, one can already work in front of a television-like display. Eventually anything that one sketches on to it will be checked, corrected and modified by the computer. All the relevant technical information will be stored in the computer—information on materials, methods of construction, the Building Regulations and so on, not to mention geographical, climatic, geological, town planning and other information on particular sites. There may well be a library of space standards, environmental requirements and circulation patterns for common human activities. Eventually, the complete form of the building will be built up, after which the computer can be asked to simulate parts of it, presenting interior and exterior perspectives into which colours, textures, etc., can be projected—each checked against the characteristics of real materials as recorded in the computer. One report (MPBW, 1969) envisages a three-dimensional display in colour. Each plane, presumably, could be varied until client and architect were satisfied; one might be able to simulate different lighting conditions and perhaps, eventually, acoustics, heating and other environmental characteristics. In the cybernetic process, it will be possible to experience, modify and adapt the building *before* it is built. It *may* be a better fit on completion, but the more convincing the simulation, the more likely it is that the client will want its details to match what he knows of buildings already, so that the new environment will match his existing sensory expectations. In other words, this most sophisticated of thing-based tools will actually encourage a people-based architecture.

Cybernetic thinking can be applied to production procedures too. The future of building certainly lies in industrialization but the computer-controlled fully automated factory suggests a very different pattern of industrialization from that which we know already. This assumes that the essence of industrialization lies in standardization and repetition. It is a Henry Ford approach, based on the premiss that methods devised for making small machine parts (bolts, pistons and so on) and for putting these together (the production line) would also be suitable for building components.

Motor car engines are built of tiny parts, each one cast and then machined. When their production was first industrialized, there were real advantages in standardization because tooling costs were high, repetitive machining brought further economies and if the parts were interchangeable then assembly was also facilitated. This is no longer true in the automated factory, where the machines which actually do the work are controlled by internal computers. Policy decisions are taken by man-computer dialogue, whilst costing, stock control and so on are also computerized. In one advanced application (Molins Machine Company Ltd., System 24) a range of specialized machines, differing in complexity, was controlled by an on-line computer. Orders were received and fed into another computer which prepared schedules so that work would be distributed between various machines, each would be utilized as effectively as possible, and each operation would take place on the simplest machine which could cope with it. This computer prepared the tape program from which the working machines were actually controlled (see Abel, 1969). Clearly a wide range of processes may be tackled when machines are controlled and interrelated in this way. Given such a system it may be *necessary*, for the efficient deployment of the different machines, that the production runs of particular components be kept as short as possible, thus encouraging variety rather than uniformity.

Beer (1968) describes the fully automated factory in which computer-operated machines are themselves controlled by other computers. He envisages a basic cybernetic component *System One* in which a lathe, Versatron, Unimate (see Figure 21.5) or some other device which actually performs physical tasks has built into it an intrinsic control system. He calls this level *A*. Once this internal computer has been programmed, then the machine will perform a certain range of actions, in a particular sequence, whenever it is instructed to do so. Its task may very well be integrated with those of other machines; Unimate, for instance, might pick a component which has been partly worked out of one machine and take it over to another, locating it in the appropriate position for further work to be

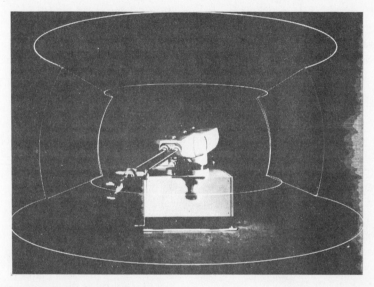

Figure 21.5—Unimation Unimate

done on it. Clearly there must be some overriding control system, level *B*, which instructs the three machines to behave in an integrated way. This sequencing activity also enables great flexibility to be built into the workings of the machines at level *A*. But the level *B* controllers have themselves to be controlled by a fourth computer at level *C*, which is concerned with costing, utilization of machinery, stock control, invoicing and so on, not to mention the continuous monitoring of work as it is carried out at the lower levels.

The three levels taken together form System One, and such control has just about been achieved, according to Beer, in the oil, chemical and automobile industries. It represents, as far as Beer is concerned, a single division in some industrial enterprise and the complete form would consist of a number of such systems interacting with each other. As these interactions become more subtle and complex, so Systems Two and Three are built up. The higher levels, Systems Four and Five etc., represent different levels of management acting in cybernetic relationship with each other.

A similar approach can be applied to the assembly line itself; the American 'Non-Linear Systems' Company uses small teams, each working on a different product and thus, again, variety is encouraged (Abel, 1969).

The case for standardizing building components (which tend to be large, crude and simple) has never been as strong as the case for standardizing car engine parts (which tend to be small, complex and highly finished). It is likely that the techniques of automation (which encourage variety anyway) will be much more appropriate for building than simple industrialization ever was. In certain cases man-like operations (such as picking work out of one machine and feeding it into another) are performed by devices such as Versatron and Unimate which, once they have been taught the job, can perform more operations per hour (typically, 25 per cent more) with fewer mistakes (typically ten or twenty times less) than a man. In addition, of course, they are untiring (Ballinger, 1968).

If Unimate, say, can lay 25 per cent more bricks per hour than the finest bricklayer, and bricks provide a better environmental filter than glass or thin concrete slabs, why not design in brick? And if that seems too anachronistic, then design a bigger and better Unimate which can handle storey-height slabs or whatever else one wants to use.

However, on the whole the concept of building as environmental filter, as intermediate system between the environmental system and the human system, might well lead to a certain conservatism. We are building for human beings, to provide conditions in which they are comfortable. Comfort is a perceptual matter, a matter of experience. You feel cold in my sitting room because yours is five degrees warmer. If people *are* to be comfortable we have to match their sensory expectations, and these expectations have been built out of years of experience, most of it gained in traditional buildings. If we are to satisfy them, we shall have to match the standards of the buildings they find comfortable and this a good deal of 'modern' architecture so far has conspicuously failed to do.

As a first step we might devote a good deal more energy to finding out what people *really* find acceptable—not by asking them, for that would build in indeterminacies, but by finding out what they *do* to buildings which do not fit their needs. They paste paper over the windows, bring in venetian blinds, plug in their own electric fires, all these are indications as to what they really needed. If we then measure systematically the conditions they have created for themselves, we might then devise some relevant standards. The buildings we build to those standards may or may not look remarkably like those we know already. But then, perhaps, my own predilections are showing through.

References

ABEL, C. (1969) 'Ditching the Dinosaur Sanctuary', *Architectural Design*, August 1969.

ABERCROMBIE, M. L. J. (1960) *The Anatomy of Judgement*, Hutchinson, London.
(1964) 'The Observer and his Errors', *Journal of Psychosomatic Research*, **8**, Pergamon, Oxford.
(1965) 'The Nature and Nurture of Architects', *Transactions of the Bartlett Society*, **2**, 1963–64, Bartlett School of Architecture, London.

ADLER, A. *The Individual Psychology of Alfred Adler* (ed. Ansbacher), Allen and Unwin, London.

ADORNO, T. W. and others (1950) *The Authoritarian Personality*, Harper, New York.

AGRAA, O. M. & WHITEHEAD, B. (1968A) 'A Study of Movement in a School Building', *Building Science*, **2**, March 1968, pp. 279–89.
(1968B) 'Nuisance Restrictions in the Planning of Single-storey Layouts', *Building Science*, **2**, March 1968, pp. 292–302.

ALDERSEY WILLIAMS, A. (1969) 'Sound 3', *Building Environment*, A.J. Handbook. *Architects' Journal*, 5 February 1969, pp. 395–404.

ALEXANDER, C. (1963) 'Determination of Components for an Indian Village' (Eds. Jones, J. C. and Thornley, D. G.), *Conference on Design Methods*, Pergamon, Oxford.
(1963) 'HIDECS 3', four computer programs for the Hierarchical Decomposition of systems which have an associated linear graph. Civil Engineering Systems Laboratory, M.I.T., Cambridge, Mass.
(1964) *Notes on the Synthesis of Form*, Harvard University Press, Cambridge, Mass.
(1966A) 'A City is not a Tree', *Architectural Forum*, April 1965; reprinted in *Design*, no. 206, February 1966, pp. 46–55.
(1966B) 'From a Set of Forces to a Form', *The Man-made Object* (ed. Keepes, G.), Braziller, New York; Studio Vista, London.
(1966C) 'The Pattern of Streets', *Journal of the American Institute of Planners*, **XXXII**, no. 5, September 1966, pp. 273–76; reprinted in *Architectural Design*, **XXXVII**, November 1967, pp. 528–531.
(1967) 'The City as a Mechanism for Sustaining Human Contact', *Transactions of the Bartlett Society*, **4**, Bartlett School of Architecture, London.
(1968) 'Systems Generating Systems', *Systemat*—Journal of the Inlaid Steel Products Co., Milwaukee, reprinted in *Architectural Design*, **XXXVIII**, December 1968, pp. 605–10.
(1971) 'The State of the Art in Design Methodology' (replies to questions by M. Jacobson). *D.M.G. Newsletter*, March 1971, pp. 3–7.

ALEXANDER, C. and others. (1969) *Houses Generated by Patterns* (report of competition entry for Proyecto Experimentale de Vivienda, Lima, Peru). Center for Environmental Structure, Berkeley, California.

ALEXANDER, C. ISHIKAWA, S. & SILVERSTEIN, M. (1968) *A Pattern Language which Generates multi-service Centres*, Center for Environmental Structures, Berkeley, California.

ALEXANDER, C. & MANHEIM, M. (1962) 'HIDECS 2', a computer program for the hierarchical decomposition of a set within an associated graph. Publication no. 160, Civil Engineering Systems Laboratory, M.I.T., Cambridge, Mass.

ALEXANDER, C. & POYNER, B. (1965/6) *The Atoms of Environmental Structure*, R & D Paper, Directorate of Development, Ministry of Public Building and Works, London.

ALEXANDER, T. (1965) 'Synectics: Inventing by the Madness Method', *Fortune*, August 1965, pp. 165–94.

ALGER, J. R. M. & HAYS, C. V. (1964) *Creative Synthesis in Design*, Prentice-Hall, Englewood Cliffs, New Jersey.

ALLPORT, F. H. (1955) *Theories of Perception and the Concept of Structure*, Wiley, New York.

ALLPORT, G. W. (1954) *The Nature of Prejudice*, Addison–Wesley, New York.

ALLPORT, G. W., VERNON, P. E. & LINDZEY, G. (1951) *Study of Values: Manual of Directions* (revised ed.), Houghton Mifflin, Boston.

ALTMAN, I. & LETT, E. E. (1967) *The Ecology of Interpersonal Relationships: A Classification system and Conceptual Model* (mimeo), U.S. Navy Department Bureau of Medicine and Surgery.

ANASTASI, A. (1961) *Psychological Testing* (2nd edn.), Macmillan, New York.

ANDERSON, H. H. (ed.) (1959) *Creativity and its Cultivation*, Harper and Row, New York.

ANGYAL, A. (1941) *Foundations for a Science of Personality* (1967 edn. consulted), Harvard University Press, Cambridge, Mass. (for the Commonwealth Fund); Oxford University Press, London.

ARCHEA, J. & EASTMAN, C. (1970) 'EDRA 2', *Proceedings of the 2nd Annual Environmental Design Research Association Conference*, October 1970. Carnegie–Mellon University, Pittsburgh, Penn.

ARCHER, L. B. (1963–64) 'Systematic Method for Designers', *Design*, 1963: April, pp. 46–9; June, pp. 70–3; August, pp. 52–7; November, pp. 68–72. 1964: January, pp. 50–2; May, pp. 60–2; August, pp. 56–9. Reprinted for the Council of Industrial Design, HMSO, London.
(1969) 'The Structure of the Design Process', *Design Methods in Architecture* (Eds. Broadbent, G. and Ward, A.). Lund Humphries, London.

ARCHIGRAM GROUP *Archigram 1* (1961); *Archigram 2* (1962); *Archigram 3* (1963); *Archigram 4* (1964); *Archigram 5* (1964); *Archigram 6* (1965); *Archigram 7* (1967); *Archigram 8* (1968).
(1965) 'Archigram Group, London: a Chronological Survey', *Architectural Design*, XXXV, November 1965, pp. 559–72.

ARCHITECTURAL DESIGN (1969) 'Treasure Island', *Architectural Design*, XXXIX, June 1969, pp. 302–42.

ARDREY, R. (1961) *African Genesis*, Atheneum, New York.
(1967) *The Territorial Imperative*, Collins (1969 edn. consulted), London.

ARGYLE, M. (1967) *The Psychology of Interpersonal*, Penguin Books, Harmondsworth.
(1969) *Social Interaction*, Methuen, London.

ARGYLE, M. & DEAN, J. (1965) 'Eye-contact, Distance and Affiliation', *Sociometry* 1965, no. 28, pp. 289–304.

ARISTOTLE (c. 335–323 B.C.) *Organon: Comprising the Categories and Interpretations* (trans. Ackrill, 1963), Oxford University Press. *Prior and Posterior Analytics* (ed. and trans. Warrington, J.), Dent–Everyman. *The Topica and Sophistici Elenchi* (ed. Ross, W. D., 1958), Oxford University Press.

ARMOUR, G. C. & BUFFA, E. S. (1963) 'A Heuristic Algorithm and Simulation Approach to Relative Location of Facilities', *Management Science*, January 1963, pp. 294–309.

ARMOUR, G. C. & CRAMER, P. A. (1965) *Computer Relative Allocation of Facilities Technique* (CRAFT), IBM.

ARNHEIM, R. (1956) *Art and Visual Perception*, Faber, London. (1970) *Visual Thinking*, Faber, London.

ASHBY, W. R. (1956) *An Introduction to Cybernetics*, Chapman and Hall, London; republished Methuen 1965.

ASIMOW, M. (1962) *Introduction to Design*, Prentice-Hall, Engelwood Cliffs, New Jersey.

AUSTIN, J. L. (1962) *Sense and Sensibilia*, Clarendon Press, Oxford.

BACON, F. (1690) *The New Organon* (ed. F. H. Anderson 1960), Bobbs–Merrill, New York.

BALLINGER, H. A. (1968) 'Machines with Arms', *Science Journal*, October 1968.

BANHAM, R. *Architecture of the Well-tempered Environment*, Architectural Press, London.
(1962A) 'Kent and Capability', *New Statesman*, December 1962.
(1962B) 'ON TRIAL: CLASP. Ill met by clip-joint?', *Architectural Review*, **131**, no. 783, May 1962, pp. 349–52.
(1965) 'A Home is not a House' (with illustrations by Dallegret, F.), *Art in America*, April 1965; reprinted in *Clip Kit* and in *Architectural Design*, **XXXIX**, January 1969, pp. 45–8. Also in Jencks, C. & Baird, G., *Meaning in Architecture*, Barrie and Rockliff, London.
(1969) 'Flatscape with Containers', in Jencks, C. & Baird, G., *Meaning in Architecture*, Barrie & Rockliff, London.

BARNLUND, D. C. & HARLAND, C. (1963) 'Propinquity and Prestige as Determinants of Communication', *Sociometry*, **26**, 1963, pp. 467–79.

BARR, J. (ed.) (1971) *The Environmental Handbook*, Ballantine/Pan, London.

BARRON, F. (1958) 'The Psychology of Imagination', *Scientific American*.

BATTERSBY, A. (1964) *Network Analysis for Planning and Scheduling*, Macmillan, London and New York.

BEACH, F. A. (1956) 'Characteristics of Masculine "Sex Drive" ', *Nebraska Symposium on Motivation*, University of Nebraska Press.
(1965) *Sex and Behaviour*, Wiley, New York.

BEAUMONT, M. J. S. (1967) *Techniques for the Synthesis of Layout and Form with Respect to Building Layout*, PhD Thesis, University of Bristol, Department of Engineering.

BEDFORD, T. (1958) *Research on Heating and Ventilation in Relation to Human Comfort Heat Pip. Air Condit.*, December 1958, pp. 127–34.

456   References

BEER, S. (1959) *Cybernetics and Management*, English Universities Press, London.
(1965) 'The World, the Flesh and the Metal', *Nature*, 16 January 1965, pp.
223–31.
(1966) *Decision and Control: The Meaning of Management*, Wiley, London.
(1968) 'Machines that Control Machines', *Science Journal*, October 1968.

BENTHAM, J. (1789) *Introduction to the Principles of Morals and Legislation* (intro.
Harrison, W. 1948), University Press, Oxford.

BEREITER, C. & FREEDMAN, M. B. (1962) 'Fields of Study and the People in Them',
The American College (ed. Sanford, N.). Wiley, London.

BERKELEY, G. (1709) *An Essay Towards a New Theory of Vision*.

BERNOUILLI, J. (1738) 'Hydrodynamica: Kinetic Theory of Gases', in Newman,
J. R., *The World of Mathematics*, vol. 11, pp. 774–7, Allen & Unwin, London,
1960.

BERTALANFFY, L. VON (1950) 'The Theory of Open Systems in Physics and Biology',
Science, 111 (1950), pp. 23–9; reprinted in Emery, W. B. (Ed.) *Systems Thinking*,
Penguin Books, Harmondsworth.
(1968) *General System Theory*, Braziller, New York.

BEVERIDGE, W. I. B. (1950) *The Art of Scientific Investigation*, Heinemann, London.

BIERSTONE, E. & BERNHOLTZ, A. (1966) 'HIDECS-RECOMP', a Computer Pro-
gram for the semi-lattice Decomposition and Hierarchical Recomposition of a
System with Associated Linear Graph. Department of Civil Engineering,
M.I.T., Cambridge, Mass.

BLAKE, P. (1960) *The Master Builders*, Victor Gollancz, London.

BLOCK, J. (1961) *The Q-Sort Method in Personality Assessment and Psychiatric
Research*, Thomas, Springfield, Illinois.

BOAS, F. (1888) *The Central Eskimo*, 6th Annual Report, Bureau of Ethnology,
Smithsonian Institute, Washington. Reprinted 1964, University of Nebraska
Press, Lincoln, Nebraska.

BOGARDUS, E. S. (1925) 'Measuring Social Distance', *Journal of Applied Sociology*,
IX.

BOHR, N. (1958) *Atomic Physics and Human Knowledge*, Science Editions, New
York.

BOOLE, G. (1847) 'The Mathematical Analysis of Logic', Cambridge; quoted in
Newman, J. R., *The World of Mathematics*, vol. 3, pp. 1856–8.

BREUIL, (1952) *Quatre cents Siècles d'Art Pariétal*, Montignac.

BROADBENT, G. (1963) 'Use of Models in Design', *Architects' Journal*, 138, no. 14,
2 October 1963.
(1966A) 'Creativity', *The Design Method* (Ed.) Gregory, S. A. Butterworth,
London. Plenum Press, New York.
(1966B) 'Design Method in Architecture', *Architects' Journal*, 14 September
1966, pp. 679–85.
(1968) 'A Plain Man's Guide to Systematic Design Methods', *RIBA Journal*,
May 1968, pp. 223–7.
(1969A) 'Design Methods in Architecture', *Design Methods in Architecture*,
(eds. Broadbent, G. & Ward, A.) Lund Humphries, London.
(1969B) 'Meaning into Architecture', *Meaning in Architecture* (eds. Jencks,
C. & Baird, G.) Barrie & Rockliff, London. Braziller, New York.

(1970A) 'Architecture in the Future', *RIBA Journal*, October 1970, pp. 457–63.
(1970B) 'Systems and Environmental Design' (eds. Archea, J. & Eastman, C.), *EDRA 2: Proceedings of the 2nd Environmental Design Research Association Conference*, Pittsburgh, 1970.
(1970C) 'Review of Canter, D.V. 1970 *Architectural Psychology*', *Architectural Research and Teaching*, **1**, no. 2, November 1970.
(in preparation) 'The Structure of Architectural Revolutions'.

BROADBENT, G. & WARD, A. (1969) 'Design Methods in Architecture', *Architectural Association Paper no. 4*, printed by Lund Humphries for the Architectural Association, London.

BROADY, M. (1966) 'Social Theory in Architectural Design', *Architectural Association Journal*, **81**, no. 88, January 1966.
(1968) *Planning for People*, Bedford Square Press, London.

BROOM, L. & SELZNICK, P. (1955) *Sociology: a Text with Adapted Readings*, Row Petersen, Evanston.

BROSS, I. D. J. (1953) *Design for Decision*, Macmillan, New York.

BROWN, J. (1966) 'Information Theory', *New Horizons in Psychology* (ed. Foss, B. M.), Penguin Books, Harmondsworth.

BROWN, J. C. (1963) *Aggressiveness, Dominance and Social Organisation in the Steller Jay*, Condor, 65.

BRUNER, J. S., GOODNOW, J. J. & AUSTIN, G. A. (1962) *A Study of Thinking*, Wiley, New York.

BUCHANAN, C. (1963) *Traffic in Towns*, HMSO, London.

BUCKLEY, W. (1967) *Sociology and Modern Systems Theory*, Prentice-Hall, Englewood Cliffs, New Jersey.

BULLOCK, N., DICKENS, P. & STEADMAN, P. (1968) *A Theoretical Basis for University Planning*, Report no. 1, Land Use and Built-form studies, Cambridge.

BULLOCK and others. (1971) 'The Modelling of day to day Activity Patterns; the Simulation of University Activities; the Timetable as a Model of "scheduled" Activities; Diary Surveys; Patterns of Student Activity', *Architectural Design*, May 1971, pp. 292–305.

BURBERRY, P. (Ed.) '*Architects' Journal* Environmental Handbook', *Architects' Journal*, 2 October 1968–July 1969.
(1970) (Ed.) '*Architects' Journal* Handbook: Building Services and Circulation', *Architects' Journal*, 1 October 1969–7 October 1970.

BURT, C. (1949) 'Alternative Methods of Factor Analysis', *British Journal of Psychology* (Statistical Section), **2**, 98.

BYRNE, D. (1955) 'A Note on the Influence of Propinquity upon Acquaintanceship', *Journal of Abnormal and Social Psychology*, **51**, 1955.
(1961) 'The Influence of Propinquity and Opportunities for Interaction on Classroom Relationships', *Human Relations*, **14**, no. 1, February 1961.

BYRNE, E. (1966) *Games People Play*, Deutsch, London

CAMARERO, E. G., SEGUI DE LA RIVA, J. and others (1972) *Analisis y generacion automatica de formas arquitectonicas*, University of Madrid, Centro de Calcul.

CAMPION, D. (1968) *Computers in Architectural Design*, Elsevier, London.

458 *References*

CANNON, W. B. (1939) *The Wisdom of the Body*, W. W. Norton, New York.

CANTER, D. V. (1968) 'Office Size: an Example of Psychological Research in Architecture', *Architects' Journal*, 28 April 1968, pp. 881–8.
(1969A) *Measurement of Verbal Response to Physical Environment* (draft), University of Strathclyde Building Performance Research Unit.
(1969B) *The Subjective Assessment of Environment* (mimeo), Report no. 42, University of Strathclyde Building Performance Research Unit.
(1970) (Ed.) *Architectural Psychology: Proceedings of the Conference* held at Dalandhui, University of Strathclyde, 28 February–2 March 1969, RIBA Publications, London.

CAP 1970 (see Stewart, Teicholz & Lee).

CAPLOW, T. (1950) 'Neighbourhood Interaction in a homogenous Community' *American Sociological Review*, 15, 13 June 1950.

CASSIDY, H. G. (1962) *The Sciences and the Arts*, Harper, New York.

CATTELL, R. B. (1952) *Factor Analysis*, Harper, New York.

CHALK, W. (1964) 'Plug-in Living Units', *Archigram 4*.

CHANDOR, A. with GRAHAM, J. & WILLIAMSON, R. (1970) *A Dictionary of Computers*, Penguin Books, Harmondsworth.

CHAPANIS, A. (1959) *Research Techniques in Human Engineering*, The Johns Hopkins Press, Baltimore.
(1967) 'The Relevance of Laboratory Studies to Practical Situations', *Ergonomics*. 10, no. 5, 1969, pp. 557–77.

CHAPIN, F. S. (1965) *Urban Land-use Planning*, Illinois University Press, Urbana.

CHERMAYEFF, S. & ALEXANDER, C. (1963) *Community and Privacy*, Doubleday, New York. Penguin Books, Harmondsworth (1966).

CHERRY, C. (1957) *On Human Communication*, M.I.T. Press, Cambridge, Mass.; Wiley, New York.

CHILDE, V. G. (1925) *The Dawn of European Civilization* (6th edn. 1957), London.

CHOMSKY, N. (1957) *Syntactic Structures*, Mouton, The Hague.
(1959) 'Review of Verbal Behaviour' by Skinner, B. F., *Language*, 35, January–March 1959.
(1965) *Aspects of the Theory of Syntax*, M.I.T., Cambridge, Mass.

CHORLEY, R. J. & HAGGETT, P. (eds.) (1967) *Models in Geography*, Methuen, London.

CHRENKO, F. A. (1953) 'Probit Analysis of Subjective Reaction to Thermal Stimuli', *British Journal of Psychology*, 44, no. 3, pp. 248–56.

CHRISTALLER, W. (1933) *Central Places in Southern Germany* (trans. Buskin, C. W. 1966), Prentice-Hall, Englewood Cliffs, New Jersey.

CHRISTOPHERSON, D. G. (1963) 'Discovering Designers': opening address to Conference on Design Methods 1962. *Conference on Design Methods* (eds. Jones, J. C. and Thornley, D. G.), Pergamon, Oxford.

CHURCHMAN, C. W. & ACKOFF, R. L. (1950) 'Purposive Behaviour and Cybernetics', *Social Forces*, 29, pp. 32–9.

CHURCHMAN, C. W., ACKOFF, R. L. & ARNOFF, E. C. (1957) *Introduction to Operations Research*, Wiley, New York.

CLARK, G. (1967) *The Stone Age Hunters*, Thames & Hudson, London.

CLARKE, S. & ENGELBACH, R. (1930) *Ancient Egyptian Masonry*, Oxford University Press. Humphrey Milford, London.

CLOUZOT, G. H. (1956) *Le Mystère Picasso*.

COHEN, M. R. & NAGEL, E. (1961) *An Introduction to Logic and Scientific Method*, Routledge & Kegan Paul, London.

COHN, D. L. (1954) 'Optimal Systems 1. The Vascular System', *Bulletin of Mathematical Biophysics*, no. 16, pp. 59–74.

COHN-BENDIT and others (1969) *Why Sociologists?*, Student Power 1969, Penguin Books, Harmondsworth.

COIA, J. (1969) Gold Medal Address, *RIBA Journal*, 76, no. 7, July 1969, p. 283.

COLLINS, B. E. & GUETZKOW, A. (1964) *A Social Psychology of Group Processes for Decision Making*, Wiley, New York.

COLLINS, P. (1970) *Architectural Judgement*, Faber, London.

COOK, P. (1964) 'Plug-in City', *Archigram 4*.
(1967) *Architecture: Action and Plan*, Studio Vista, London.

COSER, L. A. (1956) *The Functions of Social Conflict*, Routledge, London.

COUFFIGNAL, L. (1958) *Les Notions de Base*, Paris.

COURANT, R. & ROBBINS, H. (1941) *What is Mathematics?* New York.

COUSIN, J. (1969) 'Architecture et Topologie', *Habitat*, 12, no. 2, 1969, pp. 13–18; translated and reprinted in *Architectural Design*, October 1970, pp. 491–3.

COWAN, P. (1964) 'Studies in the Growth, Change and Ageing of Buildings', *Transactions of the Bartlett Society*, 1, Bartlett School of Architecture, London.

COWAN, P. & NICHOLSON, J. (1965) 'Growth and Change in Hospitals', *Transactions of the Bartlett Society*, 3, Bartlett School of Architecture, London.

CRAIK, K. (1970) 'New Directions in Psychology', *Environmental Psychology*, Holt, Rinehart & Winston, London.

CRITCHLOW, K. *Order in Space*, Thames & Hudson, London.

CROGHAN, D. (1965) 'Daylight Study: Daylight and the Form of Office Buildings', *Architects' Journal*, 22 December 1965.

CROMPTON, D. (1964) 'Computer City', *Archigram 4*.

CROOK, J. H. (1961) 'The Basis of Flock Organisation in Birds', in *Current Problems in Animal Behaviour* (eds. Thorpe, W. H. and Zangwill, O. L.), Cambridge.

DALEY, J. (1968) 'The Myth of Quantifiability', *Architects' Journal*, 148, no. 34, 21 August 1968, pp. 339–41.
(1969) 'A Philosophical Critique of Behaviourism in Architectural Design', *Design Methods in Architecture* (eds. Broadbent, G. and Ward, A.) Lund Humphries, London.

DANSEREAU, P. (1970) *Challenge for Survival*, Columbia University Press, New York.

DAVIS, T. (1960) *The Architecture of John Nash*, Studio, London.

DEAN, R. D. & McGLOTHLEN, L. (1965) *Effect of Combined Heat and Noise on Human Performance, Physiology and Subjective Estimate of Comfort and Performance*, Proceedings of Institute of Environmental Sciences Annual Technical Meeting 1965, pp. 55–65.

460 *References*

DEFFONTAINES, P. (1948) *Geographie et Religions* (9th edn. consulted), Gallimard, Paris.

DESCARTES, R. (1637) *Discourse on Method* (trans. Wollaston, A., 1960), Penguin Books, Harmondsworth.

DEWEY, J. (1910) *How We Think*, Heath, D. C., London.

DREVER, J. (1917) *Instinct in Man*, Cambridge University Press, Cambridge.

DRUCKER, P. (1955) *The Practice of Management*, Heinemann, London.

DRUMMOND, G., PATTERSON, W. & WILLOUGHBY, T. (1970) 'Computer Approach to Built-form Layout', *Operational Research Quarterly*, **21** (1), p. 91.

DUBOS, R. *Man Adapting*, Yale University Press, New Haven.

DUCKWORTH, E. (1965) *A Guide to Operational Research*, Methuen, London.

DUFFY, F. (1969A) 'A Method of Analysing and Charting Relationships in the Office', *Architects' Journal*, 12 March 1969, pp. 693–9.
(1969B) 'Role and Status in the Office', *A.A. Quarterly*, **1**, no. 4. October 1969, pp. 4–13.

DURKHEIM, E. (1895) *The Rules of Sociological Method* (trans. Catlin, E. G.; 1938 edn. consulted) Collier–Macmillan Canada Ltd., Toronto, Ontario.
Suicide (ed. Simpson 1952), Routledge, London.

ECCLES, J. C. (1958) 'The Physiology of Imagination', *Scientific American*, September 1958.

ECHENIQUE, M. (1968) 'Models: a Discussion', Working Paper no. 6. Cambridge: Land Use and Built-form Studies, reprinted in *Architectural Research and Teaching*, **1**, no. 1, May 1970.
(1971A) 'An Approach to Urban Studies', *Architectural Design*, May 1971, pp. 276–7.
(1971B) 'A Model of the Urban Spatial Structure', *Architectural Design*, May 1971, pp. 277–80.

ECO, U. (1968) *La Struttura Assente*, Bompiani, Milano.

EDER, W. E. (1966) 'Definitions and Methodologies', in *The Design Method* (ed. Gregory, S. A.), Butterworth, London.

EDGAR, C. C. (1906) *Sculptors' Studies and Unfinished Works*, Cataologue generale du Musee du Caire, Cairo.

EDHOLM, O. G. (1967) *The Biology of Work*, Weidenfeld & Nicolson, London.

EDWARDS, A. L. (1965) *Experimental Design in Psychological Research*, Holt, Rinehart & Winston, New York.

EDWARDS, E. (1964) *Information Transmission*, Chapman & Hall, London.

EDWARDS, I. E. S. (1947) *The Pyramids of Egypt* (1961 edn. consulted), Penguin Books, Harmondsworth.

EHRENZWEIG, A. (1965) *The Psychoanalysis of Artistic Vision and Hearing*, Braziller, New York.
(1967) *The Hidden Order in Art—a Study in the Psychology of Artistic Imagination*, Weidenfeld & Nicolson, London.

EHRLICH, P. R. (1968) *The Population Bomb*, Ballantine, New York.

EHRLICH, P. R. & A. H. (1970) *Population, Resources, Environment*, W. H. Freeman, San Francisco and London.

EMERY, F. E. (Ed.) (1969) *Systems Thinking*, Penguin Books, Harmondsworth.

EMPSON, W. (1930) *Seven Types of Ambiguity* (1962 edn. consulted), Penguin Books, Harmondsworth.

ENGLAND, R. (1971) 'Planning complex Building Systems', *Nature*; reprinted in *Architectural Research and Teaching*, **2**, no. 1, pp. 34–39.

L'ESPRIT NOUVEAU: *Revue Internationale D'Esthetique*, nos. 1 to 28 (1920–25), Editions de l'esprit nouveau, Paris. Reprinted Da Capo Press, New York, 1969.

EULER, L. (1735) 'The Seven Bridges of Konigsberg' (trans. Courant, R. and Robbins, H. 1941), in *The World of Mathematics* (ed. Newman, J. R.), vol. 1, pp. 573–80, Allen & Unwin, London, 1960.

EVANS, C. R., PURCELL, P. A. & WOOD, J. (1971) *An Investigation of Design Activities using Analytic Time-lapse Photography*, National Physical Laboratory, Division of Computer Science.

EVANS, R. (1969) 'Piezoelectric Structures', *Architectural Design*, **XXXIX**, September 1969, p. 470.

EYSENCK, H. J. (1967) *The Biological Basis of Personality*, Thomas, C. C., Springfield.
(1970) *The Structure of Human Personality* (3rd edn.), Methuen, London.

FALCON, W. D. (1964) *Value Analysis—Value Engineering*, New York.

FARLEY, F. H. (1966) 'Individual Differences in Solution Time in Error-free Problem Solving', *British Journal Society Clinical Psychology*, 1966, **5**, pp. 306–9.

FAST, J. (1970) *Body Language*, Evans, New York.

FEDER, D. (Ed.) (1967) Proceedings of the first International Colloquium on Pneumatic Structures, organized by the University of Stuttgart, International Association for Shell Structures, Stuttgart, Department of Architecture and Civil Engineering, University of Stuttgart.

FESTINGER, L., SCHACHTER, S. & BACK, K. (1969) *Social Pressures in informal Groups: a Study of Human Factors in Housing*, Tavistock Publications, London.

FITTS, P. Fitts List: *Relative Advantages of Men and Machines*; Singleton, W. T. 1966, *Current Trends Towards Systems Designs*, Ministry of Technology, *Ergonomics for Industry*, **12**, HMSO, London.

FLEIG, K. (1963) *Alvar Aalto 1922–62*, Guisberger, Zurich, London, New York.

FLETCHER, R. (1957) *Instinct in Man* (1968 edn. consulted). Unwin University Books, London.

FOLLETT, T. & CAVRAK, S. (1969) *COMPROGRAPH 2; COMPROGRAPH 3;* Computer programs for optimizing relationships between design elements along vectors from a point on a line, Design Systems, Boston, Mass.

FORD, L. K. & FULKERSON, D. K. (1962) *Flows in Networks*, Princeton.

FORDE, C. D. (1934) *Habitat, Economy and Society*, Methuen, London.

FOTI, M. & ZAFFAGINI, M. (1969) *La Sfida Elettronica*, Fiere di Bologna, Bologna.

FOWLER, F. G. (1962) *A Dictionary of Modern English Usage* (1961 edn. consulted) Oxford University Press, London.

FRANKL, P. (1946) 'Secrets of the Mediaeval Masons', *Art Bulletin*, **XXVII**, March 1946.

FRASER DARLING, F. (1969) *Wilderness and Plenty*, B.B.C., London.

FREUD, S. (1910A) *Five Introductory Lectures on Psychoanalysis* (1947 edn.), Hogarth, London.
(1910B) *Leonardo da Vinci* (trans. Tyson, A. 1957), Pelican Books, Harmondsworth, 1963.
(1933) *New Introductory Lectures on Psychoanalysis*, Norton, New York.
(1938) *The Basic Writings of Sigmund Freud* (ed. Brill, A. A. 1938), The Modern Library, New York.
(1952) *Delusion and Dream*, Beacon, Boston.
(1966) *The Complete Introductory Lectures on Psychoanalysis*, W. W. Norton, New York.

FROMM, E. (1941) *Escape from Freedom*, Farrar & Rinehart, New York.
(1942) *Fear of Freedom*, Kegan Paul, London.
(1956) *The Sane Society*, Routledge & Kegan Paul, London.

FULLER, R. B. (1969) *Operation Manual for the Spaceship Earth*, Pocket Books, New York.

FULLER, R., BUCKMINSTER & MCHALE, J. (1963–67) *World Design Science Decade*, 6 vols., World Resources Inventory, Southern Illinois University, Carbondale, Illinois.

GALBRAITH, J. K. (1958) *The Affluent Society*, Hamish Hamilton, London.

GALILEI, GALILEO (1632) 'Dialogue Concerning the Two Chief World Systems—Ptolemaic and Copernican' (trans. Stillman Drake), *The World of Mathematics* (ed. Newman, J. R.) vol. 11, Allen & Unwin, London, 1956.

GAMOW, G. (1958) 'The Principle of Uncertainty', *Scientific American*, January 1958.

GANS, H. J. (1967) *The Levittowners*, Free Press, New York.

GASS, S. (1958) *Linear Programming*, McGraw-Hill, New York.

GERO, J. S. & BROWN, M. (1969) 'A Selective Bibliography of Computers in Architecture', *Architectural Science Review*, December 1969, pp. 105–11.

GETZELS, J. W. & JACKSON, P. W. (1962) *Creativity and Intelligence*, Wiley, New York.

GHISELIN, B. (1955) *The Creative Process*, Mentor, New York.

GILBRETH, F. B. (1909) *Bricklaying Systems*, Myron C. Clark, New York.

GILBRETH, F. B. & L.M. (1917) *Applied Motion Study*, Sturgis & Walton, New York.

GINSBERG, M. (1955) 'Sociology', *Chambers Encyclopaedia*.

GOFFMAN, E. (1959) *Presentation of Self in Everyday Life*, Doubleday Anchor, New York.
(1961A) *Asylums. Essays on the Social Situation of Mental Patients and other Inmates*, Doubleday Archer, New York.
(1961B) *Encounters*, Bobbs-Merrill, Indianapolis.
(1966) *Behavior in Public Places*, Free Press, New York.

GOODALL, M. C. (1965) *Science and the Politician*, Schenkman, Cambridge, Mass.

GOODMAN, D. (1964) *Utopian Essays and Practical Proposals*, Vintage, New York.

GORDON, A. (1968) 'Architects' Approach to Architecture', *RIBA Journal*, **75**, no. 4, April 1968, pp. 169–78.

GORDON, A. & PARTNERS. (ND) *IBIS: the Computer as Design Aid* (K. Claxton), Alex Gordon & Partners with Richard Thomas & Baldwin, Cardiff.

GORDON, J. E. (1968) *The New Science of Strong Materials*, Penguin Press, Harmondsworth.

GORDON, W. J. J. (1961) *Synectics: the Development of Creative Capacity*, Harper & Brothers, New York.

GOSLING, W. (1962) *The Design of Engineering Systems*, Heywood, London.

GOTTSCHALDT, K. (1926) *Embedded Figures*, quoted in Macfarlane-Smith, 1964, *Spatial Ability*.

GOUGH, H. G. (1954) *The General Information Survey, Forms A and B*, Institute of Personality Assessment and Research, University of California, Berkeley (1957).

GRAUNT, J. (1662) 'Natural and Political Observations . . . upon the Bills of Mortality', in *The World of Mathematics* (ed. Newman J. R.), Allen & Unwin, London.

GREEN, A. (1965) *Sociology—an Analysis of Modern Life*, Mcgraw-Hill, New York.

GREENE, D. and others—ARCHIGRAM GROUP (1969) 'Instant City', *Architectural Design*, XXXIX, May 1969, pp. 274–80.

GREGORY, R. L. (1963) 'Distortion of Visual Space as Inappropriate Constancy Scaling', *Nature, London*.
(1966) *Eye and Brain*, World University Library, London.

GREGORY, S. A. (1963) 'Creativity in Chemical Engineering Research' (ed. Pine, J. M.), *Symposium on Productivity in Research*, Institute of Chemical Engineers, London.

GREGORY, S. A. (Ed.) (1966) *The Design Method*, Butterworth, London.

GRINKER, R. R. (Ed.) (1956) *Toward a Unified Theory of Human Behaviour*, Basic Books, New York, London.

GROPIUS, W. (1935) *The New Architecture and the Bauhaus* (trans. Morton Shand P.; 1956 edn. consulted), Faber, London.
(1956) *Scope of Total Architecture*, Allen & Unwin, London.

GRUBER, H. E., TEYRELL, G. & WERTHEIMER, M. (Eds.) *Contemporary approaches to Creative Thinking: a Symposium*, Colorado University Press, Boulder.

GUERRA, G. (1969) 'A Geometrical Method of Systematic Design in Architecture', *Design Methods in Architecture* (eds. Broadbent, G. and Ward, A.), Lund Humphries, London.

GUGELOT, H. (1963) 'Industrial Design in Practice', *Zeitschrift der Hochschule für Gestaltung*, 7, January 1963, pp. 3–5.

GUILFORD, J. P. (1950) 'Creativity', *American Psychology*, no. 5, p. 444.
(1954) *Psychometric Methods*, McGraw-Hill, New York, Toronto, London.

GULLAHORN, J. T. (1952) 'Distance and Friendship as Factors in the Gross Interaction Matrix', *Sociometry*, 15.

GUTTMAN, L. (1950) 'The Basis for Scalogram Analysis', *Measurement and Prediction* (ed. S. A. Stoffer), Princeton University Press, Princeton, New Jersey.

GUTTMAN, R. (1966) 'The Questions Architects ask', *Transactions of the Bartlett Society*, 4, 1965–66, pp. 49–82.

HABRAKEN, N. J. (1960) *Supports of the People* (mimeo), Technical University, Delft.
(1961) *The Supports and the People*, Scheltema & Holkema, Amsterdam; reprinted Architectural Press, London, 1972.
(1972) *Supports: an Alternative to Mass Housing* (trans. Valkenburg, B.), Architectural Press, London.

HADAMARD, J. (1945) *The Psychology of Invention in the Mathematical Field*, Princeton University Press, New York; republished Dover, 1954.

HADLEY, G. (1962) *Linear Programming*, Addison-Wesley, Reading, Mass.

HAGGETT, P. (1965) *Locational Analysis in Human Geography*, London.

HAGGETT, P. & CHORLEY, R. J. (1967) 'Models, Paradigms and the New Geography', in *Models in Geography* (eds. Chorley, R. J. and Haggett, P.).

HALL, A. D. (1962) *A Methodology for Systems Engineers*, Van Nostrand, Princeton.

HALL, E. T. (1959) *The Silent Language*, Doubleday & Co., Garden City, New York.
(1963A) 'A System for the Notation of Proxemic Behavior', *American Anthropologist*, **65**, no. 5.
(1963B) 'Proxemics—a Study of Man's Spatial Relationships', in *Man's Image in Medicine and Anthropology*, (ed. Galdston, I.), International Universities Press, New York.
(1966) *The Hidden Dimension*, The Bodley Head, London, Sydney, Toronto.

HALPRIN, L. (1965) 'Motation', *Progressive Architecture*, July 1965, pp. 126–33.

DE HANIKA, F. DE P. (1965) *New Thinking in Management*, Hutchinson, London.

HANSON, K. (1969) 'Design from Linked Requirements in a Housing Problem', in *Design Methods on Architecture* (eds. Broadbent, G. and Ward, A.), Lund Humphries, London.

HARDY, A. L. & O'SULLIVAN, P. E. (1967A) *Building a Climate*, Electricity Council, London.
(1967B) 'The Building: a Climatic Modifier', *Heating and Ventilation for a Human Environment*, Institute of Mechanical Engineers, London, November 1967.
(1969) *Integrated Design*, Electricity Council, London.

HARE, A. P. & BALES, R. F. (1963) 'Seating Position and Small Group Interaction', *Sociometry*, **26**.

HARE, E. M. & SHAW, G. K. (1965) *Mental Health on a New Housing Estate*, Oxford University Press, London.

HARTLEY, R. V. L. (1928) 'Transmission of Information', *Bell Systems Technical Journal*, **7**, 1928, p. 535.

HAWKES, D. (1970) *The Environmental Evaluation of Buildings*, 5; 'Explorations', Working Paper 30.
(1971) 'Building Scale: Computer Representation', *Architectural Design*, May 1971, pp. 309–12.
(n.d.) *Building Bulk Legislation: a Description and Analysis*, Working Paper 4. Land Use and Built-form Studies, Cambridge.

HAWKES, D. & STIBBS, R. (1969) *The Environmental Evaluation of Buildings*, 1: 'A Mathematical Model', Working Paper 15.
(1970A) *The Environmental Evaluation of Buildings*, 2: 'Technical Specification of the Model'.

(1970B) *The Environmental Evaluation of Buildings*, 3: 'A Worked Example', Working Paper 28.

(1970C) *The Environmental Evaluation of Buildings*, 4: 'The Description and Evaluation of Rooflights', Working Paper 29.

(1971) 'An Environmental Model: Computer Representation', *Architectural Design*, **XLI**, May 1971, pp. 309–12.

HAZARD, J. N. (1962) 'Furniture Arrangement as a Symbol of Judicial Role', *ETC: A Review of General Semantics*, **XIX**, no. 2, July 1962, pp. 181–8.

HEDGEPATH, W. & STOCK, D. (1970) *The Alternative*, Macmillan, New York.

HEIDEGGER, M. (1931) *Being and Time* (trans. Macquarrie, J. & Robinson, E., 1967), Blackwell, Oxford.

HEISENBERG, W. (1958) *The Physicists Conception of Nature* (trans. Pomerans, A. J.), Hutchinson, London.
(1959) *Physics and Philosophy*, Allen & Unwin, London.

HELMER-PETERSEN, E. (1959) 'A New Personality: Jorn Utzon', in *A Visit to Denmark* (ed. Alfieri, B.), Zodiac 5, 1959.

HILLIER, W. R. G. (1970) 'Psychology and the Subject Matter of Architectural Research' (ed. Canter, D. V.), *Architectural Psychology*.

HIPPLE, W. J. (1957) *The Beautiful, the Sublime and the Picturesque in 18th Century British Aesthetic Theory*, Southern Illinois University Press, Carbondale.

HITCHCOCK, H. R. & JOHNSON, P. (1932) *The International Style: Architecture since 1922* (ed. consulted *The International Style*, 1966), W. W. Norton, New York.

HOCHBERG, J. E. (1964) *Perception*, Prentice-Hall, Englewood Cliffs, New Jersey.

HODEIR, A. (1956) *Jazz: its Evolution and Essence*, Grove Press, New York.

HOLE, W. V. & ATTENBURROW, J. J. (1966) *Houses and People: a Review of User Studies* (Building Research Station), H.M.S.O., London.

HOPKINSON, R. G., PETHERIDGE, P. & LONGMORE, J. (1966) *Daylighting*, Heinemann, London.

HORTON, R. E. (1945) 'Erosional Development of Streams and their Drainage Basins', *Bulletin of the Geological Society of America*, no. 56, pp. 275–370.

HOVEY, H. B. (1928) 'Effects of General Distraction on the Higher Thought Processes', *American Journal of Psychology*, **40**.

HUDSON, L. (1960) 'A Different Test of Science/Arts Aptitude', *Nature*, **182**, p. 413.
(1966) *Contrary Imaginations*, Methuen, London.

HUME, D. (1739–40) *A Treatise of Human Nature* (ed. Biggs, L. A. S., 1967), Oxford University Press, London.

HUSSERL, E. 'The Philosophy of Arithmetic', 1891, quoted in Husserl, *The Idea of Phenomenology*, 1964, Martinus Nijhoff, The Hague.
(1964) *The Idea of Phenomenology*, Martinus Nijhoff, The Hague.

HYDE, R. W. & YORK, R. H. (1948) 'A Technique for Investigating Interpersonal Relationships in a Mental Hospital', *Journal of Abnormal Psychology*, 1948, **43**, pp. 287–99.

I.E.S. (1968) *The I.E.S. Code: Recommendations for Lighting Building Interiors*, Illuminating Engineering Society, London.

INKELES, A. (1964) *What is Sociology?*, Prentice-Hall, Englewood Cliffs, New Jersey.

I.R.I.A. (Ed. Maroy, J. P.) *Informatique et conception en Architecture*, Institut de Recherche en Informatique et Automatique, Rocquencourt.

JACOBS, J. (1961) *The Life and Death of Great American Cities*, Random House, New York. Penguin Books, Harmondsworth.

JAMES, W. (1890) *Principles of Psychology*, Macmillan, London.

JOINER, D. (1971) 'Social Ritual and Architectural Space', *Architectural Research and Teaching*, **1**, no. 3, April 1971, pp. 11–22.

JONES, J. C. (1963) 'A Method of Systematic Design', *Conference on Design Methods*, (eds. Jones, J. C. and Thornley, D. G.) Pergamon, Oxford.
(1965) 'Systematic Design Methods and the Building Design Process', *Architects' Journal*, 22 September 1965, pp. 685–7.
(1966) 'Design Methods Compared: 1. Strategies. 2. Tactics', *Design, 212* and *213*, August 1966, pp. 32–5, September 1966, pp. 46–52.
(1970) *Design Methods*, Wiley, London and New York.
(1971) *Contribution to Coloquio Internacional sobre arquitectura y automatica*, Madrid, 1–3 April.

JONES, J. C. & THORNLEY, D. G. *Conference on Design Methods:* Papers presented at the Conference on Systematic and Intuitive Methods in Engineering, Industrial Design, Architecture and Communications, London. September 1962. Pergamon, Oxford.

JUNG, C. G. (1923) *Psychological Types* (trans. Baynes, H. G.), Routledge & Kegan Paul, London.
(ed.) (1964) *Man and his Symbols*, Aldus, London.
(1969) *The Psychology of C. G. Jung*, by J. de F. Jacobi, Routledge & Kegan Paul, London.

KAMNITZER, P. (1969) 'Computer Aid to Design' (INTU-VAL 7 City-scape), *Architectural Design*, XXXIX, September 1969, pp. 507, 508.

KANSKY, K. J. (1963) *Structure of Transportation Networks*, Research Paper no. 84, University of Chicago, Department of Geography.

KELLY, C. A. (1955) *The Psychology of Personal Constricts*, Norton, New York.

KLIR, J. & VALACH, M. (1965) *Cybernetic Modelling* (trans. Dolan, P. 1966), Iliffe, London, 1967.

KNIGHT, C. B. (1965) *Basic Concepts of Ecology*, Macmillan, New York.

KOCH, S. (1964) 'Psychology and Emerging Conceptions of Knowledge as Unitary', *Behaviourism and Phenomenology* (ed. Wann, T. W.), Chicago University Press, Chicago.

KOESTLER, A. (1964) *The Act of Creation*, Hutchinson, London.

KOFFKA, K. (1935) *Principles of Gestalt Psychology*, Harcourt, New York.

KOHLER, W. (1929) *Gestalt Psychology* (Mentor 1947 edn. consulted), Liveright, New York.

KOWAI, C. D. (1968) 'Difficulties with Network Models in Problem Formulation', *Emerging Methods in Environmental Design and Planning* (ed. Moore, G. T.), M.I.T. Press, Cambridge, Mass., 1970.

KUTNER, B. and others. (1952) 'Verbal Attitudes and Overt Behavior Involving Racial Prejudice', *Journal of Abnormal and Social Psychology*, **XLVII**.

LAING, N. (1967) 'The Use of Solar and Sky Radiation for Air Conditioning', *Proceedings of the first International Colloquium on Pneumatic Structures* (ed. Feder, D.).

LANDAU, R. (1965) 'Towards a Structure for Architectural Ideas', *A.A. Journal*, June 1965, pp. 7–11.

LANE, B. M. (1968) *Architecture and Politics in Germany 1918–1945*, Harvard University Press, Cambridge, Mass.

LANGDON, F. J. (1966) *Modern Offices: a User Survey*, National Building Studies Research Paper 41, HMSO, London.

LANGDON, F. J. & KEIGHLEY, E. C. (1964) 'User Research in Office Design', *Architects' Journal*, 5 February 1964.

LANGER, S. (1942) *Philosophy in a New Key*, Harvard University Press, Cambridge, Mass.

LANGHAAR, H. L. (1951) *Dimensional Analysis and the Theory of Models*, Wiley, London.

LAPIERRE (1934) 'Attitudes versus Actions', *Social Forces*, XIV.

LAPLACE, P. S. DE (1812) 'Théorie analytique des probabilités'; translated as 'Concerning Probability', in *The World of Mathematics* (ed. Newman, J. R.), vol. 11, pp. 1325–33, Allen & Unwin, London, 1960.
(1814) 'Essai philosophique sur les probabilités', Paris; quoted in *The World of Mathematics* (ed. Newman, J. R.), Allen & Unwin, London.

LASDUN, D. (1965) 'Architects' Approach to Architecture', *RIBA Journal*, April 1865.

LAU, J. J. H. (1970) 'Differences between Full-size and Scale-model Rooms in the Assessment of Lighting Quality', *Architectural Psychology* (ed. Canter, D. V.), RIBA, London.

LAUGIER, M. A. (1753) *Essai sur l'Architecture*, Duchesne, Paris, reprinted Gregg Press, Farnborough, 1966.

LEAVIS, F. R. (1970) '"Literism" versus "Scientism": the Misconception and the Menace', *The Times Literary Supplement*, no. 3556, 23 April 1970, pp. 441–4. Reprinted in Leavis, F. R., *Nor shall my Sword*, Chatto & Windus, London, 1972.

LE CORBUSIER (1923) *Vers une Architecture*, Editions Crès., Paris.
(1923) *Towards a New Architecture* (trans. Etchells 1927), Architectural Press, London.
(1929) *Œuvre Complète*, vol. 1, 1910–1929 (ed. Boesiger, W.), Girsberger, Zurich.
(1958) *The Chapel at Ronchamp*, Architectural Press, London.
(1960) *My Work*, Architectural Press, London.

LEE, T. (1957) 'On the Relation Between the School Journey and Social and Emotional Adjustment in Rural Infant Children', *British Journal of Educational Psychology*, XXVII, part 11, June 1957, pp. 101–14.
(1963) 'Psychology and Living Space', *Transactions of the Bartlett Society*, 2, 1963, pp. 9–36.
(1971) 'Psychology and Architectural Determinism' (parts 1–3), *Architects' Journal*, 154, no. 31, 4 August 1971, pp. 253–62; no. 35, 1 September 1971, pp. 475–86; no. 37, 22 September 1971, pp. 651–62.

LEE, T. R. (1967) 'The Concept of Space and Control of the Environment', *Arena* (Architectural Association Journal), **82**, no. 908, 1967, pp. 172–5.
(1970) 'Do we Need a Theory? *Architectural Psychology* (ed. Canter, D. V.), RIBA Publications, London.

LEVIN, P. H. (1964) 'The Use of Graphs to Decide the Optimum Layout of Buildings', *Architects' Journal*, 7 October 1964, pp. 809–15.
(1966A) 'Decision making in Urban Design', *Building Research Current Papers*, Design Series 49, HMSO, London.
(1966B) 'Design Process in Planning', *Town Planning Review*, **37**, April 1966, pp. 520.
(1967) 'Towards Decision Making Rules for Urban Planners', *Journal of the Town Planning Institute*, December 1967.

LEVI-STRAUSS, C. (1963) *Structural Anthropology*, Allen Lane, The Penguin Press, London.

LEW, P. I. & BROWN, P. H. (1968) 'Evaluation and Modification of CRAFT for an Architectural Methodology', in *Emerging Methods in Environmental Design and Planning*, (ed. Moore, G. T.), M.I.T. Press, Cambridge, Mass.

LEWIS, P. T. (1970) 'Real Windows', *BAS Conference*, Newcastle upon Tyne, quoted in RIA Group 1970.

LIKERT, R. (1932) 'A Technique for the Measurement of Attitudes', *Archives of Psychology*, no. 140.

LINDEMAN, E. C. (1924) *Social Discovery*, New York.

LINDSAY, W. (1971) *Structural Comparisons of Three Generations of New Towns*, Working Paper 25, Land Use and Built-form Studies, Cambridge.

LIPMAN, A. (1968A) 'Building Design and Social Interaction', *Architects' Journal*, 3 January 1968, pp. 23–30.
(1968B) 'Propinquity as a Factor in Social Relations: an Example and some Inferences', *Architectural Science Review*, **11**, no. 3, September 1968, pp. 100–12.

LISTING, J. B. (1847) 'Vorstudien zur Topologie', quoted in *The World of Mathematics* (ed. Newman, J. R.), Allen & Unwin, London, 1960.

LOCKE, J. (1690) *An Essay concerning Human Understanding* (ed. Yolton, J. W.), 1961, Dent, London.

LOCKYER, K. (1964) *Critical Path Analysis*, Pitman, London.

LORENZ, K. Z. (1952) *King Solomon's Ring*, Crowell, New York.

LOSCH, A. (1940) 'Die Raumliche Ordnung der Wirtschaft', Jena, quoted in Hagget, P., 1965, *Locational Analysis in Human Geography*, London.

LOWES, J. L. (1927) *The Road to Xanadu: a Study in the Ways of the Imagination*, Constable, London.

LOWRY, I. S. (1964) *Model of Metropolis*, RAND Corporation.

LUCKIESH, M. & TAYLOR, A. H. (1922) 'Radiant Energy from Fluorescent Lamps', *Transactions of the Illuminating Engineering Society*, **17**, 1922, p. 269.

LUCKMAN, J. (1969) 'An Approach to the Management of Design', in *Design Methods on Architecture* (eds. Broadbent, G. and Ward, A.), Lund Humphries, London.

LYNCH, K. (1960) *The Image of the City*, Technology Press and Harvard University Press, Cambridge, Mass.

LYNES, J. A. (1969) *Principles of Natural Lighting*, Elsevier, London.

LYNES, J. A., BURT, W. A. & CUTTLE, C. (1966) 'The Flow of Light into Buildings', *Transactions of the Illuminating Engineering Society*, **31**, no. 3, 1966, pp. 65–9.

McCLELLAND, D. C. (1962) 'On the Psychodynamics of Creative Physical Scientists,' in *Contemporary Approaches to Creative Thinking* (ed. Gruber and others), Atherton, New York.

MacCLOUGHLIN, J. B. (1969) *Urban Regional Planning: a Systems Approach*, Faber, London.

MacCLOUGHLIN, J. B. & WEBSTER, J. (1970) 'Cybernetic and General-system Approaches to Urban and Regional Research: a Review of the Literature', *Environment and Planning*, **2**, 1970, pp. 369–408.

MacCORMAC, R. C. (1968) 'The Anatomy of Wright's Aesthetic', *Architectural Review*, **143**, no. 852, February 1968, pp. 143–6.

McCORMICK, E. J. (1957) *Human Engineering*, McGraw-Hill, London and New York.

MacCURDY, E. (Ed.) (1938) *The Notebooks of Leonardo da Vinci*, Jonathan Cape, London.

MacFARLANE SMITH, I. (1964) *Spatial Ability*, University of London Press, London.

McGILL, W. J. & QUASTLER, H. (1955) 'Standardised Nomenclature: an Attempt', in *Information Theory in Psychology: Problems and Methods* (ed. Quastler, H.), 1955.

MacINTYRE, A. (1970) *Marcuse*, Fontana/Collins, London.

McKELLAR, P. (1957) *Imagination and Thinking*, Cohen and West, London.

MacKINNON, D. W. (1962A) 'The Personality Correlates a Creativity; A Study of American Architects', in *Proceedings of the XIV International Congress of Applied Psychology* (ed. Nielson, G. S.), Copenhagen, 1961, Munksgaard, Copenhagen, 1962.
(1962B) 'The Nature and Nurture of Creative Talent', in *Personality Assessment* (ed. Semenoff, Boris, 1966), Penguin Books, Harmondsworth.

McLUHAN, M. (1964) *Understanding Media*, Routledge, London.

MADGE, J. (1953) *The Tools of Social Science*, Longmans, London.

MALDONADO, T. (1965) 'The Emergent World: a Challenge to Architectural and Industrial Design Training', ULM 12/13 *Zeitschrift der Hochschule für Gestaltung*, March 1965, pp. 2–10.

MALDONADO, T. & BONSIEPE, G. (1964) 'Science and Design', ULM 10/11, *Zeitschrift der Hochschule für Gestaltung*, May 1964, pp. 10–29.

MALINOWSKI, B. (1922) *Argonauts of the Western Pacific*, London.

MANNING, P. B. (Ed.) (1965) *Office Design: a Study of Environment*, Pilkington Research Unit, University of Liverpool Department of Building Science.
(1967A) 'Design Flow Process Chart', ULM Reporting Back Conference: *The Teaching of Design—Design Method in Architecture*, School of Architecture, Waltham Forest Technical College, London. Revised and reprinted in 'Appraisals of Building Performance: their use in the Design Process', *Architects' Journal*, 9 October 1968, pp. 793–6.
(1967B) 'Multi-disciplinary Research for Architecture', *The Architects' Journal*, **146**, no. 20, 1967, pp. 1239–43.

(1967C) *The Primary School: an Environment for education*, Pilkington Research Unit, University of Liverpool Department of Building Science.
(1969) 'St. George's School, Wallasey: Evaluation of a solar heated Building', *Architects' Journal*, 25 June 1969, pp. 1715–21.

MARCH, L. & STEADMAN, P. *The Geometry of Environment*, RIBA, London.

MARCH, L. & TRACE, M. (1968) *The Land Use Performance of Selected Arrays of Built Forms*, Working Paper 2, Land Use and Built-form Studies, Cambridge.

MARCUSE, H. (1964) *One Dimensional Man*, Routledge & Kegan Paul, London.

MARKOV, A. A. (1954) *Theory of Algorithms* (trans. Schorr-Kon, J. J., 1962), Israel Programme for Scientific Translation, Jerusalem.

MARKS, R. W. (1959) *The Dymaxion World of Buckminster Fuller*, Reinhold, New York.

MARKUS, T. A. (1967) 'The Role of Building Performance, Measurement and Appraisal in Design Method', *Architects' Journal*, 20 December 1967, pp. 1567–73. Reprinted with revisions, in *Design Methods in Architecture* (eds. Broadbent, G. and Ward, A.), Lund Humphries, London, 1969.
(1970A) Foreword to Canter, D. (Ed.) *Architectural Psychology*, RIBA Publications, London.
(1970B) 'Optimisation by Evaluation in the Appraisal of Buildings', *Building*, 21 August 1970, pp. 51–7 and 18 September 1970, pp. 91–4.

MARLER, P. R. & HAMILTON, W. J. (1966) *Mechanisms of Animal Behaviour*, New York.

MARTIN, L. (1965) *Whitehall—a Plan for the National and Government Centre*, HMSO, London.

MASLOW, A. H. (1954) *Motivation and Personality*, Harper, New York.

MASLOW, A. H. & MINTZ, N. L. (1956) 'Effects of aesthetic surroundings: 1. Initial effects of three aesthetic conditions upon perceiving "energy" and "wellbeing" in faces', *Journal of Psychology*, **41.**

MATOUSEK, R. (1963) *Engineering Design: a Systematic Approach*, Blackie, Glasgow.

MELLONE, S. H. (1934) *Elements of Modern Logic*, University Tutorial Press, London.

MERTON, R. K. & KENDALL, P. L. (1946) 'The Focussed Interview', *American Journal of Sociology*, **51,** pp. 541–57.

MESAROVIC, M. D. (Ed.) (1964) *Views on General Systems Theory*, Wiley, New York.

MEYER, H. (1926) *Die Neue Welt*, trans. in Schnaidt, C., 1965, *Hannes Meyer*, Tiranti, London.

MICHAEL, W. B. and others (1957) 'The Description of Spatio-visualization Abilities', *Educational Psychology Measurement 1957*, **17,** pp. 185–99.

MIDDLETON, (1967) *Group Practice in Design*, London.

MIES VAN DER ROHE (1960) Interview with Graham Shankland, B.B.C. Third Programme.

MILL, J. S. (N.D.) *A System of Logic: Ratiocinative and Inductive*, Longmans, London.

MILLER, G. A. (1964) *Psychology, the Science of Mental Life*, Hutchinson—Pelican, London, 1966.

MILLS, R. (Ed.) (1964) 'The Development by Le Corbusier of the Design for l'Église de Firminy, a Church in France', *Student Publications of the School of Design*, North Carolina State University, Raleigh, **14**, no. 2.

MINISTRY OF EDUCATION (1959) *Education Act 1944, Statutory Instrument no. 890*, HMSO, London.

MINTZ, N. L. (1956) 'Effects of Aesthetic Surroundings, 11; Prolonged and Repeated Experience in a "beautiful" and an "ugly" room', *Journal of Psychology*, **41**, 1956, pp. 459–66.

MITCHELL, W. J. (Ed.) (1972) 'Environmental Design: Research and Practice', *Proceedings of the EDRA 3/AR 8 Conference*, January 1972, University of California, Los Angeles, California.

MOBIUS, K. (1877) 'The Oyster and Oyster Culture', quoted in Knight C. B., *Basic Concepts in Ecology*, Macmillan, New York.

MAHOLY-NAGY, L. (1965) *Vision in Motion*, Paul Theobald, Chicago.

MOLES, A. (1958) *Information Theory and Aesthetic Perception* (trans. Cohen, J. E., 1966), Illinois University Press, Urbana and London.

MONGAIT, A. L. (1955) *Archaeology in the U.S.S.R* (trans. Thompson, M. W., 1961), Penguin Books, Harmondsworth.

MONTAGU, M. F. A. (1968) *Men and Aggression*, Oxford University Press, London, Oxford, New York.

MOORE, G. T. (Ed.) (1970) 'Emerging Methods in Environmental Design and Planning', *Proceedings of the Design Methods Group First International Conference*, M.I.T. Press, Cambridge, Mass.

MOORE, I. (1969) 'Design Methods and Development Programming', in *Design Methods in Architecture* (eds. Broadbent, G. and Ward, A.), Lund Humphries, London.

MORAY, N. (1964) 'Outside the Cave'. Commentary on Koestler, A., *The Act of Creation*, in *The Listener*, **71**, 25 June 1964, pp. 1028–9, 1032.

MORGAN, B. G. (1961) *Canonic Design in English Mediaeval Architecture*, Liverpool University Press, Liverpool.

MORGAN, M. A. (1967) 'Hardware Models in Geography,' in *Models in Geography* (eds. Chorley R. J. and Haggett, P.). Methuen, London.

MORONEY, M. J. (1951) *Facts from Figures* (1970 edn. consulted), Penguin Books, Harmondsworth.

MORRIS, D. (1967) *The Naked Ape*, Jonathan Cape, London.
(1969) *The Human Zoo*, Jonathan Cape, London.

MORSE, E. S. (1885) *Japanese Homes and their Surroundings*, Ticknor, New York.

MORSE, P. M. (1958) *Queues, Inventories and Maintenance*, Wiley, New York.

MORSE, P. M. & KIMBALL, G. E. (1951) *Methods of Operations Research*, New York.

MOSELEY, L. (1963) 'A Rational Design Theory for the Planning of Buildings based on the Analysis and Solution of Circulation Problems', *Architects' Journal*, 11 November 1963.

M.P.B.W. (1965) 'Plant Houses for the Botanical Gardens, Edinburgh', *Building and Scottish Architecture*, March 1965; *Surveyor*, 20 February 1965; *Building*, 1 December 1967; *Architects' Journal*, 1 December 1967, and *Acier/Stahl/Steel*, July/August 1968.

(1966A) *Activity Data Method: a Method of Recording User Requirements*, M.P.B.W. Directorate of Development, HMSO, London.

(1966B) *Planning a Major Building Project*, M.P.B.W. Directorate of Development. HMSO, London.

(1969) *Computer-aided Architectural Design. Part 1 Reports of Three Working Groups. Part 2*, R. & D. Paper. Directorate of Research and Information, HMSO, London.

MURPHY & MACKEY (1961) see *Progressive Architecture*.

MURRELL, K. F. H. (1965) *Ergonomics; Man in his Working Environment*, Chapman & Hall, London.

MUSGROVE, J. (1966) 'Dangers of Scientism', *Architectural Review*, July 1966.

MUSGROVE, J. & DOIDGE, C. (1970) 'Room Classification', *Architectural Research and Teaching*, **1**, no. 1, May 1970, pp. 31–6.

MYERS, I. B. (1958) *Some Findings with Regard to Type and Manual for Myers–Briggs Type Indicator, Form E*, Author, Swarthmore, Pa.

NAIRN, I. (1966) 'Stop the Architects Now', *The Observer*, 13 February 1966, p. 21.

NEGROPONTE, N. (1969A) 'Towards a Humanism through Machines', *Technology Review*, **71**, no. 6, April 1969. Reprinted in *Architectural Design*, XXXIX, September 1969, pp. 511, 512.

(1969B) 'Architecture Machine', *Architectural Design*, XXXIX, September 1969, p. 510.

(1970) *The Architecture Machine*, M.I.T. Press, Cambridge, Mass.

NEGROPONTE, N. & GROISER, L. B. (1969) 'The Semantics of Architecture Machines', *Architectural Design*, XL, September 1970, pp. 466–9.

NEUTRA, R. (1954) *Survival through Design*, Oxford University Press, New York.

NEWMAN, J. R. (1960) *The World of Mathematics* (4 vols.), Allen & Unwin, London.

NEWTON, I. (1687) *Principia Mathematica* (ed. Cajori, F.; trans. Motte, A., 1962), California University Press.

NICHOLSON, M. (1970) *The Environmental Revolution*, Hodder & Stoughton, London.

NOBLE, J. (1963) 'The How and Why of Behaviour: Social Psychology for the Architect', *Architects' Journal*, 6 March 1963, pp. 630–46.

NORRIS, K. W. (1963) 'The Morphological Approach to Engineering Design', *Conference on Design Methods* (eds. Jones, J. C. and Thornley, D. G.), Pergamon, London; Macmillan, New York.

OGBURN, W. F. & NIMKOFF, M. F. (1958) *Sociology*, Houghton Mifflin, Boston.

OGDEN, C. K. & RICHARDS, I. A. (1923) *The Meaning of Meaning* (10th edn. consulted), Routledge & Kegan Paul, London.

O.I.D.—COULSON, J. and others (1962) *Oxford Illustrated Dictionary*, Oxford University Press, Oxford.

O'KEEFE, J. P. (1971) Private communications.

OLDS, J. (1956) 'Pleasure Centres in the Brain', *Scientific American*, October 1956.

ORE, O. (1963) *Graphs and their Uses*, Random House, New York.

OSBORN, A. F. (1957) *Applied Imagination: Principles and Practices of Creative Thinking*, Scribners, New York.

OSGOOD, C. E. (1953) *Method and Theory in Experimental Psychology*, Oxford University Press, London.

OSGOOD, C. E., SUCI, G. J. & TANNENBAUM, P. H. (1957) *The Measurement of Meaning*, Illinois University Press, Urbana.

OZBEKHAN, H. (1969) 'The Future as an Ethical Concept', *Proceedings of the 6th General Assembly and Congress, International Conference of Societies of Industrial Designers*, London, September 1969.

P.A. (*Progressive Architecture*) (1961) *And Suddenly Last Summer*, description of the Climatron designed for the Missouri Botanical Gardens, St. Louis, by Murphy & Mackey. *Progressive Architecture*, April 1961, pp. 174–8; see also *AIA Journal*, May 1961, pp. 22–32.

PADGHAM, C. A. (1965) *Subjective Limitations on Physical Measurements*, Chapman & Hall, London.

PAGE, J. K. (1963) 'Review of Papers presented at the Conference', *Conference on Design Methods* (eds. Jones, J. C. and Thornley, P. G.), Pergamon, Oxford. (1964) 'Environmental Research Using Models', *Architects' Journal*, **139**, no. 11, 11 March 1964.

PARSONS, T. and others (Eds.) (1961) *Theories of Society*, Illinois Free Press, Glencoe.

PASK, G. (1961) *An Approach to Cybernetics*, Hutchinson, London.

PATTERSON, M. (1968) 'Social Factors in Social Interaction', *Human Relations*, **27**, no. 4, 1968.

PAVLOV, I. P. (1903) 'Experimental Psychology and Psychopathology in Animals', *Essential Works of Pavlov*, 1966 (Ed. Kaplan, M.) Bantam Books, New York.

PAWLEY, M. 'The Time House', *Architectural Design*; reprinted in Jencks, C. and Baird, G. *Meaning in Architecture*, Barrie & Rockliff, London; Braziller, New York. (1971) *Architecture versus Housing*, Studio Vista, London.

PAYNE, I. (1970) 'Pupillary Response to Architectural Stimuli', *Architectural Psychology* (ed. Canter, D.V.) RIBA, London.

PEANO, G. *Formulaire de Mathématiques*, quoted in Newman, J. R., *The World of Mathematics* (1960), Allen & Unwin, London.

PEARSON, K. (1948) *Early Statistical Papers*, Cambridge University Press.

PEVSNER, N. (1943) *An Outline of European Architecture* (1960, 1968 edns. consulted), Penguin Books, Harmondsworth.

PHILIPS, R. J. (1968) *Optimize Layout Program*, Department of Architecture, University of Bristol.

PITTS, F. R. (1965) 'A Graph Theoretic Approach to Historical Geography', *Professional Geographer*, **17** (5), pp. 15–20.

VER PLANCK, D. W. & TEARE, B. R. (1954) *Engineering Analysis*, Wiley, New York.

PLATO. *The Republic of Plato*, trans. with introduction and notes by Cornford, F. M., Clarendon, Oxford. *Parmenides*, trans. Warrington, J. 1961, J. M. Dent, London; Dutton, New York.

POPHAM, Sir H. (1799) *Manual of Telegraphic Signals and Marine Vocabulary*, London.

POPPER, K. (1957) *The Poverty of Historicism*, Routledge, London.
(1959) *Logic of Scientific Discovery*, Hutchinson, London.
(1963) *Conjectures and Refutations*, Routledge, London.

PRICE, C. (1964) 'Fun Palace', *Architectural Design*, November 1964.
(1966A) 'Potteries Thinkbelt', *New Society*, 2 June 1966, pp. 14–17.
(1966B) 'Life Conditioning and Potteries Thinkbelt', *Architectural Design*, October 1966, pp. 483–97.
(1967) 'Fun Palace, Camden', *Architectural Design*, XXXVII, November 1967, pp. 522–5.

PRICE, C. and others. (1965) *First Giant Space Mobile in the World*, Fun Palace Trust, London.

PROSHANSKY, H. M., ITTELSON, W. H. & RIVLIN, L. G. (1970) *Environmental Psychology*, Holt, Rinehard & Winston, London.

PUGIN, A. W. (1841) *The True Principles of Christian or Pointed Architecture*, John Weale, London.

PURCELL, P. (1970) 'Computer Graphics in Systems Building', *Industrialised Building*, March 1970, pp. 51–52.

PURCELL, P. A. (1971). See Evans, C. R., Purcell, P. A. and Wood, J., *An Investigation of Design Activities using Analytic Time-lapse Photography*.

PURCELL, P. A. and others (1970) 'Computer Graphics System for School Design', *Proceedings of Symposium on Computer-aided Design*, Delft, October 1970.

QUASTLER, H. (ed.) (1955) 'Information Theory in Psychology: Problems and Methods', *Proceedings of Conference on Estimation of Information Flow*, held at Monticello, Illinois, July 1954, Illinois Free Press, Glencoe.

RADCLIFFE BROWN (1952) *Structure and Function in Primitive Society*, Illinois Free Press, Glencoe.

RAGLAN, LORD (1964) *The Temple and the House*, Norton, New York.

RANDALL, F. E.. and others. (1946) *Human Body Sizes in Military Aircraft and Personal Equipment*, Army Air Forces Air Material Command (Wright Field, Dayton, Ohio), Technical Report no. 5501, June 10, 1946.

RAPOPORT, A. (1969A) 'The Design Profession and the Behavioral Sciences', *Architectural Association Quarterly*, 1, no. 1, 1968–69.
(1969B) 'Facts and Models', in *Design Methods in Architecture* (eds. Broadbent, G. and Ward, A.), Lund Humphries, London.
(1969C) *House Form and Culture*, Prentice-Hall, Englewood Cliffs, New Jersey.
(1970) 'Observations Regarding Man–Environment Systems', *Man–Environment Systems*, January 1970; Reprinted in *Architectural Research and Teaching*, 4, 1971.

RAPOPORT, A. & WATSON, N. (1968) 'Cultural Variability in Physical Standards', *Transactions of the Bartlett Society*, 6, Bartlett School of Architecture, London.

RASMUSSEN, S. E. (1959) *Experiencing Architecture* (1962 edn. consulted), M.I.T. Press, Cambridge, Mass.

RAWLINSON, C. & DOIDGE, C. (1971) 'Dynamic Space Allocation', *Architectural Research and Teaching*, 1, no. 3, April 1971, pp. 4–10.

REPTON, H. (1840) *The Landscape Gardening and Landscape Architecture of Humphrey Repton* (Ed. J. C. Loudon), London.

RHINE, J. B. & SPRATT, J. G. (1962) *Parapsychology*, Thomas, C. C., Springfield, Illinois.

R.I.A. (Research in Action) Group (1970) 'An Integrated Design Study applied to Schools Development', *Architectural Research and Teaching*, **1**, no. 2, November 1970, RIBA Publications, London.

R.I.B.A. (1965) *Handbook of Architectural Practice and Management*, RIBA, London.

R.I.B.A. Research Committee (1970) 'Strategies for Architectural Research', *Architectural Research and Teaching*, **1**, no. 1, May 1970, RIBA, London.

RICHARD, B. (1966) *New Movement in Cities*, Studio Vista, London.

RICHARDS, C. A. & DOBYNS, H. 'Topography and Culture: the Case of the Changing Cage', *Human Organization*, **16**, no. 1, pp. 16–20.

RICHARDS, I. A. (1936) *The Philosophy of Rhetoric*, Oxford University Press, London.

ROE, A. (1951) 'A Study of Imagery in Research Scientists', *Journal of Personality*, no. 19, p. 459.
(1953) 'A Psychological Study of Eminent Psychologists and Anthropologists and a Comparison with Biological and Physical Scientists', *Psychological Monographs*, **67**, no. 352.

ROETHLISBERGER, F. J. & DICKSON, W. J. (1939) *Management and the Worker*, Harvard University Press, Cambridge, Mass.

ROHLES, F. H. (1967) 'Environmental Psychology—a Bucket of Worms?' *Psychology Today*, June 1967, pp. 54–63.

ROHN, J. (1970) 'The CRAFT Program: Improvements and Proposed Improvements', *Proceedings of the International Symposium on Computer Graphics 70*, Brunel University, Uxbridge.

ROKEACH, M. (1960) *The Open and Closed Mind*, Basic Books, New York.

ROSENBLUTH, A., WEINER, N. & BIGELOW, J. (1943) 'Purpose and Teleology', *Philosophy of Science*, **10**, pp. 18–24.

ROSENSTEIN, A. B., RATHBONE, R. R. & SNEERER, W. F. (1964) *Engineering Communications*, Prentice-Hall, Englewood Cliffs, New Jersey.

ROSENTHAL, R. (1966) *Experimenter Effects in Behavioral Research*, Appleton-Century Crofts, New York.

RUSSELL, B. (1946) *History of Western Philosophy*, Allen & Unwin, London.

RYLE, G. (1949) *The Concept of Mind*, Hutchinson, London.

SANOFF, H. & COHNS (Eds.) (1969) *Proceedings of EDRA*, Raleigh, North Carolina.

SARGEAUNT, M. J. (1965) *Operational Research for Management*, Heinemann, London.

SAUSSURE, F. DE (1906–11) *Course in General Linguistics* (trans. Baskin, W. 1959), Philosophical Library, New York; Peter Owen, London.

SCHNAIDT, C. (1965) *Hannes Meyer: Buildings, Projects, Writings*, Tiranti, London.

SCHNEIDER, D. E. (1950) *The Psychoanalyst and the Artist* (1962 edn. consulted), Mentor, New York.

SCHOLFIELD, P. H. (1958) *The Theory of Proportion in Architecture*, Cambridge University Press, London.

SCHON, D. A. (1963) *Invention and the Evolution of Ideas* (formerly published as *Displacement of Concepts*), Tavistock Social Science Paper backs, London.

SCULLY, V. (1961) *Modern Architecture*, Prentice-Hall International, London; Braziller, New York.

SEEHOF, J. M. & EVANS, W. O. (1967) *Automated Layout Design Program* (ALDEP), I.B.M.

SEGAL, W. (1968) 'A Man on his Own', *Architect and Building News*, 23 October 1968, pp. 20–27.

SEVERUD, F. (1954) 'Structural Analogies Taken from Nature: the Structures that House us', *Architectural Record*, **115**, no. 1, January 1954, pp. 169–75.

SHANNON, C. E. & WEAVER, W. (1949) *The Mathematical Theory of Communication*, University of Illinois Press, Urbana.

SIMMEL, G. (1902–3) *The Metropolis and Mental Life*, in *The Sociology of Georg Simmel 1950* (ed. Wolf, K. H.), Free Press, New York; Collier–Macmillan, London.
(1955) *Conflict* (trans. Wolf, K. H.), Illinois Free Press, Glencoe.

SIMON, H. A. (1957) *Models of Man: Social and Rational*, Wiley, New York.

SINGLETON, W. T. (1966) 'Current Trends towards Systems Design', Ministry of Technology, *Ergonomics for Industry*, **12**, HMSO, London.

SINTON, D. & FOSBERG, S. (1969) *LOKAT: a Computer Program Which Tries to Relate Functional Requirements with Physical Layout by Random Generation of Plan Alternatives*, Perkins & Will (architects), New York.

SKINNER, B. F. (1972) *Beyond Freedom Dignity*, Cape, London.

SLANN, P. A. (1963) 'Foreword to Jones, J. C. and Thornley, D. G.', *Conference on Design Methods*, Pergamon, Oxford.

SMITH, S. (1967) In Eysenk, H. J., *The Biological Basis of Personality*, Thomas, C. C., Springfield.

SMUTS, J. C. (1961) *Holism and Evolution*, Viking, New York.

SOMMER, R. (1967) 'Can Behavioural Studies be Useful as Well as Ornamental?', *Transactions of the Bartlett Society*, **5**, 1966–7, pp. 49–65, Bartlett School of Architecture, London.
(1969) *Personal Space*, Prentice-Hall, Englewood Cliffs, New Jersey.

SONTAG, S. (1967) *Against Interpretation*, Eyre & Spottiswoode, London.

SPEARMAN, C. (1904) ' "General Intelligence" Objectively Determined and Measured', *American Journal of Psychology*, **15**, pp. 201–93.
(1927) *The Abilities of Man*, Macmillan, London.

SPRANGER, E. (1928) *Types of Men* (trans. Paul, J. W. Pigors.), Max Niemeyer, Halle, Germany.

SPROTT, W. J. H. (1958) *Human Groups*, Penguin Books, Harmondsworth.

STARLING, J. (Ed.) Ulm Group 4 (1966) *Programme for the Conference Course on The Teaching of Design–Design Method in Architecture*, organized by the Ministry of Education at the Hochschule für Gestaltung, Ulm, April 1966, School of Architecture, Waltham Forest Technical College, London.

(Ed.) (1967) Reporting Back on the Conference Course as above, School of Architecture, Waltham Forest Technical College, London.

STARR, M. K. (1963) *Product Design and Decision Theory*, Prentice-Hall, Englewood Cliffs, New Jersey.

STEINBERG, J. L. (Ed.) (1962) *The Future Implications of Creativity Research*, Los Angeles State College, Los Angeles.

STERN, W. (1938) *General Psychology* (trans. H. D. Spoerl), Macmillan, New York.

STEVENS, S. S. (Ed.) (1951) *Handbook of Experimental Psychology*, Wiley, New York.

STEWART, C. D., TEKHOLZ, E. & LEE, K. (1970) *Computer Architecture Programs*, Center for Environmental Research, Boston, Mass.

STIRLING, J. (1960) Photograph from 'The "Functional Tradition" and Expression', *Perspecta*, **6**, pp. 89–97.

STREHLOW, T. G. H. (1947) *Aranda Traditions*, Melbourne.

STRINGER, P. (1967) 'Masculinity–Feminity as a possible Factor underlying the Personality Responses of Male and Female Art Students'. *British Journal of Social and Clinical Psychology*, **6**.
(1970) 'Architecture, Psychology, the Game's the Same', *Architectural Psychology* (ed. Canter, D. V.), RIBA, London.

STURT, G. (1923) *The Wheelwright's Shop* (1963 edn. consulted), Cambridge University Press, London.

SUMMERSON, J. (1949) *Heavenly Mansions* (1963 edn. consulted), Norton, New York; Cressett, London.

SYNECTICS INC. (GITTER, D., GORDON, W. J. J. & PRINCE) (1964) *The Operational Mechanisms of Synectics*, Synectics Inc. (mimeo), Cambridge, Mass.

TABOR, P. (1969–70) *Traffic in Buildings* **1–4**, 1. 'Pedestrian Circulation in Offices', 2. 'Systematic Activity-location', 3. 'Analysis of Communication Patterns', 4. 'Evaluation of Routes', Working Papers 17–20, Land Use and Built Form Studies, Cambridge.
(1971) 'The Analysis of a Complex Web of Association', *Architectural Design*, **XLI**, May 1971, pp. 319–20.

TAVISTOCK INSTITUTE (1966) *Interdependence and Uncertainty: a Study of the Building Industry*, Tavistock Publications, London.

TAYLOR, C. W. (Ed.) (1956) *The 1955 University of Utah Research Conference on the Identification of Creative Scientific Talent*, Utah University Press, Salt Lake City.
(1958) *The Second (1957) University of Utah Research Conference on the Identification of Creative Scientific Talent*, Utah University Press, Salt Lake City.
(1959) *The Third (1959) University of Utah Research Conference on the Identification of Creative Scientific Talent*. Utah University Press, Salt Lake City.

TAYLOR, C. W. & BARRON, F. (1963) *Scientific Creativity: its Recognition and Development*, Selected papers from the first, second and third University of Utah Conferences, Wiley, New York.

TAYLOR, D. W., BERRY, P. C. & BLOCK, C. H. (1958) 'Does Group Participation when using Brainstorming facilitate or inhibit Creative Thinking?' *Administrative Science Quarterly*, June 1958.

478   *References*

TAYLOR, R. (1950) 'Comments on a Mechanistic Conception of Purposefulness' and 'Purposeful and Non-purposeful Behaviour: a Rejoinder', *Philosophy of Science* 17, pp. 310–17, 327–32.

TEICHNER, W. H. (1967) 'The Subjective Response to the Thermal Environment', *Human Factors*, 9, no. 5, 1967, pp. 497–510.

TERMAN, L. M. (1956) *Concept Mastery Test, Form T Manual*, Psychological Corporation, New York.

THIEL, P. (1961) 'A Sequence Experience Notation for Architectural and Urban Space', *Town Planning Review*, 32, April 1961, pp. 32–52.
(1962) 'An Experiment in Space Notation', *Architectural Review*, 131, no. 783, May 1962, pp. 326–9.
(1964) 'Processional Architecture', *A.I.A. Journal*, February 1964, pp. 23–8.

THOMPSON, W. D'A. *On Growth and Form*, Cambridge University Press.

THORNLEY, D. G. (1963) 'Design Method in Architectural Education', in *Conference on Design Methods* (eds. Jones, J. C. and Thornley, D. G.), Pergamon, Oxford.

THURSTONE, L. L. (1947) *Multiple Factor Analysis*, Chicago University Press, Chicago.

THURSTONE, L. L. & CHAVE, E. J. (1929) *The Measurement of Attitudes*, University of Chicago Press, Chicago.

TINBERGEN, N. (1953) *The Herring Gull's World*, Collins, London.
(1957) 'The Functions of Territory', *Bird Study*, 4, pp. 14–27.

TINKER, M. A. (1941) 'Effect of Visual Adaptation upon Intensity of Light Preferred for Reading', *American Journal of Psychology*, 54.

VAJDA, S. (1956) *The Theory of Games and Linear Programming*, Methuen, London.

VALERY, P. In *Nouvelle Revue Française*, quoted Hadamard, 1945.

VERNON, J. (1963) *Inside the Black Room*, Penguin Books, Harmondsworth.

VERNON, P. E. (1950) *The Structure of Human Abilities* (1971 edn. consulted), Methuen, London.

VITRUVIUS (1914) *The Ten Books on Architecture* (trans. Morgan, M. H.), (1960 edn consulted), Dover Publications, New York.

VOLLMAN, T. E. & BUFFA, E. S. (1966) 'The Facilities Layout Problem in Perspective', *Management Science*, 12, pp. 450–68.

VON NEUMANN, J. & MORGENSTERN, O. (1944) *Theory of Games and Economic Behavior*, Princeton, New Jersey.

VORDEMBERGE-GILDEWART, F. (1963) Obituary in Ulm 7: *Zeitschrift der Hochschule für Gestaltung*, January 1963, p. 37.

VOSCH, A. (1940) *The Economics of Location* (trans. Woglom, W. W., 1954), New Haven.

WADDINGTON, C. H. (1969) *Behind Appearance*, University Press, Edinburgh; M.I.T. Press, Cambridge, Mass.

WALLAS, G. (1926) *The Art of Thought*, Jonathan Cape, London.

WANG, J. C. (1970) *Description? Prescription? An Approach to Design Research* (mimeo), Portsmouth School of Architecture.

(1971) *Design Research, an Analysis of three Types of Field Study* (mimeo), Portsmouth School of Architecture.

(1972) *A Study of Design Decision-making*, Unpublished PhD. Thesis.

WARD, A. (1967) Private Communication.

(1971) *Contribution to Coloquo Internacional sobre Arquitectura y Automatica*, Madrid, 1–3 April.

WARNER, O. (1958) *A Portrait of Lord Nelson*, Chatto & Windus, London.

WATSON, J. B. (1924) *Behaviorism*, University of Chicago Press, Chicago and London.

WATSON, J. D. (1968) *The Double Helix*, Weidenfeld & Nicolson, London.

WEBBER, M. L. (1963) 'Order in Diversity without Propinquity', in *Cities and Spaces* (ed. Wingo, I.), Johns Hopkins Press, Baltimore.

WEEKS, J. (1960) 'Planning for Growth and Change', *Architects' Journal*.

(1965) 'Indeterminate Architecture', *Transactions of the Bartlett Society*, **2**, 1963–4, Bartlett School of Architecture, London.

(1966A) 'Hospital Design for Growth and Change', *World Hospitals*, **5**, Pergamon, London.

(1966B) 'Multi-strategy Buildings', *Architectural Design*, **XXXIX**, October 1969, pp. 536–40.

WEISEN, A. (1965) *Differential reinforcing effects of onset and offset stimulation on the Operant Behaviour of Normals, Neurotics and Psychopaths*, quoted in Eysenck, H. J., *The Structure of Human Personality*, 1970, Methuen, London.

WELBY, V. (1896) 'Sense, Meaning and Interpretation', *Mind*, p. 187 etc.: quoted in Ogden, C. K. and Richards, I. A., 1923.

WELLS, B. (1965A) 'Subjective Responses to the Lighting Installation in a Modern Office Building and their Design Implications', *Building Science*, **1**, p. 67–8.

(1965B) 'The Psycho-social Influence of Building Environment', *Building Science*, **1**, pp. 153–65.

(1965C) 'The Psycho-social Influence of Environmental Studies: a Psychologist's Contribution', *Architects' Journal*, 22 September 1967, pp. 167–71.

(1967) 'Individual Differences in Environmental Response', *Arena*, January 1967, pp. 167–71.

WENDT, P. F. (1957) 'Theory of Urban Land Values', *Land Economics*, August 1957.

WENNER, L. B. (1954) 'The Degree to which Colour (hues) are associated with Mood Tones', *Journal of Applied Psychology*, **38**, no. 4, pp. 432–35.

WERTHEIMER, M. (1943) *Productive Thinking* (1961 edn. consulted), Tavistock Publications, London.

WESTON, H. C. (1949) *Sight, Light and Work*, H. K. Lewis, London.

WHITE, M. (1955) *The Age of Analysis*, Mentor Books, The New American Library of World Literature Inc., New York.

WHITEHEAD, B. & ELDARS, M. (1964A) 'An Approach to the Optimum Layout of Single-storey Buildings', *Architects' Journal*, 17 June 1964, pp. 1373–80.

(1964B) Correspondence with P. Levin, *Architects' Journal*, 25 November 1964, pp. 1223–4.

(1965) 'Computer Program for the Planning of Single-Storey Layouts', *Building Science*, **1**, September 1965, pp. 127–39.

WHITTICK, A. (1940) *Eric Mendelsohn*, London.

References

WIENER, N. (1948) *Cybernetics* (2nd ed., 1961) M.I.T. Press, Cambridge, Mass.
(1954) *The Human Use of Human Beings*, Houghton Mifflin, Boston, Mass.

WILLIAMS, S. H. (1954) 'Urban Aesthetics,' *Town Planning Review*, July 1954.

WILLOUGHBY, T. (1970) *A Generative approach to Computer Aided Planning*, Working Paper, Land Use and Built-form Studies, London.
(1971) 'Evaluating Circulation Performance', *Architectural Design*, XLI, May 1971, p. 314.

WITTGENSTEIN, L. (1921) *Tractacus Logico-Philosophicus* (trans. Pears, D. F. and McGuiness, B. F.) (1961 edn. consulted) Routledge, London.

WITTKOWER, R. (1962) *Architectural Principles in the Age of Humanism*, Tiranti, London.

WOODBRIDGE, K. (1965) 'Henry Hoare's Paradise', *Art Bulletin*, March 1965; revised as *The Stourhead Landscape* (1971). National Trust, London.
(1970) *Landscape and Antiquity: Aspects of English Culture at Stourhead, 1718–1838*, Oxford University Press, London.

WOODWORTH, R. S. & SCHLOSBERG, H. (1954) *Experimental Psychology*, Holt, Rinehard & Winston, New York.

WOOLS, R. M. (1970) 'The Assessment of Room Friendliness', in *Architectural Psychology* (ed. Canter, D. V.), RIBA, London.

WOTTON, H. (1624) *The Elements of Architecture collected from the Best Sources and Examples*, John Bill, London. Reprinted Gregg Press, Farnborough, 1969.

WRIGHT, D. (1969) 'Sex: Instinct or Appetite?' *New Society*, 22 May 1969, pp. 791–3.

WRIGHT, F. L. (1932) *Autobiography* (rev. edn. 1943), Hawthorn, New York.
(1937) *Architecture and Modern Life*, Harper & Brothers, New York.

YUDKIN, J. (1957) 'Correlation between the Number of Radio and Television Licences and Death from Coronary Artery Disease', *The Lancet*, July 1957.

ZINOVIEFF, P. (1968) 'Two Electronic Music Computer Projects in Britain', *Cybernetic Serendipity: the Computer and the Arts* (ed. Reichardt, J.), Studio International, London.

ZWICKY, F. (1948) 'A Morphological Method of Analysis and Construction', *Studies and Essays* (Courant Anniversary Volume), Interscience, New York.

Name Index

481

General Index

Abilities, ability, 16–22, 92
 hierarchy of, 20, Fig. 1.1
 mechanical, 20, 92
 numerical, 20, 92
 spatial, 16, 18, 19, 20, 21, 92
 verbal, 12, 92, 266
Abscissa, 104, 296
Activists, student, 442–9
Activities, activity, ix, x, xiii
 and planning, 401
 and room sizes, 164–6, Fig. 9.1, 391–5,
  432
 hierarchy of, 393
 plotted into environmental matrix, 408–
  411
Activity Data Method (ADM), 287–8, 391
Act of thought, analysis of, 179–80, 181
Adaptation, 30, 122, 139–40, 150, 446
Adjacency, adjacency programs, ix, 309,
  310–11
Administration of building, 158, 159, 163,
  171–4
Aesthetics, aestheticians, 61, 73
Air houses, inflatable, 28, 417, Fig. 20.4
Algorithms, 254, 283, 306
 in design, 325, 326–7, 338
Analogic design, applications of, 121
Analogue, analogues, 34–35, 88, 329
 definitions of, 87
 take over by, 34, 272, 274, 278, 291
Analogy, analogies, 87
 creative use of, 31, 38, 325, 329–30, 338,
  440
 definitions of, 87, 329
 false, 330
 generation of, 329
 in Synectics, 350, 351
 language, uses in, 30, 88, 213–14, 222
Analysis of interconnected decision areas
  (AIDA), 269, 280–3, Fig. 14.3
Analysis/synthesis/evaluation sequence,
  256, 258, Figs. 13.1 and 13.2, 323,
  324–5, 338, 340, 356
Analytical engine, 299, 302
Animal behaviour, 136, 137
Anthropologist, anthropology, 3, 12, 83–4,
  122, 137, 254
Arab architecture, 341, 342
Architect, as artist, 3
 as scientist, 3

at work, analysis of, 204–6, Table 11
 communications with client, 221
 creative, 3, 9, 17
 role of, 361–3
Architecture, as sensory experience, 12
 nature of, 1
Artist, creative, 2, 3, 13, 17, 21, 22
Assembly effect in group working, 345,
  357
Associationism, 60–1, 177
Attitude, attitudes, 273
 judging, 18, 19
 perceiving, 18, 19
 scales, 125–31
 to daylight, 151–2
Automation, 450–2
Axiomatic method, 56, 75

Bauhaus, 66, 252, 253
Behaviour, and verbal response, 120–1
 bird and animal, 136–7
 effect of environment on, 156, 157
 exploratory, 137
 goal seeking, 371–2, Fig. 18.1
 learned, 137
 purposeful, 371–2
Behaviourism, behaviourist, 10, 21, 22,
  62–4, 72, 76, 78, 136–7, 177
 objections to, 64
Binary arithmetic, 215, 304
Biocoenosis, 366, 367
Biologists, 3, 12
Black box, 376–7
 input to, 376
 output from, 376
 protocol for, 377
Block schematic diagram, 293
 applications of, 397
Boolean algebra, 246–51
Brain, human, 314–16, 319
 compared with computer, 314–16, Table
  15.2
 pleasure centres in, 319
Brainstorming, rules of, 348, 349
Brick house project, 53, Fig. 2.16, 54, Fig.
  20.2
Brief, briefing, 257, 266, 287–8, 390–9
 activity based, 390–9, Fig. 19.1
 sensory, 405

489

Acknowledgements to Authors and Publishers

I wish to acknowledge co-operation by the following, in granting permission for diagrams, tables and passages of text from their various publications:

Dr. Jane Abercrombie
Figure 16.1 (from 'The Nature and Nurture of Architects', *Transactions of the Bartlett Society*, **2**, 1963–64. First published in Spastics International Medical Publication).

The Architectural Press
Quotations on pp. 45–8 (from Le Corbusier, *Towards a New Architecture*, translated Etchells, 1927).
Table 9.2 (*AJ Environmental Handbook*, section 5, Sound 3, *Architects' Journal*, 5 February 1969).
Figures 12.9 and 15.4 (from Whitehead, B. and Eldars, M. 'An Approach to the Optimum Layout of Single-storey Buildings', *Architects' Journal*, 17 June 1964).
Figure 12.16 (Levin, P.E., 'The Uses of Graphs to Decide the Optimum Layout of Buildings, *Architects' Journal*, 7 October 1964, pp. 809–15).
Figure 17.2 (Le Corbusier, *The Chapel at Ronchamp*, 1957, pp. 94 and 106).

Architectural Record
Figure 17.4 (from Fred N. Severud, 'The Structures that House us', *Architectural Record*, **115**, no. 1, January 1954, p. 170).

Architectural Research and Teaching
Figure 5.1 (Author's classification of models; adapted from Echenique).

Professor Reyner Banham
Figure 21.3 (drawing by François Dallegret, first published in *Arts and Architecture*, New York).

Barrie and Jenkins Ltd.
Quotations on pp. 345 (Summerson, J., *Heavenly Mansions*, Cresset Press, London, 1949).

George Braziller Inc.
Quotations on pp. 373 and 374 (Bertalanffy, L. von, *General Systems Theory*, 1968).

Building Design Partnership (N. K. Scott)
Table 11.1—Percentages of time spent in various activities by a job architect.

Butterworth & Co. Ltd.
Figure 13.2 (from Watts *in* Gregory, S. A. (ed.), *The Design Method*. Butterworth, London, 1966).
Figures 18.4 and 18.5 (from Klir, J. and Valach, M., *Cybernetic Modelling*, Iliffe Books Ltd., London, 1965).

Peter Cook
Figure 21.2 (from Archigram 4).

Professor Jean Cousin
Figures 12.17 (adapted from 'Architecture et Topologie', *Habitat*, **12**, no. 2, 1969, pp. 13–18, translated and reprinted in *Architectural Design*, October 1970, pp. 491–3).

502   *Acknowledgements to Authors and Publishers*

Professor Peter Cowan
Figure 9.4 (from 'Studies in the Growth, Change and Ageing of Buildings', *Transactions of the Bartlett Society*, 1962–83).

Department of Antiquities, United Arab Republic
Figures 2.4 and 2.5 (from *Annales du Service*, as reproduced in Clarke and Engelbach *Ancient Egyptian Masonry*).

Design Council
Figures 14.4 and 14.5 (from Alexander, C. A., 'A City is not a Tree', *Design*, **206**, February 1966, pp. 46–55).
Figure 13.1 (from Archer, B., 'Systematic Method for Designers' *Design*, 1963).

Harvard University Press
Figures 14.1 and 14.2 (adapted from Alexander, C. A., 'Notes on the Synthesis of Form'. Harvard University Press, Cambridge, Mass., 1964).

Hawthorn Books
Quotations on pp. 40 to 43 (from Wright, F. L., *Autobiography*, Hawthorn, New York, 1932).

Her Majesty's Stationery Office
Table 9.1 (from Hole, W. V. and Attenburrow, J. J., 'Houses and People: a Review of User Studies', (Building Research Station), HMSO, London, 1966).
Figure 5.1 (adapted from Echenique, M., Models—a Discussion'. Working paper 6, Cambridge, 'Land Use and Build-form Studies' reprinted *Architectural Research and Teaching*, **1**, no. 1, May 1970).

Harper
Figure 10.1 (adapted from Wertheimer, M., 'Productive Thinking').

Illuminating Engineering Society, New York
Table 8.5 (from Luckiesh, M. and Taylor, A. H., 'Radiant Energy from Fluorescent Lamps', *Transactions of the Illuminating Engineering Society*, **17**, 1922, p. 269).

Professor K. J. Kansky
Figures 12.7, 12.8 and 12.9 (from Research papers no. 84, 'Structure of Transport Networks').

The Macmillan Company
Figure 10.6 and Table 10.6 (from Bross, I. D. J., *Design for Decision*, Macmillan, New York, 1953).

Professor Peter Manning
Table 8.6 (from Manning, P. (ed.), *Office Design: A Study of Environment*, Pilkington Research Unit, University of Liverpool Department of Building Science, 1965)

Professor Tom Markus
Figure 18.7 (from 'The Role of Building Performance Measurement and Appraisal in Design Method', Broadbent and Ward (eds.), *Design Methods in Architecture*, Lund Humphries, London, 1969).

Methuen & Co. Ltd. (Associated Book Publishers)
Figure 1.1 (from Vernon, P. E., *The Structure of Human Abilities*, Methuen, London, 1950).
Figure 12.3 (from Chorley, R. J. and Haggett, P. (eds.), *Models in Geography*, Methuen, London, 1967).

Figure 18.3 (from Ashby, W. R., *An Introduction to Cybernetics*, Methuen, London, 1956).

Metropolitan Museum of Art, New York
Figure 2.5 (from *Bulletin* of Metropolitan Museum of Art).

Museum of Modern Art, New York
Figures 2.16 and 20.2 (adapted from Mies van de Rohe's Brick House design).

Arthur Niggli Ltd.
Quotations on pp. 77 and 78 (from Schnaidt, C., Hannes Meyer, *Buildings, Projects, Writings*,Neiderrenfen, Switzerland, 1965).

Kenneth Norris
Figure 17.3 (Different Transportation Systems).

W. W. Norton & Co. Inc., New York
Quotations on pp. 345 (from Summerson, J., *Heavenly Mansions*, Norton, New York, 1949).

Peter Owen Ltd.
Quotations on pp. 211–13 and Figure 11.4 (from Saussure, F. de, *Course in General Linquistics*, Peter Owen, London).

Penguin Books Ltd.
Figure 2.1 (from Mongait, A. L., *Archaeology in the USSR*, Penguin Books Ltd., Harmondsworth, 1961).
Figure 2.3 (from Edwards, I. E. S., *The Pyramids of Egypt*, Penguin Books Ltd., Harmondsworth, 1951).
Quotations on pp. 343 and 374 (from Bertalanffy, L. von: *General Systems Theory*, Allen Lane, The Penguin Press, 1972. Copyright © L. von Bertalanffy 1968).

Pergamon Press
Figure 17.3 (from Norris, K. W., 'The Morphological Approach to Engineering Design', Jones, J. C. and Thornley, D. G. (eds.); *Conference on Design Methods*, Pergamon, London, 1963).

Philadelphia Museum of Art
Figure 17.4 (Duchamp, M., 'Nude Descending a Staircase', no. 2, 1911).

Philosophical Library Inc. New York
Quotations on pp. 211–13 and figure 11.4 (from Saussure, F. de, *Course in General Linguistics*, Philosophical Library, New York, 1906–11).

Prentice-Hall Inc.
Table 9.3 (from Rober Sommer, *Personal Space: the Behavioral Basis of Design*, © 1969; by permission of Prentice Hall, Inc., Englewood Cliffs, New Jersey).

Cedric Price
Figure 17.6 (Price, C., *Fun Palace Drawing*).
Figure 21.2 (Price, C., *Potteries Thinkbelt*).

Progressive Architecture
Figure 17.3 (from Severud, F. W., 'Structural Analogies Taken from Nature: the Structures that House us', *Architectural Record* **115**, no. 1, January 1954, pp. 169–175).

RIBA Publications Ltd.
Figure 12.15 (from March, L. and Steadman, P., *The Geometry of Environment*, RIBA, London).

Spastics International
Figure 16.1 (from Abercrombie, J., 'The Nature and Nurture of Architects', *Transactions of the Bartlett Society*, **2**, 1963. First published in Spastics International Medical Publication).

James Stirling
Figures 17.2 (photographs of Peasant housing on Ischia).

Tavistock Publications Ltd.
Figure 10.1 (from Wetheimer, M., *Productive Thinking*, Tavistock Publications Ltd., London, 1943).

Unimation Inc.
Figure 21.5 (photograph of a Unimate Robot).

United States Department of the Air Force
Table 6.3 (from Randall and others, *Human Body Sizes in Military Aircraft and Personal Equipment*, Army Air Forces Air Material Command (Wright Field, Dayton, Ohio), Technical Report no. 5501, 10 June 1946).

University of Chicago, Department of Geography
Figures 12.7, 12.8 and 12.9 (from Kansky, J., University of Chicago, Department of Geography, Research Paper no. 84).

University of Illinois Press
Figures 11.2 and 11.3 (adapted from Channon, C. E. and Weaver, W., *The Mathematical Theory of Communication*, University of Illinois Press, Urbana, 1949).

University of Nebraska Press
Figure 2.2 (from Boas, F., *The Central Eskimo*, 6th Annual Report Bureau of Ethology, Smithsonian Institute, Washington. Reprinted 1964. University of Nebraska Press, Lincoln, Nebraska, 1964).

Jorn Utzon
Figure 17.1 (Utzon, J., first sketch for Sydney Opera House).

Verlag für Architektur
Figures 2.11–2.16 and 17.6 (adapted from Le Corbusier, *Œuvre Complete*, **1**).

Ronald D. Watts
Figure 31.2 (from 'Elements of Design', *The Design Method* by Gregory, S. A. (ed.), Methuen, London).

Please turn this as soon as you have it